The Papers of Dwight David Eisenhower

THE PAPERS OF DWIGHT DAVID EISENHOWER

THE CHIEF OF STAFF: IX

LOUIS GALAMBOS, *EDITOR*

ASSOCIATE EDITORS

JOSEPH P. HOBBS ELIZABETH F. SMITH

ASSISTANT EDITORS

DAUN VAN EE ELIZABETH S. HUGHES

EDITORIAL ASSISTANT

ESTHER GILLER

CONSULTING EDITORS

ALFRED D. CHANDLER, JR.

STEPHEN E. AMBROSE

THE JOHNS HOPKINS UNIVERSITY PRESS

BALTIMORE AND LONDON

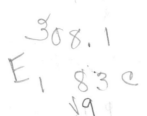

The Johns Hopkins University Press, Baltimore, Maryland 21218
The Johns Hopkins Press Ltd., London
Library of Congress Catalog Number 65-27672
ISBN 0-8018-2061-8
Library of Congress Cataloging in Publication data will be found on the last printed page of this book.

All illustrations in this volume are U.S. Army photographs unless indicated otherwise.

Contents

Volume VI

Occupation, 1945

Volume VII

The Chief of Staff

Volume VIII

The Chief of Staff

Volume IX

The Chief of Staff

The Papers of Dwight David Eisenhower

The Chief of Staff

16

A National Military Establishment

To All Members of the Army[1]   *July 26, 1947*

The President has signed the National Security Act of 1947 and unification of the armed forces will soon be an established fact.[2]

This measure is designed to integrate our military forces—Army, Navy, and Air Force—into a coordinated fighting team. It is incumbent upon all ranks to accept and to practice unification in spirit and in action as a patriotic duty. We of the Army must do our full part to insure the success of this legislation and demonstrate that it results in greater unification as opposed to separation.

There will be no change in official status of the Army with respect to the Air Force until specific orders are issued.[3] Thereafter, I am particularly anxious that the existing pleasant and friendly relations between Ground and Air personnel continue, and that every possible means be adopted to insure that legal recognition of the autonomy of the Air Force will serve only to bring us closer together in friendship and in performance of duty.

Air Force personnel will continue to enjoy the same rights, privileges and facilities to which they have always been entitled as members of the Army in such matters as command status, assignment of quarters, commissary and post exchange privileges, membership in clubs and use of recreational facilities and activities. In short, although legally they will no longer be "in the Army" they will in all ways continue to be treated as members of the "Army family".

I am equally anxious that a similar relationship be achieved with Navy personnel within the new National Military Establishment. Army personnel whose duties bring them in contact with members of the Navy and Marine Corps will make a particular effort to foster the most cordial possible relation.

Commanders of all ranks will give their personal attention to this matter, which I consider of paramount importance and the keystone of Army policy on our future relations with our sister services.[4]

[1] Colonel Bowen drafted this memorandum, which was transmitted to all Army commands on this same day (WCL 37904, same file as document).

[2] On July 26 President Truman signed both Executive Order 9877, defining the missions of the services (see no. 1269), and the National Security Act, PL 253 (U.S., *Statutes at Large*, vol. 61, pp. 495–510). The latter act was a compromise measure that set up a national military establishment consisting of three departments: Army (the old War Department), Navy, and Air. Presiding over these departments was a secretary of defense, who sat on a war council with the civilian secretaries and military chiefs of the three services. The Joint Chiefs of Staff, composed of the three service chiefs and a chief of staff to the President, were formally recognized in the new law; it was implied that the JCS would continue to

have direct access to the President. A Joint Staff would assist the JCS, and the Munitions Board and the Research and Development Board were authorized as interservice agencies. The act followed the Eberstadt recommendations (see no. 206) in trying to coordinate military and other national policies by establishing three agencies: the National Security Council (NSC); the Central Intelligence Agency (CIA); and the National Securities Resources Board (NSRB). The NSC, which was to formulate a coherent national military policy, would include the President, the secretary of defense, and other key officials. The CIA would direct intelligence activities and make recommendations to the NSC. The NSRB would coordinate plans for mobilization (Weigley, *History of the Army*, p. 493).

The new law came far closer to achieving the goals of the Navy than it did to achieving those of the Army. The Army had called for a single military establishment with a powerful secretary. Even Forrestal, who became the first secretary of defense, came to acknowledge that his office lacked power and that the military departments had to be brought under tighter central control. In 1949 Congress would thus strengthen the powers of the secretary of defense, and the Departments of the Army, the Navy, and the Air Force would lose their status as executive departments and become, instead, military departments in the single Department of Defense. Even before this change was made, however, the Army could gain some solace from the fact that at the very least "unification was law" (see *ibid.*, pp. 492, 495; and Legere, "Unification," pp. 381–82).

[3] As Hewes, *From Root to McNamara*, p. 167, points out, "The immediate impact of the National Defense Act on the Army was the final separation and independence of the Army Air Forces." Beyond that, the only effect on the Army was to change the name of the War Department to the Department of the Army. On the separation of the Air Force see no. 1727.

[4] President Truman had originally intended to sign the National Security Act and then to meet with Norstad, Sherman, and Special Counsel to the President Clark McAdams Clifford (LL.B. Washington University 1928) to work out any necessary changes in the draft of the executive order sent to him by Patterson and Forrestal on January 16. The President's mother became ill, however, and he decided to leave Washington to visit her on July 26. He therefore signed the executive order in its original form (see Forrestal to Secretaries of the Army, Navy, Air Force, and JCS, Jan. 20, 1948, P&O 320, Case 31/27; and Legere, "Unification," p. 358). On January 20, 1948, Forrestal would propose some minor corrections in the executive order to make it conform to the National Security Act, but he quickly encountered the same sort of interservice rivalry that had existed before unification. Secretary of the Army Royall would reply on January 29 (P&O drafted this message) taking exception to Forrestal's proposals. Royall said that the executive order already dwelt far more on the Navy and Marine Corps than it did on the Army and the Air Force. He understood why this was done. "However, I do not favor action which will place any additional emphasis upon the Navy and Marine Corps until the functions of all three Departments can be further determined and clarified." He proposed instead that "the Joint Chiefs of Staff should more specifically determine roles and missions for each service." (All correspondence is in P&O 320, Case 31/27.) Some months before, Eisenhower had urged the JCS to conduct a new and detailed study of this subject, but the problems had not been resolved at that time (see no. 1852).

To Edgar Hunt Wilson   *July 26, 1947*

Dear Mr. Wilson: It was very thoughtful of you to invite me to participate in the celebration of Blair Academy's 100th anniversary, and I wish sincerely that it were possible for me to accept.[1] Unfortunately, my plans for the spring of 1948 are too indefinite for me to make a commitment so far in advance. I am not too hopeful that I shall be able to fit additional commitments into a schedule that is already crowded with tentative engagements. However, if you should desire to write me again, sometime after the first of the year, I should be able to give a definite answer.[2] In any event, my best wishes both to the Blair Academy and to the success of its 100th anniversary celebration. Many thanks for your courtesy and consideration. *Sincerely*

[1] Wilson, president of Blair Academy Alumni Association, had written Eisenhower on July 23. Wilson said that almost eleven hundred men from Blair had served in World War II and that fifty-five of them had died in service. The figure eleven hundred equaled the total of all of Blair's graduates for the eighteen years preceding the war, and the number fifty-five equaled the size of the average graduating class. He invited Eisenhower to speak at the academy, which was located at Blairstown, New Jersey, on the third Saturday of May 1948. Parker drafted a response, which Eisenhower revised (McDuff Coll.).

[2] We do not have any further correspondence on this subject. This same day Eisenhower also declined an invitation from the Buffalo (New York) City Planning Association (see Guggenheimer to Eisenhower, July 23, 1947, and Eisenhower to Guggenheimer, July 26, 1947, both in COS, 1947, 080 Buffalo City Planning Association; see also a revised copy of the letter in McDuff Coll.).

To Thomas Troy Handy   *July 30, 1947*
Top secret. Priority

CINCAL,[1] *War Dept., Wash., D.C. This is PAR number two personal for General Handy*: It is my understanding that under the new bill the Joint Comdr in the Alaskan area is to be a Lt. Gen.[2] If this is true please see Spaatz at once about advisability of submitting a recommendation to the President for a recess appointment. I am informally advised that a new naval comdr is soon to report in this area who will carry the rank of Vice Admiral.

[1] Commander in Chief, Alaska. Eisenhower was in Alaska at this time (see the next document).

[2] Eisenhower was referring to the Officer Personnel Act of 1947 (see no. 1596). He was concerned because the current commander, General Howard A. Craig, was

a major general (two stars). In August 1946 Craig had been appointed commander of the Alaskan Department; since January 1947 he had been CINCAL. If he were not promoted, he would soon have a vice-admiral (three stars) as his chief naval subordinate. General Craig would receive his third star on October 1, but as it turned out, the problem anticipated by Eisenhower would not arise (see no. 1679).

1678   *Eisenhower Mss., Clay Corr.*

TO THOMAS TROY HANDY   *July 30, 1947*

Top secret. Priority

CINCAL War Dept., Wash., D.C. This is PAR number one personal for General Handy:[1] Please examine into status of District Engineer who seems to operate in his military functions completely independent of Dept. Comdr. We have always followed the principle that for military purposes all representatives of staff branches are responsible to their local chiefs. By the time I get back I should like to have an analysis of the situation with respect to the Engineer staff officers.[2] New subject. Please send following to General Clay in Berlin.

"Your reply to my message reached me in Alaska. I hope that my former telegram did not seem stuffy to you. Naturally I am highly gratified with your reply and you may be sure that I understand your situation.[3] Particularly I appreciate the necessity for forwarding you advance information regarding policy and changes therein and will do my best so far as I can in the future to make sure you are kept fully informed. You realize that I can operate only on a friend of the family basis since I have no official connection with civil government matters. My warmest regards. Sgd Ike."

[1] On Sunday, July 27, Eisenhower had left Washington, D.C., for a twenty-one-day trip to inspect U.S. Army installations in Alaska. His first stop was at Fort Riley, Kansas; from there he drove to Manhattan, Kansas, for an overnight visit with Milton Eisenhower and his family. The next day the General flew to Great Falls, Montana, and then on to Anchorage, Alaska, arriving at 6:45 P.M. on July 29. Eisenhower was accompanied by Generals Gruenther and Sayler, Colonel John Bartlett Murphy (USMA 1919), G–1, and Colonel Henry Jeffrey Matchett, a member of the Army Manpower Board.

In Anchorage Eisenhower inspected Elmendorf Field and Fort Richardson. He held a press conference and gave three separate talks to the officers and enlisted men (the texts are in EM, Subject File, Speeches). The next day, July 31, the General traveled by car to Lake Louise to fish and play bridge. On August 4 he flew to Fairbanks, where he inspected Ladd Field and held another press conference. This time, however, he reversed the usual procedure and questioned a group of Alaskan newsmen on the problems of the territory (*New York Times*, Aug. 7, 1947). On August 6, 7, and 8 the Chief of Staff and his party made consecutive stops at Point Barrow, the northernmost Alaskan settlement; Nome; and Adak, far west in the Aleutian Islands. On Saturday, August 9, the group flew to Naknek for more fishing and bridge. Three days later the party returned to Fort Richardson and continued to McChord Field, Washington, where they were met by Eisenhower's former aide, James Stack. On August 13 Eisenhower reviewed the 2d Division at Fort Lewis, near Tacoma, and held a third news conference (*New York Times*, Aug. 14, 1947). He had hoped to visit Edgar Eisenhower in Tacoma, but a cable indicates that these arrangements could not be made (Eisenhower to Stack, Aug. 6, 1947, EM, Subject File, Trips). Eisenhower left Fort Lewis on August 15, spent the night in Denver, Colorado, and arrived at National Airport in Washington, D.C., on Saturday, August 16. Itineraries and cables regarding the schedules are in *ibid.*

[2] This paragraph from Eisenhower started a new round of debate over command responsibility. At issue in particular was the lack of control by the theater commander over construction and real-estate matters, all of which involved the expenditure of funds. (For the basic unified command agreements see no. 1214; see also no. 1248.) Handy consulted Lutes, Director of SS&P, who in turn asked Wheeler, Chief of Engineers, about this question. Wheeler responded in a memo of August 1 to Lutes, who sent the report to Handy on August 11 but said he would await Eisenhower's return to discuss the matter. Eisenhower, Lutes, and Wheeler would confer on August 19. At Eisenhower's instructions, Lutes would outline the relationship between the CG of Alaska and the district engineer along these lines: General Craig, the commander, would have some say in construction, but he would not have the ultimate authority over construction funds. This policy was based on the technical branches' argument that in wartime unlimited funds, troops, and equipment were available to the theater commander, but in peacetime the work had to be done by contract with a limit on funds. In Wheeler's view, control through technical rather than command channels was thus more "economical, efficient, and expeditious." (All correspondence is in COS, 1947, 333.1.)

The matter would not end there. On September 18 Royall would write to Forrestal asking that he direct the Joint Chiefs to consider Alaska as a laboratory in which they could experiment by giving the theater commander a more centralized control of logistics and construction. On October 1 Forrestal so directed the JCS. As late as February 1948 (shortly before Eisenhower left office), however, the Joint Chiefs would write to Forrestal saying that they did not believe the problem should be resolved only for the Alaskan command; the JCS were trying to amend the Unified Command Plan to define more clearly the theater commanders' logistical and administrative responsibilities. All correspondence is in CCS 381 (1-24-42), Secs. 6–8; ABC 370.26 Unity of Command, Alaska (12-11-46); and COS, 1947, 333.1.

[3] For background on Clay's situation see no. 1671. Handy had forwarded to Eisenhower the text of Clay's July 28 cable (WAR 82925, EM). Clay's message, which is reprinted in Clay, *Papers* vol. I, pp. 389–90, reminded Eisenhower, "You could not have run the Allied Expeditionary Force if you had been kept in the dark relative to conditions elsewhere." But Clay nevertheless said, "If you think that my departure would be running out on the job and failing in my obligation to an Army which has been more than good to me, that is enough to keep me here." Handy forwarded Eisenhower's message to Clay on August 1 as W 83185 (Clay Personal Papers, Box 4).

To Thomas Troy Handy   *August 5, 1947*
Cable PAR 3. Secret. Priority

From COMGEN Ladd Field, Fairbanks, Alaska[1] *from Eisenhower to War Dept. for Handy*: For General Handy, appreciate your messages involving British intentions in Europe and relieved to learn rumors have been exaggerated.[2] Glad to know new Admiral will be of two star category but still believe Spaatz should consider question of appropriate rank for top man.[3] Learned yesterday that Army forces in this area were compelled by War Department to withdraw stevedores and truck drivers from task of unloading and transporting Army supplies in favor of unions which operate at a greater cost and less efficiency. Am doubtful that Staff has anything to do with matter but if Staff is involved at all would like to know, when I return, why Army is prohibited anywhere in world of using its own means to move Army cargos from Army ships to Army posts for Army consumption. I do not recall any civilians high pressuring the Army out of such jobs on Omaha Beach in 1944. Don't send answer here. Prefer to have it when I get back.[4]

Please send following to Mrs. Eisenhower "Wrote letters to you and to folks. Arrived here at Fairbanks Monday morning and will stay until Wednesday morning when we go to Nome, weather permitting. All in party are well. Would like to have Cannon or Schulz telephone to wives of all to say everything's fine. My letter should reach folks by 10th but if delayed please say I sent my warmest congratulations and felicitations. Much love to you. Ike."

[1] On Eisenhower's Alaskan inspection trip see the previous document.

[2] The United States and Great Britain had for some time, and with varying degrees of success, been attempting to coordinate certain aspects of their military operations, including their planning for the event of hostilities (see no. 1149; and the continuing correspondence on contingency planning in Europe, esp. Huebner to Norstad, June 13, in P&O 381 TS, Case 88). On July 31, however, Eisenhower had received a cable from Handy saying that Britain, because of its economic problems, was going to withdraw its remaining forces in Greece and Italy, leaving five thousand troops for duty in Trieste; Handy also feared cutbacks on British forces in Germany (P&O 319.1 TS, Case 42/15). Eisenhower then received another cable from Handy (WAR 83412, Aug. 2, 1947, in COS, 1947, 333.1 Alaska Trip, Messages) reporting that Secretary of State Marshall had informed the British of his concern that this decision had been made without consulting the United States. The State Department objected to the British decision on several grounds, suggesting that the economic advantages of withdrawal were outweighed by the problems the policy would create in Europe. On August 4 Handy sent a message that presented a somewhat more sanguine view of the situation (WAR 83466, in *ibid.*): He reported that the British now intended to consult with the United States before announcing any further reduction. No mention was made of a

withdrawal from Germany. Eisenhower would nevertheless be forced to confront the threatened withdrawal from Greece and Italy (see no. 1711).

[3] See no. 1678.

[4] On August 7 Colonel Godwin Ordway, Jr., Chief, Western Hemisphere Branch, Operations Group, P&O, informed Norstad that there was no law preventing the Army from using its own forces to move Army cargo. The War Department's policy, however, was to hire civilian stevedores if at all possible. This policy "has made possible peaceful relations with maritime and stevedore organizations such that Army cargo has moved everywhere in spite of national maritime strikes." If such strikes were to affect the Army, transportation would be more expensive. On August 8 Lutes sent the C/S a summary that reiterated these points and added: "The labor movement is so integrated in the Maritime industry that alienation of a particular union in one area can directly and materially effect [sic] Army shipping operations by sympathetic strikes or walk-outs in other areas where the Army must rely on commercial Maritime movements" (COS, 1947, 333.1).

1680   *Eisenhower Mss., Subject File, Trips*

To Thomas Troy Handy   *August 8, 1947*
Cable PAR 4. Top secret. Priority

From HQ Aleutian Sector, Adak Alaska[1] *sgd Eisenhower to WAR personal for General Handy*: I agree with Gruenther detail although Admiral Hill has submitted a special plea for disapproval. However I have already promised Gruenther a leave for important family reasons and he will not arrive in Washington until 23rd August.[2] In meantime other staff officers of the 3 services can be developing a proposed organization for the Joint Staff and he can make final revision before submitting to JCS. If you personally believe it to be of great importance that Gruenther reach Washington by the 15th he prefers to alter plans so that he can do so. I do not see any compelling reasons in the matter but we will be guided by your personal judgment.

I am personally opposed to wearing civilian clothes while on duty and since this is a minor detail of internal organization I do not consider that this attitude would interfere with any action the Navy might desire to take. Moreover if Secretary Royall has any strong reasons for concurring with Secretary Forrestal on this matter, I would not urge strenuous objection. I intend personally to continue to wear uniform during duty hours.[3]

Please phone Mrs. Ike that we have just landed at Adak after visits to Anchorage, Louise, Fairbanks, Point Barrow and Nome. All is well.

[1] For the schedule of Eisenhower's Alaskan trip see no. 1678.

[2] Gruenther was to assume command of the Joint Staff, created by the National Security Act of 1947 (see no. 1675). Eisenhower was responding to a cable from

Handy, who reported that the Joint Chiefs had approved Gruenther's appointment, and to a paper requesting Gruenther's proposals on the organization and operation of the new Joint Staff. Handy had indicated that Gruenther could start his new job around August 15 (WAR 83652, Aug. 6, in COS, 1947, 333.1 Alaska Trip, Messages).

[3] After Forrestal and Royall had discussed this subject on August 6, Handy said that Royall "asked me to get your views and those of the Staff, stating that he would be governed thereby." For background see no. 1354.

1681   *Eisenhower Mss.*

To Herbert Bayard Swope   *August 18, 1947*

Dear Herbert: I dashed off a short message today to be given to Mr. Baruch at his birthday party.[1] It was nice to be asked and would have been a real privilege to attend.

Regarding the presentation of the Medal of Merit: this Medal, as you know, is awarded by the President, and the only way I could present it personally would be for you to tell one of the White House staff that, provided the President could not present the Medal personally, you hoped that I could act in his stead.[2] If he so designated me we could have a small and informal ceremony here in my office, after which you and whoever might come with you might be able to have a soldier lunch with me.

Of course it is entirely possible that the President might specifically desire to present the Medal personally. You could not possibly, in such a case, suggest otherwise. If he does not so indicate, I will be flattered to officiate.[3]

With warm regard,[4] *Sincerely*

[1] Swope had called on Major Cannon on August 16 and, among other things, had invited Eisenhower to a party celebrating Bernard Baruch's seventy-seventh birthday on August 19 (Cannon to Eisenhower, EM, Swope Corr.). Eisenhower's telegram and Baruch's September 1 reply are in EM.

[2] When he saw Cannon, Swope had also asked if the Chief of Staff would present the Medal of Merit that had been awarded to Swope.

[3] In a letter of August 21 (EM) Eisenhower wrote Swope that the White House had approved Eisenhower's awarding the medal. Eisenhower would make the presentation in his office on September 8.

[4] General Eisenhower did not comment on the third part of Swope's conversation with Cannon. Swope had reported "on a confidential basis the fact that several individuals, important in both national political parties, were seriously discussing your name."

To Edwin Norman Clark   *August 18, 1947*

Dear Ed: In spite of my hopes it is out of the question for me to visit you this month.[1] My next trip in that direction will be fully occupied with a number of preliminary business details with some of the Columbia trustees. While it would be advantageous for me to go up there this week I now feel certain that I cannot leave the city before the following weekend. In other words, life seems to be the same as it has been for the past ten years; I can count on nothing so far as personal plans are concerned.

Naturally when I do get to New York I will see several houses that have been tentatively selected for my inspection.[2] Nevertheless, nothing that I have heard of sounds so attractive to me as the one you have described.[3] I can only hope that the coming weeks will develop some particular day when Mamie and I can get away to make a very hurried visit, even if we cannot spend a weekend. Even if you have moved into town, perhaps we could drive out long enough to take a quick look. The only period that promises any hope for the moment is that between September 6 and 13. It is the only 7-day period in the next several months in which I am not already tied up with some kind of firm engagement involving a trip out of town.[4]

With my warmest appreciation for your kindness and as always, with best regard,[5] *Sincerely*

P.S. I think I sent you a copy of the letter I wrote to General Hodges.[6] Since I am just back from Alaska I have not heard of any action taken in your case but when you write again you might tell me whether there have been any developments.[7]

Of course I should thank you especially for the sketches you sent along with your August 13 letter.[8]

[1] On Colonel Clark's career see no. 1456.
[2] One part of Eisenhower's agreement with the trustees of Columbia University was that he would have a private home in the nearby countryside (see no. 1565).
[3] In a long letter to Eisenhower, Clark had described a house that was for sale near his home in Westport, Connecticut. The white clapboard, Colonial-style house, called Mill House, was situated on about twenty-eight acres of land on the west bank of the Aspetuck River. The property included a pre-Revolution barn and a mill dam with a small mill house (July 23, 1947, EM). Eisenhower was anxious to see the house but skeptical about commuting between Westport and New York City (Eisenhower to Clark, July 24, 1947, *ibid.*).
[4] General and Mrs. Eisenhower would spend September 11–13 in New York as the guests of Mr. and Mrs. Thomas J. Watson. They would look at several houses, including the one Colonel Clark had suggested (see no. 1700).

[5] On September 5 Eisenhower would again write to Clark explaining that the other houses he had heard about did not compare with the one in Clark's neighborhood but that Mrs. Eisenhower was anxious to find a house no further than a thirty-to thirty-five-minute drive from upper New York. The Eisenhowers also had decided it would be wise "to rent one for six months to a year until we learn more about the area and can confirm our own desires."

[6] This letter concerned Eisenhower's recommendation for Clark's promotion (see no. 1643).

[7] For the Alaskan trip see no. 1678.

[8] Clark had enclosed sketches taken from the blueprints of Mill House, as well as a map of its immediate vicinity (see note 3 above).

1683

COS, 1947, 080 Tennessee
Education Association

To ANDREW DAVID HOLT

August 18, 1947

Dear Mr. Holt:[1] Many thanks for your thoughtful letter which was received during my absence in Alaska.

I would like very much to accept your cordial invitation to address the Annual Convention of the Tennessee Education Association in March, but it is just impossible for me to do so.[2] An overburdened schedule for the remainder of my tour as Chief of Staff has been further complicated by frequent enforced absences from Washington, and I have already been compelled to break many engagements—some of long standing.[3] It is not yet possible to forecast, with any accuracy, the date of my release from this post.

Your membership is exactly the kind with which I like to meet and frankly, I would like also to visit in your great State. Moreover, I hope you will understand that no consideration of an honorarium has swayed me in reaching the decision that I must regretfully decline your invitation. It has been my invariable practice to refuse any honorarium in fulfilling any engagement of this kind and I shall most certainly adhere to that policy as long as I occupy any type of public office.[4]

Please accept my assurances of deepest appreciation for your courtesy and my best wishes for the complete success of your Convention. *Sincerely*

[1] Holt (Ph.D. Columbia 1933) had been executive secretary-treasurer of the Tennessee Education Association since 1937 (except for the period when he was in military service during World War II).

[2] Holt had written on August 7 to ask Eisenhower to deliver the principal address at the association's annual convention on March 19, 1948 (same file as document).

[3] From this point in the text, Eisenhower entirely rewrote Parker's draft.

[4] Holt had said that the association's usual honorarium for featured speakers was five hundred dollars, but he believed they "might be justified in increasing this sum if it is necessary in obtaining your services."

TO CHARLES CRAIG CANNON   [*August 19, 1947*]

Replying further to your query—[1]

General Eisenhower states that he had a conversation with Sec. Morgenthau in the summer of 1944, during which the future of Germany was discussed. In that conversation Gen. Eisenhower expressed the same *personal* views that he did on numerous other occasions to numerous other persons. These were, briefly:

    a. The German people must not be allowed to escape a personal sense of guilt for the terrible tragedy that had engulfed the world.

    b. Germany's war making power should be eliminated.

    c. Certain groups should be specifically punished by Allied Tribunals:

        (1) Leading Nazis.

        (2) Gestapo members.

        (3) S.S. members.

        (4) Soldiers guilty of violation of rules of land warfare.

    d. The German General Staff should be utterly eliminated. All records destroyed and individuals scattered and rendered powerless to operate as a body. In proper cases more specifically punished.

    e. In eliminating German war making ability, care should be taken to see that Germans could make a living, else they could become a charitable charge and America would be the only one to assume the burden. They should not be allowed to become objects of world pity.

General Eisenhower suggested no plan and never, to anyone, expressed the opinion that Germany should or could become a pastoral state.[2] He expressed the opinion that the Ruhr should be worked by Germans, but under direct Allied supervision and control.[3]

[1] Henry Morgenthau, Jr., secretary of the treasury from 1934 to 1945, had published his proposal for the future treatment of Germany in the book *Germany Is Our Problem.* The Morgenthau Plan was to make Germany a pastoral state without the industrial capacity to wage a modern war. On August 19 Cannon wrote Eisenhower to explain that while the General was in Alaska Cannon had received a telephone call from Denys Peter Myers, of the State Department, inquiring about the origins of the Morgenthau Plan (letter from David F. Trask, Feb. 17, 1977, EP). Myers was writing an historical account of U.S. postwar policy. He said that Morgenthau's book attributed the origin of his plan to a discussion he had held with Eisenhower on August 7, 1944, and Myers asked if the C/S's office could corroborate this statement. Cannon had told Myers that there was nothing in Eisenhower's files to substantiate Morgenthau's statement. Cannon asked whether Eisenhower wanted to amplify on this response, and the General wrote this account. For background on the question see nos. 386 and 471; and John Morton Blum, *From*

the Morgenthau Diaries, 3 vols. (Boston, 1959–67), vol. III, *Years of War, 1941–1945* (1967), pp. 327–74.

[2] Eisenhower apparently ordered a more thorough search of the pertinent files for information on his involvement with the Morgenthau Plan (see Norstad to Eisenhower, n.d., and C. V. R. Schuyler to Norstad, Oct. 17, 1947, both in EM). Schuyler reported, "In brief, nothing has been found to indicate that General Eisenhower has ever taken a firm stand on these matters."

[3] During much of the immediate postwar period the Army, and especially Clay, had actually been under attack for rebuilding Germany too quickly (see for example no. 1299). Lewis H. Brown, chairman of the board of Johns-Manville Corporation, had just completed a two-month trip, made at Clay's request, to study West Germany's postwar industrial potential. On August 22 Brown sent Eisenhower a summary of his findings, including his conclusion that "we must completely abandon the Morgenthau philosophy." In a response of August 30 (drafted by Carroll) Eisenhower said he had found "your suggestions on Ruhr production and the transportation problem especially illuminating." All correspondence is in EM.

1685   *Eisenhower Mss.*

To Hugh Montague Trenchard   *August 19, 1947*

Dear Lord Trenchard: I have just returned from a trip in the Alaskan region, to find your letter of the 24th of July awaiting me. It is most interesting, particularly in view of your effort to get something specific started on what we both know would be a good idea.[1] It does pose for me certain personal problems which I shall endeavor to explain.

First and foremost, a military official in this country must be exceedingly careful to avoid even the appearance of interfering in a matter that is not strictly professional in character. I think it would be far more likely to damage than to promote the project for me to advocate publicly the writing of a Joint History. I would have no hesitancy in doing so after I once left the Army but the date of my departure from this office is still so uncertain that I cannot possibly advocate holding the matter in abeyance for that indefinite length of time.

The recently appointed Secretary of our new Department of National Defense is Mr. Forrestal, a man of vision and of influence. I can and shall suggest the matter to him as one in which he might interest himself.[2]

Naturally I do not pose as an expert interpreter of political possibilities in this country. Consequently I have no idea whether our Congress would make an appropriation available to historians completely outside the Government, no matter how worthy the project. On the other hand, if the President should direct the cooperation of the Armed Services and make available to designated historians all the documents of the war, the whole thing might then be accomplished here by executive action. This would of course presuppose the availability of private funds and just as in your country, the necessary sum might not be forthcoming from this source.

After consultation with Mr. Forrestal I shall write you further on the matter.[3]

With warm personal regard, *Sincerely*

[1] Trenchard had proposed that a joint history of Anglo-American cooperation during World War II be written. He wanted the history to be an authoritative work—by well-known historians employing large staffs—that would also be readable and inexpensive. Given the difficult economic conditions, he felt that it would be impossible to obtain private financing. He therefore wanted both governments to subsidize the study. He and a friend would rally the effort to get money from the British government, and he asked Eisenhower to take the lead in the United States. For background see no. 776.
[2] See the following document.
[3] On September 20 Eisenhower would send Forrestal further correspondence from Trenchard (EM). For later developments see no. 1934.

1686   *Eisenhower Mss.*

To James Vincent Forrestal   *August 19, 1947*

Memorandum for Secretary Forrestal:

Subject: Joint U.S.-British History of World War II.

Some months ago there was brought to me, by Lord Trenchard, a proposition that our two Governments cooperate to prepare a truly joint, popular history of the British-American part in World War II. In general his proposition is as follows:

a. Each Government to subscribe approximately $800,000 for the project.

b. Each Government to appoint a number of joint co-Chairmen of a historical committee, upon the nomination of a committee of college presidents or of some other similar body. The co-Chairmen to select equal numbers of qualified historians from each country to do the work.

c. The Governments to make available to the committee all papers, without reservation, that apply to the joint war effort.

Lord Trenchard made a rough estimate that it would take several years to complete the work with a half dozen individuals from each country working on it constantly. He indicated to me that he intended soon to introduce a resolution in the House of Lords in the purport of the outline given above.

I have told Lord Trenchard, by letter, that as Chief of Staff of the Army it was inappropriate for me to take any action whatsoever in such a matter but that I would refer it to you as our newly designated Secretary of National Defense.[1] I informed him further that, provided you thought well of the project and desired to interest yourself in it personally, you would have to decide on the various points of procedure in order to get the thing started.

Lord Trenchard stated that while in some ways it might be preferable to attempt the matter through private subscription, he believed that in England the necessary money could not be raised under current conditions and therefore felt that if one country had to do this by legal appropriation it would be advisable for the other to do the same.

I personally believe that something of this sort might do much to straighten out misconceptions that have always existed between our two countries and which are likely to be intensified by unilaterally prepared histories of the recent conflict. However, the matter so far transcends my official responsibilities as Chief of Staff that I offer nothing except this personal conviction. But if you see any virtue in the proposal I would not only be glad to discuss it with you but will forward an expression of your convictions to Lord Trenchard.[2]

[1] See the previous document.
[2] In an August 27 memorandum to Eisenhower, Forrestal said that while he was all for the project, "ways and means are another matter." He wanted to talk further to Eisenhower about it; "in the meantime, I shall explore possibilities of getting the necessary funds." For further developments see no. 1934.

1687 *Eisenhower Mss.*

To William Samuel Paley *August 19, 1947*

Dear Bill: Thank you very much for your letter of July 24th which I found awaiting me upon my return from Alaska.[1] It appears that now you have gone to Europe and I see no chance of us getting together before early October, since I have promised my wife to take the last week of September in order that we may enjoy one short vacation together.

Naturally I am flattered by your suggestion and though my first reaction is that I cannot consistently accept, it will be interesting to talk about it. Consequently, on your first trip to Washington after your return from Europe, won't you give my office a ring so that we may arrange an hour or so for a talk that may be convenient to us both?[2] *Sincerely*

[1] In his letter Paley, chairman of the board of the Columbia Broadcasting System, offered Eisenhower a position on the board of directors of CBS (EM). Paley said it was important that the ties between the universities and the primary systems of communication be strengthened; he reminded General Eisenhower that Dr. Nicholas Murray Butler had served as a director of the New York Life Insurance Company during his tenure as president of Columbia University.
[2] Paley and Eisenhower would apparently be unable to meet during October 1947, and the General would not become a director of CBS. For further developments involving Paley see no. 1863.

1688   *Eisenhower Mss., Subject File,* Crusade in Europe

TO GARDNER COWLES   *August 19, 1947*

Dear Mr. Cowles:[1] It was indeed thoughtful of you to suggest that I prepare a series of articles for "Look", and I truly appreciate your kindness.[2] It is as yet much too early for me to say when, if ever, I will be able to do any independent writing, but I shall be happy to keep your suggestions in mind.

I have been extremely reluctant to consider the possibility. However, when you are again in Washington, if you would give my office a ring, we could undoubtedly arrange a meeting convenient to us both. Certainly we could find interesting subjects to talk about—even if we don't pursue this particular one to any extent.[3] *Sincerely*

[1] Cowles, a 1925 graduate of Harvard, had begun his career in journalism that same year as city editor of the *Des Moines Register.* He was now president of the Register and Tribune Company, the Cowles Broadcasting Company, and Cowles Magazines, Inc. He was president and editor of *Look* magazine.
[2] In a letter of July 28 Cowles offered Eisenhower the opportunity to write a series of articles for *Look* over the next several years; Cowles also said he could syndicate the material. He concluded, "I would be glad to talk with you about it any time either in New York or Washington." McDuff drafted this response, and Eisenhower added the second paragraph (McDuff Coll.).
[3] They apparently did not pursue this question any further.

1689   *Eisenhower Mss.*

TO WILLIAM BENTON   *August 19, 1947*

Dear Bill:[1] Thanks a lot for the Encyclopedia Britannica which I find arrived here during my absence in Alaska.[2] I cannot tell you how pleased I am to have this replacement for my five-year-old edition. I have written a personal note to Mr. Powell in Chicago extending my thanks also to him.[3]

With warm regard, *Sincerely*

[1] Before he became assistant secretary of state in 1945, Benton had been chairman of the board of Encyclopaedia Britannica and of Encyclopaedia Britannica Films (since 1942).

[2] In a luncheon conversation on July 11, Benton had promised to send Eisenhower a set of the Britannica. Elkan Harrison Powell, president of Encyclopaedia Britannica since 1934, had written Eisenhower on July 23 to say he had forwarded the set, together with the current *Britannica Book of the Year* and a set of coupons for future yearbooks (EM).

[3] Parker drafted a note of thanks to Powell, and Eisenhower made some changes in the draft (Aug. 19, 1947, *ibid.*; and McDuff Coll.). On September 29 Powell would write Eisenhower that he was forwarding the Britannica's latest publication, a four-volume history of the period 1937–46, again with Benton's compliments. Eisenhower would thank Powell and Benton in staff-drafted letters of October 6 (EM).

1690   *Eisenhower Mss.*

To EDWIN PALMER HOYT   *August 19, 1947*

Dear Mr. Hoyt:[1] Thank you for sending me a copy of your August 16th edition. I am truly grateful for the understanding and consideration reflected in the article about me that you published on your front page that day.[2]

It was a privilege to meet you in Washington, one that I hope I may have again at an early date. *Sincerely*

[1] Hoyt, who had served in World War I as an enlisted man with the A.E.F. in France, had begun his newspaper career in 1923 as an editor on the *East Oregonian* in Pendleton, Oregon. In 1926 he had begun a long career with the *Portland Oregonian*, and he had become this paper's publisher in 1939. Since 1946, Hoyt had published the *Denver Post*.

[2] The *Denver Post* article said that Eisenhower had enjoyed a restful overnight stop in Denver following his exhausting twelve-thousand-mile inspection tour of Alaska. The article pointed out that lack of publicity and fanfare had enabled the Chief of Staff to benefit from "an uninterrupted night of splendid sleep." For details of the trip see no. 1678.

1691   *Eisenhower Mss.*

To CHARLES HENRY GOREN   *August 19, 1947*

Dear Mr. Goren:[1] Many thanks for the bridge books. I feel sure that General Gruenther[2] is sorry now that he brought them to the plane for I studied them en route and—contrary to Mr. Kauffman's[3] experience—learned how to hold some Aces and Kings. I still don't do so well with deuces and treys.

I am indeed grateful for your thoughtfulness.[4] *Sincerely*

[1] Goren was the top-ranked player in the American Contract Bridge League and author of several popular books on bridge. Since 1944 he had written a daily, syndicated column on bridge that appeared in seventy-one newspapers. For background see Richard Frey, ed., *The Official Encyclopedia of Bridge* (New York, 1971), p. 607.
[2] Gruenther and Eisenhower frequently played bridge together (see *ibid.*, pp. 592, 609; and no. 1350).
[3] Eisenhower was probably referring to New York playwright George Simon Kaufman, who had written several humorous articles about bridge for the *New Yorker* magazine and other periodicals (see Frey, *Official Encyclopedia of Bridge*, pp. 626–27).
[4] McDuff prepared the initial draft of this message for Eisenhower.

1692   *COS, 1947, 080 Republican*
                                          National Committee

To Eileen Ewing Archibold   *August 19, 1947*

Dear Mrs. Archibold:[1] Mamie has given me your cordial letter which was not sent to any of the stations I visited on my recent trip, due to the imminence of my return to Washington and the very tight schedule on which I was traveling.[2] Needless to say, I am honored that your State Central Committee should feel I might be able to contribute something to their banquet meeting in February.

I have been looking forward to an opportunity to visit Denver, and had hoped until today that I would be able to do so within the foreseeable future. However, my frequent absences from Washington have confronted me with such an appallingly heavy schedule for a considerable time ahead that it is not humanly possible for me to make additional commitments. I have just written to Mr. Bannister explaining my predicament and declining the kind invitation he had extended on behalf of the Mile High Club.[3]

Please accept my thanks for your gracious invitation. *Sincerely*

[1] Since 1944 Mrs. Archibold (B.A. Vassar 1921) had been the Republican national committeewoman from Colorado. She was a member of the executive committee of the Republican National Committee.
[2] Mrs. Archibold, a friend of Mrs. Eisenhower's, had written to her on August 4 asking her to forward to the General a letter (same date) inviting him to address a meeting of the Republican State Central Committee on February 21, 1948 (same file as document). Parker wrote the initial draft of this reply.
[3] Lucius Ward Bannister was president of the Mile High Club (see no. 1534).

TO HAROLD RUPERT LEOFRIC GEORGE ALEXANDER   *August 20, 1947*
Cable WCL 44934

U.S. Milattache Am. Embassy Ottawa Canada signed Eisenhower: Will you please forward the following message to the Governor General of Canada: Dear Alex: Morgan tells me that there is some possibility you could attend the Army Navy football game on November 29th.[1] Nothing would give me greater pleasure than to have you and Lady Alexander attend that game and I think you would find it most interesting. I have arranged with the West Point authorities to hold a box for you pending receipt of your reply. My present plans are to attend personally and I would be in an adjoining box as would also General Taylor of West Point. If you can come would a total of 4 in your party be satisfactory?[2] *With my warm regard*

[1] General William D. Morgan, the British Army member of the Joint Staff Mission in Washington, probably had discussed this subject with Eisenhower when they met at the Chief of Staff's office at 10:30 A.M. this same day.

[2] At the end of this cable, Eisenhower wrote to the U.S. military attaché: "If Field Marshal Alexander's reply is direct through you, please forward it to me promptly." (For developments see no. 1714.) The Alexanders would attend the game, which Army won, 21–0 (*New York Times*, Nov. 30, 1947). Correspondence concerning the visit is in EM.

TO JAMES FREDERICK GAULT   *August 20, 1947*

Dear Jimmy: Your note of the 14th came through speedily and was awaiting me when I returned to my office on the morning of the 18th.[1]

Frankly I am not too certain that I will be either happy or particularly useful in my new post, once I get a chance to enter upon its duties. The fact is that so many different groups began to urge me to promise to undertake some particular type of activity upon my retirement from the Army that I reached the point where I felt it easier to say "Yes" to someone.

The advantages of the Columbia post are, the opportunity it offers to continue preaching the basic principles in which I so firmly believe; it is distinctly a public service as distinguished from a commercial position; it will keep me close to many of my warm friends; and it offers some opportunity to influence the youth of the nation. Its disadvantages are that it forces me to live in or near New York City whereas I would vastly prefer a rural community; it takes me into a field so entirely new that my self-confidence is somewhat shaken; and, finally, I am afraid it is going to demand real intensity of effort whereas I had hoped, upon donning civilian clothes, to pace myself and lead a somewhat more leisurely life. However, I have made a promise and I will try to live up to it. I assume that I shall start on the new assignment sometime in the spring.

It was grand to hear news of Pug and if he is still in London give him my very best.[2]

I am very sorry to hear that you had a recurrence of the old African trouble but I am delighted that you are up and about again.[3]

My love to Peggy and, as always, warmest regards to yourself. *As ever*

P.S. I shall be on the lookout for the photographs of Culzean and thank you for them in advance of their coming.[4] I know they will be interesting.

[1] Gault had written to congratulate Eisenhower on his appointment as president of Columbia (EM). Eisenhower had been in Alaska (see no. 1678).
[2] General Sir Hastings Ismay had asked to be remembered to Eisenhower.
[3] Gault wrote that he had been ill since his return from New York in April.
[4] Gault now had the photographs of Culzean Castle that he had promised to Mrs. Eisenhower, and he said he would mail them that week.

1695   *COS, 1947, 360.33*

To Mrs. Carl Austin Russell   *August 20, 1947*

Dear Mrs. Russell: My deepest sympathy goes out to you in the untimely loss of your fine husband.[1] Throughout his long and inspired service in the Army, Colonel Russell stood in ever-increasing stature among his contemporaries. His integrity and selfless devotion to duty will long be remembered by his many friends in the service, among whom I have been proud to count myself. *Sincerely*

[1] Colonel Carl Austin Russell, Jr., had died on August 16, 1947, while serving in the Pacific Area. (For background on Russell see Chandler, *War Years.*) McDuff helped Eisenhower draft this letter of condolence.

1696   *COS, 1947, 320.2 TS*

To Lucius Du Bignon Clay   *August 21, 1947*
Top secret

Dear Lucius: I understand that you now intend to send your representatives here to discuss further the reorganization of the Constabulary, and that pending this discussion you desire that we withhold any further action on the T/O and E's[1] which you submitted in December of last year. We have, incidentally, completed study of these T/O and E's and agree with them in principle.[2]

I appreciate your need for a realistic troop basis ceiling, but I cannot make a decision on this matter until I have a better indication of our future strength trends.[3]

The recruiting campaign for Europe has been under way for too short a time to allow me to make even an off-hand estimate as to its success or failure. If total Army strength is appreciably increased as a result of this campaign, we will undoubtedly be able to maintain your Ground enlisted strength at a level in excess of the 80,000 previously discussed.[4]

Sincerely

[1] Tables of organization and equipment.

[2] Clay's letter, dated August 1947, said that he had made some further revisions in his constabulary reorganization. Clay hoped that "the new recruiting campaign will alleviate the European Command shortage" (for background see no. 1669). P&O drafted this response for Eisenhower.

[3] In his letter Clay had pressed for a realistic troop-basis ceiling. On August 22 Norstad presented P&O's study to Eisenhower, who approved it on August 30 (see Norstad to Eisenhower, Aug. 22, P&O 320.2 TS, Case 82). As Eisenhower had warned Clay in his letter of June 10 (no. 1537), EUCOM's enlisted level for June 30, 1948, was set at eighty thousand.

[4] For the Army's total strength when Eisenhower left office see no. 2039.

1697   *Eisenhower Mss.*

To Maxwell Davenport Taylor   *August 21, 1947*

Dear Max: With the Unification Law[1] on the books, a problem will arise involving the Service Academies. There will be the question of establishing a new Service Academy for the Air Forces or of devising some plan whereby the Air Forces could take, say, approximately one-third of the annual West Point output and a somewhat similar proportion of the annual Annapolis output.

Both Spaatz and I favor this latter system if it can be worked out. The reasons will be obvious to you. Under such a plan the Air Forces would, of course, be expected to provide their share of instructors and to assume a comparable portion of the annual running expenses of the Military Academy. I think that if the output should be of necessity increased in size, they would, of course, share in the expenses of plant expansion, and so on.[2]

Beyond this, I have long held an idea which I may or may not have heretofore discussed with you. It is the possibility of making practically identical the West Point and Annapolis curricula for the second and third years, and during those years accomplish a mutual exchange of half of each those two classes between the two Academies. If this were done, I think that it would also be proper to have a few Army and Air officers acting as instructors in Annapolis and vice versa.

Again, the advantages sought seem to me to be so obvious as to require no lengthy explanation. On the other hand, I know that many types of objections can be raised and I suspect that on the part of the Navy we might run into one or two individuals who would be violently opposed. However, at one time Admiral Nimitz was at least attracted to the principle of the thing but we never pushed it because of the feeling that it would be met, at that time, by defeat.[3]

Without asking you at the moment to comment on either of these ideas in detail, I should like for you to think them over with a view to future informal discussion. Moreover, if the second scheme appeals to you as having merit and being in the realm of feasibility, I wonder whether you would not, at a convenient opportunity, make the suggestion informally, as your own, to the Superintendent of the Naval Academy. If the two of you should ever agree on the wisdom of some such plan as this and at the same time declare it to be possible of accomplishment, I am certain that the rest could be done.

Naturally if you condemn the whole thought, there is no point in carrying it further. Your casual talks with the Superintendent of the Naval Academy would take place only in the event you were ready to pick up and sponsor the plan as an idea of your own.[4]

I have no idea whether or not you contemplate any trip to this city in the near future. If you should come down for any purpose, please call my aide in advance and make certain that we can have a chance to have a chat.

With warmest regards to you and Mrs. Taylor, *Sincerely*

[1] The National Security Act of 1947 (see no. 1675).
[2] After years of debate, a separate Air Force Academy would finally be established at Lowry Air Force Base, Denver, on August 15, 1954. For a history of the debate, its resolution, and the establishment of the third academy see Masland and Radway, *Soldiers and Scholars*, pp. 106–28.
[3] For background see no. 1271.
[4] General Taylor replied that he and the commandant and the dean of the U.S. Military Academy were working on a study of the implications of an exchange such as Eisenhower had suggested (Aug. 25, 1947, EM). On September 30 Taylor submitted a memorandum to Eisenhower that listed one advantage (reduction of "unwholesome service rivalry") and five major disadvantages of the proposed program. The objections centered around Taylor's view that the philosophies of the two academies were simply incompatible. Taylor wrote: " . . . I would view with the greatest concern the effect of this plan on the spiritual features of West Point training. The Honor System as it now exists could not be maintained without a complete change of attitude on the part of the naval authorities. Also, Annapolis is so different in its approach to discipline, plebe training, officer-midshipman relationships, and numerous other aspects of training that I feel it hopeless to try to

1887

bring the attitudes of the two schools together" (*ibid.*). Eisenhower noted on the attached OCS memo, "File and forget!" (Michaelis to Eisenhower, Oct. 1, 1947, *ibid.*).

1698 *Eisenhower Mss.*

TO JOHN JAY MCCLOY *August 21, 1947*

Dear Jack: Thank you for letting me read a copy of your article.[1] I consider it intensely interesting (although this may possibly be the prejudiced view of one who was something of a participant in a few of the events described) and so far as my memory serves me, I think it is accurate.

The only place where the element of possible classification of information occurred to me was where you mentioned President Quezon's proposal and President Roosevelt's reply thereto.[2] I did not know that this information had hitherto been made public but I assume that you have cleared this point.[3] All in all, my opinion is: the article is clearly and simply written and every decision you discuss was one of great importance. I am certain that the publishers and the public will agree with this.

With warm regard, *Sincerely*

[1] McCloy had sent Eisenhower the manuscript of an article, with a covering note, on August 19 (EM). The article, entitled "Important Decisions of World War II," was being prepared for the twenty-fifth-anniversary edition (October 1947) of *Foreign Affairs*, the quarterly review of the Council on Foreign Relations.
[2] McCloy wrote that on February 8, 1942, when the Battle of Bataan was nearly over but the U.S. and Filipino forces were still fighting, President of the Philippines Manuel Quezon proposed to President Roosevelt that the neutrality of the Philippines be declared and fighting cease. On February 9 Roosevelt cabled Quezon that he was unable to accept the suggestion; Roosevelt directed the American troops "to fight it out." McCloy contended that the decision was of great importance in continuing the resistance to the Japanese. "It also rendered necessary the subsequent decision to return to the attack in the Philippines in 1944, rather than, as was later urged by some, to by-pass the islands for Formosa." For an analysis of the episode see Morton, *Strategy and Command*, p. 190.
[3] McCloy's article would include the Bataan episode.

1699 *Eisenhower Mss.*

TO ROBERT EDWARD MERRIAM *August 21, 1947*

Dear Colonel Merriam:[1] I have just read a copy of your book "Dark December".[2] Since the close of hostilities I have had few opportunities to read any operational or personal accounts of the war. Yours is only the fourth that I have read completely. The others were Montgomery's "From El Alamein to the Sangre", de Guingand's "Operation Victory" and Drew Middleton's "Our Share of the Night". I cite this merely to give you some idea of my basis of comparison when I say that yours is the most satisfying war account I have seen. Its whole atmosphere is analytical and judicial and while, naturally, there are certain points in which my interpretation or recollections differ somewhat from the impressions given by your book, on the whole I consider it a remarkably accurate document.

I am quite amazed that you were able, in the time available, to consult the variety of records and the great numbers of people that you obviously have. Some day I hope I may have a chance to talk to you a bit further about points that would possibly be of no interest except to individuals who had either made a detailed study of the European operations or who were, like you and myself, participants in them.[3]

With my congratulations and with personal regard, *Sincerely*

[1] Merriam (M.A. University of Chicago 1940) had served with the National Housing Agency in Washington from 1941 to 1942. As a colonel (AUS) in the Historical Section of the War Department, he had been attached to the Ninth Army during the war. He later became Chief of the Ardennes Section of the Historical Division, ETO.
[2] Robert E. Merriam, *Dark December: The Full Account of the Battle of the Bulge* (Chicago, 1947).
[3] In a letter of September 4 Merriam said that in spite of his work on the official Army history of the battle, he had been unable to put the story together until he had been home for six months. When he sat down to write the book, "the pieces seemed to fall into place." He thanked Eisenhower for his letter and said he looked forward to discussing the events of the battle with the General (COS, 1947, 201 Merriam).

1700   *Eisenhower Mss.*

To Thomas John Watson   *August 21, 1947*

Dear Tom: There is, of course, something to be said for the idea of postponing the selection of a personal, out-of-town residence until after Mamie and I have had opportunity to settle in New York and have more leisure in which to determine our own requirements.[1] We have had several long talks about the matter, and even though it should involve the storing here of a great portion of our belongings, this would in itself be a relatively minor matter because the War Department will accomplish the transportation of our property any time within one year after my retirement.

On the other hand, as you suggested, it is at least possible that we would see a place so attractive and appealing that all the question would be instantly removed from our minds. This would naturally take all the doubt in any decision out of the problem.

In the whole thing, however, one point comes up which I have carefully avoided mentioning to date since I do not want in any slightest way to embarrass the University authorities, Dr. Butler or, indeed, myself. It is the question of the date that it may become possible for Mamie to make an inspection of the house on the campus, to gain some idea of its size, layout, and the extent of its furnishing. As Mamie sees it, she cannot possibly do this until after the place has been vacated since it would be almost rude to have to ask questions concerning items that belong to the University.

As you can understand, the determination of these things looms very large in Mamie's mind, and she feels that the time for her to come to New York to go around the countryside would be at a time when she could also, with perfect freedom, enter the town house for a quick survey.[2]

The purpose of this note is most emphatically not to suggest any pressure upon Dr. Butler. It is merely a personal query to you as to the probable date on which Mamie could accomplish what she has in mind. I sincerely feel that many of her doubts and misgivings will instantly disappear once she can begin to plan definitely on the move she will have to make.[3]

Most of my friends continue to assure me of their conviction that in the new field I will have added rather than lesser opportunity for carrying on my feeble efforts to do something in the public service. From my viewpoint it at least provides some shelter from the constant political darts that are launched in my direction by well-meaning, but I fear short-sighted, friends.

I am looking forward with real anticipation to coming up for a long talk with you and your family and friends, but your answer to this letter may indicate a somewhat more satisfactory date than the one we have already agreed upon.[4]

In this connection, could you give me some idea of whether your plans include any dinners or meetings other than on a purely "family basis"?[5] I ask the question because these things are always important to a woman when she packs for a weekend trip.

Word from General Taylor states that he had a most enjoyable time at Endicott.[6]

With warmest personal regard, *Sincerely*

[1] Watson had written to General Eisenhower about the housing situation on August 4 and had called the C/S's office on August 11 (Cannon to Eisenhower, Aug. 11, 1947, both in EM). The Eisenhowers had previously planned to visit New York in late August to look for a house (Eisenhower to Watson, July 25, 1947, *ibid.*). For background see no. 1682; for later developments see no. 1733.

² General and Mrs. Eisenhower inspected the President's House, at 60 Morningside Drive, at 10 A.M. on Thursday, September 11, during a three-day trip to New York. For details of the trip see no. 1682. Further correspondence concerning the President's House is in EM.
³ Dr. Nicholas Murray Butler died early in December 1947, and Mrs. Butler moved to a Park Avenue apartment the following spring. The Eisenhowers would occupy the President's House on May 2, 1948 (see no. 1916; also see Kevin McCann, *Man from Abilene* [New York, 1952], p. 166).
⁴ The proposed dates for the visit, August 22–25, would be changed as indicated above in n. 2.
⁵ Watson had previously indicated that the plans for the weekend would be "entirely in accord with your wishes—not too many people and no publicity" (Cannon to Eisenhower, Aug. 11, 1947, EM).
⁶ See no. 1598.

1701   *Eisenhower Mss., Routine Corr., Miscellaneous*

To Hugh P. Avent   *August 21, 1947*

Dear Hugh:[1] It was good to hear from you again and I truly appreciate your cordial invitation to visit you in Greenville.[2] I hope that I may find an opportunity to stop by to see you in the not too distant future.

I am unable to say at this time what the plans are for your brother-in-law.[3] However, a memorandum of your request is being placed in his file and will be considered when he comes up for assignment upon his return to the States.

With warm regard, *Sincerely*

¹ Eisenhower had recently seen Colonel Avent at the reunion of the West Point Class of 1915. Avent had served in the cavalry and field artillery in Mexico and Europe from 1916 to 1918. He had retired, disabled, on December 15, 1922, but during World War II he had been recalled to active duty in the Air Corps and had served from 1942 to 1946.
² Avent's August 17 letter is in EM.
³ In his letter Avent asked if his brother-in-law, Lieutenant Colonel John Hiram Lewis, Jr. (USMA 1918), could be assigned near Louisville, Kentucky, upon his return from Japan. Avent said Lewis had been overseas for two years and would be retiring within three to six months after his return. Parker drafted this reply, and Eisenhower added a handwritten postscript which read, "I will do my best for him!" This same day Michaelis sent a memorandum to Paul expressing Eisenhower's desire to have Lewis stationed near his family in Louisville (COS, 1947, 201 Lewis). Upon his return in January 1948, Lewis would be assigned to the 3d Armored Division, at Fort Knox, Kentucky. He would retire on December 31, 1948.

1702   *Eisenhower Mss.*

To Earl Marvin Price   *August 22, 1947*

Dear Mr. Price:[1] Many thanks for your stimulating letter. I am pleased to have your comments on Universal Military Training and deeply appreciate your interest in this vital aspect of the national security.[2] I am astonished that you fear I might hold my peace because of personal political implication or out of regard for the obligations of a school teacher! My sole concern is for the Army and the discharge of its important responsibilities to the country. The Army does *not* make political policy—it is an operating agency. Its military head must stay in his proper field or he will destroy the value of the Army's considered professional advice. That is the story. *Sincerely*

[1] For background on Price see Chandler, *War Years.*
[2] The staff-drafted version of this reply included only these first two sentences; Eisenhower added the remainder of the letter in longhand, making several revisions in his own draft (McDuff Coll.). General Eisenhower's reply would anger Price (see no. 1873).

1703   *Eisenhower Mss.*

To Howard Arnold Craig   *August 23, 1947*

Dear Pinkey: I have had the Staff go over the several memoranda you provided me.[1] One or two of them are still under study.

The labor questions were all settled directly by Judge Patterson when he was Secretary of War, and while I feel that a mistake was made, there is nothing to do about it.[2]

With respect to your "civil component" memorandum, I had already given you an outline of our thinking and planning on that matter.[3]

I am quite certain that I learned more from my Alaskan trip than I have from any similar inspection in my life. I believe that one of the reasons was the leisureliness with which we did it. I learned more from absorption and from my two weeks with you than I did from the more formal parts of our activities. I think I have written notes of acknowledgment to each of the various individuals who were so kind to us throughout the journey.[4]

Please remember me warmly to Mrs. Craig and her mother, and with best regards to yourself,[5] *Sincerely*

[1] Craig had forwarded these memoranda with a covering message of August 2 (COS, 1947, 333.1). His major concern was to clarify the command structure and in particular to specify the relationship between the commander and the district engineer (see no. 1678; and the papers in P&O 384, Case 80/16).

1892

² See no. 1679.
³ Craig's recommendation was to give civilian components more authority and responsibility for the conduct of their affairs and "to establish co-terminus areas of Army, Air and Navy responsibility and thus simplify manpower problems." Eisenhower had probably discussed this with Craig while visiting Alaska. These questions, especially those involving cooperation among the services, were still being studied when Eisenhower left office (see no. 1677, n. 2).
⁴ McDuff had drafted a letter of appreciation to Craig, which Eisenhower signed and dispatched on August 20 (EM). Other similar correspondence is in EM.
⁵ Other problems involving Alaska would arise during Eisenhower's remaining months as Chief of Staff. On October 6 he would sign a McDuff-drafted letter answering Craig's August 13 request for help in obtaining post-exchange merchandise and special-services equipment (COS, 1947, 333.1). On October 25 the JCS would approve Eisenhower's JCS 1259/46 (of October 20, 1947), which designated the Chief of Staff, U.S. Air Force, as executive agent for the JCS for the Alaskan Command (CCS 381 [1-24-42], Sec. 7).

Later, the Joint Chiefs would consider the secretary of the interior's proposal to build a railroad to Alaska to improve its defenses and to promote its economic development. On Eisenhower's recommendation, the problem would be referred to the Joint Strategic Plans Committee (enclosure to JCS 1818, of November 18). In a memo to the new Chief of Staff, General Bradley, Wedemeyer would sum up their report: "The above conclusions give the Secretary of the Interior mild support for the railroad without endorsing it to the extent that a decision might be made to construe the railroad as a military necessity" (Feb. 10, 1948; all papers are in ABC 617 Alaska [10-10-47]).

1704   *Eisenhower Mss.*

To TERRY DE LA MESA ALLEN   *August 23, 1947*

*Dear Terry:*¹ I hasten to answer your letter of the 19th.²

First, let me say that things said during a campaign at moments of irritation should never be taken too seriously; I regard it as most unfortunate that they should ever be said, if at all, in front of anyone whose business it is to make them a matter of record.

My own opinion of you as a combat commander is sufficiently proved by my taking you back in command of the 104th.³ I suppose you know that the War Department gave me absolute authority to veto the transfer to Europe of any commander of whom I did not completely approve. When you left Algiers, I told you that I expected you back into the battle and I was glad to have you.

You will recall that we had some very annoying, not to say destructive, results from bringing the First Division back into the Algiers area after the Tunisian campaign was completed. Very elaborate control methods had to be devised until we got it straightened up. Unquestionably it was some such thing as this that was in Smith's mind when he made the unguarded and unnecessary remarks attributed to him in the book you mention. From my viewpoint, I knew that we were still developing an army and perfection could not be expected suddenly. When you were sent back from the First Division, there were a number of reasons. Among these reasons was an agreement with the War Department that selected commanders would be sent back to improve the training of the vast number of divisions that would still have to enter the battle. Another was that you yourself told me you were somewhat tired, and I felt that a short period in training activity in the United States would bring you back freshened and with all your combat leadership qualities unimpaired. In this I think I was proved right, because I have had occasion now and then to remark upon the remarkable degree of training, particularly in night fighting, that the 104th Division had attained when it first entered battle. The final reason was after the conclusion of the Sicilian campaign. I felt that the First Division, which had performed magnificently under you, should then undergo a considerable period of training, and I felt that in Huebner we had available a man ideally suited for this role, particularly in view of his almost life-time association with the First Division.

So far as I know, I have never expressed any ideas other than those hinted at above. I have testified time and again to the qualities of the First Division and to your ability as a battle leader, and I hope that I have never been guilty, even at a time of emotional stress, of referring in derogatory tones of any of the men who were my team mates both in the Mediterranean and Europe.

There were several individuals who failed, and they were relieved from command and thereafter either reduced in rank, or were never again allowed to come into combat. Your whole record shows that you were definitely not classed in this category, but on the other hand were considered an extremely able combat commander.

I repeat that I regret the publication of something which you justifiably resent. In this connection I can say the only thing I can offer is that I, too, have been subjected at various times to most inaccurate, misleading, and sometimes actually completely false allegations.

I hope you are still able to grin about the matter a bit, and I assure you that if ever an occasion offers where I can say a word publicly, I will do my best to counteract the impressions caused by any such unfair statements as you have quoted in your letter.[4]

With warm personal regard, *Sincerely*

---

[1] In late 1943 Eisenhower had removed from the 1st Division both the commanding general, Terry Allen, and the assistant CG on the grounds that they were not enforcing good discipline among their troops while away from battle (see Chandler, *War Years*; and Bradley, *A Soldier's Story*, pp. 154–56).
[2] Allen had enclosed a copy of his letter of August 19 to Bedell Smith. Allen protested about comments allegedly made by Smith and quoted in *One Last Look*

Around (New York, 1947), a newly published book by journalist Clark Lee. Smith was quoted as having told the reporter in late 1943 that Allen had ruined the 1st Division by enforcing discipline only on the battlefield and not behind the lines. Allen contended to Smith that the reports of the activities of his troops while out of the line were *"grossly* exaggerated and many had no foundation of truth *whatsoever."* Allen quoted to Smith from the citation accompanying the DSM he had received; Smith had presented this award, and the citation praised Allen and his division for their performance in North Africa. He also quoted from the citation he had received with the Legion of Merit, awarded for his efforts in Sicily. In his letter to Eisenhower, Allen objected to Smith's statements (Aug. 19, EM).

Smith would reply to Allen on September 3 and send a copy to Eisenhower (*ibid.*). Smith denied that he had told Lee that Allen "ruined" the 1st Division. Although unable to remember specifically any conversation with Lee, Smith said that he would not have made any "gratuitous" comments, but if asked the reasons for Allen's relief, Smith would have answered "quite frankly and dispassionately." As Smith recalled, the problem had been a deterioration of discipline.

[3] On December 14, 1943, Eisenhower had answered allegations that Allen had been relieved for inefficiency; Eisenhower wrote General Surles: "The answer to this one is that I will be glad to have General Allen again as a division commander" (Chandler, *War Years*, no. 1416). Allen later fought under Eisenhower in the ETO as commander of the 104th Infantry Division.

[4] Allen thanked Eisenhower in a note of September 1, 1947. He confessed that he had been greatly annoyed by the publicity given Smith's comments: "But that's all water over the dam now and one should not let oneself be bothered by irritating trifles of that sort" (EM).

1705   *Eisenhower Mss.*

To Thomas John Watson   *August 25, 1947*

Dear Tom: I cannot possibly come to New York on November 5 even though I deeply appreciate Mr. Forbes' invitation and have the most profound respect for the character of the audience that will be gathered at his dinner.[1] The demands upon me have grown both in number and in intensity. Lately I have had to adopt a firm and fixed rule of refusing to add to my commitments, at least until the end of January next. It has been exceedingly difficult to hold to this rule and I am sure that you can understand some of the reasons why it is very wise to do so.

So won't you please express my very deep appreciation of Mr. Forbes' courtesy and explain to him that it is a real impossibility for me to accept his gracious invitation.

With warm personal regard, *Sincerely*

[1] Watson wrote Eisenhower on August 22 enclosing a copy of an August 21 letter from Bertie Charles Forbes. Forbes, who was the founder, editor, and publisher of *Forbes Magazine*, a semimonthly business and financial journal, was also the author of numerous books on business. Forbes was having a dinner in New York to honor fifty of America's leading businessmen, and he wanted to invite Eisenhower to be the speaker.

Eisenhower Mss.

To M. Burneice Larson   *August 25, 1947*

Dear Mr. Larson: I am more than delighted to provide you such information as I have concerning Brigadier General Albert W. Kenner.[1]

I first became acquainted with General Kenner in the North African
campaign where he came as the Chief of the Medical Service in the
expedition headed by General George Patton. General Kenner carried
out his difficult task in such fashion as to win the highest type of
commendation from his Commanding General, whose good opinion of
General Kenner was shared by the entire staff of the Casablanca expedition. Everything that I saw of his work tended to confirm the accuracy
of this estimate.

When preparing, in London, for the final phases of the plan for
invasion of northern Europe, I found need for a medical adviser, of
high rank, who could be disassociated from the actual operational end of
the Medical Service. For this position I chose General Kenner.
Throughout the campaign he showed a comprehension of complex and
vital issues that was remarkable and displayed qualities of tact and
leadership in assuring the accomplishment of needful measures.[2]

While I cannot, of course, comment upon General Kenner's purely
professional qualifications, I can add that he acted as my personal physician throughout the campaign with the greatest of satisfaction to myself. I consider him a man of character, ability, personality and above
all, of good judgment and common sense. In addition he is mentally
and physically vigorous.

I trust that the above will provide you with the information you need.
Sincerely

[1] Larson, Director of the Medical Bureau in Chicago, had written Eisenhower on
August 22 (EM). Larson said that General Kenner had given Eisenhower's name
as a reference and asked for a recommendation.
[2] See Chandler, *War Years.*

1707   *Eisenhower Mss.*

To Edward Everett Hazlett, Jr.   *August 25, 1947*

Dear Swede: Your note just reached me. I am delighted that we shall
meet for a few moments in Raleigh, even though I shall apparently have
the sketchiest of opportunities to talk to you.[1]

Possibly you can go along with me to my train which I understand is not to pull out until 9:45 and this might give us an opportunity to talk a bit longer.[2] I am due to go to Abilene about October 25 where I will attend a testimonial dinner to Mr. Harger.[3] I would also like to tell you about my latest visit there which took place in June.

Please don't concern yourself about the possibility that I have "changed my mind".[4] You may be certain that I have been absolutely truthful in every public statement I have made on the personal political question and you can be equally sure that I have not directly or indirectly given to anyone the right to represent my feelings and convictions differently at any place or at any time.

It is difficult for many people—particularly those who have led a political life or are engaged in newspaper or radio work—to believe anyone who disclaims political ambition. Even though they may accept without the faintest hint of challenge any statement a man might make about any other subject in the world, on this one thing they maintain a position of doubt, not to say suspicion. Frankly, if Mamie and I could have our way we would, without the slightest hesitation, retire to the quietest and least publicized neighborhood in the United States. We have become convinced that a completely private life is denied us—this conviction, as much as anything else, is at the bottom of my agreement to attempt the job in New York. Beyond this, however, I have no plans, no personal ambitions, and I am attempting to live this as honestly as I say it.

My own deepest concern involves America's situation in the world today. Her security position and her international leadership I regard as matters of the gravest concern to all of us and to our national future. Allied to these questions of course is that of internal health, particularly maximum productivity. While there may be little that I can do about such matters, I do have the satisfaction of feeling that whatever I try to do is on a national and not on any partisan basis. Moreover, I flatter myself to believe that the people who listen to me understand that I am talking or working for all, not for any political party or for any political ambition. This is the attitude I hope that I can preserve to the end of my days.

My very best to Ibby and the girls and, as always, my very best to you. *Sincerely*

---

[1] Hazlett's letter of August 23 is in EM. For background see no. 1516; and on Eisenhower's trip to Raleigh see no. 1713.

[2] Eisenhower was to leave Raleigh for New York City at 9:45 P.M.

[3] See no. 1724.

[4] Hazlett had written that several recent articles indicated that Eisenhower had changed his mind about running for President. If the reports were true, Hazlett said, he wanted to "do some missionary work in the Solid South."

To Aksel Nielsen   *August 26, 1947*

Dear Aksel: Thank you for giving me the interesting housing survey report and the letters from local groups urging me to visit Denver.[1] While my stop at Lowry was necessarily brief, it was a real pleasure to see and talk to you again.

As you know, I would need no urging to come to Denver if it were humanly possible for me to do so. I shall continue to seek an opportunity to accept your gracious invitation, but my schedule is so formidable that I cannot consider any new commitments until after relief from this assignment. I am sending short notes to those who joined in extending Denver's hospitality.[2]

My best to Helen and Virginia[3] and warmest regards to yourself. *Sincerely*

[1] Nielsen had written Eisenhower on August 16 enclosing a Denver city council report on VA housing (EM). Eisenhower had asked Nielsen for the report when they met on August 15 at Lowry Air Base, Denver; at that time the Chief of Staff was returning from his Alaskan inspection trip (see no. 1678). Parker drafted this reply, and Eisenhower added the last sentence (McDuff Coll.).

[2] In a letter of June 11 Nielsen had said that various organizations were trying to convince the public that to have good government the people must participate in the selection of candidates. He said, "We in Denver would appreciate an opportunity to have you talk to that subject."

[3] Nielsen's wife and daughter.

1709   *COS, 1947, 095*

To ——   *August 27, 1947*

Dear ——:[1] Your recent letter has just been received and I can well understand the concern that prompted it.[2]

I am informed that the investigation of your son's record was purely a matter of routine procedure. Such investigations are made of all personnel who are employed in sensitive positions in Headquarters, Army Air Forces. This one developed no derogatory information of any sort and disclosed that your son is of the highest character. As a result, we place complete confidence in him and this fact has been noted in his record.

It seems that a misunderstanding may have arisen during the course of the questioning of Mr. . . . .[3] which led him to assume that the investigator had some concern because of your past association with the American Youth Congress.[4] This, however, was not the case as that matter was fully and satisfactorily discussed with . . . .[5]

Thanks for writing to me about this matter. I sincerely trust that this letter answers satisfactorily the questions you held as to War Department attitude.[6] *Sincerely*

[1] We have deleted all of the names in this letter.
[2] The correspondent was concerned about remarks made by a War Department special investigator during a loyalty check being conducted on the correspondent's son (who was a member of the A–2 staff in the War Department). The letter to Eisenhower said: "The investigator stated . . . that there were doubts about my son since I was a communist. . . . Even were the charge against me true, which it is not, in view of his [the son's] record, it would seem he should not be questioned on those grounds." The correspondent had been in government service during the war and had himself undergone several loyalty checks. "I am, however, deeply concerned that this episode should appear to my son's Department as an adverse item on his record" (letter of July 30, same file as document). McDuff prepared an initial draft of this reply, which Eisenhower revised (McDuff Coll.).
[3] The correspondent's insurance broker.
[4] The accusation was made, the correspondent wrote, because he had signed a petition asking his congressman to vote against a continuation of the House Committee on Un-American Activities (HUAC) and because he had been "connected with" the American Youth Congress. While both charges were true, he said, "neither shows allegiance to communism."
[5] The correspondent's administrative superior.
[6] For a discussion of the concern in the United States about loyalty see Latham, *Communist Controversy in Washington*; and Alan Barth, *The Loyalty of Free Men* (New York, 1951).

1710   *McDuff Coll.*

To Beulah de Vries   *August 27, 1947*

Dear Mrs. de Vries:[0] Many thanks for your letter.[1] I am indeed sorry to hear about Grant's illness.[2]

Legally, the matter of your brother's hospitalization is under the exclusive jurisdiction of the Veterans Administration, an agency separate and apart from the War Department. Although this fact prohibits me from intervening personally, yet General Bradley is not only a great friend of mine but is always concerned about the welfare of veterans. He is in Europe right now, but I will send your letter to one of his assistants with a personal request that your brother's affliction be promptly and sympathetically considered.[3]

With best wishes, *Sincerely*

[1] Mrs. de Vries and her brother, Grant Fisher, had known Eisenhower in Abilene. Her letter of August 25, 1947, is in EM. Eisenhower made several changes in the staff-drafted version of this reply.
[2] Mrs. de Vries wrote on behalf of her brother, who was in the Birmingham (Alabama) Veterans Hospital with a severe case of bronchial asthma. She asked

that he be transferred to San Fernando Veterans Hospital, where the climate would be better for him.
[3] On September 12, 1947, Lieutenant Colonel Chester Bayard Hansen, Veterans Administration special assistant, would write to Eisenhower's aide, Michaelis, to inform him that Fisher had been transferred to the San Fernando hospital on September 10 (EM).

1711   *ABC 370.5 Greece-Italy (8-20-47), Sec. 1-A*

To Joint Chiefs of Staff   *August 28, 1947*
Memorandum. Top secret

Subject: Military Implications of Withdrawal of British Troops from Greece and Italy[1]

I recommend that the letter of the Acting Secretary of State to the Secretary of War, dated 27 August, requesting the views of the Joint Chiefs of Staff concerning the above mentioned subject be referred to the Joint Strategic Survey Committee for study and preparation of recommendations as a matter of urgency.[2]

[1] On August 22, 1947, the British had announced plans to withdraw all of their troops from Greece and to reduce their forces in Italy to the bare minimum called for in the peace treaty. (For background see no. 1679; on U.S. involvement in Greece, no. 1554; and on the Italian situation, no. 1504.) Conditions in Greece were particularly troublesome to the United States. While the United Nations was investigating the sources of support for the guerrilla movement in Greece, the State Department and American military planners were concerned that the Greek Army might be defeated before any effective action could be taken by either the United Nations or the United States. In the August 27 letter that Eisenhower mentions (Robert J. Lovett to Royall) the State Department expressed concern over "the drastically changed conditions that have occurred since March" (same file as document). The Chief of Staff had also received intelligence reports indicating that the Soviets would exert increasing pressure on the Greek government and that the Communist satellites in the Balkans would step up their aid to the guerrillas (July 9 and 24, COS, 1947, 091 Greece). P&O was already studying the possibility of increasing the size of the Greek Army, which at this point was barely maintaining the initiative against the guerrillas (see *ibid.*; and Memo for Record, Aug. 7, 1947, in P&O 092 TS, Case 95/21. See also State, *Foreign Relations, 1947*, vol. V, *The Near East and Africa*, pp. 816–89).
[2] Eisenhower's memorandum (drafted by Schuyler) was circulated as JCS 1801 and was immediately referred to the Joint Strategic Survey Committee. The JSSC reported on August 30, and the Joint Chiefs would approve the JSSC paper on September 2 (JCS 1801/1, all in the same file as this document). Royall and Forrestal sent these views to the State Department on September 5. (Their paper is reprinted in State, *Foreign Relations, 1947*, vol. V, *The Near East and Africa*, pp. 327–29.) The JCS position was that the British forces in Greece were of crucial, although largely symbolic, significance in preventing a collapse that would leave Russia in a powerful position in the Mediterranean. If the Communists controlled Greece, Turkey would be outflanked, and access to Middle Eastern petroleum

supplies would be endangered. The Western Powers' ties with Italy and Iran would be weakened. (For JCS strategic plans involving the Middle East see no. 1370.) The JCS did not, however, oppose British troop withdrawal in Italy because that action had been mooted by Yugoslavia's ratification of the Italian peace treaty (see no. 1557). After considerable negotiation the two sides would work out a compromise on the question of military support for Greece (in a series of high-level discussions in Washington—the Pentagon Talks of 1947—in mid-October), and British and American policies would once again be coordinated (see State, *Foreign Relations, 1947*, vol. V, *The Near East and Africa*, pp. 485–626). After the withdrawals agreed upon in the Pentagon Talks, the British would not reduce their forces any further while Eisenhower was Chief of Staff. For subsequent events in Greece see no. 1815; on Italy see no. 1825.

1712   *Eisenhower Mss., Family File*

To John Sheldon Doud Eisenhower and   *August 28, 1947*
Barbara Jean Thompson Eisenhower

Dear Kids: The first thing I must do in this letter is give you the address of General and Mrs. Surles. It is the "Wyoming Apartments, Columbia Road, Washington, D.C." His name is Major General A. D. Surles.

There would seem to be little profit in attempting to give you an account of my Alaska trip.[1] Travelogues are available in many places and I doubt that my observations were much different from those of the ordinary visitor. At one spot I had a chance to go fishing for two days and at another for three. These were the highlights of the whole trip. The fishing was good and we had cabins on the shore of the lake. It was so isolated from civilization that the only way to get in was by float plane—except for those who had the courage to undertake a walk of at least eleven miles over the treacherous Alaska tundra. Of course the radio-telephone was always present and this brought to me occasionally a few messages that gave me some concern, but which I did not allow to raise my blood pressure.

Upon returning home I came through Fort Lewis, but Edgar and all his family were absent on a trip, so my activities there were confined to purely professional matters.

When I arrived in Washington I found all the family in very good shape. Min has removed the last bandage from her arm and now needs only to exercise care to insure she does not injure it again.[2] She takes daily treatments at the dispensary to restore circulation and muscular strength.

From what I remember of John's program, he must be soon to enter the Motor Maintenance School. I remain certain that he will always be thankful that he decided to take the short courses he selected at Benning.[3]

Naturally Mamie and I talk often of some opportunity to see you before your anticipated arrival here in December. We are counting on spending the last week in September with the Saylers near Savannah. For the moment at least, Mamie is tentatively planning to come on over to Benning to stay a day or so, but whether or not I can make it will depend on the circumstances at the time.[4]

Every day brings fresh evidence of world unrest and tension and life in this city is anything but tranquil and serene. Sometimes I wonder, though, whether I would not be even more concerned about it if I were so far removed from direct contact that all my information would have to come through the newspapers and with the uneasy feeling that I, at least, could do nothing about the matter whatsoever! In any event I am still planning to go to Columbia sometime next spring—possibly along about April, although this is merely a wild guess.

This note, of course, brings the best from all of us. We have been particularly delighted that Barbara has found opportunities to write. In spite of the good grades Johnnie has always attained in the estimation of his parents, he has never had a high mark as a correspondent. The only thing I can say is that if you, Barbara, cannot bring about some improvement in his habits in this regard, you simply must act as his amanuensis and do the work for you both. Of course I must admit that even if you did get John all bucked up on this matter, we would still raise a lot of cain if you didn't also keep up the splendid practice you have begun.

With love to you both, *As ever*

[1] See no. 1678.
[2] Mrs. Doud (see no. 1663).
[3] See no. 1527.
[4] For subsequent developments see no. 1751.

1713   *COS, 1947, 080 National Federation of Business*
                                      and Professional Women's Clubs

To Katheryn P. Casey   *August 28, 1947*

Dear Mrs. Casey:[1] It is difficult to decline your gracious invitation to address the luncheon meeting on 11 October but, unfortunately, I am obliged to do so.[2] Personally, and because of my interest in the public service your Federation is performing, I deeply regret that this is so.

My several lengthy absences from Washington have complicated a very formidable schedule for the fall and early winter. I am already committed at the time you mention, and have been forced to avoid making any additional public engagements for the remainder of the year.

The strong support which the National Federation of Business and Professional Women's Clubs has given to the important security measures now before the nation is very gratifying. If you should desire any other member of the Army to attend one of your meetings, I should be glad to assist in making the necessary arrangements.

Many thanks for your courtesy and consideration.[3] *Sincerely*

[1] Mrs. Casey (B.A. University of California 1941) was an attorney in Washington, D.C.

[2] Mrs. Casey's letter of August 27 explained that the National Federation of Business and Professional Women's Clubs had designated October 5–11 as National Business Women's Week. Mrs. Casey was chairman of the week's activities in the District of Columbia. She asked if Eisenhower would speak "at a summing-up luncheon on Saturday, October eleventh." Casey wrote that the business and professional women were "vitally concerned . . . with the future of the United States" and that they recognized "that our future is irrevocably linked with that of the whole world." She reminded Eisenhower that the federation, founded in 1919, had a U.S. membership of 120,000 and a foreign membership of 130,000. Parker drafted a response, which Eisenhower revised extensively (McDuff Coll.).

[3] At 9:45 A.M. this same day Eisenhower left Washington by train for Raleigh, North Carolina, arriving about 4 P.M. After a press conference and a dinner at the Governor's Mansion, he went to Reddick Stadium, on the campus of North Carolina State College, to address the Farmers' and Farm Women's Convention. Eisenhower left Raleigh at 9:45 P.M. by train for New York City, arriving at 9:55 the morning of August 29. That afternoon he addressed the annual convention of the American Legion at the 71st Regiment Armory. He returned to Washington by train that same evening, arriving about 9:30. Eisenhower had submitted the text of his speech for the American Legion to the State Department on August 25 to insure that his statements agreed "with State Department doctrine" (see Bowen to Humelsine, in COS, 1947, 080 American Legion). Copies of both of Eisenhower's speeches are in EM, Subject File, Speeches.

1714   *Eisenhower Mss.*

To Maxwell Davenport Taylor   *August 30, 1947*

Dear Max: Thank you for your note with the football schedule. I see no opportunity for attending any game other than the Navy battle on November 29th. That I hope to take in this year.[1]

I saw Field Marshal Alexander at New York yesterday. He is quite steamed up about an opportunity to see one of our college games and I told him that you were planning on his coming down. I told him also that I thought your box and mine were usually right close together and that I assumed his would be in the same vicinity.[2]

Please tell whoever makes the reservation for the Field Marshal that it is quite o.k. for him to bill me for the cost of the Field Marshal's box.

Mamie and I are looking forward to seeing you and Mrs. Taylor at Tom Watson's lunch.[3]

With warm regards to you both, *Sincerely*

[1] Taylor had sent General Eisenhower the Army team's 1947 schedule with a covering note of August 27 (EM).

[2] See no. 1693.

[3] The Eisenhowers and the Taylors would have lunch at Watson's home in New York on September 13 (Taylor to Eisenhower, Aug. 25, 1947, EM).

1715 *Eisenhower Mss.*

TO GEORGE VAN HORN MOSELEY *August 30, 1947*

Dear General: It will be a real pleasure to have a visit with you when you come to Washington.[1] If you can let my office know, a bit beforehand, the advance timing of your visit, we can insure against the possibility that I might be out. Possibly we can arrange to have lunch here at my office, which would give us opportunity for a real chat.[2]

Personally, I see no objection whatsoever in filing with your official record any facts that may seem to you pertinent. I should think it would be a very simple matter.[3]

With warm personal regard,[4] *Sincerely*

[1] Moseley had written Eisenhower on August 28 that he would like to drop by to visit while he was passing through Washington in the next few days (COS, 1947, 201 Moseley). For background on Major General Moseley see no. 515.

[2] Eisenhower was out of town much of the month of September and thus may have been gone when Moseley stopped in Washington. The C/S's desk calendar does not indicate that the two men met.

[3] Moseley asked for permission to place on file in the War Department evidence to correct "certain impressions" that had been formed by the press about his activities in speaking out against what he felt were dangers within the United States (see no. 675).

[4] Eisenhower left Washington, D.C., by plane the afternoon of August 31 and arrived in Minneapolis at 4:30 P.M. The next day, Labor Day, he visited the Minnesota State Fair, where he held a press conference and addressed fairgoers (*New York Times*, Sept. 2, 1947). That evening Eisenhower left by train for the Cedar Island Lodge, near Superior, Wisconsin, to rest and to fish on the Brule River. He spent September 2 and 3 at the lodge with his host, John Gilman Ordway, president of the Crane Company, St. Paul, Minnesota. Other members of the party included Carl Raymond Gray, Jr., vice-president of the Chicago and North Western Railway System (for background on Gray see Chandler, *War Years*); Lieutenant General Walton H. Walker; Colonel Joseph C. Haw, CO, recruiting district, Minneapolis (since 1945); and Major C. Craig Cannon. On September 4 Eisenhower traveled to Chicago to address the annual convention of

the American Meat Institute. He left Chicago the next morning by air, arriving in Washington at 12:30 P.M. Eisenhower's speeches and correspondence regarding the trips are in EM, Subject File, Speeches; and in COS, 1947, 001.

1716   *ABC 014 Austria (2-2-44), Sec. 1-I*

To Joint Chiefs of Staff   *September 5, 1947*
Confidential

Memorandum by the Chief of Staff, U.S. Army:

Subject: Termination of Civil Censorship Activity by United States Forces, Austria
     References: *a.* J. C. S. 1110
                b. J. C. S. Memo for Info 257
                c. J. C. S. 1369/6
                d. C. C. S. 271

1. By virtue of paragraph 9, Instrument of Unconditional Surrender of Germany (J.C.S. 1110 and J.C.S. Memorandum for Information No. 257) military authorities were empowered to establish control over all means of civilian communications in Germany.[1] Under paragraph 2 *a* of the Enclosure to J.C.S. 1369/6 the foregoing is equally applicable to Austria.[2]

2. C.C.S. 271[3] and J.C.S. 1110 provide for the establishment and operation of civil censorship, and there is no explicit mention contained in these papers concerning the authority necessary for the termination of this censorship on a unilateral or other basis. The only known authority for the termination of civil censorship activity is contained in paragraph 5 of War Department Technical Manual 30-235, dated September 1946, which states in part, "Civil censorship will not be terminated without the prior approval of the War Department or higher authority".

3. In message No. P-7637 (CM-IN-2512) dated 13 August 1947 the Commanding General, U.S. Forces in Austria[4] reports that information gathered through U.S. civil censorship is not sufficiently valuable and essential to warrant continuance of censorship, and that its operation in Austria costs $650,000 per annum. He further states that unless otherwise instructed he intends to take action to:

     a. Eliminate by 1 November 1947 all U.S. civil censorship activity conducted unilaterally in the U.S. Zone of Austria, less Vienna;

     b. Support in quadripartite discussion the elimination of quadripartite censorship in Vienna;

     c. Withdraw by 1 November 1947 U.S. Forces in Austria from participation in quadripartite censorship if attempts to eliminate same are not successful.

4. I therefore recommend that the Joint Chiefs of Staff dispatch to the Commanding General, U.S. Forces in Austria, the message in the Enclosure hereto.[5]

[1] The Instrument of Unconditional Surrender of Germany, signed at Berlin on June 5, 1945, is printed in Leland M. Goodrich and Marie J. Carroll, eds., *July 1944–June 1945*, Documents on American Foreign Relations, vol. VII (Princeton, 1947), pp. 217–22. JCS 1110, of October 16, 1944, is in CCS 000.73 (7-20-44). Memorandum for Information No. 257, of June 28, 1944, is in CCS 387 Germany (12-17-43), Sec. 2. Major General S. J. Chamberlin, Director of Intelligence, prepared a brief and a draft of this memorandum for Eisenhower (Chamberlin to Eisenhower, Aug. 26, 1947, P&O 091 Austria, Case 11); a substantially revised version of Chamberlin's draft became the Chief of Staff's memo, as printed here. Eisenhower's paper circulated as JCS 1802.
[2] JCS 1369/6, of August 1, 1945, is in CCS 383.21 Austria (1-21-44).
[3] CCS 271, of July 6, 1943, is in CCS 000.73 (6-26-43).
[4] Lieutenant General Geoffrey Keyes had succeeded General Clark as CGUSFIA on May 17, 1947. See also no. 1155.
[5] This message authorized Keyes to take the actions he had proposed. The Joint Chiefs would approve Eisenhower's recommendation on September 16 and send the message to Keyes in WAR 86392 (see Edwards to CGUSFIA, with enclosure, Sept. 22, 1947, in CCS 000.73 [6-26-43], Sec. 2).

1717   *Eisenhower Mss.*

To Robert Wallace Berry   *September 5, 1947*

Dear Captain Berry:[1] Thank you very much for sending me the report prepared by Edie and Company.[2] I found it most interesting and instructive and am grateful to the Secretary for his thoughtfulness in making it available to me. *Sincerely*

[1] Captain Berry (USNA 1921) was special assistant to Secretary of the Navy Forrestal. During the war Berry had served in the Navy Department's Office of Public Relations in Washington (1940–43) and in the Pacific as commanding officer of the submarine U.S.S. *Proteus* (February–September 1944) and of the attack transport U.S.S. *William P. Biddle* (October 1944–January 1945). He had assumed his present position on July 15, 1947.
[2] On September 2, at Forrestal's request, Berry had sent Eisenhower an analysis of current political developments that the Lionel D. Edie Company (investment advisors in New York City) had prepared. Berry said: "The Secretary places more than ordinary emphasis on this report because this service is very highly regarded by business people. . . ." The report, dated August 28, speculated on the short-term outlook for international affairs, particularly insofar as they might be influenced by the Marshall Plan; in general the report was optimistic about what could be achieved. Eisenhower wrote at the top of the report, "Show this to O.P.D.—then put in my file."

To Joint Chiefs of Staff   *September 8, 1947*
Top secret

Memorandum by the Chief of Staff, U.S. Army:

Subject: Handover of the Italy-Yugoslav Provisional Frontier[1]
    References: a. FAN 759
                b. NAF 1360

1. Paragraph 1 of FAN 759 directs the Supreme Allied Commander, Mediterranean (SACMED), to establish the French Line as recognized by U.S., UK and French members at all points of disagreement as the official provisional boundary line for the Italy-Yugoslav frontier.[2]

2. In NAF 1360[3] SACMED proposes to hand over to the Italians on a line which is the interpretation as understood by the U.S.-UK members of the demarcation of the French Line which the Four Power Commission agreed upon.

3. The Department of State is in receipt of information which leads it to believe that SACMED's proposed line has not been established in accordance with paragraph 1 of FAN 759, and therefore does not concur in the dispatch of the message in Enclosure "A" of CCS 959/75.[4] In lieu thereof the Department of State has requested the transmittal of the message in Appendix "A" of the enclosure. This message is a reiteration of the instructions sent to SACMED in FAN 759.

4. I recommend that the memorandum in the enclosure be urgently considered for immediate presentation to the Combined Chiefs of Staff.[5]

[1] For background see no. 1557. Schuyler prepared this memorandum for Eisenhower; the paper would circulate on September 9 as JCS 1701/18.
[2] The French line is discussed in no. 1504.
[3] In this message General Lee, SACMED, pointed out that in a few sectors the Italians had not agreed to the boundary decisions of the U.S.-U.K.-French members of the Four Power Boundary Commission, even though the Yugoslavs had. SACMED was planning to turn over to the Italians the boundary acceptable to the U.S.-U.K.-French members (NAF 1360, Sept. 2, 1947, in CAD TS Message File, 1942–49; and Norstad to Royall, Sept. 11, 1947, in CCS 383.21 Italy [10-18-44], Sec. 22).
[4] In CCS 959/75 (of September 5) the British Chiefs recommended the dispatch of a message to SACMED accepting the plan outlined in NAF 1360. The U.S. State Department, however, objected ("for political reasons") to the imposition of a boundary that was not acceptable to the Italian government. Lee explained that the French line of FAN 759 had never been defined. At the request of the commander of the British element of the Trieste Free Territory Force (General Airey), the U.S. and U.K. members of the commission had marked their interpretation of the French line on a map (NAF 1368, Sept. 9); and State, *Foreign Relations, 1947*, vol. IV, *Eastern Europe: The Soviet Union*, pp. 95–96).

[5] According to Norstad's memo of September 11 the State Department continued to press its objections and asked the JCS for an estimate of the military risks involved; that same day, however, the State Department cabled the U.S. ambassadors in Italy and Yugoslavia that it had accepted the proposals in NAF 1360. Eisenhower then withdrew his own paper, and the CCS notified Lee of this action in NAF 790 of September 12 (*ibid.*; same file as document; and CCS 383.21 Italy [10-18-44], Sec. 22). The peace treaty, which would go into effect on September 15, would be followed by a series of charges and countercharges concerning border incidents (see CCS 383.21 Italy [10-18-44], Sec. 22).

1719   *Eisenhower Mss.*

To Lucius Du Bignon Clay   *September 8, 1947*
Cable *WAR 85865. Restricted*

CINCEUR, Berlin, Germany for General Lucius D. Clay: Dear Lucius: Thank you very much for your telegram about the historical activity. I quite agree that you have made generous allotment of time and I will make no further suggestions in the matter.[1]

New subject: Walter Lippmann is just starting a European tour.[2] Within a couple of weeks I think he expects to be in Berlin briefly. The results of your conferences with Taylor[3] and Childs[4] were so beneficial that I venture to suggest you have a similar type of meeting with Mr. Lippmann when he arrives. I assure you again I am not trying to impose upon you in these matters. The decision is entirely up to you and I am merely giving you a personal recommendation.

[1] On September 6 Clay had sent Eisenhower his reasons for planning to terminate the German Operational History Project, which involved the preparation of manuscript histories of the war by German generals (Clay Personal Papers, Box 4). He explained that he wanted to end the expensive project to help reduce the costs of the occupation. Moreover, he felt that the work had dragged on far too long and that the preferential treatment necessarily given to the participating German military leaders was misunderstood. Clay had sent his summary in response to an August 30 cable from Eisenhower asking Clay to reconsider his plan to close out the project by December 31. "In the absence of adequate German records," Eisenhower had said, "the reports by these German commanders of their operations are proving to be not only reliable, but the only information we will ever have as to what occurred on the German side. This is our one opportunity to prevent our own military history from being one-sided." The Chief of Staff said the entire undertaking could be finished in six months, and he asked Clay to extend it until July 1, 1948 (COS, 1947, 314.7). In his reply Clay proposed that the data gathering be continued until April 1, 1948, and that the German staff be discharged on that date; he would terminate the rest of the project on July 1, 1948. On November 19, 1947, Eisenhower would again write Clay on this subject; in an effort to prevent "this source of information from drying up entirely" he would ask Clay to see General Malony, Chief of the Army's Historical Division (WAR 90643, EM). The result of Clay's December 1947 conference with Malony was "to transfer the emphasis in the interviews of German generals and staff officers from the historical coverage of German oper-

ations to the study of special subjects of interest and value to the various staff divisions of the Army and to the service schools." Furthermore, the German officers would work in their homes rather than in POW camps (Malony to Bradley, Apr. 22, 1948, in COS, 1948, 314.7). This revised program continued until 1961 (Ziemke, *Stalingrad to Berlin*, p. 512). For a discussion of the contributions German officers made to the history of the war see Pogue, *Supreme Command*, p. 558.

[2] Lippmann had met with Eisenhower in the Chief of Staff's office at 10:30 A.M. this same day.

[3] Henry J. Taylor (see no. 1553).

[4] Marquis Childs (see no. 1664).

1720   *Eisenhower Mss.*

To Roy Allison Roberts   *September 8, 1947*

Dear Roy: It is embarrassing, if not disturbing, to realize that the possibility of a personal political career has developed to the point that you found it necessary to write an article about it. I thoroughly agree with the comment that "draft without artificial stimulus" is not possible in this country. I *know* there will be no stimulus from me; quite the contrary. [1]

In any event, I most profoundly and sincerely appreciate your understanding and particularly your conviction that I am absolutely honest in my repeated refusal to consider the possibility of any type of political career.

Many thanks for your thoughtfulness in forwarding me a copy of the article.

With warm personal regard, *Sincerely*

[1] On September 6 Roberts had sent Eisenhower a story he was publishing in the September 7 *Kansas City Star*. In the article Roberts wrote that Eisenhower was "absolutely honest" about not wanting to be President. Roberts said, however, that in his opinion, Eisenhower would accept "an honest-to-God draft that came from the people without conniving and intrigue. . . ." Such a draft had never occurred, Roberts said, and Eisenhower would not accept a Republican nomination generated by a "phony draft." For background see nos. 1538 and 1625.

1721   *Eisenhower Mss.*

To Willard R. Cox   *September 8, 1947*

Dear Willard: Your letter made me homesick for Wisconsin and the extraordinary group of fine people I met there last summer. [1] During a recent trip to Minneapolis I got a chance to fish for a day and a half on

Brule.[2] It was a most enjoyable experience but of course nothing can ever take the place of the double chance offered in the Minocqua area to spend a summer period under ideal conditions, with gorgeous friends, and with members of my own immediate family.

It was more than kind of Mr. Paget to make such a generous offer with respect to accommodations at the Pierre Hotel.[3] Actually what I rather think we shall do is to attempt to find some out-of-town house, possibly somewhere in the Greenwich area, and spend the severe winter months in the house on the Columbia campus. This would be almost necessary because of the various social demands made upon a couple occupying that position.

I feel quite certain that next summer Mamie will be ready to accompany me to Wisconsin for a short vacation. Two weeks there would, in my opinion, sell her on the delights of the place, even though she has no interest in fishing.

With warmest personal regard, *As ever*

[1] Eisenhower and his brothers had visited Cox's ranch when they vacationed at Big Lake, Wisconsin, in July 1946 (see no. 1019). Cox had written that Milton Eisenhower and his wife had enjoyed their visit this year and that they had missed the General. Cox said, "Milton had excellent fishing—that is—when I went with him" (Sept. 4, 1947, EM).
[2] See no. 1715.
[3] Frank A. Paget, manager of the Pierre Hotel in New York City, had been a summer guest of Willard Cox's. In his letter Cox said that Paget had volunteered to make special rate arrangements for Eisenhower during his tenure as president of Columbia University.

1722   *Eisenhower Mss.*

To Omar Nelson Bradley   *September 9, 1947*
Cable WAR 85895. Confidential

CINCEUR Berlin Germany personal for General Clay from General Eisenhower:[1] The combined veterans organizations in Birmingham, Alabama are staging a very ambitious Armistice Day celebration. Senators Hill and Sparkman are both sponsoring the affair and it is well supported in every direction.[2] They are very anxious to have you as their principal speaker on that day. In view of your present position and its direct connection with veterans and the plans for your coming back to the War Department, I feel that it would be most advisable for you to accept if you are not already completely tied up for that date. I told Senator Sparkman that I would send this telegram and communicate your answer to him as soon as received. I think you know that the Alabama delegation both in the Senate and in the House will be a tower of strength to you during your next 4 years. I hope you will find it possible to give this favorable consideration and will let me have your answer at your earliest convenience.[3] *Regards*

[1] The Chief of Staff asked Clay to "please have the following message transmitted to General Bradley as soon as possible. I do not know whether he is now in your area or has gone to Italy but I am anxious to reach him quickly." On Bradley's trip see *New York Times*, August 16, 1947.

[2] John Jackson Sparkman and Lister Hill, both Democrats, were the U.S. senators from Alabama. Senator Sparkman had seen Eisenhower this same day.

[3] Bradley accepted the invitation in a cable of September 12 (EM).

1723   *Eisenhower Mss., Family File*

TO MILTON STOVER EISENHOWER   *September 9, 1947*

Dear Milton: I inclose a note I have just received from Mr. Harger and a copy of my reply to him.[1] It looks to me like something is getting off the track—I thought we were going to this dinner to honor Mr. Harger. Maybe his note merely represents a successful "cover plan" that someone may have started in the knowledge that preparation for the dinner could not have been concealed from Mr. Harger. I hope that is the case.

Ordinarily I would have no objection to allowing my address at Kansas State to be broadcast.[2] However, this political talk has become so embarrassing, not to say irritating, that in keeping the engagements I have already made I have been insisting upon their remaining completely local in character. I feel and fear that if I should come to Kansas—reported to be the stronghold of sentiment in my favor—and make a talk that would be broadcast to various sections, the action would be interpreted as some kind of a bid for additional publicity, even though I should confine my remarks to the obvious subject of national security in some aspect of its implications upon our daily life. For these reasons I prefer that there be no broadcast of my talk. However, it is quite likely that I shall make my talk from a prepared paper so as to be assured that whatever thoughts I have are clearly presented to the student body. While I like talking "off the cuff" I do realize that a man frequently gets the emphasis in the wrong spot. On such an occasion I should like to avoid this so far as I can.

A note from Willard Cox gave me the impression that the fishing was better than your letter indicated.[3] In any event, you must have had a wonderful time and I envied you all. I did get to spend the afternoon of September 2nd and all day September 3rd on a river in Wisconsin. The visit was merely incident to an engagement of long standing with Carl Gray at Minneapolis.[4]

If you write to any of your Wisconsin friends, give them my warmest regards. As always, my very best to you, to Helen and the children, *Devotedly*

[1] See the following document.
[2] Eisenhower would speak at Kansas State College, in Manhattan, Kansas, on October 25 (see no. 1822).
[3] Milton Eisenhower had written, "The fishing was terrible, but we had a lot of fun anyway" (Sept. 3, 1947, EM). For Cox's opinion see no. 1721.
[4] For Eisenhower's trip to Minneapolis see no. 1715.

1724   *Eisenhower Mss., Family File*

To Charles Moreau Harger   *September 9, 1947*

Dear Mr. Harger: Thank you for your note.[1] I am planning on coming to Abilene when I visit Milton in late October, but it is amazing news to me that I am to participate in any reception as one of the "honorees." Abilene gave me the most heartwarming reception of my life; I hope now that I may be allowed to join the cheering gang for someone else. That will be great for me in one instance—in spite of the fact that he is my brother. I think that there is no man his age I admire more in this world than I do Milton.[2]

In any event, it is going to be a great treat to see you and my other friends in the old town.[3] *Sincerely*

[1] General Eisenhower sent Harger's note to his brother Milton (see the previous document). According to Milton Eisenhower, Harger would not agree to a dinner in his honor and had suggested instead that the dinner honor Milton and Dwight Eisenhower and Deane Malott, president of the University of Kansas (Sept. 16; same file as document).
[2] Milton Eisenhower would write to Harger on September 16 also objecting to Harger's suggestion. Milton recommended that they instead meet informally on October 26 (*ibid.*).
[3] For Eisenhower's visit to Abilene see no. 1822.

1725   *Eisenhower Mss.*

To Arthur Bliss Lane   *September 10, 1947*

Dear Mr. Lane:[1] Many thanks for your letter.[2] I, of course, do not remember the exact quotations you attribute to me. Since one was made to you personally, I assume that you have correctly recalled the sense of my remark and, therefore, I have no objection to its use.

In the second case, the quotation represents my *opinion*, but as a soldier, I could not, and I'm sure, did not, express the idea without the qualifying clause, "in my opinion as a soldier". This, I think, should be inserted—otherwise I would be represented as attempting, inappropriately, to speak for the American people and Government.

I shall look forward to reading your book some day.[3] I'm certain it will be interesting.

With warm regard, *Sincerely*

[1] With the approval of the President, Lane had resigned his post as Ambassador to Poland on March 26, 1947, in order to attack publicly the manner in which the Polish elections in January had been conducted.

[2] In his letter of September 4 Lane asked for permission to quote two statements he said Eisenhower had made in the fall of 1945. During Eisenhower's visit to Warsaw in September of that year, Lane had shown the General the part of the Vistula River that had been controlled by the Warsaw insurrectionists. Viewing the site where the Poles had hoped the Red Army would cross and liberate Warsaw, Eisenhower had commented, "What a perfect bridgehead." The Russian Army had not crossed the river, however, and the Germans had crushed the insurrection. The second quotation was Eisenhower's reaction to a request for American uniforms and equipment for the rebuilt Polish Army. According to Lane, Eisenhower told a visiting Polish general: "Until a true democracy is established in Poland, the American people would not countenance the granting of a credit to the Polish Army." For background on this issue see no. 304. McDuff prepared a draft of this reply, but Eisenhower used only the first sentence and wrote the remainder of the letter himself (McDuff Coll.).

[3] Lane's book, *I Saw Poland Betrayed*, would include the first quotation but not the second.

1726   *COS, 1947, 201 Barnes*

To CHARLES CRAIG CANNON   [*September 10, 1947*]

My own opinion was nothing but impressions—formed on the basis of meager reports and with no knowledge of conditions.[1] I *think* Barnes *was under* MacArthur from about Mar 1, '42.[2]

[1] This was a handwritten note on a September 10, 1947, memo from Cannon to Eisenhower. Cannon said the Personnel Records Board wanted a rating on Colonel (formerly Major General) Julian Francis Barnes. Eisenhower, who had been Deputy Assistant Chief of Staff, War Plans Division, for the Pacific theater from December 1941 to February 1942, was asked to give the rating or to recommend someone who could. Cannon had suggested Lieutenant General George Howard Brett (for background see Chandler, *War Years*) or General Brehon Burke Somervell and said, "At no time was General Barnes under the command of General MacArthur."

[2] Eisenhower was right. According to the *Army Almanac* (p. 612), Barnes had served under MacArthur when he took command of the Southwest Pacific theater

in April 1942. Barnes was Commanding General, U.S. Army Forces in Australia, until the theater was disbanded in June 1945. Barnes, who had become a major general (AUS) in January 1942, was now serving on the War Department Manpower Board. He would retire on October 31, 1947, with the permanent rank of colonel.

1727   *COS, 1947, 320 Monitoring Agency*

To KENNETH CLAIBORNE ROYALL   *September 15, 1947*

Memorandum for the Secretary of War:

Subject: Separation of the Air Force from the U.S. Army.[1]
The attached report of agreements is submitted in accordance with the oral instructions of the Secretary of War issued upon the ratification of the National Security Act of 1947, Public Law 253, 80th Congress.
These agreements are based upon preliminary studies instituted by the War Department such as the report of a Board of Officers, Major General William Hall as senior member, and upon later studies made in the office of the then Under Secretary (the present Secretary) of War. The agreements are in consonance with the testimony given before the Congress in support of the National Security Act of 1947 by Mr. Patterson, Mr. Royall, Mr. Symington, General Spaatz and myself.[2]
Upon receipt of the Secretary of War's oral instructions, General Spaatz and I directed our staffs to prepare jointly, in the form of agreements, the basic policies upon which the United States Air Force would be established separate from the Army and that if any disagreements occurred, they would be presented jointly to us for resolution.[3] I am happy to report that through the able executive direction of my Deputy Chief of Staff, Lieutenant General J. Lawton Collins[4] and the Deputy Commander and Chief of Air Staff, Lieutenant General H. S. Vandenberg and through the spirit of cooperation existing between all elements of the War Department and Air Staffs, agreements have been reached on all basic policies.[5]
General Spaatz and I are in complete accord and recommend that these agreements be forwarded to the Secretary Designate of Defense with the recommendation that he approve them upon the assumption of his duties as Secretary of Defense and that he direct their implementation by the Department of the Army and the Department of the Air Force at such times and dates as are mutually agreed upon between the Chief of Staff, U.S. Army and Chief of Staff, U.S. Air Force.[6]

[1] On September 17 James Forrestal would be sworn in as the first secretary of defense. The next day, in accordance with the National Security Act, the United

States Air Force would come into being as a separate service. (For background see no. 1675.) Stuart Symington was appointed the first civilian Secretary of the Air Force, and Spaatz became the commanding general. Eisenhower's memorandum was drafted by the Army Monitoring Agency, which had been set up to check on the progress in implementing the National Security Act.

[2] See nos. 1396 and 1449. On September 18 Royall would become Secretary of the Army.

[3] Spaatz and Eisenhower also worked on problems involving personnel. Lieutenant General Vandenberg, who had been Director of the Central Intelligence Group since June 10, 1946, had been slated to take "a high post" in the Army Air Force. Spaatz had wanted Vandenberg relieved from the CIG early in the year, but the best that Eisenhower and Spaatz could do was to have Vandenberg take up his new duties as AAF Deputy Commander and Chief of the Air Staff on June 15, 1947 (see Spaatz to Eisenhower, Feb. 13, 1947, including the C/S's pen note on the memo, and Patterson to Eisenhower, Feb. 12, 1947, both in OSW/RPP Gen. Dec. File, 334 Central Intelligence Group).

[4] Collins had replaced General Handy as Eisenhower's deputy on September 1, 1947. See also no. 1755.

[5] The agreements are in the same file as this document. Patterson had been concerned that the Air Force would set up duplicate service units in all areas (see no. 1449). The agreements specified that for the present the Army would continue to provide service support for the Air Force. Each department would try to avoid wasteful duplication. Common service-support units, such as those of the chaplains, would remain with the Army but would include Air Force officers. Only units that were organic parts of an Air Force group or wing, such as the band, would be organized as separate Air Force units.

[6] Royall and Symington would approve the agreements this same day (*ibid.*). At a news conference on September 23 Forrestal would announce that he had approved the agreements but that they were not final and were subject to adjustment. In a letter of October 14 he reminded the Secretaries of the Army and the Air Force of this and also said that the agreements themselves did not transfer any functions from the Army to the Air Force (O&T 320 [11-4-47]). Forrestal, as secretary of defense, would have to order any changes of this sort. He would issue the first such order on September 26, 1947 (P&O 320, Case 27). Other correspondence concerning the separation of the Air Force from the Army is in *ibid.*

The afternoon of September 15 Eisenhower left Washington by plane for Columbus, Ohio, where he spoke to the first national convention of the Air Force Association, a newly formed organization with an initial membership of eighty thousand. General Doolittle, president of the association, had invited Eisenhower in a letter of April 24, 1947, and Eisenhower had accepted in a note of April 28. Correspondence concerning the trip is in COS, 1947, 080 Air Force Association, and a copy of Eisenhower's speech is in EM, Subject File, Speeches.

1728   *Eisenhower Mss., Family File*

To JOHN SHELDON DOUD EISENHOWER AND   *September 15, 1947*
BARBARA JEAN THOMPSON EISENHOWER

Dear Kids: Your next few months, extending up until you finally enter upon your duties at West Point about the first of June, seem to be most terribly complicated. Of course you always have one good hole card in the fact that wherever we might be and whatever we might be doing, Barbara will always be welcomed by Mamie and me to come whenever she can and stay as long as she pleases. Consequently, no matter if we are unsuccessful in working out plans that will keep you constantly together, she can always be certain of the best that the Eisenhower tribe can put out.

One unknown factor is the date of my leaving this job. I have been thinking that I might be able to turn over to General Bradley sometime shortly after the first of the year but I am quite convinced that even if I am able to do it that early I will have to stay here for some little time to accomplish the turn-over smoothly and without a hitch. This will be particularly true because Congress will be meeting again in January. If we knew, for example, that we were actually moving to New York City by the end of January, the problem of a home for you both during the time that John will be attending Columbia would be automatically solved. The house there, as it now stands, is far from attractive—but it is most certainly large.[1] One thought that I have not yet entirely abandoned is that the necessary remodeling and redecorating *might possibly* be completed by that time and if that were the case I am quite sure the Trustees would see no objection to you living there, pending the time I could arrive. However, we cannot depend upon such faint possibilities as these and consequently I think I had better have some of my friends attempt to find a small apartment in the Morningside area that would be reasonable in cost. Unquestionably it would be tiny but certainly would not be too bad for the short period involved, provided I can find it.[2]

The next thing would be the location of Barbara, say from the middle of March onward. There is a wonderful Medical Center at Columbia and I feel that we can count upon the authorities there being more than glad to do anything in the world for a member of my family;[3] but it occurred to me that she might prefer to be near West Point at that time and it was for this reason that I suggested I might try to reserve a small apartment in the Thayer Hotel, say from the middle of March until John reported up there about May 25.

Finally, of course you are going to be concerned in a house or apartment in which to live after you go permanently to West Point. I do not know too much about the countryside but I know that many officers live in Newburgh, Highland Falls and other little towns throughout the region. It would appear that you ought to try to be certain of having one from June 1st onward and again I could have friends of mine begin looking sometime this winter with the idea of getting a nice little place beginning as of that date. If you should like me to do this you ought to tell me what area you would prefer and whether you would rather try for a small house than for an apartment, or vice versa.

I am sure you will understand that in all this I am not trying to be nosy or to interfere in your business—I simply want to be helpful at a time when you are both bound to be most unsettled and will likely have very little time in which to do these things for yourself.

To prevent the using up of too much leave in December and January, G–1 tells me that it is perfectly normal and proper for you to remain at Benning for some days after you finish your school on December 3rd. If you should leave there about the 15th and come to this region to stay with us as long as you please, you are likewise authorized to go to West Point ahead of your Columbia engagement and be there on temporary duty while you get oriented and look around somewhat on your own. In this way you could take just as much leave as might seem most convenient to yourselves and still save up a bit of credit for any emergency that might occur.

In any event, anything that you would like for me to do will be no trouble whatsoever. I have many friends in New York that will be more than glad to help out. Many of them would undoubtedly like to take you in as guests but that is something that I know neither one of you would like. After all, you are entitled to your own home and I am certain that we can get it.

When Mamie and I called you yesterday on the phone we forgot there was an hour's difference in time. That accounts for our calling you as early as we did.

Mamie and I are counting on going to Savannah about the 24th and somewhere around the 1st of October she wants to come over to Columbus to visit with you a little while.[4] It is faintly possible that I might be able to get over for a day but certainly I can't make any definite plans to that effect at this moment. Please do not even mention the possibility because in that event I would have to go through certain formalities that would consume all the time that I might have to spend with you.

Take good care of yourselves and with best love to you both, *As ever*

---

[1] Eisenhower was referring to the house on Morningside Drive that Columbia University provided for its presidents. In a September 10 memorandum (EM, Watson Corr.) Schulz informed the Chief of Staff that "to satisfy the numerous inquiries as to where the President-elect of Columbia would reside, Dr. Butler plans a press release to the effect, 'We expect General Eisenhower to take over Columbia some time after the first of the year, and when he does, we expect to turn over the Morningside Drive residence to him at that time'" (see no. 1700; and *New York Times*, Oct. 7, 1947).

[2] For later developments see no. 1862.

[3] See no. 1861.

[4] See no. 1751.

Eisenhower Mss.

To John Ogden Carley   *September 15, 1947*
Personal

Dear Mr. Carley: I am more than grateful for your understanding
editorial which I find in your issue of September 1.[1] To my amazement
I have found that people who would not think of questioning a man's
word on any other subject, adopt an attitude of complete disbelief when
the subject of personal political ambition is mentioned. For this reason I
am particularly grateful that there obviously remains one man who
continues to have some trust in my honesty; I could not help telling you
so.
    With warm personal regard, *Sincerely*

    [1] In an editorial in the September 1 *Memphis Commercial Appeal*, Carley had
    contended that those projecting Eisenhower "into the national political arena with-
    out his consent are doing him and the Army a great disservice" (EM). For previous
    correspondence between Carley and Eisenhower on this same subject see no. 1614.

COS, 1947, 350.05 TS

To Carl Spaatz   *September 16, 1947*
Top secret

Memorandum for the Commanding General, Army Air Forces:

Subject: Long Range Detection of Atomic Explosions[1]
    The Commanding General, Army Air Forces, is hereby charged with
the over-all responsibility for detecting atomic explosions anywhere in
the world. This responsibility is to include the collection, analysis and
evaluation of the required scientific data and the appropriate dissemination of the resulting intelligence.
    In carrying out this responsibility, the Commanding General, Army
Air Forces, will utilize to the maximum existing personnel and
facilities, both within and without the War Department, will establish
appropriate arrangements with other interested agencies for necessary
assistance and will effect and maintain liaison with all participating
organizations.

    [1] The AEC was concerned that no one government organization had primary
    responsibility for detecting atomic explosions. At the request of the AEC, the
    Central Intelligence Group (CIG) had established a Special Committee on Long

Range Detection of Atomic Explosions in May. The CIG said that a detection system would take two years to install, but the AEC refused to accept that timetable and appealed to the military and to the State Department. The State Department, citing the unproductive U.N. negotiations on control of atomic energy, argued that the United States must know about the Soviet Union's progress (State, *Foreign Relations, 1947*, vol. I, *General; The United Nations*, pp. 829–30; Hewlett and Duncan, *Atomic Shield*, pp. 130–31; and Lewis L. Strauss, *Men and Decisions* [New York, 1962], pp. 202–4). On June 30 the committee recommended vesting responsibility in the Air Force "forthwith" and outlined steps to create a detection system. G–2 and P&O, noting that the Air Force would be able to call upon the resources of the Armed Forces Special Weapons Project, concurred in the committee's recommendation. Royall then informed Eisenhower that he wanted the Air Force to have this responsibility (Hillenkoetter to Secretary of War, June 30, 1947; Norstad to Royall, Sept. 3, 1947; and Royall to Eisenhower, Sept. 5, 1947, all in the same file as this document). The deputy director of intelligence drafted this memorandum for Eisenhower.

1731   *Eisenhower Mss.*

To WILLARD STEWART PAUL   *September 16, 1947*

Memorandum for Director, Personnel and Administration: I have just received from General Ridgway a copy of a special report he has submitted to you on Lt. Colonel Dan Gilmer.[1]

Colonel Gilmer served in important capacities under me during the war and I endorse everything General Ridgway has to say about his unusual capabilities.[2] The only defect then noticeable was an impatience with others less gifted or less devoted to duty than himself, an impatience that sometimes expressed itself in irritation. This, I am informed, has been wholly corrected. I have never known a man more completely devoted to the service and to the constant improvement of his own effectiveness.[3]

[1] A copy of Ridgway's September 15 report on Gilmer is in EM. Ridgway praised Gilmer highly and said that as the chief of staff to the U.S. Army representative on the United Nations Military Staff Committee, Gilmer had played an "important role in the struggle to build an enduring peace." Ridgway thought Gilmer was "conspicuously superior" and recommended that he be promoted to the permanent rank of colonel as soon as possible. Gilmer (USMA 1932) had served as SGS, AFHQ, in the European and North African theaters during 1942 and 1943. A colonel in the AUS since 1942, Gilmer had been assigned as SGS, SHAEF, in 1944; later that year he returned to Washington, D.C., as Chief of the European Theater Section, OPD. In April 1946 Gilmer became Ridgway's chief of staff at the U.N. He had been reduced in rank to lieutenant colonel, AUS, in July 1947.
[2] See Eisenhower's evaluation of Gilmer in Chandler, *War Years*, no. 1767.
[3] Gilmer, who had held the rank of second lieutenant, Infantry, RA, since June 1932, would be promoted to lieutenant colonel, RA, in July 1948.

Eisenhower Mss.

To Roy Edward Larsen   *September 16, 1947*

Dear Mr. Larsen:[1] Upon returning from New York I find that my schedule for early October is not yet completely firmed up.[2] I return to this city from a visit to the south about October 3rd, but have a tentative date involving the 6th, 7th or 8th which cannot be finally fixed until my prospective host, a Chairman of one of the Congressional Committees, returns from Europe.[3]

In these circumstances I can only say that I shall come for your October 8th meeting if it is possible for me to do so. I understand that I am not to be any "principal" speaker but am merely to add my endorsement, from the standpoint of the military service, to the project that you are advancing. I would plan to speak some three or four minutes, most informally.

Unfortunately, I cannot be certain when I can give you more definite information than this; possibly not before the 2nd or 3rd of October. In the event that it should prove impossible for me to attend, would you want me to forward a short statement of endorsement?[4] My concern in your success is very real and I shall be happy to do what I can. *Sincerely*

[1] Larsen (A.B. Harvard 1921), who was president of Time, Inc., was heading the United Hospital Fund of New York. In a telegram of September 15 Larsen had invited Eisenhower to appear at the dinner celebrating the opening of the fund's campaign on October 8. The fund was seeking more than $2 million to meet expected deficits at eighty-nine New York City hospitals.

[2] Eisenhower had been in New York September 11–14 (see no. 1682).

[3] Eisenhower would leave Washington, D.C., on September 23 for a vacation trip to Savannah, Georgia. He would return on October 5 (see no. 1751). On the evening of October 7 the Chief of Staff would co-host a dinner for General Salih Omurtak, Chief of the Turkish General Staff, at the Shoreham Hotel, in Washington, D.C. Omurtak was in the United States to inspect military installations and industrial plants. On October 8 Eisenhower and Bedell Smith would dine at Quarters One, Fort Myer.

[4] On September 18 Larsen replied that he would like to have a written statement in the event that Eisenhower could not attend the dinner. Eisenhower's statement of endorsement would be dictated by Cannon to Larsen's secretary on the evening of October 3. The message read, in part: "Every participant in this campaign, everyone who helps to sustain these free hospitals, will be demonstrating a concern in the American system of individual freedom that 14,000,000 uniformed Americans sustained victoriously against direct threat from Axis powers." Correspondence regarding these arrangements is in EM; also see *New York Times,* October 9, 1947.

To James Stack   *September 16, 1947*

Dear Jim: Please do not interpret my failure to write as any lack of interest in what you're doing or any failure to appreciate the nice letter you sent me not so long ago.[1] Since you know the nature of my daily life, I feel I scarcely need apologize to you.

An hour ago I got back to my office from a trip to Columbus, Ohio. I went there to participate in the opening sessions of the Air Force Association.[2]

Mamie and I were in the New York-Connecticut area on the 11th, 12th and 13th, looking over the countryside with a view of determining where we might live when we go to that region.[3] We have virtually decided to have the town house fixed up first and move in, with the idea that thereafter we will have plenty of time and greater knowledge for the picking of a home that we might want to purchase.[4]

Love to Elsa[5] and the children, and warmest regards to yourself, *As ever*

[1] Stack had retired officially on February 28, 1947, because of poor health, but he had continued as Eisenhower's aide through part of the summer. In July he had moved with his family to Tacoma, Washington (see no. 1607). In an undated note, Stack wrote of the strong sentiment in the Northwest for Eisenhower as President. He said: "Basking in reflected glory as I do, you may be interested in knowing that I have been approached by the local Republican group asking that I run for Congress. In essence, I replied 'no dice.'" Stack asked Eisenhower to call on him if he could ever be of help (Stout to Stack, Aug. 28, 1947, EM).
[2] See no. 1727.
[3] See no. 1682.
[4] See no. 1700.
[5] Stack's wife.

To Milton Stover Eisenhower   *September 16, 1947*

Dear Milton: I did not forget that yesterday you completed your first four dozen years but as I happened to be in Columbus, Ohio, on a very busy day, I did not actually have time to send you a message.[1]

Last evening I fell by accident into a most interesting conversation with three men. One was Tom Campbell from Montana,[2] another was a cotton broker and cotton grower from Tennessee and the third was a Vice President of the Eastman Company who served with me as a general officer during the war.[3] The subject that came up for discussion was what to do about mounting costs of living, particularly food costs. Tom Campbell started us on this involved matter by the casual statement that he was on his way to Washington to testify in favor of governmental price controls for food. Someone very pointedly remarked that anyone who advocated price control also usually had in mind a price floor—and that he was actually more concerned in this guaranteed minimum than he was in the established maximum. In any event, the discussion quickly launched us into the pros and cons of governmental controls and the path toward socialism as opposed to free enterprise and personal initiative.

We covered the water front. England was put on the spit and roasted well, while France and Italy came in also for their share of scorching. It was the kind of thing you would have enjoyed to the utmost, and strangely enough, the cotton broker—who I had no idea knew you—finally brought your name into the conversation. His name is Cook and he lives at Memphis, Tennessee.[4]

The nice part about the conversation was that it was all conducted in the friendliest of tones and in the best of humor. In basic assumptions and purposes there seemed to be no differences whatsoever. The whole thing revolved around methods and particularly the danger of starting certain procedures in time of peace that could never thereafter be wholly eradicated from our economy.

I suppose that most of the conversation, in spite of its interest for me, was mostly froth. In any event, out of it came only one unanimously held opinion. It was that all of us in the United States should eat less and live more frugally. It was agreed that this would not only be better for us physically (in addition we thought also mentally and morally), but that if we could achieve real effectiveness in the saving of food through the voluntary action of the entire American population, it would be a most heartening declaration of the working ability of democracy, even in the solution of problems of an emergency character.

I read in the papers this morning that Senator Taft was castigated in some sections for urging that we do eat less. I don't know exactly what his statement was, but if it was just that, then I agree with him one hundred percent.[5]

My love to Helen and the children, and warmest regards to yourself,
As ever

[1] See no. 1727.
[2] For background on Campbell see no. 408.
[3] For background on Edward P. Curtis see no. 76.
[4] This was probably Everett Richard Cook, a senior partner since 1919 in Cook and Company of Memphis, dealers in raw cotton.
[5] In a speech at Santa Cruz, California, Taft had asked Americans to help bring down rising food prices by eating less, particularly less meat. The CIO and Henry

Wallace had criticized Taft for his statement (see *New York Times*, Sept. 13, 14, 21, 1947). Wallace, Vice-President of the United States from 1941 to 1945, had resigned from the post of secretary of commerce in September 1946. For his career during these years see Edward L. Schapsmeier and Frederick H. Schapsmeier, *Prophet in Politics: Henry A. Wallace and the War Years, 1940–1965* (Ames, 1970).

1735   *ABC 381 United Nations (1-23-42), Sec. 3-F*

To Joint Chiefs of Staff   *September 17, 1947*
Confidential

Memorandum by the Chief of Staff, U.S. Army:

Subject: Provision of Intelligence Material for the National War College[1]
References: a. JCS 369/8
             b. JCS 369/9
             c. JCS 369/10

1. The intent of the memorandum in JCS 369/9 was to disassociate the matter of furnishing intelligence to the National War College from any relationship with Joint Chiefs of Staff papers and thus from the policy in JCS 369/7.[2]

2. The memorandum in the Appendix, JCS 369/9, would authorize the Commandant, National War College, to request intelligence material from the Service best able to fulfill the requirements. I consider that the Commandant as the head of a joint school should be permitted to draw on the resources of all the Services. Therefore, I do not agree that it would be desirable to channel requests as recommended in JCS 369/10.[3]

3. Accordingly, the recommendation in paragraph 3, JCS 369/9, is reaffirmed.[4]

[1] Admiral Hill, commandant of the National War College, in a letter of August 28, 1946, had asked the JCS to direct its intelligence agencies to furnish the college with appropriate intelligence material.
[2] Joint Security Control (in JCS 369/7, of March 27, 1947) had recommended that the JCS furnish copies of selected CCS and JCS papers to the various staff colleges. On May 14, however, the JCS had turned down this recommendation and decided instead that the commandant of each school should forward his requests for such papers to the military head of the service to which the commandant belonged. On the basis of this decision, the JIC proposed that Hill's request be denied (JCS 369/8, June 27). Handy, as Acting C/S, argued against this reply to Hill. In JCS 369/9 (of August 11) Handy proposed a reply that would deny JCS materials but would advise Hill that if he wrote to the military chiefs individually, "intelligence material within the capabilities and security requirements of the individual Services will be furnished the National War College."

³ This was Vice-Chief of Naval Operations Admiral Ramsay's paper, which recommended that all such requests be channeled to the service to which the commandant belonged. Since Hill was in the Navy, all of his requests on behalf of the college would thus have gone to the Navy. All related documents are in CCS 313.5 (2-5-42), Sec. 1. Schuyler prepared a brief and Eisenhower's memorandum, which was circulated as JCS 369/11, of September 20.
⁴ On September 26 the JCS would approve Eisenhower's recommendation and forward its decision to Hill that same day.

1736   *Eisenhower Mss., Routine Corr., Miscellaneous*

To Edward Maher   *September 17, 1947*

*Dear Mr. Maher:*¹ It was nice to hear from you and to learn something of your activities since I saw you at the hospital some months ago.

Your request is one that I cannot consider at this time.² In the first place, I do not yet know when I am to be released from active service and I certainly would not express myself upon the subjects listed in your questionnaire—most of which properly pertain to the functions of the State Department—until after I had become a private citizen. I must adhere to this practice regardless of the proposed date of publication of any views I might express. Secondly, I have always observed the practice of avoiding individual interviews with representatives of the press. You will recall that when we met in the hospital you came as an editor of a magazine merely for a friendly talk involving background and both of us understood that it was not an "interview" and of course you did not treat it as such. I have never broken this rule and could be fairly charged with lack of good faith if I did so now.³

I am naturally sorry to send you such a completely unfavorable reply but I am confident that you will appreciate my position and realize that under the circumstances I can do nothing else.⁴ *Sincerely*

¹ Maher, a former editor of *Liberty* magazine, was now a freelance writer.
² Maher's letter of September 10 said that *Cosmopolitan* magazine had assigned him to do an article about Eisenhower's views on national and world affairs. The article would not be printed until the General had retired to private life as president of Columbia University. Maher, who had met Eisenhower at the Pratt General Hospital in January 1947, enclosed a set of specific questions—for example, "What are the danger signals which will indicate war is near?"
³ The Public Information Division had strongly recommended that Eisenhower refuse Maher's request (see Fitzgerald to Parks, Sept. 11, 1947, EM).
⁴ Maher acknowledged Eisenhower's reply in a letter of September 22, 1947 (*ibid.*).

To Frederick Coykendall   *September 17, 1947*

Dear Mr. Coykendall: I am truly grateful for your complete understanding of my personal position, implicit in your letter of the 15th.[1] Frankly, a brief meeting with the entire Board of Trustees at this time would do little more than to create in me the fear that I might fail to identify some one of them upon a future occasion. I understood from Mr. Dodge[2] that the suggestion concerning the dinner came from you. I am relieved to know that it was merely a passing thought of his own.

While, as you suspect, some Columbia men have approached me with ideas, the occasions for such conversations have been purely informal, with no attempt made to urge upon me specific recommendations. I think most of them realize that I would not even attempt to examine a specific suggestion, in view of my appalling ignorance of college administration.

On the other hand, I would regard it a privilege to have an hour's talk with you. Concerning a number of important details there is considerable confusion in my mind; it would be helpful to discuss them with someone in authoritative position. Should suitable opportunity appear in any of my plans for visiting New York in the future, I will send you timely notice in the hope that we can get together as you have so kindly suggested.

Incidentally, there is one invitation involving Columbia that I have tentatively accepted and in view of what you say in your letter I hope that you will advise me upon the matter either to confirm my action or to suggest that I take some means of eliminating the engagement from my schedule. It is a meeting held by the Alumni of Columbia College in honor of Dr. Fackenthal.

The invitation was issued to me not as the President-elect of the University but as Chief of Staff of the Army, the idea being that I could, in my present position, pay an informal tribute from the Army to a man who has established such a splendid name for himself in the educational world. I am not to be the principal speaker; merely one of half a dozen or so, to each of whom will be allotted one or two minutes. I believe the date is next January 15.[3]

All other invitations from local groups of Columbia alumni I have consistently declined. *Cordially*

[1] Coykendall's September 15 letter concerned a proposal for a dinner at which Eisenhower could meet the trustees of Columbia University. Coykendall wrote, "I think you are busy enough getting out of Washington without trying to acquaint yourself immediately with Columbia University's affairs and people. . ." (EM).
[2] Marcellus Hartley Dodge (see no. 1640).

[3] Coykendall replied that there was no reason for Eisenhower to attend in his capacity as Chief of Staff and that as president-elect of the university, it would be most appropriate for him to make a longer speech rather than be "an 'also ran' with a group of two-minute talkers" (Sept. 19, 1947, EM). In his reply Eisenhower reemphasized his wish to avoid a long speech; he asked that Coykendall "please take no steps to increase the importance of my role in the Alumni dinner in January" (Sept. 22, 1947, *ibid.*). In spite of this firm answer, Eisenhower would receive a December 15 letter from William J. Donovan, chairman of the committee organizing the dinner, explaining that Eisenhower, in his first appearance as president-elect, was to be the honored guest. (For background on Donovan, a New York attorney, see no. 608.) Donovan wrote that he had been told of Eisenhower's reluctance to speak at length. "However, the enthusiasm of our alumni compels me to urge you to permit us to allot you a period of from twenty-five to thirty minutes on our program." Eisenhower persisted. He wrote to Donovan saying that his letter contained "the implication of a slight misunderstanding." Eisenhower flatly refused to attend the function in the capacity of president-elect. "I would seemingly be belittling an individual [Fackenthal] to whom the university owes so much and for whom I have the most tremendous admiration" (Dec. 18, 1947, EM). This final effort on Eisenhower's part would be successful (see *New York Times*, Jan. 16, 1948).

1738

Eisenhower Mss.

To Mabel Eakin

September 17, 1947

Dear Mrs. Eakin: I [am] swamped—and this political turmoil has merely increased my difficulties. I send you the attached as something that will satisfy the club that you've done your part in issuing the invitation![1]

Hope to see you and Roy soon.

[1] Mabel Eakin had called Eisenhower's office on Friday, September 12, to ask if the Chief of Staff could speak to her women's organization, the Washington Club, on November 6 or 20. Cannon suggested to Eisenhower that he send Mrs. Eakin a personal letter explaining that it was impossible for him to accept the invitation (memo, Sept. 13). Parker drafted Eisenhower's formal reply, which was enclosed with this note. All correspondence is in EM; see also no. 1570. For background on Mrs. Eakin see no. 1117.

1739

Eisenhower Mss.

To Willard Stewart Paul

September 18, 1947

Memorandum for Personnel and Administration Division: Herewith records pertaining to the service of Colonel Sidney H. Bingham who occupied a key position in our railroad service of the ETO.[1] In the attached file is considerable evidence of the kind of work that Colonel

Bingham did, particularly in certain of the inventions for which he was personally responsible and which were of inestimable value to us in the invasion. Among these was one that permitted us to land railway equipment in France out of LST's and without the use of docks.

I personally believe that Colonel Bingham earned the Distinguished Service Medal over and over again. I desire that the Decoration Board study this file carefully to determine whether such an award can be issued.

Should the Board desire any information not available in War Department records or in the attached file, I suggest that it communicate promptly with General Carl Gray, who was the operating head of the railway service in France.[2] I am sure that General Gray will be intimately acquainted with the character of Colonel Bingham's service. Colonel Bingham is now a public official in New York City.[3]

[1] Sidney Hedley Bingham, who had been associated with the transportation system of New York City since 1915, was at this time a commissioner on the city's Board of Transportation. During World War II he had served on active military duty in London in the Office of the Chief of Transportation, ETO. He had retired as a colonel in 1945. Bingham had received a Purple Heart, the Legion of Merit, and a Bronze Star, as well as several foreign decorations, including the OBE and the Croix de Guerre avec Palme. Bingham had visited General Eisenhower the morning of September 18.
[2] For background on Gray see no. 1715.
[3] Paul forwarded Eisenhower's memorandum to Major General Bull, president of the War Department Decoration Board. In a memorandum of November 5 (COS, 1947, 201 Bingham) Bull would recommend that the DSM not be awarded. He said that awarding the DSM to Bingham would be inconsistent with previous actions by the Army concerning DSMs for those in similar or higher positions in the Office of the Chief of Transportation, ETO. For background on the questions that had arisen about the DSM see no. 1433.

1740   *Eisenhower Mss.*

To Bernard Mannes Baruch   *September 18, 1947*

Dear Mr. Baruch: Today an officer named Colonel Henry Matchett informed me that he intends soon to seek retirement.[1] He was a brigadier, I believe, during the war and is 56 years old. I know him and Mrs. Matchett very well and can vouch for both as to character and personable qualities. In addition, Matchett has been considered one of our able, splendid officers. He is not the high pressure, breast-beating type but he is thoroughly honest, efficient, and—at least as I found him in Europe—effective.

Because I promised to keep looking around for some individual who might be useful to you in your South Carolina plantation,[2] I am sending his name along to you because I believe him to be the best prospect who has yet come to sight.[3]

With warm personal regard, *Sincerely*

[1] Matchett had entered the Army as an enlisted man in 1916. He had been commissioned as a second lieutenant in 1917 (see no. 1678).
[2] See no. 1740.
[3] Matchett would not retire at this time; and we have found no further recommendations by Eisenhower for the position. Baruch acknowledged Eisenhower's assistance in a letter of September 22, 1947 (EM).

1741   *Eisenhower Mss.*

To Frank Diehl Fackenthal   *September 18, 1947*

Dear Dr. Fackenthal: Your two letters of September 15 have just come to my desk.[1] I find them both intensely interesting and I am struck by the amazing similarity between the problems that are facing you and those that I encounter day by day. Institutions that depend upon public support constantly feel the pinch of money—rather the lack of it.

I know that you sent these documents on to me merely as a matter of information, not for comment. Nevertheless, there is one question affecting the laboratory matter, that instantly occurs to me.[2] It involves the possibility that the Navy Department might find it advisable to contribute another $36,000 on this project in order to secure the added efficiency that the experts visualize. Naturally I know nothing about the legal, practical, or ethical considerations that might apply. But it does seem to me that any service that has over a million dollars invested in a project of this sort would be anxious to know the details of any difficulty, provided a small extra investment would vastly increase the prospects for beneficial results.

The other document gave me my first real information on general considerations affecting tuition levels in our colleges, particularly Columbia. I see what you are up against and though again I speak as a complete novice, I find myself, instinctively, in general agreement with your personal views as they are represented in your addendum to the report.[3]

In this connection I cannot recall whether or not you suggested that I read the recent analysis prepared for you by Mr. Booz and his associates.[4] If you think that I should do so would you please forward to me a copy at your convenience. Sometimes on trains and planes I find an opportunity for a bit of collateral reading.[5] If, however, you believe that the report would be meaningless to me until after I have had a chance to become indoctrinated under your tutelage, please exercise your own judgment in deciding whether or not to send on a copy of the report.

With respect to certain personal problems that present themselves to me from time to time as I plan for my eventual move to Columbia, my chief concern is to secure information without running the risk of appearing either too forward and presumptuous or of unconsciously ignoring the authority and position of anyone who, such as yourself, may feel that his own responsibilities are involved. I have some appreciation of the daily demands upon your time and do not wish to bother you more than is absolutely essential. Yet because I am a rather busy person myself and consequently find it impossible to come to New York to seek advice and information, I am forced to resort to the use of an emissary such as Major Schulz or some other individual in a similar capacity. I want to assure you that in no case am I doing more than to seek, in this vicarious fashion, information that is necessary to me in planning for my future moves. I wonder whether all of the requirements of the situation would be met if I should require that whenever anyone comes to Columbia on any matter connected with my personal business, he first report to you and outline the purposes of his visit. It would seem to me that under some such arrangements as this we would both be certain of staying on the rails and incidentally, of keeping you, as the central focus of Columbia responsibility, fully informed of what I am trying to do.[6]

I shall be more than happy to follow the exact path of any advice you may give me on this and related subjects.

With warm personal regard, *Sincerely*

[1] Fackenthal's letters are in EM.

[2] The Nevis Laboratories were to house a $1.4-million, Navy-funded, cyclotron. The university's Committee on Buildings and Grounds had not approved a requested appropriation to enlarge the facility. Fackenthal hoped that special funds would be made available for the project later. Other related correspondence is in *ibid.*

[3] Fackenthal thought that the tuition increase should not be a general one. Rather than have all students pay six hundred dollars, he suggested, for example, that those in medicine and dentistry pay seven hundred fifty dollars, while those in law pay five hundred dollars.

[4] Assistant Secretary of State William Benton had recommended to Eisenhower that the Chicago firm of Booz, Allen, and Hamilton conduct a study of special problems at Columbia. Coincidentally, Dr. Fackenthal had hired the same firm (see Benton to Eisenhower, Aug. 5, 1947, and Eisenhower to Benton, Aug. 19, 1947, both in *ibid.*). General Eisenhower would meet with Edwin George Booz at 9:30 A.M. on September 19.

[5] In a September 19 letter, Fackenthal promised to send Eisenhower a copy of the analysis by Booz, Allen, and Hamilton as soon as it was ready. He also wrote, "You will henceforth receive all material sent to the Trustees, and . . . I hope you will let me have your comment, whether pro or con, in regard to any matters under consideration by the Trustees." On September 22 Eisenhower replied, asking that

Fackenthal please not bombard him with mail. "While I will greatly appreciate receiving anything you think may be of real value in my education for the new job, I must beg you that under no circumstances must you send me anything except those things you think I should see." In the following months, Fackenthal and M. Hartley Dodge would periodically send Eisenhower letters involving matters of current interest at the university (see, for example, Fackenthal to Eisenhower, Oct. 21, 1947, and Eisenhower to Fackenthal, Oct. 28, 1947). All correspondence is in *ibid*.

[6] Fackenthal agreed that this would be "an excellent way to handle the matter" (Fackenthal to Eisenhower, Sept. 19, 1947, *ibid.*).

17

"I want no part of any political job"

To Walter Bedell Smith   *September 18, 1947*
Personal and confidential

Dear Beedle: Your letter of September 3 has just arrived. It equals its predecessors in interest and information.[1]

It is true that there is a very considerable amount of gossip these days revolving around the subject of my political availability.[2] You can well imagine how irksome it becomes. Harold Ickes is now a columnist and while it is very infrequently that I find myself agreeing with the views that he expresses, he has just written a column on this particular subject.[3] I forward it to you as showing that at least one person understands something of my personal position.

I do not believe that you or I or anyone else has the right to state, categorically, that he will *not* perform *any* duty that his country might demand of him. You did *not want* to become our Ambassador to Moscow. There is no question in my mind that Nathan Hale accepted the order to serve as a spy with extreme reluctance and distaste. Nevertheless, he did so serve. Now in this matter of a political role the question naturally arises, "What circumstances could ever convince you or me that it was a *duty* to become a political candidate?" Certainly I do not see how anyone could obtain a conviction of duty from a deadlocked convention that should name him as a "compromise" selection after great portions of the delegates, representing equally large portions of the population, had failed to secure the naming of their own first choices. Under such circumstances I believe that instead of feeling a call to duty a man would have to consider himself merely a political expediency or political compromise. Consequently, as long as he should feel—as I do—that he does *not* want a political office and does *not* believe himself to be particularly suited for it, I think he would be perfectly within his rights to reject the suggestion.

On the other hand, if you should assume the occurrence of an American miracle of a nature that has never heretofore occurred, at least since Washington, you might have the spectacle of someone being named by common consent rather than by the voice and manipulations of politicians. So-called "drafts", since Washington's time, have been carefully nurtured, with the full, even though undercover, support of the "victim". But I feel that if you or I or anyone else should state, a year in advance of such a faint possibility, that even under such an unmistakable call he would still insist upon following his own personal inclinations, it would be almost the same thing as a soldier refusing to go forward with his unit or a Nathan Hale refusing to carry out the desires of his commander.

This is a laborious attempt to explain something involving a hypothetical situation which, in my earnest conviction, can never occur—certainly not so long as we have eager politicians, earnestly seeking high political honor and who will do their utmost with party machines to secure their own selection. Because of all these factors you will understand also why I make no attempt to elaborate further in the public press on my position. I frequently am flayed because I insist that I do not want to have any political office and still will not use the language of Sherman.[4] The two cases are not parallel.

In any event, I have done my utmost to discourage everyone from even mentioning my name in political connections and I would regard it as the saddest day of my life if ever I should become convinced that I owed it to any considerable portion of the public to lend my name to any political purpose.

I sincerely and honestly believe that America is facing national and international problems of such grave import that little room is left for political maneuvering and struggle within the limits of the broad national interest, which must always govern. There are few people outside the armed services and the higher echelons of the State Department that are giving their full attention to American interests as a whole and refusing to color their conclusions and convictions with the interests of party politics. I should like to be numbered among this disinterested group; regardless of any lack of qualification I may have for service with them, I am still one with them in purpose and desire.

I would scarcely have the temerity to write such a letter to anyone else. You have been so long with me that you will always read from a letter only what I intend to say.

I look forward to seeing you in October. I shall be away from the city a few days in the latter part of the month but aside from that I expect to be here almost constantly. As always, you know that you are welcome in our house. Both Mamie and I would consider it an honor as well as a great privilege to have you stay with us.

My very warmest regards to Norrie and to Ruth Briggs and of course, to yourself, *As ever*

[1] Smith's letter offered his assessment of current Soviet policy (EM).
[2] For example, see no. 1614.
[3] Ickes had resigned from his position as secretary of the interior in February 1946. His column, "Man to Man," was distributed by the New York Post Syndicate. The article in question discussed a press conference at which Eisenhower had been questioned repeatedly about his availability for a nomination. Ickes said that Eisenhower had made his position clear and should now "be let alone" (*New York Post*, Sept. 17, 1947; see also no. 1762).
[4] Ickes had said: "It seems that we have reached a point where no one can be

counted out as a possible candidate for President unless he uses the formula originated by General William Tecumseh Sherman in 1884 when he declared 'I will not accept if nominated and will not serve if elected.'"

1743   *Eisenhower Mss.*

To Davenport Johnson   *September 18, 1947*

Dear Johnny:[1] Thank you very much for your very warm and appealing invitation.[2] I assure you that if ever Mamie and I get into Colorado with a day to spare we will come down to see you and Manon.[3]

You made a sad mistake when you decided that I would "rope easily".[4] There are a thousand influences pulling and tugging throughout the country today and sometimes an innocent bystander gets caught up in some of the cross-purposes. But you may be perfectly certain that Mamie and I fully intend to avoid all type of governmental activity once I have quit this job. Actually one of the big reasons for taking the post at Columbia was that because of the standing of that position we would not be forever harassed by requests to come back into the service for a variety of temporary or semi-permanent tasks.

Years ago I used to come occasionally to Colorado Springs. There was a little town just outside the city called Manitou, I think. We used to stay at a little hotel there and go walking up in the canyons or would take drives around through the various parks. We would very much like to come back to those old scenes.[5]

With warmest regards to you both, *Sincerely*

[1] Major General Johnson (USMA 1912) had served with Eisenhower in the 19th Infantry at Fort Sam Houston in 1915. During World War II he had been Assistant to the Chief of the Air Corps, Washington, D.C. (1940–41); commanding general of the Caribbean Air Command (1941–42); and commanding officer of the Sixth Air Force, Canal Zone (until November 1942). He then became Director of Military Personnel, AAF, a position he held until February 1943, when he became commanding general of the Second Air Force, Fort George Wright, Washington. From September 1943 until his retirement in November 1945 Johnson had been commanding general of the Eleventh Air Force.
[2] In a letter of September 12, 1947, Johnson had invited the Eisenhowers to spend some time at his home in Colorado Springs, Colorado (EM).
[3] Johnson's wife.
[4] Johnson said that for two years he had been telling everyone that Eisenhower had no political ambitions. Recently, however, following the "Draft Ike flurry," he and a friend "sadly came to the conclusion that, from a political standpoint, you would 'Rope Easily.'" He gave Eisenhower the following advice: " 'For God's Sake don't be a damn Fool, turn it down,' enjoy the rest of your life."
[5] Eisenhower was probably referring to his visits to the Doud family home in Colorado.

COS, 1947, 091.711

To Lauris Norstad   [*September 19, 1947*]
Secret

To OPD:[1] This accords very accurately with my current views.[2] Have
you any comment? Is there anything further to be done about it now?[3]

[1] Eisenhower wrote this message on a memorandum sent to him by Lieutenant
General Ridgway on September 19. Ridgway's memo—on the "Proposed U.S.
Contribution to the United Nations Security Forces"—was in response to a request
from Secretary of State Marshall, who wanted to know the reasons for the U.S.
offer of five air wings, one ground corps of two divisions, and one carrier task
group. Ridgway confined his answer to the Army's contribution. He said that a
corps would be "the smallest Army unit of sufficient size to accord with U.S.
power and prestige, to be capable of effective sustained combat for considerable
periods, and to include such supporting services as the American people demands
for its troops." A corps would also have a senior commander who could report
directly to the U.S. government. A division might have a Russian as an intermediate commander, in which case "the U.S. force could expect to be employed in
accordance with Russian standards, with a brutal disregard for the value of American lives and of the persons and property of civilians in the combat area." Ridgway
argued that the United States should keep its contribution "as small compared to
our total forces, as the foregoing reasons dictate." See also L. W. Truman,
Memorandum for the Secretary, Joint Chiefs of Staff, Sept. 30, 1947, with
enclosure, in ABC 334.8 International Security Organization (8-9-44), Sec. 2-H;
and State, *Foreign Relations, 1947*, vol. I, *General; The United Nations*, pp. 662–
70. For background see no. 1198.
[2] At this time neither Eisenhower nor Ridgway could have had much hope that the
long-discussed plans for a U.N. force would be realized. The United States and the
Soviet Union had continued to disagree about the organization and operation of the
proposed force. When the MSC made public its report on this question on April
30, 1947, one of the only areas of agreement was that a U.N. force should be
strong enough to provide some initial opposition to any nation deemed an aggressor
by the Security Council. Such a force, while not so strong as that of several single
nations, might serve as a deterrent and thus increase world confidence and stability,
in which case the need for armaments by individual nations would be diminished
(see United Nations, *Security Council Official Records: Second Year*, special Supp. 1;
and Harrington, *Problem of Disarmament*, pp. 30–55). Military documents outlining the JCS and MSC positions are in CCS 092 (4-14-45), Secs. 15–25; and ABC
334.8 International Security Organization (8-9-44), Secs. 2-E, 2-G, 2-H.
[3] Collins informed Ridgway on September 26 that Eisenhower agreed with Ridgway's analysis and that the JSSC was preparing a formal reply for the State
Department (same file as document). Lieutenant Colonel Louis W. Truman,
secretary of the U.S. delegation to the MSC, included the position paper to be used
in briefing Secretary Marshall on October 3 (memo, Sept. 30, 1947 [see n. 1
above]). The JSSC would approve Ridgway's figures—one element in the MSC
proposal for the entire force (JCS 1670/34, Jan. 2, 1948, ABC 334.8 International Security Organization [8-9-44], Sec. 2-H)—but the question would become
moot when the State Department decided not to press for a General Assembly
resolution calling for each nation to inform the Security Council as to what forces
it would make available to the United Nations. The proposal was dropped when the
United States could not muster the support of England or France (State, *Foreign*

Relations, 1947, vol. I, *General; The United Nations*, pp. 632–42, 677–78, 680–81. See also Wedemeyer to Chief of Staff, Jan. 5, 1948, ABC 334.8 International Security Organization [8-9-44], Sec. 2-H).

1745

Eisenhower Mss., Subject File, Atomic Weapons and Energy

To LAURIS NORSTAD

September 20, 1947

Memorandum for General Norstad: What would you think of suggesting the following for the first paragraph of the attached draft of memorandum, addressed to Lieut. General Brereton?:[1]

"In reply to your memorandum of 4 September 1947 to the Secretary of the Army on the above subject, it is of course the clear legal responsibility of the Atomic Energy Commission to store and maintain atomic weapons. These are to be turned over to the Armed Services only at the direction of the President. However, it is equally clear that the Armed Services could and possibly should act as the agent of the Atomic Energy Commission for the physical guarding and storage of bombs, and if the Commission should so decide, then it would appear easy to work out the necessary arrangements between the Armed Services and the Commission. The Department of the Army is in general agreement with the considerations you advance as applicable to this subject."[2]

It would seem to me that this substitution would make the memorandum one that could be shown to the Atomic Energy Commission in an attempt to secure an agreement. Moreover, it would have the advantage of demonstrating clearly that the Army recognizes at all times the legal responsibilities resting upon the Commission.[3]

[1] Lieutenant General Brereton had been chairman of the Military Liaison Committee to the AEC since November 1946. (For background on his career see no. 177.) At a meeting of August 13 the MLC had requested the AEC's view on a proposal for delivery of completed atomic weapons to the armed forces. The AEC had replied that it was unanimously opposed to such a proposal; nevertheless, on September 4 Brereton had written to Royall and Forrestal recommending that when ready for stockpiling, all completed atomic weapons and parts be turned over to the armed forces "at the earliest practicable date" agreed to by the military and the AEC. The Armed Forces Special Weapons Project (see no. 1520) would assume custody, and the AEC would provide technical assistance "to maintain the weapons in a proper state of readiness." This was the memorandum for which Eisenhower and Norstad were preparing a reply. Norstad had informed the Chief of Staff (brief, Sept. 12) that the AEC questioned "the readiness of the AFSWP to accept custody of the weapons." Norstad felt this view was "unfounded," since the military actually had physical custody. The Atomic Energy Act of 1946 (see no. 920) required presidential action to transfer atomic weapons to the military; a request could be submitted either by the AEC or by the Secretaries of War and the

Navy. But Norstad was worried about "political complications"—for example, if the armed forces recommended transfer of custody and the AEC opposed it. He felt that the War Department should "be more fully advised regarding the views of the AEC. . . ." All correspondence is in P&O 000.9 TS, Case 40.

2 The first paragraph of Norstad's draft had simply said that the Army agreed with Brereton's recommendation.

3 On October 7 Norstad would send Eisenhower a new draft incorporating these revisions. On October 16 Eisenhower would sign the reply to Brereton. Eisenhower's memorandum told Brereton to present any agreements or disagreements to the Army before proceeding to implement the policy. (All correspondence is in *ibid.*; and COS, 1947, 334 Military Liaison Committee TS.) On November 14 Brereton would formally request that the AEC deliver the weapons, but the commission would demur. The question of custody would still be unresolved when Eisenhower left office (Hewlett and Duncan, *Atomic Shield*, pp. 150–53).

1746   *Eisenhower Mss.*

To YOUSUF KARSH   *September 20, 1947*
Personal

Dear Mr. Karsh:[1] I have just examined the portraits in your book, brought to me yesterday by our common friend, Commander Powell.[2] On the artistic side my comment would naturally mean little to anyone, but I cannot forbear saying that, until now, I did not realize how successful the camera could be in producing "speaking" likenesses. I find that of the men you have photographed for the book, I know all but four or five; a goodly number are my warm friends. Consequently I do feel qualified to express an opinion as to the faithfulness of your work, and upon it I most sincerely congratulate you.

A further thought stems out of my belief that through universal widening of understanding and knowledge there is some hope that order and logic can gradually replace chaos and hysteria in the world. It occurs to me that in publishing this book you may have contributed in some definite way toward helping peoples of the world to a better knowledge of each other. The opportunity to examine in one volume the faces of men whose names frequently appear in our newspapers and in those of so many other countries may possibly do something to increase mutual understanding.

Personally I am flattered that you wanted to include a picture of me in your book, but the real reason of this note is to suggest the possibility of universal value in your work.[3] In addition, of course, I wanted to thank you for your courtesy in sending me a copy of the book.[4] *Sincerely*

1 Karsh was an Armenian-born photographer and portraitist who had emigrated to Canada in 1924. He had photographed numerous statesmen and celebrities, includ-

ing Winston Churchill, King George VI of England, Thomas Mann, Albert Einstein, Picasso, and Ernest Hemingway.
2 Karsh's book of photographs was entitled *Faces of Destiny* (Chicago, 1947). Eisenhower had known Captain Bonney Macoy Powell (USNR) in the Philippines.
3 On October 11 Karsh replied, "I have sent a copy of your letter to the Prime Minister of Canada who I know will find your sentiments concerning international understanding a reflection of his own hope and inspiration" (EM).
4 The next day, Eisenhower would fly to Huntington, Long Island, to attend a celebration in honor of Henry L. Stimson's eightieth birthday (see no. 1543).

1747   *COS, 1947, 602*

To Deane Emmett Ackers   *September 22, 1947*

Dear Deane:[1] Many thanks for your recent letter. It is a pleasure to give you what information I can regarding the Topeka Army Air Base.[2]

I am informed that the Air Force now plans to retain the field in an inactive status with the intention of eventually basing one of its units there. This decision would appear to clear the way for C.A.A. approval of the city's plans to repair and expand the municipal airport.

Any joint operating contract which would permit use of the Topeka Base by commercial lines would necessarily be on a temporary basis pending actual use of the field by the Air Force. However, I am advised that the Air Force would give every possible consideration to an application for a revocable agreement which would allow commercial use of their base during the period that construction and repairs were going forward at the Topeka Municipal Airport.[3]

With warm personal regard,[4] *Sincerely*

1 Ackers, president of the Kansas Power and Light Company, had been a high-school classmate of Eisenhower's. For background see Chandler, *War Years.*
2 Ackers had written to find out whether the Topeka Army Air Base would be abandoned. If not, he proposed that "the City of Topeka make a joint operating contract, so that the base could be used by commercial airlines." His interest, he said, was in maintaining good commercial airline service to Topeka while the Topeka Municipal Airport was under repair (Sept. 20, 1947, same file as document; also see *Topeka Daily Capital,* Sept. 19, 1947). Parker drafted this reply for Eisenhower.
3 There are no records at the Philip Billard Municipal Airport in Topeka indicating that this plan was ever implemented (letter from Patsy Smola, Apr. 30, 1977, EP). The Air Force transferred Topeka Air Force Base to the Strategic Air Command (SAC) and reactivated the facility on July 1, 1948 (Thompson to Chief of Staff, USAF, July 12, 1948, and Myers to Commanding General, SAC, July 13, 1948, in AF/AG, 1947, 686 Kansas).
4 Eisenhower added a postscript that read: "Thanks for your personal note. The 'best interests' of this Dickinson Co. boy point straight *away* from any political office." Ackers's personal note is not in EM.

COS, 1947, 201 Breitling

To Joseph Cushman Breitling   *September 22, 1947*

Dear Colonel Breitling: It was good of you to think of our son. We know
that when the occasion comes, he will be proud to wear the leaves you
forwarded and will appreciate greatly the sentiment attached to them.[1]
Mamie and I know well the enormity of the loss you suffered in the
death of your boy, Tod. It would be quite impossible to express the
depth of our sympathy. When our own son, whom you helped bring
into the world in 1917, died some three and a half years later we
suffered a numbing shock that still endures.[2]
Many thanks for your thoughtfulness. *Sincerely*

[1] Lieutenant Colonel Joseph Cushman Breitling, M.D., USA, ret., of Newbury,
Vermont, had written Eisenhower on September 14 (same file as document).
Breitling wanted to give his gold major leaves to John Eisenhower because General
Eisenhower had presented the leaves to him on the occasion of his temporary
promotion to that grade in January 1918. Breitling had hoped to give these leaves to
his own son, Captain George Thaddeus Breitling (USMA 1939), but Tad had died
of wounds aboard a Japanese POW ship in January 1945. Breitling, retired since
December 1938, had written to Eisenhower on this same subject on February 8,
1946. (That letter and Eisenhower's reply of March 2 are in EM, Routine Corr.,
Miscellaneous.) McDuff drafted this letter for Eisenhower.
[2] Doud Dwight Eisenhower (see no. 1667).

1749   *Eisenhower Mss., Dwight D. Eisenhower 201*

To Ho Ying-Chin   *September 22, 1947*

Dear General Ho:[1] I am indeed grateful to the Chinese Government for
conferring upon me the Order of Yun-Fei, Grand Cordon, Special
Class.[2] This is truly a great personal honor and I shall treasure the
decoration through the years to come. It was splendid of you to take the
time from your busy day to come to my office with General Pee[3] and
the officers of your staff to confer the decoration and I truly appreciate
your thoughtful kindness.
    Will you please convey to Generalissimo Chiang Kai-shek my pro-
found thanks for this symbolic expression on the part of your great
country. Also tell the Generalissimo that it is my fervent hope that
China may rapidly overcome her present difficulties and enjoy that
peace and prosperity to which she is so richly entitled.[4]
With kind personal regard,[5] *Sincerely*

[1] Ho Ying-Chin was a former commander in chief of the Chinese Armies. Since
1946 he had been chief of the Chinese Military Mission to the United States and
chief Chinese delegate to the United Nations Military Staff Committee.

² The award had been presented on September 18 at 11:40 A.M. in the Chief of Staff's office. Eisenhower made minor changes in McDuff's draft of this letter (McDuff Coll.).
³ General Peter T. K. Pee, formerly aide-de-camp to Generalissimo Chiang Kai-shek, was the newly appointed Chinese military attaché to the United States.
⁴ In a citation accompanying the decoration, Chiang Kai-shek said Eisenhower's "extraordinary ability and technical skill" had made possible "the defeat of the enemy in Europe with the minimum of losses, hastening thereby the subsequent collapse of the enemy in Asia and the conclusion of the war" (EM).
⁵ On October 6 General Ho thanked Eisenhower for his letter and said that the message had been sent to Chiang Kai-shek (EM).

1750   *Eisenhower Mss., Subject File,*
                                              Clubs and Associations

To Robert F. Warner   *September 22, 1947*

*Dear Mr. Warner:*¹ It was more than kind of your Board of Governors to extend to my family and me honorary membership in the Ardsley Country Club. We are pleased indeed to accept the honor and are very grateful to the Board for their thoughtfulness. Our brief glimpse of the club, last week, left us with a distinct impression of a wonderful setting and an atmosphere of real hospitality.² *Sincerely*

¹ Warner was president of the Ardsley Country Club in Ardsley-on-Hudson, New York.
² The Eisenhowers had undoubtedly visited the club during their weekend house-hunting trip to New York on September 11–14. (For details of this trip see no. 1682.) Eisenhower had also accepted honorary membership in the Greenwich Country Club, Greenwich, Connecticut (Eisenhower to Harvey, Aug. 27, 1947, EM). McDuff drafted these letters for the General.

1751   *Eisenhower Mss., Family File*

To John Sheldon Doud Eisenhower   *September 22, 1947*

Dear Johnnie: It is absolutely impossible for me to write you at·any length at this moment. I am still hoping I get a chance to talk to you while I am in Georgia.¹ However, I cannot count upon this for a certainty because the emergency demands for my presence in Washington are likely to be so insistent at any moment that I may have to come back here on the jump.

A short conversation with the G–1 Division convinces me that you should count upon going to parachute school after you finish at Columbia.² It would take you away from your family for eight weeks but I do not see any other way of crowding it in.

You have misunderstood me slightly about my attitude toward your writing, including a revision of the Moscow story.[3] I would have no objection whatsoever but as I recall the article I would think you would want to revise it a bit, particularly in finding a real excuse for publishing it two years after it was first composed.

If I don't get to see you within a week or two I will write you a longer letter.

Love to you both, *Devotedly*

[1] This was Eisenhower's reply to his son's long letter of September 15 (same file as document). General and Mrs. Eisenhower would visit John and Barbara in Columbus, Georgia, during a vacation trip to Savannah Beach this month (see no. 1774).

The Chief of Staff would leave the Pentagon on the morning of September 23 for a flight to West Virginia University in Morgantown. On his arrival, Eisenhower was met by West Virginia Governor Clarence W. Meadows and West Virginia University President Irvin Stewart. The party proceeded to the campus to inspect an ROTC guard of honor, to meet the university's board of governors, to hold a news conference, and to attend a reception and luncheon for some three hundred people. At 2:00 P.M. Eisenhower was driven to the stadium for a convocation at which Stewart and Raymond Earnest Salvati, president of the university's board of governors, conferred an honorary LL.D. on the General. (Eisenhower's speech is in EM, Subject File, Speeches, and it is summarized in *New York Times*, Sept. 24, 1947. Correspondence and itineraries regarding the trip are in EM; and COS, 1947, 000.8 West Virginia University.) According to Eisenhower's desk calendar, he returned to Washington, D.C., immediately after the convocation and left by plane that same evening for Savannah Beach (see *New York Times*, Oct. 5, 1947). The Eisenhowers would return from Georgia on October 5.

[2] Captain Eisenhower had written that he was interested in attending parachute school: "I have made up my mind that if a ground force officer is going to get along and get the respect an army officer should have, there is no asset like being a qualified jumper." His difficulty was in finding time for the eight-week course before he began teaching at West Point.

[3] John Eisenhower had described his August 1945 trip to Russia in a 7½-page story that he hoped to publish. He said, "I would like to break into the tight writing game and this looks like a rather good chance." He had anticipated several of his father's potential objections and emphasized that he would understand fully if the General thought the article would be inappropriate (for background see no. 704).

1752   *COS, 1947, 333*

To Kenneth Claiborne Royal   *September 30, 1947*

Memorandum for the Secretary of the Army: Attached is a detailed report of an investigation of conditions in the Mediterranean Theater of Operations, accomplished at my direction following the appearance in the public press of a series of highly critical articles written by Mr. Robert Ruark.[1]

The Inspector General invites particular attention to two considerations that, while without bearing upon specific allegations in Mr. Ruark's articles, are important to higher authority in reaching final determination. The first of these is General Lee's long and spotless record of service in the Army in peace and war. Deeply religious, meticulously correct in deportment, fully devoted to the service, his reputation as to character is unimpeachable. The Inspector General implies that such mistakes as may be noted are those of judgment, never of intent. He points out that General Lee, in a position requiring the exercise of tact, judgment, skill and courage in dealing with foreign officials and peoples, some unfriendly, has achieved a notable success for his country.

The second consideration is the special responsibilities devolving upon an army of occupation to maintain a standard of discipline and deportment that might, under different circumstances, be considered extreme if not actually harsh.

In a population composed of those who are friendly and those who are aggressively hostile, the soldier must so conduct himself as to maintain the friendship of the former and, at least, the prudent respect of the latter. I gave this particular item special attention last year during my inspection of the 88th Division in Venezia Giulia.[2] In critical incidents along the Morgan Line in this province and in heavily populated areas throughout the American Zone, the officers and men of General Lee's command have consistently performed with commendable discretion and judgment.

The Inspector General takes up one by one the charges of Mr. Ruark and finds, on the whole, that isolated incidents of maladministration have been so reported as to create the impression of general and widespread deficiencies.

He makes special note of two facts in support of this conclusion. The first is that the percentage of reenlistments from the Mediterranean Theater has been at least as high as in the Army as a whole, indicating a satisfactory state of morale. The second fact is that Mr. Ruark himself has highly complimented the efficiency of 88th Division units, which comprised approximately half of General Lee's American command. The same general theater policies and instructions apply to that Division as to other portions of the force.

The Inspector General specifically disagrees with the allegation that General Lee has lived in extravagant style, or made improper use of such facilities as trains, planes and cars. The evidence submitted seems clearly to justify the Inspector General's conclusions on these items. In this connection, the same type of facilities are used by our commanders in all theaters and, from personal experience, I can testify that without them, no single person could possibly perform the duties we expect and demand of our commanders in each of these critical spots.

The conclusion of the Inspector General is that Mr. Ruark has presented an out-of-focus picture and, stating that deficiencies discovered by official investigation have already been corrected, recommends no further action in the case.

My own comments follow:

While the Department of the Army agrees that the highest standards of conduct must obtain in armies of occupation and, indeed, has insisted that commanders give the matter their earnest and special attention, yet the evidence included in this report clearly establishes the existence of certain errors of omission or commission that could have been corrected. Of these, I note three especially:[3]

1. Undue pressure exercised by commanders to induce subordinates to join fraternal organizations.

Traditionally the Army has frowned upon any attempt to indulge in such practice and the evidence is clear that in this case General Lee did not violate the tradition. However, because he should have realized that an expression of his personal endorsement would in some instances be interpreted by subordinates as a virtual command, he should have taken special steps to see that no such misinterpretation was possible. On this point, I am sending out instructions to the Army.

2. Unsatisfactory conditions in the Theater Disciplinary Camp.

The primary purpose of such camps is to attempt rehabilitation of men who otherwise would be transferred to penitentiaries at home, suffering the stigma of such confinement together with that attached to dishonorable discharge from the Army.

In this particular function the camp in Italy has been equally successful with others established in peace and war throughout the Army organization. A study of the evidence taken by the Inspector indicates, however, that two errors were committed in the conduct of this camp.

a. Minor offenders appear to have been incarcerated where contact was possible with individuals guilty of the most serious type of crime. In view of the extreme youth of the average soldier on occupation, I regard this as a serious mistake.

b. It appears also that the daily routine required of all prisoners was of a very severe order—far more so than justified by the obvious necessity of establishing in the camp the highest possible order of discipline in the performance of daily duty. An active day of seventeen hours does not conform to my convictions of proper, even though strict, treatment of offenders.

Both these points will be brought promptly to the attention of the new Theater Commander with orders for correction.

1944

3. Indifferent or neglectful conduct on the part of some officers in requiring chauffeurs to wait unconscionably long hours to suit the social convenience of the officers.

This offense seems to be of an occasional rather than of a general nature. Officers, on the average, are intensely concerned with the rights and welfare of their enlisted men; but it is undeniably true that the negligence of a few gives substance to allegations of neglect or arrogance on the part of all. Such officers create justifiable resentment on the part of enlisted men and the special attention of the Theater Commander will be immediately directed to it.

Two additional matters of importance were noted by the Inspector General, for which the War Department, rather than the Theater, was responsible:

1. Complaints by a number of enlisted men that promises made upon enlistment have been broken by the Army.

Where such complaints are justified, the fault lies primarily with the Army in the United States. I have long made this matter one of personal attention and shall take steps again to follow up on it.[4] The Army could do no greater disservice to itself and to its personnel than to be guilty of bad faith in this matter.

2. Unfairness and instability in policies applying to the transport of service dependents to Italy.

The Inspector General recites the special uncertainties in the Mediterranean area that have made impossible the maintenance of stable policy, which has naturally caused discontent. Here the principal cause is traceable to a failure of the War Department to inform affected personnel of the reasons for changes in orders and policies. The situation in Italy was so fluid, and the possibilities of such a serious character, that insufficient attention was paid by the Department to the natural reactions of theater personnel and their dependents. Recent instructions for the concurrent movement to the European Command of service personnel and their dependents should greatly reduce such difficulties in the future.[5]

Further Action

Other than to take the corrective steps noted above, I propose no further action except to furnish a copy of the full record to General Lee. He applied, last February, for retirement as soon as his services could be spared by the Department. Because of the close-out of the Supreme Command in the Mediterranean he will soon pass from the active list.[6]

I am impelled to remark that, in a position of grave responsibility and one in which the delicate and critical interests of the United States were involved day by day, General Lee has performed a service to his country which has won the approbation of associates both civilian and military, not only of our own country but of those attempting to work with us. The errors uncovered by the original articles and by the inspection were the exception rather than the rule, and in no case could be traced to wrong intent on the part of the Theater Commander.

Although it is proper and necessary that corrective steps be taken, and that General Lee be informed concerning the Department's attitude and action, to my mind there is nothing contained in any of the evidence procured from a wide variety of sources that constitutes a basis for any further action.[7]

[1] Robert Chester Ruark was a syndicated columnist and author. He had been a newspaperman in Washington, D.C., since 1937, except for the period when he was on active duty with the U.S. Navy during World War II. In a series of five columns published between August 11 and 15, 1947 (in the *Washington Daily News* and other Scripps-Howard newspapers), Ruark had charged that while General Lee and his staff lived in luxury in Italy, the enlisted men in Lee's command lived in terrible conditions and were subjected to continuing mistreatment by their officers. Lee, he said, had condoned and fostered a lavish waste of the taxpayers' money. On August 16 Eisenhower sent Major General Ira T. Wyche, the Army's Inspector General, to Italy to investigate, and Eisenhower discussed the charges at the War Council meeting of August 18 (OSA/KCR Cent. Dec. File, 337 War Council Minutes). The IG arrived in Italy on August 20, and the August 29 *New York Times* said that enlisted men reported a sudden improvement in conditions. Wyche remained in Italy until September 15 and submitted his report to Eisenhower on September 22. Wyche reported that he had personally inspected "every administrative unit of company size and larger in the Leghorn (except unit at Pisa Air Base) and Rome Areas, and practically all of those in the 88th Division—TRUST (Trieste U.S. Troops) Area. I visited their quarters, their latrines, their mess halls and kitchens, their day rooms and clubs, and their other recreational facilities; and I conferred with all U.S. high commanders, the senior British officer commanding and his Chief of Staff, the American Ambassador to Italy, a retired American general officer in charge of CARE in Italy, many junior officers, and hundreds of enlisted men of all grades, concerning the manner in which enlisted men are being treated in the Mediterranean." Wyche and his staff took the testimony of officers and enlisted men concerning specific charges that Wyche had obtained from Ruark. Ruark had given sworn testimony to Wyche, on the condition that he need not disclose the names of his informants.

Wyche concluded that Ruark's articles "were based upon very meager information," that there had been "a few isolated cases of maladministration and probable miscarriages of justice . . . none of which were condoned and fostered by General Lee," that Lee and his staff enjoyed the perquisites of rank but no more, and "that General Lee's administration of the Mediterranean Theater of Operations has been such as to establish and maintain good relations with all Allied Governments concerned, to provide the best housing and general care of all personnel under the conditions confronting him, and to reduce to a minimum miscarriages of justice." Wyche's report is in the same file as this document.

[2] For Eisenhower's inspection trip see no. 1120.

[3] Eisenhower would send orders on these three points to Lee and other theater commanders (see nos. 1770 and 1771).

[4] On Eisenhower's concern about recruiting see, for example, no. 1696.

[5] See no. 1770.

⁶ Lee made a formal response to the IG (Sept. 3, OSW, 47–49, 327.02). Eisenhower's statement to Lee about the investigation is no. 1771. Lee would retire on December 31, 1947.
⁷ Eisenhower was on vacation when he dictated this memorandum. This same day Eisenhower and Collins discussed by phone the changes that Collins and his staff had made in the wording of the memo. Collins said that he had called Roy Wilson Howard, the president of Scripps-Howard newspapers, and "I didn't tell him what the action was—that the action would be completed, and invited him down in your name." Howard, who said he would have to think it over, then called Collins and "said that he really thought it was inadvisable for him to come." Collins had told Howard that it was up to Howard, that Eisenhower had "simply wanted to extend the courtesy to you of seeing the report before it was released. We didn't in any sense want to bargain or to attempt to put you under pressure of any sort." Howard accepted this explanation, but he still decided not to come. Collins and Eisenhower also discussed the problems caused by the fact that Lee was in the United States and wanted to remain in Washington, D.C., until the report was issued. Royall did not want to order Lee out of town, but he did not want Lee to have a press conference. Eisenhower thought that Lee could hold a press conference as an individual, but the Chief of Staff was worried about Lee's possible comments (see telecon transcript, Sept. 30, 1947, same file as document). For further developments see no. 1771.

1753   *COS, 1947, 580*

To Jacob Loucks Devers   *October 6, 1947*
Secret

*Dear Jake:*¹ I appreciate your bringing to my attention the planned allocation of transport aircraft in event of mobilization.² The picture presented was not encouraging and I referred the matter to my staff for comments and further study. I am enclosing a brief of their initial comments.³

The allocation of the capabilities of the aircraft industry to the various types of aircraft is a complex problem requiring continuous study and any decision arrived at is open to attack. Your recommendations on all these matters would be appreciated. In this connection, it may be desirable for you to appear before the President's Air Policy Commission.⁴

Copies of your letter and this reply are being furnished Secretary Royall, Secretary Symington and General Spaatz as you requested.⁵
Sincerely

¹ Eisenhower signed this letter when he returned from vacation at Savannah Beach, Georgia (see no. 1751).
² In his letter of September 20 Devers said he found "disturbing" the plans to produce only 1,085 air transports by M-day (that is, the day of mobilization) plus two years. Devers had obtained his figures "from sources within the War Depart-

ment." He felt the figures "do not reflect the importance given to the subject of air transportability by the Secretary of War and by your office" (same file as document). For background on the mobilization plans see no. 1370.
[3] O&T prepared for Eisenhower a draft response that included a breakdown of planned production. Eisenhower's office rewrote the letter and sent along with it a copy of an undated brief to Eisenhower summarizing the information in the original draft. The actual plans were to produce 2,157 air transports by M-day plus two years. In addition, aircraft would be available in the Air Transport Command, in reserve stocks, and from civilian air lines (same file as document).
[4] The President had established this commission, comprising five outstanding civilian leaders, "to formulate an integrated national aviation policy." The commission had already been in contact with the JCS on an informal basis, and Eisenhower would testify before the commission on November 11 (see Schuyler memorandums for the A/CS, Aug. 5, 15, 1947, and other papers in ABC 360.2 APC [7-15-47]; Finletter to Eisenhower, Nov. 13, 1947, same file as document; and *New York Times*, Nov. 12, 1947).
[5] Representatives of the AGF would testify before the Congressional Aviation Policy Board, and Devers would provide information on the Army's need for air transports. Secretary Royall would later revise the data provided by Devers (see Ruffner, Memorandum for the Secretary of the Army, Dec. 1, 1947; and Royall to the Congressional Aviation Policy Board, n.d., both in the same file as this document).

1754   *Eisenhower Mss.*

To Jacob Loucks Devers   *October 6, 1947*

Dear Devers: This morning the Secretary of the Army brought to me an article in the Washington Post which quotes certain criticisms you have allegedly expressed with respect to extravagance in Air Force plans.[1]

Every Army officer is of course entitled to his own convictions and it is his duty to submit these to proper authority when they have any bearing upon the national security. Where any such suggestion or comment applies to organizations other than the Department of the Army, there are means available in Washington for transmitting communications to the office bearing primary responsibility.

Only damage to the Army can result from public criticism by Army personnel of any sister service. While I have no knowledge concerning the context or purpose of the statements which are purportedly quoted in the article in question, I write this note to remind you of the implications of giving this type of opinion and comment to the press, especially when there exists a normal and effective way of having these opinions considered by responsible authority. *Very sincerely*

[1] The article, "Defense Experts Disagree on Economy—and on Atomic War" by reporter John G. Norris, had appeared in the October 5 edition of the *Washington Post*. Devers had been quoted to the effect that substantial savings could be made in costs for airplanes and for construction of air bases.

Dear Tom: I am glad that you are well settled in your new job and that your first impression is so favorable.[1]

Your leaving here was of course a shock; possibly more so to me than to any other, although the entire Staff misses your friendly guiding hand and the vast store of experience that was so valuable to all of us. Sometimes I wonder whether even my conviction that you deserved a vacation from this maelstrom was sufficient reason for letting you go to another post which, regardless of its importance, deprives us of your daily assistance and collaboration.[2]

There is no officer in the Army today who deserves better of his country than do you; no one has performed services in war and in peace more widely beneficial to all. Your wisdom, your leadership and your extraordinary loyalty and devotion to duty are something that I shall always remember with admiration and moreover, with gratitude, because you so often devoted these qualities to my personal and official assistance.[3]

The Army is fortunate that you have some years of active service still ahead of you.

With warmest personal regard, and affectionate greetings to your wife and daughter, *As ever*

[1] Handy, who had written to Eisenhower on September 19, had assumed command of the Fourth Army at Fort Sam Houston, Texas, the previous day (EM). Collins had succeeded Handy as Deputy Chief of Staff.

[2] Handy wrote, "Everything looks good to me and I couldn't be more pleased. Thanks again for sending me here."

[3] Handy had said of Eisenhower: "It is not your ability, tact, and resourcefulness, as great as they are, which most impressed me. Your great strength and the power of your leadership, I am convinced, have their source primarily in your great moral courage and integrity."

Dear Mrs. Sobolta: You may be confident that the remains to be returned to you for burial in the United States are those of your son.[1] Trained personnel of the American Graves Registration Service have established positive identification through Army identification tags and an identification bracelet found on his body when initially recovered. Identification was verified when the remains were removed to Margraten, Holland, and will again be verified at the time of disinterment for return to this country.

Identification in this case would not be considered complete unless all pertinent factors confirmed such action beyond any reasonable doubt. While I am truly sympathetic in your great loss, I must inform you that no basis exists for a belief that your son may be alive. *Sincerely*

[1] Mrs. Sobolta, of Elizabeth, New Jersey, had written the War Department several times concerning her son. Private Richard J. Sobolta, Company I, 414th Infantry, 104th Division, had died at Eibehshausen, Germany, on March 28, 1945, as a result of gunshot wounds received in action. Eisenhower's office and the Surgeon General's office had responded (see especially Eisenhower's letter of February 11, 1947). On March 4 Eisenhower met with Mrs. Sobolta in his office. After the meeting Eisenhower wrote at the bottom of a March 3 briefing paper from Stack: "Mrs. Sobolta wants her son's body brought back—Have proper person write her & tell her it will be done." On March 4 Eisenhower wrote Terry Allen, who had commanded the 104th Division at the time Sobolta died, and asked him to help gather information about Private Sobolta's death. Allen did so and communicated with Mrs. Sobolta. In a letter of September 15, however, Mrs. Sobolta said to Eisenhower, "I have expressed my doubts to you Sir before, If you recall and now I want positive evidence even if I have to go to his grave an [*sic*] my own expense for identification." All correspondence is in the same file as this document. Eisenhower added the following postscript to this staff-drafted response: "I truly regret that I can hold out to you no hope—I wish I could find any reason for doing so."

1757   *Eisenhower Mss.*

To Frank Diehl Fackenthal   *October 6, 1947*

Dear Dr. Fackenthal: Last evening I had a conference, the purpose of which was to make some estimate as to the time I might expect to be relieved from this post. While we came to no definite conclusion it appears certain that I cannot possibly join you in time to sign the diplomas for the February 1 graduation.[1]

For your information, when the Committee from the Board of Trustees was discussing with me the possibility of my coming to Columbia, it was clearly understood that I would take a period of approximately 60 days between the termination of my duty here and my actual assumption of administrative responsibility at Columbia. It was then suggested by the Committee that I come to the University for an inauguration ceremony as quickly as released here and that my vacation begin immediately thereafter. The members of the Committee expressed their hope that the inauguration could take place about the time of the initiation of the spring term. This, I believe they said, would be in early February.[2]

I assume that as quickly as I can make a really accurate estimate of my date of relief here I should communicate with Mr. Coykendall to determine what the wishes of the Trustees may be. Regardless, however, of the specific arrangements made, it is certain that we will all have to depend upon you to handle all affairs of the University until somewhere toward the end of March, as the earliest possible date that I could really go to work.[3]

With warm personal regard, *Sincerely*

[1] On September 24 Acting President Fackenthal had written Eisenhower that "students will be most anxious to have your signature on their diplomas"; he nevertheless assumed that "these should be again prepared for the signature of the Acting President."

[2] General Eisenhower would write to Thomas J. Watson on October to apologize for his inability to set a fixed date of departure from Washington. He wanted to confer with Coykendall about the inauguration date, but Eisenhower's schedule was so full that he was unable to find time for such a conference. He again mentioned Watson and Parkinson's suggestion about being inaugurated before he took his two-month vacation. Coykendall pointed out, however, that such a plan was highly unsatisfactory: ". . . your assumption of the Presidency will automatically legislate Dr. Fackenthal out of office, and thereafter he will have no administrative position. Were you then to be absent for sixty days, we would be left with no presiding officer during that time" (Coykendall to Eisenhower, Oct. 10, 1947). Eisenhower replied (Oct. 13) that he was in total agreement that fall 1948 was the appropriate time for his inauguration. He was relieved it had worked out this way: "A postponement until next fall will, among other things, permit me to enjoy whatever vacation I may succeed in obtaining for my wife and myself next spring."

[3] On November 22 Eisenhower would again write to Watson: "To my mind, the exact time selected for the formal inauguration is immaterial. It is perfectly obvious that Dr. Fackenthal has to act as President up to the completion of the current academic year, which means that when I first come up there I shall be undergoing a sort of 'indoctrination' course." All correspondence is in EM. For later developments see no. 1878.

1758   *Eisenhower Mss.*

To Arthur William Sidney Herrington   *October 6, 1947*

Dear Art:[1] Your note,[2] forwarded by Mr. Louis Johnson,[3] was on my desk upon my recent return to Washington. Needless to say, I enjoyed it immensely. It carried me back a lot of years.

I hope I may have the pleasure of talking over old times with you when I take over my duties at Columbia.

With warm personal regard, *Sincerely*

[1] Herrington had been a consulting engineer to the motor corps of the U.S. Army and Marines from 1921 until 1931, when he had become president and chief engineer of the Marmon-Herrington Company. He had been chairman of the

company's board of directors since 1940. During World War II Herrington had served for a time as technical advisor to Louis Arthur Johnson, who was President Roosevelt's personal representative in India.

2 Herrington's note read: "I'll bet ten bucks you can't shoot W. Va. jack rabbits as easily as you nailed Wyoming variety in 1919" (Sept. 18, 1947, EM). Herrington's reference was undoubtedly to an incident during a transcontinental military-truck expedition with which Eisenhower had traveled in 1919. For details see Eisenhower, *At Ease*, pp. 162–63.

3 For more background see Chandler, *War Years*.

1759   *Eisenhower Mss.*

To THOMAS STEVEN SMITH, JR.   *October 6, 1947*

Dear Mr. Smith:[1] Many thanks to you and to the students of West Virginia University for your gracious letter. Needless to say, I appreciate it immensely.

I am deeply grateful for the distinction accorded me by the University.[2] It was a real pleasure to meet such a splendid group of college people and, especially, so many veterans of World War II.

I hope you may find opportunity to extend my warm greetings to the student body. *Sincerely*

1 Smith was president of the student body at West Virginia University, where Eisenhower had received an honorary degree on September 23 (see no. 1751). Smith had written on September 30 to thank Eisenhower for the visit. On this same date Eisenhower signed a staff-drafted reply to a letter (of September 24) that he had received from the president of the university. All correspondence is in EM.

2 From this point on, Eisenhower rewrote McDuff's draft of this letter (McDuff Coll.).

1760   *Eisenhower Mss., Family File*

To MILTON STOVER EISENHOWER   *October 6, 1947*

Dear Milton: So far as I am concerned the program you have devised for my visit to Kansas State is completely satisfactory.[1] I have no objection to the open air address Saturday (although appreciating the attendant difficulties) provided, of course, the weather is favorable.

I completely agree with your attitude toward the Abilene meeting.[2] This whole matter of war mementoes is one that causes me some concern. I think your suggestion a good one to bring on a few things at present and merely mention the fact that in the future I will do something further along this line.

As you may know I am terribly rushed after just returning to my office from a 10-day leave but I did want you to know instantly that the program you suggest is O.K.[3]

My love to the family. *As ever*

[1] On September 22 Milton Eisenhower had written a five-page letter concerning the plans for General Eisenhower's visit to Kansas State University (Oct. 24–25) and Abilene (Oct. 26). For background see no. 1723.
[2] Milton Eisenhower's letter had brought his brother up-to-date on the Eisenhower Foundation. He thought it a good idea for the General to come to Abilene during this period of fund raising and to present to the trustees of the foundation a few mementoes, such as a sword or a gun. Eisenhower could then indicate his intention to turn the bulk of his collection over to the foundation at some future date. Milton urged caution: "I think that during your lifetime you should reserve the right to withdraw any particular item, just in case you change your mind regarding it."
[3] On the trip to Kansas see no. 1822.

1761   *McDuff Coll.*

To Leonard V. Finder   *October 6, 1947*

Dear Mr. Finder:[01] Thank you very much for inviting me to participate in the Manchester Community Forum.[2] I am looking forward to this visit with a group devoted to promotion of understanding of world problems. Nothing is more important to us all than development of more understanding. Naturally, I feel especially honored by the opportunity to participate in a public forum in New England, home of the town meeting that cradled our democracy.[3] *Sincerely*

[1] Finder, who had been a public relations consultant in New York City, was now publisher of the *Manchester* (N.H.) *Union-Leader.*
[2] Finder had originally invited Eisenhower to the forum in a letter of July 3, 1947; the General had accepted in a staff-drafted reply of July 10. These letters and other correspondence on the trip are in EM; and in COS, 1947, 080 Manchester Community Forum. Eisenhower revised the staff-drafted version of this letter. On this same day Eisenhower declined an invitation from John Lyon Collyer, president of the B. F. Goodrich Company, Akron, Ohio, to attend a weekend meeting of the Department of Commerce's Business Advisory Council. According to Collyer, who was chairman of the council, the session would be held from October 31 to November 2 at Hot Springs, Virginia (see Eisenhower to Collyer, same file as document; and correspondence in COS, 1947, 080 Business Advisory Council for Department of Commerce).
[3] Eisenhower would leave Washington for Manchester at 2:00 P.M. on October 16. After dinner at the country club, he would speak to the forum at the Manchester Armory and then spend the night at Finder's home. The next morning the General flew back to Washington. Eisenhower's speech is in EM, Subject File, Speeches.

Eisenhower Mss.

To Harold Le Clair Ickes   *October 6, 1947*
Personal

My dear Mr. Secretary: I am indeed grateful for the consideration that
prompted your note to me.[1] It has particular value because of its complete disinterestedness. I agree with your observation that any statement
upon a political subject is always certain to be misconstrued. *Very
sincerely*

> [1] Ickes had written on September 24 urging Eisenhower to reply "no comment" to
> questions about the General's availability for the presidency. He added, "My belief
> is that this would save you a lot of trouble and prevent much misconstruction"
> (EM). For background see no. 1742.

1763   *COS, 1947, 095 Todd*

To E. W. Todd   *October 6, 1947*

Dear Mrs. Todd: Thank you for your thoughtful letter and very generous comments.[1] I experience a feeling of deep and humble pride
whenever I receive a message such as yours, but I have absolutely no
political intentions or ambitions. I should like to keep serving my
country, but in a more nearly private capacity.

I have signed the stamps you enclosed. It was a pleasure to do so for a
Navy veteran and former Kansan—and for his wife. *Sincerely*

> [1] Mrs. Todd, of Fresno, California, had written on September 23 to urge
> Eisenhower to run for President. She asked him to sign an enclosed stamp.
> McDuff drafted a response, but Eisenhower completely rewrote it (McDuff Coll.).

1764   *COS, 1947, 334 Joint Committee
                                                      on Atomic Energy TS*

To Bourke Blakemore Hickenlooper   *October 7, 1947*
Confidential

Dear Senator Hickenlooper: In reply to your request concerning the
matter of Armed Forces' requirements for atomic weapons, I should
like to advise that the Joint Chiefs of Staff have referred this matter to
their principal advisory group, the Joint Strategic Survey Committee.[1]
The problem of estimating these requirements is now under consideration by this group, which is expected to present its recommendations to

the Joint Chiefs of Staff in the not distant future.[2] When these requirements have been reviewed and approved by the Joint Chiefs of Staff and a date for submission to the Atomic Energy Commission is established, you will be informed.[3]

Referring to our earlier conversations, I wish to assure you that I fully appreciate the importance of this matter and the urgent necessity for reaching joint agreement on requirements at an early date. *Sincerely*

[1] Senator Hickenlooper was chairman of the Joint Congressional Committee on Atomic Energy. In a September 4 letter to Eisenhower, Hickenlooper had inquired as to the status of the study on the armed forces' requirements for atomic weapons, a study to which the Joint Chiefs had referred during their meeting with the committee on July 19, 1947. He asked to be informed when the requirements were submitted to the AEC. On September 11, P&O sent Eisenhower a draft response, and on September 15 Eisenhower asked the JCS to approve his reply (JSC 1745/3, Sept. 16). The Joint Chiefs did so on September 22 (ABC 471.6 Atom [8-17-45], Sec. 10; Carroll made minor stylistic changes in the reply).

[2] The JSSC had already studied U.S. needs for fissionable material and atomic weapons during the calendar year 1947. The committee's report (JCS 1745/1, of February 25, in *ibid.*) said that the present supply of atomic bombs was not adequate to meet the security requirements of the United States. American military needs could not be met even if all of the fissionable material produced during 1947 was used in weapons. The JSSC urged early production of sufficient fissionable material. For 1947, all such materials except those needed for "essential research" in medicine and other areas should be used to make atomic bombs. Finally, the JSSC called for a report that would provide long-range estimates of military needs, including schedules for procurement. The JCS had approved this paper on February 26 (*ibid.*).

[3] On October 28 the Joint Staff Planners would give the JCS their estimate of the military requirements for atomic bombs in the event of war. The Planners recommended that the JCS send a memo to the chairman of the AEC informing him of the military's needs. They also recommended that the JCS send a letter to Senator Hickenlooper advising him that the Joint Chiefs had given this estimate to the AEC. The JCS approved the report on October 29, 1947 (CCS 471.6 [8-15-45], Sec. 7). For the Army's problems in gaining custody of atomic weapons see no. 1745. For War Department policy on the use of the bomb see no. 1386.

1765   *Eisenhower Mss.*

TO BRADFORD GRETHEN CHYNOWETH   *October 7, 1947*

Dear Chyn:[1] It would be difficult to describe the degree of interest I found in your letter. You are tackling this educational matter from the angle that I would myself prefer.[2] However, in my case I must not only plunge into a new venture without any special preparation—I have really no time to contemplate the particular type of difficulty in which I may be getting involved.

Should you ever be in Washington, won't you please give my Aide a ring to see whether we could find an hour or two for a conversation. It would be a real treat to talk to you. *Cordially*

[1] For background see no. 759.

[2] General Chynoweth had written that he was on sick leave and that he had been enrolled since February 1947 as a graduate student at the University of California. He was learning a great deal about the educational system. The job of college president, he said, would be harder than that of Chief of Staff, especially if Eisenhower intended to "dig into that racket and change the course of education." Chynoweth hoped some day to see Eisenhower and "compare notes on our educational ventures" (Sept. 21, 1947, EM).

1766   *Eisenhower Mss., Routine Corr., Miscellaneous*

To George T. Bye   *October 7, 1947*

Dear Mr. Bye: From your letter it appears that Captain Butcher has interpreted a comment of mine as a definite intention to begin some writing at an early date.[1] For the next several months I see no opportunity whatsoever to undertake such work.

During a long talk with him I merely indicated the type of arrangement with a publisher or agent that would appeal to me and I did of course state that certain things had arisen during the past two years that had almost determined me to undertake some writing when I could find the time and providing I could get the necessary help.

Under the circumstances I believe it would be almost useless to discuss the subject seriously because my ideas are too hazy to transform into any definite plan. On the other hand, should other business bring you into this city at any time, I suggest a telephone call to my office to see whether it would be possible for us to have a short general chat.

I am of course grateful for your thoughtful consideration.[2] *Sincerely*

[1] Bye, who was a literary agent in New York City, had written Eisenhower on October 3 that he had had lunch with Butcher and was "delighted beyond words to hear that you would like to talk with me about our becoming your agents in 1948" (EM). For background see no. 1405.

[2] Bye replied on October 9 that Butcher had made it clear that Eisenhower would do no writing before the summer, if then. Bye hoped that his letter was "not too impetuous" (EM, Subject File, *Crusade in Europe*). Bye would see Eisenhower in the General's office on November 8.

TO FRANK HODGES *October 7, 1947*
Personal and confidential

Dear Mr. Hodges:[1] Many thanks for your letter.[2] I truly appreciate the spirit in which it was written and am more than grateful for your interest. However, I have no political desires or intentions. Such service as I can render after leaving the Army will be performed, I profoundly hope, as a private citizen.

I thoroughly believe, with you, that the spirit of conciliation must be militantly supported—and I do not consider this statement to be a contradiction in terms.[3] *Sincerely*

[1] Hodges, who was a partner in Hodges Brothers, investors and suppliers of building materials in Olathe, Kansas, was also the editor of the *Johnson County Democrat.*

[2] Hodges's letter of September 27 advised Eisenhower not to run for President, arguing that he could garner no greater glory than he already had. Hodges added, "Great military leaders have never been successful presidents. . ." (EM). Carroll drafted a response, but Eisenhower rewrote all except the first two sentences of the letter (McDuff Coll.).

[3] On October 16 Eisenhower would send Hodges a note of sympathy upon the death of his brother, George Hartshorn Hodges, Democratic governor of Kansas from 1913 to 1915.

TO WILLIAM ELIZABETH BROOKS *October 7, 1947*

Dear Dr. Brooks:[1] Thank you very much for your book on Lee.[2] I shall start reading it almost immediately.

Naturally I have no objection to your quoting anything that I have given in a public talk. I shall examine my files to see whether I have a copy of the address I made at Morgantown and if so shall be glad to send it to you.

With renewed thanks for your courtesy and with warm regard,[3] *Sincerely*

[1] Brooks, a clergyman and author, had been pastor of the First Presbyterian Church at Morgantown, West Virginia, since 1924. He and Eisenhower had met on September 23, when Eisenhower spoke at West Virginia University (see no. 1751).

[2] Brooks had sent Eisenhower a copy of his book *Lee of Virginia*, which had been published in 1932.

[3] In a note of October 9 Brooks thanked Eisenhower and told him he planned to use the speech in his current writing (EM).

To Douglas MacArthur   *October 8, 1947*
Top secret

Dear General: Members of the General Staff who have visited your Headquarters during the past year have discussed informally with you the serious Army personnel shortages which we have been experiencing.[1]

Troop basis requirements furnished by you and other commanders have been carefully studied. As a result of our analysis, I fully agree that these stated requirements are valid and worthy of implementation, supported by every resource of the Army. These requirements can be met with an over-all Air Force and Army strength of 1,070,000 military personnel divided 401,362 Air Force and 668,638 Army.

No difficulty is anticipated in maintaining the Air Force strength for reasons well known. However, our present and predicted recruitment for the Army yields only some 10,000 men per month. We are making every effort and using all means to produce a greater flow of recruits and will continue these efforts. In spite of this, the strength of the Army at this time is 614,184. The 10,000 monthly recruitment rate combined with the great number of separations that are known will give us a strength of approximately 500,000 by June, 1949, an average strength of about 530,000 for Fiscal Year 1949.

After considering these facts, my staff has developed a prediction of personnel strengths for your command for the remainder of Fiscal Year 1948. From this study it appears that your strength may continue to drop until the end of this calendar year, stabilizing then at an Army strength of about 152,000 officers and men.[2] This predicted manning level does not affect your authorized strength which will remain as at present,[3] and you may rest assured every effort will continue to be made to obtain men in sufficient quantities to allow us to bring you back to full strength. However, in view of the anticipated shortages, I feel obligated to give you all information available here so that you may make plans now to take care of such future understrengths as may develop.[4] *Sincerely*

[1] For background on MacArthur's shortage of personnel see no. 1493. P&O drafted this letter for Eisenhower, and Carroll made some minor changes in the message.

[2] The study Eisenhower mentions is discussed in no. 1696. FECOM's manning level for the last half of fiscal year 1948 would be 138,000 enlisted men and 14,000 officers, a total of 152,000.

[3] MacArthur's authorized strength was 189,000 (see no. 1317).

For the attempt to come up with one realistic set of figures (including provision for occupation tasks) for the Regular Army see no. 1852. The strength levels at the time Eisenhower left office are in no. 2039.

1770   *COS, 1947, 333*

To Lucius Du Bignon Clay   *October 8, 1947*
Restricted

Dear General Clay: I have been concerned recently over certain criticism directed at elements of the Army. These reports charged that some officers occupying positions of authority at various levels are failing in their responsibilities toward junior officers and enlisted men. While investigation reveals that, for the most part, these charges are unwarranted, some discrepancies have been found to exist which can provide a basis for justified criticism.[1]

Instances have been reported in which military prisoners have been subjected to unreasonably long hours of activity. In some military prisons insufficient efforts have been made to separate hardened criminals from first offenders. There have been cases where, by inexperience or inadvertence, officers have given the impression, slight but subject to criticism, of using their authority to influence their subordinates to participate in charitable or fraternal organizations.

In certain commands the high percentage of courts-martial cases indicates that the commanders concerned may be placing too great reliance on courts-martial procedures as a means of enforcing discipline. By the same token, the requirements governing saluting and other military courtesies have occasionally been imposed in such a manner as to contribute to an unhealthy feeling of discontent which might impair the discipline and morale which is their only purpose.

The extensive use of government vehicles for semi-official purposes has invited criticism in some instances. The rules and customs governing such use must be based upon a policy of great discretion and a high sense of propriety and must be carefully administered to ensure their complete observance.

My daily mail usually contains several letters from dependents reporting delays encountered in allotment and family allowance payments. Every effort must be made to keep these payments current and, where delays occur, personnel affected should be given every assistance, including initial and follow-up corrective action. In a similar connection, some justifiable complaints have resulted from instability in War Department policies in such matters as transport of dependents. These subjects are receiving my personal attention.

With a million men in uniform in various parts of the world, we are under a constant observation from which we could not escape if we wished. It is not a hostile observation—our own press is as quick to commend as it is to criticize. Investigations which have been made, however, point up the fact that few and relatively minor irregularities can and do result in hasty generalizations which reflect adversely on the entire Army.

It is not intended that the above comments should be interpreted as any indication of a lowering of our traditional high military standards. I am justly proud of the behavior of our soldiers and of the impressions which they have created among the people of all nationalities with whom they have come in contact.[2] *Sincerely*

[1] Eisenhower sent this letter (drafted by Carroll) to all major commanders. See no. 1752; and the following document.
[2] Eisenhower would receive replies from the various Army commanders outlining for the C/S the remedial action being taken; see, for example, Clay to Eisenhower, Nov. 6, 1947 (all are in the same file as this document).

1771
COS, 1947, 333

To Lawrence Carmel Jaynes
October 8, 1947
Cable W 87926. Restricted. Eyes only

To COMGEN MTO Leghorn Italy from Eisenhower signed CSUSA:[1] I have studied the report arising from the recent visit of Major General Wyche to your theater.[2] I note that specific instances of irregularities he discovered have been brought to your attention and that you have already undertaken necessary corrective action. My study of this report indicates several matters which require continuing attention.

One is the necessity for avoiding any impression of the use of official position to influence enlisted personnel or junior officers to become affiliated with fraternal or charitable organizations. In the endorsement of causes, however worthy, commanders must be careful to ensure that the participation of subordinates is wholly voluntary.

While the Inspector General reported that the theater disciplinary camp was well run, I think that the schedule of daily activity, as reported, is unnecessarily long. I also feel that further efforts are required to effect the separation insofar as possible of criminals from younger prisoners serving their first sentence for minor infractions.

Thoughtlessness on the part of some officers in their treatment of chauffeurs, as well as in their extensive use of government vehicles, requires constant attention. Rules and customs concerning the use of government vehicles must be based upon a policy of great discretion and a high sense of propriety, and must be carefully administered to ensure their proper observance.

Other conditions noted may be traced to failure of the Department of the Army to keep the field informed of necessary changes in policies which have sometimes made it impossible for us to carry out promises given or implied to our personnel. These matters are receiving my personal attention.

I am confident of your ability to take care of the problems in your theater and I know you realize how important it is that we avoid giving any cause for public criticism which, though exaggerated in many instances, will at the same time be prejudicial to the prestige of the Army and to the national security.[3]

[1] For background on Major General Jaynes see no. 1397.
[2] Wyche's report is discussed in no. 1752. On October 2, in a memorandum to Eisenhower, Secretary Royall had approved Wyche's report on conditions in the Mediterranean theater. The War Department released the report on October 3. This did not immediately end the controversy, however; some newspapermen labeled the report a whitewash, and General Lee aroused further discussion of the issue when he publicly defended himself (see *New York Times*, Oct. 4, 1947). Major General Parks talked with Lee on October 8 and "strongly urged that in his future meetings with the press he not go into details, but simply state that he had nothing to add to the report of the Inspector General and the action taken by the Secretary of the Army and General Eisenhower" (Parks to Handy, Oct. 8, 1947, same file as document). In his written comment on the IG's report, Lee specifically defended conditions in his theater's disciplinary camp and the conduct of his officers toward their chauffeurs. He did not comment on recruiting for fraternal organizations (Lee to TAG, Oct. 2, 1947, same file as document). Carroll drafted this message for Eisenhower.
[3] General Jaynes replied to Eisenhower's cable on October 16 (F 77694, same file as document). Jaynes reported that "action on all irregularities called to our attention by General Wyche during his visit, as well as the matters mentioned by you, has been completed prior to or since receipt of your message." Specifically, "every semblance of sponsorship or encouragement" by commanders on behalf of fraternal or charitable organizations had been stopped, and the theater had inactivated its disciplinary camp on October 15. Furthermore, the improper use of government vehicles had been "drastically reduced" and would be "entirely eliminated" by October 25.

1772   *Eisenhower Mss.*

To Earl North   *October 8, 1947*

Dear Earl:[1] Thank you very much for your letter. You certainly don't care what kind of a prospect you wish onto a fellow—I want none of it.[2]

What Mamie and I would really like to do is to have a chance to join the colony you talk of in the Maine woods.[3] What a place to spend a summer, particularly if you could ——— [4] in the winter in Texas! It would appear that life isn't going to be that simple for us.

Incidentally, Mamie is spending a week visiting our son and new daughter-in-law in Columbus, Georgia.

With loads of love to Dorothy[5] and, as always, with warmest regards to yourself, *Cordially*

[1] North (USMA 1909) had been a math instructor at West Point from 1913 to 1917, when Eisenhower was a cadet, and had served as the academy's treasurer from 1942 to 1943, when John Eisenhower was there. He had been assigned to the Office of the Chief of Engineers in 1917, and from 1926 to 1929 he had been district engineer of the Territory of Hawaii. In 1930 he was transferred to the Office of the Assistant Secretary of War. Colonel North retired on October 31, 1943, but he remained on active duty until February 29, 1944.
[2] North had strongly urged Eisenhower to run for the presidency (Oct. 5, 1947, EM).
[3] North said he spent his summers in "a little retired Army colony" in New Vineyard, Maine.
[4] A word is blotted on our copy of the letter.
[5] North's wife, the former Dorothy Gatewood.

1773   *Eisenhower Mss.*

To MILTON RICE POLLAND   *October 8, 1947*
Personal and confidential

Dear Mr. Polland:[1] Quite naturally no man could receive a letter, such as you wrote to me on the 29th, without experiencing a sense of personal pride from its flattering implications. I would not want you to think that I am unappreciative of your high opinion but I feel it incumbent upon me to inform you that I have been completely sincere in my attitude that I neither seek nor desire political office.[2]

I most earnestly hope that in the years to come I may be of some usefulness to my country. Having been for 36 years in a service that places duty above all else, it would be entirely out of character for me to attempt completely to "quit". Nevertheless I hold a firm conviction that whatever I can contribute can be best done in a private or semi-private career; I am devoid of experience in the "political" field. Consequently, although I thoroughly understand that the purpose of your letter was not to request my consent for the specific action you propose taking, I cannot fail to tell you that it runs completely contrary to my hopes for my own future.

I repeat my expressions of appreciation for the great compliment you have paid me, just as I repeat the hope that it will go no further.[3] *Very sincerely*

1962

¹ Polland was the general agent of the Security Mutual Life Insurance Company in Milwaukee, Wisconsin. He had organized Wendell Willkie's campaigns in Milwaukee in 1940 and 1944.
² On September 29 Polland had sent a clipping from the *Milwaukee Journal*. The *Journal* story said that Polland had started a campaign in Wisconsin to nominate Eisenhower as the Republican presidential candidate in 1948. In his covering letter Polland said he thought it was much too early for news stories such as the one he had enclosed, but "since the story was to be run in any case," he had insisted that "they include the fact that the consent of the individual was not needed in order to enter a slate of delegates in his behalf" (EM).
³ For subsequent developments see no. 1847.

1774   *Eisenhower Mss., Family File*

To John Sheldon Doud Eisenhower and   *October 8, 1947*
Barbara Jean Thompson Eisenhower

Dear Kids: This is the first time I have had a chance to write a bread-and-butter note to you both so I don't want to miss the opportunity.

It was great to see you two; I wish I could have stayed with Mamie for the week.¹

Today I told Secretary Royall to send the mattress to Captain John Eisenhower at Fort Benning.² I thought that was better than to try to send it to 1336,³ even though it may be a bit of a chore to transport it in your car. Actually I suppose it will be shipped by freight in which event you will merely get a notice and will have to go to the freight depot to pick it up. Secretary Royall left here today to go down to North Carolina for a celebration to which he had invited Mamie. He decided not to bother her any more about it because he figured she would rather spend the time with you two.

Lots of love and many thanks for the nice time last weekend. *Devotedly*

¹ See no. 1728.
² Captain Eisenhower's bedroll was being shipped from Bremerhaven, West Germany, where it had been since his return from Europe (Cannon to John Eisenhower, Sept. 10, 1947, EM).
³ Captain and Mrs. Eisenhower's home address.

1775   *Eisenhower Mss.*

To Ben Hibbs   *October 8, 1947*

Dear Mr. Hibbs: Although I have as yet no definite plans for writing in the near future, I should be very glad to see you when you come to Washington.¹ I shall have to be out of town from October 23 through the 27th, but if you can manage it either before or after those dates, I should like to have you join me for luncheon in my office here in the Pentagon. When you are ready to come down, won't you give my office a call, so that we can set up the engagement.[2] By all means bring along Mr. Smith and Mr. Sommers.[3] *Sincerely*

[1] Hibbs, editor of the *Saturday Evening Post*, had written on October 6 to ask Eisenhower if he could arrange a meeting to discuss the General's writing plans. He asked if he could bring along two of his editors (EM). For background see no. 1594.

[2] Eisenhower would lunch with the Hibbs party on October 28.

[3] Beverly Waugh Smith, Jr., who had served as a second lieutenant in World War I, had obtained his law degree with honors at Oxford University in 1922. After practicing law for three years, he became a journalist, and in 1946 he was appointed Washington editor of the *Post*.

Martin Sommers, who had also served in World War I, had started his journalistic career in 1919 as a reporter for the *Parkersburg* (W. Va.) *News*. He joined the *Post* in 1936 as an associate editor. He took leave to serve in World War II as a lieutenant colonel and rejoined the *Post* in 1945 as foreign and military editor. For later developments see no. 1945.

1776   *COS, 1947, 095 Kittrell*

To W. H. KITTRELL   *October 8, 1947*

Dear Kittrell: Many thanks for sending me the copies of your column and the editorial.[1] I enjoyed them very much. Your Algiers story took me back to those days so completely I could believe we were there yesterday. I'm glad you use the facetious touch on the political angle—I have no intention of getting mixed up in that kind of business.[2] *Very sincerely*

[1] Kittrell, of Dallas, Texas, had written on October 2 enclosing some clippings of the articles he had done on Eisenhower for the *Dallas Times Herald*. He also sent an editorial from the newspaper. McDuff drafted a reply, but Eisenhower rewrote everything except the first two sentences (McDuff Coll.).

[2] Kittrell had written: "As your sincere admirer I note with interest the increasing discussion of you as a presidential possibility, despite your discouragement of such movements. As a sincere Democrat I cannot help but feel a certain uneasiness about it too."

1777   *Eisenhower Mss.*

To JOHN RUPERT COLVILLE   *October 10, 1947*

Dear Mr. Colville:[1] The two charming watercolors of Culzean Castle arrived today and I am more than grateful to you for sending them to me. It was most generous of your cousin to part with them, and I wish you would convey to him an expression of these sentiments. I shall have them framed at once to occupy a prominent place in my library.[2]

Of course I remember you. I should think your present position as Private Secretary to the Princess Elizabeth would be about as interesting (and demanding) as any post to be found anywhere today. If you think it appropriate I would appreciate your presenting to Her Royal Highness my sincere and respectful greetings.[3]

Again, many thanks for your thoughtfulness. *Sincerely*

[1] Colville had met Eisenhower during World War II, while Colville was serving as one of Churchill's secretaries. He was now private secretary to Princess Elizabeth.

[2] In a letter of September 15 Colville had said he was sending two paintings his grandfather had done of Culzean Castle. Colville's cousin, who owned the paintings, thought Eisenhower might like to have them (EM).

[3] In a reply of October 16 Colville said he had conveyed Eisenhower's message to the Princess, "and her Royal Highness desires me to thank you most warmly" (EM).

1778   *Eisenhower Mss.*

To Mabel Frances Doud Moore,   *October 11, 1947*
George Gordon Moore, Jr., Richard Gill, Jr.,
Michael Doud Gill, Ellen Doud Moore,
and Mamie Eisenhower Moore

Dear Mike, Gordon, Richard, Michael, Ellen, Mamie: What a nice surprise to receive today the birthday cards you sent me![1]

I want particularly to congratulate Richard on his elevation to Eagle Scout on the 13th. It is a great honor and all the more notable because it cannot be achieved unless it is *earned*. I shall brag about him to all the people I meet.

Mamie will probably accompany me when I come to Texas early in November. Unfortunately our time will be short; we shall be in Fort Worth throughout the day of the 4th and the next morning early we must take off for Little Rock. From there we return here.[2]

Has Gordon yet received his specific orders for foreign service? If so, when does he leave and by what route will you all travel?[3]

With much love and again, many thanks to each for remembering me so nicely, *Devotedly*

[1] Eisenhower would celebrate his fifty-seventh birthday on October 14. For background on the Moores (whose cards are not in EM) see no. 604. In a note of October 14 (drafted by McDuff) Eisenhower also thanked Major and Mrs. Moore for a gift of a soft leather bottle guard.

[2] For the trip see no. 1839.

[3] Major Moore had been ordered to Panama and would depart from New Orleans on January 24, 1948 (Dept. of the Army, Special Order No. 56, Dec. 5, 1947, and Paul to Crittenberger, Dec. 22, 1947, both in Moore Corr., EM).

1779   *ABC 334.8 Telecom (10-29-43)*

To Joint Chiefs of Staff   *October 13, 1947*
Memorandum. Restricted

Subject: Principles for Joint Communications[1]
        Reference: JCS 1799
    1. I do not consider it appropriate for the Joint Chiefs of Staff to forward the conclusions in paragraph 3, JCS 1799 to the Director (designate) of the Joint Staff.[2] Such action might be interpreted as indicating Joint Chiefs of Staff approval of such conclusions and thus prejudice the freedom of the Director (designate) in formulating his recommendations regarding reorganization of the Joint Staff structure. However, there appears to be no objection to the Joint Communications Board furnishing the Director (designate) its views regarding future organization for coordination of joint communications problems.
    2. With regard to the last line of paragraph 3 of the Principles For Joint Communications in the Enclosure to JCS 1799, I consider this statement might well be deleted since it touches on the functions of the Joint Communications Board, a matter which is already under consideration.
    3. In light of the above comments I recommend, in lieu of the recommendations in paragraph 4, JCS 1799, that the Joint Chiefs of Staff:
    a. Advise the Joint Communications Board that there is no objection to the Board furnishing the Director (designate) of the Joint Staff its views regarding future organization for coordination of joint communications problems.
    b. Approve the Principles for Joint Communications subject to the deletion of the final line of paragraph 3 in the Enclosure to JCS 1799: "...should be made by, a commander senior to those vitally interested, ~~or by the Joint-Chiefs-of Staff-(Joint Communications Board)~~:"[3]

[1] In JCS 1799, of August 22, the Joint Communications Board had argued the case for maintaining a joint communications agency. The board wanted the JCS to forward its arguments to General Gruenther, director of the newly created Joint Staff. (On the Joint Staff see no. 1781.) The JCB also included an enclosure, "Principles for Joint Communications," which it wanted the JCS to approve (CCS 334 CCB [6-25-42], Sec. 8). Schuyler prepared a brief for Eisenhower and drafted

the Chief of Staff's memo. Major William A. Knowlton, Assistant Secretary, General Staff, forwarded the memorandum to the JCS, where it became JCS 1799/2, of October 16 (same file as document; and CCS 334 CCB [6-25-42], Sec. 8).
[2] Paragraph 3 urged the maintenance of "a strong over-all agency, such as the present Joint Communications Board."
[3] Eisenhower wanted the phrase "or by the Joint Chiefs of Staff (Joint Communications Board)" deleted. On October 28 the JCS would approve Eisenhower's recommendations and forward an appropriate memorandum to the JCS (CCS 334 CCB [6-25-42], Sec. 8; and CCS 311 [7-16-47], Sec. 1).

1780

ABC 370.26 Unity of Command, Atlantic (12-11-46)

To JOINT CHIEFS OF STAFF

October 13, 1947

Top secret

Memorandum by the Chief of Staff, U.S. Army:

Subject: Modification to the Unified Command Plan
    Reference: a. JCS 1259/27

1. I note that in JCS 1259/27 the Joint Chiefs of Staff agreed upon the establishment of a Caribbean Command, to include forces in Panama and the Antilles.[1] None of the members of the Joint Chiefs of Staff has, since the date of approval of JCS 1259/27, indicated any change in viewpoint as to the desirability of establishing this command. Although I recognize the fact that there is no military urgency involved, nevertheless, it appears to me that final action implementing the decision of the Joint Chiefs of Staff on 11 December 1946, has already been too long delayed. I therefore, am of the opinion that orders establishing the Caribbean Command should be issued without delay.

2. With reference to the proposed establishment under the Joint Chiefs of Staff of a naval command in the Eastern Atlantic and Mediterranean, this action appears to be in consonance with the policy enunciated in JCS 1259/27 that "all action of strategic significance will be referred to the Joint Chiefs of Staff."[2] Since any movement of our naval forces in the Mediterranean during the present critical period is of considerable strategic significance, I consider it entirely appropriate that the naval forces now in this area be placed under the Joint Chiefs of Staff.

3. I note that the Joint Staff Planners are in disagreement concerning the proposed establishment at this time of an Atlantic Command under the Joint Chiefs of Staff.[3] This disagreement is, in effect, a difference of opinion as to the best type of command structure for forces

operating in the Atlantic and now under the Joint Chiefs of Staff. Since the proposal to establish this command contemplates merely a revision of the command structure already approved in JCS 1259/27 and since all concerned are equally desirous of insuring the most effective operations of U.S. forces in that area, I am confident this problem can be resolved. To this end, I plan to submit in the near future my views on this subject.

4. I recommend that:

a. The Caribbean Command be implemented as a unified command under the provisions of JCS 1259/27.[4]

b. The naval forces of the Eastern Atlantic and Mediterranean be established as a naval command under the Joint Chiefs of Staff with the Chief of Naval Operations designated as the executive agent of the Joint Chiefs of Staff for this command.[5]

c. The decision of the Joint Chiefs of Staff on the question of establishing an Atlantic Command be deferred.[6]

[1] The implementation of the agreement to form a unified Caribbean command awaited a decision by the Army and the Navy as to which naval bases would be exempt from control by the Caribbean commander. (For background see no. 1214.) By late August 1947 the Army felt the planners had resolved the issue, and the chief of the Strategic Plans Branch prepared a memo that included the draft of a JCS paper on this question. The draft of August 21 expressed the same conclusions as this document, but the effort to resolve the issue stalled at this point. Finally, on October 13, General Schuyler, of P&O, prepared a brief, along with a draft of this document, for the Chief of Staff and a covering memo for the Assistant SGS's signature. Eisenhower's paper became JCS 1259/45, of October 16, 1947. All correspondence is in the same file as this document; and CCS 381 (1-24-42), Sec. 7.

[2] Admiral Nimitz had proposed that the U.S. Naval forces in the Eastern Atlantic and the Mediterranean be placed directly under the JCS and that the CNO (Nimitz) be designated as the executive agent of the Joint Chiefs for this command (JCS 1259/38, Aug. 6, 1947, same file as document). The command directive of December 11, 1946, had ordered that any forces not specifically assigned to a unified command would remain under operational control of the separate services, with the proviso that Eisenhower quotes here. Neither the Army nor the Air Force disagreed with this part of Nimitz's proposal (see Schuyler to C/S, Oct. 13, 1947, same file as document).

[3] In JCS 1259/38 Nimitz proposed that the Joint Chiefs transform the Atlantic Fleet into a unified command, the Atlantic Command. When first confronted with this proposition, Schuyler argued that the Atlantic Fleet "should be kept as a strategic striking force and not tied down to any geographical command." Later Schuyler noted that the Army and Air Force planners had raised other questions about the proposal: The limited capability of the Soviet Union in the Atlantic argued against the plan, as did the lack of agreement on means and methods for joint antisubmarine operations; furthermore, there was the possibility that a unified command would hinder air-ferrying operations in the Atlantic (Schuyler to Norstad, July 25, 1947, ABC 370.26 Unity of Command [3-16-42], Sec. 1-B; and Schuyler to Eisenhower, Oct. 13, 1947, same file as document).

[4] The JCS would approve all of Eisenhower's recommendations on October 27. The Joint Chiefs modified the Caribbean agreement on October 29 by approving Nimitz's JCS 1259/47, of October 27, which made clear that the Caribbean

commander could come from the Army, the Navy, or the Air Force. In JCS 1259/48, of October 30, 1947, the JCS made the necessary changes to the Unified Command Plan and informed the commanders of this action in WARX 89419 (also Oct. 30). General Crittenberger was named Commander in Chief, Caribbean (CINCARIB), and Eisenhower was designated as executive agent for the JCS. All correspondence is in CCS 381 (1-24-42), Sec. 7.

⁵ The Joint Chiefs appointed Admiral Richard Lansing Conolly as the commander in chief of the new Eastern Atlantic and Mediterranean Naval command (CINCNAVEASTLANTMED). Conolly had served with the Amphibious Forces, Pacific Fleet, from October 1943 until October 1945. In January 1946 he became Deputy Chief of Naval Operations (Administration), and later he was designated as commander of U.S. Naval forces in Europe and commander of the Twelfth Fleet. Conolly's title was changed on March 15, 1947, to Commander, U.S. Naval Forces, Eastern Atlantic and Mediterranean, and it would be changed again on November 1, the date the JCS directive became effective. For further information on Conolly's wartime service see Chandler, *War Years*. The CNO would be the executive agent for the JCS in this new command.

⁶ At this same time the Joint Chiefs established the Atlantic Fleet as a naval command over all U.S. naval forces in the Atlantic and the Caribbean except those under Conolly and Crittenberger. The JCS named Admiral William H. P. Blandy as commander in chief of the Atlantic Fleet (CINCLANTFLT) and the CNO as executive agent for the JCS. In December 1946 Blandy, who had been Deputy Chief of Naval Operations and commander of Joint Task Force One, assumed command of the Eighth Fleet (later called the Second Task Fleet), operating in the Atlantic. For further background on Blandy see no. 773.

On November 6 Nimitz would renew his proposal for a unified Atlantic command (JCS 1259/49, CCS 381 [1-24-42], Sec. 7). This time the Army retreated. Schuyler advised that "P&O believes that a unified command in the Atlantic is not necessary at this time and its establishment may unduly influence later command arrangements required to implement operational plans. However, P&O considers that in the absence of sound and compelling reasons for opposing the establishment of an Atlantic Command, the Chief of Staff should take no strong position" (Memo to C/S, Nov. 19, same file as document). In the absence of Army or Air Force opposition, the JCS would approve Nimitz's proposition on November 26, 1947. The JCS informed the commanders in WARX 91186 of November 26 and WARX 91239 of November 28. The Joint Chiefs would appoint Blandy as the commander in chief of the Atlantic (CINCLANT). The CNO (Nimitz) would serve as executive agent for the JCS. A press release of December 1 noted that for the time being, Blandy's new command would not carry with it "control over materially larger forces than formerly." All papers are in CCS 381 (1-24-42), Sec. 7.

ABC 321 Joint Staff (7-26-47), Sec. 1

To Joint Chiefs of Staff   *October 13, 1947*
Memorandum. Restricted

Subject: Organization and Functions of the Joint Staff¹

1. The Joint Chiefs of Staff in their directive of 25 August to the Director (Designate) of the Joint Staff indicated his appointment as Director would become effective on a date fixed by the Joint Chiefs of

Staff.[2] I consider General Gruenther's appointment as Director should become effective with the approval of his statement of functions and proposed organization.[3]

2. In referring to the Joint Strategic Survey Committee (paragraph 5 of JCS 1794/4), the Director (Designate) indicates that:

a. He has not shown the location of the Joint Strategic Survey Committee on his proposed chart pending decision by the Joint Chiefs of Staff as to whether the Committee will operate directly under the Joint Chiefs of Staff or the Director. Either arrangement is satisfactory to him.[4]

b. The membership of the Joint Strategic Survey Committee should consist of three or six officers, but for the present it should remain at four (two Navy, one Army and one Air) until further experience has indicated the nature of the workload under the new organization.

3. I consider that:

a. Initially, the Joint Strategic Survey Committee should operate directly under the JCS with provision for a possible later change as the nature of the work of the Joint Staff develops.

b. The membership of the Joint Strategic Survey Committee should be three or six officers, but for the present it should remain at four until further experience has indicated the nature of the workload.

4. I recommend that:

a. The Director (Designate) be appointed the Director concurrently with JCS approval of his recommended statement of functions and organization.

b. Initially, the Joint Strategic Survey Committee operate directly under the JCS with provision for a change at a later date if the nature of the work of the Joint Staff warrants it.

c. The membership of the Joint Strategic Survey Committee be set at three or six, but for the present remain at four until not later than Jan. 1.

d. Recommendations in JCS 1794/4 be approved.[5]

[1] The National Security Act (see no. 1675) had established a Joint Staff to perform "such duties as may be directed by the Joint Chiefs of Staff." The staff, which was not to exceed one hundred officers, was to be apportioned among the three services on an approximately equal basis. The Joint Chiefs would appoint the director, who would be junior in grade to all members of the JCS.

[2] This directive (the enclosure to JCS 1794/1, of August 6) called upon the director (designate) of the Joint Staff, General Gruenther, to prepare a statement detailing the staff's organization and functions (CCS 300 [1-25-42], Sec. 11). Schuyler drafted this memorandum for Eisenhower and also prepared a brief and a covering memo for the C/S.

³ Gruenther had made his recommendations in JCS 1794/4, of October 10 (*ibid.*). Gruenther proposed that the Joint Staff, in conjunction with the JCS committees, function as a planning and coordinating agency of the JCS. The Joint Staff would consist of the director, his two assistants, the secretary, and the following three groups: a Joint Strategic Plans Group (JSPG), a Joint Intelligence Group, and a Joint Logistics Plans Group. A fourth working committee, Joint Security Control, would be abolished, and the JIG and JSPG would take over its functions. A deputy director would head each group. In addition to the JSSC, there would be three senior JCS committees: the Joint Strategic Plans Committee (formerly the Joint Staff Planners); Joint Logistics Plans (formerly the Joint Logistics Committee); and the Joint Intelligence Committee. Each of these senior committees would include the deputy director of the corresponding group of the Joint Staff, and each would be under the authority of the director of the Joint Staff.
⁴ The JSSC was the senior policy planning committee.
⁵ Eisenhower's memorandum, with minor stylistic changes, became JCS 1794/6, of October 15. The JCS would approve Eisenhower's recommendations on October 22. On October 31 the JCS would circulate a memo establishing the three new groups and changing the names of the two senior committees. All papers are in the same file as this document.

1782   *Eisenhower Mss.*

To Bernard Law Montgomery   *October 13, 1947*
Private and top secret

Thank you very much for your letter of September 30.¹ I am more than delighted to accept your invitation for the Army and since you suggested also an Air officer, I will clear the matter with Spaatz who, I am sure, will feel as I do.²

You did not mention a Naval officer and I assume that if the Exercise covers Naval matters, a similar invitation will be sent to Admiral Nimitz.³

The two Army officers and the Air Force officer will be selected at an early date and Bissell will be notified of their names so that the usual arrangements can be made.⁴

With warm personal regard, *As ever*

¹ Montgomery had invited Eisenhower to send two general officers from the Army and one from the Air Force in May 1948 to attend a British Command conference and a training exercise similar to the one Montgomery had conducted in May 1947 (see no. 1622). The exercise, Operation BAMBOO, would simulate mobile operations in the Burma-Siam-Malaya area. Montgomery said that although British commanders from all over the world would attend, "as was the case last year, I cannot let the representative[s] of Foreign Powers attend the exercise. But I always regard the United States as *not* being a Foreign Power. . . ." Montgomery would prefer that Eisenhower send officers who had been in the Far East during World War II. As had been the case the year before, they would have to wear civilian clothes (EM).

² P&O would deal with the Air Force on this matter (see Muir to Wedemeyer, Nov. 4, 1947, P&O 354.2 TS, Case 1/5).
³ General Bissell, the American military attaché in London, would inform Eisenhower in a letter of October 29 that Montgomery did not want a naval officer because the exercise involved only army and air forces. Bowen informed Eisenhower that he would pass the information on to P&O, and Eisenhower responded: "Right—I think that we should notify Sec. Natl. Def. of plan, as matter of secret information" (undated memo). Bowen notified Secretary of Defense Forrestal's office in a top secret memo of December 2 (all correspondence is in EM). Forrestal, who apparently did not receive Bowen's memo, asked Eisenhower on January 23, 1948, about sending a naval officer (COS, 1948, 091.713 Montgomery TS). On January 26 Eisenhower explained the situation to Forrestal (EM).
⁴ The officers would be selected after Eisenhower was no longer Chief of Staff (see no. 2010).

1783   *COS, 1947, 201 Siegel*

TO ARTHUR R. SIEGEL   *October 13, 1947*

Dear Mr. Siegel: Nothing ever causes me greater distress than to be unable to help any veteran, particularly one who has suffered disability in combat, when he makes upon me such a reasonable request as yours.[1] I thoroughly understand your feelings and except for the fact that it would be a violation of existing law, I assure you that I would find some way by which we could take you to visit the grave of your brother. Of course if you were still a soldier we could solve the problem but there is no way, under the law, that we could take you in for the brief period necessary for you to accomplish your purpose.

    I hope you will accept my most profound sympathy in the loss you and your parents have suffered in the death of your brother. I repeat that I fully sympathize with your desire and am truly sorry I cannot do anything. *Sincerely*

[1] In a letter of October 8 Siegel (who lived in New York City) had asked Eisenhower to provide him with transportation "to pay his religious respects" to his brother Jack, who had been killed in France (COS, 1947, Index, 201 Siegel).

1784   *Eisenhower Mss.*

TO ROBERT MAYNARD HUTCHINS   *October 13, 1947*

Dear Dr. Hutchins:[1] It would be futile to attempt to express my appreciation for the time you gave me the other day.[2] It is no exaggeration to say that you provided me with the most interesting hour I have had since my return from Europe. As would be expected, there have since occurred to me numerous topics on which I should have liked to have obtained your views: I have the uneasy feeling that I might have profited more had I talked less and so given you more time to carry the conversational ball.

Over the weekend I read a short article from the Saturday Review of Literature, dated January 13, 1945.[3] Its author was Joseph A. Brandt, who was then, and may still be, the director of the University of Chicago Press. His article was packed full of suggestions and comments that were brand new to me. I don't mind telling you that it succeeded in frightening me very definitely, as I contemplate my next year's change in activity. He ended up with two paragraphs that I wish he had expanded into definite and concrete recommendations. Out of these two paragraphs I quote the following:

"Perhaps the greatest anomaly of democratic America is the continuance of the monarchical system which fetters our colleges and our universities. * * * Courageous educational leaders here and there are making some progress toward breaking the system, and in doing so, liberating the faculty and thus giving the students an example of democracy in action."

"The most important question facing any board of trustees seeking a new president should be * * how clearly he sees the need for educational reform and a restoration of democratic ideals, and how courageously he is willing to battle for them. * * *"

In writing this letter I don't mean to make further inroads on your time, but it occurred to me that if Mr. Brandt is still a member of your organization and if he occasionally comes to Washington, you might suggest to him that I should be more than grateful if he could drop in at the Pentagon to talk to me about some of the matters raised in his article.[4]

Among other things, he frightens me with an implication that the president and his wife, in a university, are more involved in social activity than in anything else! I happen to be one of those who believes that the "fried shirt" dinner is still one of the most abominable tortures that civilization has persisted in carrying over from the Dark Ages.

Again let me express my gratitude for your kindness to me.

With warm personal regard, *Sincerely*

[1] Hutchins (LL.B. Yale 1925) had been a member of the Yale Law School faculty from 1925 until his appointment as president of the University of Chicago in 1929. He had become chancellor of the University of Chicago in 1945.
[2] Eisenhower and Hutchins had had lunch in the Chief of Staff's office on Tuesday, October 7.
[3] The article, entitled "Poison in the Academic Ivy," had been sent to Mrs. Eisenhower by the general secretary of Columbia University, Paul H. Davis. Davis

noted that both the title and some of Brandt's statements were extreme. "But I think his emphasis on the importance of the President's wife is correctly made" (Davis to Mrs. Eisenhower, Oct. 6, 1947, EM).
[4] Hutchins replied that Joseph August Brandt had left the University of Chicago to become president of Henry Holt and Company in New York. "Please see him," Hutchins wrote. "He knows the racket from inside and out" (Oct. 17, 1947, *ibid.*).

1785   *Eisenhower Mss.*

To Robert Sharon Allen   *October 13, 1947*

Dear Colonel:[1] Your letter presents me with a bit of a dilemma for the reason that I have never yet consented to meet any single representative of the press on an "interview" basis or to give any special quotable statement.[2]

I have tried to be perfectly straightforward in the matter and while I have often had personal conversations with individuals of the press, it has been on the definite understanding that no direct quotes were involved and the whole conversation should be treated as background material. On the basis of such interviews, of course, these individuals have often stated that they knew my views to be so and so.

Although, therefore, I would be guilty of bad faith with many others if I should agree to your specific request, I would, on the other hand, have no hesitation in talking to you personally about military subjects, and on the same understanding that I have had with others. If you should wish to pursue this method as an alternative to your original suggestion, it would be simple enough to ask General Parks or somebody in my office to arrange a meeting convenient to us both.

I am sorry I do not feel at liberty to give you a more definitely favorable answer.[3] *Sincerely*

[1] Robert Sharon Allen, a syndicated columnist and author, had begun his career in journalism in 1919 as a reporter for the *Capital Times* in Madison, Wisconsin. He had served on active duty in both world wars. He had drawn upon his experience as a member of General Patton's staff in writing his most recent book, a history of Third Army headquarters entitled *Lucky Forward: The History of Patton's Third U.S. Army* (New York, 1947).
[2] Allen had written Eisenhower on October 3 requesting a statement he could use in an article for *Liberty* magazine on the imminence of war. In a memorandum to SGS, Parks said Eisenhower should not give Allen a statement or any exclusive material. He added, "However, in view of the high standing of Mr. Allen in the writing profession, it is believed that an interview on an 'unattributable' basis may be granted by the Chief of Staff" (Oct. 9). Parks enclosed a draft reply to Allen, but Eisenhower did not use it. All correspondence is in EM; and in COS, 1947, 095 Allen.

Allen replied that he would be "delighted to have the opportunity to talk to you under the conditions you specify" (Oct. 14, EM). Eisenhower and Allen would meet in the Chief of Staff's office on Saturday, October 18.

1786   *COS, 1947, 080 Ta–Tg*

To Texas State Fair Association   *October 13, 1947*
Cable WCL 29255

Texas State Fair Association, Dallas, Texas signed Dwight D. Eisenhower:[1] I regret sincerely that I cannot be present for the Veterans Day ceremonies at the Texas State Fair, but I want to extend my warmest greetings to the Veterans assembled[2] from the state where I was born. It is my great pride that I was permitted to serve with them in a national crisis. My profound admiration and gratitude will always be theirs.

[1] Dale Miller, the Washington representative of the Dallas Chamber of Commerce, had written to General Parks, Chief of the Public Information Division, asking him to forward an attached letter of the same date from Miller to Eisenhower (Oct. 3, 1947, same file as document). Parks and Miller had already discussed the matter. Miller asked for a two-hundred- to three-hundred-word statement from Eisenhower that could be read during the Cotton Bowl ceremonies honoring veterans on October 14. The event would be part of the Texas State Fair exposition. In his letter to Eisenhower, Miller said, "I am fully aware of your reluctance to participate prominently in public affairs particularly at this time, but I am sure you will be equally aware that a purely unselfish tribute to the Veterans of your native State could not possibly be subject to any misinterpretation." Parks advised General Eisenhower not to provide the statement. Parks wrote that he had told Miller that not only would it be inconsistent with previous Eisenhower practice, but "any statement which you might make now would add to the impression on the part of many people that a carefully planned political campaign was being conducted for you. I pointed out that you had drastically curtailed your public appearances in view of this and therefore I was sure you would feel you must decline. . ." (Oct. 3, *ibid.*). Despite Parks's misgivings, Eisenhower had Carroll draft a statement.
[2] From this point on, Eisenhower rewrote Carroll's draft.

1787   *Eisenhower Mss.*

To James Vincent Forrestal   *October 14, 1947*

Memorandum for Secretary Forrestal: I have been considering your proposal to hold an "orientation" meeting for key members of the combined organization that you now head.[1] While I have already expressed to you my approval of the idea, my later reflection has been turned more to your questions as to the composition of the body that should be gathered together for such a meeting.

I feel that the first question that presents itself is whether or not to include key members of all groupments with which you are closely associated as well as those over which you exercise authority, or whether it would be preferable to limit the meeting largely to the military elements of your organization.

I favor the latter course because of the feeling that it will permit a more intimate presentation of your personal and official views. Consequently, aside from key military and civilian members of the Army, Navy and Air Forces, I would recommend that there be included the Executive Committee of the Munitions Board, the Chairman and the Executive Secretary of the Research and Development Board, the members of the Military Liaison Committee (AEC), and the Director and three Deputy Directors of the Joint Staff.

In addition to the above, Admiral Leahy might be invited to the meeting if you should so desire.

For the Army, I would suggest the following:

Secretary	Kenneth C. Royall
Under Secretary	William H. Draper, Jr.[2]
Assistant Secretary	Gordon Gray[3]
Special Assistant to the Secretary	Edwin W. Pauley[4]
G/A Dwight D. Eisenhower	Chief of Staff
Gen. Jacob L. Devers	Commanding General, Army Ground Forces
LG J. Lawton Collins	Deputy Chief of Staff
LG Charles P. Hall	Director, Organization & Training Div.
LG LeRoy Lutes	Director, Service, Supply & Procurement Div.
LG Lauris Norstad	Director, Plans & Operations Division[5]
MG Willard S. Paul	Director, Personnel & Administration Div.
MG Stephen J. Chamberlin	Director, Intelligence Division
MG Henry S. Aurand	Director, Research & Development Div.
LG R. A. Wheeler	Chief, Corps of Engineers
MG Manton S. Eddy	Chief of Information
MG Floyd L. Parks	Chief, Public Information Division
MG Edmond H. Leavey[6]	Chief, Transportation Corps

MG Spencer B. Akin[7]	Chief, Signal Corps
MG Raymond W. Bliss	Chief, Medical Department
MG E. S. Hughes	Chief, Ordnance Department
MG Thomas H. Green	Judge Advocate General
MG Alden H. Waitt[8]	Chief, Chemical Corps
MG Luther D. Miller[9]	Chief, Corps of Chaplains
MG T. B. Larkin	Chief, Quartermaster Corps
BG Cortlandt V. R. Schuyler	Chief, Plans & Policy Group, Plans & Opns. Div.

For the Navy and for the Air, I suggest somewhat similar groups. I realize that at some future time it might be wise to have a meeting that would include representatives of the Department of State, of the Central Intelligence Agency, of the Atomic Energy Commission, and of the National Security Resources Board, but at such a meeting I think that the military representation should be limited to a maximum of five or six for each service. In the present instance I believe that to include all these associated groups would merely compel such a diffusion of interest as partially to defeat the purpose of a "team" talk.[10]

[1] Secretary of Defense Forrestal had probably talked previously to Eisenhower about this meeting. The Chief of Staff had asked General Gruenther for a list of those who he felt should attend. Gruenther sent a list of ninety-two persons, including representatives from the Navy and the Air Force, as well as the organizations listed in the last paragraph of Eisenhower's letter (Oct. 13, COS, 1947, 337).
[2] Major General Draper had been economic advisor to the commander in chief of the ETO before he assumed his present position on August 29, 1947. For background see no. 397.
[3] Gordon Gray (LL.B. Yale 1933) had practiced law in North Carolina (1933–37) and had been president and publisher of the Piedmont Publishing Company, the *Winston-Salem Journal*, and the *Twin City Sentinel* (1935–47). On September 24, 1947, he had become Assistant Secretary of the Army.
[4] Pauley had served as an advisor to Secretary of State Marshall on questions involving reparations. He had been appointed special assistant to Royall in September. For background see no. 793.
[5] On October 1, 1947, Norstad had been promoted to lieutenant general.
[6] Edmond Harrison Leavey (USMA 1917; C. E. Rensselaer Polytechnic Institute 1922) had served during World War II in the European, African, and Pacific theaters. In May 1945 he became deputy commander and Chief of Staff of the U.S. Army Forces in the Western Pacific. Leavey had become Chief of the Transportation Corps in December 1945. For further background see Chandler, *War Years*.
[7] On April 1, 1947, Akin had become chief signal officer. For background see no. 537.
[8] Alden Hardy Waitt (M.S. Massachusetts Institute of Technology 1926) had become Chief of the Chemical Corps on November 29, 1945. From 1941 to 1942 Waitt had served with the WDGS G–3 Division, and subsequently he had been executive officer and then Chief of the Field Service in the Chemical War Service. In 1943 he had become Assistant Chief of the Chemical War Service in charge of field operations.
[9] Luther Deck Miller (B.D. Chicago Theological Seminary 1917) had been com-

missioned a first lieutenant in 1918. He had served in the southwest Pacific during World War II, and had been named Chief of Chaplains on July 9, 1945.
[10] Forrestal would hold a "unification team get-together" on November 20. The meeting proved somewhat disappointing, however, because the participants congregated "at the bars at the two extreme ends" of Forrestal's Pentagon suite, and the Secretary of Defense was forced to go "back and forth between the two groups at either end" (see Buchanan to McNeil *et al.*, Oct. 28, 1947, OS/D, Aides' Chron. File, 47–50, Buchanan; and Buchanan to Royall *et al.*, Nov. 10, 1947, and Buchanan to McNeil *et al.*, Nov. 21, 1947, OS/D, Reading Files, 46–50, Buchanan).

1788   *Eisenhower Mss.*

To John Heddon   *October 14, 1947*

Dear Mr. Heddon: I do not know how to thank you for sending me the fine fishing rod for my birthday. It is truly a splendid gift and I am more than grateful for your kindness.[1]

The rod is beautifully balanced and I shall have a struggle with an impatient temperament until I get to use it. I have never before had a rod with a name plate; think of the fun I'll have showing it off! Thank you again for remembering me so nicely. *Sincerely*

[1] John Heddon was president of James Heddon's Sons of Dowagiac, Michigan, makers of "high grade fishing tackle and steel golf shafts." Heddon wrote, ". . . this rod is called 'The Rod with the Fighting Heart' and is therefore quite appropriate for 'fighting General Ike'" (Oct. 13, 1947, EM). McDuff drafted this reply, and Eisenhower extensively revised the second paragraph (McDuff Coll.). This same day and the next, Eisenhower acknowledged numerous birthday gifts and greetings (see the correspondence in EM; and in McDuff Coll.).

1789   *Eisenhower Mss.*

To Hjordis Swenson   *October 14, 1947*
Telegram

Because of my earnest belief in the worthiness of your work for peace, it is with sincere regret that I must tell you I cannot attend your dinner on December tenth.[1] Demands upon my time have resulted in a congested schedule that permits no added commitments. I wish you every success, not only in your ceremony commemorating Alfred Nobel but in progress toward the great objective of world peace. I deeply appreciate the honor of your invitation.

[1] Mrs. Swenson, chairman of the American Nobel Anniversary Committee, had asked Eisenhower to be the principal speaker at the seventh annual Nobel anniver-

sary dinner (Oct. 10, EM). The dinner commemorated the date of Alfred B. Nobel's death and was held on the day the Nobel prizes were awarded in Sweden and Norway. Eisenhower's staff drafted a short reply, but Eisenhower rewrote the message (McDuff Coll.).

1790   *ABC 370.5 Germany (10-1-47)*

To Joint Chiefs of Staff   *October 15, 1947*
Secret

Memorandum by the Chief of Staff, U.S. Army:

Subject: Military Implications in an Early Withdrawal of Occupation Forces from Germany[1]

The possibility is being suggested in State Department despatches that the Soviets may propose, at the Council of Foreign Ministers scheduled for 26 November 1947 in London, an early withdrawal of occupation forces from Germany.[2] The recent Soviet proposal of a joint withdrawal from Korea lends credence to this possibility and suggests the advisability of examining the implications which would thus be raised from the military and security point of view.[3] It is accordingly recommended that the Joint Chiefs of Staff request the Joint Strategic Survey Committee to prepare a study developing the military and security implications involved in a possible Soviet proposal for the early withdrawal of occupation forces from Germany.[4]

[1] The United States and the Soviet Union had been unable to agree on troop levels in Germany (see nos. 1429 and 1537). In early October 1947 a Paris newspaper had reported that the Soviets would shortly propose the withdrawal of all occupation troops from Germany. A State Department representative in Berlin gave little credence to the report, pointing out that the German Communists, including those in the Soviet zone, were too weak to risk withdrawal of the Red Army (State, *Foreign Relations, 1947*, vol. II, *Council of Foreign Ministers; Germany and Austria*, p. 896, n. 89).
[2] For the meetings see *ibid.*, pp. 676–830. Schuyler, who drafted this memorandum for Eisenhower, also prepared a brief and covering memo for the General. The paper circulated, after minor stylistic changes, as JCS 1811, of October 23 (CCS 383.21 Germany [2-22-44], Sec. 19).
[3] For the Soviet proposal on Korea see no. 1900.
[4] On October 23 the JCS would order the JSSC to prepare this study (CCS 383.21 Germany [2-22-44], Sec. 19). For later developments see no. 1875.

To Hamilton Holt   *October 15, 1947*

Dear Dr. Holt:[1] I am embarrassed to have to tell you that while you were in my office a couple of hours ago I had totally forgotten a tentative commitment made on October 12th for the evening of February 23rd in Baltimore. While I had told my prospective host, as I do all others, that I could not make a definite commitment to come, yet I did promise that if I could make any engagement whatsoever for that evening I would come to that city. This rules out coming to Florida for that date.

I can explain my lapse of memory only by the fact that I signed the Baltimore message during a very busy period; my error was brought to my attention by a secretary shortly after you left. You will, I am sure, accept my very humble apologies and I can only say that I am glad the mistake came to my attention so quickly.

Permit me again to express my deep and lasting appreciation of the honor you had in mind for me.[2] *Sincerely*

[1] Holt, an educator and author, had been president of Rollins College, in Winter Park, Florida, since 1925. He had been active in international affairs and had received decorations from various governments. Holt had visited Eisenhower to urge him to accept an honorary degree from Rollins and to visit the school.
[2] Holt replied that he understood Eisenhower's situation and issued a new invitation for June 1948 or February 1949. Eisenhower said he would consider the February 1949 date (Oct. 27; all correspondence is in EM).

To Thomas Jefferson Davis and   *October 15, 1947*
Nina Eristova-Shervashitze Davis

Dear T.J. and Nina: Some days ago I ran into a friend—I believe it was Littlejohn—who had recently seen you in the Carolina area. Until that moment I had not known where you were but I instantly made a resolution to write to you. As seems usual these days, the intention became a victim of procrastination but when your birthday telegram arrived yesterday the intention became a determination.

Whoever my friend was that told me about you, said that you were raising poultry, looking fine and seemingly very happy. I should think that all three would be true because of my own longing to get a little piece of ground, retire from the regions where one seems always to be on the spot, and live the simplest possible life.

From time to time old friends of SHAEF days drop in to see me. Within the past few months both Freddie de Guingand and "Bomber"

Bert Harris have been in. Both are now out of the service and living in the southern part of Africa. They are doing splendidly in civil life.

A few weeks ago I was in Minneapolis and had a visit with Art Nevins. He has a job there with the Community Chest. About two weeks ago Butch dropped in to see me and we talked for a couple of hours.

John and his new wife are still at Fort Benning where John is taking a motor mechanics course. Mamie is quite well but complaining about her weight. I keep struggling along but sometimes lose the bloom of my optimism.

This letter will reach you by the 19th and so gives me an opportunity to send my warmest regards and best wishes to T.J. on his own birthday. I hope the day will be a fine one for the entire family and that the future will bring you many more even happier ones.

Love to Nina and the children (wherever they may be) and, as always, warmest regards to you, T.J.[1] *As ever*

[1] For background on Davis and the other persons mentioned see no. 248; and Chandler, *War Years*.

1793   *Eisenhower Mss.*

To ALFRED M. WOLF   *October 15, 1947*

Dear Mr. Wolf:[1] Many thanks for your letter. I truly appreciate the spirit in which it was written and am more than flattered by your opinion of my qualifications. However, I assure you that I am completely sincere in stating that I have no political desires or intentions. Such service as I may be able to render after leaving the Army will be best performed as a private citizen.[2] *Sincerely*

[1] Alfred M. Wolf, of New York City, had written Eisenhower on September 3 urging him to run for President. Wolf said, "Strictly in the interest of our country is this letter written to you." McDuff drafted a reply, which Eisenhower substantially revised (McDuff Coll.).
[2] On this same day Eisenhower signed a similar letter to Edward G. Petrillo, general chairman of the Veterans Non-Partisan Political Committee in Erie, Pennsylvania (EM, Routine Corr., Miscellaneous).

1794   *Eisenhower Mss.*

To JOHN OGDEN CARLEY   *October 15, 1947*

Dear Mr. Carley: I cannot remember when I have seen a more effective and appropriate cartoon than the one you sent me from your issue of

October 12.[1] This morning I showed it to a group of visitors in my office, one of which was a Congressman, and all agreed with me that it was timely and carried for all of us a real lesson.[2] Not only do I congratulate its author—I think you are fortunate to have a man on your staff who possesses so much feeling and common sense.

With personal regard, *Sincerely*

[1] The cartoon, from the *Memphis Commercial Appeal*, had the caption "Home." It depicted a soldier who had given "that last full measure of devotion," asking "Remember me?" of civilians scurrying along amidst such labels as "Self-Pity" and "Malcontents." A copy is in EM. For background on Carley see no. 1614.
[2] According to Eisenhower's desk calendar, his visitors that morning included "Mr. Con Lanier of Senator Hoey's office with delegation from North Carolina." Clyde Roark Hoey, a Democrat, who had been governor of North Carolina from 1937 to 1941, had been elected to the U.S. Senate in 1944.

1795   *Eisenhower Mss.*

TO MARK WAYNE CLARK   *October 15, 1947*

Dear Wayne: I would see no objection to your making visits to Hawaii and to Alaska.[1] I believe, however, that you should write to Devers about the matter; I think that all such activities on the part of Army Commanders come within the general area of his responsibilities.[2]

So far as I can see there is no chance of Mamie and I coming West unless we should do so next spring during a leave that we earnestly hope to take.[3] After I turn over the reins here I am certainly going to hold out for a short period of doing as I please before I plunge into another difficult job.

My very best to Renie and to Ann[4] and as always, with warm regards to yourself, *Cordially*

[1] In a letter of October 13 Clark had said he planned trips to Hawaii and Alaska both for recreation and "to familiarize myself with the situations in both those outposts" (EM).
[2] See the next document.
[3] Clark hoped the Eisenhowers could visit him and his wife in San Francisco.
[4] Clark's wife and daughter.

1796   *Eisenhower Mss.*

TO JACOB LOUCKS DEVERS   *October 15, 1947*

Dear Jake: I just had a note from Wayne Clark who wants to take short trips to Hawaii and to Alaska. I told him that while I had no personal objection to such a thing, it was my understanding that such movements on the part of Army Commanders came within the realm of your responsibility.[1]

I hope this is right.[2] *Sincerely*

[1] See the previous document.
[2] Devers responded that he had wired permission to Clark and that he agreed "that such movements of Army Commanders are a matter of concern to me" (Oct. 17, EM).

1797   *ABC 370.26 Unity of Command,*
                                                     Alaska (12-11-46)

To Joint Chiefs of Staff   *October 16, 1947*
Confidential

Memorandum by the Chief of Staff, U.S. Army:

Subject: Designation of the Chief of Staff, U.S. Air Force, as the Executive Agent for the Joint Chiefs of Staff for the Alaskan Command.

Reference: JCS 1259/27

1. In recognition of the significant interest of the Department of the Air Force in Alaska and the areas adjacent thereto, and as a step in the implementation of the separation of the Air Force from the Army, I recommend that the Chief of Staff, U.S. Air Force, be designated as the executive agent for the Joint Chiefs of Staff for the Alaskan Command vice the Chief of Staff, U.S. Army, and that JCS 1259/27 be amended accordingly.[1]

2. If you approve, I further recommend that the attached draft message be dispatched.[2]

[1] Eisenhower's memorandum was part of a general effort to unify the various elements in the military command structure. The air command had a primary role in the operations centered in Alaska. JCS 1259/27 was the basic directive on unified command (see no. 1214; see also no. 1780). Schuyler prepared a brief and covering memo and drafted Eisenhower's memorandum. The Chief of Staff's memo, with minor changes, circulated as JCS 1259/46, of October 20, 1947 (CCS 381 [1-24-42], Sec. 7).
[2] The Joint Chiefs would approve Eisenhower's recommendation on October 25, and the message would be sent that same day to Air Force Lieutenant General Nathan Farragut Twining, the newly appointed Alaskan commander. Twining had served in the South Pacific and in Europe during World War II. (For further background see Chandler, *War Years*.) On November 15, 1947, the Army contingent that had formerly been the Alaskan Department would be redesignated United States Army, Alaska, or USARAL (*Army Almanac*, p. 306).

To JOINT CHIEFS OF STAFF   *October 16, 1947*
Secret

Memorandum by the Chief of Staff, U.S. Army:

Subject: Security Aspects of Current Isthmian Canal Studies (JCS 1778/2)[1]
I have studied JCS 1778/1 and 1778/2, and am in agreement with these papers except for the use of the word "reasonable" in paragraph 8 on page 4 and paragraph 6 on page 8 of JCS 1778/1.[2] I suggest the word *complete* be substituted in place of "reasonable" as I do not believe the statements as they stand.

With exception of the comments stated above I approve JCS 1778/2.[3]

[1] For background see no. 1487. The governor of the canal and a joint ad hoc committee of the JCS were studying the prospects for the Panama Canal and its relationship to our national security. The committee and the governor were agreed that the canal was essential to U.S. commerce and national defense; the Panama Canal Zone, they said, was still the best location for such a waterway (see the draft of the governor's report in P&O 381, Case 89/9; and JCS 1778/1, Oct. 1, 1947, same file as document). General Spaatz had agreed to accept the committee's report, providing that certain paragraphs were deleted (see JCS 1778/2, Oct. 15, CCS 821.1 [5-12-47], Sec. 1). These paragraphs stated that the canal's strategic value would diminish when either the United States "or a potential enemy" had the capability to attack "with long-range airborne weapons of mass destructiveness." The report said, however, that such a capability was not "sufficiently proximate" to affect the canal's current strategic importance or to influence the decision to modernize its facilities.

[2] Both of these paragraphs said that a lock canal could not be protected well enough "to afford *reasonable* assurance against the interruption of traffic..." (italics added).

[3] Eisenhower's memo (which had been drafted by Schuyler) circulated as JCS 1778/3, of October 25 (*ibid.*). On November 4 the Joint Chiefs would approve Eisenhower's recommendation and forward the report of the ad hoc committee to the Secretary of the Army. The governor's report, approved by the JCS, would advocate a sea-level canal (P&O 381, Case 89/16).

1799   *Eisenhower Mss.*

To JOSEPH LAWTON COLLINS   *October 16, 1947*

Memorandum for the Deputy Chief of Staff: The trial in which General DeWitt has been engaged has finally been settled by the refusal of the Supreme Court to review the findings of the Circuit Court of Appeals.[1]

This case serves in all its stages to clarify the standing and authority of an Area Commander in time of war to carry out executive orders in protecting the country against those suspected of disloyalty or of subversive action.[2]

Because of its importance, it is my belief that The Judge Advocate General should be required to make a short digest of the essentials of the case together with the findings of the courts so that in any future emergency everybody from the highest executive authority on down to the soldier in the field would have a clear understanding of his own position and authority together with the limitation on that authority.

Such a digest should not only be available to important commanders in time of war but I think an understanding of the case might be taught in appropriate places in the Army school system.[3]

[1] Lieutenant General John Lesesne De Witt, who had served in the Office of the Chief of Staff from November 1945 to April 1947, had retired from active duty on June 10, 1947. (For background see no. 307.) On February 14, 1942, General De Witt, the commanding general of the Western Defense Command and the Fourth Army, had, in the words of his final report, "recommended to the War Department that the military security of the Pacific Coast required the establishment of broad civil control, anti-sabotage and counter-espionage measures, including the evacuation therefrom of all persons of Japanese ancestry." Five days later President Roosevelt issued Executive Order 9066 authorizing these actions, and on February 20, 1942, Secretary of War Stimson gave De Witt the authority to exercise the delegated powers. To quote De Witt, "Among the steps taken was the evacuation of Japanese from western Washington and Oregon, California, and southern Arizona." De Witt said: "There was neither pattern nor precedent for an undertaking of this magnitude and character; and yet over a period of less than ninety operating days, 110,442 persons of Japanese ancestry were evacuated from the West Coast" (U.S. Army, Western Defense Command and Fourth Army, *Final Report: Japanese Evacuation from the West Coast, 1942* [Washington, D.C., 1943], pp. vii–viii). Approximately 112,000 persons (of whom over 70,000 were American citizens) would be evacuated. Several cases were brought to the courts, including some that alleged denial of the due process guaranteed to all American citizens. For a concise summary see Donald Teruo Hata, Jr., and Nadine Ishitani Hata, *Japanese Americans and World War II*, The Forum Series, ed. Franklin Mitchell (St. Charles, Mo., 1974). See also Milton R. Konvitz, *The Alien and the Asiatic in American Law* (Ithaca, 1946); Roger Daniels, *Concentration Camps USA: Japanese Americans and World War II* (New York, 1971); and Morton Grodzins, *Americans Betrayed: Politics and the Japanese Evacuation* (Chicago, 1949).

The case to which Eisenhower refers is *De Witt* v. *Wilcox (Federal Reporter,* 2d ser., vol. 161 [1947], pp. 785–91), which reversed *Wilcox* v. *Emmons et al. (Federal Supplement,* vol. 67 [1947], pp. 339–73). In December 1942 De Witt, acting under the authority of Executive Order 9066, had ordered Homer Glen Wilcox to leave the West Coast. Wilcox, an opponent of the war who had been accused of disloyal and subversive activities, refused to obey the order, and in September 1943 De Witt's soldiers removed Wilcox from his San Diego, California, home and transported him to Las Vegas, Nevada. Claiming that De Witt had exceeded his authority, Wilcox brought suit in the District Court for San Diego, California. There he won a summary judgment for one hundred dollars. De Witt

appealed to the federal circuit court of appeals, which reversed the judgment (Green to Collins, Jan. 20, 1948, P&O 371, Case 17).
[2] De Witt and Eisenhower had conferred that morning.
[3] This same day Lutes, as Acting Deputy Chief of Staff, issued to the JAG a directive embodying Eisenhower's orders (COS, 1947, 201 De Witt). The JAG completed its resumé of the De Witt case shortly before Eisenhower left office. In a covering note General Green stated that the case had settled only one "very narrow point" and could not be used "as a vehicle for the instruction of military personnel as to the authority of commanders in combat areas." The Deputy Chief of Staff nevertheless directed that the resumé be sent to theater and army commanders, General and Special Staff division directors, and joint and Army service schools (Green to Collins, Jan. 20, 1948, P&O 371, Case 17; and Bowen to Witsell, Feb. 3, 1948, COS, 1948, 201 De Witt).

1800   *Eisenhower Mss., Family File*

To Milton Stover Eisenhower   *October 16, 1947*
Personal

Dear Milton: I think that nothing would please me more now than a chance to go to some isolated ranch in Texas at least 100 miles from a railhead and stay there for one solid year. This gossip around the country that I am an aspirant for Republican nomination or at least have a receptive mood with respect to the prospect, is beginning to damage my disposition—at times it becomes positively insulted.

Only this morning I noticed an account of a radio broadcast in which I was accused of having held a long and secret conference with Mr. Wallace and two of his colleagues, the alleged purpose of their visit being to persuade me to declare for the Democratic nomination with the purpose of ousting Mr. Truman.[1]

Not only is the entire story fantastic—the only one of the individuals mentioned in the story that I personally knew was Mr. Wallace—but the implication that I had even countenanced people talking to me about a subject like this while I am still in the Army is very close to a challenge to a soldier's loyalty. The commentator did end his story with the conclusion that I had given Mr. Wallace no satisfaction because—according to him—I was personally hoping for the Republican nomination! The fact is that I have not even seen Mr. Wallace at a distance since he left the administration and I have never had a private talk with him in my life. Moreover, I have never mentioned the word "politics" to him, nor he to me.

In any event, I merely cite these things to show you that I am getting very close to violating the one underlying principle that I have always believed to be binding on every American. That principle is that every citizen is required to do his duty for the country no matter what it may be. While I am very clear in my own mind that no man since Washington has had any occasion to feel that it was his *duty* to stand for or to accept political office, yet the principle remains valid. Because of this feeling I have so far been unwilling to say exactly what I'd like to say but I do know this. I would never feel any sense of duty from a situation that saw a convention deadlocked for some days and which would finally, in desperation, turn to some name that might be a bit popular around the country, in the effort to drag a political and partisan organization out of the hole. That is exactly the kind of thing that Sherman answered so emphatically; under the same circumstances I would do the same.

However, we are not children and we know that under the political party system of this country it would certainly be nothing less than a miracle if any group of delegates assembling for a convention felt such a terrific popular pressure behind them that they would instantly cease any effort to handle their work on a political basis and would respond to such a general sentiment. Since those are the only circumstances that I believe could impart a sense of duty to a normal human being, I come around again to the conclusion that by [declining?], in advance, to use words similar to Sherman's, I am merely punishing myself for adhering to a principle that has become certainly academic so far as any application to the present case is concerned.

I realize that a man should hold on to a sense of humor with sufficient strength to be able to laugh at the annoyances that I feel out of this whole thing. I believe that what irritates me more than anything else is the veiled, sometimes open, charge that I am being dishonest. I am certain that 99% of the press representatives that I have ever met would accept instantly and without question my statement on any subject I could speak of in the world except only this one. It has become so much a practice in this country for political candidates to be coy and to try to preserve the illusion that "The office seeks the man, not the man the office" that it is difficult for anyone to carry conviction in his words when he is perfectly honest in saying that he wants nothing whatsoever to do with politics—well, I suppose there is no use pursuing this subject further. I doubt that in this letter I have told you anything that I haven't said to you often before. It is merely inspired by the fact that this morning I am a bit more irked than usual by the constant hammering.

My love to Helen and the children and, as always, best to yourself.[2]

As ever

[1] For background on Henry A. Wallace see no. 1734. For an analysis of Wallace's differences with Truman, especially over foreign policy, see Richard J. Walton, *Henry Wallace, Harry Truman, and the Cold War* (New York, 1976).

1801   *Eisenhower Mss.*

To Jack Ellis   *October 16, 1947*

Dear Jack:[1] I have just mailed to you a few cigars that have come to me from Cuba. Since I do not smoke cigars I cannot give you an expert opinion but I am told that they are among the finest you can get in Havana. I truly hope you like them.

In the package you will find a smaller one wrapped in white paper. That was put in by Mamie who asks that you hand it to your daughter.

Mamie reports to me that your fishing trip was washed out by a hurricane. I am of course sorry—I expected her to bring a tale of worlds of fish with none less than five pounds.

Would you mind giving me again the name on that new reel you bought and the address of the maker?

This gives me an opportunity to tell you again how grateful Mrs. Eisenhower and I are for the hospitality shown us by the Ellis family. Even more we are grateful for the many kindnesses you showed to our children. We shall always be in your debt.[2]

With warm regards, and better luck the next time we go to Florida. *Cordially*

[1] Ellis was associated with Southern Foods, Inc., in Columbus, Georgia.
[2] John and Barbara Eisenhower lived at the Ellis home during their stay in Columbus. General and Mrs. Eisenhower had recently visited their son and daughter-in-law there. For background on the trip see no. 1751.

1802   *Eisenhower Mss.*

To Bolling Raines Powell, Jr.   *October 16, 1947*

Dear Mr. Powell: Thank you very much for your birthday greetings.[1] It is nice to know that you are back in law practice and that you are in business here in the city.[2] Actually I have never had a chance even to glance at my income tax records of the war years and if ever the Internal Revenue people question me about them I shall come arunning to you. Mrs. Eisenhower and I will always be in your debt for your great courtesy to us in helping out on such a difficult matter during the war.[3]

With warm personal regard, *Sincerely*

[1] Eisenhower's birthday was October 14.
[2] Powell had recently become an associate with the Paul V. McNutt law firm in Washington, D.C. (Powell to Eisenhower, Oct. 28, 1947, EM).
[3] Powell, who had been a major in the AUS during World War II, had prepared the Eisenhowers' income tax returns for 1942–45.

1803   *Eisenhower Mss.*

To Ruby Norman Lucier   *October 17, 1947*

Dear Ruby: Your nice letter added greatly to the pleasure of my birthday and I am grateful to you and Ralph for remembering the occasion.[1] The cake with "several candles" is appealing; maybe one of these days I'll take you up on the offer.

Johnnie and Barbara are very happy and still walking on clouds. They are at Fort Benning where Johnnie is in school. Thanks very much for your congratulations on their wedding. Here are my congratulations to you both as grandparents—actual and prospective.

Please forget all about any political position for me. I have absolutely no ambitions along those lines and do not intend to get mixed up in anything like that. I hope to be perfectly happy at Columbia University when I assume my new duties there.[2]

Thanks again for your thoughtful letter. Mamie joins me in warm regard to you and Ralph. *Sincerely*

[1] Mrs. Ralph F. Lucier had been a close friend of Eisenhower's in high school (see Eisenhower, *At Ease*, p. 3). McDuff prepared a draft of this letter for Eisenhower.
[2] Mrs. Lucier had sent birthday greetings from her and her husband. She said that if Eisenhower were near, "I'd make you a cake with *several* candles on it." The Luciers had heard that Eisenhower was being urged to run for President, and they hoped he would (Oct. 13, EM).

1804   *COS, 1947, 201 Gay*

To Mary Louise Doud   *October 17, 1947*

Dear Louise:[1] I can easily understand your interest in the case of Colonel Elmer D. Gay and appreciate your writing to me about the matter.[2] I directed that the records be examined and am inclosing a copy of our reply to Colonel Gay.[3] He is not eligible for retirement under current policy[4] of the Department and there is no way in which I could personally intervene.

Mamie joins me in love to you, *As ever*

[1] Miss Doud was Mrs. Eisenhower's first cousin. For background see Chandler, *War Years*.

[2] Miss Doud's September 22 letter on behalf of Colonel Gay is in the same file as this document. She had been a patient of Colonel Gay's uncle, a physician specializing in asthma treatment.

[3] After fifteen years of service Colonel Gay believed he was eligible for retirement under a provision requiring the approval of the Secretary of the Army. Gay had been a member of the Medical Corps on duty in Hawaii at the onset of the war; he had subsequently served with the Third and Ninth armies while commanding the 5th Auxiliary Surgical Group (Gay to Eisenhower, Sept. 22, 1947, same file as document). The War Department reply said that while Gay had more than fifteen years of service, he had slightly less than the fifteen years of active federal service required before one could be eligible for retirement (Carroll to Gay, Oct. 16, 1947, *ibid.*). Gay would resign his commission on November 9, 1947.

[4] From this point on, Eisenhower rewrote McDuff's draft of this reply (McDuff Coll.). A copy of the letter was sent to Mrs. Eisenhower.

1805   *Eisenhower Mss., Family File*

To MILTON STOVER EISENHOWER   *October 18, 1947*
Cable WCL 31084

Herbert Huston, a friend of Tom Watson, is quite anxious to talk to you about certain new methods he is sponsoring for world education.[1] Mr. Huston is addressing a convention in St. Louis and will be at the Jefferson Hotel.[2] He will come to Manhattan[3] if you will have time to see and talk to him. I told him that I would inform you of his intention. He is a very interesting gentleman of 70 with very wide international connections.

[1] Herbert Sherman Houston had chaired a committee that developed and tested a weekly radio program on world news that was broadcast to the New York City schools. Houston and others wanted to expand the program and to organize world trade exhibits to show how commerce united nations. An exhibit in each state would show the trade of that state with the world and the relevance of that trade to the welfare of the state. Eisenhower had seen Houston this same day.

[2] On October 21 Houston would address the World Trade Convention in his capacity as chairman of the School World Friendship Plan for the United States. A copy of his speech is in the same file as this document.

[3] Manhattan, Kansas, where Kansas State College was located.

1806   *COS, 1947, 000.8 Yale University*

To CHARLES SEYMOUR   *October 18, 1947*

Dear President Seymour:[1] Thank you for your letter endorsing the invitation from the editors of the "Yale Daily News."[2] I am inclosing a copy of my reply, and I assure you that my regret is very real that I have not found it possible to accept.³

Needless to say, I am doubly honored that you should add your personal invitation to that of the editors. I am looking forward to an opportunity of meeting and talking to you, and for this reason I have additional disappointment in the necessity of forgoing this chance to come to New Haven.

With assurances of highest personal esteem, *Sincerely*

P.S. It is faintly possible that I may get to see the Yale-Princeton game.⁴

¹ Seymour, who had received his Ph.D. in history from Yale in 1911, had joined the Yale faculty that same year. He had published numerous books on American diplomacy, and after World War I, he had been a member of the U.S. delegation to the Paris Peace Conference. Since 1937 Seymour had been president of Yale University.

² In a letter of October 13 Seymour had urged Eisenhower to accept a forthcoming invitation from the editors of the *Yale Daily News*. John Grandin Rohrbach, chairman of the student newspaper, wrote on October 14 to invite the General to speak at the newspaper's annual banquet.

³ In his reply to Rohrbach, Eisenhower explained: "Pressure of official duties, together with commitments of long standing, have forced me to decline to make additional engagements for the remainder of my tour as Chief of Staff" (Oct. 18; all correspondence is in the same file as this document).

⁴ Eisenhower would be unable to attend the football game. The Chief of Staff made minor changes in a draft of this letter and added the postscript (see draft in *ibid.*).

1807   *Eisenhower Mss.*

To Louis Francis Albert Mountbatten   *October 20, 1947*

Dear Dickie: Many thanks for the copy of your Report to the Combined Chiefs of Staff. Needless to say, I am very grateful for your kind inscription.¹

The Report will be of great interest to me. I am informed that copies are currently being studied by our Army, Air and Navy staffs, and am requesting that the various comments be completed before January 1948 so that they may be available at the time you suggest.²

I know you have been working under tremendous pressure in the past months. Your efforts to instill calm and reason during India's trying period are an outstanding contribution to the future of India and Pakistan.³ *As ever*

¹ Under a covering letter of October 2 Mountbatten had sent a personal copy of his "Report to the Combined Chiefs of Staff by the Supreme Commander, South-East Asia, 1943–1946." Mountbatten had asked Eisenhower to "accord some slight

measure of priority in the War Department to the reading of this Report" in order that the U.S. Chiefs of Staff could clear it by January, when the British Chiefs would finish their examination of the report (EM). Eisenhower wrote at the bottom of the letter: "For General Norstad. Please save attached copy for me. Note this letter and see me about it at your convenience." P&O drafted Eisenhower's response, which Carroll rewrote (COS, 1947, 319.1). For background see no. 1161.
² On October 20 Eisenhower signed letters to Nimitz and Spaatz asking them to expedite their comments (P&O and Carroll drafted these notes [COS, 1947, 319.1 TS; and P&O 319.1 TS, Case 57/2]). The British staff was delayed in getting the manuscript to the United States, however, and this slowed the clearance process (summary, Dec. 3, 1947, by Clark, in COS, 1947, 091.713 Alexander). In a staff-drafted letter of December 5 Eisenhower would inform Mountbatten of the delay (EM). For further developments see no. 2041.
³ Mountbatten had been Governor General of India since August 1947.

1808   *Eisenhower Mss.*

To James Bryant Conant   *October 20, 1947*

Dear Dr. Conant: Thank you very much for your kindness in sending along to me a copy of your talk before The National War College. By coincidence, only five minutes before your letter arrived at my desk I had sent word to an aide that I wanted a copy of your talk.¹

I used my lunch hour to read it. I must say that I invariably find your comments on this subject to be stimulating even if sometimes I become fearful. I have read stories of people who at the time of the building of the railroads expressed a longing for the "good old days." I am beginning to have more sympathy with them.²

Anyway, I agree with you that study, patience, open-mindedness and at least a modicum of optimism are necessary to us in these conflicting times.

Hoping that it will not be too long until I see you again, *Sincerely*

¹ Eisenhower had written this note: "Col. Michaelis—Please obtain for me a copy of *address* made recently by *Dr. Conant* to Nat. Def. College. I believe the subject dealt with atomic weapons." Conant had sent Eisenhower a copy with a covering letter of October 16 (EM). Conant asked that Eisenhower read in particular "what I say about the long-range planning and particularly the implications for the international situation." He said that one day when he was in Washington he would "like to amplify in conversation certain aspects of the problem of the international control of the atomic bomb." Conant's address was entitled "The Atomic Age—A Preview 1947 Edition."
² Conant's address alluded to the revolutionary consequences of atomic energy and stressed that the major discoveries were yet to be made. In fact, the world was not even yet in the atomic age, for "I would define this age as coming into being only when two or more powers had a sufficient stock of atomic bombs to make a use of

atomic bombs in war a likely contingency." It was still feasible that atomic controls could be introduced before the Russians obtained a stock of bombs, but military planners should look to the day when Russia might have sufficient atomic weapons "to constitute a military menace to the United States. . . ." On current Army planning for this eventuality see no. 1668.

1809   *Eisenhower Mss.*

TO ROBERT PORTER PATTERSON   *October 20, 1947*

Dear Bob: I have read the comments you furnished Mr. Brown.[1] I think that they are applicable as well as clearly stated. Thank you for sending them to me. With cordial personal regard, *Sincerely*

[1] Patterson had sent Eisenhower a copy of a letter he had written that same day to Lewis H. Brown, who had recently released a report on his mission to Germany. (For Brown's report see no. 1684.) Patterson agreed with Brown's stress on the effect on Western Germany of Russian and Polish control of the breadbasket of Germany. He took issue, however, with other aspects of Brown's report. Patterson thought most of the problems in Germany "flow directly from Russia's non-observance of the rule of economic unity of Germany as laid down in the Potsdam Agreement." The State Department was nevertheless "loath to cut loose from the Potsdam Agreement, even though they knew well that Russia was not observing it. They hoped that if we were patient, the Russians would change their behaviour." Patterson concluded: "Even with the use of hindsight I cannot say that I blame them, in view of the tremendous importance, in the interest of lasting peace, of coming to an understanding with Russia. Thus far, the progress of economic recovery in Germany has been sacrificed to the objective of One World" (Patterson to Eisenhower, Oct. 17, with enclosed letter to Brown, EM).

1810   *Eisenhower Mss.*

TO CHARLES MOREAU HARGER   *October 20, 1947*

Dear Mr. Harger: Thank you very much for your letter.[1] I am looking forward with pleasure to seeing you at the Foundation Dinner on 26 October. At that time I shall turn over to the Foundation some samples of the mementos and souvenirs you mentioned. As you may know, Milton is making the arrangements for my visit to Abilene—which, I understand, is to be on the simplest possible basis. With warm personal regard, *Sincerely*

[1] Harger's October 13 letter (EM) confirmed the arrangements for Eisenhower's visit to Abilene on October 26 (see no. 1760). Eisenhower made some changes in a draft of this reply prepared by McDuff (McDuff Coll.).

Eisenhower Mss.

To William Edward Robinson   *October 20, 1947*

Dear Mr. Robinson:[1] Thank you very much for your letter. I shall place it in my file with the understanding that if I ever decide to engage in writing and have the opportunity to do so, you will be promptly informed.[2]

Naturally I am deeply appreciative of your kindness in outlining the various prospects and considerations that would apply. While I find myself too pressed and driven to give objective thought to the matter, I do assure you that your advice and comment will be valuable.

It was nice seeing you the other day; I hope it will not be too long until we may meet again.[3] *Sincerely*

[1] Robinson, who had been with several newspapers in New York City, had joined the *New York Herald Tribune* in 1936. He had been a vice-president and business manager of the paper since 1945. Robinson visited with Eisenhower in the General's office on October 17, and on the next day Robinson wrote to offer an arrangement whereby the New York Herald Tribune Syndicate would handle Eisenhower's publications (EM).

[2] In *At Ease* (pp. 324–26) Eisenhower says he was dissatisfied with his previous publishing offers and explains why he came to be particularly interested in the proposals he received from the *Herald Tribune* and from Doubleday & Company. Instead of stressing the financial rewards, the representatives of these firms emphasized that Eisenhower would provide future historians with a personal memoir that would help them evaluate the wartime histories, which Eisenhower had found to be "riddled with inaccuracies" (see for example no. 1826). Eisenhower did not want to start writing until he left active service. He also wanted a package arrangement under which he would not have to concern himself with the details of various forms of publication. For subsequent developments see no. 1945.

[3] On October 22 Eisenhower would write in longhand an informal document to Mrs. Eisenhower establishing, in the event of his sudden death, her "clear ownership of certain papers which I have personally written" (General Eisenhower to Mrs. Eisenhower, EM, Subject File, *Crusade in Europe*). The Chief of Staff would meet with Robinson again on December 5 in his Pentagon office.

ABC 000.9 SANDSTONE *(10-1-47), Sec. 1*

To Joint Chiefs of Staff   *October 21, 1947*
Memorandum. Top secret

Subject: Armed Forces Participation in Proof-Testing Operations for
    Atomic Weapons[1]

1. Report of the Joint Proof-Test Committee on this subject, JCS 1795/6,[2] contains the recommendation that one of the Joint Chiefs of Staff be designated as the Executive Agent for the Joint Chiefs of Staff

for the Joint Task Force organized to conduct proof-tests of atomic weapons pursuant to JCS 1795/1.[3] The Report of the Joint Proof-Test Committee was approved by the Joint Chiefs of Staff on 18 October 1947.

2. In view of the designation of an army officer to command the Joint Task Force (JCS 1795/4), it is believed appropriate for the Chief of Staff, U.S. Army to be designated as the Executive Agent for the Joint Chiefs of Staff for this Task Group.[4]

3. I, therefore, recommend that the Joint Chiefs of Staff designate the Chief of Staff, U.S. Army as the Executive Agent for the Joint Chiefs of Staff for the Joint Task Force organized pursuant to JCS 1795/1.[5]

[1] On June 27, 1947, President Truman had approved SANDSTONE, a series of atomic tests that the AEC had proposed for April 1948. A Joint Proof-Test Committee—including representatives of the three services, the MLC, and the AEC—would draw up recommendations for military participation in the operation and for the organization of a Joint Task Force to conduct the tests (Hewlett and Duncan, *Atomic Shield*, pp. 47, 55, 65, 84–85, 138–41). Schuyler drafted this memorandum for Eisenhower; the paper circulated as JCS 1795/8, of October 24.

[2] JCS 1795/6, of October 14, contained the committee's detailed recommendations concerning the tests (CCS 471.6 [8-15-45], Sec. 7).

[3] In JCS 1795/1, of September 3, the Joint Staff Planners had recommended the establishment of a Joint Task Force and a Joint Proof-Test Committee, which would set policies for armed forces participation. The Joint Chiefs had approved this paper on September 10, 1947 (*ibid.*, Sec. 6).

[4] The JCS had appointed Lieutenant General John E. Hull as the commander (JCS 1795/4, Oct. 1, 1947, in *ibid.*).

[5] The JCS would approve Eisenhower's recommendation on November 4 (same file as document), and the tests would be conducted at Eniwetok Atoll in the Marshall Islands in April 1948 (see Hewlett and Duncan, *Atomic Shield*, pp. 161–65).

1813   *Eisenhower Mss.*

To Harry Cecil Butcher   *October 21, 1947*

Dear Butch: Of course I appreciate your long letter giving an account of your conversation with the Chicago publisher.[1] I must say that the real news in your letter is the "expectancy" in your family. May I salute you?

I regret that you agreed to write a magazine article on the subject you mention. Certain as you are a foot high, someone will instantly jump to the conclusion that it is inspired—that it is merely additional evidence that I am conniving to get something that I publicly state I don't want. Since you so clearly understand the honesty of my convictions in this regard, it is possible that my fears are groundless. However, I am still hoping that the whole thing dies a natural death, or as some of the commentators put it, that the "bubble will be pricked."[2]

With best regards, and thanks again for your newsy letter. *As ever*

[1] We have been unable to locate the incoming letter.
[2] Butcher replied that the article would contain a disclaimer stating that Eisenhower had not read the piece and that the General "probably will give me hell when and if" he reads it (Dec. 5, 1947, EM). The article, entitled "Why I Like Eisenhower for President," would appear in the February 1948 issue of *Coronet*.

1814   *McDuff Coll.*

TO THOMAS JOHN WATSON   *October 21, 1947*

Dear Tom:[0] I am most grateful for your handling of the real estate offerings which have been made to you in my behalf.[1] I hope it has not proven too much of an inconvenience.

Ambassador Pell was kind indeed to offer me such an attractive homesite and I have written him a note to thank him for his thoughtfulness.[2] A copy is attached.

I do hope that we can get together soon; it is always a great pleasure to see you.

With warm regard, *Cordially*

[1] Eisenhower had considered buying a house in the countryside near New York City (for background see no. 1682). The General made two changes in the staff-drafted version of this letter.
[2] Herbert Claiborne Pell, Jr., had been appointed U.S. Ambassador to Portugal in 1937 and to Hungary in 1941. In 1943 he had become the American member of the United Nations Commission Investigating War Crimes. Pell had also been a Democratic congressman from New York's Seventeenth District (1919–21). Eisenhower's note to Pell is not in EM.

1815   *COS, 1947, 091 Greece TS*

TO KENNETH CLAIBORNE ROYALL   *October 22, 1947*
Top secret

Memorandum for the Secretary of the Army:

Subject: Report on Greece

Reference is made to the report of General Chamberlin to the Chief of Staff, U.S. Army, concerning Greece, copy attached. Your attention is invited to the conclusions and the recommendations of the report as summarized on page 9 to 12, inclusive.[1]

I attach great significance to General Chamberlin's recommendation in paragraph 6 *a* to the effect that a broad definition on the highest level of U.S. objectives in Greece is required in order to permit timely provision of adequate means of assistance. I feel very strongly that unless a clear-cut definition of the U.S. objectives in Greece can be determined on the highest level indicating a definite U.S. commitment to assure the survival of a democratic Greece in the interest of our own national security, it would be unwise, and possibly even dangerous, to commit ourselves further militarily in Greece.[2] Subject to formulation of such a statement of U.S. objectives in Greece, my views with respect to the remaining recommendations of General Chamberlin's report are as indicated in the following paragraphs.

I concur in the following of General Chamberlin's recommendations as they are stated in his report. Implementation is contingent upon approval of the Department of State and upon the availability of necessary Greek aid funds. The Army is prepared to take necessary implementing action in conjunction with the other departments and agencies concerned.

Recommendation 6 *b*—Approval of the formation of approximately 50 Home Guard Battalions.[3]

Recommendation 6 *d*—Provision of additional machine guns for the Greek Army and the substitution of U.S. mountain artillery for 25 pounders and British mountain guns (both subject to further study and coordination with the Greek Army and USAGG to determine quantities and effect on organization).[4]

Recommendation 6 *f*—Advice to the Greek Army to cease the arming of civilians for the present.[5]

Recommendation 6 *g*—Release the Gendarmerie from Greek Army control and effect a suitable reduction in strength.[6]

Recommendation 6 *h*—Augmenting of USAGG by 8 officers and 12 enlisted men. (Already accomplished.)[7]

Recommendation 6 *i* and 6 *j*—Establishment of a U.S. Advisory and Planning Group in Greece, under the nominal control of the Ambassador and reporting directly to the JCS, to advise on and coordinate military matters; and to furnish U.S. observers with Greek Army units in the field.[8] (Total Army personnel: approximately 69 officers and 83 enlisted men initially.[9] Navy and Air Force contingents to be determined by the JCS.)

In the case of the following recommendations no action in addition to what is already being done appears necessary at this time. However, the Army will maintain each matter under continuing study with a view to prompt action should the British indicate their later intentions of altering the present status quo of their forces in Greece:

Recommendation 6 c—Retention of the British Training Mission.[10]

Recommendation 6 e—Retention of the British combat forces.[11]

Recommendation 6 g—Retention of the British Police Mission.[12]

As to recommendation 6 k, I consider that the decision to form the proposed US-UK Committee should be held in abeyance pending the establishment of the U.S. Advisory and Planning Group in Greece.[13]

In his letter of transmittal forwarding his report General Chamberlin expresses three thoughts, which, although pertaining to matters within the province of the Department of State, have a direct bearing on the efficient implementation of the military assistance program. Although these subjects are beyond the purview of the military, I recommend that they be called to the attention of appropriate officials. General Chamberlin points out that there are, as you know, two agencies of the State Department operating in Greece, both of which are vitally interested in the military objectives. He states that the solutions he has recommended in the military field have necessarily taken into consideration this situation as it exists, but he is of the opinion that coordination in the military field would be simpler and more certain should unification be effected on the diplomatic level.[14] Secondly, General Chamberlin points out that the short range character of the present aid program makes it difficult to render sound decisions as to the relative emphasis to be placed on the military and the economic rehabilitation programs. In fact, this consideration creates doubt in his mind as to the efficacy of conclusions and proposed actions based solely on military factors if, promptly on 1 July, 1948, the financial aid of the U.S. is to be withdrawn abruptly. General Chamberlin is of the opinion that the administrators of the aid program could act with more assurance if, after a firm executive estimate and decision, key Congressional leaders could be approached for a declaration of support of the aid program subsequent to 1 July, 1948.[15] Thirdly, General Chamberlin indicates that the Greek Government should establish a state of emergency in Greece in order to impress upon the Greek people the peril of their position and to facilitate all out efforts to eliminate the guerrilla bands.[16]

I am aware that should the foregoing recommendations be approved there will result additional transfers of funds now earmarked for economic purposes to use in support of the military assistance program. However, the military situation in Greece has deteriorated to a marked degree since the initial allocation of funds was made to the military and economic programs. Until the military situation is improved, it appears extremely unlikely that the economic program, as originally planned, can be implemented successfully. I therefore feel that the transfer of funds is not only justified but essential.[17]

With respect to increasing the number of military personnel in Greece, it may have been previously brought to your attention that Secretary of War Patterson on 11 April, 1947, in an Executive Session of the House Foreign Affairs Committee stated that the Committee would be advised if and when the Army Advisory Group to Greece exceeded 40 in number. The Committee should therefore be informed of any increase in the number of military personnel in Greece.[18]

General Chamberlin's report is based on the current situation. The measures which he advocates, and in which I concur, do not insure success but, if taken at this time, they should create conditions favorable to the achievement of our announced intentions in Greece.[19]

The urgency of the situation in Greece is such that I believe early action is required. Since the Secretary of State is charged with overall responsibility for the program of aid to Greece you may wish to take appropriate action to bring it to his attention without delay. I am prepared to initiate such implementing action as may be required by the Army as soon as decisions are reached regarding the above recommendations.

I enclose for your approval and signature a suggested letter to the Secretary of Defense.[20]

[1] The war in Greece was not going well for the government forces, and in late September Eisenhower had sent his director of intelligence, Major General Chamberlin, to make a personal survey of the situation. (For background see no. 1711.) Chamberlin's report of October 20 is in CCS 092 (8-22-46), B.P., and his recommendations are reprinted in State, *Foreign Relations, 1947*, vol. V, *The Near East and Africa*, pp. 375–77. Norstad prepared a brief for Eisenhower and drafted this letter to Royall.

[2] The National Security Council discussed the Chamberlin report on October 27. The acting secretary of state objected to Eisenhower's proposed statement on the grounds that it would constitute a commitment to use U.S. troops if necessary, and that was impossible without the consent of Congress. Forrestal suggested a milder statement, which the Council accepted (Schuyler, Memo for Record, Oct. 28, 1947, ABC 400.336 Greece [3-20-47], Sec. 1-B). The statement that was adopted "committed" the U.S. to "help," rather than to "assure the survival of a democratic Greece . . . " (State, *Foreign Relations, 1947*, vol. V, *The Near East and Africa*, pp. 391–93). The President would approve the National Security Council memo on November 3.

By this time the United Nations had also taken action on the situation in Greece. On September 25 the United States had introduced a motion in the General Assembly censuring Albania, Bulgaria, and Yugoslavia for supporting the Greek guerrillas; the motion called upon these nations and Greece to settle their disputes peacefully and provided for a special committee to observe whether the countries were complying with this resolution. The committee was to report back to the General Assembly. The General Assembly adopted the U.S. proposal on October

21, 1947, and established the United Nations Special Committee on the Balkans (UNSCOB). This committee would issue its first report on December 31, 1947, and through 1948 it would continue its efforts to end the hostilities (see United Nations, *Official Records of the Second Session of the General Assembly: First Committee, Summary Record of Meetings, 16 September–19 November 1947* and *Resolutions, 16 September–29 November 1947*, pp. 12–14 [both Lake Success, N.Y., 1947]; and State, *Foreign Relations, 1948*, vol. IV, *Eastern Europe; The Soviet Union*, pp. 222–78).

[3] Chamberlin recommended that these units—some 25,000 men—be organized to free elements of the Greek Army from static defense. Greece would provide part of the funds for the new battalions, and the rest would come from the $6 million recently transferred from the American Mission to the Department of the Army for the purpose of augmenting the Greek Army (see correspondence in P&O 091 Greece TS, Case 3/9, esp. Memo for Record, Nov. 26, 1947). In subsequent discussions the United States agreed to authorize one hundred divisions of what came to be called the National Defense Corps (see State, *Foreign Relations, 1947*, vol. V, *The Near East and Africa*, pp. 466–69, 478–80).

[4] This action also required the United States to use for military assistance funds that had been appropriated for economic aid (see Arnold to Schuyler, Oct. 28, 1947, in P&O 091 Greece TS, Case 8/3).

[5] Little progress had been made on this recommendation by the time Eisenhower left office (see Griswold to Secretary of State, July 1, 1948, in State Department Decimal File, 868.00/7-148). For the conditions that made this a difficult task see Edgar O'Ballance, *The Greek Civil War, 1944–1949* (New York, 1966), pp. 141–54; D. George Kousoulas, *Revolution and Defeat: The Story of the Greek Communist Party* (London, 1965), p. 237; and State, *Foreign Relations, 1947*, vol. V, *The Near East and Africa*, p. 428.

[6] By February 1948 this still had not been accomplished (see Griswold to Marshall, Dec. 2, 1947, State Department Decimal File, 868.00/12-247; Livesay to Wedemeyer, Dec. 10, 1947, and Jan. 13, 1948, both in P&O 091 Greece, Case 63; and State, *Foreign Relations, 1947*, vol. V, *The Near East and Africa*, p. 428).

[7] For P&O's action see Arnold to Schuyler, Oct. 28, 1947, P&O 091 Greece TS, Case 8/3.

[8] This was the most controversial of the recommendations. If U.S. military personnel provided operational advice in the field, they might be wounded or killed. The proposal would nevertheless be implemented (see no. 1990).

[9] Norstad's original draft had called for *eighty-nine* officers and eighty-three enlisted men. Chamberlin's report had recommended that twenty officers be sent initially, to be followed by sixty-nine more officers and the enlisted men. Eisenhower wrote to Collins: "I've signed letter to Sec. Royall *but*, I do not understand discrepancy in recommendation checked on page 2 of that letter & Chamberlin's statement that initially *20* officers are sufficient. Please check." The letter was then changed (P&O 091 Greece TS, Case 8/2). By November 12, P&O had selected all of the officers (see Arnold to Schuyler, Oct. 28, 1947, and P&O to P&A, Nov. 12, 1947, both in *ibid.*, Cases 8/3 and 3/11, respectively).

[10] See for example State, *Foreign Relations, 1947*, vol. V, *The Near East and Africa*, pp. 116–17, 148–49, 277–80, 419–20.

[11] See no. 1711.

[12] Chamberlin recommended this, even though he also wanted the gendarmerie to perform only police functions.

[13] Chamberlin wanted such a committee to effect high-level military coordination. Eisenhower would shortly attempt to allay British anxieties on this point (see no. 1903).

4 On the continuing jurisdictional squabbles between the American Ambassador
o Greece and the chief of the American Mission to Aid Greece see for example
tate, *Foreign Relations, 1947*, vol. V, *The Near East and Africa*, pp. 361–63,
95–96, 404–7.

5 The National Security Council called on the secretary of state, subject to the
pproval of the President, to ask Congress to declare its support "at an appropriate
ime" (*ibid.*, pp. 392–93).

6 Under American prodding, the Greek government would take increasingly
arsh measures (O'Ballance, *Greek Civil War*, pp. 154–61).

7 The National Security Council stressed the need to divert aid to military oper-
tions against the guerrillas (State, *Foreign Relations, 1947*, vol. V, *The Near East
nd Africa*, pp. 391–93).

8 The National Security Council directed Secretary of Army Royall to inform
oth the House Foreign Affairs Committee and the Senate Foreign Relations
Committee (see also Marshall to Royall, Nov. 7, 1947, *ibid.*, p. 393n). Royall's
discussions with the congressmen did not all go smoothly. At Royall's request,
P&O drew up a memorandum for record (Nov. 13, in P&O 091 Greece TS, Case
3/12) describing his conversations with the congressional leaders. According to the
memo, he had difficulty with Senator Vandenberg, who "made the remark that if
he Congress had been informed of our present intentions last May, there was a
chance that the legislation [that is, for the Truman Doctrine] would not have been
passed." Vandenberg at first demanded a letter; later, however, the Undersecretary
of State said that this would not be necessary and that the Army should prepare a
brief press release for November 14. On that day the Army released the story,
including the information that U.S. military advisors would be stationed at division headquarters in battle areas (*New York Times*, Nov. 15, 1947).

19 One option not called for by Chamberlin but discussed by the JCS during this
period involved the sending of U.S. combat troops (see esp. the JCS 1798 series in
ABC 370.5 Greece-Italy [8-20-47], Sec. 1-A). Later in November the JCS would
also comment (at Forrestal's request) on a State Department position paper stressing
the importance of the eastern Mediterranean and the Middle East. In the draft
response to Forrestal, Eisenhower let stand a sentence attesting to the area's importance, but the Chief of Staff rewrote the remainder of the message as follows:
"Insofar as the military implications are concerned, the J.C.S. advise that: *a.* Any
additional deployment of American [this was later changed to read "U.S."] armed
forces to this area will, in view of our present extended position, automatically
raise the question of [later changed to read "the question of the advisability of"]
partial mobilization, and *b.* Any deployment of appreciable strength in this area
will make a partial mobilization a necessity" (see JCS 1819, of November 19). All
correspondence is in CCS 381 Eastern Mediterranean and Middle East Area (11-
19-47); and ABC 381 Eastern Mediterranean and Middle East (11-19-47).

20 The suggested letter from Royall to Forrestal (not printed here) would simply
forward Eisenhower's letter and Chamberlin's report. Royall would sign and dispatch the letter on October 24 (same file as document).

Memorandum by the Chief of Staff, U.S. Army:

Subject: Proposed Oil Pipeline to the Mediterranean from the Middle
East Oil Areas[1]
References: *a.* JCS 1754
b. JCS 1754/1
c. JCS 1754/2
d. JCS 1754/3
e. JCS 1754/4

1. The Commander of the British Army Staff has presented to me an
aide memoire, copy attached, embodying a request from the British
Chiefs of Staff for reconsideration by the Joint Chiefs of Staff of their
stand concerning the strategic implications of the location of a proposed
Anglo-Iranian/Standard Oil Company of New Jersey pipeline from the
Persian Gulf area to the Mediterranean.[2]

2. On 4 August 1947, by JCS 1754/4 the Joint Chiefs of Staff
stated to the State-War-Navy Coordinating Committee their opinion
that they "perceived no overriding military consideration justifying exception to established State Department policy in this instance." However, in view of the numerous recent changes in the international
situation, I consider it appropriate for the Joint Chiefs of Staff to
comply with the current British request for reconsideration of the matter.[3]

3. I recommend that the Joint Chiefs of Staff direct the Joint
Strategic Survey Committee to restudy the question of the military
implications involved in the matter of the location of the proposed
pipeline, with a view to recommending appropriate action by the Joint
Chiefs of Staff in the light of the British request.[4]

[1] On March 8, 1947, in JCS 1754, the British Chiefs advised the JCS that the
British government-owned Anglo-Iranian Oil Company, in partnership with a
U.S. oil company, planned to build a pipeline from the Persian Gulf to the
Mediterranean. The BCOS considered a route through Saudi Arabia and southern
Trans-Jordan, with a terminal at Gaza, desirable from a military point of view,
even though such a line would be more expensive to construct and operate than one
following a more northerly route to a point on the coast of either Lebanon or Syria.
The British Chiefs wanted the Joint Chiefs to convince the involved U.S. oil
interests that they should concur in the proposed southern route. The JCS replied
that due to the commercial and political aspects of the problem, the question should
be referred to the British Foreign Office and the State Department (JCS 1754/1, of
March 29). The Joint Chiefs told SWNCC that it was "desirable from the military

point of view that pipe lines through the Middle East area be located as far to the southward as is compatible with the other considerations involved." Since the locations of the oil fields and other facilities would not change in either event, however, and since the distance between the proposed routes was relatively short, the Joint Chiefs concluded that the U.S. government should not take an interest in the decision (JCS 1754/4, approved August 4). State Department policy was that the selection of a pipeline route was a commercial decision that should be made by the company involved. All correspondence is in CCS 678 (3-6-47); and ABC 463.7 (4-29-44), Sec. 1-C. See also State, *Foreign Relations, 1947*, vol. V, *The Near East and Africa*, pp. 660–63.

[2] The Standard Oil Company, which was the American concern involved, preferred the less expensive, northern route. Thus, the British Chiefs again approached the JCS on this problem when the joint British-American military talks on the eastern Mediterranean and the Middle East got underway in Washington (see no. 1711). In an October 8 note, Eisenhower forwarded to Norstad a new British *aide-mémoire* on the subject and said that "the propriety of reopening the matter would seem to be unquestioned in view of the uncertainties in the international situation" (same file as document). The result was this Eisenhower memorandum, which was circulated as JCS 1754/5, of October 30 (ABC 463.7 [4-29-44], Sec. 1-D). Schuyler prepared the memorandum and a brief for General Eisenhower (same file as document).

[3] In their *aide-mémoire* the British again stressed the strategic considerations and urged the JCS to take "appropriate steps to influence the American partners of the Anglo-Iranian Oil Company to adopt the more southerly route" (*ibid.*; see also State, *Foreign Relations, 1947*, vol. V, *The Near East and Africa*, pp. 613–14).

[4] The JCS would approve Eisenhower's recommendation on November 6. On November 19, however, the JCS would also approve a reply (drafted by the JSSC in JCS 1754/6, of November 14) informing the BCOS that "the United States Chiefs of Staff regret that they are unable to change their position regarding the location of the proposed oil pipeline from the Middle East Oil area to the Mediterranean." All correspondence is in CCS 678 (3-6-47). According to Henrietta M. Larson; Evelyn H. Knowlton; and Charles S. Popple, *New Horizons, 1927–1950: History of Standard Oil Company (New Jersey)* (New York, 1971), p. 747, the firm would drop this project because of "difficulties in getting rights of way across some countries and in arranging transit payments...."

1817

TO AKSEL NIELSEN

Eisenhower Mss.

October 22, 1947

Dear Aksel: Thank you for your letter of the 18th.[1] As long as the young bull is not developing into the type you desire, I think that you are absolutely right in selling him off as quickly as possible. As you must suspect, I have taken a great deal of pride in boasting about my "stock" holdings so I am bold enough to say that some day I want a replacement. I really believe I should prefer to stick to the bull for the reason that one of these days I can always have the hope of possessing a champion and go around collecting a lot of blue ribbons. Of course, in this matter, you are the expert and I must look to you for a decision. I am merely expressing sentimental preference.

I admit all this is on the brassy side. There was no reason in the first place why you should have presented to me such a fine product of your ranch; and as long as he failed to turn out correctly that should simply wash out the deal. But nevertheless, while I cannot escape a feeling that I am a bit of a heel, I want to wait until the cows produce a replacement.

All are well here—I do hope that come spring we can at long last return to Denver for a visit with our family and friends. Possibly you should tell me what is the earliest date we can count on getting up into the mountains or getting a little fishing in that wonderful club of yours. Confidentially I have been rather counting on our anticipated leave covering the months of February–March. That may be far too early for going up over the passes.

With warm regard, *Cordially*

[1] Nielsen had written, "I have now definitely decided that your bull is not good enough to fit and keep" (EM). For background see no. 1158.

1818   *Eisenhower Mss., Routine Corr., Miscellaneous*

To Isaiah Bowman   *October 22, 1947*

Dear Dr. Bowman:[1] Through Secretary Forrestal I have just come into possession of a copy of a talk you recently made before the incoming class at Johns Hopkins.[2] I liked it so much that I cannot refrain from sending you this note to say that you packed into a very brief statement a lot of good horse sense. *Sincerely*

[1] Bowman (Ph.D. Yale 1908), the author of several books on geography, had interrupted his academic career during both world wars to serve as an advisor on various diplomatic missions. Since 1935 he had served as president of The Johns Hopkins University. In a letter of October 9 Bowman had invited Eisenhower to attend the university's convocation on February 23, 1948, but Eisenhower was unable to do so (Eisenhower to Bowman, Oct. 16, Dec. 31, 1947; all correspondence is in EM).
[2] Forrestal's forwarding note of October 17 and Eisenhower's reply of October 22 are both in *ibid*. Bowman's September 22 address was entitled "Discovering Your Place in This Complex World." There is a copy in the Milton S. Eisenhower Library, at The Johns Hopkins University.

To Bernard Samuel   *October 22, 1947*

Dear Mr. Mayor:[1] Thank you very much for your letter of October 20
endorsing the invitation extended to me by the Philadelphia Club Printing House Craftsmen.[2]

I am flattered by the invitation itself and its implications, as well as
by your own thoughtful interest. My only difficulty, which I explained
in some detail to the committee that came to see me, is in the matter of
dates. The latter part of February promises to be a very involved period
for me and I am almost prevented from making definite personal plans
for any specific day around that time. However, I am examining my
whole situation as carefully as I can from this distance and have promised to give a final answer to the committee by the end of this month.[3]

I explain this to you in some detail because I profoundly appreciate
the personal compliment implied by your letter. *Sincerely*

[1] Bernard Samuel had first been elected to the Philadelphia City Council in 1923.
After nearly twenty years on the council, he had become acting mayor of Philadelphia in 1941 and then mayor in 1944.
[2] Samuel's letter said that "a warm and cordial welcome" awaited Eisenhower in
Philadelphia (COS, 1947, 080 Philadelphia Club Printing House Craftsmen).
The General had been invited by Samuel J. Mink, who was the president of the
club (which comprised the leading printing and publishing houses in the Philadelphia area). In a letter of September 23 Mink had told Eisenhower that he had been
selected to receive the club's "Share Your Knowledge" Gold Medal Award for
1948. Eisenhower had responded on October 10 that he was "deeply grateful" but
probably could not come to Philadelphia on the desired date, February 28, 1948.
He would, however, meet with a delegation from the club in his office, as Mink
had suggested. The meeting would take place on October 21. All correspondence is
in EM.
[3] In letters to Mink of October 28 and November 12, Eisenhower said that he
would be unable to go to Philadelphia on the suggested date (EM).

1820   *Eisenhower Mss.*

To Paul Alfred Hodgson   *October 23, 1947*

Dear P.A.: I am flattered that your memory should retain the date of
my birth. Personally I try to forget them but on the other hand I can
stand them if they serve to bring me messages from my old friends.[1]

To settle one thing once and for all, as far as the one subject mentioned in your letter goes—I don't want any part of a political position.
That is completely sincere and honest and there are no mental reservations either real or implied.

A group of Army couples occasionally have a bit of bridge and the number available for play is sufficiently large to have one man's game. Usually Al Gruenther, Henry Sayler,[3] Bob Littlejohn and I have a foursome at the modest sum of a tenth a point. Very occasionally Omar Bradley or a Colonel named Henry Matchett[4] is either added as a fifth member to the game or replaces one of the regulars. Al Gruenther plays a really topnotch game and is guilty of fewer mistakes than almost any person I know. This is because he never makes an impulsive, quick, or careless play. He watches every moment for useful evidence and is, in addition, a very pleasant type to have in the game. He and I have lots of fun when we are partners but this occurs only when the cut brings it about. We have never had opportunity to play together enough to develop the detailed understandings that are so essential to really good teamwork. Henry Sayler plays sort of a slapdash game and frequently takes terrific sets. He is bright and quick enough but careless. He won't go to the mental effort of counting out a hand even when he has conclusive evidence—nevertheless he is lots of fun and we like him in the game.

Littlejohn is the good average player and so is Henry Matchett. Bradley is very considerably above average but plays with us less than any of the others. In fact, we rarely have a game more often than once every two weeks; that is about the best I can manage. For myself, I still retain my keen interest in the game and enjoy it thoroughly, but I sometimes think I am too tired to devote to it the concentration that I once did with great zeal and enthusiasm. This of course is reflected in play and sometimes I wake up to find myself guilty of the grossest error. The only saving grace is that I usually recognize it before my partner can cut my throat and so I spend the rest of the hand trying to conceal it.

I doubt that I have written you since last June when we had a reunion at West Point.[5] I pushed pretty hard to get as many of our class there as could come because we had missed our 30th reunion due to the war. I believe that some 32 or 33 attended and, all in all, it was a most enjoyable meeting. There are not too many classmates around here. Offhand I think of Blister Evans, Henry Aurand, Sayler, Larkin and Sid Graves.[6] Undoubtedly there are others that would come to mind if I stopped to think long enough but certainly the total in the city would not run over a dozen.

There was one very funny incident at the June meeting. It involved getting together a class organization which it appears we have lacked since the day of our graduation. Two or three made violent speeches to have me as president of the class and I, supported by at least one faithful adherent, as violently objected. I maintained that to nominate me as permanent president, which was the proposal, was to place all the emphasis on rank and was foolish; that I was entitled to belong to something where I was one of the crowd rather than its eternal center. The darn thing created more froth and fury than was warranted by such an inconsequential matter but it ended up in electing me an "honorary" president, while the real president is to be nominated and elected from time to time.

Life goes on as hectically as ever. There is constant pressure to make speeches and attend all sorts of meetings, and appeals to support numbers of movements of an altruistic or charitable nature. Added to all this type of pressure is that of ordinary business, including interminable conferences, committee meetings and so on. Possibly I will be just as hard-worked when I go to Columbia but at the very least it will be a change and possibly I will not be so constantly frightened by lugubrious staff officers.

Mamie is in better health I think than for a long time, although she worries about increasing weight. She is around the 130 mark which means that all her clothes that are more than a few months old are too small. I assume that, so far as she is concerned the changing styles make no difference; she would probably be compelled to consider a new wardrobe anyway. This last year we had an unusual little windfall and since that time I have been urging her to fulfill a long-held ambition, namely, to buy herself a good fur coat. Today she got around to the matter and I believe has finally settled on one. The final struggle was between a "natural" wild mink and a ranch-bred mink. The latter type is darker and she thought she liked the lighter one better, possibly because it cost twice as much. The eventual decision was in favor of the darker one because of its nicer texture and lesser weight. In any event, that great problem is now apparently solved.

We were invited to the wedding of the Princess in London and I confess to just a shade of disappointment that I cannot go.[7] I like her and her family tremendously and I should like to see just once how such an affair would be conducted. In addition, of course, a visit there would give us a chance to see many old and fine friends. However, it is out of the question.

Undoubtedly there are a thousand other details of Washington news and gossip that might be of interest to you but I believe I have exhausted the list so far as my memory will serve me at this instant.

My very best love to Anne and, as always, with warmest personal regards to you, *As ever*

P.S. Your own birthday on Nov. 19th of next month will bring you up again to just one year younger than I. If I fail to write you again before that time, please remember that I always wish for you the best of everything there is.

[1] In a letter of October 10 Hodgson had sent best wishes for Eisenhower's birthday. Although Hodgson thought Eisenhower would make an excellent President, h said he was "not sure you'd be very happy doing it. However, I'm for you in an case."
[2] Hodgson had written, "I don't suppose you can find much time for bridge. . . ."
[3] See no. 1227.
[4] See no. 1678.
[5] For background on the reunion of the West Point Class of 1915 see nos. 153 and 1544.
[6] Major General Vernon "Blister" Evans had been Deputy Chief of Staff and the Chief of Staff of the China-Burma-India theater during World War II. Since 194 he had been commanding general of the Southeast Asia Command. For back ground on Aurand see no. 876; on Sayler see n. 3 above; and on Larkin see no 648. Sidney Carroll Graves (USMA 1915) had served in the infantry in Europ during World War I and then in Siberia. He had resigned from the Army in 1920
[7] See no. 1841.

1821

To Clara B. Gebsen

Dear Mrs. Gebsen:[1] It was good to receive your letter and I appreciate your generous remarks about my new position at Columbia.[2] Personally, I am rather doubtful that the University has served herself well in this instance.

I am sorry that Mamie and I missed seeing you and Emma while you were in Washington;[3] we seem to be always on the jump.

Your question about membership in the club at Barksdale is one I cannot answer.[4] As a general rule, club by-laws prescribe eligibility for membership and this differs at various stations. I suggest you see the Commanding Officer at Barksdale.

Send along the etching; I will be happy to inscribe it.[5] Warm regard and the best of good wishes, *Sincerely*

[1] Mrs. Clara Gebsen, of Shreveport, Louisiana, was the wife of a retired naval officer. She had met Eisenhower in 1941 during Army maneuvers in Louisiana.
[2] In her October 14 letter Mrs. Gebsen said, ". . . you will please note that no congratulations are forthcoming from these quarters on your new venture. The *University* is to be congratulated, sir, *not* their new President!" (EM). Eisenhower made several changes in a reply drafted by Carroll.
[3] For background on Emma Michie see no. 1420. Mrs. Gebsen wrote that on their way home from a trip through New England and eastern Canada, they had stopped in Washington to see the Eisenhowers.
[4] She asked whether retired naval officers were eligible for membership in the Barksdale Officers' Club. She wanted to give such a membership to her husband as a Christmas gift.
[5] The Gebsens had acquired a signed, original etching of Eisenhower through the

American Art Association. They wanted the General to autograph it before they had it framed.

1822   *COS, 1947, 080 Military Order*
                                                           of the Purple Heart

To Irving Jerome Davis   *October 23, 1947*

Dear Mr. Davis:[1] The invitation to address your annual Purple Heart Dinner is most appealing.[2] I would consider it a privilege to accept and sincerely wish I could do so.

As matters stand, however, I am confronted with a mounting pressure of official duties and a heavy schedule of long-standing engagements for my remaining months as Chief of Staff. At some undetermined time after the first of the year, I will face the dual problem of moving to Columbia and at the same time clearing up the final phases of this assignment. Under these circumstances, I am not in a position to make any new commitments for the winter or spring.[3]

Thank you very much for the honor of your consideration. I am very sorry that my answer cannot be an acceptance.[4] *Sincerely*

[1] Davis was chairman of the dinner committee of the Military Order of the Purple Heart, Department of New York. He had served overseas during World War I as a member of Company C, 108th Infantry. He was wounded on October 17, 1918, at St. Souplet, France, and received a Purple Heart with two Oak Leaf Clusters.
[2] Davis wrote Eisenhower on October 21 to invite the Chief of Staff to be the honored guest at the annual dinner on December 7 (same file as document). Parker drafted this reply.
[3] This same day Eisenhower also declined an invitation for cocktails from Mrs. Eleanor Roosevelt, widow of the late President (McDuff Coll.).
[4] In a handwritten postscript Eisenhower said: "There is no organization with which I would rather meet. My best to everyone of you!"
    On October 24 General Eisenhower would leave for his trip to Kansas State University and Abilene. At the university on the twenty-fourth he would participate in a groundbreaking ceremony for a memorial meditation chapel and speak informally at a dinner on behalf of the chapel workers. On the twenty-fifth he would attend a breakfast given by the business community, review a parade, give a formal address on the college green, lunch at the university with the governors of Kansas and Nebraska (among others), and attend Kansas State's homecoming football game with the University of Nebraska. Eisenhower's remarks at the chapel dedication and his address are in EM, Subject File, Speeches (see also Milton S. Eisenhower to Dwight D. Eisenhower, Sept. 22, EM, Family File). On the twenty-sixth Eisenhower would make a brief stop in Abilene to present a collection of war decorations and other mementoes to the Eisenhower Memorial Foundation. He would then spend the night at the home of his brother Milton, in Manhattan, Kansas, and fly from Fort Riley, Kansas, to Washington, D.C., the morning of the twenty-seventh.

To Chester William Nimitz   *October 27, 1947*
Top secret

Memorandum for Admiral Nimitz:

Subject: Naval Officers Commanding the Naval Forces, Far East, in the Event of an Emergency[1]

1. With reference to your recent memorandum, I recognize the problem confronting you under CINCFE's emergency plan in the relationship between the Commanders, Naval Forces, Western Pacific and Naval Forces, Far East.[2]

2. In an attempt to resolve this question, I am forwarding your memorandum to General MacArthur for his comments. Upon receipt of his comments, I shall inform you of the action I propose to take toward solving the problem.[3]

[1] The theater commanders had been directed, in JCS 1259/27, to prepare integrated emergency plans (see no. 1214). On February 24 the War Department had reminded MacArthur, Commander in Chief, Far East (CINCFE), that his plan had not been received (P&O 370.02 TS, Case 10/2). MacArthur's chief of staff finally forwarded the plan, BAKER 65, with a covering letter of August 18. On August 25 Knowlton wrote the JCS that Eisenhower wanted the Joint Staff Planners to study the report and make recommendations, and the Joint Chiefs accepted this proposal that same day. In the course of their deliberations the Planners met several times in September with their counterparts from MacArthur's headquarters. According to an undated, unsigned memo written after one such meeting, MacArthur did not envision reequipping "a Jap Army even in event of a war"; yet the Joint War Plans Committee "still feels that war plans should include use of trained Jap manpower. However, it is not believed advisable to tell MacArthur to do any such planning at this time." (All correspondence is in ABC 381 Far East [8-1-47].) On October 7, in JCS 1259/43 (CCS 381 [1-24-42], Sec. 6), the Planners concluded that formal JCS comment on BAKER 65 had to wait until the plans submitted by CINCPAC and CINCAL had been reviewed (see WARX 88651, Oct. 20, 1947, in ABC 381 Far East [8-1-47]). The Joint Chiefs approved this recommendation on October 18.

[2] Nimitz, in his memo of October 4 (same file as document), pointed out that BAKER 65 called for the Commander, Naval Forces, Far East (COMNAVFE), to direct the forces of the Commander, Naval Forces, Western Pacific (COMNAVWESPAC), and to exercise unified command (through COMNAVWESPAC) of U.S. forces in China. But, Nimitz said, COMNAVFE was at present junior to COMNAVWESPAC. Nimitz proposed that MacArthur, as CINCFE, issue orders directly to COMNAVWESPAC or that Nimitz, as CNO, issue orders to the effect that the senior naval officer involved would become COMNAVFE in an emergency. Schuyler prepared a draft of Eisenhower's document, but the paper was then revised in the office of the Chief of Staff (ABC 381 Far East [8-1-47]).

[3] On this same date Eisenhower sent the memo to MacArthur, who responded on November 9 that "the strategic plans for this theater are based upon basic principles and are not determined by the accident of personnel assigned to the various echelons of command involved." He wanted COMNAVFE to be the overall sea commander

in the Far East. COMNAVWESPAC, as a sector commander exercising control of all air, sea, and ground forces in the China sector, would report directly to MacArthur. (All correspondence is in the same file as this document.) MacArthur's change solved the problem. On November 28 Eisenhower proposed to Nimitz that the command relationships proposed in the November 9 letter be approved (same file as document). The Navy accepted this position (see Wedemeyer to C/S, Jan. 27, 1948, ABC 381 Far East [8-1-47]), and on February 3 the JCS approved the change in BAKER 65 (JCS 1259/55, Jan. 19, 1948, CCS 381 [1-24-42], Sec. 9).

1824   *Eisenhower Mss.*

To AKSEL NIELSEN   *October 28, 1947*

Dear Aksel: Thank you very much for inviting me to meet with your Association on the night of September 24, next year.[1] Your associates were very kind to suggest that you ask me to be there and, since any organization that you would join must constitute a pretty fine group of men, I confess it would be fun to attend.

However—and here is the rub—I do not see how I could possibly foretell with any degree of confidence just where I will be and what I will be doing next September. Presumably I then shall have joined the Columbia staff; but I know so little about the requirements of the Columbia job that it would be foolish for me to make a firm commitment at this time. For example, the date you give might coincide with some personal obligation connected with the opening of a new school year at Columbia. Such an engagement I could not avoid and there are other possibilities of a similar character.

Please let your committee members know that I am honored by their consideration and explain why it is totally impossible for me to do anything other than to decline.[2]

With warm regard, *As ever*

[1] Nielsen would be installed as president of the Mortgage Bankers Association of America at a dinner in New York City; he had invited Eisenhower to speak on that occasion (Oct. 21, 1947, EM).
[2] In his response of October 30 Nielsen said he would not yet accept Eisenhower's rejection as final (*ibid.*).

1825   *ABC 371.2 Italy (9-15-47)*

To JOINT CHIEFS OF STAFF   *October 29, 1947*
Memorandum. Top secret

Subject: The Position of the United States with Respect to Italy[1]
    1. In my opinion J.C.S. 1808/1 deals with a number of aspects of

J.C.S. 1808 which are not of strictly military significance and, hence, are beyond the purview of the Joint Chiefs of Staff.

2. Accordingly, I recommend that the enclosed reply be forwarded by the Joint Chiefs of Staff to the Secretary of Defense in lieu of that proposed in the Enclosure to J.C.S. 1808/1.[2]

MEMORANDUM FOR THE SECRETARY OF DEFENSE

In compliance with your oral request to the Director (Designate), Joint Staff, the Joint Chiefs of Staff submit herewith their comments on NSC 1.

1. In so far as the military aspects of NSC 1 are concerned, the Joint Chiefs of Staff are generally in agreement with the views expressed therein.

2. In addition, the Joint Chiefs of Staff, from the military point of view, desire to point out the following considerations:

a. With reference to paragraph 8 a (3) of NSC 1, it should be noted that there are not presently available any substantial amounts of equipment surplus to the needs of U.S. armed forces of the types required by the Italian armed forces.

b. At the present time there are immediately available only three divisions (one Army and two Marine)[3] to meet any additional requirements for U.S. ground forces over and above the present commitments. An additional Army division could be made available within two or three weeks. It is, therefore, of great importance to avoid committing these ground forces in an area where they may suddenly find themselves confronting enemy forces overwhelmingly superior in strength and with no possibility of early and adequate reinforcements. Any such reinforcement, if provided, would require at least a partial mobilization.[4] The U.S. Navy could deploy sufficient naval strength in the Mediterranean to overcome any naval opposition which could be brought against it unless opposed by a significant proportion of the available U.S.S.R. air strength. The U.S. Air Force has available sufficient combat, troop carrier, reconnaissance and liaison groups to gain and maintain air supremacy in Italy unless opposed by available U.S.S.R. units. However, considerable time would probably be required to repair existing airfields in Italy before more than a small portion of available U.S. air units could be deployed in that country.

c. From the military point of view it is potentially dangerous to adopt policies and plans concerning the Eastern and Central Mediterranean area which may require commitment of U.S. forces without adequate assurance that passage through the Straits of Gibraltar will not be denied to our forces.[5]

[1] Under the terms of the Italian peace treaty, all foreign troops would leave the country by December 15, 1947, but the U.S. government, especially the State Department, was concerned about the political, economic, and military stability of the Italian government. The major concern was that the Communists might attempt to seize power illegally in advance of the elections scheduled for March 1948. (For background see no. 1504.) On October 15, 1947, the executive secretary of the National Security Council circulated NSC 1, "A Report to the National Security Council by the Executive Secretary on the Position of the United States with respect to Italy." The paper concluded that the United States had primary security interests in Italy and should assist the government in several ways: The United States would not withdraw its forces if the Italian government was unable to carry out the terms of the peace treaty. The U.S. position would be that unless all parties to the treaty were able to carry out its terms, the treaty was no longer binding. The United States should not use troops in a civil war in Italy, but if a Communist government was established by civil war or illegal means, the United States would assist the legal government and maintain the position of the U.S. forces in that country. Forrestal referred this paper to the Joint Chiefs for comment (JCS 1808, Oct. 16, 1947), and the JCS sent the report to the JSSC. The JSSC reported in JCS 1808/1, of October 23, which included a draft reply to Forrestal. Eisenhower's response to the JSSC proposal was drafted by Schuyler and was circulated as JCS 1808/2, of October 29. All correspondence is in the same file as this document; and CCS 092 Italy (10-2-47), Sec. 1. See also State, *Foreign Relations, 1947*, vol. III, *The British Commonwealth; Europe*, pp. 988–90; and *1948*, vol. III, *Western Europe*, pp. 724–89.

[2] Eisenhower objected to several of the JSSC's comments, including the following: that the JCS agreed with NSC 1 that the rise to power of communism in Italy would seriously menace U.S. security interests; that legislation should not be sought to permit transfer to Italy of equipment now held by U.S. forces because this might weaken the Italian government; that the JCS agreed that U.S. armed forces should not intervene in a civil war; that the U.S. should counter Communist aggression in Italy by certain steps "which would facilitate the extension of the strategic disposition of United States armed forces in Italy and adjacent Mediterranean areas, and that, in order to prepare for such extension, the United States should now request the Italian government to make available Italian air bases for training flights by United States air units"; that the JCS agreed that the Communists would not attempt to seize control until U.S. and British troops had been withdrawn and that if Communists seized control of any part of Italy, U.S. troop withdrawal should be suspended; that it was potentially dangerous to adopt plans for the eastern and central Mediterranean which might involve U.S. forces "without simultaneously implementing a plan of action designed to align Spain with the United States."

[3] This would be amended to read "one Army division and two marine divisions, reinforced, less one Marine regimental combat team now on duty in China."

[4] For a similar statement by Eisenhower see no. 1815.

[5] The Joint Chiefs approved Eisenhower's paper on October 29 and the next day forwarded the memo to Forrestal, who transmitted it to the National Security Council. The revised NSC paper, NSC 1/1, of November 14, which the President approved on November 24, was not substantially different from NSC/1. On December 1 the State Department would ask Forrestal to have plans drawn up for the implementation of military aid, including the strategic deployment of U.S. armed forces in Italy and other parts of the Mediterranean. For the result see no. 1919. The text of NSC 1/1 is in State, *Foreign Relations, 1948*, vol. III, *Western Europe*, pp. 724–26.

Dear Beedle: I find that the age limitation for the appointment of nurses to the Regular Army was established by law.[1] This does not mean that the decision was a correct one and I am informed that both the Personnel Division and the Surgeon General are convinced that a mistake was made. They intend to ask for amendment and I will follow up the matter.

My days since you left have been as busy as ever. I went out to Kansas hoping that on at least one day there I would get a chance to loaf. I was on the jump every minute.[2]

Right now the local excitement centers around an investigation by a Congressional Committee into Communism in Hollywood.[3] I am not exactly sure what the Committee hopes to accomplish; I have not been able to follow the details of the matter. I am quite certain, however, that such matters have to be handled with great wisdom and delicacy. We must not, in our own country, establish practices that by their very nature would interfere with legitimate rights of individuals. On the other hand, where it can be proved that an individual has taken an oath or has become a member of a party which is openly dedicated to destruction of our form of government, by force, it would appear that some sort of decent defense should be available to us. I simply have not had time to study the pros and cons in the current instance so as to have a worthwhile opinion regarding them but it is making interesting reading in the newspapers.

Out in Utah we had one of our most serious airplane accidents when a DC-6 crashed into a mountainside.[4] In Maine we had terrific forest fires that resulted in the death of a number of people and some thirty million dollars in loss.[5] A plane going to Alaska with 18 aboard has disappeared.[6] As a result of these incidents and others, numbers of people are of course hinting darkly at "sabotage" and it is always possible that there may be something of this sort involved. While my own belief—in the absence of any proof to the contrary—is that they are accidents and nothing more, they are added fuel to the smouldering doubts and fears that are plaguing this country if not the whole world today. It would indeed be a blessing if the country could regain a bit of serenity and peace of mind even if the price were somewhat lowered standards of living.

I do not recall at the moment any local news or gossip that might be of interest except that George Patton's memoirs are just now coming out in book form. An early excerpt, published in the Saturday Evening Post, alleges vehemently that SHAEF prolonged the war and lost thousands of additional lives when we "prevented George Patton from winning the war in September, 1944".[7] I am beginning to think that crackpot history is going to guide the future student in his study of the late conflict.

With warm regard, *As ever*

[1] Smith, who was returning to Moscow after a short visit in the United States, had written to Eisenhower on October 21 (EM). He inquired about the age limitation on appointments of nurses because this regulation had prevented a nurse he had known throughout the war from obtaining a permanent commission. For the act, PL 36, of April 16, 1947, see U.S., *Statutes at Large*, vol. 61, pp. 41–52.

[2] See no. 1822.

[3] For background see no. 1709. At an October 28 hearing a witness who had refused to identify himself with the Communist party had mentioned Eisenhower's refusal to name his political party (*New York Times*, Oct. 29, 1947).

[4] On October 24 a United Air Lines plane with fifty-two aboard had crashed in Bryce Canyon, Utah (*New York Times*, Oct. 25, 1947).

[5] On October 29 rains would stop the fires and ease the drought that had caused them (see *New York Times*, Oct. 17–30, 1947).

[6] The wreckage of the Pan American World Airways plane would be found on October 31 (*New York Times*, Nov. 1, 1947).

[7] The excerpt was published in the November 1, 1947, edition. The full memoir, *War As I Knew It*, would be published by Houghton Mifflin Company, of Boston, later in the year.

1827   *Eisenhower Mss.*

TO EDWARD EVERETT HAZLETT, JR.   *October 29, 1947*

Dear Swede: While I have not been invited to the meeting of the North Carolina Press Association in January, it will be impossible for me to attend even if I am asked.[1] My life is just as hectic as ever and I have flatly refused, for many weeks past, to add a single engagement to my schedule. In fact, I have had to break three or four of long standing. At the end of this week I must make a run to Texas and stop at Little Rock on the way back.[2] I am desperately trying to make those my only public appearances during the month except for a two-minute appearance here in the city in an effort to help out the Community Chest campaign.

All the so-called experts in the field of political analysis continuously point out that without artificial stimulus all these "boomlets" for particular individuals sooner or later collapse. I have been pinning my faith and my hopes on the correctness of this assertion—I have made my position very clear and still feel sure that I am not going to be faced with an impossible situation.[3] It has been a most burdensome, not to say annoying, development. It has even resulted in bringing down on my naked head a lot of attacks from people who would ordinarily have no reason for concerning themselves about me one way or the other. But because they see in me some possible thwarting of their own purposes, they use the method of cursing anyone that gets in their way.

Personally I feel that there are a number of candidates in the field who would make acceptable political leaders and I cannot conceive of any set of probable circumstances that would ever convince me that it was my duty to enter such a hectic arena.

I am counting on going to the Army-Navy game this year, primarily because Lord Alexander, Governor General of Canada, is going to attend and I am rather in the position of being one of his hosts.[4] Frankly, I think I would far rather have the day just to sleep, and read about the results the following morning in the papers. In any event I shall not attend any of the other games.

In Abilene I found that my circle of old acquaintances and friends seems gradually to contract.[5] On this trip I did see Lois Harger Parker—the first time I have seen her since we graduated from high school in 1909. I saw no significant physical change in the town—that is one corner of the country that seems to drift along in the even tenor of its ways, and its people are the happier for it.

It is nice to know that you and your family had such a fine time at the beach. When a whole family loves the sea, the sunlight and deep-sea fishing, it certainly simplifies the vacation problem. With us the matter is somewhat more difficult because Mamie has no interest in outdoor life. I am perfectly ready (always assuming we can get any kind of an opportunity) to go to a mountain stream or a farm with some birds on it or to the seashore. But since none of these places has a definite attraction for Mamie, we always have a big discussion and end up by traveling around and tiring ourselves out. In any event, we are going to take 60 days between the termination of this job and the beginning of the next and incidentally, during that time, I am going to be careful to retain my active duty status.

Give my love to Ibby and the girls, and with warmest regards to yourself, *As ever*

[1] In his letter of October 25 Hazlett said that he understood that the North Carolina Press Association had invited Eisenhower to speak at its meeting in January. Hazlett hoped that Eisenhower could attend the meeting (EM).
[2] See no. 1839.
[3] Hazlett, wondering if Eisenhower could resolve the questions over his political future, had inquired, "... shouldn't you make an unequivocal statement on the subject—one that no one can shoot holes in?"

2016

[4] See no. 1714.
[5] See no. 1822.

1828   *Eisenhower Mss.*

To Cornelius Vanderbilt, Jr.   *October 29, 1947*

Dear Mr. Vanderbilt: I deeply appreciate the kindness and disinterestedness of your letter of October 20.[1]

As an individual I am, of course, interested in the broad observations
you make; it would be sheer hypocrisy to pretend indifference to such a
report as yours.

With respect to popular sentiment against war; no man could more
fully share it than myself.[2] Indeed I think this view is deep in the mind
of every responsible person that is compelled seriously to contemplate
the possibility. I believe that few people have any real understanding of
the grim potentialities of such a disaster, even if the outcome should be
military victory. The great question is,—what to do about it? I cannot
subscribe to the theory that weakness on our part would tend to
minimize the danger. On the contrary I believe that moral, industrial
and political strength, properly buttressed by a sensible military structure, represents our best hope of maintaining our security now, and of
progressing toward worthwhile agreements involving world stability and
disarmament.

Regarding your more personal comments, I assure you that there has
been nothing evasive or equivocal in the statements I have made in
expressing my earnest desire to lead a semi-private life after leaving the
Army. I have been honest and straightforward and since, to my knowledge, no man since Washington has been elected to political office
unless he definitely desired it, I have felt perfectly secure in my opportunity to realize my ambition. As long as this point is understood, I
would be glad if you find it convenient to write to me from time to time
as you suggest.[3]

Thank you again for your consideration and thoughtfulness. *Sincerely*

[1] In his letter Vanderbilt had said that based upon his travels around the country,
he had concluded that Eisenhower could be elected President on any ticket (EM).
For background on Vanderbilt see no. 1215.
[2] Vanderbilt had written: "Oddly enough the second most popular man in the
country today as I sense it is Henry Wallace. I guess this is because of his 'peace'
issue. General, *the American people dont want another war now.*"
[3] Vanderbilt, who was leaving on another trip, said he would like to report to
Eisenhower on popular sentiment in the southern and eastern parts of the country.

To Robert Sharon Allen   *October 29, 1947*

Dear Colonel:[1] It was more than kind of you to pass on to me the information contained in your note of the 27th.[2] The news you give me is somewhat astonishing; I had thought that the speaker's spot on that particular program was always reserved for a prominent figure in the political party to which the President does not belong. That just shows how poorly I keep track of such matters.

In any event, I am grateful for your warning.[3]

Drop in to see me sometime when you are going through the Pentagon hallways. *Sincerely*

[1] For background on Allen see no. 1785.

[2] Allen had reported to Eisenhower that the Gridiron Club of Washington, D.C., was planning to ask the General to be the principal speaker at its annual winter dinner in December. He warned: "You are being invited primarily because of the political conjectures that continue to swirl around your head. They won't put it that way when they invite you, but it will amount to your being put on the spot as a presidential possibility" (EM). The Gridiron Club, a social organization comprised of newspapermen, sponsored semiannual dinners and satirical programs about top government officials and current news events.

[3] Eisenhower would not address the club.

To Francis Pendleton Gaines   *October 29, 1947*

Dear Dr. Gaines:[1] Naturally I feel a high sense of honor and distinction in the decision of your board of Trustees to accord me an honorary degree if I find it possible to be with you on January 19.[2] I assure you that any degree of that type I accept has a very great deal of significance for me and if I should be unable to come such inability should never be interpreted as evidence of a lack of appreciation.

Actually the pressures building up on me make it more and more doubtful that I shall find it possible to give you an affirmative answer. Nevertheless, I am holding the matter open as long as you can allow me to do so in the hope that some development will give me a bit more freedom.[3]

With many thanks to you and to your Board of Trustees, and with warm personal regard, *Sincerely*

[1] Dr. Gaines (Ph.D. Columbia 1924) had taught English at several colleges and for a year had been literary editor of the *Greenville* (S.C.) *Piedmont*. From 1927 to 1930 he had served as president of Wake Forest College, and since 1930 he had been president of Washington and Lee University, in Virginia.

1831   *ABC 471.6 Atom (8-17-45), Sec. 4-F*

To Joint Chiefs of Staff   *October 30, 1947*
Memorandum. Top secret

Subject: Proposed Release of an Extracted Version of the Final Report of the JCS Evaluation Board on Operation Crossroads and the Related Proposed Press Release[1]
        Reference: JCS 1691/7

1. I believe that the Joint Chiefs of Staff should obtain the comments of the Chairman, Joint Chiefs of Staff Evaluation Board, prior to reaching a decision on JCS 1691/7.[2]

2. JCS 1691/7 suggests that policy decisions be reached on certain controversial subjects prior to release of the extract report to the public.[3] The position of the National Military Establishment on these politico-military issues can best be finalized by submission of the extract report to the President through the Secretary of Defense, thereby making possible discussion of the matter in the War Council.

3. Based on the above, I recommend that the recommendations in paragraph 4 of JCS 1691/7 be replaced by the following:

"4. It is recommended that:

a. The memorandum in Enclosure "A" be approved and forwarded to the Chairman, Joint Chiefs of Staff Evaluation Board for comment.

b. Upon receipt, the reply from the Chairman, Joint Chiefs of Staff Evaluation Board, be forwarded to Joint Security Control for the preparation of an appropriate recommendation to the President through the Secretary of Defense regarding release of Enclosures "C" and "D" to the press.[4]

c. Approval by the Joint Chiefs of Staff to Enclosures "C" and "D" await the action in *a* and *b* above as well as final Joint Chiefs of Staff decision on the complete Joint Chiefs of Staff Evaluation Board Final Report."[5]

[1] For information on Operation CROSSROADS, the 1946 atomic-bomb tests, see no. 1002. The final report of the JCS Evaluation Board is discussed in no. 1846. Schuyler prepared this memorandum for Eisenhower, and the paper circulated as JCS 1691/8, of November 3.
[2] In JCS 1691/7, of October 16, Joint Security Control had sent the JCS its recommendations, including four enclosures: A, a proposed memorandum to the

chairman of the JCS Evaluation Board; B, a discussion; C, a draft press release, prepared by the Evaluation Board but modified by the JSC; and D, an extracted version of the final report originally prepared on June 30 (same file as document).
[3] The most controversial subject involved the degree of discretionary authority to be given the President to order the use of the atomic bomb prior to an actual atomic attack upon the United States. The report also recommended that Congress review the Atomic Energy Act, with the implication that the military should have a larger role in the AEC.
[4] The Joint Security Control paper recommended that the Joint Chiefs approve the revised press release and extract (enclosures C and D, respectively) after consideration of the Evaluation Board's final report. Then the JCS should forward the material to Dr. Karl T. Compton, chairman of the board, for comment. Upon receipt of the board's comments, Joint Security Control would prepare appropriate recommendations to the President regarding release of the material. Eisenhower's proposal was that the JCS approve the material after Dr. Compton had commented on it.
[5] Admiral Nimitz recommended deletion of the comments on the need for congressional determination of what constituted aggression or imminent or incipient attack (JCS 1691/9, Nov. 6, same file as document). Schuyler advised General Eisenhower to oppose this deletion and said that the question could be discussed with the secretary of defense (memo, Nov. 12). On November 14 the JCS sent the two documents to Compton (as Eisenhower had suggested), and on December 18 Dr. Compton would forward his approval, with minor modifications, to the proposal that the extracted version and accompanying press release be sent to the President through the secretary of defense. The "political" portions would be set off in brackets to alert the President to the fact that the Joint Chiefs considered these questions beyond their purview. On January 8, 1948, the JCS would send to Forrestal the extracted report, the press release, and Compton's letter, together with a covering message. (All correspondence is in the same file as this document.) After checking with the State Department, Forrestal would decide not to release the extract because of the "tense international situation" and the possibility that it might be interpreted "as a preface to some brusk action. . ." (see correspondence in CCS 471.6 [10-16-45], Sec. 9, esp. Forrestal to Bradley Dewey, Sept. 21, 1948).

1832   *Eisenhower Mss.*

TO HENRY MAITLAND WILSON   *October 30, 1947*
Personal and confidential

Dear Jumbo: There were many reasons underlying my decision to go to Columbia sometime next year.[1] In the first place, I could scarcely stay in the Army longer than the end of 1949 since the Chief of Staff's tour ordinarily has a legal limit of four years and it would be awkward for any new Chief of Staff to hold me in the Army when his own personal rank would be junior to mine. Not that such a thing would make any very great difference to me, but it would probably to many individuals in the service.

Faced with the certainty that I was to go out within the next couple of years, Mamie and I began to consider the various localities in which we might settle down and lead a quiet life with my own activities confined to a bit of writing. As soon as others learned that we had begun thinking about our post-Army life a number of individuals visited me to point out what I should do when I became a civilian. Each of them seemed to be perfectly clear as to the nature of my duty. This whole thing became rather pressing and finally Mamie and I came to the sad conclusion that the quiet and secluded life we sought would be denied to us. In these circumstances I decided that, whatever activity I entered, I would want some kind of an organization that would serve as a shield against the interminable and pressing demands that I do this and that and the other. All things considered, I finally came to the conclusion that Columbia would offer me opportunity for some kind of public service and would provide about as good protection as anything else. When the pressure from the Trustees got too great I merely said "Yes"—but since that time I have had only a few moments even to contemplate the type of thing into which I am getting. I may be the biggest flop in history but I haven't time to worry about that right now.

I agree with you that it seems a great pity that the world cannot regain some peace of mind, some ability to gaze at our immediate problems objectively and to relieve ourselves of the fears and hatreds that are generating among us all a near hysteria. There is so much to be done in the world in straightening out local messes, in increasing production, in providing for sustenance and health and education, that it is more than tragic that we have to spend our time worrying about the fear of attack, the unbridled ambitions of politicians and a thousand other things that should be thrown into the scrap heap. I think that one of the best services any individual can do these days is to preach sanity—to attempt to preserve some attitude of balance and judgment in the midst of argument, criticisms, and namecalling that are usually senseless.

Of course the big obstacle is Russia. It is difficult indeed to understand why a country that is now controlling as much of the earth's surface as she is, and which has already absorbed great parcels of humanity, should find it necessary at this moment to keep up such an aggressive attitude. To the end of my days I shall always wonder whether something specific, even though small, did not happen in the late fall of 1945 that inspired Russia to adopt the attitude she now so clearly shows to all. I shall always be convinced that Zhukov wanted to be friends with the Western democracies and I am almost equally sure that at that moment (summer of 1945) Stalin agreed with Zhukov's viewpoint.[2] The Generalissimo himself recited to me specific instances in which his country needed Western help. He talked about the fields of agriculture, manufacturing, public works development, and in fact, all of the sciences except medicine, asserting that the good of his own people demanded that they import rapidly our techniques and practices. He even said "We must be friends, even if we don't want to." Within a few short months thereafter he had already adopted the attitude he now shows to the world and it is of course possible that he was merely being hypocritical when he talked to me and others at the close of the European hostilities. There is room to believe, however, that either something occurred to arouse his fear or anger or that he discovered that the great part of his Politbureau was determined to pursue without pause the old Communistic doctrine of world revolution. In this latter case, he would have, in character, immediately taken the lead to become the greatest "hate" of all.

In any event, the world is in a rather sorry mess and there seems no better prescription, for the moment, than to be patient and conciliatory, but to be certain that we are strong enough politically, economically and militarily so that conciliation and patience will not be mistaken for fear and weakness. If all the free countries could present a united front in this regard we would breathe easier; the great obstacle is the shattered economies of so many countries that would otherwise be an effective bar to the realization of Communistic ambition.

The issues are involved and the proper path is certainly far from clear. Anyone who today would deliberately seek a decisive role in the business of conducting national or world politics must certainly be more than self-confident—he must believe himself practically omnipotent.

I believe that one of the great anchors we have now is the certainty that the English-speaking race will never give up the individual liberties they fought so long and hard to secure and maintain. Another encouraging factor is the great interest that every individual citizen is today taking in world problems and in the security of his own country. Still another encouraging thing that we must never forget is the fact that in free countries the unrestricted genius of all the people will in the long run be responsible for constructive development beyond that possible in a regimented and policed state.

There are other important factors working on our side. I merely mention two or three that seem often to be overlooked.

I don't know why I got started on such a rambling presentation of ideas that have certainly not been coordinated or even well thought out. I suppose it is merely that since it was always fun to talk to you when you were here I am continuing the practice.

With warm regard, *Cordially*

---

[1] Field Marshal Wilson had written to wish Eisenhower success in the academic world. He thought that Eisenhower's move would be a good thing because in many cases "those who have had the great responsibilities of command are out of adjustment with the stresses and pulls of the post-war situation that the world is in today"

(n.d., EM). In the spring of 1947 William D. Morgan had succeeded Wilson as head of the British Joint Staff Mission in Washington.

[2] See no. 1327.

1833   *Eisenhower Mss.*

To Miles Christopher Dempsey   *October 30, 1947*

Dear Bimbo:[1] I am flattered that you should want my photograph.[2] It is coming by the next boat. Likewise I feel honored that the Royal Berkshires should want some memento in their headquarters and for want of anything more appropriate—at least until my imagination can do a better job—I am sending two of the items you suggested. One is an outsize photograph that my Aide seems to think would be better for your purpose than would a size more in keeping with a sense of modesty. The other is a signed copy of my final Despatch. I shall write to Max Taylor at once. He is now Superintendent of our Military Academy at West Point, New York, and was the Commander of the 101st Airborne Division during the war. I shall suggest to him that as soon as the history of the 101st Division is completed, he forward you a copy suitably inscribed to the Royal Berkshires.[3]

It was delightful to hear from you and you owe me no apology whatsoever. I know of nothing from which I derive greater pleasure than a word from my old teammates. Within the past few months I have had visits with Freddie de Guingand and with "Bomber" Bert.[4] Both were in top form and I had a grand time with each of them. Freddie stayed with me a day or two and if ever you get to this country you must do the same.

Please remember me to any of our old friends that you may happen to encounter, and with warm personal regards to yourself,[5] *Cordially*

[1] Dempsey had been colonel commandant of the Corps of Royal Military Police (Royal Berkshire Regiment) since his retirement from the British Army in 1947. In 1946 and 1947 he had served as Commander in Chief, Middle East, and A.D.C. General to the King. For further background see no. 177.

[2] In a letter of October 16 Dempsey had asked Eisenhower if he would send one of the following: an inscribed photo; an inscribed and bound copy of Eisenhower's report to the CCS on the campaign in Europe; or an inscribed history of the 101st Airborne Division. Dempsey said that the Royal Berkshire Regiment now occupied barracks formerly used by the 101st and that the regiment would especially like some memento associated with that division.

[3] This same day Eisenhower sent Taylor a copy of Dempsey's letter, with a covering note. Taylor replied on November 3 that he had sent a pictorial history of the 101st to Dempsey and would send him the formal history when it was published. Both letters are in EM.

[4] Air Marshal Harris.

[5] Dempsey thanked Eisenhower in a letter of November 25 (*ibid.*).

To James Lawrence Walsh   *October 30, 1947*

Dear Colonel Walsh:[1] I am delighted that the Councillors, Directors and Officers of the Army Ordnance Association are to hold their annual meeting at West Point. The place of the meeting should typify the acute need in this country for close and continuing cooperation between our organized military services and the vast American industry that supports them.

In response to your suggestion that I send a brief message, I am inclosing a copy of a talk I once made on this general subject.[2] But as an added thought I submit the following for any use you can make of it:

"On the modern continental battlefield a decisive factor in the attainment of victory is the perfection of coordination between the ground-air team, and the efficiency with which their every material need is satisfied by service organizations. In the same way, the security of this country depends directly and inescapably upon effectiveness of coordination between the industrial fabric of the country and the fighting forces which, even in war, are merely the cutting edges of a great machine for which the power is supplied by the productiveness of the entire population.[3] To assure the integration of these vast organisms in time of great emergency, foresight and common planning during years of peace are mandatory. Every individual in our productive processes, particularly the leaders of our great industrial organizations, must feel as direct a responsibility for the present and future security of the country as does any soldier in uniform. In turn the soldier, recognizing the direct dependence of all forms of military effort upon adequate weapons and supply, must make it his own duty to cooperate with and to assist the industrialist in preparing for grave contingencies. In the discharge of these responsibilities the Army Ordnance Association has always taken a leading part; to it and to all its members and to all those with whom it works, I send my greetings and best wishes for their continued success."

I truly trust that you will find the above useful. I will get it off as quickly as I can by air mail because I note that your meeting is tomorrow night.

With warm personal regards, and my thanks for providing me this opportunity, *Sincerely*

[1] Colonel James Lawrence Walsh (USMA 1909) had founded the *Army Ordnance* magazine in 1920 and had edited it until 1922. He had retired from active duty in 1930, but he had served as a special advisor to the Chief of Ordnance during World

War II. As president of the Army Ordnance Association, he had written on October 28 asking Eisenhower for a brief message to be read at the association's annual meeting on October 31 (COS, 1947, 080 Army Ordnance Association).
[2] We have been unable to locate a transcript of this talk.
[3] According to Walsh, the association's membership included "approximately 40,000 scientists, engineers, and industrialists. . . ."

1835   *Eisenhower Mss.*

To Pelagius Williams   *October 30, 1947*

Dear Mr. Williams: Your note carried me back, for a moment at least, over a stretch of 40 years. I remember you perfectly; I have often felt, as I look back, that you and your associates must have had a trying time with a group of healthy, vigorous Kansas boys who were far more interested in football and shooting rabbits than they were in the knowledge and sense that you tried to cram into our heads.[1]

I regard it as one of the most fortunate things in my life that I spent my boyhood in a region and in a situation that provided both a healthy outdoor existence and a need to work. These same conditions were responsible for the existence of a society which, more nearly than any other I have encountered, eliminated prejudices based upon wealth, race or creed, and maintained a standard of values that placed a premium upon integrity, decency, and consideration for others. The democracy of our schools and the understanding of our teachers helped likewise to emphasize the dignity of work and of accomplishment. I shall always believe that any youngster, boy or girl, who has the opportunity to spend his early youth in an enlightened rural area has been favored by fortune and has obtained something that will never desert him throughout his life.

I truly appreciated your letter. From time to time I have heard from some of my other high school and grade school teachers and I never fail to draw some inspiration from their messages.

With warm personal regard, *Sincerely*

[1] Williams had written to Eisenhower: "Perhaps you will recall that I was your high school principal and history teacher at Abilene in 1907–08." Williams was now living in Bellingham, Washington, and was to address the Hobby Club there on November 10. Since Williams's hobby was history and biography, he was going to present a paper on Eisenhower. He asked if he "might have from you (a very busy man I know) a few lines expressing your idea of some of the factors in your early life that have brought you to the outstanding position you now occupy or any other personal message you may wish to give to this group" (Oct. 27, EM).

To Ruth Noyes McDowell Sheldon   *October 30, 1947*

Dear Mrs. Sheldon:[1] My interest in the Soldiers, Sailors and Marines Club has not abated, and I am deeply appreciative of the work it is doing. I earnestly hope it will continue to receive the support of the Community Chest of the District of Washington because no other organization offers to the enlisted men of our military forces the facilities that it does.

However, I do not feel that it is appropriate for me to suggest to the officers and men of the Army that they single out the Soldiers, Sailors and Marines Club in their contribution.[2] Such a suggestion is too likely to be interpreted almost as an order—in other words, an attempt to interfere in individual personal matters. I feel, of course, that the Chest should continue to support the Club. I have no objection to your using this expression of opinion in any way you may deem proper and appropriate. *Sincerely*

[1] Mrs. Sheldon, the wife of Rear Admiral Luther Sheldon, Jr., was a vice-president of the Soldiers, Sailors and Marines Club of Washington. On October 23 she had written, "Following my recent conversation with Mrs. Eisenhower, I am writing to ask your help for our club in the Community Chest drive." Mrs. Sheldon asked that Eisenhower suggest to Army personnel that they indicate their support merely by placing a check mark beside the name of the club when they make their contribution to the combined-charities drive. Michaelis (in a note of October 25 to the Chief of Staff) pointed out that Mrs. Eisenhower was also a vice-president of the club but had committed General Eisenhower "in no way." He recommended that Eisenhower reject the request. Eisenhower wrote at the bottom of Mrs. Sheldon's letter, "What does Gen. Parks think of this?" On October 28, in a memorandum to Michaelis, Parks sent a suggested reply. All correspondence is in the same file as this document.

[2] From this point on, Eisenhower rewrote the draft (McDuff Coll.).

1837   *Eisenhower Mss.*

To Earl Marvin Price   *October 31, 1947*
Personal and confidential

Dear E.M.: It seems to me you have developed quite a high blood pressure out of the simple accident that in answering your last summer's letter—which I did personally—I overlooked the fact that you were the same fellow that I have known for 36 years.[1] Without attempting to defend my carelessness or to present an alibi, it is still true that the number of letters that I write is, to say the least, unusual. No old friend of mine has ever had justifiable reason for believing that I was trying to give him the brush-off. Naturally, had I not missed this important point at the time, I would have answered more fully, because I suppose that not more than 1% of the communications I receive are from old friends—and more especially, from old soldiers and classmates.

First of all, you seem to think that I have been rather a shrinking violet in supporting Universal Military Training.[2] I could send you a whole list of Congressional hearings, public speeches and records of press conferences in which I have battled for UMT ever since our 1943 campaigns in Africa. In fact, I kept talking when many real friends of UMT suggested that I keep still—their advice being based on their own conclusions as to expediency at a moment when so many other subjects were engaging the attention of the Congress and the public. I have not waited for anyone else to suggest a lead in this line—in fact, except for a few other soldiers and one or two devoted friends, for a long time I felt very much alone in the struggle.

I do not resent, of course, your holding any opinion you please. That is your personal right. But when you intimate that any cause for which I have labored so long and so hard has only recently been undertaken as a matter of convenience, there is plenty of evidence in the record to show that you are mistaken.

What I had to say about "policy" in my former letter most certainly does not apply to anything that is involved in the security of this country. I was talking merely about subjects that are non-military in character and which do not come within the scope of the Army's responsibilities. For example: any comment on the New Deal![3]

You devoted a considerable portion of your letter to discussing political affairs, more particularly as they might affect me personally. It is true that numbers of friends, acquaintances, or old associates around the country have done some talking about the possibility of my standing for political office. This has happened to every man who ever had his name favorably mentioned in the newspapers and I see no reason for my getting particularly excited about it except to say what I have already said, and mean, that *I want no part of any political job.* Since no man—at least since Washington's day—has ever gone into high political office except with his own consent, indeed with his own connivance, I feel perfectly secure in my position and I do not consider it either appropriate or in good taste that I say another word about it. If ever you find any statement anywhere that purports to quote me as saying that I want a political office, and I mean now or in the future, then you send it on to me and remind me of this statement.[4]

You seem to be impressed greatly with what Sherman said as applicable to any citizen whose name might be casually mentioned (at any time) for political office. Did you ever look up the circumstances under which he said it? For 20 years many people hounded Sherman to take a part in politics and he steadfastly refused. Finally in 1884 a political convention was actually in session. It deadlocked. The bosses communicated with him and asked him to step in as the one person around whom all might unite. Of course, under those circumstances, it was appropriate and proper for him to say exactly what he did. He was definitely offered something but certainly he did not have to feel any personal duty about engaging in an activity which was distasteful to him when he clearly understood that political leaders were merely trying to make him a convenience to pull the party out of a hole.

Frankly, the reason I am trying to point out these things in some detail is because you state that I have been guilty of double-talk. I am astonished that at this distance and considering the number of years that have elapsed since last I saw you, you should feel yourself so competent to pass such firm and unfavorable judgment upon an old classmate. Although I can agree with your generalization that plenty of double-talk does come out of Washington, I do not see why that circumstance alone convicts everyone who is compelled to serve here. I have never evaded a legitimate question or consciously lied to the press or the public— regardless of your interpretation of whatever you may have seen as quotes from me. Enough of that!

There is to be a joint luncheon of the Army and Navy classes of 1915 within a matter of a week or so. It is the first one that I have found myself able to attend for many months but I will give to all the Army side your best wishes and greetings. If you should get back this way by all means drop in to see me. I assure you that all anyone has to do to get in here is to tell an Aide that he is an old classmate or an old friend of mine in the Army.

I hope that you will consider this letter entirely personal and confidential, which it is, but I also hope that when next you have the impulse to accuse an old friend of things of which you yourself would not be guilty, you try to avoid jumping at conclusions.[5] *Cordially*

[1] Price had written on October 25 (EM). He was angry because Eisenhower's reply to his previous letter was headed "Dear Mr. Price" and gave no indication that the two men had known each other for many years. He wanted Eisenhower to tell whoever was signing his letters that he had a Christian name, which he thought his classmates should use. For background see no. 1702.

[2] Actually, Price had expressed his point much more strongly than this. He had scolded Eisenhower for not speaking out forcefully for UMT. As recently as October 21, however, the General had issued a public statement strongly supporting the Compton Commission report on UMT (EM). A copy showing Eisenhower's changes in the draft is in the McDuff Collection. For later developments on UMT see no. 1980.

³ Price had referred to Eisenhower's comment that the Army did not make political policy. Price had denounced the New Deal several times.

⁴ Price thought Eisenhower was being deliberately vague as to his willingness to run for President. Like many others, he referred to the unequivocal position taken by General William Tecumseh Sherman in 1884.

⁵ Price sent a long and conciliatory response on November 11 (EM). He told Eisenhower that he would not, however, be coming to Washington.

1838   *Eisenhower Mss.*

To Joseph Lawrence Lehner   *October 31, 1947*

Dear Joseph: Naturally I shall be delighted to do what I can in helping you get an appointment to West Point.¹ I have some good friends in the State of Washington and I shall ask them to help in the matter also.

I assume that your official residence is still Tacoma or the Fort Lewis area and it is for that reason that you are requesting your appointment from that District. Also I assume that you have a presidential appointment to enter the competitive examinations but that you would like to get the congressional appointment in order that a passing grade will secure your entrance into West Point.²

You need feel no sense of obligation in asking me to help because I assure you it will always be a pleasure to do whatever I can for the son of people that have been such good friends as have your father and mother.³

Wishing you the best of luck, *Sincerely*

¹ Lehner, who was at the USMA preparatory school at Stewart Field, in Newburgh, New York, had written Mrs. Eisenhower on October 28 (EM). He asked if she would write three of the congressmen from the state of Washington in support of his request for an appointment to West Point. Lehner's parents had been friends of the Eisenhowers' at Fort Lewis before the war.

² Lehner replied that Eisenhower was correct on all the points in this paragraph (Nov. 4, *ibid.*).

³ See the next document for further developments.

1839   *Eisenhower Mss.*

To James Stack   *October 31, 1947*

Dear Jim: I am inclosing a letter I have received from young Joseph Lehner, son of the Lehners who served with us at Fort Lewis.¹ Because you know personally the Senators and the Congressmen that the boy desires to contact I am hopeful that you can do something to help him in the matter, primarily because I liked his father and mother so much.

I shall not write personally to any of these until I am advised to do so by you—this in the thought that it might be more effective if you carry the ball rather than myself. Please understand that I am perfectly ready to write such letters. I merely want your suggestions as to what would be the most helpful thing to do. It is possible also that Edgar might help out. I believe he is a very good friend of Senator Cain's.[2]

Herb Blunck came to lunch with me today and we had a nice visit extending over an hour and a half.[3] It is the first time I have seen him for quite a while and naturally you became one of the subjects of our conversation. We worried some for fear you were attempting to get active in business too quickly; the news that you were coming East to a couple of conventions didn't sound too good since both of us have some idea of what these conventions ordinarily turn out to be.[4] However, when you get to Washington I hope that you and Elsa[5] will count on staying with us. Mamie and I would be more than delighted to have you, as you well know.

Some time back you were a bit disturbed by a Drew Pearson column reporting that the politicians of the State of Washington had approached you on the proposition of standing for Governor. You seemed to think that someone might find a close connection between your position and my future intentions.[6] As you know, I have been perfectly honest in all that I have had to say about this irritating business and I merely want to assure you that from my viewpoint you are as free as air to do whatever you think you should—although I must say that I think you would find a business career far more attractive than a political one, assuming that the doctors finally give you a good bill of health to do anything active.

Recently I was out to Kansas and for once I made a visit where the people were kind enough to lay off personally embarrassing questions.[7] Consequently the trip, though tiring, was enjoyable.

Tomorrow night Mamie and I leave by train for Fort Worth, Texas, and on the way home will stop briefly at Little Rock, Arkansas, where I will address some veterans. At Fort Worth I am to dedicate a statue to Will Rogers, which I shall do in a very simple, homely little talk.[8]

Life here is as hectic as ever and the prospect of a special session of Congress adds nothing to my anticipation of a peaceful fall. I have become perfectly hardboiled in the matter of accepting invitations over the country and have not added a single commitment to this year's calendar during the past three months. I think I have hurt some feelings but at least I am saving myself a lot of hard work. I still think it will be as late as February before I turn over this job to my successor and then I am going to take a 60-day leave.

Please let me know about the Lehner matter as soon as you can—I should really like to help the boy if he is as fine a character as his father and his mother.[9]

Give my love to Elsa and the children and, as always, with warmest regards to yourself, *Sincerely*

[1] See the previous document. Stack now lived in Tacoma, Washington.

[2] The General's reference was to his brother Edgar. Senator Cain was a Republican who had represented the state of Washington since 1946. On November 10 and 14 Eisenhower would write to Senator Cain on Lehner's behalf (EM).

[3] Herbert Christopher Blunck was the manager of the Statler Hotel in Washington, D.C.

[4] Stack was coming to Washington for two weekends in January.

[5] Stack's wife.

[6] Stack had enclosed a copy of the column in his letter of October 5 (EM).

[7] See no. 1822.

[8] Eisenhower would leave Washington the next evening by train for Chicago, arriving Sunday morning, November 2. He left Chicago by train for Fort Worth, Texas. On November 4, the sixty-eighth anniversary of Will Rogers's birth, Eisenhower unveiled a bronze statue of Rogers on his horse, Soap Suds. Eisenhower then proceeded to Little Rock, Arkansas, where at the invitation of local veterans organizations, he addressed a public gathering. He arrived back in Washington the night of the sixth. Copies of Eisenhower's speeches at Fort Worth and Little Rock are in EM, Subject File, Speeches. Documents concerning the trip are in EM; and COS, 1947, 080 Greater Little Rock Chamber of Commerce.

[9] Stack would describe his efforts on Lehner's behalf in a letter of November 17 (EM). Lehner would not receive an appointment (see Cain to Stack, Aug. 13, 1948, *ibid.*).

VIII

"I was their fellow-soldier"

NOVEMBER 1947 TO FEBRUARY 1948

18

The Three-Service Concept in Theory and Practice

To James Vincent Forrestal   *November 1, 1947*
Secret

Memorandum for the Secretary of Defense:

Subject: Tactical Air Support

At the meeting of the War Council on 21 October, you requested that I submit to you a brief statement of my views as to whether or not so-called tactical air units supporting Army forces should be under the command of the Army commander, and hence, whether or not the Department of the Army should include within its organization the tactical air units for this purpose.[1]

The Army concept of the land, sea and air principle of organization of the armed forces is well-known; this Service accepts without reservation the concept of complementary roles—air, ground and sea—and consequent mutual dependence of the three components of the armed services. Under this three service concept it is axiomatic that no single service should acquire forces or equipment necessary to accomplish joint missions singlehanded, if such forces or equipment unnecessarily duplicate those characteristic of and fundamental to either of the other two services. The experiences of this war have indicated that in many operations, if not in the majority, the task was of necessity accomplished by contributions from two or three services acting under the principle of unified command. Furthermore, the welding of the forces resulted in the greatest possible concentration of combat power at the decisive point while at the same time permitting the greatest economy of force on lesser tasks.[2]

Employment of tactical air in World War II is an outstanding illustration of the application of this concept to a specific problem. Battle experience proved that control of the air, the prerequisite to the conduct of ground operations in any given area, was gained most economically by the employment of air forces operating under a single command. This assured a maximum of flexibility, providing a command structure under which all forms of available air power could be concentrated on tactical support missions or on strategic missions, as the situation demanded—in other words, it permitted the maximum concentration of combat air power at the decisive point at the decisive time. Throughout the war, the Army depended on the necessary tactical air support from a practically autonomous Air Force. This type of close, accurate, and effective support of the front-line fighting units *was* provided and proved an essential element in the achievement of the Army objectives.

The case for the concept that tactical air units belong under the Air Force rather than under the Army is supported by the abundant evidence of World War II, but does not rest on this evidence alone. Basically, the Army does not belong in the air—it belongs on the ground. Planes are but a facet of the over-all problem, which is basically much broader and includes responsibilities now involving approximately one-third of the Air Force. Control of the tactical Air Force means responsibility, not merely for the fighters and medium bombers themselves, but, as well, for the entire operating establishment required to support these planes. This includes the requisite basic air research and development program necessary to maintain a vital arm and the additional specialized service forces to support the arm; for example: air maintenance units, aircraft warning units (radar, DF stations), tactical air communications nets, etc. In short, assumption of this task by the Army would duplicate in great measure the primary and continuing responsibilities of the Air Force and, in effect, would result in the creation of another air establishment.

To the foregoing, I would add one final thought. The question of whether or not the tactical Air Force should be included within the Department of the Army was thoroughly explored in both the House and Senate hearings on Public Law 253, National Security Act of 1947, and solutions which would have placed this function under the Department of the Army were rejected by the Army, by the Air Force and by the Congress. To include now within the Department of the Army the tactical air units required for support of the Army would, to my mind, be contrary to the letter and spirit of the National Security Act.[3]

I have full confidence that the Air Force can and will furnish with full effectiveness this vital support to the Army. I, therefore, recommend adherence to the proved and accepted concept that the Air Force furnishes tactical air support to the Army.[4]

[1] Secretary of the Air Force Stuart Symington raised this question because Forrestal had "evidently become aware of adverse comments by some ground officers on having tactical air under the Department of the Air Force rather than under the Department of the Army" (Norstad to Royall and Eisenhower, Oct. 20, 1947, OSA/KCR Cent. Dec. File, 334 War Council). At the October 21 meeting Forrestal agreed with the principle of Air Force responsibility for tactical air. The Secretary of Defense, however, wanted to make certain that vital close air support would be provided in such "dispersed and scattered operations" as the United States had undertaken in the Pacific during World War II. He asked Eisenhower and Spaatz to tell him whether "all elements in the Services" were satisfied with the existing and proposed arrangements (Forrestal, *Diaries*, pp. 333–34; see also notes from the War Council meeting of October 21 in OS/D, 47–49, Cent. Numeric File, D 2-1-3).
[2] This question had been one of the central issues in the debate over unification of the services; for background see no. 1325.
[3] The act creating the Department of Defense is discussed in no. 1675.
[4] On November 3 Collins, Eisenhower's deputy chief of staff, forwarded

Eisenhower's memorandum to Forrestal with a note that read, "Prior to his departure on 1 November for absence of a few days, General Eisenhower dictated the
substance of the attached memorandum and directed that it be delivered to you this
date." For information on Eisenhower's trip see the previous document.

1841   *Eisenhower Mss.*

To Jock Rupert Colville   *November 1, 1947*

Dear Mr. Colville: Today there is going forward to London a small gift
from Mrs. Eisenhower and me to The Princess.[1] It is nothing but a
silver ash tray made in the form of a wedding ring. The reason for its
selection is that for some years it has constituted the standard little
wedding present that Mrs. Eisenhower and I have sent to the children of
our dearest friends. Because of our affection and admiration for Her
Royal Highness, we chose to avoid changing our practice, thus including her, in our minds, at least, among those we hold most dear.

We postponed, as long as possible, informing the Lord Chamberlain
that we could not come to the wedding, because we continued to hope
that something might turn up to make attendance feasible.[2] It was with
very real and lasting disappointment that we had to conclude that we just
could not do so. I can assure you that, through the future years, no one
will be ahead of Mrs. Eisenhower and myself in continuing to wish for
The Princess and Lieutenant Mountbatten every possible happiness and
success.

I shall be grateful if you can explain to Her Royal Highness the
special sentiments that come with our little gift.[3]

With personal regard, *Sincerely*

[1] Princess Elizabeth of England would marry Lieutenant Philip Mountbatten on
November 20, 1947 (see *New York Times,* Nov. 20, 1947). On October 29
General and Mrs. Eisenhower regretfully declined the invitation to attend the
wedding. A typed copy of their handwritten letter and related correspondence are in
EM. For background on Colville see no. 1777.
[2] See no. 1820.
[3] On November 12 Princess Elizabeth would send Eisenhower a handwritten note
of thanks (a typed copy is in EM).

1842   *Eisenhower Mss.*

To James Phinney Baxter III   *November 1, 1947*

Dear Dr. Baxter: It would be difficult to tell you how flattered I feel by
the suggestion made to me in your letter of October 12.[1] You may be
certain that I will come to Williams next June if it is humanly possible.

The only condition I must make is that you let me know the final date on which I could give you a firm answer, since the period promises to be one of extraordinary activity for me, including as it probably will the early days of my transfer to Columbia.

Frankly, one of the appealing features of your suggestion—quite aside from my affection for Williams and my admiration for you—is found in the fact that I shall not be expected to make an address. I like very much to attend college functions as long as I am not called upon to expose my woeful failings in all those qualities characteristic of the scholar.

If it is understood, then, that I may answer conditionally, with the understanding that you will notify me when I must give you a definite answer, I assure you again that I am delighted at the prospect.[2]

With kind personal regards, *Sincerely*

[1] Baxter received his Ph.D. in history from Harvard University in 1926. He was on the Harvard faculty from 1925 until 1937, when he became president of Williams College. During World War II he served as deputy director of the OSS and then as historian of the Office of Scientific Research and Development. In his letter of October 12 Baxter invited Eisenhower to Williams to receive the honorary degree of Doctor of Laws on June 20, 1948 (EM).

[2] Eisenhower would go to Williamstown, Massachusetts, on June 20 to receive the degree at the annual commencement ceremonies.

1843   *Eisenhower Mss.*

To Alden Hatch   *November 1, 1947*

Dear Alden:[1] I have hastily run over your article on General Bradley and as you suggested, have sent it on to Colonel Hansen.[2] I can understand what you say about the mild criticism involving V.A. as a means of providing obvious authenticity for the whole article, but as to its applicability I have nothing to say. If there is any comment on it I suppose Colonel Hansen will provide it.

When you get your manuscript back you will find that I have made one or two corrections in pencil, merely factual in character. For example, on page 8 you classed Bradley as a Personnel Inspector when he was really a Tactical Inspector. Also you state he was Deputy Commander of the II Corps in the final attacks in northern Tunisia when actually he was the Corps Commander. At the bottom of the same page it is more accurate to say that Bradley was responsible for all American "tactical ground" plans; this for the reason that there were many naval and air phases to the plan for which others were responsible. Your statement as it stands would be objected to by such individuals.

There is only one statement you make to which I make objection. On page 4 I quote: "He seemed to think he could win the war with Third Army alone—*and maybe he could have.*" I am astonished that you could have included in the sentence the last clause. You have been an observer of things military for a long time and you have lost sight of the position that Patton occupied in Europe. He was merely an Army Commander, always operating under Bradley's direction. Within the Twelfth Army Group only Bradley was responsible for the allocation of air power, of supply, of transport facilities, and for cooperation among neighboring Armies. All the material paraphernalia of war were at that time in short supply and even had Bradley given to Patton everything that he had in his whole Army Group, indeed, if he could have given him everything in the whole ETO, it is clear that Patton's few divisions would certainly have had to stop within a short space of time. He could have gone further than he did, possibly even up to the Rhine, but the implication of your statement, particularly in the light of the fact that the German still had strong reserves within his own country, is, I repeat, astonishing. Remember, we did not yet have *Antwerp*, and without that port (or its equivalent) no major invasion of Germany was possible. When Bradley was commanding the Army Group he always had at least one and sometimes two Armies in addition to Patton's. Just as I was responsible for the over-all strategy, Bradley was completely responsible for *the grand tactics, direction* and *coordination* of *this huge ground force.* At all times Patton had exactly the strength and *carried out exactly the missions that Bradley laid down for him.*[3]

On the bottom of page 11 you refer to the "largest *field* command." The term may be a bit misleading. Strictly speaking, any theater commander is a field commander, so I think it would be more accurate to say "battle line" command. This is, of course, a very minor point.

Generally speaking, I liked the article and assure you that it is far from being overdrawn in its sympathetic approach.[4]

With personal regard, and my best to Ruth,[5] *Sincerely*

[1] For background on Hatch see no. 1481.

[2] Hatch had sent Eisenhower an article he had written on General Bradley, with a covering letter of October 29 (EM). Hatch intended to withhold the manuscript until Bradley's appointment as Chief of Staff was announced. He said, "The very mild criticism of some aspects of V.A. is merely to give an air of objectivity to the piece...." He asked Eisenhower to read the article and then to pass it on to Lieutenant Colonel Chester B. Hansen, who was Bradley's special assistant at the Veterans Administration. Michaelis would forward the article to Hansen with a note of November 3. On November 6 Hansen would send Michaelis a copy of a letter (same date) recommending certain changes to Hatch. All correspondence is in EM.

[3] Hatch would write Eisenhower on November 5 thanking him for examining the manuscript; he said he was deleting the statement to which Eisenhower had objected (EM).

[4] The article, "Eisenhower Views His Successor," would be published in the February 1948 issue of *True* magazine.

[5] Hatch's wife, formerly Ruth Brown.

1844   *Eisenhower Mss.*

To Marie Fisher La Guardia   *November 1, 1947*

Dear Mrs. LaGuardia:[1] It was more than kind of you to write me such a nice letter about Miss Steinberg and, needless to say, I am flattered by her desire to be associated with me in the work at Columbia.[2] There is no doubt that anyone who was so valuable to your late husband is a person of the highest ability and character.

My difficulty is that I cannot foresee the nature of my staff organization at Columbia. It is possible that the University already has assembled the individuals necessary to allow the President to function efficiently; on the other hand, it is just as possible that I myself will be expected to collect such a group. In these circumstances it is not possible for me to give Miss Steinberg any definite answer. I can only say that when I finally do come to that institution—assuming she would then be free to take a position at the University—I shall be more than happy to have a conference with her.

While I realize that this answer is, from her viewpoint, most unsatisfactory, I do not see how I can say more at the moment.

Thank you again for your kind interest.[3] *Sincerely*

[1] Mrs. La Guardia was the widow of Fiorello La Guardia, formerly mayor of New York City and deputy general of UNRRA. Mayor La Guardia had died on September 20, 1947.

[2] Mrs. La Guardia had written to Eisenhower on behalf of Ceil Steinberg, who had been secretary and assistant to her late husband. She described Miss Steinberg as a college graduate and a former WAC with "an excellent background in both public affairs and academic interests" (Oct. 28, 1947, EM).

[3] Eisenhower responded similarly in a December 2 letter to Major General Walter Francis Kraus, a retired Army officer who wished to become associated with Columbia. General Kraus had taught engineering at Columbia before joining the Army. He had served in the Air Corps from 1920 to 1946. Eisenhower wrote: "If you should desire to write me a personal letter on the matter sometime next June, after I have arrived at Columbia, I could undoubtedly have the situation examined to determine whether or not there exists any opportunity for your employment." In his December 21 reply Kraus assured Eisenhower that he would take his suggestion. All correspondence is in COS, 1947, 201 Kraus. Columbia University records indicate that neither Steinberg nor Kraus would be employed there during the period 1948–50 (letter from Paul R. Palmer, Apr. 25, 1977, EP).

To Joint Chiefs of Staff   *November 5, 1947*
Memorandum. Confidential

Subject: Informal Staff Conversations with Argentina

THE PROBLEM

1. To determine an over-all military program for the Argentine Army.

FACTS BEARING ON THE PROBLEM

2. At a conference with representatives of the State, War, and Navy Departments held on 11 September 1947, the representative of the Department of State informed those present that authority was granted by his Department for the National Military Establishment to conduct staff conversations with Argentina, if such were necessary to implement an over-all military program for that country. This action was prompted by the Department of State to demonstrate to Argentina our sincerity in relations with them.

3. Previously, during 1944–1945, staff conversations, which were basically exploratory, not involving any commitments by the United States Government, were concluded bilaterally between the United States and all Latin-American nations, except Argentina.[1] These conversations were carried out under the supervision of Headquarters, Caribbean Defense Command, heretofore commanded by Lieutenant General Willis D. Crittenberger.[2] Similar conversations, held on a governmental level involving actual commitments, must be held subsequent to passage of the Inter-American Military Cooperation Act, with each of the Latin-American nations.

4. An over-all military program with Argentina must be determined as a basis for intermittent decisions to be made by the Department of the Army on repeated requests for authority by that country to procure items of equipment in the United States.[3] Likewise, equipment now being procured intermittently and made available to Argentina as and when requested, is not necessarily preventing the purchase of additional equipment by Argentina from other nations.

5. Previously, repeated requests by Argentina for Lieutenant General W. D. Crittenberger to visit there have been deferred each time due to the peculiar relationship existing between our respective countries. Now it has become possible to permit acceptance of this invitation and General Crittenberger will be in Argentina on or about 25 November 1947. It is most essential that he be provided with instructions upon which to base conversations with their representatives. Prior to his

arrival, the United States Department of State will inform the American Embassy, Buenos Aires, that General Crittenberger is prepared for such discussions with the Argentines, preferably upon the latter's initiation.

CONCLUSIONS

6. That exploratory conversations in the immediate future with military representatives of Argentina are most essential to accomplish the following:

> *a.* Determine the approximate over-all requirements of the Argentine Army;
>
> *b.* Obtain an indication from the Argentine representatives that their country will agree, in the later formal staff conversations, to limit their procurement to sources in the United States and to confine their purchases to standard United States items.

7. That Lieutenant General Willis D. Crittenberger, as a representative of the Department of the Army, and assisted by officers from the appropriate divisions of the General Staff, United States Army, should be directed by an appropriate letter of instructions to accomplish the purposes outlined above during his forthcoming visit by means of informal conversations with their representatives.

RECOMMENDATION

8. That the Joint Chiefs of Staff note the enclosed letter of instructions which is to be dispatched by the Chief of Staff, United States Army, to Lieutenant General Willis D. Crittenberger.[4]

[1] These staff conversations and the U.S. policy toward equipping Argentina are discussed in nos. 918 and 1272. Wedemeyer, who on October 31 became Director of Plans and Operations, prepared this memorandum and a brief on November 5, when Eisenhower was in Little Rock, Arkansas (see no. 1839). The Chief of Staff would approve the paper on November 7, after he returned to his office, and the memorandum would circulate as JCS 1815 on the same day (P&O 091 Argentina, Case 10).

[2] On Crittenberger see no. 528.

[3] In its most recent proposal (October 30) the Army had advanced recommendations as to what size of tank forces Argentina should have (State, *Foreign Relations, 1947,* vol. VIII, *The American Republics,* p. 231). For the debate during 1947 over the types of weapons to send to Argentina see *ibid.,* pp. 101–30, 215–38.

[4] The enclosed letter of instructions (not printed here) embodied the specific conclusions of Eisenhower's paper. The letter instructed Crittenberger to make no commitments involving arms or equipment, to obtain a list of the arms Argentina needed, and to ascertain whether Argentina would agree—subsequent to the passage of the Inter-American Military Cooperation Act—"not to purchase equipment from nations other than the United States, and to acquire therein only standard United States equipment." The JCS would approve Eisenhower's recommendation on November 10 (CCS 092 Argentina [3-16-44]). For Crittenberger's report see no. 1967.

846   *ABC 471.6 Atom (8-17-45), Sec. 4-F*

To Joint Chiefs of Staff   *November 5, 1947*
Memorandum. Top secret

Subject: The Final Report of the Joint Chiefs of Staff Evaluation
Board for Operation Crossroads (JCS 1805 and 1805/1)[1]

1. With reference to JCS 1805 and 1805/1, it now appears that the
memorandum to the Secretary of Defense will be at marked variance
with parts of Enclosure B to JCS 1805 (Discussion).[2] I concur in
recommendation of the Chief of Naval Operations in JCS 1805/1 that
Enclosure B then not be forwarded to the Secretary of Defense.[3] I
suggest, however, that the memorandum to the Secretary of Defense be
revised to include all 15 of the recommendations contained in the Final
Report of the JCS Evaluation Board on Operation Crossroads, and that
the following be substituted for the initial paragraph of this letter (Enclosure A to JCS 1805):

"The final report of the Board appointed by the Joint Chiefs of
Staff to evaluate the results of Operation Crossroads contains
twenty-two broad conclusions, together with fifteen recommendations which the Board considered necessary if the implications of their conclusions were to be implemented. These recommendations, together with comments of the Joint Chiefs of Staff
where appropriate, are as follows:"

This revision will also involve deletion of the penultimate paragraph
of Enclosure A to JCS 1805 and the incorporation into Enclosure A of
appropriate recommendations and comments thereto from Enclosure B
of JCS 1805, with resultant elimination of the latter.

2. With reference to amendments to Enclosure A to JCS 1805
proposed by the Chief of Naval Operations in paragraph 3 of JCS
1805/1,[4] I concur in all these amendments subject to the following
comments or exceptions:

a. Regarding proposed substitute comment to Recommendation 4
(page 23, JCS 1805/1),[5] it is considered that the political considerations concerning implementation of this recommendation are
not within the purview of the Joint Chiefs of Staff. However, it
would appear quite appropriate for the JCS to comment upon the
operational significance of this recommendation and to leave for
decision of the Secretary of Defense the desirability of initiating a
request for the necessary legislation. It is, therefore, my view that
the comment to this Recommendation on page 5, Enclosure A to
JCS 1805, (with "Secretary of Defense" substituted for "Sec-

retaries of the Army, Navy[6] and Air Forces"), is preferable t
that proposed in JCS 1805/1.

b. Regarding revised comment to Recommendation 10, page 2
and 25, JCS 1805/1,[7] I concur in the general thought expresse
by the Chief of Naval Operations but suggest that the last sentenc
of the revised comment be deleted and the following substitute
therefor: "The Joint Chiefs of Staff consider that existing agencies
including the Research and Development Board, the National Re
search Council, the Atomic Energy Commission, and the Arme
Forces Special Weapons Project, are now giving adequate attentio
to the *military aspects of the* problems outlined in Recommendatio
10. *The civilian defense aspects should be a responsibility of whateve
agency is designated or established to assume responsibility for civi
defense. Specific recommendation on this subject is being submittec
separately to the Secretary of Defense.*"

c. Regarding paragraph 5 concerning protection of the Unite
States against clandestine delivery of atomic weapons in period
of nominal peace (page 26, JCS 1805/1),[8] the Joint Research an
Development Board has requested the Armed Forces Specia
Weapons Project to investigate the potentialities of sabotage b
atomic weapons, and possible countermeasures. It is considere
that action in this matter by the Joint Chiefs of Staff is not require
at this time.

3. I recommend the following additional changes in Enclosure A to
JCS 1805 and to portions of Enclosure B to JCS 1805 which I propose
in paragraph 1 above to be incorporated into Enclosure A:

a. Add to paragraph 5 *a.*, page 2: "The Air Intelligence Group
will be reorganized to include Army representation" and revise the
third sentence of comment to Recommendation 6, page 12 to read:
"The section would be suitable as a nucleus for a group to make
the study called for in Recommendation 7 below, *but should be
reorganized to include Army representation.*"[9] The Air Intelligence
Group is presently staffed by Air Force and Navy personnel. It is
now proposed that the functions of the Group be expanded to
include exploration of the psychological aspects of atomic warfare,
including analysis of targets which will affect the will of a nation
to make war. Psychological warfare requires integration of the
activities of all services. It is, therefore, considered that the Air
Intelligence Group in undertaking this work should include representation from the Department of the Army.

b. Revise first sentence of comment to Recommendation 12, page
6 to read: "As of 16 September 1947, the Chief of Staff, U.S. Air
Force, is charged with the over-all responsibility for detecting

atomic explosions anywhere in the world *by long-range detection devices*".[10] The letter of 16 September 1947 to which reference is made pertained to long-range detection of atomic explosions. It is possible the original wording could be misinterpreted to include espionage activities.

4. In view of the many revisions proposed for Enclosure A to JCS 805, I recommend that, after consideration by the Joint Chiefs of Staff of the comments of the Chief of Naval Operations contained in JCS 805/1 and my comments contained herein, these papers be returned to the Joint Strategic Survey Committee for reediting and resubmittal to the Joint Chiefs of Staff.[11]

---

[1] The subject under discussion was "An Evaluation of the Atomic Bomb as a Military Weapon," the final report submitted by the JCS board evaluating the atomic tests at Bikini. (For background see no. 1831.) The report contained twenty-two conclusions and fifteen recommendations. The recommendations were as follows: (1) The JCS should work for "an acceptable guaranty of international peace"; lacking this guaranty, the United States should (2) stockpile atomic weapons, (3) continue R&D, and (4) enact legislation "establishing new definitions of acts of aggression and incipient attack, including the readying of atomic weapons against us." This legislation would require the President, after consulting the Cabinet, "to order atomic bomb retaliation when such retaliation is necessary to prevent or frustrate an atomic weapon attack upon us." The report also recommended that (5) atomic-weapons systems be coordinated and integrated and that the JCS (6) direct the appropriate service organization to select atomic-bomb targets and (7) establish a temporary board to study the psychological aspects of atomic warfare. The board said that (8) passive defense (dispersion and concealment) was "practical for relatively small facilities" but not for "urban and industrial areas." Studies should be undertaken (9) to determine how to protect important targets and (10) to find techniques for reducing casualties. Further, (11) the United States should "maintain an intelligence service with a far greater effectiveness than any such service this country has had heretofore in peace or war"; (12) responsibility for detection of atomic bursts should be clearly established; and (13) weapon testing should be coordinated with R&D and with the development of appropriate tactics and trained personnel to use the weapons. (14) The AEC should reclassify the Bikini test data so as to make some of it available to the military and other data open to the public. Finally, (15) Congress should review the statement of policy upon which the Atomic Energy Act was based (CCS 471.6 [10-16-45], Sec. 9).
[2] On October 1 Schuyler had prepared for Eisenhower a draft of a response to JCS 1805, the JSSC's September 23 comment on the board's report. Schuyler had revised the draft, however, in light of Nimitz's comments (in JCS 1801/1, of October 18). The present memorandum was drafted on November 5, while General Eisenhower was out of town (see no. 1839), but the paper would not be cleared by the Chief of Staff's office until after he had returned. With minor revisions, the document would circulate as JCS 1805/2, of November 13. All papers are in the same file as this document; and CCS 471.6 (10-16-45), Sec. 9.
[3] The JSSC had provided a memorandum to be sent to Forrestal (Enclosure A to JCS 1805) and a long discussion of the board's report (Enclosure B). Nimitz had proposed a number of changes in the message to Forrestal; since these revisions, if accepted, would leave the message at variance with the discussion, Nimitz recom-

mended that the message not be sent to the Secretary of Defense. Eisenhowe
agreed.

[4] Nimitz had commented on recommendations 4, 5, 10, 11, and 14. The Air Forc
and the Navy representatives on the JSSC had disagreed as to which service c
agency should have primary responsibility for coordinating atomic-weapon systen
(recommendation 5); Nimitz wanted to vest authority in the Research and De
velopment Board set up under the National Security Act of 1947. He also wante
to add a statement to the effect that no new intelligence organization should b
created (recommendation 11) and a clarifying comment upon the current status c
the efforts to reclassify the test results (recommendation 14). Eisenhower agree
with these last three proposals by Nimitz, but the Chief of Staff made counter
proposals (as follows) about recommendations 4 and 10.

[5] Nimitz had wanted to eliminate any comment on recommendation 4
Eisenhower accepted the JSSC view that the Joint Chiefs should in fact commer
on the need to give the President authority to order retaliatory use of the atom
bomb "when such retaliation is necessary to prevent or frustrate an atomic weapo
attack upon us."

[6] John Lawrence Sullivan (LL.B. Harvard 1924) had been appointed Secretary o
the Navy in September 1947. He had been assistant secretary of the treasury fron
January 1940 until November 1944; in July 1945 he had become the Nav
Department's assistant secretary for air. From June 1946 until he assumed hi
present position, Sullivan had served as the under secretary of the Navy.

[7] Nimitz had disagreed with the recommendation that the President appoint
special civilian-military board to study means of achieving protection from atomi
attack.

[8] According to Nimitz, the Joint Chiefs had already turned this problem over t
the Armed Forces Special Weapons Project; he proposed that they now merely ad
a paragraph noting that this action had been taken.

[9] The JSSC had advocated using the Air Intelligence Group as the nucleus for th
unit charged with implementing recommendation 6 (on selection of atomic-bom
targets).

[10] Eisenhower was adding the italicized words. The document of September 16
1947, which gave the Air Force this responsibility, is no. 1730.

[11] Eisenhower's paper elicited a number of responses and counter-responses. Th
first reaction came from Nimitz in JCS 1805/3, of January 14, 1948. The debate
which would still be going on when Eisenhower left office, can be followed i
CCS 471.6 (10-16-45), Sec. 9.

1847   *Eisenhower Mss*

To Milton Rice Polland   *November 7, 194*

Dear Mr. Polland: Please let me assure you that I understand th
disinterested attitude and sincere motives that have prompted your lette
to me. My own attitude was, I think, well expressed in my former not
to you.[1]

Quite naturally, it would be a personal pleasure to have a talk wit you. However, I know that any such meeting would be misinterpreted and much as I dislike to appear rude in the eyes of anyone who obviously has such a flattering opinion of my character and abilities, I feel that it would be unwise to arrange such a meeting.

I do hope you will understand my position; I have earnestly tried to be straightforward in this whole matter and have expressed to no one in the world any thought or idea that differs in the slightest degree from what I have told you.[2] *Most sincerely*

[1] General Eisenhower's previous letter was no. 1773. Polland belonged to a group in Wisconsin that was urging Eisenhower to run for President. Polland had written on November 3 asking Eisenhower if they could meet in Washington "completely divorced from press notoriety... " (EM).

[2] Polland replied, "Please rest assured that I respect your wishes and that I shall do nothing that would in any way indicate a relationship between us" (Nov. 12, EM). Polland would write Eisenhower again on November 28 and send a clipping about the Wisconsin campaign efforts. The Chief of Staff wrote on Polland's letter, "This stuff is treason" (see *Milwaukee Journal*, Nov. 19, 1947).

1848   *COS, 1947, 095 Knox*

To WILLIAM EDWARD KNOX   *November 7, 1947*

Dear Bill:[1] I'll take you at your word on this nickname business![2]

Naturally, I am honored by your cordial invitation to the pre-Christmas luncheon and would consider it a privilege to attend. It sounds like a thoroughly enjoyable occasion. As matters stand, however, I am faced with a formidable December schedule and have already been compelled to decline a New York engagement for the 18th. I feel, therefore, that I have no alternative but to decline your gracious offer of hospitality.

Thank you for your kindness in thinking about me. I wish my answer could be different, but it is one where necessity outweighs my personal desire. *Sincerely*

[1] Knox (B.S. University of New Hampshire 1921) had begun his career with Westinghouse Electric International Company in 1921. Since 1946 he had been the firm's president.

[2] In a letter of October 29 Knox had invited Eisenhower to a small pre-Christmas luncheon at the Wall Street Club. He said that even though the two had not met, he had addressed his letter "Dear Ike" and hoped Eisenhower would call him Bill. On Knox's letter, Eisenhower wrote the first sentence of this reply, and at the bottom he noted: "*Nice letter.* Have already declined New York engagement for that date. Too crowded, etc." Carroll drafted the remainder of the reply, on which Eisenhower made one minor change (McDuff Coll.).

1849

To Aksel Nielsen

Dear Aksel: Upon my return from Texas I find two notes from you awaiting me.[1] I thank you particularly for the little picture of the bull—I will keep it in my records.

Give my office a ring as quickly as you get in town. I will arrange a date even if I have to break some engagement.[2] *Sincerely*

[1] Nielsen's letter of October 30 had pressed Eisenhower about a dinner Nielsen wanted him to attend (see no. 1824). With his letter of November 1 Nielsen had enclosed a picture of the bull that Eisenhower owned—for the moment (see no. 1817). Both notes are in EM.
[2] Nielsen had said he would be in Washington soon. He would see Eisenhower on November 11.

1850

To Patrick Jay Hurley

Dear Pat: After you visited me the other day I had the Decorations Board review an old recommendation involving a Distinguished Service Cross for you.[1] The Board came to a finding somewhat similar to the original decision which was that for the specific service the Distinguished Service Cross is not considered applicable. I am told that for services covering that particular period you have been awarded an Oak Leaf Cluster to your Distinguished Service Medal and the Distinguished Flying Cross. Also I believe you were given the Purple Heart.

Of course I could personally argue this matter with the Decorations Board, but in view of your request that I take it up in a routine manner and make no special point of it, I have gone no further in the matter.[2]

Sometime when you are in the Department I will be glad to have an aide get out the entire file and show it to you.

With warm regard, *Sincerely*

[1] Eisenhower's desk calendar does not include the visit from former Ambassador Hurley. (On Hurley's career see no. 520.) In a memorandum to Eisenhower of October 27 Michaelis traced the history of the recommendation and the reasons the award had not been made (COS, 1947, 201 Hurley).
[2] In a note of November 19 Hurley said, "Your action is completely satisfactory to me" (EM).

To Edward Arthur Evans   *November 8, 1947*

Dear General Evans:[1] It is gratifying to know that in 1948 the Reserve Officers Association will continue its traditional practice of sponsoring a National Security Week.[2] An alert and unified America has proved its strength time and again in momentous undertakings. On the issue of national security there is no question that Americans will remain alert and unified, provided only that all of us understand the basic factors in the problem facing us.

The security we seek cannot be maintained merely by military force, although in the present state of the world's development adequate and efficient armies, navies and air forces are mandatory. Security in its larger sense is the responsibility of every individual; it involves our moral, economic and social strength as fully as it does a reasonable state of military preparedness.

The Reserve Officers Association, in sponsoring National Security Week, does a great service in reminding our people that each of us has a responsibility to bear, each some task to perform, if we are to continue to develop as the great and unchallengeable stronghold of human freedom—a prosperous and mighty example of democracy at work.

I wish you every conceivable success in the progress of your campaign. *Sincerely*

[1] Brigadier General Evans was the executive director of the Reserve Officers Association of the United States, Washington, D.C. Evans had served in the Coast Artillery in World War I and was honorably discharged in 1919. He had been commissioned a captain in the Coast Artillery Reserve in 1919 and had risen through the ranks to colonel by 1936. In 1940 Evans was recalled to active duty, and in 1942 he was promoted to brigadier general. During World War II he held various assignments in the ZI. He was relieved from active duty in May 1945.

[2] Evans had written on October 15 asking General Eisenhower to endorse the association's program (COS, 1947, 080 Reserve Officers Association). Colonel James Robinson Pierce (USMA 1922), Deputy Chief of the Public Information Division, drafted a reply (Pierce to Carroll, Oct. 24, 1947, in *ibid.*; Eisenhower's handwritten changes are on a draft in the McDuff Collection).

Memorandum by the Chief of Staff, U.S. Army:

Subject: Correlation of Budgets of Army, Navy and Air Force With Strategic Planning[1]

Reference: a. JCS 1800/1

1. I agree that the procedure proposed by the Director of the Joint Staff is suitable with respect to both the FY 1949 budget estimate and the FY 1950 presentation to the Budget Bureau.[2] However, I consider that the procedure with respect to the basis of the FY 1950 budget does not carry the solution of the problem to its ultimate objective and thereby will establish an undesirable precedent, since the budgets of the three services should be correlated upon an agreed basis which goes into greater detail than a joint strategic concept and a joint strategic outline war plan. The requirements of each Service individually arrived at from these broad considerations will be difficult to defend.[3] On the other hand, an agreed statement of military requirements, prepared from the strategic concept and the joint strategic outline war plan as well as our present national security commitments, will provide the Services with a firm foundation for the submission of their budget estimates.

2. This statement of requirements prepared by the Joint Staff should include missions, priority of missions, required strength of the military forces, the allocation of this strength to the Army, Navy and Air Force, deployment of forces, employment of forces by component, programmed development of military installations and bases, as well as policies on equipping and maintaining the military forces.[4] In order to prepare this additional statement, the Joint Staff should be permitted to submit their proposal on 1 February 1948.

3. Therefore, I recommend that paragraph 4 of JCS 1800/1 be amended to read as follows:

> *b.* By 1 ~~January~~-*February* 1948, the joint strategic concept, ~~and~~ joint strategic outline war plans, *and a statement of military requirements* which, when approved, will constitute the basis for the preparation by the Services of their respective 1950 budget programs.[5]

[1] In 1946 and again in 1947 efforts had been made to prepare a coordinated budget (see no. 1102 and the correspondence in ABC 121.4 [9-29-42]; CCS 300 [1-25-42], Sec. 8; and Budget Division Decimal File, 1942–47, 110.01 [7-11-47]). All of these endeavors had been crippled, Forrestal's assistant said, because the services had failed "to develop a single integrated concept for the conduct of a future war

and a single war plan based on such a concept" (see Ohly to Forrestal, Oct. 15, 1947, and Royall to Forrestal, with enclosure, Oct. 3, 1947, both in OS/D, 47–49, Clas. Numeric File, CD 12-1-8 and 12-1-6). Forrestal was upset because the services, in spite of unification, had yet to produce a joint war plan that could be used in connection with the budget for FY 1949. As a result, the JCS ordered the JSP to prepare a statement of the major forces and supporting establishments needed during FY 1949; the JSP in turn directed the JWPC to prepare a joint outline war plan and a statement of needs (see Schuyler to Eisenhower, Sept. 2, 1947, and H.C.D. memo to Schuyler, Sept. 11, 1947, same file as document; and JCS 1800, approved Sept. 4, 1947, in CCS 370 [9-19-45], Sec. 6. On the previous efforts to devise a joint war plan see no. 1370).

[2] The director, General Gruenther, had proposed that the Joint Staff prepare a summary and projection describing the world situation, as well as a discussion of America's basic strategic concept, to support the FY 1949 budget requests of the three services. Gruenther also wanted a joint statement of the country's strategic concept and a joint strategic outline war plan that could constitute the basis for the preparation of the FY 1950 budgets (JCS 1800/1, Oct. 23, 1947). But Schuyler gave Eisenhower a brief that pointed out that FY 1949 budget estimates were so far along that the Joint Chiefs could only give Congress general background material that established the relationships between the budget figures and the country's basic military strategy. Schuyler nevertheless felt that in order to have a truly coordinated FY 1950 budget, the Joint Staff should prepare an even more detailed statement of military requirements than Gruenther proposed. Schuyler drafted this memorandum for the Chief of Staff; the paper circulated as JCS 1800/2, of November 17.

[3] For background on the Army's own budget planning see no. 1371. The Haislip Board had been charged with the responsibility for reviewing all War Department programs and policies to provide a basis for the FY 1949 budget and future budgets. The board's final report, dated August 11, 1947, is in P&O 020 WD. In most regards, the board's view of the future was not very different from those expressed in previous Army plans (see for instance nos. 925 and 1250). The fate of UMT was, the report said, crucial to the future of the Army; despite its misgivings about the prospects for UMT, the board rejected all other alternatives. The board wanted a permanent Regular Army strength of 877,000 (+ 400,000 civilians). This Regular Army could be supplemented by UMT, so that at the beginning of any future war, the Army could have in units its desired total figure of 1.75 million. The board feared that the Army could not achieve its required strength through recruiting; hence UMT was of vital importance.

On September 23 Eisenhower had directed (verbally) that the board's recommendations, with the exception of all references to the Navy and the National Guard, be implemented. On November 7 Collins had issued a directive assigning to specific staff divisions the tasks of revising current plans and conducting further studies (COS, 1948, 111 TS; the studies are in P&O 020 WD). By the time Eisenhower left office, however, the foundation stones of the Haislip Board's report still had not been laid; UMT—indeed selective service—had not been adopted.

[4] Eisenhower had called for such a statement previously (see no. 1325). He would be unable to persuade the services to adopt more precise statements of their respective missions.

[5] Eisenhower made this change in dates so that these JCS statements would be as up-to-date as possible. Further correspondence in the files cited above indicates, however, that the necessary agreement would not be reached before Eisenhower left office.

1853

To Olive W. Hammer   *November 10, 1947*

Dear Mrs. Hammer: Your interesting letter has just reached me, having
been forwarded to Washington from Columbia University.[1] It is
gratifying indeed to learn the Santa Claus Mail Association will make a
special effort this Christmas to dispatch warm clothing and bright toys
to thousands of little children in war-torn Western Europe. Your effort
will certainly bring some happiness and comfort to innocent sufferers;
perhaps even greater good may flow from it.

My best wishes and deep appreciation are with you and your associates. *Sincerely*

[1] Mrs. Olive Hammer, of Jenkintown, Pennsylvania, was head of the Santa Claus
Mail Association, which was sending clothing and toys to children in Europe. She
had written Eisenhower on November 7 to ask for a letter supporting the association's work. Carroll drafted a reply, which Eisenhower rewrote almost entirely.

1854

To James S. Beattie   *November 10, 1947*
Confidential

Dear Mr. Beattie:[1] I find that it is impossible for me to participate in
your splendidly conceived program of November 21st.[2] A period including that date has been reserved for me to undergo a short period of
hospitalization and it is impracticable to find an alternate time for this
purpose on my schedule.[3] While I hope you will keep this reason
confidential, I did want you to know the true cause of my inability to
accept your gracious invitation.

I am sorry to have delayed a day or two, since my return from the
West, to answer your letter but I was attempting to find some way in
which I could comply with your request. *Sincerely*

[1] James S. Beattie was president of the Washington, D.C., Junior Board of
Commerce and also chairman of that city's Youth Day Committee.
[2] The American Heritage Foundation had established the Freedom Train, a mobile
exhibit of historical documents that was touring the United States in an effort to
make citizens more aware of American ideals and history. To celebrate the arrival
of the Freedom Train in Washington on Thanksgiving Day, the Youth Day
Committee planned a television broadcast entitled "An American Freedom Program." The program, slated to feature the leaders "in the major phases of American endeavor which are inspirational to youth," would be broadcast to school
assemblies throughout the Washington area. In a November 3 letter Beattie had
invited Eisenhower to take part in the telecast, speaking briefly about the preserva-

tion of American freedom by military force. Other national leaders invited to participate were FBI Director J. Edgar Hoover, football player Sammy Baugh, and Secretary of Commerce W. Averell Harriman. For background on Harriman see no. 110. He had served as Ambassador to the Soviet Union until April 1946, when he had become Ambassador to Great Britain. In October 1946 he was named secretary of commerce. For the Freedom Train's visit to Washington, D.C., see *Washington Post*, November 27, 1947.

[3] See no. 1857.

1855   *Eisenhower Mss.*

To Raymond Weeks   *November 11, 1947*
Cable WCL 36952

Mr. Raymond Weeks, Director, National Armistice Day, 2108 Fifth Avenue, North, Birmingham, Alabama signed Dwight D. Eisenhower:[1] Your World Peace dinner demonstrates the realization of the Birmingham veterans that peace is something to be secured and perpetuated by thought and work and sacrifice. Everyone of us has the personal task of supporting our country's continuing efforts to establish a world system characterized by justice and respect for the rights of all. America must remain the leader and champion of all who likewise seek to eliminate force as the decisive element in relationships with others, and to exercise that leadership under conditions of today she must be strong morally, economically and militarily.

I wish you every success in your purpose of arousing all American citizens to the need for cooperating among ourselves to the utmost so as to achieve the greatest of all goals—assurance of enduring peace.[2]

[1] Weeks cabled Eisenhower on November 9 asking for a message to be read at a dinner for world peace to be held in Birmingham on Armistice Day, November 11. Carroll drafted a reply, which Eisenhower rewrote (COS, 1947, 006).
[2] This same day Eisenhower went to Arlington Cemetery to attend the traditional Armistice Day ceremony, in which the President placed a wreath on the grave of the Unknown Soldier.

1856   *Eisenhower Mss.*

To Frederick Coykendall   *November 12, 1947*

Dear Dr. Coykendall: I do not recall writing to you since Mamie and I had the pleasure of having you and Mrs. Coykendall with us for an evening.[1] In the meantime I have made two or three trips and have been as busy as ever.

When you and I were talking at my house, I gathered the impression that certain points involved in my early conferences with Mr. Parkinson's Committee may never have come specifically to your attention. I am attaching copies of one or two letters written at that time, merely to give you some idea of a few of the subjects we discussed. I assume that copies are filed with the records of the Trustees.[2]

Everybody at Columbia, from yourself on down, has been exceedingly kind and considerate. Mamie and I have had great difficulty in believing that I possess any particular qualifications for the distinguished position to which the Trustees have appointed me, and this universal attitude of helpfulness, on the part of the University family, has done much to reassure us. Personally, I had the feeling, and so expressed myself, that Columbia should select an experienced educator for that post and I had the temerity to undertake the assignment only because I was informed that the Trustees were unanimous in their conviction that I could render useful service. If I am in the slightest degree mistaken in my assumption on this point, I should know it at once—it would be unfair both to Columbia and myself to allow me to come up there in the face of doubts or mental reservations on the part of any important person in the institution.

As you know, the life obviously in store for us at Columbia is radically different from that we had so long planned for our future. While I have never had any intention of going into a hermit-like retirement, we did plan to pace ourselves more deliberately than we have been able to do in the past. Both in our official and social life we shall be on a more intensive schedule than would have been the case had I merely accepted one or more of the attractive offers made to me by prominent publishers. Your Committee convinced me that duty pointed to Columbia—and, accepting that judgment, we mean to do the best we can, enthusiastically.

In line with your suggestion, we are planning on arriving at Columbia in April, or at least by May 1st. Dr. Fackenthal will continue as Acting President through the current academic year and I will spend the month of May "getting acquainted." By April the house will surely be completely renovated and furnished, and we can move in with a minimum of confusion. I understand that Mr. Black is the Trustee that my aide is to contact concerning any detail regarding the house.[3] Is this correct?

I did not mean to draw this letter out to such length. Since having that enjoyable meeting with you and Mrs. Coykendall, I am encouraged to attempt to keep you fully acquainted with my thoughts and feelings regarding the future, in which my association with you is bound to be a close one.[4] *Cordially*

[1] Mr. and Mrs. Coykendall had arrived in Washington at 5:30 P.M. on October 22 (for background see no. 1757; Mrs. Coykendall was the former Mary Beach Warrin). Eisenhower and Coykendall conferred in the General's office at 9:00 the next morning. Later that afternoon the Eisenhowers entertained the Coykendalls at Quarters One.
[2] See nos. 1551 and 1565.
[3] Douglas M. Black was president of Doubleday & Company (see no. 1621).
[4] On November 17 Eisenhower received a three-page reply in which Coykendall assured the General of unanimous support by the trustees of Columbia University and of their agreement to the requests Eisenhower had specified in the earlier letters. There would be no problem about Eisenhower's military aide, he wrote; he did wonder, however, if it would be necessary to have a second military man to assist in University functions, since Columbia already provided such a person. Coykendall pointed out that the provost of the university, Professor Albert Charles Jacobs, "is a Navy-trained man and will give you all the immediate assistance you need in academic matters." Any questions Eisenhower had about alteration and furnishing of the president's house, which the Eisenhowers would occupy on May 1, should be taken up with Henry M. Schley, the comptroller of the university. For later developments see no. 1878.

1857 *Eisenhower Mss.*

To Kathleen McCarthy-Morrogh Summersby *November 12, 1947*

Dear Kay: I am grateful to you for informing me about the change in your wedding plans but I am most sorry to say that it is absolutely impossible for me to come to New York at any time during that particular period.[1] Actually, I am to go into the hospital at that time for my annual check-up and will be there several days.[2] This will further complicate my schedule and already it is so congested that I have had to break a number of engagements for late November and early December, two of which involved a New York trip.

Needless to say, I wish for you and your new husband every possible happiness. You served so long and so faithfully with the American forces and more particularly as one of my personal assistants,[3] that I shall never lose the intense desire to see everything work out for the best for you and those close to you.

I have just heard that Sue has a new baby, and this has the entire office force all excited.[4] After you are married I think that Nana Rae will be the only one of the WAC's that served in my office during the war who has not taken that step.[5] She is in New York and undoubtedly will be at your wedding.

Again, the very best wishes possible. *Cordially*

P.S. Why don't you get married on your birthday? That would make both dates easy for your husband to remember! ! !

[1] The wedding to which Eisenhower was referring would not take place. In 1952 Kay Summersby would marry Reginald H. Morgan, a Wall Street stockbroker.
[2] Eisenhower would enter Walter Reed Hospital on November 20 for a physical examination (see *Washington Post*, Nov. 20, 1947).
[3] See *New York Times*, January 21, 1975; also see Summersby, *Eisenhower Was My Boss* and Morgan, *Past Forgetting*.
[4] Sue Sarafian Jehl, a member of Eisenhower's office staff at SHAEF (see no. 1307), had given birth to Roland Roy Jehl, Jr., on October 20. Eisenhower's letter of congratulation is in EM (Nov. 10, 1947).
[5] Nana Rae had been Eisenhower's chief stenographer. For background see no. 607.

1858   *Eisenhower Mss., Family File*

TO JOHN SHELDON DOUD   *November 13, 1947*

Dear Pupah: Another anniversary rolls around for you—and along with my congratulations I send my fervent hope that you have many more happy ones.[1]

1915—when I first met the Doud family is a long way back—but I am astonished how swiftly the time has vanished. You weighed 240; I was a second Lieut! We have both changed![2]

We hope that you and Min will be with us for Xmas. We want to stage a real family reunion. Gordon and Mike are apparently ready to drive up here with their whole brood![3]

Aksel was here a day or so ago—looking well as ever.[4]

Love to mother—and again "Happy birthday to you!" *As ever*

[1] The original of this note—written by Eisenhower on the occasion of Mr. Doud's seventy-seventh birthday on November 15—was in longhand.
[2] For background see Eisenhower, *At Ease*, pp. 113–18.
[3] See no. 1956.
[4] See no. 1849.

1859   *Eisenhower Mss.*

TO FLOYD TAYLOR   *November 14, 1947*

Dear Mr. Taylor:[1] No invitation that I have received in a long time carries the appeal that does the one contained in your letter of November 11.[2] I should like very much to come—the difficulty is that I am caught up in circumstances where, virtually, my integrity is involved. Some weeks ago in response to a very urgent and persistent invitation to come to New York on December 15, I replied that I could not possibly do so;

I gave as my reason the factual one of the press of official business. Nevertheless, for a meeting such as yours I would have arbitrarily made room on my schedule, and except for the fact that I would now be guilty of bad faith I would do so, with a very definite sense of privilege.

In these circumstances I suggest that Lieutenant General A. C. Wedemeyer be invited to be at your Seminar. He is very well known by reason of his war and post-war services in the China region and is a most able and highly qualified man in every respect. He is now in charge of Operations in the Department of the Army and as such is in full contact with our broad defense problems.[3] He has marked ability to handle himself well in public gatherings.

I assure you of my gratitude for thinking of me in this connection and for once it is accurate to say that I unqualifiedly regret that I am unable to attend.

If you should want to ask General Wedemeyer you may contact him directly by writing here to the Pentagon Building or you could send word to me and I would arrange it. Moreover, if there is any other individual that you would prefer in his stead, I would be quite ready to do my best in meeting your exact desires.[4] *Very sincerely*

[1] Floyd Taylor had started his journalism career in 1923 as a reporter for the *New York Herald*. He had joined the Columbia University faculty in 1944, and since 1946 he had been director of the university's American Press Institute.
[2] Taylor had invited Eisenhower to lead a discussion of national defense at the institute's seminar for editorial writers on December 15. Writers would come from all regions of the United States. All sessions would be "off the record and we have had no trouble with leaks." Taylor asked Eisenhower to recommend a substitute if he could not come. In a November 13 note to Eisenhower, Carroll said that the Public Information Division "feels this is a very important group and recommends that the Seminar be handled by General Collins or General Wedemeyer, if you cannot do it personally" (both in COS, 1947, 080 American Press Institute).
[3] Wedemeyer had assumed this position on October 31.
[4] In his response of November 18 Taylor said that Wedemeyer would be "excellent" (EM).

1860   *Eisenhower Mss., Routine Corr., Miscellaneous*

To Hugh Meglone Milton II   *November 14, 1947*

Dear President Milton:[1] I am truly grateful for the cordiality of your invitation to visit the campus of the New Mexico Military Institute.[2] For many years I have heard much of your institution—all of it good. Consequently I would count myself fortunate if I could work out a program permitting me to make you a visit.

Under present plans I am counting on taking an extended leave in the late winter or early spring. The only opportunity that could possibly arise for my coming to the Southwest would be during that time. These plans are, however, so hazy and so uncrystallized that I could not possibly suggest a definite date at this time or even promise unequivocally that I could come between given limiting dates.

In these circumstances I wonder whether it would be possible for me to communicate with you again about January 15, at which time my spring schedule should be firming up more definitely. Should this be acceptable to you I will be glad to charge myself with the responsibility of writing to you again in about 60 days' time.[3]

Because of the complete uncertainty of my plans, might I suggest that we keep the matter relatively confidential unless and until I can promise definitely to come.

Thank you again for the graciousness of your invitation. *Very sincerely*

[1] Milton (M.E. University of Kentucky 1922) had recently become president of the New Mexico Military Institute, in Roswell, New Mexico. From 1924 to 1947 he had been associated with the New Mexico College of Agriculture and Mechanic Arts as professor, dean of engineering, and later (1938) as president. On leave from the university during the war, Milton had advanced to the grade of brigadier general (AUS) by 1944 and had served as Chief of Staff, XIV Corps, in the Pacific Area.

[2] In a letter of November 10 Milton had invited Eisenhower to visit the military institute (EM).

[3] On December 31, in a letter drafted by Carroll, Eisenhower would inform Milton that he would not be able to come (EM).

1861   *Eisenhower Mss.*

To WILLARD COLE RAPPLEYE   *November 14, 1947*

Dear Dr. Rappleye:[1] My son, Captain John Eisenhower, will be a student at Columbia from January 25 until the end of the school term. The present prospects are that there will be an infant born in the family along about the first of April. The purpose of this note is to ask whether my son and his wife can count on necessary hospital care through your medical center or would it be more appropriate for us to make arrangements elsewhere.[2]

You can understand my concern since I am anticipating the arrival of my first grandchild and so you will realize that I am merely taking every precaution to assure the finest kind of attention for my daughter-in-law during that period.[3]

With my thanks for the trouble I am causing you to answer this note, and with warm personal regard,[4] *Cordially*

¹ Rappleye (M.D. Harvard 1918) was professor of medical economics and dean of the College of Physicians and Surgeons at Columbia University.
² Rappleye would reply on November 22 that Dr. Howard Canning Taylor, Jr., professor of obstetrics and gynecology and director of the Obstetrical Service at Presbyterian Hospital, would be delighted to care for Barbara Eisenhower. In a letter of November 26 Eisenhower thanked Rappleye for making the necessary arrangements and asked him to extend the General's gratitude to Dr. Taylor.
³ The grandchild, Dwight David Eisenhower II, would be born on March 31, 1948.
⁴ Eisenhower forwarded copies of this correspondence to his son and daughter-in-law at Fort Monroe, Virginia, where they were visiting (Eisenhower to Thompson, Nov. 28, 1947). All correspondence is in EM.

1862   *Eisenhower Mss., Family File*

To John Sheldon Doud Eisenhower   *November 14, 1947*

Captain John Eisenhower, 1336 Third Avenue, Columbus, Georgia: Please write letter immediately to Dr. Frank D. Fackenthal, Acting President of Columbia University, telling him you would like to apply for housekeeping suite at Butler Hall for period during which you expect to be a student.¹ Suggest that you state your readiness to take the apartment from first of January. Suggest you do this without delay because he has informed me he will be glad to place matter into official channels instantly. Believe you should send application airmail special delivery because I understand Butler Hall is located in very heart of University center.² Although I understand your student period there covers only from January 25 to May 25 I think even if we have to rent a place for a full five or six months it would still be fine thing.³

¹ Preliminary inquiries regarding housing for John Eisenhower at Columbia had been made through correspondence with Dorothy Mills Young, wife of Brigadier General Gordon R. Young (see no. 1581), and her sister, Katherine Mills, of New York City. Miss Mills indicated that the Eisenhowers would probably be best satisfied by handling the matter themselves through conventional channels (Eisenhower to Young, Nov. 7, 1947; and related correspondence in EM).
² We can not find a copy of Captain Eisenhower's November 15 letter to Fackenthal; however, Fackenthal's reply (of November 17) is in the Columbia University Archives, Special Manuscripts Collections. Fackenthal agreed to forward Captain Eisenhower's request to the persons in charge of Butler Hall, a university-owned apartment building located on the Columbia campus. He warned, however, that there were no vacancies at that time.
³ As it turned out, Captain and Mrs. Eisenhower would find an off-campus apartment with the help of Thomas Parkinson (Eisenhower to Parkinson, Dec. 8, 1947). In a letter to Philip M. Hayden, secretary of the university, General Eisenhower would explain his son's change of plans: "... I felt that as long as applications would apparently outnumber the availability of quarters, he was probably in far better position to seek an apartment elsewhere than would be many of the others attending school at that time" (Dec. 22, 1947, both in EM).

1863 *Eisenhower Mss.*

To James Vincent Forrestal   *November 17, 1947*
Confidential

Memorandum for Secretary Forrestal:

Subject: Psychological Warfare.

Bill Paley came to see me recently to discuss psychological warfare, probably as the result of your note on that subject to him.[1]

He expressed readiness to assist and participate actively in the task of psychological warfare planning, even to the extent of doing so in uniform. He would prefer, however, to serve as a civilian consultant. I believe that this would be preferable inasmuch as the sense of the discussions among interested agencies has been to the effect that civilians should control and predominate in the current organization and planning.[2]

I realize that there are high-level committees considering the subject, but it seems to me that the military must give continued impetus to the organization and realistic functioning of this important activity.[3] Further, the Armed Services should prepare plans now involving enunciation of policy and methods applying to actual war. I do not know whether the responsibility for this planning should be referred to the JCS or to an ad hoc committee under your immediate supervision. In the latter event, I could, if you so desire, detail as the head of a combined committee, a brigadier general—(Robert A. McClure) who had extensive experience in this field during the war in Europe. He was closely associated with Bill Paley and others of similar qualifications. He is therefore in a position to crystallize the experience and knowledge acquired during the past war and should facilitate the development of a workable plan for the future employment of psychological warfare under conditions of actual war.[4]

This note has no other purpose than to express readiness to be helpful. If the matter is completely in hand through the processes of the high-level committees, my suggestions may not be pertinent.[5]

[1] Paley had seen Eisenhower on November 12 (for background see no. 1556). Forrestal had sent the Chief of Staff a copy of his November 1 note to Paley (EM). Forrestal wrote that he and Eisenhower had been discussing "certain subjects with which you were concerned during the war" and that Eisenhower might ask Paley to return to active duty for a short time to develop "certain plans." Paley had served as chief of radio in the Psychological Warfare Division of SHAEF in 1945 (see no. 1687). Wedemeyer drafted this memorandum for Eisenhower.
[2] United States officials had been discussing the means of employing covert action, initially psychological action, since late 1946, when Secretary of War Patterson had suggested that a study be conducted of "this form of war for future use." In January 1947, SWNCC adopted guidelines for the conduct of peacetime and

wartime psychological warfare. On April 30, 1947, SWNCC established a sub-committee to plan U.S. psychological warfare. By the summer, "the fact that the U.S. would engage in covert operations was a given; what remained were decisions about the organizational arrangements and actual implementation." On November 4, SANACC (State-Army-Navy-Air Force Coordinating Committee, the successor to SWNCC) recommended that the secretary of state be responsible for the general direction of the program—which was to be started immediately (U.S., Congress, Senate, Select Committee to Study Governmental Operations with Respect to Intelligence Activities, *Supplementary Detailed Staff Reports on Foreign and Military Intelligence, Book IV*, 94th Cong., 2d sess., 1976, S. Rept. 94-755, pp. 26–27). The SANACC proposal was discussed in the War Council meeting of November 4 (see Blum to Ohly, Nov. 11, 1947, in OS/D, 47–49, Clas. Numeric File, CD 23-1-1; see also the notes from the War Council meeting of October 21 in OS/D, 47–49, Cent. Numeric File, D 2-1-3).

³ For Eisenhower's impatience with the lack of a coordinated psychological-warfare program see P&O memorandum of November 12, "Conversation with General Collins," P&O 337, Case 82/2.

⁴ McClure was presently chief of the New York Field Office of the Civil Affairs Division. Eisenhower, who had already been in contact with McClure, envisioned "the formation of a small group of selected personnel shortly after the first of the year for the purpose of evolving psychological warfare measures that might reasonably assist in the problem presented by current campaign of the USSR in that field" (see Wedemeyer to Chief, Plans and Policy Group, Dec. 6, 1947, in P&O 091.412, Case 30; and McClure to Eisenhower, Nov. 5, 1947, *ibid.*, Case 50/2). From September 1950 through March 1953 McClure would serve as Chief of Psychological Warfare at Army Headquarters, Washington, D.C.

⁵ On November 18 the War Council decided to postpone action on Eisenhower's recommendations until the National Security Council had considered the matter (Ohly memorandum to the Secretary of the Army *et al.*, Nov. 18, 1947, in OSA/KCR Cent. Dec. File, 334 War Council). On November 24 Truman would assign the coordination of psychological warfare to the State Department, but Marshall objected that if such activities were associated with the State Department, American foreign policy would be discredited. Marshall thought that the State Department should provide guidance but that operational responsibility for covert activities should be placed elsewhere. On December 14 the National Security Council would give the CIA responsibility for "covert psychological operations," and the program would actually get underway. The director of the CIA was to insure that such activities were consistent with U.S. foreign policy and with other information activities (U.S., Congress, Senate, Select Committee on Intelligence Activities, *Supplementary Detailed Staff Reports on Foreign and Military Intelligence, Book IV*, 94th Cong., 2d sess., 1976, S. Rept. 94-755, pp. 28–29).

1864   *Eisenhower Mss.*

To Lauris Norstad   *November 17, 1947*

Dear Norstad: Although I feel that in the Air Forces your talents will continue to be devoted to the support of the entire security establishment as they have in the past, yet I cannot see you terminate your official connection in the Department of the Army without some attempt to express to you my appreciation and gratitude for your outstanding service therein.[1]

There would be little point in using a multitude of words to describe the qualifications you possess, which have been so valuable to the Army while you were serving as the Director of Operations in the General Staff. Likewise with respect to a tabulation of your accomplishments; I think it more appropriate merely to say that from the time I first met you, near the beginning of the war, you have, through a series of positions of increasing importance and responsibility, constantly demonstrated your capacity for filling a still higher one. It is my conviction that, short of posts requiring special technical training, there is no assignment in America's security establishment for which you are not eminently qualified. I count the country fortunate that for another score of years you will be available for service in positions of gravest responsibility.

The entire General Staff is regretful that you must leave our midst; all of us will look forward with keen anticipation to a continuation of our association with you.

The best of luck in all that you do.

With warm personal regard, *Cordially*

[1] With the separation of the Air Force from the Army, Lieutenant General Norstad had become Deputy Chief of Staff of the Air Force's Operations Division on October 30.

1865   *Eisenhower Mss.*

To Thomas John Watson   *November 17, 1947*

Dear Tom: The name of the man of whom I spoke to you is John H. G. Pierson.[1] His proposal to me was that a Graduate School of Labor should be established at Columbia University and concerning this I told him that as yet I had absolutely nothing to do with that school. Moreover, I told him that for a long time I would not know enough about the institution to make any such definite proposals and the only man who was in a position to confer with him was Dr. Fackenthal.

On the other hand, I told him that numbers of people were interested in the general problem of studying and improving labor relations in this country, among whom you were one. I therefore suggested that upon his return from Havana he might call upon you, not to discuss the matter of establishing a college at Columbia but of preparing an exact plan that could be considered by any school which might be interested. My own thought is that until Mr. Pierson's idea is translated into a specific plan or program no institution would be in a position to take positive action in the matter.

Naturally I know nothing about the whole business; I was interested in listening to Mr. Pierson because of his long experience in the Labor Department and because he seems genuinely interested in making a positive educational approach to a matter that is of such great importance to the entire country.

I merely wish to make clear again that in asking you to see Mr. Pierson sometime next January I did not do so with any specific reference to Columbia, only with the thought that ways and means might be found of helping him prepare a plan that could receive specific analysis and consideration.[2]

With warm personal regard, *Cordially*

P.S. It was odd that after your exhortations to me on Saturday to "have nothing to do with this political business", you should be accused by a Sunday night commentator of holding a dinner somewhere to promote my active participation in politics and I hope you can take all this stuff with a grin.[3]

[1] John Herman Groesbeck Pierson (Ph.D. Yale 1938) had held several teaching positions before he became associate director of the Institute for Applied Social Analysis at Columbia in 1939. In 1941 Pierson had joined the Bureau of Labor Statistics, and in 1943–44 he had headed its Postwar Labor Problems Division. He was consultant to the acting commissioner of the bureau from 1944 to 1946 and economic advisor to the assistant secretary of labor from January to June 1947. He had written two books and several articles on the problem of achieving full employment. Pierson had met with Eisenhower in his office at 10:00 A.M. on November 14.
[2] Watson replied: "I shall be very pleased to talk with Mr. Pierson in January and learn more about his plans. This might be a fine opportunity for Columbia to do some pioneering work along very constructive lines" (Nov. 22, 1947, EM).
[3] Watson's letter explained that "the Monday night affair was a public dinner in honor of James G. K. McClure, who has been doing a very outstanding job in assisting the mountain farmers of western North Carolina. . . ." Watson said that the one thousand people attending the dinner thought the commentator's announcement was amusing because the purpose of the affair was "so far removed from anything political." Personally, Watson took the remarks "not only with a grin, but it gives me a real laugh."

1866 *Eisenhower Mss., Routine Corr.,*
Miscellaneous

To Edward John Noble *November 17, 1947*

Dear Mr. Noble:[1] Tom Watson came to see me the other day to tell me about your rally for the Salvation Army on January 6.[2] Since then I have gone over my schedule of engagements and find it simply impossible to add this one.

As you know, all soldiers hold the Salvation Army in the greatest admiration and affection—the proposal you make, therefore, has a very marked appeal and my inability to attend causes me real regret. However, you will understand that entirely aside from the constant pressure of ordinary official requirements, I shall be facing a very intensive period during early January incident to the opening of the next session of Congress and in preparation for my own termination of active duty thereafter. Because of these circumstances I have already declined to accept a very considerable number of engagements and feel that in good faith I can scarcely add further to them.

I repeat that I am truly sorry I cannot come and I most certainly wish your campaign every success. *Cordially*

P.S. You have set a fishing record at St. Catherine's that looks to me as if it would stand for some time. Nevertheless, I will go after it as hard as I know how the next time I am fortunate enough to visit that delightful spot.[3]

[1] Noble (A.B. Yale 1905) was chairman of the board of the American Broadcasting Company. He also headed Life Savers, Inc., and was chairman of the 1948 fund-raising campaign for the Salvation Army.
[2] Noble's letter of November 12 asking Watson to talk to Eisenhower is in EM. The Chief of Staff's desk calendar does not show the date of Eisenhower's meeting with Watson.
[3] Noble had asked Watson to tell Eisenhower that he had broken the General's fishing record at St. Catherine's Island, a resort off the coast of southeast Georgia. In two and one-half hours he and two others had caught 240 fish, with a combined weight of six hundred pounds.

1867   *Eisenhower Mss.*

TO WILLIAM WALLACE CHAPIN   *November 17, 1947*

Dear Mr. Chapin:[1] Thank you for your very interesting letter.[2] When next you come to Washington I do hope that opportunity will be afforded us to have a chat. If you will merely phone my office, upon arrival, it is possible we can get together for a bit of lunch in my office—which would be a break for me.[3]

With warm personal regard, *Sincerely*

[1] William Wallace Chapin had formerly owned eight large metropolitan newspapers. He now owned and published the *Argonaut*, a San Francisco weekly.
[2] In a letter of November 12 Chapin said that he had met Eisenhower at a luncheon given by Secretary Forrestal and would like to call on the Chief of Staff in early December. Chapin remarked that he was a supporter of UMT and of Eisenhower

for the presidency: "I only hope you will be drafted, for you will certainly sweep this nation."

³ The Chief of Staff's desk calendar does not mention a meeting with Chapin.

1868   *Eisenhower Mss.*

To Thomas Jean Hargrave   *November 18, 1947*

*Dear Mr. Hargrave:*¹ Since my return to the city, I have had an opportunity to study the tentative copy of your 1947 Industrial Mobilization Plan.² My comments are of necessity limited to a very brief survey of the plan and will, therefore, be limited to comments on fundamentals. With your approval, and providing you can allow time for it, I would like to have a more detailed study of the plan made by appropriate sections of my staff.

I consider the plan an excellent approach to the problem of industrial mobilization based upon our World War II experience. More than this, I consider the attached documents to be an important and comprehensive piece of work that certainly reflects most favorably upon the Munitions Board. For the moment I should like to confine my comments to the following observations:

a. I believe that all planning should stress the time element, with particular reference to the possibility that in any future emergency we may be denied the opportunity to do much of our preparatory and organizational work, after the beginning of the war. This suggests the advisability of making sure that there exists in peace, even if only in embryo, every agency or office that planning demonstrates will be necessary after the war starts.

b. A further implication of the time element is that there should possibly be on the books, in time of peace, a comprehensive and coordinated act covering the whole subject of war-time industrial mobilization and which would contain the proviso that it becomes effective only upon the declaration of war by constitutional methods.³ In the years between the two world wars this issue was always conveniently sidetracked on the basis of political expediency; however, since such a law would permit authoritative and specific preparation in time of peace as opposed to "conditional" planning, the question arises as to whether it is not an essential factor in any reasonable program.

c. Another consideration is that organizational planning must be particularly clear and definite as to lines of authority. So far as it is possible the power of decision should reside in key individuals and we should attempt to confine committee, conference and consultative action to the advisory field.

In all this work it should be clearly understood that we are planning only for a country mobilized for war and not one for carrying on the business of peace under democratic concepts. But we must always remember that so long as we are faced with the possibility of global war, this preparatory work is necessitated by the basic impulse of survival. Unless plans are developed in this concept we are likely to miss our target.

When the staff has made its comments on your plan I will forward them to you.[4]

Again let me congratulate the Board on this extraordinary piece of work. *Very sincerely*

[1] Hargrave (LL.B. Harvard 1915) was president of the Eastman Kodak Company. He had joined the company in 1928 and had become its president in 1941.

[2] Hargrave had written in his capacity as chairman of the Munitions Board, which had been charged with the responsibility for drafting an industrial mobilization plan (see no. 1370). Hargrave had forwarded the plan to Eisenhower with a covering letter of October 30 (COS, 1947, 091.33). SS&P drafted a response for the Chief of Staff, but Carroll and Eisenhower rewrote the message.

[3] The question of how the next war might commence was under active consideration (see no. 1846).

[4] This phase of planning would still be underway when Eisenhower left office. On November 19 the JCS would approve Eisenhower's recommendations stemming from the annual review of merchant shipping requirements. Eisenhower had noted (in JCS 1454/12, of November 4) that each request for shipping should be handled on its own merits and not turned down simply because it would be needed for other purposes under war emergency conditions (CCS 540 [8-9-45], Sec. 4).

1869   *Eisenhower Mss.*

To LeRoy Lutes   *November 19, 1947*
Confidential

Memorandum for the Director, Service, Supply & Procurement Division: At the War Council meeting November 18, Secretary Forrestal brought up the matter of inventories. Conversation about the table developed that some of the Services at least have placed procurement orders for very considerable sums of items in which they actually had an overage and which records failed to disclose. During the discussion Secretary Forrestal made the remark that he heard, for example, that the Army had 100,000 shotguns in storage in Philadelphia.

If there is any doubt about the accuracy of our inventories, particularly in the ZI, the Chiefs of Services should take the matter in hand as quickly and effectively as possible.

Please give me your comment on the adequacy of our current stock records.[1]

[1] Lutes replied, "It is considered that our stock records, if determined to be adequate, indicate that our inventories are accurate." The most recent inspection had turned up only a 1-percent error in the stock records. Lutes acknowledged that the chiefs of technical services at times procured items substantially the same as those being disposed of, but he said that this was justified by such factors as improvements in equipment. He said the report about the shotguns was not accurate (Nov. 24, 1947). Eisenhower passed Lutes's memorandum along to Royall with an undated note saying, "You may wish to show Sec. Forrestal this paper." In a follow-up memo of December 5 Lutes said that a check with the chiefs of the technical services confirmed that with minor exceptions, "there have been no major items purchased which were actually surplus in stock." All correspondence is in COS, 1947, 400.

1870

Eisenhower Mss.

To Robert Porter Patterson
for the National Conference
of Christians and Jews

November 19, 1947

Dear ———:[1] The single purpose of this letter is to tell you why my experiences in the war have excited my interest in Brotherhood Week, sponsored by the National Conference of Christians and Jews.[2]

In its basic philosophy and its waging among nations, war is a renunciation and a denial of human brotherhood. But those who bear its heaviest brunt gain a deep and enduring appreciation of the ties that join them with their fellows. I have seen and marveled at the flawless human unity it has wrought among men whose common denominator was comradeship in the defense of freedom.

In the assembly area before a dawn assault, on the ready line of a forward airfield, there was no thought of a man's antecedents, creed or race. It was enough then that he was an American—that his heart was strong, his spirit willing—that he was big enough to place the cause above himself.

It is in such a spirit of brotherhood that Americans must unite to combat the problems of the peace. Our own tranquillity and continued productiveness can be assured only through harmony and fellowship, and these attributes, faithfully sustained, may well prove our greatest contribution to a civilization paralyzed and wasted by dissension.[3] *Sincerely*

[1] The National Conference of Christians and Jews had selected Patterson as chairman of its annual Brotherhood Week, to be held in February. In a letter of October 7 Patterson had asked Eisenhower to sign a letter soliciting "support in

spirit and also in contribution." The letter would be mailed to about one hundred thousand people.

[2] Eisenhower added the first paragraph to this staff-drafted letter, made some other minor changes, and eliminated a final paragraph that referred to the work of the organization. The letter, together with a short covering note drafted by Carroll, is in EM and in the McDuff Collection.

[3] Patterson thanked Eisenhower in a letter of November 21 (EM). For later developments see Eisenhower to Patterson, Feb. 26, 1948, and Patterson to Eisenhower, Mar. 1, 1948, both in *ibid.*

1871   *Eisenhower Mss.*

To Kenneth Safford Parker   *November 19, 1947*

Dear Kenneth: Thanks for your excellent suggestion for increasing Army enlistments. As a matter of fact, it closely parallels a program which we have already instituted and your letter makes me feel the more certain that we are on the right track.[1]

Our present high school graduate enlistment program permits qualified young men to enlist in the Army for the specific purpose of attending Army technical schools. The program is now operating at top capacity to provide trained specialists in all of the various categories we need for current operation. It embraces such subjects as general electricity, railway bridge construction, radio operation and engineer drafting, just to mention a few.

While I agree fully with your feeling that extension and expansion of this type of program would be eminently desirable, such action at this time would place an additional burden on the Army when manpower requirements are extremely critical. However, the matter will receive continuing consideration as we hope to do more along this line when current commitments are reduced.

I sincerely appreciate the interest you have shown in this problem. I hope you will never hesitate to bring your suggestions to my attention. When I go to Columbia—or right now for that matter—I would be very pleased if you would call me "Ike".[2]

Thanks again for your interest and, with warm regard and the best wishes, *Sincerely*

[1] Parker's letter suggested that the Army "offer enlisters who have the aptitude and a high school education the equivalent of a Junior College Pre-Engineering course... " (Nov. 11, EM). On the letter, Eisenhower wrote, "To G-1 for comment." On November 17 Paul prepared a draft, but Carroll rewrote the reply (COS, 1947, 342).

[2] Parker had written: "When you are no longer a General and go to Columbia, what should I then call you? Of course I hope it is not Columbia that you become President of."

1872   *Eisenhower Mss.*

To Charles P. Ritter   *November 19, 1947*

Dear Mr. Ritter: Thank you very much for your letter. I was highly interested to read of your suggestion as to the possibilities for oil storage in exhausted metal mines.[1]

There is no need for me to disclaim any knowledge on the technical phases of such problems as the one we discussed in Secretary Forrestal's office. My ignorance is appalling but it is encouraging to know that people, who do have the requisite professional training, are vitally interested in assuring to this country adequate supplies of raw materials. Our metal resources, including petroleum, directly and vitally affect the entire security problem just as they affect our economic position.

I am grateful for the trouble you took to write to me and for sending along to me additional data and opinion bearing on the subject.[2] *Very sincerely*

[1] In his letter of November 12 to Eisenhower and Forrestal (OS/D, 47–49, Cent. Numeric File, D 36-1-18), Ritter, who was associated with the Consolidated Petroleum Company of Beverly Hills, California, recalled their suggestion that he put in writing his "ideas of stockpiling vital raw materials, particularly petroleum, for defense purposes." At a previous meeting the three men had discussed the possibility that oil "could be stored in partially exhausted oil and gas fields by introducing it in wells no longer commercially productive." Ritter proposed the storage of foreign crude oil in old metal mines; such mines, he believed, were "remote from the thickly settled sections of the country which would be vulnerable to attack." Ritter enclosed two letters from petroleum engineers who thought the proposal was feasible. Ritter was also concerned about "the continued depletion of the supplies of vital raw materials in this country, in our efforts to put the rest of the world back on its feet." In particular, he objected to the export of steel products for petroleum development abroad. In wartime, he believed, "these facilities and the production itself would soon become the property of the enemy, as in the case of the Rumanian Oil Field now dominated by Russia."

[2] Eisenhower sent Ritter's letter to Forrestal with a covering note of November 18 (EM). Forrestal thanked Ritter for his suggestion and told him that the National Security Resources Board would consider his ideas (Forrestal to Ritter, Nov. 25, 1947, OS/D, 47–49, Cent. Numeric File, D 36-1-18).

1873   *Eisenhower Mss.*

To the Directors of Army   *November 20, 1947*
General Staff Divisions and the Chiefs
of Army Special Staff Divisions
Memorandum

Subject: Policy Concerning Release of Information from Historical Documents of the Army—With Special Reference to the Events of World War II[1]

In the following memorandum, standing verbal instructions, which have been fully approved by the Secretary of the Army, are repeated for the guidance of the staff:

The Army possesses no inherent right to conceal the history of its affairs behind a cloak of secrecy, nor is such conduct conducive to a sound and healthy approach to the day to day performance of its duties.[2]

The historical record of the Army's operations as well as the manner in which these were accomplished are public property, and except where the security of the Nation may be jeopardized, the right of the citizens to the full story is unquestioned. Beyond this, the major achievements with which the Army is credited are in fact the accomplishments of the entire nation. The American public therefore should find no unnecessary obstacle to its access to the written record. The history of the Army in World War II, now in preparation, must, without reservation, tell the complete story of the Army's participation, fully documented with references to the records used.[3] The preparation of this history does not, however, constitute any reason or excuse for denying to the public immediate access to facts and records, where they deal solely with the operations of the Army, and where the security of the Nation is not involved.

In light of the foregoing I consider it appropriate to set forth as a guide, the following, which will govern the release to the public of information from documents pertaining exclusively to the Army:

a. Consistent with existing binding agreements with other agencies, and Governments, the maximum downgrading of all information on military subjects will be accomplished, except only when to do so would *in fact* endanger the security of the Nation.[4]

b. All appropriate members of the Army Staff are charged with facilitating the efforts of individuals who desire access to military information of historical character.

The foregoing directive will be interpreted in the most liberal sense with no reservations as to whether or not the evidence of history places the Army in a favorable light.

[1] Over one hundred copies of this memorandum were distributed, chiefly among the General and Special Staff divisions, the Historical Division, and the Public Information Division. Eisenhower also requested that copies be sent to the Secretary of Defense, Admirals Leahy and Nimitz, and General Spaatz (J.A.C. to Bowen, n.d., COS, 1947, 380.01).

[2] Eisenhower made numerous changes in the draft of this memorandum that General Schuyler of P&O had prepared (*ibid.*).

[3] The United States Army in World War II was projected as a series of about one hundred volumes, to be divided into thirteen sub-series. For the story of this official history see Kent Roberts Greenfield, *The Historian and the Army* (New Brunswick, N.J., 1954).

All documents containing information regarding joint or combined agencies had to be cleared by all the agencies (or governments) concerned, as well as by the U.S. Army. For Eisenhower's attempt to change these declassification procedures see no. 2017.

1874   *COS, 1947, 314.7*

To Joint Chiefs of Staff   *November 21, 1947*

Memorandum by the Chief of Staff, U.S. Army:

Subject: Downgrading of Captured German Documents of Joint and Combined Interest
        Reference: J.C.S. 950/15

1. Under the provisions of J.C.S. 950/15, certain groups of joint and combined records were allocated for custody to the Department of the Army. Within this group are collections such as the records of Supreme Headquarters, Allied Expeditionary Force, and South East Asia Command, but by far the largest group consists of captured records of the German Army. The entire German collection is classified, although it has never been carefully reviewed. The Department of the Army is receiving numerous requests from interested persons not in the government service for access to this German material. At present these requests cannot be granted because of the classification of the records.[1]

2. It would be most advantageous to make as much of this material as possible available to persons desiring it. Personnel familiar with the collection estimate that a major percentage could be downgraded to unclassified and made available to the public without risk of diplomatic embarrassment or breach of security. This would foster the increased public interest in military affairs which is now evident and which the services should make every effort to sustain. The lack of interest and the misunderstandings by the American public of military affairs and military problems during the years between the wars is in large measure traceable to their exclusion from war records on which research could be done and material drawn for articles, histories and other items of public interest. The Department of the Army and the other services are already downgrading their records of World War II for this purpose.

3. This collection of German documents totals over 10,000 file drawers and is administratively difficult and expensive to maintain. It is estimated that about fifty per cent of the total is of no value either for intelligence or historical purposes, and could be transferred to the National Archives or to some other suitable agency. The remainder is very

valuable for military historians and will be used by the Department of the Army and other government agencies for five to ten years.

4. Present arrangements for review and declassification of these documents are cumbersome and unsatisfactory. It is impracticable to translate and circulate the material for necessary concurrences from the three services and the British. If the German documents are ever to be made available to private researchers and writers, a centralized agency must be established to deal with them on the spot and in their context. The Central Intelligence Agency has expressed no interest in handling the downgrading of these documents and making them available for public use.

5. I therefore recommend that consideration be given to the establishment of a committee by the Joint Chiefs of Staff, with a member from each service, and a British member, which shall be directed to review the German documents and declassify such of them as do not warrant continued classification. The State Department should be requested to designate a part-time member for consultation on matters affecting that department. The members should be authorized to act on their own responsibility in the name of their service, and the committee as a whole empowered to act in the name of the Joint Chiefs of Staff. They would operate in accordance with such policy directives as might be furnished them, consulting their own services for advice in doubtful cases. But only with broad authority to act on their own responsibility can this immense collection be reviewed and acted upon with the necessary dispatch. The committee must be assisted by a staff of competent civilian or military linguists. In order to complete the review in about five years it is estimated that about twelve such assistants will be required.

6. Although such a committee could also serve as a central review and declassification agency for such other joint and combined documents as may be referred to it from time to time by the Joint Chiefs of Staff or the services, in my opinion no systematic review of groups of joint or combined records, other than the German, should be considered at this time.[2]

[1] Eisenhower had earlier taken an interest in the German records of the war (see no. 1719). JCS 950/15, of August 13, 1946, a report by the Joint Logistics Committee, is in CCS 313.6 (7-11-44), Sec. 6. Paragraph *e* of that document stated that captured German records then in the custody of the War Department would be retained by that agency. General Malony, Chief of the Historical Division, prepared a brief and a draft memorandum for the JCS on October 24 (same file as document). Malony's draft was rewritten in the Office of the Chief of Staff and sent to the JCS on November 21 (see COS, 1947, Index, 314.7).

[2] This same day Eisenhower's memo was referred to the JIC as the enclosure to JCS 950/17. On June 4, 1948, the JCS would approve an alternate JIC proposal

and reject Eisenhower's recommendation as too costly; the JIC proposal called for the assignment to and review by each service of documents appropriate to its interest (CCS 387 Germany [12-17-43], Sec. 14).

1875   *ABC 370.5 Germany (10-1-47)*

To Joint Chiefs of Staff   *November 21, 1947*
Secret

Memorandum by the Chief of Staff, U.S. Army:

Subject: Military Implications in an Early Withdrawal of Occupation Forces From Germany[1]

1. In paragraph 10 of J.C.S. 1811/1 the Joint Strategic Survey Committee states that " . . . the people most capable of ultimately providing effective resistance to forceful Soviet expansion into Western Europe are the Germans". Although the Germans have the military and economic *potential* for providing effective resistance to Soviet expansion, I feel that this potential could only be realized if the Western Allies radically changed their position of disarming and demilitarizing Germany. The U.S. clearly and fully supports the present position of the Western Allies. Hence it is misleading to indicate that the Germans are potentially capable of effective resistance to *forceful* Soviet expansion as long as the U.S. maintains its present position.[2]

2. I therefore recommend approval of the Joint Strategic Survey Committee recommendation in J.C.S. 1811/1 subject to changing paragraph 10 of the discussion as indicated below.

"10. . . . ~~But~~ The *German* people ~~most capable~~ *have the potential* of ultimately providing effective resistance to forceful Soviet expansion into Western Europe ~~are the Germans~~. *If they should be permitted to develop their military potential by the Western Allies*, they are the people most likely to provide such resistance unless the United States abandons them to Soviet domination before a German Government is set up which is capable of effectively resisting Soviet penetration."[3]

[1] For the manner in which this question had arisen see no. 1790. The JSSC had made their recommendations in JCS 1811/1, of November 14, 1947 (CCS 383.21 Germany [2-22-44], Sec. 19). The JSSC report acknowledged that Western forces could not even significantly delay an attack by the Soviets in Europe. The Russians would not, however, deliberately start a war with the United States anytime soon, the report said, and thus keeping a small number of forces in vulnerable positions in Europe "is militarily acceptable. . . ." If the United States and the Soviets both withdrew, U.S. forces would of course be very far away, while the Soviets would still be on the Continent. The JSSC continued: "It is United States policy to

oppose the spread of communism. United States troops in Germany further this policy and by so doing contribute to the future security of the United States." While Russia would not at this time seek further expansion by way of a major war, it would seek the same goal by using fifth columns and political weapons. The committee was particularly worried about a German army being formed within Russia and sent into Germany after Allied withdrawal. The United States could best avoid war, the committee said, by stopping Soviet acquisition of the resources of western Europe. If the United States withdrew, western Europe would have to align with the Soviet Union in order to avoid complete subjugation. If war did come in the near future, "the Soviets would most probably occupy Europe to the English Channel in the West and the Pyrenees in the South before the United States could seriously interfere." Initial U.S. attacks would be primarily by air, and the JSSC held out the hope that "a major atomic offensive might possibly result in Soviet capitulation." But the United States would be better off if friendly forces could keep the Red Army away from the beaches in western Europe where the United States could land troops. The Germans would be the best source of support for this plan, and the United States should work "for the re-establishment of a German government based on the right of self-determination." The JSSC stated flatly that "it would be detrimental to the future security of the United States to agree to a Soviet proposal for the early withdrawal of occupation forces from Germany." For the State Department's view of Russian intentions see no. 1883.

[2] On November 6, in SX 3741, Eisenhower had received Clay's recommendations (made in response to a P&O request of October 30) about troop strength and U.S. policy toward a withdrawal. The day before, Clay had sent to the U.S. delegation at the Council of Foreign Ministers, meeting in London, a long letter giving his views on the entire German problem. Clay called for an occupation force of 100,000 from the United States and the same number from the United Kingdom, 60,000 from France, and 150,000 from the Soviet Union. (For Clay's previous views see no. 1537.) He thought acceptance of the Soviet proposal for withdrawal would be "disastrous"; it would destroy any opposition to Soviet expansion. Soviet troops would be a short distance away, and the European nations would have little choice but to yield to Russian pressure. Clay again urged withdrawal from Austria (CCS 383.21 Germany [2-22-44], Sec. 19; and Clay, *Papers*, vol. I, pp. 479–90, 492–93).

[3] Admiral Leahy, in JCS 1811/3, of December 2 (CCS 383.21 Germany [2-22-44], Sec. 19), would argue against JCS approval of the JSSC recommendations at this time; they should merely be "noted." In a memo to Eisenhower of December 17, Schuyler (who had drafted the C/S's document) pointed out that the Council of Foreign Ministers meetings had ended without a proposal by the Soviet Union that the occupation forces be withdrawn early (same file as document). On December 23 the JCS would approve Leahy's recommendation (CCS 383.21 Germany [2-22-44], Sec. 19).

Subject: Allied Screening Commission Records
  References: *a.* J.C.S. 950 series
  b. C.C.S. 701/50

THE PROBLEM

1. To make available to the Director of Central Intelligence microfilmed copies of those files of the Allied Screening Commission, Leghorn, Italy pertaining to case histories of assistance given escapees and evaders in Italy.[1]

FACTS BEARING ON THE PROBLEM

2. There exist in the files of the Allied Screening Commission, Leghorn, Italy detailed case histories of assistance given escapees and evaders in Italy, giving names of persons assisted, locations, dates and other pertinent data. The records constitute a complete list of persons in Italy who might be useful in covert intelligence operations. It is estimated that five weeks' time and approximately $5,400 will be required to microfilm the files (see Enclosure "A").

3. In accordance with a directive from the Combined Chiefs of Staff (Appendix "A" to C.C.S. 701/50) in reply to message in Appendix "B" to C.C.S. 701/50, Allied Force Headquarters is currently engaged in preparing the records for transmittal to the United Kingdom for permanent retention without microfilming that portion referred to in paragraph 2 above.[2]

4. The Director of Central Intelligence has requested the microfilming of that portion of the files referred to in paragraph 2 and has agreed to bear the cost thereof (see Enclosure "B").[3]

RECOMMENDATIONS

5. *a.* That authority be granted the Commanding General, U.S. Army Forces in the Mediterranean Theater of Operations to microfilm for the Director of Central Intelligence that portion of the Allied Screening Commission records containing detailed information regarding assistance rendered escapees and evaders in Italy.

b. That, if action on this subject is not completed prior to the inactivation of the Mediterranean Theater of Operations on 2 December 1947, authority be granted to the Commander in Chief, European Command, to discharge this function as a residual activity of the Mediterranean Theater of Operations.[4]

[1] The Allied Screening Commission, a subordinate agency of AFHQ, dealt with the claims for compensation and recognition of Italians and Austrians who had assisted Allied soldiers behind enemy lines. The CG, MTO, in his FX 77707 of October 25, 1947 (Enclosure A to this paper), noted that these files were to be shipped to London and suggested that because of their potential value, they should be microfilmed by U.S. intelligence agencies before they were sent to London. Eisenhower's memo, drafted by P&O, was circulated as JCS 950/18.
[2] CCS 701/50 (of May 24, 1947), a report by the combined administrative committee on personnel requirements for microfilming Allied forces records, is in the same file as this document. Appendix A contained the CCS approval of SAC-MED's proposal to microfilm the records of the Allied Force Headquarters (Appendix B, NAF 1300, Mar. 25, 1947). The CCS directed SACMED to ship the Allied Screening Commission records to the United Kingdom without microfilming them.
[3] Rear Admiral Roscoe Henry Hillenkoetter (USNA 1920) had been Director of Central Intelligence since May 1, 1947. His request is dated October 28, 1947.
[4] On December 12 the JCS approved Eisenhower's recommendations and directed CINCEUR (in WARX 92208) to do the microfilming "as a residual activity of MTO." All correspondence is in the same file as this document.

1877   *Eisenhower Mss.*

To Joseph Lawton Collins   *November 22, 1947*

Memorandum for the Deputy Chief of Staff: With the consent of General Ridgway I have informed Secretary Royall that Brigadier General Hertford[1] can be made available for duty as an assistant to Mr. Gray.[2]

Hertford is presently in rather poor health and I have notified the Secretary that upon his arrival in Washington he must under no circumstances be placed on duty immediately and that for some time he would have to work at a very reasonable pace. He informed me that he already understood this.

Please make arrangements to effect the transfer and find an appropriate replacement for Ridgway.[3]

[1] Brigadier General Kenner Fisher Hertford (USMA 1923) had served during World War II as Chief of the Latin American Section, Theater Group, in OPD, and then as Deputy CG, U.S. Army Forces in the South Atlantic. In 1946 he attended the National War College and then joined Ridgway's staff at the U.N.
[2] For background on Gordon Gray see no. 1787.
[3] This would be unnecessary because Hertford would remain on the Military Staff Committee at the U.N.

1878   *Eisenhower Mss.*

To Frederick Coykendall   *November 22, 1947*

Dear Mr. Coykendall: Thank you very much for your very informative and cordial letter.[1] I am afraid that my former letter may have carried an unfortunate implication that I was somewhat disturbed; I certainly did not mean it to do so. As I told the Committee many months ago, the most important factor in my decision to accept the Columbia post was my respect for and my confidence in the Trustees. I hoped, in my letter to you, only to list some of the things, possibly inconsequential, that we talked about when we were trying to decide to make this revolutionary change in our lives.

With respect to the individual that I asked the Committee to engage as a special assistant for the President; it was agreed that he would have nothing whatsoever to do with University matters.[2] I have found from a considerable experience that there is a great volume of correspondence and incidental work that falls upon me because of the amount of publicity that has been centered around my name for the past several years. Invitations for speeches at important functions average some 40 a week, and there seems to be no indication that these will fall off markedly in the near future. Such correspondence as this, to say nothing of a great number of contacts that reach all over the country and beyond, will require the full time of some individual, so that I may devote my own efforts to University affairs. That individual has necessarily to be acquainted with my attitudes, ideas and purposes. It was for this reason that I asked them to set up a position at a reasonable salary, expressing the hope that to fill it, I could obtain some recently retired officer so that with his pension he could live reasonably comfortably in New York.

If I should retain with me, for a period, any of the military individuals authorized by regulations, they will be engaged exclusively in work pertaining to the Army, work that will not completely cease, merely because my active duty service will be terminated. These will cost the University nothing because if I should find it necessary to supplement their rather meagre Army pay in order that they could live in New York City, I would consider this my personal obligation. So to answer your question, the only individual of whom I spoke to the Committee was the one who would be working with me in order to take care of matters that I consider definite obligations to American citizens.

Incidentally, my meetings with Mr. Jacobs[3] have given me a most favorable impression of him and his abilities. I am delighted that he will be with me.

There is one matter that is of little personal importance to me but which is presented differently in your letter from what I thought you said when you were here. I think you said that it would be most convenient for me to arrive there no later than May 1st and probably take over, officially, a day or so after Commencement: Your letter states that I would not take over officially until July 1st. This is completely satisfactory to me unless you and the Trustees would think it simpler and better to tack on the Inauguration as a ceremony immediately following the Commencement. My only purpose here is to say that whatever the Trustees find to be most desirable along this line will meet my wishes exactly.[4]

President Truman has now made public announcement that my successor as Chief of Staff will be General Bradley.[5] Consequently the last barrier to Columbia making an announcement about the date of my arrival has been removed, except for the faint possibility that something unforeseen might occur to postpone it.[6] However, since such things are always understood whenever an announcement is made, the Trustees, if they so desire, may follow their own judgment in this matter, without further reference to me.

I shall inform my aide that any questions he has concerning the house will be taken up directly with Mr. Schley. My whole concern, in this matter, is to see that Mrs. Eisenhower is happy.

I am currently in the hospital undergoing a check-up[7] and so may have missed some of the points in your letter but I think this covers most of them.

I repeat that I am looking forward with great anticipation to participating with you and your associates in the work of Columbia. Mrs. Eisenhower joins me in cordial greetings to you and Mrs. Coykendall. *Faithfully*

[1] Coykendall's letter of November 17 is summarized in no. 1856, n. 4.

[2] See no. 1551.

[3] For background on Jacobs see no. 1856.

[4] In a note to Eisenhower, Coykendall pointed out that the current academic year would run through the end of June. He suggested that Eisenhower take over shortly after commencement, which would take place on June 1, but Coykendall thought the inauguration ceremony should not take place until October. In his answer of November 28 Eisenhower agreed to take over on June 7. Both letters are in EM.

[5] See *New York Times*, November 22, 1947.

[6] The press statement released by Columbia on December 10 said that Eisenhower would assume his presidential duties on June 7. See no. 1916. The related correspondence is in EM.

[7] See no. 1857.

1879   *Eisenhower Mss.*

TO NICHOLAS MURRAY BUTLER   *November 22, 1947*

Dear Dr. Butler: Under present plans I shall be in New York for a reception and dinner on December 13.[1] I am hopeful that this journey will provide me with an opportunity to fulfill my long-deferred desire to call upon you.

If it would be possible for you to see me sometime in the afternoon of

December 13 I will make arrangements to leave Washington in time to keep such an engagement. If, on the other hand, you already have commitments for that afternoon, I shall probably arrive in New York only in time for my evening engagements.

May I ask that if you find some free time on your calendar for that afternoon, you drop me a note with an indication of the time and place that would be most convenient to you. Because of the reception and dinner that evening I could scarcely come at an hour later than 4:30 P.M.[2] *Sincerely*

[1] See no. 1916, n. 4.
[2] Butler invited Eisenhower to call at 3:30 P.M. on December 13. He wrote that he would be in the process of moving from the president's house at Columbia to an apartment on Park Avenue at that time. He would contact Eisenhower when he was certain as to where he would be on December 13 (Nov. 24, EM). Eisenhower's pen note at the bottom of Butler's letter read, "Arrange Dec. 13 trip so as to reach N.Y. by 2:00 or 2:30." The two men would never meet due to Butler's sudden illness and his death on December 7 (see no. 1916).

1880   *Eisenhower Mss.*

To Edward Martin   *November 22, 1947*

Dear Senator Martin:[1] Thank you for your kind note conveying Mr. Robinson's invitation to luncheon on 13 December.[2] I am sure the occasion will be most enjoyable, but I must decline because I have appointments that will not allow me to reach New York in time.

Your interest is indeed considerate and I hope you will tell Mr. Robinson how grateful I am for his thoughtfulness. *Sincerely*

[1] Edward Martin (A.B. Waynesburg College 1901) had been governor of Pennsylvania from 1943 to 1947 and Republican senator from Pennsylvania since January 1947. Eisenhower made some changes in a draft of this reply prepared by Carroll.
[2] J. French Robinson (M.S. West Virginia University 1918), of Cleveland, Ohio, was having an informal luncheon in his apartment at the Waldorf Astoria Hotel in New York for twenty-five Pennsylvanians who would be attending the Pennsylvania Society dinner that evening. Senator Martin had extended the invitation in a letter to Eisenhower of November 19, 1947 (EM; also see no. 1916, n. 4).

1881   *COS, 1947, 020 Chief of Staff*

To Kenneth Claiborne Royall   *November 28, 1947*

Memorandum to the Secretary of the Army:[0]

Subject: Recommended Length of Service for Any Individual as Chief of Staff

In reply to your request for my views on the length of tour for the Chief of Staff, I recommend that if the matter is to become one for legislative action, the following be the stand of the Department of the Army:[1]

"In time of peace the length of tour for any individual as Chief of Staff of any of the services is fixed at three years unless sooner terminated by the President, and provided that, upon recommendation of the appropriate Secretary and of the Secretary of National Defense, the President may extend the tour of duty of an individual as Chief of Staff to a maximum length of four years."

For any man coming into the office, the first year must be largely a period of settling down and orientation, with frequent trips and visits to home installations and overseas commands. It is a period also in which the new Chief of Staff will bring in such principal assistants as he desires to form his staff team.

The second year normally would see the initiation of programs based on his conception of current needs and his observations during the first year. Much of the implementation, of course, would extend beyond a twelve-month period. For this reason, I believe that a two-year tour would not be a long enough cycle to assure reasonable continuity of policy and program. My idea is that a fourth year could normally be approved only when some unusual circumstance should indicate the wisdom thereof.[2]

[1] Royall's request had probably been verbal. The Chief of Staff extensively revised a draft of this memorandum (McDuff Coll.), and the message was hand-delivered this same day.

[2] In 1950 Congress would stipulate that the normal term of office of the Chief of Staff would be four years (see U.S., *Statutes at Large*, vol. 64, p. 266).

1882   *Eisenhower Mss.*

To Jacob Loucks Devers   *November 28, 1947*
Restricted

Dear General Devers: I am deeply appreciative of your memorandum of the 25th of November on the subject, "Proposed Project for Joint Research and Development Board."[1] The subject you discuss has been one of the most intense interest to me ever since the beginning of the war and not only have I devoted considerable attention to it but have conferred with numbers of government officials and with educators concerning the problem.

This problem has always been dramatized for me by the contrasting morale and attitude found among front-line soldiers with the fear and defeatism encountered in the rear hospitals where were concentrated those suffering from psycho-neurosis and from self-inflicted wounds.

Your search for a solution has led you into a slightly different direction than I myself have thought applicable. Believing that the matter extends very far back into the environment and early training of our youth, my mind turned instantly to the responsibility of our educational institutions and therefore I have suggested to several university officials that they seek to investigate this whole matter with a view to corrective action.

To assist in such an effort I have offered to make available our great mass of records on the individuals classified as psychoneurotics. While we had recognized psychiatrists and psychoanalysts working on this problem during the war, these individuals have returned to civil life and about the only man remaining who is completely familiar with the records and at the same time can talk the language of the psychiatrists, is Major General Howard Snyder, Retired.[2] I have been particularly hopeful that some major university would pick up him and this problem and, through analysis of our statistical records, begin to trace out the causes of these tragic failures and so do the preliminary work that would enable our educational system as a whole to act effectively in the matter.[3]

Naturally I have no objection to referring the matter also to the Research and Development Board because the problem is so serious that we should try every possible type of approach. Certainly the cure is never going to be found until we have a more realistic attack in the educational system as well as drastic revision in the military training of the recruit. Our service schools should emphasize the necessity of every officer being prepared to do his part not only upon mobilization but during all his contacts with recruits and students during times of peace. Something will be accomplished if we do nothing more than to impress upon every officer that in this field will lie one of his greatest responsibilities, the second that mobilization takes place. I thoroughly believe that if we can get concerted action both in the educational and in the military institutions of the country a tremendous improvement can be realized.

I shall send your letter, together with a copy of my reply, to the Research and Development Division. *Sincerely*

[1] In his memorandum to Eisenhower, Devers had said: "It is painfully apparent that an improvement must be made in our methods of inuring the soldier to withstand the strain of modern battle. It is the mental toughening, not the physical, that concerns me most." Devers said the high rate of battle-induced neuropsychiatric cases during World War II demonstrated that current mental conditioning was a failure. He recommended that the Joint Research and Development Board study the attitudes of American youth toward patriotism, devotion to coun-

try, and military service in peace and war (COS, 1947, 334 Joint Research and Development Board). For the Army's efforts in this area during World War II see U.S. Army Medical Service, *Zone of Interior*, ed. Robert S. Anderson, Neuropsychiatry in World War II (Washington, D.C., 1966), pp. 392–96, 402–6.
[2] For background see no. 1234.
[3] In May 1948 Eisenhower would initiate an intensive study of this subject (see no. 1005, n. 3). For Eisenhower's involvement in the project see also McCann, *Man from Abilene*, pp. 167–69.

1883   *Eisenhower Mss.*

To Walter Bedell Smith   *November 28, 1947*
Personal and confidential

Dear Beedle: Within the past two days I have had two communications from you. The first was the copy of the estimate on Russian intentions (which I found profoundly interesting)[1] and the second was your letter of November 17 which was equally intriguing.[2]

With respect to some of the so-called "histories" now being written, I have the feeling that many of them carry their own evidence of error, even prejudice.[3] However, there have been so many of these put out—Ingersoll, Allen, Patton, Moorehead and others—that there should exist alongside of them factual accounts that are plain, unvarnished stories of what actually occurred. I felt that the articles you published in the Saturday Evening Post carried a very definite atmosphere of authenticity and I believe that their expansion into a book or the writing of a book that might cover the whole period of '42 to '45 could not fail to be beneficial to a future historian.[4] I think that in such a book more references to appropriate SHAEF directives would cut the ground completely away from some of the arguments made by partisans. In any event the truth itself is an interesting and absorbing story and while such a book might not have the great sale that an argumentative, prejudiced account sometimes achieves, in the long run its value would be definitely recognized. From all this you will gather that I approve of your idea.

You will recall that during the war we often used to say: "No one thinks clearly when he's scared."[5] There is possible application of that old saw to the present day. It is a grievous error to forget for one second the might and power of this great republic. Admitting the enormity of the problem we have if Western Europe is to be saved from Soviet domination and if it is again to become a productive area in the whole world complex, yet we must realize that, assuming a cooperative attitude on the part of the peoples of that region, accomplishment lies within our power. Beyond this, although we must never lose sight of the constant threat implicit in Soviet political, economic and military aggression, we must remember also that Russia has a healthy respect for the power this nation can generate. Unless they had such a respect they would go right ahead and do as they please in Europe and wouldn't spend their time in piling hysterical charge upon hysterical charge and, in general, showing their own doubts and fears by lying when they know that we know they are lying.

I assume that Norrie is going to London with you, because you told me that she wanted to go there for some kind of medical attention. If this is true then your visit should not be as irksome and accompanied by so much loneliness as would otherwise be the case. My warmest regards to her and to any and all of our old friends of the war days that you may happen to meet.

With my very best to yourself, *As ever*

P.S. A note from Louis Marx today says that his new wife is "expecting." X-rays indicate twins!![6]

[1] Smith's paper of November 5, "Evaluation of Present Kremlin International Policies," had been written amidst growing concern on the part of many in the United States that the Soviet Union was now ready to exploit the poor economic conditions in Europe by taking more aggressive action. The Soviets in turn had characterized recent U.S. actions, such as the Truman Doctrine, as acts of aggression. The worsening atmosphere was dramatized on September 18 when the Soviet delegation to the U.N. General Assembly introduced a resolution condemning the United States, Turkey, and Greece for conducting "a new war . . . by the dissemination of all types of fabrications through the press, radio, cinema, and public speeches, containing open appeals for aggression against the peace-loving democratic countries." Smith argued that Russia was probably prepared to take more militant action but that if the West stood firm, stabilized economic conditions, and demonstrated the advantages of western democracy, "we have little to fear." Smith's paper is in State, *Foreign Relations, 1947*, vol. IV, *Eastern Europe; The Soviet Union*, pp. 606–12; the State Department's analysis is in *ibid.*, vol. I, *General; The United Nations*, pp. 770–77. For U.S. reactions to the Russian moves in the U.N. see *ibid.*, pp. 76–256. See also David E. Sumler, *Europe and the Cold War* (St. Charles, Mo., 1974).

[2] In his letter (which was in response to Eisenhower's no. 1826) Smith had said that while in the United States, he had been "impressed with the growing uncertainty, even hysteria, which prevails at home. It is paralleled by the overpowering fear of imminent war in a large part of Europe, particularly Western Europe" (EM). For the Army's plans to meet this threat see no. 1875.

[3] Smith had written that he was "getting a little bit irritated with the continuing reports of the various times that SHAEF prevented people from winning the war." He now planned to write his own book.

[4] For Smith's articles and book see no. 786; on Ingersoll see no. 900; on Allen, no. 1785; and on Patton, no. 1826. Alan Moorehead's *Montgomery: A Biography* was published in 1946 (see no. 1170).

[5] Smith had stated: "Our Soviet friends here are fully alive to the powerful influence exerted by the threat of another war, hence the 'anti war mongering campaign' which they are pressing with redoubled violence."

[6] Marx's note of November 25 is in EM (see no. 1902).

Dear P.A.: I have had the case of Captain K . . . looked up and have a report on the matter.[1] The commissioning of air officers is something with which I have nothing to do. Nevertheless they are always glad to answer any of my inquiries.

The report is that his composite score was too low to secure him a commission in the Air Forces. You understand that the whole matter of awarding commissions was handled by means of a very elaborate set-up in which War Department influence was minimized. This does not mean that the results were necessarily correct in all instances; it merely means that we took the fairest and best scheme we could develop and then refused to interfere with it so that no one could claim "special privilege."

Captain K . . .'s second choice was Cavalry, but because he had no experience whatsoever in the ground arms and because his composite score was too low to secure him a commission in the Air Forces, the Ground Forces rejected him also.[2]

In spite of all the above, I will write a personal note to General Spaatz calling attention to the Captain's special qualifications in the matter of languages. It is just possible that this point was overlooked and that the Air Department may desire to go further into it. This is the most I can do.[3]

I was interested in the account of the bridge hand.[4] Personally, I would criticize Anne for getting a bit impatient with her powerhouse. Because of your lack of great length in hearts it would seem to me that you should have ended up in seven no trump, a bid that should not have been too difficult to arrive at and which would have protected you against the possibility of one opponent's having the hearts massed against you. Of course it is easy to criticize after the cards are all laid down and I hasten to remark that I would always be delighted to take Anne as a partner in the games in which I play (especially true if she makes a habit of holding such hands).

The other evening I played a game with Al Gruenther, Averell Harriman and Ely Culbertson.[5] I was the only loser. Mr. Culbertson plays aggressively and quickly. He has a nice personality and is perfectly willing to play for any size stake, including the smallest. Al is likewise a top-notch player—a bit on the deliberate side. Averell loves the game but seems to me to be a bit unsure of himself. On the other hand his seeming hesitance may be nothing but a continuing revision of his analysis to assure that he makes no mistakes. I often wish that I were a bit more deliberate myself.

The only hand of any real interest was one that I picked up toward the end of the game and tried to bombard my partner, Mr. Culbertson, into going to a slam with it. A slam in either of my two suits, hearts and diamonds, was unbeatable, but he did not feel strong enough to carry me that far, although he had the Ace, Jack and two small diamonds. My own first bid was a double of an opponent's club bid, in which I was blank. At the end of the hand, Mr. Culbertson told me that had I bid two hearts instead of my double he would have carried me to a slam because the two-suited nature would have been more evident. However, it was fun.[6]

My warmest regards to you and Anne, *As ever*

[1] Colonel Hodgson had asked Eisenhower (Nov. 17, EM) if he would find out why the Air Force had not given a Regular commission to this officer. The captain, who had been born in Connecticut, was the son of Russian immigrants who were naturalized U.S. citizens. In 1941 he had enlisted in the Army, and he had gone overseas in 1944.

[2] Michaelis gave Eisenhower this information in a memorandum of November 24 (EM).

[3] See next document.

[4] Hodgson described a bridge hand in which he and his wife Anne had been partners.

[5] Ely Culbertson, an author and lecturer, had written several books on bridge, in addition to his publications on international politics.

[6] On November 14 Eisenhower had written to noted bridge expert Charles H. Goren about a particular hand the General had played (and about which he and Gruenther had disagreed).

1885   *Eisenhower Mss.*

TO CARL SPAATZ   *November 28, 1947*

Memorandum for General Spaatz: A friend of mine has appealed to me to see whether I could intervene in the case of Captain George K . . ., who has been rejected for commission in the Air Forces.[1] I have made reply that all these matters were handled by a system and that in any event there was nothing I could do since the separation of the two services.

However, in going over the record, I found one thing that may have been overlooked. It is that this man seems to have an unusual fluency in the Russian language. Because we are struggling so hard in the services to get linguists and a knowledge of the Russian language is something we consider most important, it occurred to me that you might like to look into the case again.

I do not expect any answer to this note.[2]

[1] See the previous document.

[2] The captain would not receive a Regular commission.

To WILLIAM PEARSON TOLLEY   *November 28, 1947*

Dear Dr. Tolley:[1] It goes without saying that I am tremendously appreciative of your kind invitation to come to Syracuse on June 14.[2] Whether or not I find it possible to attend, I do hope that you will convey to the Board of Trustees my sentiments of gratitude for their thoughtfulness and for the honor they have tendered me.

My difficulty in answering definitely is, I think, almost obvious. In June I shall have been at Columbia only a few brief weeks and whether or not I shall be able to get away for the day is something I cannot foretell. In these circumstances I am sure that you will agree that it would be wholly inadvisable for me to accept your additional invitation that I make a Commencement address; a later compulsory cancellation would be most embarrassing to both of us.

With regard to actual attendance at the Commencement, I do not know how long you can conveniently wait for a firm answer. If you must have a definite reply at this moment I would be compelled to decline. I am anxious that I place no burden upon you of holding up your arrangements for the graduation. Consequently, unless it is completely convenient to you to allow me to give my final answer sometime in the spring months, I must ask you to exclude me from consideration. If you find it necessary to do so I shall understand and shall be no less appreciative of the honor implicit in your invitation.[3]

I trust that in the not too distant future I may be able to meet you and to express in person my very great satisfaction. *Very sincerely*

[1] Tolley (Ph.D. Columbia 1930) had served as president of Allegheny College from 1931 until 1942, when he became chancellor of Syracuse University.
[2] In a letter of November 24 Tolley had invited Eisenhower to visit Syracuse on June 14 to receive an honorary Doctor of Laws degree.
[3] Eisenhower would be unable to make the trip to Syracuse on June 14.

To CLYDE MCKAY BECK   *November 28, 1947*

Dear Clyde: Thank you very much for your nice letter.[1] Mamie and I were deeply sorry that we were allowed such a short visit with you in Memphis. In fact, we were embarrassed at having asked you to come down on an expectancy of more than a half hour's stay when we actually had to leave as quickly as the baggage could be loaded. In spite of our embarrassment it was grand to see you both.

Not long ago I had a chance to endorse an application by Eleanor and her husband to join Chevy Chase.[2] That was one time that I didn't have to hold back.

I have just come out of the hospital after a week there of check-ups.[3] I cannot possibly remember all of the tests that I took but throughout the week I had the feeling that they were sparing me nothing. I haven't heard the final verdict based upon all of the accumulated records but when I left there I was told that they had found so little that they doubted the necessity of my even coming back to listen to the completed report. Anyway, Howard Snyder will go out and get the bad news—if any.[4] Actually I am feeling splendidly and I shall be astonished if they report anything except of a minor character.

This year we are going up to the Army-Navy game.[5] I haven't seen one in many years and while I think it should be a fine contest I am naturally hoping that the Army can bust through with a win.

Take care of yourselves and please remember it's always nice to have news of you. *Cordially*

[1] For background on Beck see no. 1367. Colonel and Mrs. Beck had visited Eisenhower when the General's train stopped at Memphis—while Eisenhower was on a trip to the Southwest—in early November (see no. 1839). Beck's letter of November 14 is in EM.

[2] The Becks' daughter, Mrs. John Freeman Kerkam.

[3] See *New York Times*, November 20, 1947.

[4] On Snyder, Eisenhower's personal physician, see no. 1234.

[5] As was his custom, Eisenhower spoke by telephone to the cadet pep rally (held on November 26) before the Navy game. A copy of his exhortation is in EM, Taylor Corr. On Saturday, November 29, Eisenhower would attend the game, which Army won, 21–0. For background see no. 1693.

1888   *Eisenhower Mss.*

To WILLARD STEWART PAUL   *December 1, 1947*
Confidential

Memorandum for the Director, Personnel & Administration Division:

1. This memorandum will be made of record in the Personnel and Administration Division as the action of the Secretary of the Army upon the proceedings of the General Officers Selection Board which has just terminated its duties.[1]

2. The Secretary of the Army has approved without change and will forward to the President the recommendations of the Board for permanent and temporary promotions.

3. No action will be taken for the present upon those parts of the recommendations that involve forced retirement or the reduction of any officer, except those recommended for reduction because of ineffectiveness.[2] These parts of the recommendations will be kept as Top Secret documents in the Personnel and Administration Division to be presented to the Secretary when and if such action is believed to be desirable or necessary.

4. The Secretary has no objection to the reduction of the eight officers found by the Board to be relatively ineffective, such reduction to take place whenever such action appears to be most desirable, between now and June 30, 1948. Under no circumstances will he approve the reduction of any other officer until those listed as relatively ineffective have all been reduced.

5. With respect to forced retirements, the Secretary believes it is highly unwise to promote to a permanent position a relatively young officer and then to compel retirement of such an individual within a matter of months. He would of course approve the application of any such officer for voluntary retirement. By the expression "relatively young" the Secretary apparently means any officer under the age of 56 or 57.[3]

[1] The selection board was composed of Devers, Bradley, Handy, Hodges, Eichelberger, and Haislip. (For background see no. 1596.) Eisenhower and Royall had discussed the board's recommendations during a War Council meeting this same day (see War Council Minutes, Dec. 1, 1947, OSA/KCR Cent. Dec. File, 337).
[2] The board had recommended that twenty-five generals be reduced so that the Army could meet the limit set for July 1, 1948. Of the twenty-five, the board had found eight to be "ineffective." Eisenhower told Royall, "As to the others there may be no necessity to reduce if certain retirement applications of permanent Generals are filed prior to that date." Royall said that for the present he would act only on the eight.
[3] Eisenhower would soon be forced to reduce the number of four-star generals (see no. 2038).

1889   *COS, 1947, 351*

To Kenneth Claiborne Royall   *December 1, 1947*

Memorandum for the Secretary of the Army:

Subject: Advisability of Seeking Legislation Enlarging West Point Appointments

I refer to your recent memorandum concerning the advisability of seeking legislation to increase the number of appointments to the Military Academy.[1]

As you know, we are currently procuring less than half of our new Second Lieutenants from West Point. Of those graduating, one-third go to the United States Air Force. The remainder of our vacancies are filled directly from the Reserve Officers Training Corps or from civilian component officers on active duty. This system has two important advantages; it provides incentive to members of the ROTC and the civilian components and, at the same time, it gives the Regular Officers Corps a broader structural base.

These advantages will still obtain, of course, if the Corps of Cadets were to be enlarged so as to provide say fifty per cent of the Army's annual needs in new officers. However, I am informed that existing facilities at the academy are inadequate even for the presently authorized Corps of Cadets. Based upon present construction plans and foreseeable appropriations, it is anticipated that the facilities there will continue to be inadequate for a number of years.

Although it may be necessary to enlarge the Military Academy at some time in the future in order to assure that the required number of graduates can be allotted to the United States Air Force without reducing the number required by the Army, I believe that maximum use should be made of the existing facilities of the United States Military Academy, and I do not recommend that legislation be sought, at this time, to increase the number of appointments.[2]

[1] In his November 12 memorandum Royall had asked about the advisability of seeking legislation to increase the number of appointments that the Army awarded to enlisted men and civilians on the basis of competitive examinations. Paul rewrote his draft of this reply as directed by the Chief of Staff. All correspondence is in the same file as this document.

[2] West Point's current authorized strength was 2,496, with an actual strength of 2,173. Annapolis's authorized strength was 4,382, with an actual strength of 2,865 (see Hollis to Bowen, Nov. 13, 21, 1947, same file as document).

1890   *ABC 093 Trieste (7-3-46), Sec. 1-D*

To Joint Chiefs of Staff   *December 1, 1947*
Top secret

Memorandum by the Chief of Staff, U.S. Army:

Subject: Yugoslav Participation in Administration of US/UK Zone of
        the Free Territory of Trieste[1]
    1. Since their failure to establish troops in the US/UK Zone of the Free Territory of Trieste by direct action on the night of the 15/16

September, the Yugoslavs have resorted to political infiltration which to date has made practically no headway.[2]

2. In TAF 52[3] General Airey indicates that a share in the control of the US/UK zone of the Free Territory of Trieste is now a matter of paramount importance to the Yugoslavs and that it is equally important to interests of the U.S. and U.K. that no form of Yugoslav participation in the government of the zone should be allowed. To this end he is planning as a last resort to use force to prevent the Yugoslavs from penetrating the US/UK Zone by the use of force.

3. The Department of State has proposed a message to General Airey which concurs in his views and conclusions as expressed in TAF 52 and provides guidance for him in the event the Yugoslavs attempt to establish troops in the US/UK Zone of Trieste by direct means.[4]

4. I recommend that the memorandum in the enclosure be considered for presentation to the Combined Chiefs of Staff.[5]

[1] For background see no. 1718.

[2] The Italian peace treaty had gone into effect on September 15, and U.S. troops would withdraw from Italy on December 13; however, five thousand men would remain in the Free Territory of Trieste until the United Nations established a territorial government (see no. 1504; and *Department of State Bulletin* 17, no. 442 [1947], 1221, and no. 443 [1947], 1269). Schuyler prepared this memo, which went to the JCS as 1701/19, of December 8, 1947 (CCS 383.21 Italy [10-18-44], Sec. 25).

[3] The message (dated November 22) sent by General Airey, commander of the British-U.S. forces in Trieste, is in the same file as this document and is also reprinted in State, *Foreign Relations, 1947*, vol. IV, *Eastern Europe; The Soviet Union*, pp. 126–27.

[4] The proposed message informed General Airey that the United States and Great Britain would not agree to participation by the Yugoslavs in the U.S.-U.K. zone and that he should resist with force attempts by Yugoslavs to enter the zone.

[5] Eisenhower enclosed a memorandum to be presented to the British Chiefs informing them of the position taken by the JCS and the State Department. That memo in turn enclosed the proposed CCS message to General Airey and a CCS memo to the State Department and the British Embassy requesting appropriate diplomatic representations to the Yugoslavian government. The Joint Chiefs approved Eisenhower's memorandum on December 12, and in CCS 959/90, of December 15, 1947, the CCS approved the recommended action and dispatched the messages. All correspondence is in the same file as this document. The message to Airey is reprinted in State, *Foreign Relations, 1947*, vol. IV, *Eastern Europe; The Soviet Union*, p. 131. For developments in Trieste see no. 1958.

1891   *Eisenhower Mss.*

To Leslie Cornelius Arends   *December 1, 1947*

Dear Les:[1] As I promised, when you were in my office this noon, I have again reviewed my February schedule, because of your personal interest in the nice invitation I have received from the Inland Daily Press Association.[2]

The fact is that I have not only been unable to make additional commitments for that period, I have found it necessary to cancel several of long standing. It promises to be a period of extreme personal activity, involving as it will the problem of turning over to my successor the details of my present job and preparing to go on a much-needed leave preparatory to undertaking new duties at Columbia University.

In the circumstances I hope that you will understand my position. May I ask you to convey again to the officials of the Association an expression of my appreciation for their courtesy. I should like them to know that I feel deeply honored that they should want me to appear at their meeting and that it is only the circumstances briefly outlined above that force me, most regretfully, to decline.

With warm personal regard, *Sincerely*

[1] Congressman Arends, a Republican, had represented the Seventeenth District of Illinois since 1935.
[2] The Inland Daily Press Association comprised 414 daily newspapers of the middle western and Rocky Mountain areas. On this same date Michaelis wrote the association declining the invitation (Nov. 26, 1947) that asked the C/S to speak at a luncheon meeting on February 10, 1948. All correspondence is in COS, 1947, 080 Inland Daily Press Association.

1892   *Eisenhower Mss.*

To Francis De Lashmutt Thomas   *December 1, 1947*

Dear Mr. Thomas:[1] Thank you very much indeed for your nice invitation, which Jack Eakin brought to me personally.[2] Your party sounds wonderful—if it is humanly possible I shall certainly give myself the pleasure of attending. Currently my calendar looks like I should be able to be there a couple of hours at least, possibly from something like 3:00 to 5:00.[3]

In any event, I am really grateful to you for your thoughtfulness. *Cordially*

[1] Thomas, a Washington, D.C., attorney, wrote Eisenhower on December 1 inviting him to a stag party at Thomas's farm in Warrenton, Virginia, on December 6. The guests at the annual party included members of the Gridiron and Alfalfa clubs and men in public life.
[2] John R. "Jack" Eakin, a long-time friend of Eisenhower's, was Milton Eisenhower's brother-in-law. Eakin, who had served in The Adjutant General's Department during the war, was also the brother-in-law of Francis Thomas.
[3] Eisenhower planned to attend the party but was unable to go due to the death of General Alexander Surles (see no. 1916).

1893

Eisenhower Mss.

TO LUCIUS DU BIGNON CLAY

December 2, 1947

Dear Lucius: When you left here it was understood that sometime in the late winter you would send in an official letter of application for retirement, fixing the effective date sufficiently in the future to allow us to send a suitable replacement to overlap the last few weeks of your own tenure. The purpose of this letter is to ask you whether you could give me informally some indication of the date you may have in mind.[1]

Let me hasten to assure you that I am not suggesting an early date for your retirement. Far from it! So long as you have determined to go out in 1948, my own choice of date—a feeling that I know is shared by the Secretary of the Army and by Bill Draper[2]—would be December 31. Among us in the Army there is no question as to your pre-eminent suitability for the task you have and my question is prompted merely by the necessity that always faces me of planning in advance for the shifting of senior officers. So if you can (but always with the understanding that we want you to stay as long as you can cheerfully consent to do so) give me a rough approximation of the date you have in mind, it will be extremely helpful to me.[3]

I trust that both you and Marjorie are in good health. You will recall that when she was here I urged her to start putting on a bit of weight. Tell her that a short report as to whether or not she is following my advice and instruction would be very much appreciated.

With warm personal regard, *As ever*

[1] Clay had visited the United States in the early fall. For background on this question see no. 1678.
[2] For background on Major General William H. Draper see no. 1787.
[3] For further developments see no. 2003.

1894

Eisenhower Mss.

TO ALFRED WILLIAM JONES

December 2, 1947

Dear Bill: You must accept my apologies for failure to answer sooner your nice letter of November 18.[1] Aside from a week spent in a hospital for a check-up I have been more than ordinarily busy and have simply had no time for correspondence.

Your invitation has the strongest possible appeal both to Mamie and to me. Our difficulty has been that the late winter and spring months hold for us so many uncertainties that we have been unable to plan with any assurance. I am, however, quite certain that we would not be able to come down to Sea Island before February 15, so the quail shooting would be out. One other complication has been a tentative arrangement to go to Hawaii about the first of March, a visit that would involve a recreational leave and an item or two of business.

Piled on top of the above is the great hope—rather expectation—that we shall be grandparents about the first of April, so you can understand that Mamie is attempting to arrange all her spring activities around this particular event.

I should think that within a matter of three or four weeks the uncertainties would begin to disappear and we should be able to foresee with some accuracy what we may be able to do. I hope, therefore, that you will allow me to give a final answer shortly after the first of the year. If it is at all possible we should more than appreciate the opportunity of spending a week or two in Mr. McElwain's house, as your neighbor. Because he has been so kind as to offer his house until March 1st I am writing him a personal note and am inclosing it with this letter with the request that you forward it to him.[2]

Both of us send to you and Mrs. Jones our warmest regards together with our deepest gratitude for your thoughtfulness and extraordinary courtesy.[3] *Cordially*

[1] Jones was chairman of the board of the Sea Island Company, which developed resorts. Prior to becoming chairman Jones had served as president of the company from 1928 to 1944. Eisenhower had vacationed at Sea Island the previous winter, and Jones had written on November 18 inviting Eisenhower to spend the month of February 1948 on Sea Island at the cottage of James Franklin McElwain, owner of a shoe-manufacturing firm in Boston.
[2] Eisenhower's letter of December 2 to McElwain is in EM.
[3] On December 23 Eisenhower would write to Jones and to McElwain to inform them that he would be unable to accept their invitation (both in EM).

1895 *Eisenhower Mss.*

To John Elmer McClure *December 2, 1947*

Dear John: I cannot recall receiving any recent note that astonished me quite so much as did yours. The thought that the Burning Tree Club might want a caricature of me was about the screwiest idea that I could imagine.[1]

However, as I view it, the Committee has Spoken—therefore you will find attached my check for the sixty-five bucks. The Club and its officials have been far more than courteous to me—to them I feel a sense of obligation that will never be discharged by any contribution of such doubtful value as this one.

As you suggested, the check is made out to Mr. Dunn.[2]
With warm personal regard, *Sincerely*

[1] McClure, in his capacity as chairman of the Burning Tree Country Club's committee on pictures, had written Eisenhower on November 20 (EM). (For background on McClure see no. 1025.) The committee had decided to add Eisenhower to those whose caricatures had been drawn for the club by Washington, D.C., artist Charles Arthur Ray Dunn. Dunn's paintings had been exhibited in the various national galleries in Washington, D.C. His cartoons and illustrations had appeared monthly in the *Nation's Business* since 1920.
[2] On February 3, 1948, Dunn would sketch Eisenhower in the Chief of Staff's office. The artist has kindly sent the Eisenhower Project a copy of this caricature (letter of July 27, 1977, EP).

1896   *Eisenhower Mss.*

To Anna Maria Rosenberg   *December 2, 1947*

Dear Anna: Since you called me the other day I have been trying to find some way to accept the invitation you extended for January 14 in New York.[1] You know how deeply there appeals to me anything that has to do with the welfare of our children; I am sure you realize that except for the extraordinary situation in which I shall be involved in the late winter months I would gladly accept.

I simply cannot do it. I would even break my January 15 date except that it is one of long standing and is the sole remaining one on my schedule out of a number that I had originally made with Columbia associations.[2] The hours are too short and the days are too few for me to crowd into them all the things that I must be doing.

I know you will understand my great embarrassment and will explain the matter to your associates in this most worthy cause.

With warm personal regard, *Cordially*

[1] Mrs. Rosenberg had called to invite Eisenhower to attend a dinner to raise money to aid needy children; the dinner was being given as a memorial to late New York mayor James John Walker. For background on Mrs. Rosenberg see no. 1039.
[2] An undated staff memo pointed out, "She knows he is to be there on the 15th" (EM). For Eisenhower's January 15 visit to Columbia see no. 1993.

1897   *COS, 1947, 080 Good Neighbor Foundation*

To Benjamin Edwards Neal   *December 2, 1947*

Dear Mr. Neal: Thank you for your cordial letter. I was flattered to learn of the honor the Good Neighbor Foundation wishes to extend to me.[1]

My present outlook is such, however, that I feel I cannot possibly participate in a radio broadcast or a dinner during December or early January. With a formidable array of official demands, along with several commitments of many months standing, I have been forced to call a halt on any additional engagements for the next six weeks. Since I have already declined dozens of worthy invitations and several of national and international significance, I cannot, with propriety, accept yours.

I do wish I could comply with your desires. I appreciate deeply the honor the Foundation has offered me and I trust you will understand that my negative answer is dictated by necessity. *Sincerely*

[1] Neal was president of the Good Neighbor Foundation and the composer of patriotic songs such as "I Am an American" and "My Heart Is in America." In the depths of the depression of the 1930s he had proposed that each employed American be a good neighbor by providing a meal to some less fortunate person on New Year's Day. The organization formed to promote this kind of personal act of good neighborliness had become national and then international. As part of its program the foundation had established two annual awards in 1946, one to an American and one to an international good neighbor. The first year's recipients had been Bernard Baruch and U.N. Secretary-General Trygve Lie. In a November 30 letter Neal had written that the foundation wanted to honor Eisenhower in 1947. Neal asked if the General could arrange to accept the award at his "earliest convenience." Carroll drafted this reply, and Eisenhower made minor changes in the letter (McDuff Coll.).

1898   *Eisenhower Mss.*

To Hubert G. Larson   *December 2, 1947*

Dear Mr. Larson:[1] Only today there came to my attention, through the kindness of Miss Nason, your letter to me of last July.[2] I am embarrassed that I should have been so negligent in expressing to you my very deep appreciation for your kind thoughtfulness.

Under present plans I shall not be coming to New York until May 1st and up to this very instant I had not yet concerned my mind with the acquisition of an automobile—though naturally I shall need one. Because I have not heretofore considered the matter, I naturally have no answer ready at this instant. I wonder how soon you would need to have a firm reply, on the basis that I would be coming to New York at the beginning of May?[3]

Again let me say that I am deeply grateful for your courtesy.[4] *Sincerely*

[1] Hubert G. Larson was the owner of the Larson Buick Company, of Long Island City, New York. On July 24 Dr. Fackenthal had written to Eisenhower that

Larson was "an active and useful alumnus of Columbia" who was "very anxious to serve the new President of the University."
[2] Fackenthal had forwarded Larson's letter in July. It had arrived while the General was on an inspection tour of the Alaskan Command and apparently had been misplaced. Larson said that if Eisenhower did not have satisfactory transportation, he would be "happy to see that he gets prompt delivery of any model and color Buick that he wants" (Larson to Fackenthal, July 22, 1947).
[3] Larson replied that he would be able to get the automobile Eisenhower wanted within a week or two of his order (Dec. 5, 1947). Eisenhower penned at the bottom of the page: "File where I can find it when needed." All correspondence is in EM.
[4] Eisenhower ultimately purchased a Chrysler Crown Imperial limousine.

1899   *CCS 314.7 (8-10-46), Sec. 2*

To Joint Chiefs of Staff   *December 3, 1947*

Memorandum by the Chief of Staff, U.S. Army:

Citation of JCS and CCS Documents as Sources in Official Histories[1]
    1. The Joint Chiefs of Staff previously granted permission for the official historians of the Department of the Army and of the other services to have full and complete access to JCS and CCS documents in the preparation of the histories, subject to review prior to publication (Appendix A). In the review of the first completed volume of the Department of the Army's history in which JCS documents were consulted, Joint Security Control directed that *all* references to JCS documents be deleted (Appendix B).
    2. The Department of the Army is attempting to prepare and publish a complete and factual account of its operations, fully documented in every respect, which will be of value to the public and to the Army. This directive from Joint Security Control prevents the full documentation essential to such a history. General claims that the historians have had access to JCS documents are of little value; almost every author of a war book has made the same claim, based upon his position in some staff during the war. We are dealing with subjects which are frequently controversial, and the best way in which the public can be assured of the authenticity of our work is for our historians to cite the exact document, with its title, date, and file number.[2]
    3. I see no security risk involved in citing specific documents. Textual material, as well as the citations, will continue to be carefully reviewed by the JCS to be certain that nothing of a classified nature is published. If persons apply for permission to inspect specific papers as a result of the publication of documentary sources, the same rules will

apply on access to classified documents as have always applied regardless of the form of the request.

4. In my opinion this policy of refusing to allow citation of JCS and CCS sources will substantially discredit the histories in preparation by all three services. Unsupported statements will only call forth accusations of "cover up" and "whitewash" from those critics who will be looking for just such an opportunity. I believe that the American public deserves the best possible histories of the war and to give them anything less than that is indefensible.

5. I therefore recommend that authority be granted to the three services to cite JCS and CCS documents as necessary in the published official histories.[3]

[1] Eisenhower was strongly committed to declassification, and he had assigned P&O responsibility for implementing his orders to allow the release of information (for background see nos. 1478 and 1873). Eisenhower's efforts to provide a freer flow of information had stalled, however, where JCS records were concerned. Although the JCS had granted access to its records to service historians (Jan. 22, 1947, Appendix A, this document), Joint Security Control had reviewed an Army manuscript (which would become the first volume in the U.S. Army in World War II series) and on October 28 had refused to allow any references to specific JCS and CCS papers (Appendix B, *ibid.*). General Malony, Chief of the Historical Division, prepared a brief and a draft of this memorandum for the Chief of Staff on November 24 (P&O 313.5, Case 118). Eisenhower's memo circulated as JCS 1738/2, of December 4, 1947.
[2] At this time General Eisenhower was also attempting to have declassified a broad range of other records pertaining to World War II (see no. 2017). In his brief Malony had said that lack of authority to cite these documents would place the official historians in a position "comparable to that of Mr. Ingersoll and other writers who have published books based upon their war experiences" (see no. 1039).
[3] On December 4 Eisenhower's memo was referred to the JIC, which recommended acceptance of his proposal (JCS 1738/3, of February 24). The JCS, upon the recommendation of the BCOS, amended the proposal to allow only a shortened title to be used, along with the file number and date. The short title would enable the government to conceal any signal intelligence or attempted deception in a paper. On June 16 the JCS would approve the amended proposal, as would President Truman on June 18. All correspondence is in the same file as this document.

1900   *COS, 1947, 091 Korea TS*

To George Catlett Marshall   *December 3, 1947*
Cable WAR 91489. Top secret

U.S. MILATTACHE Amembassy London, England. Military Attache please pass to General Marshall by hand. Eyes only for General Marshall from Eisenhower: Inasmuch as the decision has been reached by UNO to hold general elections in Korea March 1948, and also information from the State Department indicates that the withdrawal of American Forces presently in South Korea will be initiated July 1948,[1] I discussed the relief of the American Commander, General Hodge, with Mr. Lovett in order to ascertain your particular desires in the premises.[2] Mr. Lovett suggested that I communicate direct with you and express my views that it might be advantageous to continue General Hodge as Commander in Korea for the limited duration of American occupation.[3] In the light of his long experience and knowledge in the area, I feel that Hodge would fulfill our mutual requirements more effectively than any replacement, no matter how highly qualified. However if you are apprehensive about Hodge's ability to cope with problems which will be presented during the remaining period of American occupation, I will take prompt steps to effect his relief, submitting a list of nominees for your consideration.[4]

[1] By August 1947 the Joint Commission on Korea seemed hopelessly deadlocked (for background see no. 1492). After high-level diplomatic efforts to break the impasse failed, Secretary of State Marshall submitted the problem to the U.N. General Assembly on September 17. The Soviets objected that this action violated prior agreements and on September 26 formally proposed mutual withdrawal by January 1, 1948. Secretary of Defense Forrestal wrote Marshall, "The Joint Chiefs of Staff consider that, from the standpoint of military security, the United States has little strategic interest in maintaining the present troops and bases in Korea. . ." (Sept. 26, 1947). On the twenty-ninth, at a meeting in Marshall's office attended by Marshall, Lovett, Kennan (Director, Policy Planning Staff, Department of State, since May 1947), and other State Department officials, "It was agreed that . . . ultimately the US position in Korea is untenable even with expenditure of considerable US money and effort. . ." (State, *Foreign Relations, 1947*, vol. VI, *The Far East*, pp. 817–21). On October 17 the United States submitted its comprehensive recommendation, which the General Assembly approved (with some revisions) on November 14, 1947. Now the United Nations, and not the great powers, would assist Korea toward independence. A U.N. Temporary Commission on Korea would observe Korean elections and aid in establishing a national government and independence. Elections were to be held by March 31, 1948, with adult suffrage and by secret ballot. The representatives chosen would constitute a national assembly, which would have the authority to establish a national government. This government would arrange for the withdrawal of the occupying powers. Omitted was the original American proposal for election by the occupying powers on a zonal basis, and the resolution did not specify whether the elections would be valid if they were not held throughout Korea. See Leland M. Goodrich, *Korea: A Study of U.S. Policy in the United Nations* (New York, 1956); State, *Foreign Relations, 1947*, vol. VI, *The Far East*, pp. 596–889; and United Nations, *Official Records of the Second Session of the General Assembly—Plenary Meetings, 16 September–29 November 1947* (Lake Success, N.Y., 1947), vols. I and II. Subsequent developments are in no. 2039.
[2] At a War Council Meeting of December 1 Eisenhower reported, "State wants General Hodge relieved in Korea; considering General Haislip and General Ridgeway [*sic*] as replacement" (War Council Minutes, Dec. 1, 1947, OSA/KCR Cent. Dec. File, 337). Lovett was acting secretary of state while Secretary Marshall was in London for the meetings of the Council of Foreign Ministers (see

State, *Foreign Relations, 1947,* vol. II, *Council of Foreign Ministers; Germany and Austria,* pp. 676–830).
[3] General Hodge's reports on his problems in Korea are in CCS 383.21 Korea (3-19-45), Sec. 12. See also State, *Foreign Relations, 1946,* vol. VIII, *The Far East,* pp. 605–12, 639–43, and *1947,* vol. VI, *The Far East,* pp. 596–879 *passim.*
[4] This message, which Bowen drafted, is reprinted in State, *Foreign Relations, 1947,* vol. VI, *The Far East,* pp. 868. For background see no. 1103. On December 4 the assistant secretary of state for occupied areas cabled Marshall recommending that if U.S. troops were to leave shortly, Hodge should be permitted to stay. His relief "would be considered a victory by extremist political elements in Korea, notably, Syngman Rhee and his followers, who have been attacking General Hodge continuously." On that same day Marshall informed Eisenhower that if the troop withdrawal was forthcoming, Hodge should retain his command (State, *Foreign Relations, 1947,* vol. VI, *The Far East,* pp. 869–70). For developments see no. 1913.

1901   *Eisenhower Mss.*

To Harold Rupert Leofric Alexander   December 3, 1947

Dear Alex: Thanks for your note. My only regret is that we had such a short time for a real visit—and even that time interrupted by touchdowns, yells, songs and general confusion.[1]

Last eve I carried home with me a copy of your despatch on the period July 10–August 11.[2] So far as my memory serves me there are no mistakes in it, unless it be in the degree of credit you give to me. For that—my gratitude! I am to return the despatch to the War Office promptly.[3]

Needless to say I'm delighted that you and your party enjoyed the game, and otherwise had a good time.

With warm regard, *As ever*

[1] Eisenhower and Field Marshal Alexander had attended the Army-Navy football game on November 29 (see no. 1693). In a note of November 30 Alexander had thanked Eisenhower for his hospitality (EM).
[2] Alexander had sent Eisenhower copies of the reports he had prepared on the campaigns in North Africa, Sicily, and Italy (see Letson to Eisenhower, Nov. 3, 1947, and Eisenhower to Montgomery, WAR 90127, Nov. 11, both in *ibid.*).
[3] For Eisenhower's formal comments on Alexander's dispatches see no. 1914.

1902   *Eisenhower Mss.*

To Louis Marx   December 3, 1947

Dear Louis: It is too bad that in the rush for the train Saturday afternoon we had no time for a chat.[1] I would have particularly liked to congratulate you and your wife on the expected event in your family. I know how pleased you both must be at the prospect.[2]

Two or three weeks ago Mamie received boxes of toys from you and since then has been busily engaged in making up her lists for children on the Post and in various hospitals here where she thinks they will bring the most happiness to youngsters. I know that last year there was many a little child that felt most grateful to you for toys that otherwise they never could have enjoyed.

Recently I wrote a letter to Beedle, who is now in London. I passed on to him the news you gave me in your letter although it is possible he already has it.[3]

On December 13 I am due to come to New York for a few hours but my time looks like it will be completely absorbed, involving as it does a call on Dr. Butler and an appearance that night at the dinner of the Pennsylvania Society.[4] Nevertheless, if I get a chance I will give you a ring. I think my next trip to New York will be about January 15 and thereafter I probably will go on leave and come to the city for permanent residence about May 1.

Even if Mamie has not had an opportunity to write to you about the toys, please rest assured that she is profoundly grateful for the opportunity this gives her to bring, in your name, some Christmas pleasure to large numbers of worthy children.

Please remember me to your two Barbaras[5] and, as always, with warmest regards to yourself, *Cordially*

[1] Eisenhower had seen Marx at the Army-Navy football game on November 29 (see no. 1693).
[2] Marx had written that his wife was expecting twins (Nov. 25, 1947, EM). For developments see no. 2008.
[3] No. 1883. Eisenhower had reported to Smith that Mrs. Marx was expecting twins.
[4] For the trip see no. 1933.
[5] See no. 1499.

1903   *COS, 1947, 091 Greece*

To WILLIAM DUTHIE MORGAN   *December 4, 1947*
Secret

Dear General Morgan:[1] I am writing to inform you of recent events which directly or indirectly concern the U.K. and the U.S. Military Missions in Greece.[2] These happenings have received wide and sometimes inaccurate publicity, including misplaced emphasis on certain aspects.

As you know the U.S. Government made available in May 1947 some $300,000,000 for the purpose of aiding Greece. These funds were intended to provide aid in economic rehabilitation and to provide necessary support to the Greek armed forces in order that the disruptive influence of guerrilla bands could be eliminated.

To administer the overall aid program, the American Mission for Aid to Greece (AMAG), under Mr. Griswold,[3] was established in Greece. Concurrently, the U.S. Army Group American Mission for Aid to Greece (USAGG), under Major General Livesay, was organized as a part of AMAG to handle all military aspects of the program. From the beginning, the concept of USAGG's operations has been to supplement the functions performed by BMM(G)[4] and in no sense to take over any functions performed by BMM(G). This basic concept is still completely valid.

The close relationship and spirit of cooperation which exists between BMM(G) and USAGG is a source of much gratification to the Department of the Army. The aid provided by BMM(G), especially during the initial phases of USAGG existence, has been invaluable. The continuation of this close relationship is essential to the successful implementation of any program for military assistance to Greece.

Due to various factors, the Greek armed forces anti-guerrilla campaign has deteriorated to an alarming degree in recent months. Despite the excellent training guidance provided by BMM(G), the Greek National Army appears unable to generate any offensive when on its own in the field. Since the elimination of guerrilla bands is a prerequisite to the economic rehabilitation of Greece, it is apparent that the Greek armed forces must be provided with military advice of an operational nature. Accordingly, USAGG is now in the process of being augmented to include a Joint American Military Staff which will provide advice to the Greek military staffs down to and including divisions. This operational advice, of course, will have to be predicated on the training given to the Greek Armed Forces by BMM(G). It is contemplated that USAGG, as augmented, will continue to be headed by Major General Livesay.

We understand that the British Government's policies prohibit your officers in Greece from giving official military advice of the type outlined above. Thus, there appears to be no possibility of a conflict in functions. One of the first duties of the Joint American Military Staff will be to recommend to the U.S. Joint Chiefs of Staff any necessary arrangements for clarification of relations between BMM(G) and USAGG, whereupon JCS will complete arrangements with the appropriate British authorities.[5]

I hope this information will be of value to you. If there are any other

details I can supply, I shall be only too glad to be of service to you.
Sincerely

[1] General Morgan commanded the British Army Staff in Washington and was the Army member of the Joint Staff Mission. A veteran of both world wars, he held the Military Cross, the Companion of the Distinguished Service Order, and the Belgian Croix de Guerre. Prior to coming to Washington he had served for two years as SACMED (see no. 1504).
[2] For background see no. 1815. The British military missions in Greece were confused as to what their role would be in the plans announced by the United States (State, *Foreign Relations, 1947*, vol. V, *The Near East and Africa*, pp. 419, 433–34). Eisenhower signed this letter on December 2 but did not mail it until the fourth. Michaelis sent a note to Wedemeyer (who had drafted the letter) saying that Eisenhower wanted Wedemeyer to consider whether or not Royall or Forrestal should sign the communication (same file as document).
[3] In June 1947 Dwight Palmer Griswold, former governor of Nebraska, had been named chief of AMAG.
[4] British Military Mission, Greece.
[5] The Joint Chiefs would still be working out the details of coordinating the activities of the U.S. military groups and the British military missions in Greece when Eisenhower left office (see the correspondence in CCS 092 [8-22-46], Sec. 10, and P&O 091 Greece TS, Case 3/15). Eisenhower would be able, however, to establish the new U.S. group before he completed his service as Chief of Staff (see no. 2040).

1904   *Eisenhower Mss.*

To James Vincent Forrestal   *December 4, 1947*

Memorandum for Secretary Forrestal:

Subject: Civilian Board for Investigation of Disability Retirements in the Services

1. In conformity with verbal instructions, the following is submitted in confirmation of my informal report to you as of yesterday, 3 December.

2. I believe that whenever administrative errors, such as occurred in the Meyers case,[1] come to the attention of responsible authority, immediate and exhaustive investigation should be instituted. However, in this case I consider it inadvisable for any executive agency of government to appoint a Civilian Commission to investigate into facts and circumstances connected with retirement of officers of the Army, Navy and Air Force who have been placed on the retired list by reason of physical disability.[2] My reasons are:

    a. A committee in each House of Congress has already announced its intention of inquiring into this matter. We should fully and freely cooperate in those investigations. Any move now by the

Executive Department to appoint a civilian board for the same purpose would at the very least be a duplication of effort and would probably be interpreted as an effort to anticipate the action of the Congressional Committee.[3]

b. In the Army, Mr. Tracy Voorhees, as Special Civilian Assistant to the Secretary of War,[4] began conducting investigations of this type as long ago as the summer of 1945 and has kept in close touch with the matter since that time. He is confident that the requirements of the law have been fully met, except possibly in isolated cases.

c. In the opinion of the Army staff, concurred in by Mr. Voorhees, there are definite defects in the law, which result in unreasonable exemptions from normal tax obligations. There are already prepared studies and recommendations which will seek to remedy those defects.

d. I believe that the great mass of administrators, in this case mainly medical, have striven honestly and fairly to carry out the provisions of the law as it exists and to protect the interests of the government as well as the individual. The practice of convening a civilian board each time one or all of the services may be subjected to criticism because of the errors of some individuals does not, in my opinion, serve any useful purpose. In fact, it tends to weaken public confidence in the normal administration of the armed services.

3. None of the above precludes opportunity to direct additional investigations by appropriate service agencies if deemed desirable. In the case of the Army, I feel that Mr. Voorhees has already attained any results that could be expected through such action.[5]

[1] Major General Bennett Edward Meyers had entered the Army as a private, first class, in 1917. He had become a pilot during World War I and had been commissioned as a first lieutenant in 1918. He had risen through ranks, becoming a major general in February 1944. During World War II he had served as Deputy Assistant Chief of the Air Staff, Army Air Forces, in charge of purchasing and maintaining aircraft for the Army. He then had become Deputy Director of the Air Technical Service Command and had retired because of a physical disability on August 31, 1945, in the grade of major general. Meyers was involved in an investigation of irregularities in wartime airplane-construction contracts. On December 19 he would be indicted by a federal grand jury on six counts of perjury and subornation of perjury. The ensuing case was covered extensively in the *New York Times*.

[2] On November 26 President Truman had announced that he had asked Forrestal to begin an inquiry into the retirement pay of military officers. Truman later told Forrestal that he was "considering seriously the advisability of a survey by a Civilian Commission and having that Commission decide just what disability is, and how it can be rated on a percentage basis" (Truman to Forrestal, Feb. 4, 1948, OS/D, 47–49, Cent. Numeric File, D 56-2-7).

[3] See U.S. Congress, Senate, Special Committee Investigating the National De-

fense Program, *Hearings on S. Res. 46*, 80th Cong., 1st sess., 1948, pt. 43; and Leva memorandum, Dec. 13, 1947, P&O 337 TS, Case 26/4.

[4] Tracy Stebbins Voorhees had received his law degree from Columbia in 1915. He had been a member of a New York law firm and had served as a special assistant to the secretary of war since 1945.

[5] In January 1948 Forrestal recommended that Congress change the laws regarding retirement for physical disability, and in February Truman abandoned the idea of appointing a civilian commission to study the matter (see press release, Feb. 11, 1948, and Leva to Forrestal, Feb. 12, 1948, both in OS/D, 47–49, Cent. Numeric File, D 56-2-7; see also Paul to Eisenhower and Royall, Dec. 6, 1947, COS, 1947, 210.85, for details of the proposed changes).

1905   *Eisenhower Mss.*

To Aksel Nielsen   *December 4, 1947*

Dear Aksel: Thank you very much for your letter of the 28th.[1]

With respect to manganese deposits in the United States, I am certain that the Bureau of Mines and the Army-Navy Munitions Board have the complete records of all these resources. The trouble has been that the manganese discovered in the United States has either been in such small quantities or of such low grade ore that the cost of using it has been far greater than to import. Of one thing I am sure: the Army-Navy Munitions Board follows up every bit of information of this kind very closely so as to lessen our dependence—at least under emergency conditions—on outside sources.

As to planning for my vacation, I have been very anxious indeed that Mamie and I go together somewhere for a good rest. Unfortunately, the time of year is an awkward one so far as outdoor sports are concerned and it has been exceedingly difficult for us to make up our minds as to what we should like to do. One thought that has occurred to us is to go to Hot Springs, Arkansas, for about a month, taking the baths there and hoping that I could get to play a bit of golf. In any event, I doubt that it would be convenient for me to go down to the Mexican coast, even though the prospect you hold out is a most delightful one.[2] It is even possible that we might come to Denver for a week in spite of the fact that March is ordinarily one of your most disagreeable periods of the year from a climatic standpoint.

I had never before seen the words of the song that you sent to me. The writer very obviously felt that the Navy had been overlooked in the great "return."[3]

I am sorry to hear that you and Helen expect to be in Washington only a few hours. Be sure to let me know in advance the exact time of your arrival so that Mamie and I can have the maximum amount of time with you. Please remember me to Helen, and with warmest regards to yourself, *As ever*

[1] Nielsen's letter said he had been thinking about the manganese shortage and had learned that there were several mines in Colorado and New Mexico that were not being worked. He wondered if "the interests are not deliberately holding back domestic production" (EM).
[2] Nielsen had suggested that Eisenhower join him and some friends in Tampico, Mexico, where they could catch tarpon, yellow-tail, and sea bass.
[3] Nielsen had enclosed the words to a parody of "When Johnny Comes Marching Home Again," entitled "I Have Returned." The song gave song credit for the liberation of the Philippines to the Navy and the Marines, not MacArthur. The closing lines read: "God sent Kinkaid, Halsey and Nimitz / And the General went along to kibitz / Singing, 'I have returned.' "

1906   *Eisenhower Mss.*

To QUENTIN REYNOLDS[1]   *December 4, 1947*
Telegram

Message to Columbia's 1947 Football Team and Lou Little

Give my greetings and warm congratulations to Lou Little and the men of Columbia's 1947 Football Team.[2] I have followed their exploits with great pride this season, but confess to a lingering small regret that Army failed to kick that extra point to gain the tie.[3] I expect to qualify next year as the Columbia Team's most faithful kibitzer, right from the opening scrimmage.

[1] Quentin Reynolds (Ph.B. Brown University 1924) had been a reporter for the International News Service and an overseas correspondent until 1933, when he became an associate editor of *Collier's* magazine. He wrote numerous books and published short stories in *Collier's* and other national magazines. Reynolds was also active in radio and later appeared on television. For background see no. 1098; and Chandler, *War Years.*
[2] Lou Little, Columbia's football coach, was an old friend of Eisenhower's. For background see Eisenhower, *At Ease*, pp. 345–47.
[3] Eisenhower was referring to the October 25 Columbia-Army game, which Columbia won 21–20, breaking Army's thirty-two-game winning streak (see *New York Times*, Oct. 26, 1947).

1907   *Eisenhower Mss.*

To CARL RAYMOND GRAY, JR.   *December 5, 1947*
Personal

Dear Carl: Welcome to Washington's bureaucracy.[1] My only word of advice is, "Don't forget your sense of humor!"

Inadvertently, I heard this morning that General Hawley, who I understand has submitted his resignation at Veterans Administration, would probably stay on for several months if personal request were made upon him to do so.[2] This may look like sticking my nose in someone else's business; I pass it on merely because I happened to hear it and because I thought the item might be of some interest to you. Certainly I cannot vouch for its accuracy.

The first chance you get, please drop in at my office. Maybe we can even have lunch together.[3] *Sincerely*

[1] General Gray would shortly arrive in Washington to take up his duties as head of the Veterans Administration, replacing Bradley. For background on Gray see no. 1739.

[2] Eisenhower held Hawley in high regard and had previously tried to get him to accept the position of Surgeon General (see no. 1364). Hawley would stay on as chief medical director of the Veterans Administration only through the end of December.

[3] Gray, who acknowledged Eisenhower's letter in a note of December 15 (EM), would take the oath of office at the Veterans Administration on December 31, 1947.

1908   *COS, 1947, 201 Groves*

To James Vincent Forrestal   *December 5, 1947*

Memorandum for the Secretary of National Defense:

Subject: Major General Leslie R. Groves

There were no officers junior to Groves selected for permanent major general.[1] He was selected as a permanent brigadier general, and will retain his temporary appointment as a major general. This action does not constitute a passing over of General Groves. He is eligible for consideration by subsequent selection boards for recommendation to promotion to a higher permanent grade.[2]

[1] For background on the selection of permanent generals see no. 1888. In regard to Groves's career see no. 1192.

[2] For subsequent developments see no. 1918.

1909   *Eisenhower Mss.*

To Maxwell Davenport Taylor   *December 5, 1947*

Dear Max: I am more than grateful to you for the trouble you took to make Field Marshal Alexander's visit to Philadelphia so enjoyable.[1] It was obvious that he and his party had a wonderful time and it was equally obvious that all this resulted from the care you took to make him feel at home.

It seems a considerable time since I had a chance to talk to you. Possibly I shall see more of you after I have gotten out of the Army than I have been able to do during the past many months.

My very warmest regards to you and to your good wife. *Cordially*

P.S. I am writing a note to Red Blaik, another to Captain Steffy. I thought their performance last Saturday was a brilliant one. I merely want to tell them so.[2]

[1] Eisenhower and Alexander had gone to the Army-Navy game on November 29 (see no. 1693). Taylor had written Eisenhower on December 1 saying that he was sorry he had missed seeing the Eisenhowers at the game (EM).
[2] Army had won the game. See the next two documents.

1910   *Eisenhower Mss.*

To EARL HENRY BLAIK   *December 5, 1947*

Dear Red: I know that it must have been a tremendous satisfaction to you to wind up your season so brilliantly.[1] My outstanding impression at the game was the evidence of the success you had attained in bringing your crowd to a psychological and physical peak. That is real leadership and I, together with everyone else in the Army, have nothing but admiration for what you accomplished.

I am writing a short note to Captain Steffy[2] but I should be most appreciative if you would, when convenient, pass on my felicitations and congratulations to your assistant coaches. Under present plans I shall be out of uniform when next football season rolls around but I shall be just as violent a rooter for you and your Army team as ever before.

Again my very best wishes, and for you and yours, a Merry Christmas and Happy New Year.[3] *Cordially*

[1] See the previous document.
[2] The next document.
[3] Blaik thanked Eisenhower in a letter of December 12 (EM).

1911   *Eisenhower Mss.*

To JOSEPH BENTON STEFFY, JR.   *December 5, 1947*

Dear Captain Steffy:[1] I should like to join the others who have expressed to you their admiration for the quality of your play throughout a difficult football season and for the leadership that brought such a satisfactory result in the Navy game last Saturday. I have never seen an Army team that I thought was operating at a higher peak than yours did in the crucial game and as a result you gave the whole Army renewed reason to be proud of the Corps of Cadets and the team.

I assure you that in solving the problems that will come to you in your future years in the service you will look back upon your football training as a most valuable experience. You and your mates have fine equipment on which to build and I confidently anticipate splendid careers for all of you.

May I ask that, if convenient, you pass on to all the other members of the squad, my congratulations on their fine season and particularly upon their performance in their climactic game.

With best wishes for Christmas and the New Year, *Sincerely*

[1] Cadet Steffy, captain of West Point's football team, would graduate from the academy in 1949.

1912   *COS, 1947, 032.2 Representatives*

To Joseph Lowell Stockman   *December 5, 1947*

Dear Mr. Stockman: I received your recent letter and appreciate the spirit in which it was written.[1] Obviously I could not help feeling deeply flattered by the sentiments expressed in the accompanying clippings. However, I assure you that I am completely sincere in stating that I have no political desires whatsoever, and do not want to participate in political activity. I hope my friends will cooperate with me in discouraging any contrary purpose.

With warm regard and good wishes, *Sincerely*

[1] For background on Congressman Stockman see no. 1484. On December 1 Stockman had sent Eisenhower two newspaper clippings that quoted Stockman as urging the Republican party to nominate Eisenhower for President in 1948. Stockman wrote that in his opinion the only thing that might endanger Eisenhower's chances for the nomination would be a premature espousal of interest on the part of the General. For background on Eisenhower and the 1948 election see no. 1614. Eisenhower made several changes in Carroll's draft of this reply (McDuff Coll.).

1913   *Eisenhower Mss.*

To Matthew Bunker Ridgway   *December 6, 1947*

Dear Matt: Just a note to tell you that the whole Korea matter has been postponed, at least until the middle of next summer.[1] Because I had already "threatened" you a bit in this regard, I thought you would like to have this piece of news.

Thank you very much for telling me about the hospital service at Totten.[2] I have already spoken to Roy Lutes and he will make arrangements to reserve quarters for an aide and a non-commissioned officer. I cannot tell you how delighted I am that you brought these possibilities to my attention.

Last evening I was at a dinner party where I saw Senator Warren Austin.[3] He took several minutes to praise you in warm terms. A specific statement, expressed with great emphasis, was: "He is far more than merely a soldier; that man is a statesman!"

With warm regard, *Cordially*

P.S.: I suppose you heard that Day Surles died last evening.[4] We are all deeply saddened.

[1] Ridgway had been under consideration as a replacement for Hodge in Korea (see no. 1900). Wedemeyer had asked Ridgway if he could turn his U.N. duties over to someone else within a short time, and Ridgway had said he could (Wedemeyer to Eisenhower, Dec. 1, 1947, EM). Eisenhower wrote on the memo: "Keep this until final decision has been made."

[2] Ridgway's letter of December 5 said the service at Fort Totten, Long Island, New York (in which Eisenhower had expressed an interest), would be back in full operation by mid-January (EM). Eisenhower probably had in mind the check-up he was scheduled to have as he left active service.

[3] U.S. Ambassador to the United Nations.

[4] See no. 1915.

1914   *Eisenhower Mss.*

To Harold Rupert Leofric Alexander   *December 6, 1947*

Dear Alex: As soon as copies of your despatches were received, I forwarded them to the Army's Historical Division for study.[1] Since then, I have looked over the African and Sicilian despatches, but I do not feel qualified to comment on the Italian report since I left the Mediterranean Theater before most of the action took place.

I think your treatment of the campaigns is excellent, and that the despatches are accurate and well written. Such comments as I have are minor and in no way alter the general meaning of the narrative. Further detailed comments will be forwarded in due course, since the British Staff Mission here has just requested official review by the three services, but again I am sure that they will be minor since our Historical Division has studied all the despatches and found nothing serious on which to comment.[2]

On page 22 of "The African Campaign from El Alamein to Tunis, Chapter I, The Conquest of Libya," you state in reference to the

TORCH Operation: "The landing was to be under United States Command and, although the main forces were to be provided by the British First Army and the Royal Navy, the operation. . . ." Taking TORCH as a whole, from Algeria to Casablanca, the preponderance of ground and air strength was U.S. while that of the naval elements was British. You are correct in your statement that the operation was to be represented as almost entirely American in character, although it actually contained substantial British Forces. But to make the statement correct in every sense, it should be modified.

In Chapter II, "The Conquest of Tunisia," the statement is made on page 3 that I "hoped to be able to mount an offensive by United States troops against the southern Tunisian port of Sfax. . . ." An additional word of explanation seems indicated. Actually, the basic purpose of attempting to assemble II Corps in the Tebessa region was to provide a strategic flank guard for the northern Tunisian line and to assure early junction with you as you came through Mareth. The Sfax project, which looked so good to the staff, was to be undertaken only *after* the main purpose of the concentration had been achieved.

Your mention of the capture of Pantelleria in "The Conquest of Sicily," fails to take into consideration the effect of the heavy bombing the island was subjected to which enabled the infantry to land virtually without opposition. I think this passage should be corrected to place the action in its proper perspective.[3]

Thank you very much for your courtesy in permitting me to see these reports prior to publication.

With warm regard,

[1] Eisenhower had already written to Alexander about the reports (see no. 1901).
[2] U.S. approval would not be obtained as easily as Eisenhower hoped. On December 9 Lieutenant Colonel Allen Fraser Clark, Jr. (USMA 1932), of the Historical Division, wrote Eisenhower that he had received copies of the dispatches from three agencies. One copy came from the British Joint Staff Mission, which requested that the JCS clear the dispatches. Clark recommended that permission to publish and official comments should actually come from the Joint Chiefs. Clark attached a draft of a letter informing the British War Office to this effect. After having the letter rewritten, Eisenhower signed it on December 11. (All correspondence is in COS, 1947, 091.713 Alexander.) On December 26, in a staff-drafted cable (WCL 47793), Eisenhower would respond to a December 24 cable from Montgomery, head of the British General Staff, who had inquired about the delay (both cables in EM). On December 30 the War Office would inform Eisenhower that comments by the JCS had already begun to arrive (COS, 1947, 091.713 Alexander).
[3] Eisenhower and Alexander disagreed on the relative merits of air operations (see no. 1993).

General Eisenhower enjoys golfing and fishing in Coral Gables, Florida, January 1947.

General Eisenhower presents retiring Secretary of War Patterson with a scroll in recognition of his distinguished service to the War Department, the Pentagon, July 24, 1947. President Truman looks on.

Party in honor of former Secretary of War Henry Stimson's eightieth birthday, September 21, 1947, at Huntington, Long Island. *Seated, L to R:* Generals Spaatz and Eisenhower, Mr. Kenneth Royall, Mr. George Marshall, Mr. Stimson, Mr. James Forrestal, Mr. Robert Patterson, Mr. Ralph Lovett, General Hodges. *Standing:* General Surles, Mr. McGeorge Bundy, Colonel W. H. Kyle, Generals Kirk and Somervell, Mr. George Harrison, General McCoy, Mr. Arthur Page, Mr. Goldthwaite Dorr, Mr. Allen Klotz, Mr. Harvey Bundy.

James Byrnes, General Eisenhower, Bernard Baruch, and Herbert Swope, September 8, 1947.

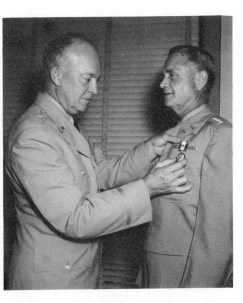

W. Averell Harriman   General Thomas T. Handy

General Eisenhower meets with Congressman Carl Mundt and Assistant Secretary of State for Public Affairs William Benton, 1947.

General and Mrs. Eisenhower with the Sword of Honor, a gift from Queen Wilhelmina of the Netherlands, Washington, D.C., October 14, 1947.

The General Officers Board meets with General Eisenhower at the Pentagon, on November 13, 1947. *Standing, L to R:* Colonel L. E. Nobles, Generals Eichelberger, Hodges, Devers, Bradley, Handy, and Haislip.

Secretary of the Army Kenneth C. Royall with members of his staff, the Pentagon, October 29, 1947. *Seated, L to R:* General Eisenhower, Mr. Royall, and Mr. William H. Draper. *Standing:* Mr. Gordon Gray, General J. Lawton Collins, and Mr. Edwin W. Pauley.

Generals Eisenhower and Bradley, Washington, D.C., January 1948.

General Bradley is sworn in as U.S. Army Chief of Staff by General Eisenhower at the Pentagon, February 7, 1948. President Truman (*center*), General Edward F. Witsell (*left*), and Kenneth C. Royall witness the ceremony.

General and Mrs. Eisenhower at Fort Myer, Virginia, February 1948.

President Truman presents a fourth Distinguished Service Medal to retiring Chief of Staff General Eisenhower at the Pentagon, February 7, 1948.

To Anne Lee Gaines Surles *December 6, 1947*

Dear Annalee: I have just heard the heartbreaking news and have telephoned to Mamie.[1] Both of us are shocked, and it is quite impossible for us to hint at the depth of our grief—and our sympathy for you. I am rushing this note out to you with an aide, and he will tell you what you must already know; that is, that the whole staff stands ready to do anything it is possible to do for you at this moment. If you desire any errands run or any help given, please just give the matter to Colonel Michaelis, who will bring this to you. He will stand by you for the day or for as long as you could possibly want.[2]

I think Mamie will be over to see you as soon as she can, and sometime during the course of the day I shall drop in if you are at home. However, don't see either one of us unless you feel like it.[3]

With all our love, *Always*

[1] General Surles had died at Walter Reed General Hospital on December 5 following an illness of several weeks.
[2] On December 15 Lieutenant Colonel Alexander Day Surles, Jr. (USMA 1937), wrote Eisenhower: "The sympathy, understanding and help which you and Mrs. Eisenhower have given to Mother since Dad's death have gone a long way towards making it possible for her to keep going. Please accept my sincere thanks for everything you have done" (EM).
[3] After writing this message, Eisenhower had his staff notify former Secretary of War Stimson of Surles's death in a cable of this same date (EM). Eisenhower also wrote a tribute (using a draft by Carroll), which was published the next day (see Michaelis to PRD, Dec. 6, 1947, *ibid.*; and *New York Times*, Dec. 7, 1947). The statement emphasized Surles's work in developing the Armored Force and his performance as the Army's Chief of Public Relations. On December 8 Eisenhower attended the funeral at Fort Myer Chapel.

1916 *Eisenhower Mss.*

To Thomas John Watson *December 8, 1947*

Dear Tom: I know what a shock it must have been to you to lose your old friend, Dr. Butler.[1] I have just written to Mr. Coykendall confirming a telegram I sent him yesterday, with an explanation of why it was impossible for me to come to the funeral.[2]

These days it seems difficult to encounter any piece of information that could be called "good" news. This afternoon I must go to Arlington to the funeral of one of my oldest and dearest friends,[3] while on the international front it is only rarely that a gleam of light seems to pierce the forbidding clouds on the horizon.

However, I always remind myself that pessimism can never win a vital struggle—we must never forget what this country is and, equally important, what it stands for.

My very best to you and Mrs. Watson and the children.[4] *Cordially*

P.S. I expressed to Mr. Coykendall my gratitude for the invitation of the Trustees to sit with them at the funeral tomorrow. It was more than kind of them to think of me in this way.[5]

[1] Nicholas Murray Butler had died the morning of December 7 in St. Luke's Hospital, New York City, where he was being treated for pneumonia. He was eighty-five years old (see *New York Times*, Dec. 7, 1947).

[2] Eisenhower wrote: "I . . . regret sincerely that my engagements for Tuesday are of such character that they cannot be postponed or broken much as I would like to attend the services at St. Paul's" (Eisenhower to Coykendall, Dec. 7, 1947, EM).

[3] The Chief of Staff was referring to Major General Alexander D. Surles. In his tribute to Surles, Eisenhower said, "In the death of General Surles, the army has lost one of its most valuable senior officers—I, personally, have lost a close friend and trusted adviser" (see previous document).

[4] This same day Eisenhower wrote a letter to Thomas I. Parkinson, a Columbia trustee, expressing his sympathy and his regret that he would be unable to attend Dr. Butler's funeral (Eisenhower to Parkinson, Dec. 8, 1947, EM). See nos. 1550 and 1933. Eisenhower would see Parkinson on December 13 at the annual dinner of the Pennsylvania Society.

[5] Eisenhower would be able to attend Dr. Butler's funeral. The General traveled by plane and returned to Washington immediately following the services, which were held in St. Paul's Chapel on the university campus. That afternoon Coykendall announced Eisenhower's plans to move to New York and take up residence at the president's house, 60 Morningside Drive, about May 1; he would not assume his duties as president, however, until June 7 (see *New York Times*, Dec. 10, 1947).

1917   *Eisenhower Mss., Morgenthau Corr.*

To John Hersey Michaelis   *December 8, 1947*

We now have a Dept. of Nat. Defense. Such conversations therefore should be held with someone above me—I represent only one service.[1]

[1] Eisenhower wrote this message on a memorandum from Michaelis transmitting a request by Henry Morgenthau, Jr., that Eisenhower see the political advisor for the Jewish Agency for Palestine. Michaelis had told Morgenthau that such a conversation would place Eisenhower in a difficult position. Morgenthau said, however, that the discussion would be off-the-record. It would center on the defense of the Jewish and Arab states in view of the pending British withdrawal. On December 9 Cannon indicated on this same memorandum that Morgenthau was disappointed but would call Forrestal. (For background on the Palestine question see no. 1568.) The British were going to withdraw from the area because on November 29, 1947, the U.N. had voted to partition Palestine into six principal parts, three of which would constitute a Jewish state and three an Arab state. In addition, Jerusalem would be an international zone under U.N. control. See the

following volumes in United Nations, *Official Records of the Second Session of the General Assembly: Supplement No. 11: United Nations Special Committee on Palestine* (Lake Success, N.Y., 1947), vols. 1–5; *Resolutions, 16 September–29 November 1947*; and *Plenary Meetings*, vol. II, *13 November–29 November 1947*. See also State, *Foreign Relations, 1947*, vol. V, *The Near East and Africa*, pp. 1113–1328. For a map showing the partitioned area see John and Hadawi, *Palestine Diary*, vol. II, p. 269.

1918   *Eisenhower Mss.*

To James Vincent Forrestal   *December 8, 1947*

Memorandum for Secretary Forrestal: Saturday I sent to you a memorandum of facts bearing on the case of General Groves.[1] This morning there has come to my desk a transcript of a conversation you had with Senator Hickenlooper.[2]

I am sure you are aware of the method, rigidly prescribed by law, under which the recent selections to general officer were made. Those methods preclude the use of influence by the Secretary of the Army or the Chief of Staff in favor of any individual.[3] This is indicated by the fact that several good friends who served close to me during the war and for whose efficiency I have the deepest respect, failed even to make the grade as permanent Brigadier Generals.

While I do not agree in detail with all the selections made by the Board, the whole system was devised so as to minimize the effects of personal acquaintanceship, friendship, and prejudice.

Senator Hickenlooper is right in his conviction that General Groves performed a most unusual and outstanding job during the war. Personally I agree with the Senator that it would have been completely fitting—and from my viewpoint, desirable—for Groves to have been included in the permanent list of Major Generals. However, I am informed that no one permanently junior to him in rank was made a permanent Major General. Secondly, by naming him as one of the permanent Brigadiers to be retained as a temporary Major General, the Board has, in effect, placed him on a preferential or eligible list and his promotion to permanent Major General within the reasonable future should be assured. This arrangement has one distinct advantage for anyone who wants to stay in the Army. Under the law, any permanent Major General, with five years' service as such and 35 years' aggregate service, is *forced* to retire. We had one officer who requested that he be *kept off the permanent Major General list* in order that he would not run the risk of having his service terminated within the next five years.

In any event, the Board was composed of the most responsible, senior, and able officers in the Army, and I find it difficult indeed, from my purely personal viewpoint, to quarrel with the mass of their selections. There are no abler or more selfless men in the entire Government than Generals Devers, Bradley, Handy, Haislip, Hodges, and Eichelberger. All these were on the Board, and they gave to the work many weeks of study and analysis. Each of them bore weighty responsibilities during the war, and the breadth of their war experience covered the European Theater, Pacific Theater, the Mediterranean Theater, and War Department activities here at home. In spite of my feeling that General Groves could logically have been selected for permanent Major General—and in my opinion should have been so selected—I cannot fail to express my complete confidence in the integrity, judgment, and disinterestedness of the men who made up the selection panel. Moreover, assuming that General Groves wants to stay in the service until statutory retiring age, I feel that he has not been hurt in the slightest degree.[4]

[1] See no. 1908.
[2] Senator Bourke B. Hickenlooper, of Iowa, was chairman of the Joint Congressional Committee on Atomic Energy.
[3] On this same date Eisenhower sent Forrestal a detailed explanation of the methods used by the General Officers Selection Board (EM).
[4] On December 13 Secretary Royall would send a memorandum to President Truman recommending that the Army member of the Military Liaison Committee to the AEC be given the rank of lieutenant general and that Groves be given the appointment. Forrestal concurred in a memorandum of December 16. (Both are in COS, 1947, 201 Groves.) Groves would be appointed to the position, with the rank of lieutenant general, on January 28, 1948. He would retire on February 29, 1948, with the rank of brigadier general but on the same day would be promoted to major general and would draw retirement pay at the higher rank. By a special act of Congress (PL 394A, of June 24, 1948, U.S., *Statutes at Large*, vol. 62, p. 1393) he would hold the honorary rank of lieutenant general, to date from July 16, 1945, the date of the first atomic explosion.

1919   *OS/D, 47–49, Clas. Numeric File, CD 6-1-34*

To JAMES VINCENT FORRESTAL   *December 9, 1947*[1]
Top secret

Memorandum for the Secretary of Defense:

Subject: Immediate U.S. Military Capabilities in Italy (Revised)[2]

1. The following is a brief estimate of the apparent possibilities which might arise in Italy, and which might make military action desirable, and the capability of the U.S. to take such action. In view of

the limited time available, this brief is not as complete as I would desire. However, as you know, a further study on this subject is being prepared in more detail by the Joint Chiefs of Staff in planning for the implementation of paragraph 12 of NSC 1/1.[3]

2. *U.S. Military Resources in Italy today.*

a. *Army.* Approximately 2,000 U.S. Army administrative personnel are presently at Leghorn, Italy. These are residue forces of Headquarters Mediterranean Theater of Operations and do not include any combat type troops. They were due to leave Italy 3 December but were held, on request of the Italian Government. In addition, the following forces will remain in Italy after 15 December 1947: Military Liquidating Agency (160); Army Graves Registration Service (140). In addition the U.S. has 5,000 troops nearby in Trieste. All military supplies and equipment which were in Italy have been shipped elsewhere to Europe or to the U.S. or have been disposed of through surplus disposal procedures.

b. *Air Force.* No Air Force units are presently stationed in Italy. However, there are a few liaison personnel stationed at Ciampino Air Field, Rome.

c. *Navy.* The Naval Forces in the Mediterranean area are: 1 Carrier (CVB);[4] 3 Cruisers (CL);[5] 10 Destroyers (DD);[6] and 1/3 Squadron Aircraft (VP–HL)[7] Port Lyautey.

3. *Possible Future Conditions under which U.S. Military Assistance Might be Desirable.* In preparing plans for possible future military action as a result of the Italian situation, the following possible developments must be given consideration:

a. Establishment of a separate Communist Government in northern Italy.

b. Overthrow of the legal Government by the Communists by civil war or illegal means.

c. Open Yugoslav military action on the Italo-Yugoslav frontier (possible but considered improbable at the present time).

4. *Military Action Open to the United States:*

a. NSC 1/1, the National Security Council position paper on Italy, recently approved by the President, supplies the basic pattern for possible military action in the event that a Communist-dominated Government is set up in all or part of Italy by civil war or illegal means. Paragraph 12 of this document provides the outline for a specific plan for diplomatic and military assistance by the United States. The Joint Chiefs of Staff are now studying the military implications of this matter and are expected to propose further details of this plan shortly. In case any one of the three eventualities mentioned in paragraph 3, above, led to a decision to commit U.S. forces in Italy, U.S. Army participation might be as follows:

(1) A U.S. Constabulary Regiment in Italy from EUCOM in approximately 10 days; a reinforced Regimental Combat Team in Italy from EUCOM in 10 days, in Libya or Sicily in 24 days; a reinforced Regimental Combat Team from the Zone of the Interior in Italy, Libya or Sicily in 10 days by air.

(2) Provision of a reinforced Division assembled at the New York Port of Embarkation ready for staging within 15 days. The New York Port of Embarkation estimates that five days staging time will be required. Sailing time to Italy is approximately 18 days. Hence, assuming that necessary shipping can be immediately assembled by the Navy, the Division should arrive in Italy in 38 days.

(3) A combination of the forces mentioned in (1) and (2) above.

(4) The above, if implemented, will force certain retrenchments in Zone of Interior operations which, however, will not be of a critical nature.

5. *Other Military Measures*:

In addition to the capabilities for military action mentioned in paragraph 4 above, other military capabilities now under study by the Joint Chiefs of Staff, such as the extension of the strategic dispositions of the U.S. Armed Forces in the Mediterranean area and assistance to the Italian armed forces in the form of equipment and technical advice, should be thoroughly considered. Before reaching any conclusions regarding military assistance to Italy it therefore appears advisable to await the completion of the studies now being undertaken by the Joint Chiefs of Staff, and the current review by the National Security Council of the possibility of furnishing military equipment to Italy.[8]

[1] Copies of this memorandum in various files are dated either December 8 or 9. We have used the copy signed by Eisenhower and received by Forrestal.

[2] For background see no. 1831. This memo was a revised version of one dated December 5, also signed by Eisenhower and sent to Forrestal (P&O 091 Italy TS, Case 3/3). Bowen sent Forrestal's office a covering memorandum that pointed out the revisions that had been made. All of the changes involved paragraph 4; the revisions made more specific the transportation time for forces sent to Italy and made less specific the impact of their diversion on the ZI (Dec. 11, 1947, same file as document). P&O drafted this message for General Eisenhower.

[3] Eisenhower is referring to the JCS 1808 series, a study that would still be under way when Eisenhower left office (see CCS 092 Italy [10-2-47], Sec. 1).

[4] Large aircraft carrier.

[5] Light cruisers.

[6] Destroyer (as distinguished, for instance, from a destroyer escort).

[7] Patrol squadron of heavy land planes.

[8] U.S. forces would be withdrawn from Italy as scheduled by midnight, December 14, 1947 (see State, *Foreign Relations, 1948*, vol. III, *Western Europe*, pp. 765–71; and the papers in ABC 371.2 Italy [9-15-47]).

1920 *Eisenhower Mss., Family File*

To Milton Stover Eisenhower *December 9, 1947*

Dear Milton: Your good friend, Sir John Maud, has just been in to call on me.[1] By a series of questions I learned something of the life you led in Mexico City, including your siege of illness.[2] I don't know why it is so difficult to make an otherwise intelligent man understand that his own efficiency and his own ability to render useful service depend upon his own good health. Activity must be paced to the capacity of the physical machine to support it and I don't know why you don't apply this simple truth to yourself.

I must admit that Sir John's account of your performance was a glowing one. He is quite certain that you not only did a remarkable job but says that your retort in the final stages of the conference, to the unwarranted Polish attack, was a masterpiece. He thought that what you said and the way you said it were both worthy of the most brilliant statesman of any era.[3]

On a number of subjects we had a very pleasant conversation and I was impressed with his integrity as well as his enthusiasm.

My days are as busy as ever, and frankly, if it were not for my definite plan of taking a two-months leave between quitting this job and going to Columbia I would take ten days off this instant just to go somewhere and sleep. I had a week in the hospital for a routine check-up but far from constituting a rest, the doctors worked me so hard that I was glad to get out of the place. Yesterday I went to the funeral of Day Surles, whom you knew. He was one of my warmest friends, and his death was a shock. It was caused by a failure in the lungs; some type of obscure disease that makes the lungs powerless to expel the air and therefore the victim finally dies through lack of oxygen in the system.[4]

This morning I rushed up to New York to attend Dr. Butler's funeral and got back in my office at 2:00 P.M.[5] So it goes, day by day.

A succession of rainy and cloudy but somewhat mild days was succeeded this morning by a clear, cold spell which may last for two or three days. So far we have had no snow in this region. I imagine that Kansas is anxiously looking for some precipitation, particularly in the western portion. The prospect of a renewed dustbowl is one to frighten us all.

Returning to my original subject, I expect a return answer from you saying that you are taking immediately a week's vacation—even if you spend it in your bedroom reading—and that aside from completely free Sundays you are taking at least two one-half days a week to do exactly as you please. After all, at this time of year you can take a little shotgun and go out into the fields of Kansas and see if you can shoot a few cottontails. Maybe you don't like to eat them, but there are plenty of people in the town that would like them. It's lots of fun and it provides a good, mild exercise in the tramping you would do through the fields.

I have already written you a Christmas note but this letter renews my best wishes for a fine holiday season for you and all the family. *As ever*

[1] Sir John Primatt Redcliffe Maud, after an academic career, had entered government service during World War II. Since 1945 he had been Permanent Secretary of Great Britain's Ministry of Education. He and Milton Eisenhower were both members of the executive council of UNESCO and had attended a UNESCO conference in Mexico City in November.
[2] In a response of December 18, Milton Eisenhower said that he indeed had not felt well but that he was now taking it easier and was having a check-up (EM).
[3] At the conference, Milton Eisenhower had stressed the need for agreement on the meaning of freedom of information. For an account see *New York Times,* November 25, 1947.
[4] See no. 1915.
[5] See no. 1916.

1921   *Eisenhower Mss.*

To John William Leonard   *December 10, 1947*

Dear John: Thank you for your note.[1] You have clearly earned everything that has come to you in the Army and you need feel obligated to no one. The only thing I did back in 1941 and 1942 was to make a few individuals understand that they had to go a little bit beyond ritualistic procedures in the selection of battle commanders.

I still hope to visit Knox before I cease operating as Chief of Staff. In the meantime, Mamie joins me in best wishes to you and yours for a fine holiday season and a good New Year. *As ever*

[1] For background on Major General Leonard see no. 202. Since July 1946, Leonard had commanded the Armored School at Fort Knox, Kentucky. In a note of December 6 he had thanked Eisenhower for giving him an armored division early in the war and for proposing that he command a division in the projected invasion of Japan (EM).

To WALTER BEDELL SMITH *December 10, 1947*

Dear Beedle: It was indeed nice of you to send me your impressions of the Conference and of the obvious difficulties we are having. I appreciate the trouble you took and am passing on your ideas to one or two people where I know they will do some good.[1]

The other evening at dinner I ran into Julius Holmes.[2] Our conversation turned to you and we reviewed many of the incidents of African and European days. Later I ran into some newspapermen who had been fortunate enough to attend a conference that you held, apparently when you were here a couple of months ago. They had nothing but praise for the keenness of your observations and the soundness of your judgments—to say nothing of your skill in presentation.

My stay in Walter Reed was for check-up purposes and so far as I know I came off with a very good verdict.[3] My "ringing" ear bothers the doctors a lot and of course my tendency to run up a bit of blood pressure when I get angry or irritated causes them to shake their heads. Aside from these things they seem to think that for an old fellow I am plugging along pretty well. . . .

I am delighted that Bradley's succession to this office was announced by the President, as I requested.[4] This makes it easy to assign him to duties that are specifically preparatory to his taking over. Mamie and I still don't know where we want to go for our two months' leave—but so far as I'm concerned I'd like to go on a foreign trip, just to get away from the interminable political gossip.

Please remember me to any and all of my old friends that you may happen to see. One place that you could easily go for a nice evening, I recommend most highly. It is to Sir Louis Greig's home in Richmond Park.[5] He is Deputy Constable there and has a nice home and a most delightful family. If you would give him a ring and tell him that you and Norrie want to come out for drinks some afternoon, you would not only please him immensely but much more to the point, you would run into a person with whom you would like very much to spend an evening. You will remember him from war days but I thought it possible that you would not recall him sufficiently well to remember where he lived. Incidentally he, along with Jimmy Gault, is a member of the Committee that represents me in England on all matters respecting the apartment in the Scottish Castle of Culzean.[6] If you and Norrie, together with two or three other couples, should like to run up to see that part of Scotland, you could easily find out from Sir Louis whether the place is now habitable (sufficient furniture, etc., etc.). If it is, he or

Jimmy would make all the arrangements quickly and I assure you that for two or three days you would have one of the most delightful and secluded visits to a countryside that you could possibly have. It may not be pheasant or partridge season (Sir Louis could also tell you this) but there would almost certainly be something that you could do. Anyway, if you could possibly go I should be delighted because then when I saw you again we would have another piece of common background.

Take care of yourself. We can't spare you these days. *As ever*

[1] Smith was in London for the fifth session of the Council of Foreign Ministers. In a letter of December 2 he had reported "no progress." Later Smith again referred to the lack of progress but said that the Russians would not permit a formal breakdown while they were in a minority position. Smith then gave his assessment: "The difficulty under which we labor is that in spite of our announced position, we really do not want nor intend to accept German unification in any terms that the Russians might agree to, even though they seemed to meet most of our requirements, since, as they have declared war on European recovery, we know very well from past experience that they would operate to prevent the resources of Germany from contributing. However, this puts us in a somewhat difficult position and it will require careful maneuvering to avoid the appearance of inconsistency if not hypocrisy" (Dec. 10, 1947, EM). See also State, *Foreign Relations, 1947*, vol. II, *Council of Foreign Ministers; Germany and Austria*, pp. 676–830, 896–98. For the Russian proposal to withdraw all occupation forces from Germany see no. 1875.

[2] For background on Julius Cecil Holmes see Chandler, *War Years*. Holmes had served on active duty in the Civil Affairs Section of Allied headquarters in the Mediterranean and in Europe. During his long career he had been alternately in foreign service and in private business, and he was at this time president of an airline in South America.

[3] Smith said he had heard that Eisenhower had been at Walter Reed General Hospital. Eisenhower had entered the hospital on November 20 for a routine physical (see no. 1887).

[4] Truman had announced Bradley's appointment on November 21 (see *New York Times*, Nov. 22, 1947).

[5] For background on Greig see no. 541.

[6] For background on Gault see no. 1156; on Eisenhower's arrangements at Culzean Castle see no. 482.

1923   *Eisenhower Mss.*

To Ben Hibbs   *December 10, 1947*

Dear Mr. Hibbs: It would be quite convenient for me to see you and Mr. Fuller at any time you might like to come down.[1] I am planning on no protracted absences from Washington this month.

I could suggest that each of you give my office a ring a day or two before you would expect to be in the city so that appointments can be made. I would not want either of you to come and encounter a situation that would force you to wait unnecessarily. For your own visit I would suggest Thursday, December 18th, at 10:00 A.M., or Friday, the 19th, at 11:00 A.M. However, if these are unsuitable, I think I could arrange almost any other day except Wednesdays—they are usually bad ones for me. As suggested above, a telephone call ought to fix the matter definitely.[2]

With personal regard, *Sincerely*

[1] For background see no. 1775. In a letter of December 8 Hibbs had asked if he could visit Eisenhower to continue their discussion of the possibility that the *Saturday Evening Post* would publish Eisenhower's memoirs. Hibbs asked if he might bring along Walter Deane Fuller, president of Curtis Publishing Company, which owned the *Post*. Fuller, who had started in the publishing business as a salesman in 1904, had been president of Curtis since 1934.

[2] Eisenhower would meet with the two men on the eighteenth. For further developments see no. 1945.

1924   *Eisenhower Mss.*

To Robert McLean   *December 10, 1947*

Dear Mr. McLean:[1] First, I want to emphasize my personal gratitude for your generosity in providing a magnificent visit in Philadelphia for my friend the Governor General. A letter since his return to Ottawa is replete with superlatives for the weekend with you and your friends.[2]

As to the Poor Richard Club presentation,[3] I have not yet been able to determine certainly that I can be in Philadelphia on January 17 but I told Mr. Slocum[4] that if it were humanly possible I would be there, with the proviso that *I do not have to make a speech.* Within a short time I should be able to give him a definite answer but I rather suspect that I shall have to make the visit as brief a one as possible, leaving directly after lunch. In this event I doubt that Mrs. Eisenhower will be with me.[5]

Nevertheless, both of us are grateful for your nice invitation and as soon as my plans firm up a little better, I will let you know the result.[6]

With warm personal regard,[7] *Cordially*

[1] For background on McLean see no. 1012.
[2] For the Philadelphia visit of Eisenhower and Alexander see no. 1693. For Alexander's letter see no. 1901.
[3] McLean, who published the *Philadelphia Evening Bulletin,* had written on December 4 to congratulate Eisenhower on being selected to receive the medal of the Poor Richard Club at the Franklin Memorial on Benjamin Franklin's birthday, January 17. The club, organized in 1906, derived its name from the Poor Richard of Franklin's *Almanac* and was a vehicle for charitable work by advertising men of Philadelphia (see *New York Times,* Jan. 18, 1948).
[4] Richard William Slocum had received his law degree from Harvard in 1925. After practicing law for twelve years, Slocum had joined the *Evening Bulletin* in

1938, serving as general manager, secretary, and a member of the board of directors. He and the president of the club, Harry Linton Hawkins, had visited Eisenhower in the Chief of Staff's office on December 3.

[5] McLean had invited the Eisenhowers to spend the night of the seventeenth at his home.

[6] The Chief of Staff went to Philadelphia to receive the award but did not spend the night (see no. 1993). Mrs. Eisenhower accompanied the General.

[7] On December 9 Eisenhower had written to Gideon Numsen Stieff, president of the Stieff Company, Baltimore silversmiths and goldsmiths, to thank him for the silver pocketknife Stieff had sent (EM). In reply to Stieff's luncheon invitation (Dec. 6, 1947, *ibid.*) Eisenhower declined because of his crowded schedule. Carroll drafted this letter, and the C/S added one sentence (McDuff Coll.).

1925 *Eisenhower Mss.*

To James Keller Beach *December 10, 1947*

Dear Jim:[1] Needless to say, I appreciate the spirit in which your letter was written, but I assure you that I have been completely sincere in stating that I have no political desires whatsoever, and have no intention of participating in political activity.[2]

With the final phases of this job and my transfer to Columbia, the months ahead will be crowded. I don't know when I may be in Dallas again but, should I come through there, will give you a ring.

Best wishes for Christmas and the New Year.[3] *Sincerely*

[1] Beach and Eisenhower had been friends when the Chief of Staff was stationed at Fort Sam Houston in San Antonio, Texas. Beach was now branch manager with the Liquid Carbonic Corporation, of Dallas, Texas. Eisenhower made numerous changes in the staff-drafted version of this letter (McDuff Coll.).

[2] Beach wrote that Eisenhower was the only man in America who possessed the qualifications necessary to lead the country and urged him to put his "Country and its good above all else" (Dec. 6, 1947, EM).

[3] In a reply of December 16 Beach thanked Eisenhower for his letter and wrote, " . . . the whole world knows you are not seeking any kind of political office, but I believe that the political office will seek you and it will be presented to you on such a basis that you would have some pangs of conscience if you did not accept it" (*ibid.*).

1926 *Eisenhower Mss.*

To Arthur Krock *December 10, 1947*

Dear Mr. Krock: Thank you very much for your kind note. It gave me a lift.[1]

On such occasions as the dinner the other night, I normally succeed in keeping my mouth closed about matters concerning which soldiers re not expected to have opinions. It happened that something suddenly touched upon one of my deep-seated convictions and I was guilty of very warm advocacy of a particular idea. Possibly I was stupid in not realizing that the dinner was not the completely private social affair that I had supposed. Anyway, you have seen in the press how badly my simple little idea was distorted and misrepresented. But I still believe that some really big man in the industrial world has an opportunity, or at least a chance, by sincere, even dramatic action, to help halt the inflationary spiral.[2]

In any event, if you feel any impulse to make use of the thought I express, you are certainly at complete liberty to do so. My only request is that you make no mention whatsoever of my name in connection herewith.

It was nice to see you again—especially to know that you are trying to think earnestly and objectively about issues basic to our country's security and welfare.[3] *Sincerely*

[1] Krock, of the *New York Times* Washington bureau, had written on December 6 to compliment Eisenhower on the remarks he had made at a dinner on December 5 at the 1925 F Street Club. The dinner, given by two Pennsylvanians, had brought together some of the top industrialists of that state, as well as the governor and congressmen, General Eisenhower, and leading Republican political figures. Krock and other journalists were present. After dinner, informal conversation turned to the problem of inflation. Eisenhower said that personal sacrifice was required. Senator Robert A. Taft of Ohio asked if Eisenhower had a more specific suggestion. Eisenhower then said that some leading industrialist, for example, the president of United States Steel, should announce that his company, regardless of profit or loss, would not raise prices for one year. The group had, however, reacted negatively to this proposal. On December 6 someone leaked one version of the incident to Fulton Lewis, Jr., who broadcast that Eisenhower had called for the top industrial leaders to reduce all prices for two or three years in order to eliminate all profits. If the industrialists balked, the government should level a confiscatory tax on all corporation profits and use that money to force a reduction in prices (see Krock, *Memoirs,* pp. 282–83; Marquis Childs, *Eisenhower, Captive Hero: A Critical Study of the General and the President* [New York, 1958], pp. 103–5; and Lyon, *Eisenhower,* pp. 377–78).

[2] The affair commanded much newspaper attention, and Eisenhower spent some time trying to clear up the matter (see for example Eisenhower to Relman Morin, Dec. 12, 1947, EM). Lyon, *Eisenhower,* pp. 378–79, argues that the incident made Eisenhower more hostile to politics.

[3] Krock and Eisenhower had not always been on such friendly terms (see no. 1601).

1927   *Eisenhower Mss.*

To Kenneth Dewey Johnson   *December 11, 1947*

Dear Mr. Johnson:[1] I am grateful for your note even though the occasion for its writing is a disappointment to your associates in the Army.[2]

All of us will miss our daily contacts with you but hope that in your new post opportunity will frequently be afforded us to see and talk to you.

It seems scarcely necessary to assure you that you have left nothing but friends in the Department of the Army, as well as lasting gratitude for the cheerfulness and efficiency that have characterized your stay with us. *Cordially*

[1] Johnson had been a special assistant to the Secretary of the Army since the end of the war. He had served overseas as an enlisted man during World War I. After receiving his law degree from Harvard in 1924, he had practiced law until World War II, when he had returned to the service, this time as an officer.

[2] Johnson had resigned on December 9 to accept the position of general counsel for the National Security Resources Board. His note of December 10 thanked Eisenhower for embodying the qualities that made Johnson proud of having served with the Army (EM).

1928   *Eisenhower Mss.*

TO ROBERT L. MCWILLIAMS   *December 11, 1947*

Dear Mr. McWilliams:[1] As I told you on the telephone, circumstances already beyond the possibilities of control compel me to decline your very cordial invitation.[2] Needless to say, I am highly honored that the Detroit Junior Board of Commerce should wish to present me an award,[3] while the warmth of your invitation increases my regret that I cannot come.

Because of the pressure of duties, intensified by the fact that during late January I shall be going through the throes of turning over my official duties to General Bradley, I have been compelled not only to decline any additional commitments for that month but have actually cancelled several of long standing. All this would make me almost guilty of bad faith if I should accept another invitation, even one so appealing as is yours.

I hope that on the night of your dinner you will convey my very warmest congratulations to the winner of your annual award[4] and express to him my sincere regrets that I cannot be there to meet in person the individual so signally honored by the young businessmen of Detroit.[5] *Most sincerely*

[1] McWilliams was president of the Detroit Junior Board of Commerce.

[2] On this same date Eisenhower signed letters to several other prominent citizens of Detroit, acknowledging their messages in support of the invitation (see COS 1947, 080 Detroit Junior Board of Commerce; and EM, Henry Corr.).

[3] McWilliams had written on December 8 that his group wanted to give Eisenhower a special distinguished-service award at its annual banquet on January 22, 1948 (COS, 1947, 080 Detroit Junior Board of Commerce).

[4] The board would, on the same night, present an award "to the young man under 36 years of age who has made the most outstanding contribution to our community." In past years the recipients had included Henry Ford II and Dr. Paul Henry, president of Wayne University.
[5] Eisenhower wrote to McWilliams again on December 16 after Senator Homer Ferguson, Republican from Michigan, endorsed McWilliams's invitation. Attached to the letter the Chief of Staff sent a congratulatory message to the young businessman who would receive the board's annual award. It read, in part: ". . . the confidence we hold in the brilliance of America's future is based upon the certainty that young leaders, such as yourself, will meet every new national and world problem with courage, resolution, and unshakable faith in the free system that has made this country what it is today" (EM).

1929   *Eisenhower Mss.*

To Harry Pulliam Cain   *December 11, 1947*

Dear Harry: Thank you very much for passing along to me greetings from my friends whom you met in New York. I am sure you enjoyed your appearance before the Calvin Bullock Forum.[1] When I went there some months ago I did so in fear and trembling and found to my delight a most sympathetic group, earnestly concerned with the security and welfare of the country.[2]

Your note reminds me that it has been too long a time since I have had a chance to talk to you. If anything should bring you to the Pentagon Building, won't you please drop into my office?[3] *Cordially*

[1] For background on the Calvin Bullock Forum see no. 1228. Senator Cain, who had addressed the group on December 5, had written Eisenhower that he "was simply delighted by the number of friends you had in the audience" (Dec. 9, 1947, EM).
[2] Eisenhower had spoken to the group on December 3, 1946 (see no. 1220).
[3] In a letter of December 12 Cain promised to "make it my business between now and the time you leave the Pentagon to drop in and pay my respects." At the bottom of the page, Eisenhower wrote, "Fine!" (EM).

1930   *ABC 381 United Nations (1-23-42), Sec. 3-F*

To Joint Chiefs of Staff   *December 12, 1947*

Memorandum by the Chief of Staff, U.S. Army:

Subject: Request by the National Archives for General Information Regarding the Joint Chiefs of Staff and Combined Chiefs of Staff Organizations and Their Respective Committees.[1]
References: JCS 1803
            JCS 1803/1

1. I do not entirely agree with the conclusions and recommendations of JCS 1803/1 because it proposes to restrict unnecessarily the information to be furnished to the National Archives. The policy of the Department of the Army in this regard is to make every effort to make available to the American public the full story of the war by allowing maximum access to historical records.[2] As long as the security of the nation is not adversely affected and no agreements with other nations are abrogated, every effort should be made to accomplish maximum downgrading of historical documents of World War II in order to facilitate their availability to the American public.

2. The proposed brief (page 10) on which to base the ultimate reply to the Archivist of the United States fails to cover his specific request for general information on the files of the JCS and CCS. Such general information on the scope, general description, systems of filing, and bulk of the documents is not of itself classified and there is no *security* reason to withhold its release.[3] Furthermore, no cogent reason is apparent why information of this kind should be withheld. It is not desired to raise the question of access to JCS records as a part of this paper. However, further study should be made of the possibility of downgrading JCS documents and of making available unclassified documents for consultation of interested members of the public.[4]

3. Accordingly, I recommend that paragraph 3 of Inclosure B (page 10) be amended to read as follows:

"3. Records Combined Chiefs of Staff—Joint Chiefs of Staff: - - - - a brief statement ~~to the effect that, for security reasons, the records of the Joint Chiefs of Staff and Combined Chiefs of Staff can not be made accessible to outside-agencies or individuals.~~ *setting forth the type of records, systems of filing, general description of groups, and bulk involved.*"

4. Subject to the foregoing, I approve JCS 1803/1.[5]

[1] On September 5, 1947, the acting archivist of the United States had asked the JCS to allow one of his staff members, Dr. Martin Paul Claussen, to study JCS records in order to assemble general organizational information on the Joint Chiefs (JCS 1803). The National Archives was gathering data for a two-volume handbook of information on federal military and civilian agencies of World War II. On September 11 the JCS assigned the request to the Joint Logistics Committee, in collaboration with Joint Security Control and the JCS Historical Section. The JLC recommended that for security reasons, outside agencies or individuals should not be granted access to JCS and CCS records (JCS 1803/1, Nov. 14). Instead, the Historical Section should draw upon unclassified material for any information considered appropriate. The Joint Intelligence Committee should then clear that information and forward it to the Archives. The JLC asked the JCS to approve its conclusions, send an interim reply, and direct that the material be prepared. Schuyler drafted this response for Eisenhower and sent it to him with a covering memo and a brief on the problem. The Chief of Staff's paper—with stylistic changes—became JCS 1803/2, of December 17. All correspondence is in CCS 000.7 [1-26-42], Sec. 3; and same file as document.

[2] For the Army policy see no. 1873. On Eisenhower's previous efforts to open material for research see no. 1899.
[3] The paper Eisenhower is discussing had called for "a brief statement" to the effect that the records of the JCS and the CCS could not be made available.
[4] For Eisenhower's next effort to promote a more liberal policy on declassification see no. 2017.
[5] On January 9, 1948, the JCS would approve Eisenhower's recommendation and forward the reply to the Archives on January 12 (CCS 000.7 [1-26-42], Sec. 3).

1931   *Eisenhower Mss.*

To FELIX FRANKFURTER   *December 12, 1947*

Dear Justice Frankfurter:[1] There was nothing specially commendable in my effort to see Sir John Maud.[2] From what you had told me, I knew I would have a pleasant few minutes—which I did. Moreover, I am not only deeply interested in the progress of UNESCO, but I was anxious also to have whatever news he could bring to me of my brother. Incidentally, I cannot help saying that based upon one short visit, I conceived a most hearty liking and admiration for your friend.

With best wishes and—if I do not see you before that time—Holiday Greetings to you and yours. *Most sincerely*

[1] Frankfurter (LL.B. Harvard 1906) had been an associate justice of the U.S. Supreme Court since 1939. He had been an assistant U.S. attorney for the Southern District of New York from 1906 to 1910; a law officer with the War Department Bureau of Insular Affairs from 1911 to 1914; and a professor at the Harvard Law School from 1914 to 1939 (Harlan Phillips, ed., *Felix Frankfurter Reminisces* [New York, 1960]).
[2] For Sir John Maud's visit see no. 1920. In a note of December 9 Justice Frankfurter had thanked Eisenhower for seeing his friend and had noted, "You give new proof to an old conviction of mine that no matter how busy he may be a truly civilized man can somehow or other manage to squeeze in a humanly desirable act" (EM).

1932   *Eisenhower Mss.*

To MAUD ROGERS HURD   *December 12, 1947*

Dear Maud: I am most grateful to you for sending along to me the clippings and copies of old letters.[1] I am having them filed away in the family historical records.

When I was last in Abilene I inquired about you from my various friends and sought an opportunity to come by your room in the hotel.

However, it had been so long since I had stopped in to see my aunt and uncle and Gladys Brooks[2] that finally I had to use up my remaining few minutes in a visit to their houses in the northern part of town. The next time I get there I will arbitrarily set aside an hour or two to come to see you, because it's always fun to talk with you about the old days.

Right now I am as busy as ever, but of course I am hopeful that after I once get broken in at Columbia my schedule will not be the backbreaking thing it is here in Washington. If I find that in Columbia I have as little time as now to go see the people that are old and good friends, I will simply quit.

This note brings best wishes and Christmas greetings to you, which I hope you will pass on also to George and Janet[3] and their families.[4] *Cordially*

[1] For background on Mrs. Hurd see no. 1567. Her letter of December 7 is in EM.
[2] A high-school sweetheart of Eisenhower's (see Chandler, *War Years*).
[3] Mrs. Hurd's son and daughter, George Arthur Hurd and Janet Hurd Kent.
[4] Mrs. Hurd has asked Eisenhower if he would send her an autographed picture. Eisenhower sent three photographs under separate cover, two of them inscribed to Mrs. Hurd's grandsons. In an undated note (EM) Mrs. Hurd thanked the General for the pictures.

1933   *Eisenhower Mss.*

TO THOMAS I. PARKINSON   *December 15, 1947*

Dear Tom: This is just a note to tell you how thoroughly I enjoyed the party night before last, to say nothing of the sense of distinction I felt in the receipt of the Society's medal.[1] Incidentally, your handling of the ceremonies was expert to a degree; I should say you have had lots of practice in that sort of thing.

One personal disappointment was my failure to get to talk to you personally. I was hopeful that after the dinner we would have some time for a chat, but I was shy about asking you to come up to the apartment after the banquet because I knew you had much to do.

In any event, the whole affair went off most pleasantly, and I shall hope to have my visit with you sometime in the near future. If you should be coming down this way, please give me a ring so we could have lunch together.

With warm personal regard and best wishes for a fine holiday season,[2] *Cordially*

[1] Eisenhower had received the Gold Medal for Distinguished Achievement from the Pennsylvania Society at its forty-ninth annual dinner on December 13 (for background see no. 1550). In accepting the medal, the General said that he did so

as a representative of the Americans who "placed their all" at the disposal of their country. The text of his impromptu speech is in EM. Also see *New York Times*, December 14, 1947.
[2] On December 16 Eisenhower received a letter from Parkinson thanking him for his participation in the dinner and ceremonies (Dec. 15, 1947, EM).

1934   *Eisenhower Mss.*

To Hugh Montague Trenchard   *December 16, 1947*

Dear Lord Trenchard: Your letter[1] is such a clear exposition of the joint historical project that I am taking the liberty of having copies made of it to circulate among friends that may be in position to do something about it.[2] In making the copies I am eliminating only the paragraph that refers to my possible future connection with the matter. My feeling in this regard is that the man selected should be one with a very high reputation in the cultural world; after all, I am not only a soldier but one whose past acts and decisions will be a part of the material that the historians will be called upon to study. This feeling will not prevent me, however, from continuing to take the liveliest interest in the whole affair.

Among those to whom I think I shall send a copy of your letter are Dr. Conant of Harvard, Dr. Baxter of Williams and Professor Allan Nevins of Columbia.[3] In the Government, to Secretary Symington of the Department of Air, Secretary Sullivan of the Department of Navy and Secretary Royall of the Department of the Army. I shall include also Secretary Forrestal as well as Under Secretary Lovett of the Department of State. While I do not anticipate that all of these people will become militant supporters of the idea, it is well to let them have some information concerning it.[4]

With warm personal regard and my very best wishes for a fine holiday season and a Happy New Year,[5] *Sincerely*

[1] Trenchard's December 11 letter explained that he was seeking support for the project in England and outlined the basic nature of the undertaking (EM). See no. 1685.
[2] Copies were dispatched from the Office of the Chief of Staff under Eisenhower's December 16 covering letter, which expressed his enthusiastic support of the project (see the following document).
[3] Allan Nevins (M.A. University of Illinois 1913) was an author and journalist. He had been a professor of American history at Columbia since 1931.
[4] Eisenhower's correspondence on this subject with Symington, Lovett, and Conant is in EM. Symington was enthusiastic and suggested several other people who might be interested in the idea (Dec. 18, 1947). Lovett replied that Professor William Leonard Langer, of Harvard University (Ph.D. Harvard 1923), was writing a history of diplomatic relations in World War II under the auspices of the

Council on Foreign Relations. Lovett suggested that some such responsible organization be contacted in regard to the proposed joint history (Dec. 29, 1947). Conant wrote that he thought it was a sound idea "but I must say that my friends who are professional historians do not seem to agree with me." He was afraid, therefore, that he would not be of much help (Jan. 6, 1948).

[5] The Historical Division asked twenty-four prominent historians for their opinions of the project. The summary report, prepared by Malony (Jan. 5, 1948, COS, 1947, 314.7), listed their major objections to the proposal: (1) Funding of the project by the two governments would create the risk of political interference and the suspicion of bias; (2) the top-flight historical personnel required by the project would probably not be available; and (3) the project would duplicate much of the research already being done by the military services and therefore should be delayed until the mass of military documents under study had been screened, evaluated, and published. The opinion of the Historical Division itself was that "to undertake this project in the immediate future would be unwise and uneconomical." The proposal would not come up again while Eisenhower was Chief of Staff.

1935   *Eisenhower Mss.*

To Kenneth Claiborne Royall   *December 16, 1947*

Dear Mr. Secretary: Attached is a letter from Lord Trenchard which you may or may not find time to read.[1] It concerns the proposal to write an authentic, joint history of the American-British effort in World War II. It is, of course, true that various departments of our Government are now engaged in writing official histories of the war but each of these is written largely from the viewpoint of the appropriate department.

The idea of the joint American-British history, written in popular style, but completely authentic in content, originated with Lord Trenchard and because I have so enthusiastically agreed with him as to the value of such an accomplishment, I have had some personal correspondence with him about it. However, it is a matter for civilian functionaries, governmental or educational, and I am merely passing this information along for such use as it may be to you in the future. No answer to this note is therefore expected—I am merely hopeful that it may create some interest, on your part, in the project. *Sincerely*

P.S. I am writing identical letters to a few other people, both in the Government and in the university world.

[1] See the previous document.

Dear Milton: When I leave Washington I expect to take 60 days' leave, arriving at Columbia about the first of May.[1] Thereafter I shall occupy a sort of "observer" capacity and will not assume responsibility for supervision of University affairs until June 7. This will allow Dr. Fackenthal, as Acting President, to complete the academic year, including the presiding over the Commencement exercises.

Mamie and I have not yet formed a definite plan for our vacation. Naturally we should like to go to the South where we can get some balmy days and of course I should personally like to find a place where I could play golf rather steadily.

As soon as we make any definite decision I will let you know. With holiday greetings to all the family, *As ever*

[1] This letter was sent in reply to a note from Milton Eisenhower that read: "The press has carried a story to the effect that you will begin your work at Columbia on June 7. Does this mean that you expect to take a three to four month vacation? If so, what are your plans?" (Dec. 11, 1947, EM). See no. 1916, n. 5.

Dear Peg: I appreciated very much your nice letter which came today, and reciprocate many times your friendly holiday greetings.[1]

You had better not bank too much on my introducing any radical reforms at Columbia—when I take stock of my academic qualifications for that post, I begin to have the feeling that Columbia will probably be doing a reform job on me![2] But I have the greatest interest in the teachers and their problems, and what I *can* do to help, I certainly will.

I saw Kay the other day. I thought she looked very well, in spite of the many difficult things she has encountered in the past two or three months.[3] I am sure there is going to come a time soon when she will get herself established and really settled in something she will like, and where she will be happy.

As to political affairs, what I told you in my letter of last May is just as true and applicable now as it was then, and I haven't any doubt that you can see my point and my stand on the subject. It's not for me![4]

With warm regard, and very best wishes for a Happy Christmas and many good things in the New Year, *Sincerely*

[1] For background on Margaret Chase see no. 1629. Her December 12 letter is in EM.
[2] Chase wrote: "Quite selfishly I hope that I can call on you as president of Columbia. I'd love to give you a few ideas about reforming *Teacher's College* for the benefit of us poor teachers who have to take too many dull and stupid educational? courses for advancement."
[3] Chase said that Kay Summersby had broken her engagement "to a fine young man whom I have known for years. However, they had very little in common so perhaps it is best that they did not marry." She thought that living in a foreign country and adjusting to civilian life had been difficult for Kay. See no. 1857.
[4] See no. 1629.

1938

ABC 014 Austria (2-2-44), Sec. 1-I

To Joint Chiefs of Staff

December 17, 1947

Secret

Memorandum by the Chief of Staff, U.S. Army:

Subject: Critical Food Situation in Austria[1]

1. The Department of the Army was relieved of financial responsibility for providing civil relief items for Austria on 30 June 1947. Since that time the Department of State has undertaken to provide for the essential needs of Austria until such time as Congress determines the degree of U.S. participation in the European Recovery Program.[2]

2. Brigadier General J. D. Balmer, U.S. Deputy Commissioner for Austria,[3] has analyzed the food program for Austria for the coming winter months and has come to the conclusion that by utilizing all available sources there will be sufficient food available only until 23 May 1948. Since the European Recovery Plan may in all probability *not* be operable by that time the food situation in Austria will become critical. To prevent such an occurrence *it is essential that supplementary aid be provided*. Procurement for such additional aid must be initiated by March 1948 if the food program is to be continuous.

3. Food is the main weapon used by the U.S. in Austria to maintain our position there. Without food in sufficient quantities, U.S. forces of occupation may soon become incapable of accomplishing the main U.S. objectives in Austria, those of reconstituting Austrian sovereignty and economic self sufficiency. The net result of lack of sufficient food for Austria might be the loss of an important U.S. strategic position on the Continent. In addition, the drastic reduction of the daily ration from 1700 calories to approximately 822 calories, caused by cessation of U.S.

food shipments, would deprive the people of Austria of both the hope and the energy to resist effectively the pressure of Soviet expansion.[4]

4. Sudden reduction of the Austrian people to a starvation diet will likely cause riots and violence beyond the capabilities of U.S. forces to contain under such conditions. Not only will it become impracticable for the U.S. to achieve its occupation objectives, but also the safety of U.S. occupation forces will be jeopardized.

5. I therefore recommend that the attached memorandum be approved and forwarded to the Secretary of Defense.[5]

[1] As of December 31, 1946, UNRRA had officially ceased to be responsible for civil relief and rehabilitation in Austria, even though it continued to furnish aid until the end of March 1947. (For background on the occupation see no. 1344.) On February 15, 1947, in response to pleas from General Clark, the JCS (after obtaining SWNCC's approval) had authorized the War Department to assume responsibility for civil relief until June 30, 1947. The State Department agreed to seek congressional approval for assistance (JCS 1369/15, CCS 400 [5-16-43], Sec. 16), and on May 31, 1947, President Truman signed Public Law 84, which authorized the use of $350 million for the relief of peoples devastated by the war. Of that amount, $115 million was to go to Austria (U.S., *Statutes at Large*, vol. 61, pp. 125–28; and State, *Foreign Relations, 1947*, vol. II, *Council of Foreign Ministers; Germany and Austria*, pp. 1176–79). On June 25 the United States and Austria concluded a relief agreement implementing PL 84 (see State, *Foreign Relations, 1947*, vol. II, *Council of Foreign Ministers; Germany and Austria*, pp. 1184–85; and Eisenhower to Keyes, May 22, 1947, in COS, 1947, 003 TS. For the texts of the agreements see *Department of State Bulletin* 17, no. 418 [1947], 39–41, 45). Public Law 389, the Foreign Aid Act of 1947, also authorized (on December 17, 1947) additional expenditures of $597 million until March 31, 1948 (U.S., *Statutes at Large*, vol. 61, pp. 934–39).

[2] Congress would not approve the European Recovery Program (the Marshall Plan) until April 3, 1948 (see no. 1482, n. 6).

[3] Brigadier General Jesmond Dene Balmer had entered active service in 1918 as a second lieutenant. He had served with the 28th and 4th divisions during World War I. During World War II he had commanded the Field Artillery School at Fort Sill, Oklahoma, before serving as CG and then deputy CG of the XXIII Artillery Corps. After the war he had been a military advisor at the council of Foreign Ministers in Paris and New York and at the Paris Peace Conference; he assumed his present post in 1947. His report of December 9, 1946, was attached as an enclosure to Eisenhower's memo.

[4] Balmer had calculated that the ration would have to be cut by this much. The State Department had rejected Keyes's request of December 10 to increase the ration to 1800 calories (State, *Foreign Relations, 1947*, vol. II, *Council of Foreign Ministers; Germany and Austria*, pp. 1217–18, 1220).

[5] Schuyler prepared Eisenhower's document and a draft memo to Secretary of Defense Forrestal asking him to forward (to the secretary of state) another draft memo embodying the JCS's views. The issue would still be under review when Eisenhower left office. (For later developments see State, *Foreign Relations, 1948*, vol. II, *Council of Foreign Ministers; Germany and Austria*, pp. 1346–47.) On January 21, 1948, Keyes would thank Eisenhower for his efforts to ease the crisis (see no. 2004).

To Mame McInerney Riordan   *December 17, 1947*

Dear Mame: It was good to hear from you, but it has always been my recollection that you sat in front of me in study hall. In fact, I had always attributed a certain amount of credit for my scholastic advancement to that arrangement.[1]

Will you please tell Mr. Bakke that, although I would like to attend the Brotherhood Week luncheon, it will be impossible for me to do so.[2] The pressure of business incident to turning over this job to General Bradley and transferring to Columbia University constitutes a most difficult schedule for the early months of 1948. Actually, I have already had to cancel several engagements of long standing and could well be accused of bad faith if I should make an exception in this instance.

Thanks for thinking about me and for taking the time to write. You have my hearty good wishes for the Christmas season and the year ahead. *Sincerely*

[1]Mrs. Riordan, who now lived in Solomon, Kansas, had written: "You won't remember—I sat right behind you in Study Hall—Of course everyone in Abilene sat right behind you[.] But I really did—I don't remember any great thrill—and I know I never, never, saw anything on your paper, I was safe in using—" (n.d.). Carroll assisted Eisenhower in drafting this response.

[2] Mrs. Riordan's letter said that "Norris Bakke of the Federal Deposit something wants you to speak at the Luncheon of Brotherhood Week—I don't know why or why he would ask me to write you—I spoke once in Denver & was introduced as coming from the same town as Buffalo Bill & Dwight E—This man was at the dinner—Thats all." Norris Conroy Bakke had received his law degree from the University of Chicago in 1919. He had served on the Colorado Supreme Court from 1936 until 1947 and had become its chief justice in 1945. He was at present associate general counsel for the Federal Deposit Insurance Corporation. Bakke was serving as the Protestant cochairman of the Washington Round Table of Christians and Jews. He would write on December 19 asking Eisenhower to be the speaker on February 23 or 24, 1948, at a luncheon inaugurating the organization's annual Brotherhood Week. Eisenhower declined the invitation in a letter of December 26 (drafted by Carroll). All correspondence is in the same file as this document.

1940   *Eisenhower Mss.*

To Edward Vernon Rickenbacker   *December 17, 1947*

Dear Eddie: Thank you very much for your inspiring Christmas message. I wish that every citizen could get a copy.[1]

I hope I won't appear presumptuous in suggesting the addition of one little thought to the truths you so eloquently express: We hurt ourselves through failure to realize that no individual or no special group can prosper in the long run unless the great country, of which we are all a part, remains prosperous. Cooperation for the good of the country is the only formula for permanent advance of individual good.

Thank you for thinking of me at this season. I scarcely need assure you that I reciprocate your good wishes for a happy holiday season and a bright New Year. *Cordially*

[1] Rickenbacker, who had been awarded the Congressional Medal of Honor, had been America's leading air ace in World War I. During World War II Captain Rickenbacker had served on special missions for the Secretary of War inspecting American air bases in England, the South Pacific, North Africa, Iran, India, China, Russia, Iceland, Greenland, and the Aleutians. In 1942 he had survived three weeks in the Pacific on a life raft. He now headed Eastern Air Lines. In his letter, dated Christmas 1947, Rickenbacker said that many of the difficulties in the nation and the world were caused by individual selfishness and the refusal to work hard in order to achieve "progress and prosperity."

1941   *Eisenhower Mss.*

To Miles Willard Jones   *December 17, 1947*

Dear Mr. Jones: In attempting to answer your gracious letter it is difficult to reconcile my continuing dislike of even momentary contemplation of a possible political career with your obviously sincere and warm interest in the subject.[1] As you possibly know, I have consistently adhered to my determination to keep aloof from political struggles. It is my conviction that such service as I might be able to render in the future can be best done in a field entirely removed from the political.

There is no possible opening on my calendar that would permit me to plan on a trip to upper New York. Actually, for the months of January, February, and March I have been forced to cancel all out-of-town engagements except two. These, of long standing, I shall be forced to keep—otherwise my time is completely absorbed in the requirements of this office.

I deeply appreciate your invitation but from the above you can see that it is out of the question for me to consider such an engagement. *Very sincerely*

[1] Jones, an attorney in Utica, New York, had written Eisenhower before to urge that he run for the presidency (see no. 975). In his letter of December 11 he said: "I have continuously talked of your candidacy." He urged Eisenhower to visit upstate New York (EM).

To THOMAS DONALD CAMPBELL   *December 17, 1947*

Dear Tom: Thank you very much for your long and newsy letter.[1]
I was particularly interested in your account of the rock well. The
stuff in which you are digging must be flint if it will yield to you only
10 or 12 inches a day. At the very least, you are carrying on a fascinating
experiment, and even if you lose, you will have proved something that
will be valuable to you in all your later planning for future production.

Your explanation concerning the distortion of your testimony—
indeed your obvious irritation over it—gave me a chuckle, though
possibly a sardonic one.[2] I happened to be present in Cleveland at the
Aviation Party[3] when you were on your way to Washington, and I
heard you expound at great length your conviction that prices, including
that of wheat, had to be kept down. I well understand your sense of
frustration at the misinterpretation of your statements, but after all, you
were suffering from something that many people have had to endure.
Only recently they took me for a great ride, except that they went so far
as to attribute to me views and ideas that I never even heard of.[4]

Mamie and I hope to take a 60-day leave in the late winter and early
spring. One spot that we have been viewing with some interest is
Tucson. We want to go to a place where the altitude is a maximum of
some 2500 feet where the weather is nice and I can play golf. In
addition, it may turn out that at some nearby hotel I would want to put
up a small staff to help me in some writing that publishers want me to
do.[5] Another place we are thinking about is the Georgia coast, but after
all, the seashore is not too nice a place at that time of year. All in all, we
are pretty much in the air about it, but if anything brings us through
New Mexico, we will certainly take advantage of your invitation to stop
off for a lunch with you.

My very best wishes for good luck in the great experiment, and as
always, warmest regards to yourself. *Cordially*

[1] For background on Campbell see no. 408. In his letter of December 13
Campbell summarized the efforts by his company to drill a new type of water well
that would "produce primary water from rock chemistry. . . ."
[2] Campbell said that news reports had presented an inaccurate account of his stand
regarding the price of wheat.
[3] See no. 859.
[4] See no. 1926.
[5] See no. 1977.

To George Catlett Marshall   *December 17, 1947*

Dear General: It gives me great pleasure to send you the first American Campaign Medal which has been struck. As you know, we had considerable difficulty in obtaining appropriate designs but finally settled on one which we feel is representative of all the services.

I am also inclosing an Asiatic-Pacific Campaign Medal,[1] the first of which has been sent to General MacArthur.[2] *Sincerely*

[1] Both of these medals are described in *Army Almanac*, p. 681.
[2] Secretary Marshall acknowledged the receipt of his medals in a note of January 12, 1948 (same file as document).

To Kenneth Arthur Noel Anderson   *December 17, 1947*

Dear Kenneth:[1] Mr. Fletcher dropped in to see me with your note and Christmas card.[2] It was like a breath of fresh air to have an opportunity to talk about you and our days together in Africa. I truly hope that you and your Lady enjoy your present post and are deriving some happiness from service there.[3]

About ten days ago I saw Field Marshal Alexander, who had come down to Philadelphia from Ottawa to see the Army-Navy Football Game.[4] We sat together during the afternoon and had a good time talking over the old days. He looks well and seems to be in splendid spirits. He has frequently asked me to come to Canada where in appropriate season the fishing is excellent. I never seem to get the time to do such things, but how I would love it!

This note brings to you and to Lady Anderson best wishes for a fine Christmas and bright New Year.

With warm personal regard, *As ever*

[1] For background on General Anderson see no. 1115.
[2] Anderson's note of November 24 and his card are in EM. They had been delivered by Cassius Paul Fletcher (B.S. University of Illinois 1914), a career foreign-service officer. Fletcher had served as U.S. consul at Basra, Iraq, from 1942 until 1944, when he had become consul at Gibraltar. He had seen Eisenhower on December 15.
[3] Anderson was presently governor and commander in chief of Gibraltar.
[4] See no. 1901.

To William Edward Robinson   *December 17, 1947*

Dear Mr. Robinson: As you suggest I will keep confidential the contents of your recent letter[1] except that I assume you have no objection to my informing Joe Davies of its general content.[2] He, I know, will respect your desires in the matter. I understand from your letter also that if either the representatives of Simon and Schuster or the Harper Company should come to see me, the secrecy restriction does not apply.

Tomorrow one of the "magazine" group is coming to see me[3] and I suppose that sooner or later I shall have to redeem my promise to let other people in the field know about the matter.[4] However, I have simply been too busy to do so.

It was nice to see you and quite naturally I am flattered by the interest you continue to take in anything I may be able to write.[5]

With warm personal regard, *Sincerely*

[1] Robinson's December 16 letter outlined a specific offer under which the New York Herald Tribune Syndicate, in conjunction with a book-publishing firm of Eisenhower's choice, was prepared to serialize and publish the General's account of the war. For Eisenhower's thoughts on writing *Crusade in Europe* see *At Ease*, pp. 324–29. For background see no. 1811.

[2] A long-time friend of Eisenhower's, attorney Joseph E. Davies, would serve as the General's "counsel" in the negotiations for publication rights. For background on Davies see no. 123. For Davies's further involvement with Eisenhower's publishing arrangements see no. 1960.

[3] On December 18 at 10:00 A.M. Eisenhower would meet with Walter D. Fuller and Ben Hibbs of the Curtis Publishing Company, which published the *Saturday Evening Post*. For background see no. 1923.

[4] See no. 1951.

[5] Eisenhower had seen Robinson on December 5 and would meet with him again on December 22.

To Carl William Ackerman   *December 17, 1947*

Dear Dr. Ackerman:[1] From your letter I assume that you wanted me to autograph my own likeness on the second page.[2] However, since the picture of Independence Hall on the front page carries a far greater amount of "eye appeal" I have autographed that side also—with the suggestion that it would make a better entry into your Hall of Fame than would the opposite side of the page. In any event it is an honor to comply with your request. *Sincerely*

[1] Ackerman had received his Bachelor of Letters degree from the Columbia University School of Journalism in 1913. After a newspaper and public relations career, he had become dean of Columbia's Graduate School of Journalism in 1931. He was the recipient of several honorary degrees.
[2] Ackerman had asked Eisenhower to autograph the program of the Pennsylvania Society dinner at which the General had been honored (see no. 1933). Ackerman wanted to frame the signed program for the school's hall of fame of distinguished Americans (Dec. 15, 1947, EM).

1947   *Eisenhower Mss.*

To Hastings Lionel Ismay   *December 18, 1947*

Dear Pug: Yesterday when I heard some people talking about the possibility of organizing a governmental secretariat in the city,[1] I advised them strongly to call on you for advice.[2] You may never hear from them but since it happened that two or three present had known you during the war I am sure it would have warmed your heart to have heard the enthusiastic support to my suggestion.

I think I wrote you a Christmas note some days ago but in any event, again, I hope that you and Lady Ismay will have the happiest of New Years. *As ever*

[1] On December 17 Eisenhower had met with a delegation led by Senator Clyde R. Hoey, Democrat from North Carolina. Senator Hoey was a member of the Senate Committee on Expenditures in the Executive Department, and his party is perhaps the one to which Eisenhower was referring.
[2] In 1939 Ismay had served as head of the Secretariat of the Committee of Imperial Defence, which became the military wing of the War Cabinet Secretariat. For Ismay's experience in this field see Ismay, *Memoirs*, pp. 45, 89, 98.

1948   *Eisenhower Mss., Family File*

To Milton Stover Eisenhower   *December 18, 1947*

Dear Milton: Our thoughts will be with you on Christmas morning. I will be thinking, also, of that Christmas, following Pearl Harbor, that I spent in your home.[1]

To you and Helen and the children, Mamie and I send the heartiest greetings of the season and the wish that your New Year will be the brightest ever. *As ever*

[1] Carroll drafted this message. Eisenhower, who made several changes, added the reference to the Christmas following Pearl Harbor (McDuff Coll.). Many other Christmas greetings that Eisenhower sent at this time are in EM.

1949   *Eisenhower Mss.*

To George Fielding Eliot   *December 18, 1947*

Dear Major Eliot:[1] I had quite a chuckle over the little poem you sent me from the Tribune.[2] I think one of the difficulties that so many critics are having these days is to realize that a person can really be so simple as to tell the truth and feel that the truth needs no explanation. They cannot believe a man who happens not to want what so many others do want.

With a Merry Christmas to you, *Sincerely*

[1] Eliot, who had received his B.A. from Melbourne University, Australia, in 1914, was an author and journalist. He had been a military and naval correspondent with the *New York Herald Tribune* from 1939 to 1946 and had joined the *New York Post* in 1947.

[2] With a covering note of December 12 Eliot had forwarded a poem by Melville Cane entitled "As to Ike." The poem, which had appeared in the *Herald Tribune* that day, speculated on Eisenhower's thoughts about the 1948 presidency, asking (in part): "Where or whom will lightning strike?/What goes on inside of Ike?"

1950   *Eisenhower Mss.*

To Amon Giles Carter   *December 18, 1947*

Dear Amon: A very happy Christmas to you and your family and all the best wishes of the season. Our visit with you was one of the bright spots of the past year and I appreciate sincerely your many kindnesses.[1]

With warm regard, *Sincerely*

P.S. The Rolls Royce people are soon to have an exhibit in your area. I told them to call you up and insist that you get one of them as a present for your new bride. If they pull some high-powered salesmanship on you, this note may give you a key to the reason.[2]

[1] For Eisenhower's trip to Forth Worth see no. 1839. For background on Carter see no. 678.

[2] On September 16, 1947, Amon Carter had married Minnie Meacham Smith in Fort Worth, Texas. McDuff drafted this letter, and Eisenhower added the postscript.

To John Neville Wheeler   *December 19, 1947*
Personal and confidential

Dear Mr. Wheeler:[1] I am conscious of the fact that during the past years I have, in reply to your courteous suggestions, promised you that if ever I should even tentatively decide to write any kind of personal account of the war I would let you know.[2] Due to a great deal of insistence that I have encountered since announcement was made of my probable date of retirement, I have come to the conclusion that I shall probably make this attempt.

The purpose of this note is merely to redeem my promise to you.[3] I want to assure you most emphatically that I am doing everything to avoid placing myself in a position where I could even appear to be seeking "competitive bids." One reason why I have considered it undesirable and unwise to give any distribution to my intention is that I have determined that in the event I do make any arrangement with a publisher, it must be on a basis of complete disposition, in one bundle, of all rights present and future of every kind. Since only some combination of publishing interests could deal on this basis, I have felt it better merely to consult with those who have informed me of an intention to meet this fixed requirement of my own. This explains why I have not followed the normal procedure which involves the use of an agent.

I have earnestly tried to postpone decisions in this matter, as well as definite consultation concerning it, but now, to keep good faith with you, I feel I must write this letter because it is beginning to become apparent that I shall probably have to give a final decision within a matter of a very few days. I assure you also that had I anticipated the terrific rush of events, I would have written to you earlier, even though I understand that under the situation I have described I would doubt that you have any particular interest in the matter.[4] *Very sincerely*

[1] Wheeler (A.B. Columbia 1908) was general manager and director of the North American Newspaper Alliance and Associated Newspapers.
[2] The North American Newspaper Alliance, which had published General Pershing's memoirs following World War I, had indicated an interest in General Eisenhower's story as early as October 1946. Wheeler had written to Eisenhower three times during August 1947 asking that his syndicate be considered when the appropriate time came. All correspondence is in EM.
[3] For similar letters to other interested publishers see Eisenhower to John L. B. Williams, Dec. 20, 1947, and Eisenhower to Harold K. Quinzburg, Dec. 23, 1947, both in the same file as this document.
[4] On December 23 Wheeler replied, "Max Schuster [of Simon & Schuster], an old friend of mine, has been discussing with me the serial rights for the North

American Newspaper Alliance, so we may be able to work something out" (in *ibid.*). For further developments see no. 1989.

1952   *Eisenhower Mss.*

To [Norma Bowler] Lewis   *December 19, 1947*
Personal and confidential

Dear Lady Lewis: I find it will take me a little time to dig to the bottom of the matter you phoned to me about.[1] From a hasty glance it appears that General Harrison is instantly due for foreign duty and since we follow a roster on such details in order to avoid injustice to anyone, I am not certain that anything can be done.[2] However, I am getting all the facts assembled so I may examine them to see whether or not it is proper and feasible to change his orders. I should say that even if any change can properly be effected it would constitute nothing more than a deferment for a brief number of months.

I shall give you a full report when I have all the facts. *Sincerely*

[1] We have been unable to locate any records relating to this letter. The message was sent to Lady Lewis, who was probably the wife of Sir Willmott Harsant Lewis, a newspaper correspondent.
[2] Eisenhower was undoubtedly referring to Brigadier General Eugene Lynch Harrison (USMA 1923), who was Chief of Information at AGF and would soon become Chief of Staff, I Corps, in Japan.

1953   *Eisenhower Mss.*

To Frances McKinney Smith   *December 19, 1947*

Dear Mrs. Smith: Your letter with the news of Dan's death has just arrived and Mamie and I hasten to extend our heartfelt sympathy in your great loss.[1]

I do wish that I could have seen him before his passing. His letters to me over the years were bright spots and I have always had the greatest respect for his ability, character and sincerity, to say nothing of a great affection for him and you.

I pray that the knowledge of his fine and full life will be of everlasting comfort to you. *Sincerely*

[1] In her letter of December 13 Mrs. Smith said that her husband had died on December 8. For background on Dan Smith see no. 181. Carroll prepared an initial draft of this reply for Eisenhower.

To William Edward Robinson   *December 20, 1947*

Dear Mr. Robinson: I have attempted to get you on the phone this morning without success. Because I have run into a piece of information that will be of importance to you, I send it to you by the fastest means available to me.

The Treasury Department informs me that the capital gains treatment of a sale such as we have in mind where the entire bundle of rights is involved is absolutely applicable.[1] The one hitch in the proceedings is that six months must elapse from the time of the completion of the document or the securing of the copyright before the actual sale can take place.

Consequently, assuming even the most rapid kind of work on my part, it would appear that the final sale could not be made before, say, six months from April 1st, and even this assumes that after asking for the copyright there is no objection to authenticating the document through records and so on.[2]

I have sent similar information to the only other individuals who have definitely interested themselves with me in this project.[3]

With cordial personal regards, *Sincerely*

[1] On this same day Eisenhower had written to Under Secretary of the Treasury Archibald Lee Manning Wiggins (A.B. University of North Carolina 1913) inquiring whether his publishing transaction could be classified as a capital gain. Wiggins referred the letter to George Jeremiah Schoeneman, commissioner of internal revenue. Eisenhower's letter and Schoeneman's December 22 reply are in EM, Presidential Papers, Official File. For background on the transaction see no. 1945.

[2] For developments see no. 1960.

[3] One copy of the Treasury Department letter was forwarded to Joseph Davies (see no. 1960).

1955   *Eisenhower Mss.*

To Henry Spiese Aurand   *December 20, 1947*

Dear Henry: As you point out, the record itself amply evidences the implication that you have "done all right."[1] I think you know me well enough to realize that your new assignment also proves that I know you will continue to do so.

Today the Army needs, as never before, vision, determination, and broad understanding of our country's position. In no other phase of our activities are these qualities more needed than in the field of materiel. It is because I believe you possess these qualities in superlative degree that you have been assigned to your present post, one of the most important in the entire Army. I shall not have many months to serve with you, but I shall most certainly continue to watch with absorbed interest your accomplishments and your progress.[2] *As ever*

[1] In a note of December 19 Aurand thanked Eisenhower for giving him various assignments, especially the one he was now starting as director of the Army's Service, Supply and Procurement Division. He said: "In 1933, you got me a job on the War College Faculty—the only one I tried to get, or asked for, in my career. My friends tell me I did all right. In 1946, you gave me the R&D Division. You must have thought I did all right there. . . ." For background on Aurand see no. 882.
[2] For Eisenhower's letter to Aurand's predecessor see no. 1965.

1956   *Eisenhower Mss.*

TO JACK ELLIS   *December 20, 1947*

Dear Jack: The arrival of your letter was a bright spot in the Eisenhower household yesterday.[1] You realize, of course, that Mamie and I will never forget our great sense of obligation to you and your family for the generous and hospitable way in which you took our children into your home. We have not yet seen them but we expect them to arrive at Fort Myer on the 23rd. They will stay with us a few days and soon after that John will go to West Point for a brief orientation before he enters Columbia in late January.

In the meantime, Mamie's father and mother as well as her sister and brother-in-law and their four children have all arrived at our house. The prospects are that for the first time in many years we are all going to have a very merry Christmas.[2] I think the whole household is already working on procuring and setting up the tree and I imagine that Christmas morning in our house should be a hectic affair. Our nieces and nephews range in age from five to sixteen so there is certain to be a bit of pandemonium, but it will be great fun.

Your suggestion that I come down for a few days fishing is most appealing. For the moment I cannot get away, but I am now planning on a sixty-day leave, probably covering the months of March and April. Is there any fishing in your region during that time? If there is no change in our plans, we may simply make this city our headquarters during our leave, but it will be easy enough for me to scoot down there for several days if we could arrange a time convenient to us both and if it is a good fishing period. You understand, of course, that a dozen things could happen to wreck our plans but at least there remains the possibility I have described.

On the political front, my attitude has not changed one iota.[3] I want to be a private citizen of the United States just like anyone else and I most emphatically do not want to get tangled up in political activity or office.

Mamie phoned me especially this morning to tell me to be sure to give you and your nice family her greetings and her love. Just when she will get a chance to write to you personally I cannot say because her household of guests is really occupying her time at the moment. In any event, this note brings to all of you our very best wishes for a fine Christmas and a bright New Year.[4] *Cordially*

[1] Ellis's letter of December 16 is in EM. For background see no. 1801.

[2] Mrs. Eisenhower's sister and her husband, Major Moore, were on their way to a new assignment (see no. 1959).

[3] Ellis said that he found the progress of the Eisenhower for President movement "encouraging."

[4] In a letter of December 26 (EM) Eisenhower would thank Ellis for his gift, a rod and reel.

1957   *ABC 092 (7-18-45), Sec. 1-B*

To Joint Chiefs of Staff   *December 22, 1947*
Memorandum. Top secret

Subject: Report of the JSSC to the JCS on Strategic Guidance to Facilitate Planning Within Joint Agencies (JCS 1630/6)[1]

1. The General assumptions in JCS 1630/6 are considered suitable in the light of present day conditions,[2] with the exception of the following:

a. It is believed that the British Commonwealth of Nations are fully aware that in the event of war between the U.S. and USSR, any position they assume other than allying with us would be gravely prejudicial to their own future national independence. Therefore, our plans should be based on the assumption that the British Commonwealth will ally with us in the event of a major war. Consequently, it is proposed that subparagraphs 1*b*(1), 1*b*(2), and 1*b*(3) be deleted and the following be substituted therefor, and renumber paragraphs 1*b*(4), 1*b*(5), and 1*b*(6) to 1*b*(2), 1*b*(3), and 1*b*(4) respectively:

b. Allies

(1) The English speaking nations of the British Commonwealth will ally with the United States in the event of a major war.[3]

2. Although Spain would likely seek to remain neutral in the event of a major war, the strongly anti-communist Franco Government would welcome assistance from the U.S. in opposing a positive military invasion threat. It is therefore proposed that paragraph 1*b*(4) be changed to read as follows:

> *(2)* In the event of major war within the next few years the United States will not have the active support of any of the European nations, *with the exception of Spain which, if attacked, will ally with the U.S.*[4]

3. It is believed that the time period during which an enemy power may possess the capability of major external interference with our mobilization (delivery of an atomic bomb, for example) should be expressed in specific rather than general terms. It is therefore proposed that paragraph 1*b*(6) be changed to read as follows:

> *(4)* Allies cannot be depended upon to protect the United States during mobilization. *Prior to 1952, no enemy power will possess the capability of major external interference with our mobilization. After 1952, an enemy may possess this capability.* Internal interference inspired by our enemies may be formidable *in the event of war at any time in the future.*[5]

4. Observed activity in the jet plane and A/A weapons fields show that the Soviets are placing great emphasis on those items. As regards the Soviet Navy, intelligence estimates conclude that the Soviets do not possess the capability of becoming a first rate sea power for years to come. They do have the capability, however, of expanding their submarine fleet and it is believed that their main effort in way of naval development will be directed towards this arm. Consequently, the following changes to paragraph 1*c*(1) are proposed:

> (1) Our probable principal opponent will concentrate meanwhile on developing and equipping his armed forces with those offensive elements presently lacking in his military establishment, notably atomic weapons, *jet planes and A/A defense,* sea power (*principally submarine*), and long range airpower.

5. The following minor changes are proposed:

> (1) Rewrite par. 1*c*(2), Page 18, to read:
>
> In the event of war, our probable principal opponent *might use biological and chemical warfare subject to considerations of retaliation.*[6]
>
> (2) Rewrite par. 5*a*, Page 20, to read as follows:
>
> *a.* Until, and possibly after occupation requirements are ended our military establishment will be capable of handling, *with conventional weapons,* only minor emergencies.[7]

(3) Rewrite par. 5*b*, Page 20, to read as follows:

The United States will maintain some advantage in the technical development and potential capacity for production of atomic weapons. Until such time as *the use of* atomic weapons *is* limited by international agreement *and effective safeguards are established* such weapons *will* be used by *one or both sides* in a major war.

(4) Rewrite par. 5*f*, Page 20, to read: *Biological and chemical warfare might be used by the U.S. subject to considerations of retaliation.*[8]

6. Future periodic revisions of the general assumptions by the JSSC should be made in collaboration with the Joint Staff Plans Committee. With the exceptions noted above, the proposed list of general assumptions are concurred in.[9]

[1] In 1946 the Joint Chiefs had approved a set of assumptions to guide joint military planning for a possible war (see no. 720). Since that time, the planners had continued to work on the specific joint plans that were to be based on these assumptions. Meanwhile, the JSSC had reviewed the assumptions in light of the changing international situation and on September 24 had submitted a revised set of assumptions in JCS 1630/6 (same file as document; see also Schuyler to Eisenhower, Nov. 12, 1947, and Schuyler to Wedemeyer, Nov. 17, 1947, both in ABC 381 Global Estimate [7-16-47]; and Bowen, Memorandum for Record, Nov. 20, 1947, P&O 370.01).

[2] The JSSC assumed that even though the United States would provide armed forces for the U.N., the international organization "will probably not function to prevent or to localize minor war, and it is not empowered to prevent war among the great nations." The United States could, however, be drawn into war in the course of meeting its U.N. responsibilities. "We may be involved in a major war by being attacked or by being drawn into a conflict among foreign powers." Wedemeyer prepared a brief and this memorandum for General Eisenhower; the paper became JCS 1630/8, of January 20, 1948 (CCS 381 [2-18-46], Sec. 1).

[3] The JSSC had proposed in 1 *b*: "(1) Great Britain and the Union of South Africa will probably seek to remain neutral in the event of major war within the next few years. (2) In the event of major war within the next few years Canada will be an active ally of the United States. (3) In the event of major war within the next few years Australia and New Zealand will seek to remain neutral unless the war entails a threat to their immediate security."

[4] Eisenhower was adding the italicized material to the JSSC proposal.

[5] Eisenhower was adding the italicized sections and deleting the following: "Although for the next several years no enemy power will possess the capability of major external interference with our mobilization, internal. . . ."

[6] The JSSC version read: "In the event of war, our probable principal opponent will not hesitate to initiate bacteriological or gas warfare if he considers it to his advantage."

[7] Eisenhower added the italicized words to JCS 1630/6; the JSSC had originally proposed the following: "Our normal peacetime military establishment will be capable of handling any emergency short of threatened major war" (1630/1, Apr. 26, 1946, same file as document).

[8] The JSSC proposed: "The United States will not engage in gas or bacteriological warfare except in retaliation."
[9] Nimitz also proposed certain amendments to the JSSC report (JCS 1630/7, Nov. 12, 1947). He thought "the position of Canada may vary from benevolent neutrality to that of active ally. This position will be in direct proportion to the immediate threat to the North American Continent." Nimitz would accept all of Eisenhower's suggestions except the Chief of Staff's statement about the probable action of the British Commonwealth (JCS 1630/9, Feb. 10, 1948). In its final version the paper said merely: "The British Commonwealth of Nations in all probability will be our allies in the event of major war within the next few years." The Joint Chiefs would approve the amended version of JCS 1630/6 on February 26, 1948. (All papers are in the same file as this document or in CCS 381 [2-18-46], Sec. 1.) The effort to achieve agreement on specific joint plans using these assumptions would continue after Eisenhower left office. By that time some progress had been made in drafting an acceptable short-range plan, but conflicts between the services continued to hamper the planners. As one OPD officer commented: "We can say that the Short-Range Plan, although not approved, is nearing completion. The first draft of the Mid-Range Outline Plan is about to be published. It is many months behind the Short-Range Plan in its development. The Long-Range Plan has served its immediate purpose [furnishing a basis for aircraft requirements for a war in 1955–56] and in its very incomplete state has been relegated to a low priority position" (speech drafted by Tarrant, Feb. 27, 1948 [marked "too controversial"], in ABC 350.001 Speeches [10-26-46], Sec. 1-A).

1958   *ABC 093 Trieste (7-3-46), Sec. 1-D*

To Joint Chiefs of Staff   *December 22, 1947*
Confidential

Memorandum by the Chief of Staff, U.S. Army:

Subject: Report on the Administration of the US/UK Zone of the Free Territory of Trieste

1. Pursuant to assurances given to the Security Council of the United Nations by the U.S. Government on 15 November 1947, the Department of State now desires that General Airey be directed to submit a report on his administration of the US/UK Zone of the Free Territory of Trieste for the period 15 September 1947 to 31 December 1947.[1] Accordingly the Department of State requests the despatch of the message in enclosure "A" to General Airey.

2. The British Embassy has informed the Department of State that the Foreign Office and the British Chiefs of Staff are prepared to agree to the despatch of the message in Enclosure "A".

3. I therefore recommend approval of the attached memorandum as a matter of priority.[2]

[1] For background on the Trieste situation and General Airey's role see no. 1890. The State Department's instructions to the U.S. representative at the U.N. are in

State, *Foreign Relations, 1947*, vol. IV, *Eastern Europe; The Soviet Union*, p. 124. Wedemeyer drafted this memorandum for Eisenhower, and the paper would become JCS 1701/21, of December 27, 1947.

[2] The Joint Chiefs would approve this memorandum (and hence the proposed message to Airey) on December 31, 1947; the CCS took similar action (CCS 959/94) and dispatched the message the same day (the correspondence is in the same file as this document). After Airey submitted his report, Wedemeyer would prepare comments for Eisenhower (Feb. 5, 1948); the memo, which became JCS 1701/22, would not be circulated, however, until February 9, after Eisenhower left office. Disagreement would continue over the appointment of a governor for the Free Territory of Trieste, and on March 20, 1948, the United States, Great Britain, and France would recommend that the Free Territory be returned to Italy (Allied Military Government, *Trieste Handbook, 1950*, pp. 8–14). For later developments see also State, *Foreign Relations, 1948*, vol. III, *Western Europe*, pp. 530–70 *passim*.

1959   *Eisenhower Mss.*

To WILLIS DALE CRITTENBERGER   *December 22, 1947*
Cable WCL 46856

CINCARIB Quarry Heights CZ personal to Crittenberger from Eisenhower:
Dear Critt: Major Moore from San Antonio has been ordered to Panama and will depart from New Orleans in January. He is of course anxious for his family to accompany him and I believe that an official inquiry has gone forward to your headquarters today to determine the availability of quarters. However the Moores are spending the holidays with Mamie and me and it would be a great convenience if you could send me direct information on the matter.[1]

Merry Christmas and best wishes to you both from Mamie and me.

[1] For background on Major Moore see no. 604. Paul, in cable WCL 46951 (same date), also inquired about Moore. The next day Crittenberger, who commanded Army forces in the Caribbean, responded that quarters would be available in the latter part of January. Major and Mrs. Moore would sail for Panama from New Orleans on January 24. All correspondence is in EM.

1960   *Eisenhower Mss.*

To JOSEPH EDWARD DAVIES   *December 23, 1947*

Dear Joe: Mr. Robinson told me that he was going to telephone you yesterday afternoon. If he succeeded in doing so, you already have the information concerning the offer which is made to me through the Doubleday Company. I am very hopeful that no other offers of any kind come in so that I can simply tell them the whole thing is settled so far as I am concerned.[1]

The only question remaining to be resolved, so far as I can foresee, is that of determining when we can call the script a finished one. The six months' period of ownership begins on that date as you will see from the copy of the Treasury Department letter, which I enclose.[2] However, I am happy to say that Mr. McCormick of Doubleday Company[3] stated that the time element was not of primary importance to them, and they seem perfectly ready to allow me whatever time is necessary to get the book done properly. On the other hand, since the next three or four months will be the only time available to me for intensive work, I do want to get my part of it finished as quickly as possible.[4] I think that some time soon I will see Mr. Richburg of your office[5] to determine whether the six months' period cannot begin running from the moment I have really completed my narrative. I think this will be perfectly satisfactory, because after all, it will be the publisher who will be engaging the checkers and researchers to determine the complete historical accuracy of every statement made before they actually accomplish its purchase.

In any event, I wanted you to know that to date, at least, the whole matter has worked out exactly as you hoped and planned. Now if I can only find the time to get going so as to make the whole book a really worthwhile, authentic, historical document, everything should be lovely.

With love to Marjorie,[6] and warmest regards to yourself. *As ever*

[1] Eisenhower would accept the Doubleday offer to publish his book (see no. 1977).
[2] For background see no. 1954.
[3] Kenneth Dale McCormick (A.B. Willamette University 1928) had been editor in chief since May 1942.
[4] Eisenhower's plan was to write the bulk of his story during the three-month terminal leave between his retirement from the Army and the beginning of his term as president of Columbia University (see Eisenhower, *At Ease*, p. 326).
[5] Attorney Donald Randall Richberg (A.B. Chicago 1901; LL.B. Harvard 1904) had become a partner in the Washington, D.C., law firm of Davies, Richberg, Beebe, Busick, and Richardson in 1936. For his work under President Franklin Delano Roosevelt in the early New Deal see Arthur M. Schlesinger, Jr., *The Age of Roosevelt II: The Coming of the New Deal* (Boston, 1958), pp. 92–175.
[6] Mrs. Davies.

1961   *Eisenhower Mss.*

TO SHIRLEY N. ROBERTS   *December 23, 1947*

Dear Mrs. Roberts: I assure you of my deep interest and concern in the personal problem described in your letter of December 15.[1] Likewise I assure you that I derive a great deal of satisfaction out of the feeling that when American soldiers or their families believe that they have exhausted every local opportunity to solve such problems, they take steps to give me the chance to see what I can do.

You understand that, from Washington, I cannot possibly intervene in the administrative arrangements that the Commanding General at Lee may find it necessary to make. Nevertheless it is entirely possible that some phase of your acute personal problem or some fact connected with your husband's claim to quarters may have been overlooked. Consequently I am sending your letter directly to General Graham with the request that he deal with the matter on a sympathetic basis;[2] I assure you that no disadvantage will accrue to you or your husband because of your letter to me. I know that our Commanding Officers are always anxious to do the best they can for loyal and efficient soldiers. After the Commanding General at Camp Lee has gone over this case in person, considering it with due regard for the claims of all others, he will be able to settle the matter with your husband in such a way that I am sure you will be convinced of the complete justice and fairness of his decision.

I earnestly hope that you and your family will soon be able to get out of the quarters where vermin make it almost dangerous to let your baby crawl about the floor.

With best wishes and hopes that the holiday season will be a bright one for you and your family, *Sincerely*

[1] Mrs. Roberts, wife of Technical Sergeant George H. Roberts, of the Quartermaster Demonstration Unit at Camp Lee, Virginia, had written Eisenhower to complain about their inability to secure NCO quarters at the camp (Dec. 15, 1947). The couple had two small children, and Mrs. Roberts had been told that they stood quite high on the waiting list. Recently, however, they had fallen to a lower position on the list. They were living in a substandard civilian apartment that was so infested with roaches and mice that the Robertses had put out poison and now could not allow their baby to be on the floor. Eisenhower made numerous changes in a draft of this letter. All correspondence is in COS, 1947, 201 Roberts.
[2] Brigadier General Roy Charles Lemach Graham had received his B.S. from New Hampshire College and his commission as a second lieutenant in 1917. He had served in the supply field and had been G-4 of the Persian Gulf Command from 1942 to 1945. He had assumed command of Camp Lee in 1946.

1962   *Eisenhower Mss.*

To LEROY HUGH WATSON   *December 23, 1947*

Dear Leroy: I am glad that you took the trouble to give me such a complete explanation of your case.[1] So far as I am concerned the sentiments expressed in my letter to you dated 11 November 1944 are still valid.[2] I think that your entire conduct during the war, and more especially since the date of your relief from command of the 3rd Armored Division, has been exemplary.[3] Frankly I have been proud of the fact that you are a classmate of mine.

I suppose you know the method under which general officers are now selected for promotion. The matter is taken completely out of the hands of the Chief of Staff, the Secretary of the Army and even the President, none of whom can do more than to remove a name from the list. None has any power to add to it. Actual selections are made by a Board of officers, established by law. On the Board this year were the best and most widely experienced officers that I could find. They were Devers, Bradley, Handy, Hodges, Eichelberger, and Haislip. They of course had many hundreds of names from which to choose and some were bound to be disappointed.

All I can say in the circumstances is that I hope that a future Board will find it proper to pick you up for transfer to the permanent list. I intend to send to the Personnel Division the file that was attached to your letter on the chance that some one of these letters of special commendation may not now be included on your official file.[4]

With best of luck and with the hope that you do not allow this disappointment to affect you too much, *As ever*

[1] In a letter of December 15 Brigadier General Watson had protested his exclusion from the list of permanent general officers (see no. 1888).
[2] See Chandler, *War Years*.
[3] See *ibid*.
[4] Eisenhower did so this same day; he also attached a copy of this letter to Watson (EM).

1963   *Eisenhower Mss.*

To Ely Culbertson   *December 23, 1947*

Dear Ely: The two articles you sent to me were full of interest but I must say that the North Carolina editor took considerable space to expound an idea which in the most favorable sense would have to be classed as academic. He certainly cannot be accused of lacking imagination.[1]

I am passing them on to Al[2] as you suggested. At the very least he will get a chuckle out of the one.

With the season's greetings and best wishes from Mamie and me to you both,[3] *Cordially*

[1] With a covering note of December 18 Culbertson had sent Eisenhower copies of two recent newspaper editorials—from Salisbury, North Carolina, and Sioux City,

Iowa. Both editorials concerned the possibility of Eisenhower's running for President, and the one from North Carolina speculated on a joint nomination by both political parties. For background on Culbertson see no. 1884.
[2] General Gruenther.
[3] In numerous other letters at this time Eisenhower tried to dampen the enthusiasm of his supporters. See for example his letters to Edgar Eisenhower on December 23 and to Colonel Douglas H. Gillette on the twenty-fourth (both in EM).

1964   *ABC 014 Japan (4-13-44), Sec. 16-C*

To Joint Chiefs of Staff   *December 24, 1947*
Secret

Memorandum by the Chief of Staff, U.S. Army:

Subject: Reduction in the United Kingdom Contingent of the British Commonwealth Occupation Force.[1]

1. The Department of State has received a memorandum (Inclosure B)[2] from the Australian Government requesting governmental agreement to a proposal to reduce progressively the UK contingent of the British Commonwealth Occupation Force from its present strength of 3800 to 750 key personnel. This proposal is made because of the grave situation regarding finance and manpower confronting the British Government. The State Department has informally requested the Department of the Army for information on which to base a reply.

2. In accordance with the MacArthur-Northcott Agreement on this subject,[3] British Commonwealth Occupation Forces in Japan may be withdrawn wholly or in part upon agreement by the Governments of the U.S. and Australia, or upon six months notice by either party. Thus the State Department must indicate to the Australian Government that the U.S. agrees to its proposal; else the British troops could not be withdrawn for six months.

3. General MacArthur states that although this proposed withdrawal will reduce the efficiency of the occupation somewhat, he does not propose to object (Incls C and D).[4]

4. This plan will result in the withdrawal of two RAF fighter squadrons and most of the British service troops, or a reduction from total British Commonwealth Occupation Forces strength of approximately 16,000 to 13,000. This constitutes a further withdrawal, since portions of the British Commonwealth Occupation Force have been previously withdrawn (JCS 1398/23 and 1398/24).

5. In light of the foregoing, it is recommended that the Joint Chiefs of Staff offer no objection to this proposal and that the memorandum in

Inclosure A be dispatched to the State-Army-Navy-Air Coordinating Committee.[5]

[1] For the text of the agreement under which the British participated in the occupation of Japan see State, *Foreign Relations, 1946*, vol. VIII, *The Far East*, pp. 117–18, 121. For background on the occupation see no. 1144. The Joint Chiefs had initially agreed to limit the size of the occupation forces of the three allies—the United Kingdom, the Soviet Union, and China—to 20,000–30,000 in order to allow U.S. "to retain dominant voice in control." The British had subsequently reduced their share of the force on several occasions (see JCS 1398/23, Jan. 2, 1947, and JCS 1398/24, Jan. 15, 1947). There was discussion of other withdrawals throughout 1947 (see for example Eisenhower's JCS 1398/26, of Feb. 11, 1947). All correspondence is in the same file as this document. See also State, *Foreign Relations, 1947*, vol. VI, *The Far East*, pp. 300–301. P&O prepared this document and a covering brief for Eisenhower; the memo became JCS 1398/29, of December 31.
[2] Attached to the document but not printed here.
[3] The agreement referred to in note 1 above had been signed in Tokyo on December 18, 1945, by General MacArthur and General Sir John Northcott, commander in chief of the British Commonwealth Occupation Force in Japan.
[4] Attached to the document but not printed here.
[5] The memo in Inclosure A said that the JCS had no objection to the withdrawal. The Joint Chiefs would approve Eisenhower's memorandum on January 7, 1948; the next day the message went to SANACC, which forwarded the information to the State Department on January 9. The State Department would inform the Australian government on January 20 (WAR 94519; see also Memo for Record, Jan. 26, and other correspondence in the same file as this document).

1965   *Eisenhower Mss.*

To LeRoy Lutes   *December 24, 1947*

Dear Lutes: On your departure from the Army General Staff, I extend my heartiest congratulations on your selection for a new post of the utmost importance to the country's security.[1] With you goes the gratitude of the entire Army for your personal contribution to the supply of the wartime Army, deployed beyond two great oceans.

As Commanding General of Army Service Forces in the postwar period, your judgment, foresight and rich experience have been invaluable assets to the efficient and orderly conduct of global demobilization, the scope and speed of which involved unprecedented logistical problems.

Never has the Army produced, in the whole logistic field, an officer of greater brilliance or one more outstanding than yourself. Personally and officially, I will keenly feel the loss of your daily counsel and advice. But I feel also that in your higher position the Army will continue to benefit from your unusual qualifications and abilities.

With warm personal regard,[2] *Sincerely*

[1] Lutes was leaving SS&P to become deputy director of the executive committee of the Munitions Board on January 5, 1948. (For background see no. 1955.) Eisenhower's extensive handwritten changes in the initial draft of this letter are in Lutes Personal Papers Scrapbook.

[2] On December 30 Lutes acknowledged the General's letter and said it had been "a high honor" to serve with Eisenhower (EM).

1966   *Eisenhower Mss.*

To FREDERICK EDGWORTH MORGAN   *December 26, 1947*

Dear Freddie: Thank you very much for your letter. With respect to any delay in the publication of your book that our staff here may be responsible for, I have already directed an inquiry to the proper people. I did not know that the text of your book had come over here—I am not certain of it yet. I will promptly forward to you any information I may uncover.[1]

I can well imagine what fun you had in chatting over old times with Generals Marshall and Smith. Among other things you must have touched upon the quirks of fate that have brought two of your old wartime comrades into such positions as the American Secretary of State and the American Ambassador to Moscow.[2] I have no doubt that you got an additional chuckle from the thought of my assuming the presidency of a great American university. Even yet I am frequently puzzled as to the particular arguments that led me to succumb—the only thing I can assure you is that whatever those arguments were, they involved no mistaken notions as to my standing in the world of the scholar and educator. On one point I am determined. It is that I must convince myself within a year that I am doing some good in the place or they shall simply have to find a new president of the university.

With respect to your terrifying implication that I have a possible governmental duty, I hope you will keep such unholy thoughts well locked up in your own breast.[3] I agree that the only worthy ambition for people as old as you and I are is to struggle toward stabilizing conditions so as to give our youngsters a chance to work out world improvements. Unless we can forget lesser motives and put behind this effort a truly unified will and determination we shall be doing far less than our duty. On the other hand I incline to the view that we often overemphasize difficulties and obstacles. We forget the tremendous nature and size of the forces that work for decency, for stability and for a brighter future. It is often the same in battle. You will remember the dire forebodings expressed to us over and over again, in the early war days, concerning the certain fate of OVERLORD.[4] I think that we never undertook any operation in the war when the same type of doubt was not expressed to me, often with the greatest emphasis. This applied very definitely to TORCH,[5] Sicily and Italy. I even had to face it in the case of Pantelleria, although this particular operation finally came off so easily and successfully that those who expressed earlier and doleful doubts were later prone to forget.[6]

Consequently, without minimizing the great need for clear thinking, for positive leadership throughout all levels and kinds of activity, for some enlightenment and understanding and finally for extraordinary determination and persistence, still I have the firm conviction that both our countries, internally and externally, will rise to the requirements of the situation and that forward progress will result.

I have already written a Christmas note to you[7] but this letter renews my very best wishes for a bright and prosperous New Year.

With warm personal regard, *As ever*

[1] Morgan's letter of December 19 said that "the British want me to believe that delay is probably due to the activities of your boys over there. This I will not accept but I'm telling you" (EM). (For background see no. 1444.) Eisenhower had Bowen investigate, and on January 9, 1948, the General informed Morgan of the results of the inquiry in a letter drafted by Carroll (using information supplied by the Historical Division). Neither the Army nor the JCS had yet received the manuscript. On February 14 Morgan wrote that Eisenhower had misunderstood his note. The manuscript was not yet in the United States; but Morgan had been told that there would be a delay on the part of the United States. On February 27, however, Eisenhower would inform Morgan that the manuscript had been cleared. Morgan's book would be published in 1950. All correspondence is in EM.
[2] Morgan had visited with Marshall and Smith when they were in London for the fifth session of the Council of Foreign Ministers, from November 25 to December 15.
[3] In his letter of December 19 Morgan urged Eisenhower to run for President.
[4] The invasion of northwest Europe in 1944.
[5] The landings in North Africa in 1942.
[6] For Eisenhower's comments on the capture of Pantelleria see Eisenhower, *Crusade in Europe*, pp. 164–66. All of these operations are discussed in Chandler, *War Years*.
[7] In EM.

1967   *Eisenhower Mss.*

To WILLIS DALE CRITTENBERGER   *December 26, 1947*

Dear Critt: I have carefully perused the fine report concerning your Argentine mission.[1] You were not only highly successful in accomplishing your primary mission, but I am convinced that you have contributed to America's ultimate objective—a realistic hemispheric solidarity, based on mutuality of interests and respect. I appreciate the difficulties inherent in the situation in Central and South America and feel that your understanding of the Latin temperament, your good judgment and tact made possible the success that the mission enjoyed.

You realize that there are many facets to the problems presented by requests on the part of Latin-American countries for United States military equipment and manufacturing facilities. Appropriate agencies within the Department of the Army are carefully studying the requests submitted by the Argentine Government through you. Every effort will be made to insure that definite decisions will be reached prior to the 60 to 90 day notice that you promised in your recent conferences.

With sincere good wishes for good health, happiness and continued success in the new and ensuing year.[2] *Sincerely*

[1] The United States had launched staff discussions with Argentina in order to pave the way for a program of military assistance. (For background see no. 1845.) Lieutenant General Crittenberger had gone to Argentina on November 25 and had remained there until early December; he had discussed Argentine needs for arms and equipment and had reported on his mission to Eisenhower on December 15 (copy in P&O 091 Argentina, Case 11). For background on Crittenberger see no. 528. Carroll drafted this letter for General Eisenhower.

[2] For the immediate steps taken to implement the U.S.-Argentine understanding see Wedemeyer to Eisenhower, Dec. 29, 1947, and Wedemeyer to the DC/S, Jan. 12, 1948, both in P&O 091 Argentina, Case 11.

1968   *Eisenhower Mss.*

To Robert Porter Patterson   *December 26, 1947*

Dear Bob: Thank you very much for sending me a copy of your talk.[1] I am profoundly grateful that you should have seized an opportunity to express admiration and esteem for the great body of Army officers with whom you have come in contact so intimately during your years of public service. It is heartwarming to know that we have staunch friends during these days when isolated cases like the dirty Meyers fiasco[2] tend to cast a cloud of suspicion over so many people who struggle hard to do their duty.

With very best wishes for a fine and prosperous 1948, *As ever*

[1] Patterson had written on December 24 and enclosed a copy of an address he had made before the New York County Lawyers' Association on December 10, 1947. In the talk he had outlined some of his impressions of the Army, emphasizing the high quality of its personnel from the "top brass" down to the junior officers and enlisted men.

[2] See no. 1904.

To Joe W. Howe *December 26, 1947*

Dear Joe:[1] Let me assure you that if, as you suggest, I am ever caught in the "whirlwind of politics" it will be because I have lost my sense of proportion and values! I dislike intensely the very thought of entering partisan argument in this country; if I have any further usefulness to this country I want every citizen to have the right to believe that whatever I might say will be free of partisan considerations. I hope that this does not sound stuffy to you because entirely aside from personal inclination this truth underlies my fixed purpose of remaining completely aloof from all such activity.[2]

To what extent I may be able to do any good at Columbia is of course a matter for the future to determine. Obviously I am not a scholar nor educator. I have deep and definite convictions about Americanism as I understand it; about the responsibilities of American citizenship as well as privileges and rights. It is these simple convictions that will guide my conduct in the educational world and I shall certainly measure, in my own conscience, my success by the degree in which I am able to induce others to guide their own efforts by those same simple truths.

I recall boyhood days in The News office both vividly and often.[3] There can be no question of the lasting influence that you had upon all the boys that used to gather there. At least I can testify that in my case this is definitely true. It would be great fun today to meet you to talk over all those experiences of some 40 years ago and particularly to trace out the path that each of that boyish group has followed during the intervening years.

This letter brings not only my thanks and appreciation for the trouble you took in writing to me but my best wishes for a fine holiday season and a bright New Year. I am distressed to learn from your letter that your health is not too good but I sincerely hope this is only a passing condition.

With warm personal regard, *Sincerely*

[1] Howe, who was an old friend of Eisenhower's, had for many years been editor and publisher of the *Dickinson County News*, a weekly Abilene newspaper. He was presently a real-estate agent in Emporia, Kansas.
[2] In his December 20 letter Howe had advised Eisenhower not to get involved in politics. Howe said that because of the chaotic state of domestic affairs, the man who would be President of the United States for the next four years would be harrassed, discredited, and blamed for everything on every side: " . . . if it were you, in that place my feelings would be of sadness. . . " (EM).
[3] See Davis, *Soldier of Democracy*, pp. 88–95.

To Glenn Woodward Davis   *December 26, 1947*

Lt. Glenn Davis: Normally in time of peace the Army accepts without
hesitation any application for resignation by regular commissioned
officers in the certainty that to do otherwise would eventually damage
the high standards of duty and service demanded of the officer corps.[1]
The operation of this rule is habitually suspended in time of national
emergency, until conditions permit the maintenance of the officer corps
on a completely volunteer basis. At present there are still on active duty
certain officers of the emergency army whose services cannot be spared
and who are retained therein regardless of any desire to return to normal
civilian pursuits. So long as this situation prevails, the Army cannot,
except in cases involving extreme hardship or other humanitarian reasons, approve the resignation of any officer who, in good faith, entered
its professional, commissioned ranks. Your application for resignation,
after full consideration of all factors involved, is therefore disapproved.[2]

[1] Football star Glenn Davis had applied for a resignation (for background see no.
1233). On December 27 the Secretary of the Army's Personnel Board would
unanimously disapprove Davis's application for resignation. On that same day
General Parks would forward Eisenhower's letter to Davis by wire. All correspondence is in COS, 1947, 201 Davis.
[2] Davis, "Mister Outside" of the Army's mid-forties football team, would later
resign his commission, but "Doc" Blanchard ("Mister Inside") would become a
career officer.

To Mary Thompson Horkan   *December 26, 1947*

Dear Mary: Not only did the Doud-Eisenhower tribe thoroughly enjoy
your party—as we proved by staying so late—but the Western story you
picked out for me was truly a nice Christmas present. I have already
read a good portion of it and found it to be right down my alley.[1]

My thanks to the whole family and especially to you because I know
that the engineering of the whole business fell to you.

With best 1948 wishes to all of you. *As ever*

[1] The party had been on Tuesday evening, December 23. For background on the
Horkans see no. 546.

1972   *Eisenhower Mss.*

To Floyd Lavinius Parks   *December 26, 1947*

Dear Floyd: Thank you very much indeed for the "neck warmer".[1]
Along with it Mamie gave me quite the nicest V-neck sweater I have
ever seen so now I have the perfect combination for chilly golf, but I
am afraid one of my alibis for my usual game is forever gone.

I spent most of the day practicing on my putting machine. To match
it I received a brand new putter of a different type than I have ever used.
Since nothing can possibly hurt my putting I immediately adopted the
new one as my "regular" and worked with it all day. Maybe I was no
better by evening than when I started—but I thought I was.

I am truly grateful that you remembered me so nicely and generously. *As ever*

[1] For background on Major General Parks see no. 373. On this same date
Eisenhower acknowledged presents from the Benjamin F. Caffeys, the John B.
Hulls, Jessie D. D. Sayler, and the Howard M. Snyders. All correspondence is in
EM.

1973   *Eisenhower Mss.*

To Julius Earl Schaefer   *December 27, 1947*

Dear Earl:[1] Thank you very much for your interesting report on progress in the development of the XL–15.[2] I was interested in the account
of your struggle to meet every performance specification that you had set
for yourself. Yet, I find it hard to believe that a 15,000-foot service
ceiling adds any advantage to such a plane. There may be some reason
for this particular specification that escapes my mind, but normally such
a plane is used at very low altitudes. In fact, I once flew a considerable
distance in a liaison plane below the floor level of the surrounding
desert. We deliberately followed the course of a dry ravine in order to
minimize chances of encounter with German fighters.

I have always felt that the governing characteristics of such a plane
should be very short take-off and landing distance, reliability, good
visibility and, so far as possible, built at low cost and with the least
possible drain on critical raw materials.

So far as I am concerned, these particular characteristics can be
embodied in the conventional type plane much more satisfactorily than
in one with the rotating wing. The only defense such a ship has against

an attacking fighter is to get speedily to the ground without injury to the occupants. It is used for contact purposes and for observation, and I believe that after any ship goes to 15,000 feet in the air, a man in a fighter could observe just as well as a man in a slower-moving ship.[3]

All this is not to discourage you in the slightest degree in what you are doing. I am merely repeating some things that I shouted as loudly as I could all through the war. Since the close of hostilities I have run into no argument sufficiently convincing to cause me to change my mind.

When I saw the XL-15 at Riley I must say that it performed beautifully.[4] It is entirely possible that it may be the best answer we can develop at the moment, but I do hope that the general guide for all future research in this line will be to get maximum performance in the particular characteristics I have set down above.

I have already sent a copy of your letter to Bradley and will forward it later to Devers.[5] All of us are, of course, delighted that you are working so hard on this project. In the American Army we have never yet had a satisfactory liaison plane and it is high time that we were getting one. With warm personal regard and best wishes for 1948, *Cordially*

[1] Schaefer, vice-president and general manager of the Boeing Airplane Company, was an old friend of Eisenhower's (see no. 193).

[2] In a letter of December 22 Schaefer had summarized the progress to date on a plane that Boeing and the Air Force were developing for the ground forces. Schaefer said that up to this point Boeing had met all the Air Force specifications except a ceiling of fifteen thousand feet. The company also wanted the plane to have a cruising speed of 101 mph. At present the plane could climb to only twelve thousand feet and cruise at only 91.5 mph. Schaefer said he was convinced that Boeing would overcome these problems.

[3] Schaefer replied that the climb rate was important and was already quite good; it would not change very much if the service-ceiling specification was met. Schaefer was confident, however, that Boeing would meet the 16,400-foot level that the firm had set as its own target. The company had already met the cruising-speed specification (Dec. 30, EM).

[4] Eisenhower had visited Fort Riley on October 27.

[5] In his letter of December 22 Schaefer had asked Eisenhower to pass the information along to Bradley and had added his hope that Devers, commander of the ground forces, had been kept up-to-date.

1974   *Eisenhower Mss.*

To James Bradshaw Mintener   *December 27, 1947*

Dear Brad: Thank you very much for your letter.[1] It is gratifying to know you liked the sauerkraut well enough to want my recipe and I am inclosing a copy of the detailed instructions.[2]

Be sure to give us a ring when you come to Washington. The house is full of relatives, but we can somehow get together! *Sincerely*

[1] James Bradshaw Mintener had received his law degree from the University of Minnesota in 1929. He had taken a position at Pillsbury Mills in 1933, and since 1946 he had been vice-president and general counsel of the firm. In his letter of December 22 he asked Eisenhower for "the recipe for the sauerkraut which you made and which I enjoyed so thoroughly at your home the other evening." At the bottom of Mintener's letter Eisenhower wrote, "Prepare draft—(call us up when he comes) House full but we can get together!" Carroll drafted this response.
[2] The next document.

1975   *Eisenhower Mss.*

To James Bradshaw Mintener   *December 27, 1947*

RECIPE FOR SAUERKRAUT[1]
15 heads of cabbage
Salt
Wooden stamper
Round board and heavy stone
Small square of cloth (to cover whole batch)
6-gallon stone jar

Select large heavy cabbage, removing outer leaves, cut in quarters, remove core, slice very fine on a large cabbage cutter. Into large granite pan place 5 lbs. of shredded cabbage, sprinkle with 1/4 cup salt, mix thoroughly and then pack into large crock; pound and stamp down the cabbage with wooden stamp until the brine flows and covers the cabbage.

Mix another 5 lbs. of cabbage and 1/4 cup of salt and pack again into crock; pound as before until covered with brine. Continue until all cabbage is used, always pounding until covered with brine.

Now cover with cabbage leaves, lay on the fitted square of cloth and then the board and stone to help keep the contents under brine. Use large crock and leave enough space on top for the cabbage to swell or ferment without overflowing.

Put in warm place to ferment. In 2 weeks examine, remove the scum, if any; wash off, pick up at corners to catch all of the scum. Wash board, stone and sides of crock. Cover again with cloth, board and stone, then remove to cool place and remove scum and wash cloth, etc., weekly.

Or pack when fermented, in jars, cover with the brine, heat thoroughly in water bath, and seal. If not enough kraut brine, mix 1/4 cup salt with one quart of water.

(FOR HOT PACK)
Put sauerkraut in saucepan, cover with its own brine, heat to boiling and pack in clean, scalded jars, adding salt water if necessary to cover. Close jars tightly and process immediately.

[1] See the previous document. Eisenhower added at the bottom: "Best temperature of room-85°. Skim *every day* after it starts to ferment. I favor hot pack method of putting up the kraut after fully fermented, which is 10 days to 2 weeks; if temperature is lower, say 80°, may take 3 weeks." On the General's cooking see Eisenhower, *At Ease*, pp. 90–92, 381–82.

1976   *Eisenhower Mss.*

To Thomas Troy Handy   *December 29, 1947*

Dear Tom: Incident to my impending departure from Washington there are, of course, members of my personal staff whose future is of concern to me. The aides are all fairly well taken care of since two of them are soon to go to school and the other one probably does not intend to make the Army his career in any event. Likewise the two Master Sergeants who have been chauffeurs and general helpers are pretty well fixed.[1]

There remains my group of personal secretaries, and I have a hunch that Bradley may bring in one of his own from the Veterans Bureau. I think that under Civil Service rules Miss Nason is a fixture—she has been here so long that the office would probably be lost without her.

But you will probably remember Miss Hays, who was the first WAC to come into my office as a replacement after the war.[2] She is a Warrant Officer, AUS, and thoroughly capable. Her present intention is to remain in the Army indefinitely and she would be a tremendous asset to any headquarters in the Army. I find also that she would really prefer to leave this city, and upon finding this out my mind instantly turned to you.

The question is, have you a vacancy for her in your own personal staff and would you like to have her transferred there somewhere around early February? Frankly, if Columbia were not already staffed with stenographic secretaries, I would try to get her to leave the Army and go along with me, but I understand that there is no prospective vacancy at the University.

I shall not write to anybody else about her case until I hear from you, because if you do need someone, I think I would be doing you both a favor to arrange for her transfer before I leave here.[3]

At lunch today I got into the dining room when only John Martyn was present.[4] We had scarcely started lunch when he said, "Great guns, how I miss Tom Handy around this place. It doesn't seem natural any more!" This started a lot of conversation—none of it was derogatory, I assure you.

I trust that you are having a fine holiday season and that 1948 will prove to be your best year yet. *As ever*

[1] Aides Cannon, Michaelis, and Schulz would all remain in the Army. Schulz would accompany Eisenhower to Columbia, where he would serve as the General's administrative aide. Sergeants Moaney and Dry would also move to New York with the Eisenhowers.

[2] Warrant Officer Junior Grade Margaret Hays had been in the Women's Army Corps since March 23, 1945.

[3] For the outcome see no. 2001.

[4] John Wesley Martyn had been administrative assistant and chief clerk to the Secretary of War since 1930. He now held the same position in the Department of the Army (see *New York Times*, Oct. 27, 1947).

1977   *Eisenhower Mss.*

To Joseph Edward Davies   *December 31, 1947*

Dear Joe: By this time you may have heard from Don Richberg that all is settled on a "gentlemen's agreement" basis.[1] Don is collaborating with the Treasury Department and with the Doubleday people to see how a tentative instrument can be drawn up that can in no wise be interpreted either as a bona fide sale or as a "contract for services."

I must say that it is a relief to have all this indecisive talk completed. I will go to work on an intensive basis as soon as I can.

Mr. Robinson will place a secretary or two in Washington on whom I may call for help during odd hours. After February 15th, the drive will really be on.[2]

In contemplating the whole business, I realize that except for your needling and pushing, I would never have had the courage to bring the matter to a definite conclusion. I think you, more than anyone else, convinced me that I might have something worth saying. Moreover, it was because you took the lead in "negotiation" that I had the patience—possibly the ego—to talk to publishers at all.

This is written on the last day of the year. It gives me renewed opportunity to say Happy New Year to you and Marjorie and to both your nice families.

With best of luck and warm regard, *Cordially*

¹ On December 30 Eisenhower had met in his office with William Robinson, vice-president of the New York Herald Tribune Syndicate (see no. 1811); Douglas M. Black, president of Doubleday & Company (see no. 1621); Kenneth McCormick, Doubleday's editor in chief; and attorney Donald Richberg (see no. 1960).
² In *At Ease*, Eisenhower said, "On February 8, 1948, I started on a writing program, at a speed that a soldier would call a blitz" (p. 326; see also pp. 327–29). The book would be published in 1948 as *Crusade in Europe*.

1978   *Eisenhower Mss., Routine Corr., Miscellaneous*

To Walter Deane Fuller   *December 31, 1947*

Dear Mr. Fuller: Your letter places a rather difficult decision before me, because of my complete inability, this far in advance, to plan definitely for details of personal activity next spring.¹ As I think I told you, I hope to go on leave toward the end of February and to stay on leave until the first of May or shortly thereafter. Until that date additional commitments are definitely out of the question.

While I have tentatively accepted one invitation for the month of May, I must confess that I have not the remotest idea of the intensity of demand that may be made upon my time during my first month at Columbia. Because of all this inescapable uncertainty, I should much prefer now to make a firm engagement with your association for January, 1949, if you should still then want me to appear before it. If we could agree on such a suggestion, then you could go ahead with your January plans for 1948, without all the trouble incident to making radical changes in your arrangements. This would also eliminate all doubt and confusion revolving around the feasibility of my personal attendance next spring.

If after consideration of the above you still feel that my appearance before your group next spring is so desirable as to warrant changing all your arrangements on the probability that I can attend, then I would have to suggest the May 28th date of the two you suggested. I do not expect to arrive in New York by April 29.

I truly hope that this letter does not sound ungracious and that it does not convey any lack of appreciation of your courtesy. It is merely that innumerable pressures incident to my leaving the Army, the need for a considerable period of recreation, and the problem of beginning an entirely new type of life, all combine to make next spring an unusually difficult one for me. Add to all this my desire, for obvious reasons, to avoid public appearances for the next few months and you can see why I would personally prefer to come to your 1949 meeting rather than the impending one.

However, in the assurance that with this explanation you will sympathetically understand my situation, I will attempt to conform to whatever your desires in the case may be.[2] *Sincerely*

[1] Fuller had written on December 26 in his capacity as chairman of the National Association of Magazine Publishers. He asked Eisenhower to address a meeting of the association in New York and suggested that the group could meet on either April 29 or May 28. Fuller and Eisenhower had met on December 18, and the General had indicated that he was unable to speak at any time during January 1948, the month originally scheduled for the association meeting. For background on Fuller see no. 1923.

[2] Fuller replied that the association would seek another speaker for 1948 and would contact Eisenhower again about the 1949 meeting (Jan. 2, 1948, EM).

1979   *Eisenhower Mss.*

To James Stack   *December 31, 1947*

Dear Jim: I have neglected to answer your latest note, except that I believe I did send a message to thank you for the smoked salmon.[1] In any event, when you come to Washington, please get in touch with me at once. The whole family is here, but I shall have plenty of time to see you. I am looking forward to an interesting visit.

With best wishes to you and Elsa for a Happy New Year, and to the two girls (with special emphasis for my godchild). *Cordially*

[1] We do not have a copy of Stack's note. Eisenhower had sent Stack a holiday greeting on December 17, and the General had thanked Stack for the salmon in a note of December 26. Both letters are in EM. For background on Stack see no. 1733.

19

"Upon termination of my active service"

To Howard Charles Petersen   *January 2, 1948*

Dear Pete:[1] Thank you for your letter of the 31st. I am delighted to know that the project for Universal Training has such warm supporters in Philadelphia.[2]

So far as my January 17th appearance is concerned, I have been assured that I am expected to speak only very briefly and extemporaneously. Emphasis will be on my gratitude for the distinction accorded me and stressing my family association with Pennsylvania. However, I can probably insert some comment on the project of Universal Military Training even though I am not scheduled to make a formal address.[3]

It was good to hear from you; I hope that the new year has started off well for you and that each day will bring improvement.

With warm personal regard, *Sincerely*

[1] Shortly after leaving his post as assistant secretary of war in July 1947, Petersen had become executive vice-president and director of the Fidelity Philadelphia Trust Company.
[2] Petersen's letter said that he hoped Eisenhower would devote some attention to UMT when he spoke to the Poor Richard Club in Philadelphia on January 17 (EM). For the talk see no. 1993.
[3] For background on UMT see no. 1473. Eisenhower would include some comments on UMT in his speech (see *New York Times*, Jan. 18, 1948). Despite the efforts of General Eisenhower, President Truman, and many others, however, Universal Military Training would not be adopted. See Weigley, *History of the Army*, p. 500, for an analysis of the reasons why the public did not support UMT at this time.

To Harold Vincent Smith   *January 2, 1948*

Dear Mr. Smith:[1] There arrived at my desk a day or so ago a letter written to you by Mr. Thompson of Seattle.[2] I assume, therefore, that you were the one who forwarded it to me. Naturally I am flattered by the things that Mr. Thompson has to say about me, but I hope that in reply you have explained to him how determined I am to stay out of the political arena.

The scrapbook—though it seems almost a desecration to call it that—continues to occupy the same place in my office.[3] It never fails to bring forth expressions of admiration and of wonderment from visitors. Right now one volume is down at the Archives Building to determine the possibility of treating the clippings in the book so that they will endure permanently. I feel that the whole set will be such a valuable thing for the future that I want, if possible, to assure that it will not deteriorate.

I trust that the new year has started off well with you and will continue to grow better.

With cordial personal regard, *Sincerely*

P.S. I am returning Mr. Thompson's letter.

[1] On Smith see no. 1663.
[2] We have been unable to identify Mr. Thompson.
[3] See no. 1663.

1982   *Eisenhower Mss.*

To Thomas Anthony Amatucci   *January 2, 1948*

Dear Mr. Amatucci:[1] I tried to telephone you this afternoon, only to find that you were engaged. I wanted to thank you for the information you sent me by my son, John, and to tell you that I am not considering hasty trade-in of my car. However, if, in the near future, I decide to get a new Chrysler, I would most certainly do so only from you.

With best wishes for 1948, and with personal regard, *Sincerely*

[1] Amatucci was president of Tom's Auto Service, a Chrysler dealership in Washington, D.C. His reply of January 23, 1948, is in EM.

1983   *Eisenhower Mss.*

To George Maurice Morris   *January 2, 1948*

Dear Mr. Morris:[1] Thank you very much for forwarding to me the copy of the paper called "The Broom."[2] While I am not disturbed by the type of misrepresentation and falsehood that characterizes the article in that paper, yet it is cause for wonderment that anyone should find it desirable to say such things. It is amazing to what lengths hatred and prejudice will lead some people, and it is even more amazing when they allow their hatreds and prejudices to make statements that are so wholly baseless as is the one they make about me.

Thank you again for your courtesies. *Sincerely*

[1] Morris (J.D. University of Chicago 1915) had practiced law in Chicago before moving to Washington, D.C., in 1919. Since 1934 he had been a member of the law firm of Morris, Kixmiller & Baar.
[2] Morris, who had met Eisenhower at a recent social occasion, had forwarded the publication with a letter of December 31, 1947 (EM).

To Mrs. Reeve Claxton   *January 2, 1948*

Dear Mrs. Claxton: I appreciate your concern over your husband's bursitis condition and send you such information as I can on the treatment that helped me so much.[1]

Approximately a year ago, I was treated with deep X-ray therapy in connection with several other types of treatment, including daily massage for more than a month.[2] My condition improved materially, but my physician informs me that it is impossible to prescribe medical treatment in a particular case unless the individual undergoes a period of observation.

I earnestly hope that Mr. Claxton will find relief from this affliction in the near future. *Sincerely yours*

[1] In a letter of December 26 Mrs. Claxton, of Hood River, Oregon, had asked Eisenhower for this information. Her husband had been suffering with bursitis for a long time, and several doctors had been unable to help him. She said, ". . . in desperation I am writing you to see if you would tell us what helped you." Mrs. Claxton's letter is in the same file as this document. Carroll drafted a reply to be signed by Michaelis, but Eisenhower made several changes in the draft, and the letter was sent over his signature.

[2] For Eisenhower's hospitalization see no. 1234.

To Arthur Seymour Nevins   *January 3, 1948*

Dear Art:[1] This letter will have no meaning whatsoever if your current job is one that ties you down pretty tightly. It is written on the chance that you might be able to take a couple of months leave soon without damage to the permanency of your position.[2]

Very soon, possibly about February 15th, I will unquestionably have need for someone to do research work on a document I am preparing. It would be desirable for the man doing this work to be an experienced staff officer, and on top of this to have personal knowledge of the operations in the Mediterranean and in Europe with which I was connected. All this, of course, instantly suggests you as the number one choice.[3]

However, it is entirely possible that the work will not require more than two or three months, since, of course, whoever may undertake it will be supported with the necessary stenographic help, etc. The eventual publishers of the document would probably be the direct employers, and while I do not know what they would be prepared to offer, I am certain that the fee would be a relatively generous one.

As you know, I thought at one time that I might be able to retire on a rather leisurely basis and undertake historical writing as a sort of permanent occupation. In this way I would have permanent positions to offer to two or three assistants. With the Columbia problem facing me, this no longer seems possible, and it appears that my writing efforts will be confined to the attempt to publish one rather complete war memoir.

I understand fully that on the basis described the chances of your being able to do anything about it are very remote indeed, but I did want to tell you about the matter so that if by chance you could be available, we could go ahead with the necessary arrangements.[4]

With warm personal regard,[5] *Sincerely*

[1] For background on Nevins see no. 1615.
[2] Nevins had been working for a bank in Minneapolis since July 1947.
[3] For background see no. 1044.
[4] Nevins replied that Eisenhower's proposal had come at a most opportune time. Nevins said his job in Minneapolis was no longer as attractive as it had been originally, and he was most interested in helping the General write his memoirs (Nevins to Eisenhower, Jan. 6, 1948, EM). On January 13 Eisenhower wrote back, "Your letter delighted me" (EM). A follow-up letter by Eisenhower (of January 19) and other correspondence regarding Nevins's employment by Doubleday and his move to Washington, D.C., are in EM.
[5] See Eisenhower, *Crusade in Europe*, p. 480.

1986   *Eisenhower Mss., Subject File,* Crusade in Europe

To Archibald Lee Manning Wiggins   *January 3, 1948*

Dear Mr. Wiggins: Thank you for your continued courtesy toward me.[1] I greatly appreciate your offer of continued assistance if such should be necessary. The information supplied by you and your office has been of material assistance to me in determining my future plans, and if need arises, I shall not hesitate to ask for additional advice.

With best wishes for the new year, *Cordially*

[1] For background see no. 1954. In a letter of December 30 Wiggins had offered to provide Eisenhower further assistance if he needed it. He said, " . . . it is the duty of the Treasury Department to advise any taxpayer on tax matters. . ." (EM). Michaelis prepared an initial draft of this reply for Eisenhower.

1987   *Eisenhower Mss.*

To Edwin Aloysius Lahey   *January 5, 1948*

Dear Mr. Lahey:[1] I'm dashing off on a short trip[2] and am handing your letter to an assistant for more specific answer.[3] There's little I could say in any event—not only because of the technicalities of dealing with the press but because I'm not and shall not be a politician. Your situation appeals to me—and your request is understandable. I hope you will understand, also, my own position.

With best wishes for your quick recovery,[4] *Sincerely*

[1] Lahey was a columnist and reporter for the *Chicago Daily News* and the Knight Newspapers. He had begun working for the Chicago paper as a general assignment writer in 1929 and had specialized in reporting on developments involving labor since 1937. In February 1941 Lahey had moved to Washington, and since then he had concentrated primarily on the national labor scene.

[2] The Chief of Staff's desk calendar does not indicate what trip Eisenhower had in mind.

[3] General Parks, Chief of Public Information, would handle this request for Eisenhower. Lahey wanted to know what Eisenhower had said at a dinner at the F Street Club on December 5 (see no. 1926), and he asked when Eisenhower would announce his political affiliation (COS, 1947, Index, 095 Lahey). With his January 7 letter Parks sent copies of the clippings and speeches he felt would be most useful to Lahey, who was writing a profile of General Eisenhower.

[4] Lahey, who was ill, had written to the General from a sanitarium in Wisconsin (Dec. 28; we do not have a copy of this letter, which was given to Parks). Eisenhower wrote his reply in longhand. A typed copy is also in COS, 1947, 095 Lahey.

1988   *Eisenhower Mss.*

To Alan Frederick Lascelles   *January 6, 1948*

Dear Sir Alan:[1] Mrs. Eisenhower just recently received, through the American Embassy in London and the State Department here, a beautiful Christmas card from Their Majesties. We are deeply touched, the more so because the card is signed by the King and Queen in person.[2]

While I have already sent off a message to the American Embassy acknowledging receipt of the card,[3] I wanted to send to you a personal note of thanks because of the certainty that your personal consideration was responsible. The card will have a permanent place among our cherished souvenirs of The Royal Family.

With the hope that the New Year started off well for you and that each day will bring added contentment and happiness. *Cordially*

¹ For background on Lascelles, who was private secretary to the King of England, see no. 290. Eisenhower wrote this letter in longhand.
² A note on the letter of transmittal says that the card was delivered to Eisenhower's quarters at Fort Myer (Dec. 17, EM).
³ In EM.

1989   *Eisenhower Mss., Subject File,* Crusade in Europe

To JOHN NEVILLE WHEELER¹   *January 6, 1948*
Telegram

Thank you for your courteous suggestion.² I have now determined upon the publisher who will take over the book when, as, and if I can produce anything I believe satisfactory.³ While further discussion on this point is now out of the question, I would always be glad to see you on personal basis.⁴ *Cordially*

¹ For background see no. 1951.
² In his January 5 letter Wheeler had said that the North American Newspaper Alliance and the New York Times Company were interested in making an offer for the rights to Eisenhower's memoirs. Eisenhower wrote this reply in longhand on Wheeler's letter, and the telegram was sent that same day.
³ Eisenhower had agreed to sell his manuscript to Doubleday & Company and the New York Herald Tribune Syndicate (see no. 1977).
⁴ Similar letters to other interested publishers are in EM. See, for example, Eisenhower to Cass Canfield, Dec. 23, 1947, and Eisenhower to Ward Greene, Dec. 24, 1947.

1990   *Eisenhower Mss.*

To GEORGE CATLETT MARSHALL   *January 7, 1948*
Personal and confidential

Dear General Marshall: This afternoon I have been looking over the list of officers that I can recommend for assignment to Greece and who are reasonably available for that task.¹

With respect to McAuliffe:² We have just reorganized the Research and Development Division in the War Department and have assigned him as its head. Because of many contacts with Dr. Vannevar Bush and other scientists of the country, it would be extremely awkward to relieve him at the moment. In his stead, I suggest any of the following, some of whom you undoubtedly know:

1. Major General Ernest Harmon.³ He is a bull-in-the-china-shop, but shrewd. He is the nearest thing we have to the George Patton type;

in fact, it is my opinion that he has always aped and imitated George Patton. He wears lots of ribbons and is a bold, raucous-voiced type, but possesses a native canniness that never deserts him.

2. Major General E. H. Brooks.[4] I believe you know Brooks very well as I think he served in the Secretariat in the early days of your tour of duty as Chief of Staff. He commanded a corps in action and is possessed of very considerable ability. He is far more of a diplomat than are most Army officers. He is now in foreign service, but I would relieve him if you should consider him your number one choice.

3. Major General Charles L. Bolte.[5] I believe that you are likewise acquainted with this man. He is very able, sincere, and direct, and is much more of the Brooks' type than of the Harmon.

4. Major General I. D. White.[6] He is a cavalryman who commanded the Second Armored Division in the late stages of the war. He is direct and hard-working, but is possibly somewhat lacking in imagination. I would class him as somewhat of a mean between the extremes, let us say, of Harmon and of Brooks.

5. Major General James A. Van Fleet. The only officer we had in the war who fought his way all the way from regimental to corps commanding. He is definitely *not* the intellectual type, but is direct and forceful and has a fighting record that would make anyone respect him.[7]

You could give me your answer on this either by note or by telephone, and I will set the ball rolling.[8] *Sincerely*

[1] On December 31, 1947, the JCS had issued the directive formally establishing the Joint U.S. Military Advisory and Planning Group in Greece (JUSMAPG). (For background see no. 1815.) The directive placed the new group, which included army, air, and naval personnel, under AMAG but authorized it to have direct communication with the Joint Chiefs (JCS 1798/3). The JCS designated General Livesay, already in Greece as head of the War Department group of AMAG, as director of the new organization (JCS 1798/4; both documents are in ABC 400.336 Greece [3-20-47], Sec. 1-B). Eisenhower and Marshall decided, however, that Livesay should concentrate on the problems of supply and that the military direction should be provided by another officer (State, *Foreign Relations, 1948*, vol. IV, *Eastern Europe; The Soviet Union*, pp. 36–37).

[2] McAuliffe had served as Army Secretary of the Joint Research and Development Board from August 1946 until he assumed his present position in December 1947. For further background see no. 307.

[3] In 1946 Harmon had assumed command of the U.S. constabulary in Germany, and in 1947 he became deputy commander of the Army Ground Forces. For further background see no. 289.

[4] See no. 1452.

[5] See no. 1133.

[6] For background on Major General Isaac Davis White see Chandler, *War Years*. After July 1945 White had been at Fort Riley, Kansas, serving as commandant of the cavalry school until December 1946; at that time he became commandant of the ground general school.

[7] See no. 76. Van Fleet had headed the 2d Service Command from February to

June 1946. He had then served as Deputy CG, First Army, until December 1947, when he had been named Deputy Chief of Staff, Headquarters, EUCOM.
[8] Van Fleet would receive the assignment, see no. 2040.

1991   *Eisenhower Mss.*

TO WALTER JOHNSON ROBB   *January 7, 1948*

Dear Mr. Robb:[1] Your letter took me back, for a moment, to the Luneta—I could almost see the Escolta and hear the turmoil of traffic that always jammed the streets.[2]

Naturally I am flattered by the kind things you had to say about me. I know of nothing so satisfying as a realization that old friends stick! You'd be interested in knowing that T. J. Davis had to retire; bad heart.[3]

Needless to say, I found Mr. Brier's column extremely interesting, as, indeed, I did your remarks on the possibility of my doing a memoir.[4] I have tentatively made up my mind to do so; but you may be sure that it will be a carefully authenticated document, having some right to pretend to the title of "history." It will be no self-defense! . . .

Thanks again for your nice letter and please accept my best wishes for the year ahead. *Sincerely*

[1] Robb had lived in the Philippines for over thirty years prior to the outbreak of World War II. During most of that time he had been a newspaper correspondent, and he had written and lectured widely on the Philippines. In a letter of January 1 Robb had reminded the General that he had covered Eisenhower's Manila service and said that he had followed with interest Eisenhower's subsequent career. He asked the Chief of Staff not to discourage those urging him to run for President.
[2] The Luneta is a large public park in Manila. The Escolta is a shopping district in downtown Manila.
[3] See no. 311.
[4] Robb had sent a copy of an article that Royce Brier had published in the January 1 edition of the *San Francisco Chronicle.* Brier, who had joined the *Chronicle* as a reporter in 1926, had been editorial director since 1942. In the article Brier commented on the possibility of Eisenhower's writing a book. Robb said that publishers' "ulterior motives are sordid." He urged: "Please write nothing, please write no book; but continue, as you do now, and have done always, to give the people your heart, and share with them your soul. Let the reporters do the writing."

1992   *COS, 1948, 000.8 Mt. Rainier Elementary*

TO VIVIAN MARSHALL   *January 7, 1948*

Dear Miss Marshall: Admiring as I do the charitable spirit manifested by you and the children of your class in seeking aid for the town of

Bohars, I sincerely wish I could accept your invitation to participate in the parade on the 31st of January.[1] I would be proud to assist in such a splendid project.

As matters stand, however, I shall be very heavily involved throughout this month in the final phases of this assignment. There is so much to be done that I feel I simply cannot take on another commitment. I have even had to cancel several of long standing.

Please express my earnest thanks to the children for thinking about me.[2] Far from feeling any need to apologize for writing to me on behalf of the young Americans in your class, you may be assured that I derive from your action a deep sense of pride. I send best wishes for success in your worthy cause.[3] *Sincerely*

[1] Miss Marshall was a teacher at the Mt. Rainier Elementary School, in Mt. Rainier, Maryland. Her second- and third-grade classes had "adopted" Bohars, a small French village that had suffered greatly during the war. The children planned a parade to raise money for their project, and Miss Marshall had sent her December 28 invitation "very humbly, as a very small and unimportant citizen" (same file as document).
[2] In addition to revising the staff-drafted version of this reply. Eisenhower inserted the next to last sentence (McDuff Coll.).
[3] In Marshall's reply of January 10 (same file as document) she thanked Eisenhower for his interest.

1993   *Eisenhower Mss.*

To Bernard Law Montgomery   *January 10, 1948*
Cable WAR 93790. Restricted

U.S. MILATTACHE American Embassy, London, England. Bissell please pass to Montgomery. Personal for Montgomery from Eisenhower: Dear Monty: The official comments previously forwarded had my personal okay and of course the dispatches as presently cleared have my personal approval for publication.[1] We have already heard from your JSM[2] and have agreed with your plans. The comment on the weight given to air was passed along for whatever value it might have. Your observation is certainly logical. In any event from my understanding of your radio the matter is now settled.[3] *With warm regards*

[1] For background on Alexander's dispatches on the Mediterranean campaigns see no. 1914.
[2] The British Joint Staff Mission in Washington, D.C.
[3] Eisenhower added this last sentence to the staff-drafted cable. His disagreement with Alexander was over the relative importance of air power, especially in the capture of Pantelleria in 1943. In a cable of January 7 Montgomery said that Alexander had agreed with all of Eisenhower's comments on the dispatches except those on this issue. Montgomery suggested to Eisenhower that the difference was one of perspective—Alexander was writing about a period when he had been the

Army commander and Eisenhower, the supreme commander. For Eisenhower's views on this question at the time Pantelleria was captured see Chandler, *War Years*.

From January 8 through the thirteenth Eisenhower had a severe cold that kept him out of the office most of the time. He would return to full-time duty on the fourteenth. On January 15 the General would leave for New York, where he would speak that evening at a Columbia College alumni dinner honoring Dr. Fackenthal. On the seventeenth Eisenhower would go to Philadelphia to receive the Poor Richard Award. He would return that same day. Copies of his remarks in New York and Philadelphia are in EM, Subject File, Speeches. Other correspondence concerning the trip is in EM. For background on the Poor Richard Award see no. 1924.

1994   *ABC 352.1 (10-9-42), Sec. 2-C*

To Joint Chiefs of Staff   *January 16, 1948*
Memorandum

Subject: Allocation of Quotas to the Reserve Components for the Joint
          Colleges (NWC, ICAF, AFSC)

1. Prior to unification of the Armed Services, the War Department policy with regard to Reserve Components provided for inclusion of officers from those components as students in the joint colleges.[1] Prior to the current year, implementation of these policies has not been pressed. The problem now arises in the Department of the Army of extending quotas to the National Guard and the Organized Reserve so that officers from those components may attend the joint schools.

2. Prior to any unilateral implementing action by the Department of the Army, it is felt that the problem should be studied by the Joint Staff to determine whether or not a unified policy should be adopted.

3. a. Currently, Armed Services basic quotas* at the joint colleges are:

	NWC^2	$ICAF^3$	$AFSC^4$
Army	30	57	50
Navy	30	35	50
Air Force	30	23	50
(State Department)	(19)		
Total	109	115	150

*Subject to variance by inter-service agreement.

b. It is my view that the problem should be explored with a view to not reducing the already small service quotas now in effect.

2188

4. Accordingly, I recommend approval of the attached memorandum to the Director, Joint Staff.[5]

[1] For background on the joint colleges see no. 307, n. 13. Wedemeyer prepared a brief and a draft of this document (and the attached memorandum) for Eisenhower (same file as document). The Chief of Staff would approve the paper when he returned to Washington following his trips to New York and Philadelphia (see no. 1993). Eisenhower's memo would be circulated as the enclosure to JCS 962/45 (Jan. 23, 1948, CCS 352 [7-14-44], Sec. 3).
[2] National War College.
[3] Industrial College of the Armed Forces.
[4] Armed Forces Staff College.
[5] The memorandum, which directed the Joint Staff to study the problem, was attached to this document but is not printed here. On January 23 the JCS Secretariat forwarded Eisenhower's memorandum to the Joint Staff; on April 22, however, the JCS would approve a recommendation by the Joint Strategic Plans Committee to defer extending quotas to the reserve components (JCS 962/51, of April 2). The JSPC believed that some "limited participation" was "desirable," but there was simply no room. Each service could educate annually in the joint colleges no more than one-fifth of one percent of its planned officer strength (CCS 352 [7-14-44], Sec. 7).

1995   *Eisenhower Mss.*

To Edward Peck Curtis   *January 19, 1948*

Dear Ted: You have devised a fine slogan for your Cine-Kodak but it is only fair to warn you that you must wait to witness the product before you make such a bold statement.[1] The first bright day that I can get away from this desk I am going to shoot all over the place and I will have you view the results even before they are sent back to me.

I am truly grateful for the five Magazines—I really thought that you understood a bit of pleasantry when you encountered it. I am glad that you are of such a serious disposition because I shall enjoy greater freedom in shooting these five Magazines than I ever will with any that I purchase myself.

I saw Toohey this morning.[2] He seems in fine form.

With warm personal regard, *Cordially*

[1] In a letter of January 14 Curtis, who was now with Eastman Kodak, had welcomed Eisenhower to the list of people who owned Kodak's new camera (EM). He said the company was thinking of adopting the slogan "So Simple Even Eisenhower Can Operate It." He said that he was sending Eisenhower five rolls of Kodachrome film. For background on Curtis see no. 1734.
[2] General Spaatz.

To Robert Clarkson Clothier   *January 20, 1948*

Dear Dr. Clothier: After reading your cordial letter[1] and discussing your invitation with Representative Case and Mr. Moreland,[2] I am happy to say that, except for some unforeseen obstacle, I shall be able to attend the Commencement Exercises at Rutgers University on 13 June.

When Dr. Fackenthal wrote last week, I told him that only the fact I had previously declined a number of similar invitations deterred me from accepting your gracious hospitality.[3] However, since this is, after all, a renewal of an invitation I was forced to decline last year, I feel that acceptance does not imply discourtesy to others. Moreover, I agree that the historic association between Rutgers and Columbia fully justifies an exception in this instance.[4] A final and important factor is that I do not have to make a speech!

It was very thoughtful of you and Mrs. Clothier to invite Mrs. Eisenhower also. I cannot say at this early date whether or not she will be able to accompany me, but I know the invitation will appeal to her. With warm regard,[5] *Sincerely*

[1] On January 17 Dr. Clothier, president of Rutgers University, had renewed his invitation to Eisenhower to receive an honorary degree from Rutgers (EM). For background on Clothier and the original invitation see no. 625.

[2] Representative Clifford Phillip Case, Republican from New Jersey's Sixth District (B.A. Rutgers 1925; LL.B. Columbia 1928), was a trustee of Rutgers University. Although Eisenhower wrote *Moreland,* his desk calendar indicates that Mr. *Morgan* accompanied Congressman Case on a January 19 visit to the Chief of Staff's office.

[3] On January 9 Fackenthal had conveyed President Clothier's invitation, which Eisenhower declined (Eisenhower to Fackenthal, Jan. 14, 1948, both letters in EM). Eisenhower had also declined an invitation to receive an honorary degree from the Jewish Theological Seminary in New York City (Eisenhower to Fackenthal, Sept. 19, 1947, *ibid.*), and on January 23 he would turn down a similar invitation from Franklin and Marshall College, in Lancaster, Pennsylvania (Eisenhower to Distler, *ibid.*).

[4] In his letter Fackenthal said, " . . . Rutgers was established as Queen's College at approximately the time as Columbia was established as King's College and there has always been a close relationship between the two. . . ." Fackenthal had received an honorary degree from Rutgers.

[5] Eisenhower extensively revised Parker's original draft of this letter (McDuff Coll.).

To Gordon Garbedian   *January 21, 1948*

Dear Mr. Garbedian:[1] Thank you for your kind letter inviting me to attend the annual dinner of the Alumni Association of the School of Journalism of Columbia University. The occasion appeals to me greatly, but I am sorry to say that it is too far in advance for me to give a firm reply.[2]

While I expect to move to New York about May 1, I cannot possibly foresee the nature and intensity of my schedule. Would it be effrontery on my part to suggest that, for this year, you invite someone else as your guest of honor and speaker and then permit me to attend as another guest if, upon arrival at Columbia, I find it possible to do so? I assure you that, under these conditions I shall most certainly make the attempt.[3]

Again my thanks for your courtesy and consideration.[4] *Sincerely*

[1] Garbedian, who was co-president of the alumni association of the Columbia University School of Journalism, was a member of the editorial staff of the *New York Times.*

[2] The dinner had been tentatively scheduled for May 12 (Garbedian to Eisenhower, Jan. 14, 1948, EM) but would actually be held on May 19 (*New York Times,* May 20, 1948). Eisenhower made extensive changes in Parks's draft of this reply (McDuff Coll.).

[3] The meeting would be addressed by Douglas M. Black, president of Doubleday & Company and alumni trustee of the university, and by Neil MacNeil, assistant night managing editor of the *New York Times.* Eisenhower apparently would not be able to attend the dinner (see *New York Times,* May 20, 1948).

[4] Eisenhower had declined similar invitations to speak at the Columbia Alumni Federation's annual holiday luncheon (Eisenhower to Keeler, July 8, 1947, same file as document) and at the annual convention of the American Association of School Administrators (Eisenhower to Hunt, Sept. 8, 1947, COS, 1947, 080 American Association of School Administrators).

To Leonard V. Finder   *January 22, 1948*

Dear Mr. Finder: Your letter and editorial have been on my desk more than a week, while I pondered the reply merited by your obvious concern for the nation's welfare and, from a personal standpoint, by the honor you have done me.[1] Months ago I thought that unqualified denial of political ambition would eliminate me from consideration in the coming campaign for the Presidency, because that office has, since the days of Washington, historically and properly fallen only to aspirants.

That some few would misinterpret or look for hidden meanings in my past expressions was expected and discounted, but my failure to convince thoughtful and earnest men, such as yourself, proves that I must make some amplification.[2] This will necessarily partake of the laborious, due to the complexity of the factors that have influenced me to say no more than I have, but which dictate my decision that I am not available for and could not accept nomination to high political office.[3]

I have heretofore refrained from making the bald statement that I would not accept nomination, although this has been my intention since the subject was first mentioned to me. This omission seems to have been a mistake, since it has inadvertently misled sincere and disinterested Americans. But my reticence stemmed from cogent reasons. The first was that such an expression would smack of effrontery. I had and have no desire to appear either as assuming that significant numbers of our people would actively interest themselves in me as a possible candidate, or to appear as lacking in respect and regard for the highest honor American citizens can confer upon one of their own body.

A second and even deeper reason was a persistent doubt that I could phrase a flat refusal without appearing to violate that concept of duty to country which calls upon every good citizen to place no limitations upon his readiness to serve in any designated capacity. On this point it is my conviction that, unless an individual feels some inner compulsion and special qualifications to enter the political arena—which I do not—a refusal to do so involves no violation of the highest standards of devotion to duty. It was only the possible misinterpretation of my attitude that caused me concern and so long as I could believe that mere denial of political ambition would prevent serious misunderstanding and misdirected effort, I was reluctant to say more. It would seem almost superfluous for me to add that as long as I live I shall hold myself in instant readiness to respond to any call by the government to military duty.

In full awareness then, and not in violation of my own sense of duty, I have developed the following conclusions, which are responsible for my negative decision.

It is my conviction that the necessary and wise subordination of the military to civil power will be best sustained, and our people will have greater confidence that it is so sustained, when lifelong professional soldiers, in the absence of some obvious and overriding reasons, abstain from seeking high political office. This truth has a possible inverse application. I would regard it as unalloyed tragedy for our country if ever should come the day when military commanders might be selected with an eye to their future potentialities in the political field rather than exclusively upon judgment as to their military abilities.

Politics is a profession; a serious, complicated and, in its true sense, a noble one. In the American scene, I see no dearth of men fitted by training, talent, and integrity for national leadership. On the other hand, nothing in the international or domestic situation especially qualifies for the most important office in the world a man whose adult years have been spent in the country's military forces. At least this is true in my case.

I am deeply regretful if a too simple faith in the effectiveness of a plain denial has misled any considerable number concerning my intentions and so allowed them to spend time and effort under erroneous impressions. At the risk of appearing pompous, I must say that the honor paid me cannot fail to spur me, in future years, to work the more diligently for America, her youth, her veterans and all her citizens, and for the continuance of peace.

I trust that this rather lengthy explanation will convince you that my conclusions are not only sound but have been arrived at objectively and have not been unduly influenced by my own desires and convenience. In any event, my decision to remove myself completely from the political scene is definite and positive. I know you will not object to my making this letter public to inform all interested persons that I could not accept nomination even under the remote circumstance that it were tendered me.

With warm personal regard,[4] *Sincerely*

[1] On January 9, 1948, a group of New Hampshire Republicans formally entered a slate of delegates pledged to Eisenhower in the March 9 primary in that state. Finder, publisher of the Manchester, New Hampshire, *Union Leader,* sent Eisenhower a copy of his evening paper's endorsement (also January 9). In his covering letter of January 12 Finder said: "As you once told me, no man should deny the will of the people in a matter such as this. All that we are attempting is to have the will of the people made so clear that it cannot be obviated by the usual politicians assembled in convention." Eisenhower wrote on the letter, "We'll have to answer—but I dont know what to say!" Michaelis informed the General (in a memo on Finder's letter) that Finder had also written him, enclosing a series of editorials and asking for "any off the record enlightening comments from time to time." Michaelis said that he had responded on January 14 "with a *simple* 'thanks for clippings' hoping it will end there." All correspondence is in EM. For background on Finder see no. 1761.
[2] Finder's letter prompted Eisenhower to make a final decision. The General's initial reaction to the news from New Hampshire had been announced in a statement issued by General Parks, Chief of the Army's Public Information Division; the statement said that Eisenhower had "reiterated on many previous occasions that he wants nothing to do with politics. He has not changed his mind" (*New York Times,* Jan. 13, 1948). Eisenhower personally drafted this stronger response (EM) and then incorporated suggestions from several others, including Forrestal, in his statement (see Lyon, *Eisenhower,* pp. 379–80).
[3] Numerous responses to Eisenhower's statement are in EM. President Truman, in a handwritten note of January 24, said that he had not seen Eisenhower's letter

to Finder before responding to the General's formal letter of resignation as Chief of Staff (see the next document). Truman said his response nonetheless "would have been just as it was. . . ." He added, "I am sure that you and I understand what politicians are doing."
[4] At 11:30 A.M. on January 23 General Parks called Finder and obtained his permission to release to the press that noon both Finder's letter to Eisenhower and the Chief of Staff's reply. Parks then read Eisenhower's letter, and Finder responded, "I wish you would tell the General that he makes me feel like bawling . . ." (EM). The letters were released that day (New York Times, Jan. 24, 1948). For further developments see no. 2005.

1999   Eisenhower Mss.

To Harry S. Truman   January 22, 1948

Dear Mr. President: You will recall that, somewhat more than two years ago, when I undertook the duties of Army Chief of Staff, it was understood between us that when you might find it possible to relieve General Bradley as Veterans Administrator, and he and I should subsequently agree upon his readiness to serve as my successor, you would approve my request for retirement to civil life. This note is to inform you that, in our judgment, that date is now at hand.

Accordingly, the Secretary of the Army will shortly forward to you General Bradley's nomination as Chief of Staff and, provided we have your consent, we shall fix a convenient date sometime shortly after February 1, for my relief from duty and his simultaneous assumption of office.[1] Thereafter he intends to place me on a temporary duty status during the remainder of February to allow me a short period of hospitalization and to make such use of me as he may desire for his own orientation purposes.[2] My terminal leave would begin, under this arrangement, and with your approval, on March 1.

I scarcely need assure you again of the high sense of distinction and privilege I have felt in the opportunity to serve under you. Your encouragement, understanding, and, above all, your friendship, have been priceless to me. You are likewise aware that I shall always hold myself available for any military duty that the Government may require of me.

With best wishes and respectful regard,[3] Sincerely

[1] Bradley would assume command at noon on February 7, 1948.
[2] Eisenhower would go to Hot Springs, Arkansas, for treatment of his recurring bursitis (New York Times, Feb. 8, 1948).
[3] In a handwritten note of January 23 President Truman acknowledged Eisenhower's letter and said: "I am sorry you are leaving. But I know that eventually your retirement must come. You have my heartiest good wishes in whatever you may decide to do—and my friendship and admiration always" (EM).

Eisenhower Mss.

To Lloyd Washington Lambert   *January 23, 1948*

Dear Lloyd:[1] Some months have passed since last I heard from you, a fact of which I was reminded by a recent visit from Alex Frieder.[2] Naturally, as is usual when two old Manila residents get together, we talked over the old days and all the people that we then knew so well. . . .

I shall not be actually in the War Department very much longer but mail addressed to me either here or at Fort Myer will always reach me.

Give my very best to Betty[3] and when you write to Manila remember me to any of our old friends that happen to be there, including particularly Clyde DeWitt and Pete Grimm.[4]

With warm personal regard, *Cordially*

[1] For background on Lambert see Chandler, *War Years.*
[2] Frieder had visited Eisenhower on January 12. For background on Frieder see no. 502.
[3] Lambert's wife.
[4] In the late 1930s, when Eisenhower was stationed in the Philippines, Clyde DeWitt had been an associate member of the Manila law firm of DeWitt, Perkins, and Ponce-Enrile. He had also been secretary and director of the Manila Gas Corporation (see letter from Federico J. Galang, Oct. 3, 1977, EP). We have been unable to identify Grimm.

2001   *Eisenhower Mss.*

To Thomas Troy Handy   *January 26, 1948*

Dear Tom: Thank you very much for your note about Miss Hays.[1] At the proper time all the necessary orders will be issued here and she will report for duty sometime in the late winter or early spring. I haven't had a chance to talk to her for some days and so I cannot give you the exact time.

The German assignment is still in the discussional stage although it looks to me that unless General Marshall should change his mind you would be leaving for Germany somewhere between the end of February and the end of April.[2] If you were to go on that job I am anxious that we do not have to go through the agony of reducing you on June 30 (to comply with the law) and then later promoting you again.[3] Clay naturally thinks that he has a right to retain his four stars until he is actually retired from the Army and consequently if we allow his leave to stretch over into the next fiscal year someone would have to be reduced to take care of him. Since he wants, in advance of his leave, a month to come home, complete his records, get hospitalized and so on, it means that we may have to relieve him over there by the first of April. You should certainly have a couple of weeks' overlap. There is a possibility that he will take terminal pay for two months in lieu of terminal leave. This would make it unnecessary to take him out of Berlin until June 1.

The whole prospect of service in Germany is a much brighter one because of the State Department's agreement—at long last—to take over the job of Military Government.[4] The Army Commander will be merely the Commander of the troops and a supporter rather than the director of Military Government. I cannot picture, from this viewpoint, a more desirable station.[5]

With warm regard and best wishes, *As ever*

[1] In a letter of January 3 Handy had said he would assign Warrant Officer Hays to his own office (EM). She would begin work at the headquarters of the Fourth Army, at Fort Sam Houston, during August 1948 but would retire from active duty in November of that same year. For background see no. 1976.

[2] Clay was planning to retire (see no. 1893). The transition in command would be easier to make now because the Army's tasks in Germany were being reduced; Secretary of State Marshall had announced at a press conference on January 8 that the State Department would assume responsibility for the occupation by June 30 *(New York Times,* Jan. 9, 1948).

[3] For background see no. 1888. As of July 1, 1948, the Army would be limited to five generals of four or five stars. The Army currently had eight such officers, and three of these, including Handy, were Army commanders. Under the new policy the seven Army commanders would be lieutenant generals. For further developments in regard to this policy see no. 2038.

[4] The Army had been attempting for some time to persuade the State Department to take over the task of military government (see no. 626).

[5] Despite Eisenhower's optimism, there was some consideration at this time of serious problems that might arise in Germany in the near future. In January 1948 there was already speculation about what the United States could do "in the event the Soviets attempt to force us out of Berlin." According to Wedemeyer's memo to the Secretary of the Army, the Russians could impose "administrative difficulties, in the expectation that the resulting inconveniences will influence the withdrawal of allied forces. . . ." The Soviets could, for instance, "cause 'unavoidable' incidents, such as the hampering of communications. . . ." In this event, Wedemeyer said, the United States should focus attention on Russia's responsibility for the problem while "utilizing every available means to transport supplies, etc. to Berlin in an effort to maintain our position" (Jan. 2, 1948, ABC 387 Germany [12-18-43], Sec. 4-I). For the events that would dash Eisenhower's hopes that Germany would be a "desirable station" see no. 2003.

2002   *Eisenhower Mss.*

To Edward Everett Hazlett, Jr.   *January 26, 1948*

Dear Swede: By this time you have possibly noted in the public press that all your remaining questions about a political career for me have been definitely answered.[1] Several of my warm friends—men whose judgment I completely respect—differed from me sharply as to the wisdom of issuing such a statement. In fact, I had only two real supporters, among all my friends, in my belief that I must do so. There were many factors other than those mentioned in my letter to Mr. Finder[2] that had some influence with me but I think I am honest in saying, as I did in the letter, that personal desire and convenience were not predominating among them. Now that it is done, I can at least devote my mind unreservedly to a number of other important things and will not feel like I am constantly on the "witness stand".

I read the letter from your friend Whicker and I must say that I found it most interesting and intriguing.[3] Discounting or even eliminating his over-generous opinions concerning my personal characteristics and qualifications, the letter is indicative of the thinking of a very, very large number of people in this country today.[4] Most of them, however, have not Mr. Whicker's ability to express himself. Incidentally, some of his sentences are a little on the lengthy side for my simple mind but even so he succeeds in expressing himself clearly and forcefully.

I also read his letter on our educational institutions.[5] You have asked me to return it and I shall do so in a few days but first I think I should like to have a copy of it made because I shall want to refer to it from time to time. My most persistent reaction to his two documents is that it is a tremendous loss to our country that he is a confirmed invalid.[6] We need crusaders; he is obviously the type of man that would never give up in his pursuit of an objective and even though some would certainly accuse him of lopsidedness (I am speaking now particularly of his castigation of our educational system) he would certainly make a lot of complacent, ritualistic people most uncomfortable. If ever I get out in that region I am going to look him up because I have the feeling that an hour's conversation with him would be truly stimulating. When you write to him please assure him of the profound impression his effort made upon me and tell him that the highest praise I can give is: "Our country needs more of his type".

Washington is undergoing a touch of real winter. The temperature must be somewhere around 15 or 20 today and we have quite a bit of snow. The forecaster says we shall continue to have no change for two or three days. I suppose that you have gotten a touch of the same thing down at Chapel Hill.

I have seen pictures of Dick Scott of the Navy and from them I should say he is a fine-looking boy.[7] I should like to get a chance to have a real talk with him because I should like to subject to microscopic examination every young man fortunate enough to run around with the Hazlett girls.

I do not remember whether I have told you that Mamie and I are counting on being grandparents in early April. Far beyond this, we are already counting on the selection of the school the young grandson or granddaughter (I wish we could figure on twins) is going to attend. Within ten days or two weeks I expect to turn over this job but I shall be around the city until May 1st, when I go to New York. Right this minute we have a household upset with sickness—Mamie's Dad became quite ill while visiting us. However, anytime you have a chance to get up this way send us a wire and count on staying with us, certainly up to the middle of April—after that we'll always have an extra room in New York.

With love to Ibby[8] and the girls, *As ever*

P.S. Tell Whicker to get a description of the effort being made at Amherst to revitalize educational processes.[9]

[1] In a letter of January 15 Hazlett had discussed Eisenhower's presidential possibilities (EM). For background on Hazlett see no. 775.

[2] No. 1998.

[3] Hazlett had forwarded two letters from Harold Wave Whicker, of Guemes Island, Anacortes, Washington. Hazlett described Whicker, in almost mythic terms, as a man who had served in the Navy as a gunner's mate during World War I, wrestled professionally, and taught English at Washington State University. Along the way he had written, hunted, fished, painted, and logged 30,000 miles in Alaskan waters in a canoe without an upset. Unfortunately, Whicker's letters are not in EM.

[4] One of the letters apparently discussed Eisenhower's political future.

[5] Hazlett thought that Eisenhower would be interested in Whicker's comments, since the General was "one of the country's foremost educators-to-be."

[6] Hazlett had explained that Whicker had suffered two severe heart attacks.

[7] Hazlett's daughter was at present "romancing" with Richard Underhill Scott. Hazlett pointed out that Scott was the Naval Academy's class president, regimental commander, football captain, and an All-American center, "so I can't be too downcast about it."

[8] Hazlett's wife.

[9] In September 1947 Amherst College had introduced an experimental curriculum to help counteract "the trends which are today lowering the educational level of colleges" (see *New York Times*, Mar. 23, 1947).

2003   *Eisenhower Mss.*

To Lucius Du Bignon Clay   *January 27, 1948*

Dear Lucius: Remembering our talk of Saturday night I started this morning to make a survey of factors bearing upon your personal problem.[1]

These facts apply:

You want to leave the Army as a 4-star General and want to leave Germany at or before the time that the State Department appointee actually takes over as Military Governor.

Your Army relief should report in Germany at least a couple of weeks before you leave and he should have 4-star grade.

Starting at the time you leave Germany you want a month on active duty, to be followed by two months' terminal leave.

After June 30, which is the target date for State Department assumption of responsibility, the Army is allowed a total of five Generals in 4-star grade.

Under present law any officer leaving the Army who does not take his terminal leave is given active duty pay for a two months' period.

These seem to be the salient points in the case and the following would seem to represent logical, alternative courses of action:

You could, with State Department approval, be relieved from duty by April 1. To do this we would have to send over Handy (the only other possibility would seem to be Clark), or any other person upon whom the State Department and we would agree, by early March. This would allow you to have your full three months in your 4-star grade because, until June 30, the legal limitation on numbers does not apply.

Another solution would be that in lieu of two months' leave, you take the pay for an equivalent time. In this case you would not have to be relieved until June 1, with your replacement arriving there during the previous month. This would still allow you to retire on June 30.

I do not consider it an acceptable solution to keep you there until June 30 and begin thereafter your period of temporary duty and leave (assuming you would want to take leave instead of pay). To do this would require us on June 30 to reduce Handy, after he had arrived in Germany, to remain in a lower grade for three months and then again to promote him. This would be a shattering blow to his morale and prestige and we could not afford it. I do not see how any other individual could be reduced because the ones involved are Bradley, MacArthur, Devers, Collins, and whoever is in Germany, possibly Handy. The Judge Advocate General in a recent opinion ruled that a man actually on terminal leave necessarily would be charged against our allotment of generals.[2]

As a consequence of all the above, it would seem to me that the only question that you need to resolve is your choice between taking two months' leave or your pay. If you should forgo the leave, you would be retired earlier but the pay would be clear gain since during that period you would draw retired pay. When we get the answer to this one we can proceed, with the State Department, to making necessary arrangements.

Quite naturally all of us are anxious to meet your wishes in the matter and have every intention of doing so. The problem merely becomes one of doing it in the best possible way.[3]

Please remember me to Bob[4] and give my affectionate regard to Marjorie. *As ever*

[1] Clay had returned to the United States briefly to testify before the congressional committees considering appropriations for Germany. In a letter of January 5 Clay had said he would like to stay in Germany until late in 1948. He was worried because "the atmosphere is rather tense." He said, however, that "we should certainly know the situation in as far as our relations with the Soviet Union are concerned some time in the early part of 1948." By taking appropriate actions at that time, the United States could "achieve stability in the next several months." Clay felt that he could leave when that goal had been attained. For background see no. 2001.

[2] See Paul to Eisenhower, Jan. 26, 1948, EM.

[3] In *Decision in Germany*, p. 240, Clay says that he set up a committee to work with State Department officials on the transfer of responsibility for the occupation. "Then in March came the first Soviet blockade move [against Berlin]." Because of the blockade, Clay would not leave Germany until May 15, 1949. For an account of U.S. policy during 1948 see State, *Foreign Relations, 1948*, vol. II, *Germany and Austria*.

[4] Ambassador Robert D. Murphy.

2004   *Eisenhower Mss.*

To Geoffrey Keyes   *January 27, 1948*

Dear Geoffrey: Thank you very much for your nice letter of the 21st. I was interested in the account of affairs in your command and particularly in the difficulties you have with the unfavorable rate of exchange.[1] It was a subject that plagued us all during the war but I must say that when the differential between the international rate and the official rate reaches the ratio of 10 to 1 it must be difficult indeed to do anything about black marketing.

Another phase of this same subject was brought out by the recent French action in devaluating the franc. Apparently the money markets all over the world were vastly disturbed by that action. International exchange seems to be one of the headaches of the world today and a lot of people are caught up in the problems so presented. So far as I am concerned the subject is very abstruse.[2]

I shall probably turn over to Bradley early in February. I want to get a reasonable rest although I shall use part of the time before I go to Columbia in working on a war memoir for which I have lots of notes. I shall never publish it, however, until I can get it properly and thoroughly annotated and checked against the records by reputable historians. I have no desire to write just another lopsided "War from my viewpoint".[3]

As you can well imagine I will never truly leave the Army. One reason I so flatly refused to have anything to do with politics was so I could continue to devote my time and effort to the teaching of a very few simple and basic truths by which we in the Army have been living for a long time. If I can do any good at all it is certainly along the lines in which I have had some experience and training.

Washington is having a touch of winter weather with considerable snow and the thermometer ranging for several days between 10 above and 20 above. This doesn't prevent a feverish interest in personal and party politics. It seems to me that half our newspapers are taken up with the efforts of the various candidates to get into a favorable position to seize the Republican nomination next summer. I don't think anyone will make any serious guesses as to who will win but there are a lot of them that are hopeful.

This letter brings to you my very deep appreciation for the fine way you have handled your difficult job in Austria as well as for the splendid services you rendered to the Army throughout the European war. While it will be a jolt for me to sever official connection with you and all the others with whom I have been so closely associated all these years—particularly since the beginning of the war—yet I hope that the future will bring us many opportunities to get together and chin over old times.[4]

Please remember me kindly to Mrs. Keyes and with warmest personal regards to yourself, *Cordially*

[1] Keyes had complained that at the international rate of exchange, eighty to one hundred schillings equaled a dollar, but at the U.S.-Austrian official rate, the exchange was ten to a dollar. Thus, a dollar paid by an American to an Austrian servant was easily turned into ten dollars on the black market. See State, *Foreign Relations, 1947*, vol. II, *Council of Foreign Ministers; Germany and Austria*, pp. 1208–17.

[2] On January 25 the French—despite British objections—had announced they were going ahead with their plan to create a two-value franc; outside of France the franc would be devalued by 40 percent.

[3] On Eisenhower's writing plans see no. 1977.

[4] Keyes said that he particularly appreciated Eisenhower's efforts in the food crises (see no. 1938) and that "we regret your departure from the Army."

To Leonard V. Finder   *January 27, 1948*
Personal and confidential

Dear Mr. Finder: Following the exchange of our public letters I was
delighted to receive your more personal and intimate reactions to what I
considered to be a necessary move on my part.[1] Frankly, I selected you
as the individual to whom my reply should be directed because out of
the entire number of individuals who were interesting themselves in a
possible political career for me, your own position from the beginning
has struck me as the most disinterested and most definitely inspired by
concern for the national welfare.

It was a difficult letter to write. I carried the draft home with me
evening after evening, not so much because of concern as to wording as
anxiety to explain exactly what I thought to be the pertinent factors
and considerations. One danger I ran was that personal inclination
dovetailed so nicely with the conclusions that I reached; I have long ago
learned that when this is the case a man should scrutinize his own
analysis with a jaundiced eye.

One factor that had some weight with me and which I did not
mention in the open letter was the fact that my name has become so
closely associated with the Army that in any future personal activity,
regardless of its nature, any blame and criticism directed toward me will
almost certainly encompass the Army. Opposition would be directed as
much to the "military mind," to the "philosophy of force" and so on, as
it would against the validity and honesty of my own deductions. The
health, efficiency and strength of the Army are important to this country; in spite of my fanatical devotion to the purpose of perpetuating
peace, indeed, rather, because of that devotion, I feel that the Army
must be projected into the public mind constantly in its true proportions
and perspective. Under no circumstances must it suffer because one of
its own number might find himself in a position where he necessarily
had to make decisions in domestic and political controversy.

In any event I have had my say and I know you thoroughly trust the
objectivity of my attitude. Naturally I am flattered by and very proud of
the sentiments you have expressed and continue to express. I assure you
again that so long as I remain active there will never be any diminution
in my readiness to work for the good of this country. My decision
merely inhibits me from directing these efforts to the strictly political
field.

Please remember me kindly to Mrs. Finder, and with warm personal
regard to yourself,[2] *Sincerely*

[1] In his letters of January 24 and 26 Finder had expressed his disappointment at Eisenhower's decision to remove himself from the 1948 presidential campaign. Finder said he was not abandoning his efforts, especially since many people wanted Eisenhower to change his position (EM). For background see no. 1998.
[2] Finder continued to press his case (letters, Jan. 30, Feb. 5, EM). He asked to meet with Eisenhower. The two men would get together on February 10 but, as Peter Lyon observes, by that time "the Eisenhower boom of 1948 was finished" (*Eisenhower*, p. 380).

2006   *Eisenhower Mss.*

To ALBERT JESSE BROWNING   *January 27, 1948*

Dear Al:[1] Many thanks for your letter.[2] For some strange reason, it did not reach me until yesterday, four days after the publication of my letter to New Hampshire.[3] However, I read your views with the keenest interest and appreciation.

I could not help but be highly flattered by the qualities you ascribe to me. Whatever they are, they will still be fully available to the nation in my capacity as a private citizen.[4]

The story of the dinner at the F Street Club reached variations, fully as surprising to me as they were to you.[5] It would have been impossible for me to think of some of the ideas attributed to me—much less say them. To eliminate the profit motive would be to scuttle our form of government and our concepts of living; to these things I am fanatically devoted. I need no selling on personal incentive and initiative. If I would do any single thing for the Army during these last few weeks, it would be to increase incentives for diligence and performance of duty.

This will reach you, no doubt, on your long-awaited vacation. I do hope you and Mrs. Browning[6] will make the most of it. We are looking forward to one in March and April, hoping to get a complete rest for a fresh start at Columbia.

Again, thank you for writing me such a thoughtful letter. I place a high value on your friendship.

With warm regard, *Sincerely*

[1] Browning was a vice-president of the Ford Motor Company. He had graduated from M.I.T. in 1922 and had headed United Wall Paper Factories, Inc., before serving on active duty in the Army during World War II. For further background see Chandler, *War Years.*
[2] Browning had written on January 15 (EM). Eisenhower made several changes in Carroll's draft of this letter (McDuff Coll.).
[3] No. 1998.
[4] On this same date Eisenhower responded in a similar vein to a letter of January 11 from attorney Robert C. Baker of San Francisco. Both letters are in EM.

⁵ See no. 1926. In his letter Browning said, "I am continually hearing reports of a statement that you were supposed to have made that business should give up all of its profits for two years in an effort to stem inflation."
⁶ Formerly Ruth Sears.

2007   *Eisenhower Mss.*

To Richard Leo Simon   *January 27, 1948*

Dear Dick: Within a matter of ten days or two weeks I think I should have a chance to take specific advantage of the nice suggestion made in your letter of the 23rd.¹ Before long I will turn this job over to General Bradley and then I hope to be able to give my time exclusively to the "Memoir" job.

The evening bridge game sounds very good indeed. I think we can work something out that might provide an evening's good fun. When I get to the point that I can make a definite plan even for a single day I shall write to you again.² *Cordially*

¹ Simon had offered to spend an afternoon helping Eisenhower start his book (see no. 1977). He suggested that they might follow up the afternoon with an evening of bridge (EM). For background on Simon see no. 799.
² On the previous day Eisenhower had replied to a January 20 letter from Roger Williams Straus, Jr., of Farrar, Straus & Company, publishers; Straus had informed the Chief of Staff about his company's plan to publish a book of Eisenhower's speeches and messages entitled *Eisenhower Speaks*. In his letter Eisenhower thanked Straus for the careful way the book was being done. All correspondence is in EM.

2008   *Eisenhower Mss.*

To Louis Marx   *January 27, 1948*

Dear Louis: Inclosed is a note in which I have tried, though most inadequately, to tell Barbara something of the depth of my sympathy.¹ Will you please pass it on to her. I know that you also have suffered a great shock and that some of your fond hopes are dashed to the ground. I want you to know that to you also I extend assurances of a deep and understanding sympathy. Our own first son died when he was quite a little boy and to this day I cannot think of it without experiencing again, at least in part, the very great grief that then seemed insurmountable.² Nevertheless, receding time does bring at least a philosophical resignation.

Please keep me informed of Barbara's progress in her return to health

and keep reminding her that all her friends will be thinking of her.[3]
Cordially

[1] Idella "Barbara" Marx had been expecting twins (see no. 1902). In a letter of January 26 Louis Marx told Eisenhower that his wife had lost the twins during childbirth (EM). A typed copy of Eisenhower's handwritten note to Mrs. Marx is in EM.
[2] See Eisenhower, *At Ease*, pp. 180–82.
[3] In a letter of February 5 Marx reported that his wife was much better (EM).

2009   *Eisenhower Mss.*

TO WALTER BEDELL SMITH   *January 28, 1948*

Dear Beedle: Your letter of the 17th reached me today, the 28th.[1] That means that yours was written before I finally made public a letter in which I completely and finally removed myself from the national political picture.[2] I do not know, of course, whether that letter received any publicity whatsoever in your corner of the world, but I can tell you that since its publication, I have experienced a great sense of personal freedom that I was rapidly losing. It created quite a sizeable stir in the American press because recent Gallup polls had been putting me at the top in popular choice for the Presidency. From this I assume that hopeful candidates are as much relieved as I am by the finality of my letter.

You are well acquainted with the reasons that have always made the prospect of a political career repugnant to me, but just to let you see what I had to say about the matter, I shall enclose a copy with this note. (If all this sounds a bit stuffy to you, I remind you your desk is probably situated close to your waste basket.)

Apparently the job that Kay thought she had obtained through Anna Rosenberg has not materialized.[3] At least it is not to do so for some months. It seems that it involved the development of a new type radio program in which she was to have a part because of her British accent. In any event, she is now applying to get back in the Wac's with the Air Force; my aide tells me that there is every possibility that she will be re-absorbed. She seems to live in hard luck.

Possibly you have already had a letter from Louis Marx telling you that just at the moment of birth, an accident happened to the expected twins and both were stillborn. I have written notes both to Louis and to his wife because they must be feeling terribly about the unfortunate accident.[4]

I have made up my mind to turn over to Bradley very soon. He has had plenty of opportunity to orient himself, and I think it would be far better for him to get into the swing of things now, just as budget hearings are beginning before Congress, than it would be to attempt to take over in the middle of them. During February I shall be on a temporary duty status and on leave during March and April. During all of this time, my address will remain at Fort Myer, but I may go to Hot Springs, Arkansas for a week or so of hospitalization, just to get a boiling out.[5] My reports from Walter Reed Hospital, where I went for a complete survey, are all most encouraging. They say that I am not as old as the calendar proves.

I have written to Jimmy Gault telling him that you and Nory have a permanent invitation to Culzean dating from the moment it is fit for habitation.[6] At any time that you may desire to go there, you have nothing further to do except to send a wire to Jimmy and fix it up with him. He will know whether the apartment has been completed and, if it has, your welcome will be sincere and complete. In fact, I would be highly delighted if my first guest in Culzean could be my Chief of Staff and my best friend of World War II.

Please remember me kindly to Ruth Briggs,[7] give my love to Nory, and as always, warmest regards to yourself, *Cordially*

[1] Smith's handwritten letter reported on his recent activities and said that he had "developed the nasty mind of a diplomat. . . ." He was now suspicious and not flattered when he received attention. "How our illusions disappear," he said, "as we grow older."
[2] See no. 1998.
[3] Smith had written that Anna Rosenberg had given Kay Summersby a job. On Rosenberg see no. 1039.
[4] See no. 2008.
[5] See no. 1999.
[6] The letter to Gault is no. 2011. Smith had asked Eisenhower if he and his wife might spend some time at Eisenhower's apartment in Culzean Castle.
[7] Smith's secretary (see no. 1040).

2010   *Eisenhower Mss.*

To Arthur William Tedder   *January 29, 1948*
Secret

Dear Arthur: Thank you very much for your letter of the 21st. We are sending to England in May two of our very best officers for participation in an exercise that Monty is to conduct. I think I shall merely send them ahead of time to participate first in your exercise, which sounds to me most interesting. The interval between the two exercises will give both these officers the chance to renew acquaintanceships with old friends in the UK, and I think will be a nice arrangement.[1]

Of course, Bradley may have different ideas and change this arrangement, but in any event, I can assure you that he will take advantage of your most generous offer.[2] I think I shall turn over to him about the 10th of February, but thereafter I shall be around here very closely until about May first.

Naturally I am grateful to you for giving us this chance.[3]

With warm regard, *As ever*

[1] Tedder had explained that he would conduct exercise PANDORA in early May. The purpose of PANDORA was to examine "the operational implications of scientific and technical developments affecting air warfare." The exercise would be set in 1955 and would take into consideration, separately, the conditions that would exist (1) if only conventional weapons were employed and (2) if weapons of mass destruction were used. On December 1, 1947, Eisenhower had approved Wedemeyer's recommendation (of November 28) to send Generals Gillem and McClure (COS, 1947, 091.713 Montgomery TS). For background on Gillem and McClure see no. 652. For Montgomery's training exercise scheduled for late May see no. 1782.

[2] Bradley did change the arrangement. He would send Generals Gillem and Beightler to Montgomery's exercise and Generals Taylor and Bolté to PANDORA. On March 23 Wedemeyer would direct the officers to take civilian clothes. Correspondence is in COS, 1948, 091.713 Montgomery TS. For background on Beightler see no. 832; on Taylor, no. 277; and on Bolté, no. 1133.

[3] On January 30 Air Chief Marshal Sir Guy Garrod, British Joint Services Mission, forwarded to Eisenhower a message from Air Chief Marshal Sir John Slessor, the commandant of the United Kingdom's Imperial Defence College; Slessor wanted the commandment of one of the U.S. war colleges to visit the IDC. Eisenhower wrote on Garrod's letter, "Wedemeyer—I think you'd better take charge of this from any standpoint." After Eisenhower left office, General Lyman Louis Lemnitzer would accept Garrod's invitation. Lemnitzer had been deputy commandant of the National War College since 1947. Prior to that he had been a member of the Joint Strategic Survey Committee of the JCS. (For his wartime service see Chandler, *War Years*.) Lemnitzer's visit would be scheduled to coincide with the PANDORA exercise. All correspondence is in EM.

2011   *Eisenhower Mss.*

To JAMES FREDERICK GAULT   *January 29, 1948*

Dear Jimmy: I have your two letters. Quite naturally I have no hesitancy in giving Dr. Dunning a little testimonial that he can use confidentially.[1] I would not, of course, want it to be used on a public basis, but if my bearing witness to the help he gave me will be of assistance to him, I am quite ready to have him use it in private correspondence or conference.

A note from Beedle says that he had a chance to talk to you in England and he seems quite pleased by the prospect of a possible future visit to Scotland.[2] I shall tell him that whenever he may have a chance to get over there he is simply to communicate with you, and that he has my personal standing invitation to go to Culzean whenever he can. Incidentally, I think I have emphasized to you time and again that if you should have some warm personal friend who might need a place like that for a few days, you may always, in my name or your own, extend an appropriate invitation to him. The same goes for Louis Greig.[3]

I have come to the conclusion that I should attempt to publish a war memoir.[4] My engagement to do so, however, is conditioned upon two things: First, that I myself shall become satisfied that the document I prepare is satisfactory to publish and is a worthwhile contribution to our war record; and secondly, I shall not publish anything unless some disinterested historian or technician has a chance to check the book against existing records and annotate it in such a way as to remove the suspicion that it is just another lopsided, *personal* story.

It would be great fun to talk to you and Peggy.[5] Just when Mamie and I may get a chance to come again to the UK, I cannot even guess. However, until we do, we shall continue to look forward to a chance to see you both again.

Give Peggy my love, and as always, warmest regards to yourself. *As ever*

P.S. I am enclosing the letter I am writing to Dr. Dunning.[6]

[1] Gault had forwarded to Eisenhower a request from Dr. John Jacob Dunning for a testimonial letter that would help him obtain a license to practice for six months in Monaco. (For background on Dunning and his treatment of Eisenhower see no. 627.) Gault explained that the medical trade union in Monaco was so strong that entry into practice in that principality was difficult. Thus, Dr. Dunning had been advised to apply as *Mister* Dunning to practice manipulation and physiotherapy, rather than as a doctor to practice osteopathy. Gault's two letters, both dated January 23, are in EM.
[2] See no. 2009.
[3] For background on Greig see nos. 541 and 1922.
[4] See no. 1977.
[5] Gault's wife.
[6] The next document.

2012   *Eisenhower Mss.*

To John Jacob Dunning   *January 29, 1948*

Dear Mr. Dunning:[1] During the progress of the European campaign, I came to you, upon the recommendation of friends, for treatment to relieve distress I was experiencing in joints and muscles. Through manipulation and physiotherapy you were completely successful in keeping me in a state of good health and vigor. You will recall that during the war I seized every opportunity to obtain one of these treatments because of my conviction that through them I retained a high state of physical well-being.

You are at liberty to use this letter in any private or confidential manner that you may deem suitable.[2] *Sincerely*

[1] See the previous document.

[2] In his covering letter Eisenhower repeated the request that Dunning use this testimonial in a confidential manner only. Eisenhower said, "I remain in your debt, and if this little act will help discharge even a small portion of it, I am delighted" (EM).

2013 *Eisenhower Mss.*

To Mary Watson *January 29, 1948*

Dear Miss Watson: I have your note asking for an estimate on the ability of Mrs. Mary Naiden to be of service in your bureau.[1]

I have known Mrs. Naiden for many years, and since I know nothing of the required qualifications for work in your bureau, my endorsement will necessarily be of a general nature.

Mrs. Naiden is an individual of character, discernment, good taste, and general ability. She is earnestly and sincerely interested in the welfare of this country and is intensely human and sympathetic in her approach to problems.

While it has been some years since I have had the pleasure of talking to her, I am certain that you will find the above description to be reasonably accurate today.[2] *Very sincerely*

[1] Mary Watson, Director of the Bureau of Occupations in New York City, had written Eisenhower on January 27 (EM). She asked about Mary Francis Naiden, the widow of Eisenhower's West Point classmate Brigadier General Earl Larue Naiden (who had died in 1944).

[2] This same day Eisenhower wrote in regard to another classmate, Ernest F. "Ike" Miller, whose wife had died in New York City while Miller was in Mexico (see Eisenhower to Aurand, Jan. 29, 1948, EM, Miller Corr.). For background on Miller see no. 1038.

2014 *Eisenhower Mss., Family File*

To Milton Stover Eisenhower *January 29, 1948*

Dear Milton: Thank you for your note.[1] You may be interested to know that out of all my friends only you and two others really thought I had a right to make the statement I did—and to publish it.[2]

The way it looks to me now we shall probably be in Washington during the period of your visit. Anytime you would like to see me will be O.K. If my plans firm up enough so that I can give you any exact information I will send it on to you. The reason for the uncertainty is the condition of Mamie's Dad who does not seem to be improving very much and cannot yet get out of bed. All of us will be looking forward to seeing you.[3] *As ever*

[1] Milton Eisenhower's letter of January 26 is in EM. He had forwarded a letter (dated January 24) that he had received from a friend of General Eisenhower's, Thomas D. Campbell. Despite Eisenhower's published disavowal (see no. 1998), Campbell said Eisenhower should accept a draft for the nomination. Campbell also wrote directly to Eisenhower (see no. 2020).

[2] Eisenhower replied on this same date to favorable notes about his statement from Gladys Harding Brooks (Jan. 25) and Major General Percy Poe Bishop (Jan. 26). He also answered a letter of January 25 from Henry J. White, of Sedgwick County (Kansas) Draft Eisenhower for President, Inc. All correspondence is in EM.

[3] Milton Eisenhower would be in Washington in mid-February.

2015   *Eisenhower Mss.*

To William H. Burnham   *January 29, 1948*

Dear Mr. Burnham:[1] Thank you very much for your forthright letter, which I am delighted you wrote.[2] I read it with the keenest interest. I shall always be grateful to you for the effective steps you and your associates took, during the life of the League, to keep the whole matter on the highest plane. It will never be possible for me to express the pride I have felt that so many sincere and patriotic citizens should have believed that I might serve the country effectively as its President, and worked so unselfishly in that belief.

I most earnestly hope that the public explanation I made of my convictions and of my attitude will be convincing to all Americans, particularly to those who, like yourself, ascribed to me qualities and abilities they desire in their President. They will understand, I feel sure, that in closing the door to all such prospects, I did it out of conviction and out of deep concern for what I believed best for the country—and its Army. Whatever these qualities may be, I assure you they will be fully available to the nation in my capacity as a private citizen.

Again my thanks for the honor you have paid me. I hope I may have the opportunity in the future of meeting you to express my gratitude personally.[3]

With best wishes, *Sincerely*

[1] Burnham was an investment banker in New York City and one of the leading directors of the National Draft Eisenhower League. For background see no. 2005.

² In his long letter of January 23 Burnham had analyzed the league's past and planned actions and his own role in the organization. He stressed the spontaneity of the entire Eisenhower for President movement. Burnham, who had never met Eisenhower, said that when he was asked to join the league he went to Washington, "talked with some of my Army friends and yours also, who informed me that the group running the movement in Washington on a national level would harm your reputation with the public whether you retired to private life, became the President of Columbia, or of the United States." Burnham decided to join, and he and other leaders in New York determined the movement had to be centered there, and not in Washington. "For some reason I have never been able to discover," he said, "the Washington organizers, under pressure but still voluntarily, withdrew from the scene of action with no unpleasantness and no publicity." One of those with whom Burnham had consulted in Washington was the late General Surles (see no. 1915).

³ In his response of February 9 Burnham discussed the league's decision—prompted by Eisenhower's public statement—to endorse the candidacy of the former governor of Minnesota, Harold Edward Stassen.

2016   *Eisenhower Mss.*

To Lynn Townsend White, Jr.   *January 29, 1948*

*Dear President White:*¹ I am quite overwhelmed by the kind sentiments expressed in your letter.² While I had not thought of my recently published statement as anything of lasting value, it is quite true that I worked on it very hard in an effort to be completely honest and straightforward and without seeming to deny the principle of readiness to respond to duty. There is, I believe, always a personal obligation implicit in our form of government and, even at the expense of verbosity, I felt it necessary to show why, in this particular instance, the door leading to a political career could be shut without violating a fundamental.

Naturally I doubt that Mr. Aldrich will look upon the document with the same generous eyes as you do.³ However, in the event that he should do so and wants to follow your suggestion, I could not, in all good conscience, object. To get the original of the letter, he would have to apply to Mr. Finder, to whom it was written.

Please let me assure you that the receipt of such a letter as yours from any American—and more particularly when it comes from one of your distinguished record—gives to me a sense of pride that is probably close to sinful, but it is certainly heart-warming. *Very sincerely*

¹ White, president of Mills College, had received his Ph.D. in history from Harvard in 1934. He had taught at Princeton and Stanford before assuming the presidency of Mills in 1943.

² White had forwarded a copy of a letter he had written to Winthrop Williams Aldrich, who was chairman of the board of trustees of the American Heritage

Foundation, which sponsored the Freedom Train. (For background on the train see no. 1854.) White asked Aldrich to consider including Eisenhower's statement about withdrawing from the election (no. 1998) as an exhibit. He characterized Eisenhower's act as "paralleled only by Washington's refusal of a third term..." (White to Eisenhower, with enclosure, Jan. 26, 1948, EM).
³ Aldrich (LL.B. Harvard 1910) was chairman of the board of the Chase National Bank of New York.

2017   *P&O 313.5, Case 115/5*

TO JOINT CHIEFS OF STAFF   *[January 30, 1948]*
Confidential

Memorandum by the Chief of Staff, U.S. Army:

Subject: Release of Information to the Public From Historical Documents of World War II[1]
    Reference: JCS 802 series

    1. The inclosed memoranda (Annex A & B) set forth the Army policy and procedure with respect to public right of access to the historical records of the Army's operations.[2] I believe that you will agree that the right of our citizens to the full story of our national war effort applies with equal effect to all three of the armed forces.

    2. The major campaigns of the Army in the last war were parts of a pattern of coordinated action by our own ground, air and naval forces and those of our allies. They were executed under Supreme Allied Commanders or Commanders-in-Chief responsible to the Combined or to the Joint Chiefs of Staff, respectively. As a result most historical records of major commands of Army Forces contain information which United States or Allied authority outside the jurisdiction of the War Department has safeguarded from disclosure. These safeguards, even the ones that are manifestly obsolete, the Department of the Army as successor to the War Department has a duty to respect.

    3. The Army, working to the full extent of its authority, has systematically cleared security classification from a large measure of its historical records of most interest and value to the public. However, it is hard to conceive of any comprehensive history of the Army's major operations in World War II which might be compiled without reference to Army papers now safeguarded in the interest of other agencies or governments. Public access to such of those papers as no longer require protection is hampered by lack of a uniform policy among the armed forces, lack of an efficient means of downgrading security classifications of joint interest, and lack of a policy agreement between the National

2212

Military Establishment and the corresponding agencies of our principal allies with respect to release of information of interest to United States Forces but safeguarded by direction of Inter-Allied Organization.[3]

4. I therefore recommend that the Joint Chiefs of Staff:

a. Adopt a uniform policy with reference to public access to information in the records of World War II pertaining to all three Departments similar to that expressed in the attached annexes and examine existing policy with a view to liberalization.

b. Designate an agency empowered to review and regrade the security classifications of documents classified by elements of the National Military Establishment and to represent the Joint Chiefs of Staff in negotiating agreements for downgrading the security classification of information safeguarded by direction of Inter-Allied agencies.[4]

[1] For background on this issue see no. 1899. Wedemeyer had sent Eisenhower this document, together with a covering memo and a lengthy staff study of the problem, on this same day. Knowlton forwarded the memo to the JCS, where it became JCS 802/6, of February 6. Two previous memoranda on this subject—protesting cuts in a manuscript submitted by the First Army—had been drawn up on December 2 and 8, but neither memo had been sent to the Joint Chiefs (ABC 380.01 [5-10-43], Sec. 1-C).

[2] Appendix A was a copy of Eisenhower's directive of November 20, 1947 (no. 1873). Appendix B was a proposed directive governing access to the Army's World War II records by "responsible historians and writers." On this same day Eisenhower had approved the directive and a press release announcing that about 80 percent of the Army's official documents pertaining to operations of the Army in World War II were now available for research. The War Department had already published general guidelines on the release of military information in Memorandum No. 360-25-1, of January 7, 1948 (CCS 380.01 [12-30-43], Sec. 2).

[3] In his memo to Eisenhower, Wedemeyer argued that the current difficulties "arise principally from the cumbersome and ineffective machinery available for obtaining the necessary declassification agreements in connection with documents of joint and combined interest in Army custody."

[4] On February 6 the JCS would refer Eisenhower's memo to the JIC (CCS 311.5 [6-9-42], Sec. 5). When Eisenhower left office there was still no single agency with the authority to declassify or even to coordinate the declassification of documents. For an indictment of the declassification policies see Carol M. Barker and Matthew H. Fox, *Classified Files: The Yellowing Pages* (New York, 1972).

2018 *Eisenhower Mss.*

To WALTER GRESHAM ANDREWS *January 30, 1948*

Dear Ham: For some months I have been most hopeful that one of the pieces of legislation that would be on the books before my retirement as Chief of Staff would be the WAC Bill. It is now too late for that but I retain my deep interest in this necessary piece of legislation.[1]

Attached to this personal note is a letter which I have written to you on a more formal basis as I thought it might be of some use to you when you come to take up the matter—which I trust will be very soon.[2]

I am sending a short letter also to Mr. Vinson, as the ranking Democrat on your Committee, expressing ideas similar to those that are in the attached communication to you.[3]

With warm personal regard,[4] *Sincerely*

[1] For background see no. 1666.

[2] The next document.

[3] The letter to Congressman Carl Vinson, of Georgia, is in EM. On February 7 Eisenhower also wrote a letter supporting the bill to the chairman of the subcommittee considering the legislation (see Eisenhower to Shafer, in COS, 1947, 324.5 WAC).

[4] Public Law 625 would be signed by the President on June 12, 1948. The act established the WAC as part of the Regular Army and the Army Reserve and made similar provisions for the Air Force, the Navy, and the Marines. Under this law the Regular Army WAC could not exceed 2 percent of the authorized total strength of the Regular Army (U.S., *Statutes at Large*, vol. 62, pp. 356–75).

2019   *Eisenhower Mss.*

To WALTER GRESHAM ANDREWS   *January 30, 1948*

Dear Mr. Chairman:[1] The so-called WAC Bill, now in your Committee, is designed to provide the Army with assistance that it sorely needs. It is one of the pieces of legislation that I had earnestly hoped would be enacted before my forthcoming retirement as Chief of Staff. While I realize that this cannot now come to pass I am writing this letter to urge early and favorable consideration on the part of your Committee.

It is clearly evident that for some years to come the Army must remain relatively strong. To execute our occupational duties effectively, to say nothing of keeping prepared—even in the most sketchy manner—to meet security problems of the post-war world, our currently authorized strength of 670,000 is truly a minimum. At the beginning of 1947 it was decided that we should return to a voluntary method of sustaining the Regular Army. All of us realize that to achieve even approximate success we must widen, so far as is feasible and practicable, the base of recruitment. We must not exclude capable, qualified women who volunteer services which the Army so urgently needs. As of this date we are approximately 110,000 short of the minimum total number we need in the Army, and the result has been that occupational commanders, particularly General MacArthur, have reported to us in the most urgent terms that something must be done to reinforce them quickly unless serious circumstances are to develop.[2]

At the beginning of the war, I was among those who opposed the formation of the WAC. I first met them in Africa and every phase of the record they compiled during the war convinced me of the error of my first reaction.

In tasks for which they are particularly suited, WACs are more valuable than men, and fewer of them are required to perform a given amount of work. As telephone operators, clerks, stenographers and secretaries, as statisticians, interpreters of aerial photos, and as technicians in various types of hospital and other work, their performance was and continues to be outstanding.

In the disciplinary field they were, throughout the war, a model for the Army. Throughout three years' experience with them in Europe I cannot recall but one case among the WACs that was serious enough to be brought to my personal attention. More than this, their influence throughout the whole command was good. Carefully supervised, presenting a picture of model deportment and neatness, their presence was always reflected around a headquarters in improved conduct on the part of all.

In the event of another war, which would be even more truly global than the last in its effects upon the entire population, it is my conviction that everybody in this country would serve under some form of call to duty. The services then of women, both in uniform and in essential industry, would be mandatory. In order to be ready to absorb that portion of American womanhood which would be serving in uniform, we must maintain in time of peace a suitable nucleus. These individuals will not only serve as the framework for absorbing hundreds and thousands of women and utilizing them more effectively and quickly, but they will likewise, in peace, be developing plans, regulations, and methods that apply peculiarly to the women in uniform.

As matters now stand, the WAC will cease to exist on June 30, 1948. This means that in the occupational areas WACs must begin coming home no later than the month of March. To replace them from enlisted men of the Army *is an impossibility* not merely from the standpoint of equal standards in the work that they perform but from the standpoint of numbers. This indicates not only the need for the legislation but for speed in its enactment.

I assure you that I look upon this measure as a "must", because the Corps is necessary both as a measure for assisting the Army during these troubled and almost chaotic times and as a guarantee that we will be better prepared in the event another grave emergency should strike. You are at perfect liberty to quote me privately and publicly in this matter. I should like to say also that even after I have retired as Chief of Staff, in the event that your Committee should want me to appear before it, I will always do so gladly and promptly in order to express my earnest conviction that in enacting this legislation the Congress would be acting in the best interests of the country. *Sincerely*

[1] See the previous document.
[2] See for example no. 1493.

2020 *Eisenhower Mss.*

To THOMAS DONALD CAMPBELL *January 30, 1948*

Dear Tom: Thank you very much for your long letter which, as is usual with your communications, was packed with interest.[1]

I am sorry that you were disappointed in my decision. I felt that it was one I should make and the only question was the advisability of its publication. I did what I thought was correct under the circumstances and I cannot agree with you that the country will suffer as a result of it.

I continue to have the liveliest interest in the results of your experiment in getting water out of solid rock.[2] I don't know whether I'll ever be able to come and see the test with my own eyes but I shall certainly expect you to give me the details of whatever results you obtain.

It now looks as if I would stay around in this region during my leave. I have finally made up my mind to do some writing and it is almost impossible to accomplish this except in close proximity to War Department records. Since I shall have to accumulate a little staff to help me I cannot get up and run around with the abandon that I should really have liked to exercise. Consequently if you are in this region at any time up to the first of May you can get in touch with me either by calling Fort Myer or by calling my old office here in the War Department. Someone will be bound to know where I am.

With warm personal regard, *Cordially*

[1] For background see no. 2014. Campbell, in his letter of January 28, had said that Eisenhower's decision not to seek the presidency "affected me second only to the death of President Roosevelt" (EM).
[2] Campbell had brought Eisenhower up-to-date on his continuing efforts in this field.

2021 *Eisenhower Mss.*

To ROY ALLISON ROBERTS *January 30, 1948*

Dear Roy: Thank you very much for your note and for the understanding implicit in the newspaper piece you wrote about my public statement.[1] Frankly, during the days that I was trying to decide whether or not it was wise to make an additional public statement, I felt a great desire to confer with you. In all our talks, on every subject, you have always shown to me such a broad and common sense attitude toward intricate problems that I should have liked very much to have had the benefit of your counsel.

Essentially it was of course a question that I had to decide for myself. You will be interested to know, however, that out of all my friends, political and non-political, only two stood firmly by me in my decision that I should make a statement, but I believe I was right in doing so. In addition to the reasons given in the letter to Mr. Finder,[2] you know of some of the others that troubled me in this connection; particularly my concern for the eventual reaction upon the Army itself. In any event, I tried very hard to keep personal desire and convenience out of my mental processes.

You can imagine that I have been experiencing a great sense of relief the past few days.

Thanks again for your thoughtfulness in writing to me. *Sincerely*

[1] Roberts had written on January 27, forwarding a copy of an article he had published in his paper, the *Kansas City Star*. Roberts called Eisenhower's withdrawal from the presidential campaign "the statement of a patriot." Roberts's letter and the article are in EM. For background on Roberts see no. 1538.
[2] No. 1998.

2022   *Eisenhower Mss.*

To Joseph Hudson Short, Jr.   *January 30, 1948*

Dear Mr. Short: This note is to confirm my acceptance of your invitation to come to luncheon on February 5.[1] I profoundly hope that nothing much is expected in the way of a "speech". Certainly I shall have no time to prepare anything and shall, as usual, have to talk off the cuff. Also, as usual, I shall be very glad to subject myself to a question period if that should fit in with your plans.[2] *Sincerely*

[1] Short received his B.A. from the Virginia Military Institute in 1925 and began his newspaper career that same year as a reporter for the *Jackson* (Mississippi) *Daily News*. Since 1943 he had been with the Washington bureau of the *Baltimore Sun*. As president of the National Press Club, he had written to confirm Eisenhower's verbal acceptance of this invitation (Jan. 28, 1948, EM).
[2] In response to one of the questions at the luncheon Eisenhower said that he did not believe the Soviets intended to provoke a war deliberately. "We are afraid of stupid things starting a stupid war. Little sparks start big fires." In response to another question Eisenhower pointed out that "Europe, west of the Volga, is the most important area of the world from our viewpoint" (*New York Times*, Feb. 6, 1948).

Memorandum for Secretary Forrestal: Mr. Eberstadt's[1] memorandum makes sense to me.[2]

I now see that I have been assuming too much in the way of crediting the existence and prior approval of a plan roughly conforming to the points made by Mr. Eberstadt. In conversations with numbers of governmental and other people, they have constantly emphasized that the whole Marshall project is based upon the theory that 16 countries will get together, will accomplish among themselves the greatest possible degree of self-help, and that the American loans will be applied to the net deficit in the rehabilitation of Europe, rather than in meeting the sum total of separately calculated and uncoordinated requirements.[3] To me this has always meant a virtual economic union with realistic rates of international exchange among all.

The argument that to require these things as conditions precedent to the employment of American dollars would constitute unwarranted interference in domestic economics and would be an infringement of sovereignty is, to me, completely academic and invalid. On the other hand, it is obviously important that ideological enemies are not given the chance to use this argument as a means of beating out our brains while we pour out the dollars. The need, therefore, for the most skillful coordination between State Department policy and administration of these loans is abundantly clear.

If I were in a position of responsibility with regard to this matter, I think I would try to force Bernie Baruch to undertake the initial job of administration. In spite of his age, he has realism, the ability to attach to himself skillful and devoted technical advisers, *a commanding presence*, and an extraordinary ability in negotiation. Added to all this, his partial deafness would make him impervious to many of the whimperings, whinings, and pleadings that will be poured, from all sides, upon the man who is going to have control of so many millions and billions of dollars. I know of no man who, I believe, would have more influence than would he in wheedling and forcing the countries of Europe to do their part in this great program, or who would be more adamant in protecting our own interests.

Incidentally, here is another thought that may not have so far occurred to you. Some kind of *political* accord may have to be achieved among these European countries before they will be willing to make the required economic concessions. In each country every economic concession will be bitterly opposed by whatever segment of the population feels itself thereby damaged. To blunt the virulence and effectiveness of their attacks, governments should be able to point to some kind of political agreement, because thus each will be able to say that it is helping Allies and, therefore, itself. A possible practicable approach would be to establish a Combined Chiefs of Staff for the study of common defense problems; to such a body, even though consultative only, each country could point as evidence of a definite accord.

It is useless to minimize the tremendous political obstacles that each government will have to surmount in order to implement sound economic concessions, and I believe that some approach similar to the one suggested might be of assistance.

These things are none of my business and my ideas may be completely screwy. Anyway, they are communicated only to you and you are quite free to aim this at the wastebasket.[4]

[1] For background on Eberstadt see no. 206.

[2] Eberstadt apparently had brought to Forrestal's attention a letter written by William Chamberlain and published in the *Commercial and Financial Chronicle* (Dec. 25, 1947). Chamberlain's letter was critical of the proposals to aid Europe, as set forth in the Marshall Plan. He said that "the principal countries of Western Europe are in economic chains of their own forging. . . . they cannot recover until freed, and their freedom is to be had only through drastic political and economic reforms." Forrestal sent Eisenhower the article and a note on January 20 (OS/D, 47–49, Cent. Numeric File, D 19-1-44), and Eisenhower returned both with the following handwritten comments: "The piece is well worth reading. It is forceful, but lopsided. The true answer, it seems to me, lies somewhere between the 'do nothing but lecture Europe on "freeing her people"' advocated here—and the unwise giving of gratuity without demanding, as its price, the doing of some of the things herein advocated. The cost should be much less." Forrestal passed Eisenhower's reaction on to Eberstadt on January 23, and Eberstadt replied with a January 27 letter and the memorandum to which Eisenhower refers (in *ibid.*).

Eberstadt's letter said that he had been "very much interested" in Eisenhower's comments. Eberstadt did not think "that Chamberlain would differ with the General." Chamberlain's article, said Eberstadt, was "a sort of protest" concerning the "reluctance to attach reasonable conditions to the aid" that the United States was then considering for Western Europe (see n. 3 below). Eberstadt, for his part, feared that "in our eagerness to lend our money, or to give it away, we are failing to attach such reasonable conditions as are essential to rendering the aid effective and to reaching the great objective that we have in mind, namely, the restoration of the Western European economy." In his memorandum he listed four preconditions for American aid to Europe: currency stabilization; establishment of realistic exchange rates; removal of trade barriers; and acceptance of the idea that the aid should be in the form of loans rather than grants. If the Europeans met these preconditions, Eberstadt predicted, exports and private capital would furnish "substantial additional sums," and the United States would not have to advance excessive amounts to achieve recovery. Forrestal had sent Eberstadt's letter and memorandum, together with a covering note, to Eisenhower on January 29 (EM).

[3] For background on the Marshall Plan see the sources cited in no. 1482, n. 6. Also see Ernst H. van der Beugel, *From Marshall Aid to Atlantic Partnership: European Integration as a Concern of American Foreign Policy* (Amsterdam, 1966);

and Daniel Yergin, *Shattered Peace: The Origins of the Cold War and the National Security State* (Boston, 1977).

Responding to Secretary of State Marshall's speech of June 5, 1947, representatives of sixteen European nations had met to formulate a plan for using American aid to reconstruct their economies. They completed their work in September, and in December President Truman sent to Congress a bill calling for $17 billion in aid for Europe. The Senate Committee on Foreign Relations heard testimony on the European Recovery Program throughout January 1948. The European Recovery Act, authorizing an initial appropriation of $5.3 billion to carry out the Marshall Plan, would be passed after Eisenhower left office.

[4] On January 31 Forrestal sent Eisenhower's letter and the communication from Eberstadt to Undersecretary of State Robert Lovett.

2024 *Eisenhower Mss.*

To John Hennessy *January 31, 1948*

Dear Mr. Hennessy: The copy of your report[1] reached my desk only an hour before I received further word that you were awaiting its return so that it could go to the printer. Consequently, I have no time for detailed comment; on the other hand, I have read it hastily and see no reason why you should not publish it exactly as it is.

So far as the Department is concerned, I think the only point that will be seriously argued is the advisability of expanding the Quartermaster General's exclusive authority over Army schools.[2] Within recent weeks we have been trying hard to achieve a greater degree of decentralization to the Army Commands and, of course, this particular recommendation would, if adopted, be a step in the other direction. However, a re-study of the whole matter may prove it to be necessary. In any event, all these things can be finally determined after your report has reached the hands of the staff.[3]

Certainly we are again indebted to you and to your group for your constant readiness to cooperate with us in this important matter. I hope that all of you know that I am personally very deeply appreciative. *Sincerely*

[1] "A Report of Army Food Service Controls" (Jan. 26, 1948, in COS, 1948, 430). For background on Hennessy and the attempts to improve the Army's food-service program see nos. 835 and 1311.

[2] Eisenhower had questioned this recommendation before (see no. 1311). According to War Department Circular 8, of January 13, 1948, each Army commander was responsible for the operation and administration of the food-service schools within his area (COS, 1948, 430).

[3] The report was printed; on March 19 Eisenhower's successor, General Bradley, would send letters to the Army commanders urging them to make further improvements in food service (*ibid.*).

To Thomas Jefferson Davis   *January 31, 1948*

Dear T.J.: It has been so long since I have been able to pry a word out of
you that I have some misgivings as to your current state of health.[1] I
hope that you will reassure me instantly that you are feeling fine and
that you and Nina[2] and the girls are all happy and well.

I am counting on stepping out of the Chief of Staff job next Saturday, the 7th. In going back over the many pleasant things that happened
to me in the Army, none of them looms up as of more importance than
my long friendship with you.

I am certainly looking forward to an opportunity, one of these bright
days, to spend some time with you, either in a fishing boat, or maybe
with our feet propped up on a convenient railing.

With love to your family, and as always, warmest regards to yourself. *Cordially*

[1] Brigadier General Davis had retired on October 31, 1946, and was now farming
in South Carolina. For background on Davis see no. 1006.
[2] Davis's wife.

To Edgar Newton Eisenhower   *January 31, 1948*

Dear Ed: Yesterday I learned that Bernice has had to go back to the
hospital, this time with terrific complications to her former illness.[1] I
know how terribly you must be feeling, particularly because of your
entire inability to do anything about it.

When any individual is undergoing such a trial, ridden by grief and
distress, he is likely to be entirely unappreciative of any philosophical
words from friends and relatives. I shall not attempt to write any such;
but I do want you to know how earnestly I sympathize with you and
how sincerely I wish there were something I could do to help.

I hope that the knowledge that you have done and are doing all that is
within your power will prevent you from allowing your burden to grow
completely unbearable.

Mamie and I send to you and yours our deepest affections and regard.[2] *As ever*

[1] Eisenhower had learned of Mrs. Edgar Eisenhower's illness in a letter from
James Stack (see the next document).
[2] Bernice Eisenhower died on March 13, 1948.

2027 *Eisenhower Mss.*

To James Stack   *January 31, 1948*

Dear Jim: Thank you very much for writing me the letter about Ed.[1] I have dispatched a note to him.[2]

With regard to yourself, I hope that you will not allow yourself to become so immersed in Red Cross activity that you damage your health.[3]

Give my love to Elsa and the children, and as always, with warmest regard to yourself. *Cordially*

[1] Stack's letter of January 28 is in EM.
[2] The previous document.
[3] Stack said he had agreed to head the annual Red Cross drive in Pierce County, Washington, which included Tacoma, where Stack now lived.

2028 *Eisenhower Mss.*

To James Vincent Forrestal   *January 31, 1948*

Memorandum for Secretary Forrestal: Perhaps I can go to Chicago but, if so, it will have to be in May.[1]

I shall write a letter to Mr. Trees.[2]

[1] Forrestal had asked Eisenhower to accept an invitation to speak at the Commercial Club of Chicago, an organization of business leaders (memorandum, Jan. 29, 1948). Eisenhower had already been in correspondence with the group and had written on January 20 and 21 that he could not come in March. Forrestal said he wanted Eisenhower to accept this speaking engagement so that he could counter the charges leveled by the *Chicago Tribune*, which was "constantly slamming the defense set-up." All correspondence is in EM.
[2] Eisenhower would write Mr. Merle Jay Trees, president of the club, on March 10 to say that he would address the group in May. All correspondence is in EM.

2029 *Eisenhower Mss.*

To Henry Maitland Wilson   *February 2, 1948*

Dear Jumbo: Thanks so much for your nice letter.[1] Your friendship has been one of the fine things the war brought to me.

At the end of this week, I shall turn over to Bradley, and Mamie and

I will be free for the first real vacation in many years. Then off to new adventure in education. I think I will like it very much, but the prospect is naturally challenging to an old soldier.

I hope the future will be good to you and that it may bring you again to this country before many months have elapsed.

With warm regard,[2] *As ever*

[1] Field Marshal Wilson had written on January 25 to wish Eisenhower success and good luck in his "new assignment" at Columbia (EM).

[2] Eisenhower signed this letter after returning from a trip earlier in the day to Norfolk, Virginia, where he addressed the incoming class of the Armed Forces Staff College. Correspondence concerning the trip is in EM.

2030   *Eisenhower Mss.*

To Cornelius Wendell Wickersham   *February 3, 1948*

Dear Neil:[1] Entirely aside from the problem of writing a definitive history of the American Military Government development in World War II I have been puzzling over what I could say on this subject in a memoir I am trying to write. From my viewpoint I should like to have, say, two or three paragraphs dealing with the Mediterranean campaign which would tell about the concept of the Military Government organization, the method of approach, and the results accomplished, particularly in their effect upon the furtherance of the military operation. Later, in dealing with the European campaign, I should like to put in a page or two to show the planning for that military occupation and, very briefly, some of the problems encountered.[2]

My own difficulty is that I am frightened of saying something that might not conform to fact and, on the other hand, omitting features that may have been, from the viewpoint of the Military Government people, the most critical part of the whole thing.

Naturally I am not attempting to write a history of that particular development but I do not want my account to be badly out of balance, which it would be if I don't include a little story of the great place Military Government had in attaining and stabilizing the victory.

I hope you can give me a suggestion as to what I should do.[3] *Sincerely*

[1] For background on Wickersham see no. 1373.

[2] For Wickersham's service in military government during World War II see Chandler, *War Years.*

[3] In a letter of February 6 Wickersham offered to draft some comments. The letter, his draft, and further correspondence are in EM.

2031 *Eisenhower Mss.*

To Mrs. Russell J. Plue *February 3, 1948*

Dear Mrs. Plue: I was touched by the sincerity of your letter, and have had your husband's case re-examined.[1] I do not mind telling you that had the selection of officers for the Regular Army been in my personal hands, the record he has established would have been practically overwhelming evidence in his favor. The process of selection was, however, removed completely from the hands of any individual—I assure you that it was so arranged that no amount of political pressure or pull could have any possible effect.[2] This does not mean that mistakes could not have been made but the provisions of the law were carried out in strict compliance with all of the regulations necessary to insure complete freedom from any type of outside influence.

Because of your husband's splendid combat record and the straightforwardness of your letter I am particularly distressed to have to tell you that I know of no way in which the matter can be reopened. I am glad that you wrote to me so as to give me a chance to explain the method used in absorbing wartime officers in the Regular service and to extend to you and your husband my very earnest wishes for success in some other line of endeavor. *Sincerely*

[1] Mrs. Plue, of Frankfort, Kentucky, had written Eisenhower on January 27 to ask if he could help her husband obtain a commission in the Regular Army. She said that Captain Plue had been discharged from the Army on January 3, 1946. He had passed examinations for reentry into the Army, but The Adjutant General had informed him that he was ineligible (COS, 1948, Index, 201 Plue).
[2] On the process of selection see no. 783.

2032 *Eisenhower Mss.*

To Frank Copeland Page *February 3, 1948*

Dear Frank:[1] No letter that I have received made me feel better than did yours.[2] You revealed the habitual characteristic of a friend, which is to be over-generous in his praise. Nevertheless I must say that I like to read it.

The last time I saw Arthur[3] he told me you were coming along very well. I sincerely trust that you are on the road to full and complete recovery. I am looking forward to seeing you often when I come to New York, which should be about May 1.

Mamie is ill for the moment but when I go home this evening I will tell her of your message. She will be delighted, because the Page family ranks awfully high with her.

With warm personal regard, *Cordially*

[1] For background on Page see no. 764.
[2] Page's January 28 letter said that Eisenhower had "made a very wise move" in withdrawing his name from the presidential race (see no. 1998). Page said that "no man in the United States has had any finer career than yours" and added that he believed that Eisenhower would contribute a great deal to the country and the world as president of Columbia University (EM).
[3] Arthur Eisenhower.

2033   *Eisenhower Mss.*

To VERNON ASHTON HOBART STURDEE   *February 3, 1948*

Dear General Sturdee:[1] General Chapman has just brought your very kind message to my office.[2] I am touched by your thoughtfulness and truly appreciate your good wishes and felicitations.

Although I soon shall go off the active list, in a very real sense I shall never really retire from the Army. For many years I have lived by certain simple principles and truths that I cannot possibly desert merely because of an impending change in occupation. Many of these principles involve purposes that encompass, of course, all democratic nations. I assure you that I will watch the development of your great country and its security forces with continuing and sympathetic concern.

One of the fine things the war brought to me was friendship with many individuals of various countries. Among these I treasure highly those that I made with your own armed forces.

Again my thanks for your thoughtful message. *Sincerely*

[1] Lieutenant General Sturdee had been Chief of the Australian General Staff since 1945. He had headed the Australian Military Mission to Washington from 1942 to 1944 and had subsequently commanded the First Australian Army.
[2] Major General John Austin Chapman had delivered Sturdee's message of appreciation (of February 3) for Eisenhower's services during World War II. Chapman had been Chief of the Australian Military Mission since 1946. Before assuming that post, he had been Deputy Chief of the Australian General Staff.

2034   *Eisenhower Mss.*

To EDWARD GILL SHERBURNE   *February 3, 1948*

Dear Eddie:[1] As always, it was a great pleasure to hear from you.

You are putting your hand to a good cause as Chairman of the Red Cross Drive in your district.[2] Everyone appreciates the outstanding work of the Red Cross in alleviating hardship and disaster within our own country but the veteran has a special esteem for the organization that followed him the world over with its heart-warming services.

I wish you good luck and every success in the 1948 Campaign. With warm regard,[3] *Sincerely*

[1] Colonel Sherburne, a West Point classmate of Eisenhower's, had served in the Island Base Command and the 3d Service Command during World War II. He had retired on May 31, 1946, due to a disability.
[2] In a letter of January 27 Sherburne had asked Eisenhower to send him a message that he could use in the Red Cross drive in Rock Hill, South Carolina, where he now lived. Carroll drafted this reply.
[3] Eisenhower added a postscript: "Use this note in any way you choose!" Sherburne had the letter published in the February 28 Rock Hill *Herald* (copy in EM).

2035   *Eisenhower Mss.*

To Louis Alfred Merillat, Jr.   *February 4, 1948*

Dear Merry:[1] I was shocked and distressed by your letter which was the first inkling I had of your serious illness.[2] I am terribly sorry and can only hope that possibly something could be done to clear up your condition.

I have directed the Surgeon General to investigate immediately the matters you report. It will take a little time as they don't have your records here, but in the meantime I will ask General Walker in Chicago to have his Surgeon come to see you, just in case he can help in some way.[3] I hope you won't consider it an intrusion.

With warm regard and boundless sympathy in your burden,[4] *Sincerely*

[1] Colonel Merillat, a West Point classmate of Eisenhower's, had been wounded in action in World War I. He had left active service in 1922, but he had returned to active duty during World War II. He was now living in Chicago.
[2] We have been unable to locate Merillat's letter. Carroll drafted this response for General Eisenhower.
[3] General Walker was the commander of the Fifth Army, in Chicago (see no. 1146). Eisenhower's letter of February 4 and Walker's affirmative response of February 9 are both in EM.
[4] Eisenhower added this postscript: "I turn over to Brad next Saturday. If there is the slightest thing we can do, write to either of us. As always—and with sincere prayers for your recovery." Merillat, who had cancer, died on April 26 and was buried on April 28 at Arlington Cemetery. Eisenhower was an honorary pallbearer.

2036   *Eisenhower Mss.*

To Marion H. Huff   *February 4, 1948*

Dear Marion:[1] Your letter reminds me to what extent we allow preoccupations and daily duties to lead us into a seeming neglect of old friends.

Frankly, in late years it has become so difficult to carry on a satisfactory correspondence with anyone that I suppose I could be charged with indifference.[2] That, however, is not the reason. Until the past few years I've always carried on a lively correspondence. Now, I seem to do nothing except what the Army demands.

I quite agree with what you had to say about the importance of attempting to lead young Americans into the habit of thinking of our national problems from the basis of simple, honest principles, so that they may face anything that comes with the certainty that they are standing on a firm foundation and not merely whirling around in a state of complete mental confusion.[3] While I do not anticipate that at Columbia I shall be too directly concerned with details of instruction and other activities that are the specific concern of deans and professors, I do hope that the preaching of a few simple, basic truths will have some gradual effect in assisting toward the main goal of getting the future leaders to think clearly and objectively.

With respect to my recent public statement,[4] I never at any time had the slightest intention of becoming involved in partisan politics. The only real problem I had to solve was how to state my position on the matter without seeming to be a very egotistical, even selfish, individual. I hope I have said all on this subject that I shall ever have to say.

With thanks for your nice letter and the wish that you may soon be fully recovered in health.[5] *Sincerely*

[1] For background on Mrs. Huff see no. 624.
[2] Mrs. Huff had expressed disappointment that the passage of time had caused their friendship to wane (Jan. 31, 1948, EM).
[3] She wrote, "To have the opportunity to encourage and direct intelligent young minds and instil them with realism, without sacrificing idealism, is an enviable challenge."
[4] See no. 1998.
[5] Mrs. Huff said she was "laid up with the Flu bug."

2037   *Eisenhower Mss., Family File*

To Arthur B. Eisenhower   *February 4, 1948*

Dear Art: . . . I cannot recall whether I wrote to you after receiving your note about my "public" letter.[1] In any event I am glad that you approved the course I took. My critics are continuing to look for the "loophole" because they say there is bound to be one in an 800-word letter. Others—and quite a number of them—have challenged the right of any American to say what he would or would not do for his country. As to the first group of critics, I can only say that they apparently like the smart Aleck type of statement rather than an honest explanation of the factors that must appeal to an honest man as applicable in such a situation. As for the second group, I think they are straining at a principle that, no matter how sound it may be, is still an academic one when applied to every special case, such as, for example, to a professional soldier. On the whole, however, I have been highly gratified to find that my correspondence, as well as the mass of editorial comment, approves of the sentiments I expressed.

Please give my very best to George Dillon[2] and to any others I may know in the Bank. *As ever*

[1] Arthur Eisenhower's January 23 letter said, "Congratulations on your great decision. George Dillon wants to join me in this statement" (EM). The public letter is no. 1998.
[2] George Wesley Dillon was a vice-president and director of Arthur Eisenhower's firm, the Commerce Trust Company of Kansas City, Missouri.

2038   *Eisenhower Mss.*

To Mark Wayne Clark   *February 5, 1948*

Dear Wayne: Even though I've already informed you verbally of what I shall tell you in this letter, its writing is such a disagreeable task that I hesitate to pass it on to Brad.

Effective 30 June of this year, the Officer Personnel Act limits the number of four-star generals and above on active duty to five. This means that three generals will have to be reduced to lieutenant general by that date. Having only five of the four-star grade authorized, the seven Army Commanders will necessarily have to be lieutenant generals, as I told you even before you came home. You must expect, therefore, to be reduced to lieutenant general on 30 June of this year.[1]

It's always a disappointment to go backward. But I think that the Army has, following this war, done a decent job as compared to what happened to all our officers right after World War I.

In any event, your reputation and record are secure—the requirements of peacetime law will have no effect.[2]

With warm personal regard, *As ever*

[1] For background on this problem see no. 2001. Clark commanded the Sixth Army. Eisenhower wrote a similar letter this same day to Hodges, who was commanding the First Army (EM). He had written to Handy, who commanded the Fourth Army, on January 26.
[2] The law would be changed in 1948, and neither Clark, Handy, nor Hodges would be reduced to lieutenant general on June 30 (see U.S., *Statutes at Large*, vol. 62, p. 1069).

To Joint Chiefs of Staff   *February 6, 1948*
Top secret

Memorandum by the Chief of Staff, U.S. Army:

Subject: Troop Strength in Japan and Korea[1]

1. In light of the critical manpower shortages of the Army, I have had prepared the inclosed study for priority consideration by the Joint Chiefs of Staff.[2] The Department of the Army is prepared to have repeated for the Joint Chiefs the troop deployment presentation on which was based the decision relative to FECOM strength, 30 June 1948.[3]

2. I recommend vigorously that the conclusions of the inclosed study be approved and that the message to CINCFE in Appendix C of the study be dispatched by the Joint Chiefs of Staff as a matter of priority.[4]

[1] When selective service ended, the Army was concerned that actual strength would drop below the authorized levels (see no. 1769). These authorized limits were already lower than Eisenhower and others felt they should be, given the Army's responsibilities (see for example no. 1696). At Eisenhower's direction, P&O had undertaken a new study of the troop allocations and missions of its various commands in January 1948 (Seedlock, Memo for Record, Feb. 6, 1948, and other documents in P&O 320.2 TS, Case 87/2). P&O's study of February 5, 1948, predicted that on June 30, 1948, the Army would be some 140,000 below the desired strength of 669,000 (these figures did not include the Air Force). In light of this situation, President Truman would ask Congress for immediate legislation authorizing either UMT or selective service (Clyde Edward Jacobs and John F. Gallagher, *The Selective Service Act: A Case Study of the Governmental Process* [New York, 1968], pp. 43–44).
[2] Wedemeyer prepared this memorandum, a covering memo, and a brief for Eisenhower. Knowlton forwarded Eisenhower's memorandum to the Joint Chiefs, and it became JCS 1834, of February 7, 1948. All papers are in the same file as this document. The appendices are not printed here.
[3] On January 1, 1948, the Far East Command's actual strength was 142,000, or 10,000 below the strength forecasted for that date. The Army forces in Korea had assumed the bulk of the deficit. Eisenhower, after listening to P&O's presentation on February 3, had approved a troop strength of approximately 134,000 for the Far East Command (FECOM); this was more than 53,000 below MacArthur's currently stated requirements. Eisenhower had directed that this problem be explained to the JCS at their February 11 luncheon. Wedemeyer felt it was important to stabilize the forces in Korea, where the United States was confronted with an especially volatile situation. On January 23, 1947, the Soviet Union had officially refused to allow the U.N. temporary commission to enter northern Korea. On February 6 the commission announced in Seoul that it would report its failure to the U.N. General Assembly, and on the following day there was a wave of rioting and sabotage in southern Korea (Brookings Institution, *Summary of Developments in Major Problems of United States Foreign Policy* 1, no. 5 [1948], 16, and no. 6

[1948], 15. See also State, *Foreign Relations, 1947*, vol. VI, *The Far East*, pp. 843–46).

[4] On February 11, 1948, the Joint Chiefs would refer Eisenhower's paper to the director of the Joint Staff, with instructions to prepare for the secretary of defense an analysis of the present and prospective sizes of U.S. forces in relationship to their missions. The director was to specify "the implications inherent in continuation of [the] attempt to fulfill existing missions with forces presently and prospectively available" (same file as document).

2040   *ABC 400.336 Greece (3-20-47), Sec. 1-B*

TO JOINT CHIEFS OF STAFF   *February 6, 1948*
Memorandum. Top secret

Subject: Director, Joint U.S. Military Advisory and Planning Group in
          Greece

1. JCS 1798/4 dated 31 December 1947 designated Major General W. G. Livesay as Director of the Joint U.S. Military Advisory and Planning Group in Greece.

2. The Department of the Army desires that Major General James A. Van Fleet, U.S. Army, be designated Director of the Joint U.S. Military Advisory and Planning Group in Greece vice Major General W. G. Livesay relieved.[1]

3. I therefore recommend approval of the attached memorandum[2] as a matter of urgent priority.

[1] For background on this issue see no. 1990. Wedemeyer drafted this memorandum for Eisenhower; the paper would circulate on February 10 as JCS 1798/6, and the Joint Chiefs would approve the recommendation on February 17 (same file as document).

[2] The memorandum (not printed here) expressed JCS approval of this change in command.

2041   *Eisenhower Mss.*

TO LOUIS FRANCIS ALBERT MOUNTBATTEN   *February 6, 1948*

Dear Dickie: As you requested, I have had my staff examine your despatch with care, but as a matter of some urgency. Their comments have been submitted in more detail than could be included in a letter, and I will simply give some of my personal views concerning them.[1]

I agree that the despatch does not give due weight to the American effort in India and Burma. At its peak strength in March 1945, our India-Burma Theater included 215,000 officers and men, of which half were air force troops. These, you will recall, furnished a substantial portion of the air support available to your troops, and most of the air supply, without which the re-conquest of Burma would not have been possible. Of the remainder of the American Forces, more than half were service and supply personnel, supporting the air forces in Burma as well as several Chinese units. By any standard, this was a major effort exerted 12,000 miles from the United States.[2]

I can well understand that the presentation of your differences with General Stilwell is a matter of some delicacy, and I would not want any expressions of mine to deter you from a frank and full presentation of your views as against those expressed by General Stilwell. However, it seems to me that General Stilwell's relations to his Government and to the Chinese and British Governments were entirely apart from the difficulties that arose during the campaign. From the despatch, a reader might conclude that the course taken by General Stilwell was chosen independently, and that the policies followed and advocated by him as Commanding General, China-Burma-India Theater, were not necessarily those of the United States Government. In a combined command, there are bound to be diverging opinions between Allies, but in this case I believe it should be made clear that General Stilwell was following directives of the Joint Chiefs of Staff. Any discussion of your disagreements with General Stilwell might well be balanced by an account of those with your other commanders-in-chief.[3]

We were rather taken aback by one portion of the despatch, wherein parallel expressions were chosen to describe the American and Japanese attitudes toward the civil population of Burma:

"on the whole, the Japanese appeared to have shown hardly any concern with the health of the local population, *except in so far as the safeguarding of their own troops was concerned.*" Page 239.

"The attitude of the U.S. commanders directing operations in Northern Burma was different from that of the British commanders; and it was understandable that they should be concerned with the tasks of restoring public order, caring for refugees, and organizing medical service in British territory *only in so far as these commitments affected N.C.A.C.* military operations." Page 242.

The paragraph on page 242 goes on to say that General Stilwell took action which effectively barred any relief personnel whatever from the forward areas. Officers who served in Northern Burma tell me that these statements are in error, that relief and civil personnel were at the front, and that the medical care given the population of Burma went far beyond the bounds of military necessity.[4]

There is no doubt that your despatch is most comprehensive, and will provide a valuable source for future historians. However, I think the comments I have outlined here indicate that from our point of view some improvement could be achieved through a more considered balance in the roles of the Allied Forces in SEAC.

It seems to be an inopportune time to send you these comments, for I fully appreciate the pressures under which you are now working. You have my best wishes for complete success. *Sincerely*

[1] For background on Mountbatten's report to the CCS on the campaign in Southeast Asia see no. 1807. In January Mountbatten had again asked Eisenhower to expedite his comments on the SEAC report. Eisenhower had replied that the JCS could not concur in publication of Mountbatten's despatch until the BCOS had formally requested clearance. In the meantime Eisenhower promised to give Mountbatten his comments "on a personal basis" (Mountbatten to Eisenhower, Jan. 24, 1948, and Eisenhower to Mountbatten, WCL 25365, Jan. 27, 1948, in COS, 1948, 091.713 Mountbatten). General Wedemeyer, however, questioned "the advisability of either the Joint Chiefs of Staff, or of any individual U.S. officer, submitting detailed comments to Admiral Mountbatten," since the report was "obviously 'slanted' to paint British efforts in this area in the best possible light" (Wedemeyer to Malony, Jan. 15, 1948, P&O 319.1 TS, Case 57/3). The Historical Division prepared Eisenhower's comments and cleared them with Colonel Bowen.

[2] In his reply of March 7 Mountbatten said that he would insert the figures on troop strength provided by Eisenhower (EM).

[3] Mountbatten said that on this point, "I am in partial agreement with you only." He would make clear that there were high-level differences and that Stilwell was not operating independently. He would not, however, talk about his disagreements with his other commanders. Unlike Stilwell, they had been entirely subordinate to him in the chain of command; more importantly, their differences with him had not been publicized, whereas Stilwell's had been published in a one-sided book. Mountbatten's reference was to a book by Fred Eldridge (Stilwell's former public relations officer) entitled *Wrath in Burma: The Uncensored Story of General Stilwell and International Maneuvers in the Far East* (New York, 1946). For background on Stilwell see no. 1755.

[4] Mountbatten agreed that the juxtaposition was "unfortunate" and that he would rewrite page 242.

2042   *Eisenhower Mss.*

To Joseph Edward Davies   *February 6, 1948*

Dear Joe: Tomorrow at noon I turn over my job to General Bradley. In spite of the pressure of last-minute "tag-end" problems, I could not let the opportunity slip to acknowledge your nice letter of the 3rd.[1]

There is one thing I can say to you that I can scarcely tell anyone else because I would be accused either of pomposity, of egotism, or of chicanery. It is that the only ambition I have left in life is to be of service, particularly to the health and strength of democracy as I think I understand it. My problem was to decide under what conditions I could actually be of most service and events were piling up that seemed to compel me to make a far more definite statement on my plans than I had originally intended. There are a few circumstances connected with the whole matter, factors that influenced my decision, which I shall not attempt to explain until I see you again. I do believe though that, all things considered, I did the right thing.[2]

It would be difficult to tell you what your friendship and wise counsel have meant to me all these past many months, since I first met you in Europe. This again is a subject that I certainly cannot do justice to in a letter. I hope, though, that sometime when we are alone I can really make you understand a little bit of how greatly I value your kindness, your disinterestedness and your unfailing generosity.

We have had the longest spell of winter weather that I can recall experiencing in Washington. While we have been spared the really bitter temperatures of the Northwest, the thermometer has frequently hovered around zero and we have had, for this section, a great deal of snow.

I do not know how much activity the doctors permit you but if they do allow you to go fishing occasionally, I urge that you go out for a little bonefishing.[3] On the Miami Herald there is a fishing editor, Al Corson, who knows the best bonefish guide in that region.[4] The fish are not large but they are most terrific fighters and the best part of it is that you have to go only about half an hour from the pier in Miami in order to get to the fishing grounds.

Mamie has been quite ill with streptococci throat and while the doctors seemingly have conquered the infection with penicillin, she is now suffering the reaction from the drug. She will be in bed another week or so. More serious than her illness is the condition of her father who was taken quite ill while visiting us. He is 78 years old and his heart practically played out on him after a bad bout with the flu, complicated with the gout. He must stay flat on his back without moving for three weeks and then is to be allowed gradually to stir around the house. All this means that Mamie and I will spend our leave largely at Fort Myer.

Give our love to Marjorie and, as always, warmest regards to you. *As ever*

[1] Davies had said that in spite of Eisenhower's recent disavowal of political ambitions, the General was "destined to be called for still greater service to our country" (EM). For background on Davies see no. 124.
[2] See no. 1998.
[3] Davies suffered from chronic diverticulitis and had experienced a severe attack in July 1947 (see *New York Times*, July 4, 1947).
[4] For background on Eisenhower's bonefishing expedition in Florida see no. 1267.

2043   *Eisenhower Mss.*

TO WILLIAM D. SIMMONS   *February 6, 1948*

Dear Bill: As I prepare to leave this job, no message I have received gave
me a finer feeling than did yours. In all the times that I have visited the
White House during the past years, I have always counted, with certainty, upon finding, at your desk, a cheerful welcome and an obvious
spirit of helpfulness. It has meant much to me.[1]

    This note brings to you my good wishes for health and happiness—
and a lasting gratitude for your unfailing kindness. *Cordially*

    [1] William D. Simmons was the executive-office receptionist. Eisenhower wrote
this letter in longhand. Simmons's message is not in EM.

2044   *Eisenhower Mss.*

TO PAUL ALFRED HODGSON   *February 6, 1948*

Dear P.A.: Tomorrow, the 7th, I quit the job of Chief of Staff—that
is, unless some most unexpected catastrophe happens in the meantime.
Bradley is taking over, a circumstance which is of great gratification to
me. Throughout the war he was not only an outstanding commander,
but he was my warm friend and close adviser. I think I may claim some
right to at least a casual recognition in the field of strategy, organization,
and in developing Allied teamwork. Bradley was the master tactician of
our forces and in my opinion will eventually come to be recognized as
America's foremost battle leader.

    I shall not go to Columbia until the first of May. In fact, until that
time there will be no place in New York for me to live.[1] However, I
shall not get to use the intervening period for the complete and absolute
rest that I had always hoped to have. I am going to plunge into the
preparation of a memoir—a job that has already been developed to a fair
degree—and these coming three or four months will be the only ones
that I will have free for this task.[2] Because, however, I shall for once in
my life be working for myself and on an entirely different type of job, I
think the general effect will be almost as good as a complete avoidance
of all work.

    Until May 1st, therefore, my address will be Fort Myer, Virginia.
After that, it will be Columbia University.

    Our household is practically a hospital. Mamie has been quite ill, but
today shows improvement. She had a streptococcic infection in her
throat. Her father and mother are both ill, the former, seriously. His

difficulty is a heart ailment complicated by age. We will not be able to move him at all for several weeks. After that, he will have to get on to his feet quite slowly and carefully. It is a godsend that we do not have to get out of our house until May 1st.

We are glad, of course, that Anne is better.[3] Give her our love, and with warmest regards to yourself, *As ever*

[1] See no. 1700.
[2] For background see no. 1615.
[3] Hodgson had written that his wife's bursitis seemed to be entirely cured. His chatty, handwritten letter of January 26, 1948, is in EM.

2045   *Eisenhower Mss.*

To Olivette Obitts   *February 6, 1948*

Dear Miss Obitts: Many thanks for your letter. I remember your Uncle Harry very well as I used to go to the barbershop where he worked.[1] I am distressed to learn of his affliction.

When you next write to your Uncle, kindly extend my greetings and best wishes. *Sincerely*

[1] In her January 29 letter Olivette Obitts, of Newington, Kansas, reminded the General that her uncle, Harry George, had cut Eisenhower's hair when he was a young boy in Abilene. Her uncle said that he had given Eisenhower a haircut just before he left for West Point and that Eisenhower had been a pallbearer at his son's funeral. Harry George was now almost eighty years old, blind, and living in California. Miss Obitts asked if Eisenhower remembered him and the incidents. At the bottom of her letter Eisenhower wrote: "I remember him and used to go to shop where he worked. Cannot verify specific incidents of funeral & *final* hair cut—give him my greetings etc." Carroll drafted this reply.

2046   *Eisenhower Mss.*

To Ellen Gordon Allen   *February 7, 1948*

Dear Ellen: Of course I have known for these past many months how disappointed Honk would naturally feel at the Army's seeming lack of appreciation of his service, and particularly of his war record.[1] Along with this I have known that you would worry because of your anxiety for Honk.

I am not going to philosophize too much. All of us know how much such items as opportunity, propinquity, and just sheer luck mean in this business of promotion. But I am going to offer one piece of advice. It is that neither of you take this thing too seriously and that above all you never talk about it, even among yourselves, unless and until you can do so with honest amusement—even a giggle. You know, Ellen, there is almost as much disadvantage in getting too much rank as there is in receiving too little. At this minute I would not have to leave the Army merely because I cease to be Chief of Staff if I did not have a rank that precludes any other appropriate assignment for me. I think that you have also known of some of the embarrassments and problems that have come to me over these past two years merely because of too much recognition.

After all this: I most fully and unequivocally agree with your estimate of Honk's services. The best I can do is to place on his record, for the attention of the next Selection Board, a record of my opinion.[2] For your information, I am enclosing a copy of what I am saying. More than this I do not see what I can do, except to add once more that by no means should either you or Honk look upon his career as a failure. His own conscience is clear, you two have a wonderful family, you have a wonderful home and a good life. There is little more to ask.

With affectionate and lasting regard, *Cordially*

[1] For background see no. 75. Mrs. Allen was the wife of Colonel Frank A. "Honk" Allen, Jr., who had seen Eisenhower in the Chief of Staff's office on February 4.
[2] The next document.

2047 *Eisenhower Mss.*

To WILLARD STEWART PAUL *February 7, 1948*

Memorandum for Director, Personnel and Administration: Before leaving the post of Chief of Staff, I want to file with the official records of three officers my considered opinion concerning their abilities, because of a feeling that in the 1947 selections to Brigadier General the true value of these officers may possibly not have been fully appreciated. They are:
Colonel Frank A. Allen, Jr.
Brigadier General (Colonel, Regular Army) B. F. Caffey
Brigadier General (Colonel, Regular Army) J. J. O'Hare[1]

Colonel Frank A. Allen, Jr.
Colonel Allen was transferred from command of a combat team in an Armored Division to become the G–2 for the Sixth Army Group in the European campaign. My own headquarters took him from that assignment to become the Public Relations Officer of SHAEF. This was done after a thorough search of all available material, both in the European

Theater and through inquiry to the War Department, failed to uncover any other available officer considered to be his equal for the position. The task was an exceedingly difficult one and required the constant application of tact, administrative ability and understanding of operations, and above all, the highest kind of devotion to duty. He displayed all these qualities in ample degree and performed his duties to my eminent satisfaction. Colonel Allen was then a Brigadier General, but because he was on a special staff far removed from the normal activities of a headquarters, I doubt that the true worth of his services was ever understood by direct reporting officers. If I have ever reported differently on his services than is indicated in this paragraph, it was because the insistent press of duties led me to overlook a matter which was vital to him and important to the service. I strongly recommend that Colonel Allen be considered favorably for promotion to Brigadier General, Regular Army, in 1948.

Brigadier General B. F. Caffey

Colonel Caffey led the 39th Combat Team at the capture of Algiers. Soon thereafter he was made a Brigadier General, Assistant Division Commander, in the 34th Division. He served in all the campaigns of that Division until he was evacuated because of badly frozen feet. There is no question in my mind that except for this disabling occurrence he would have become a successful Division Commander. After evacuation he served in important staff positions in the Mediterranean and was eventually brought back to the United States where he soon assumed an even more important staff position in the expediting of demobilization. General Marshall and many others have told me that on this assignment he performed services of outstanding value to the Army. Some months later, after I had become Chief of Staff, he was assigned to the Operations Division of the General Staff because of our need in that Division for younger, capable men of broad experience and real ability. Throughout his service, General Caffey has been known as a most able, even brilliant officer. I definitely rate him among the upper third of the Brigadiers I met in the war and have served with since. I urgently recommend that he be favorably considered for promotion to Brigadier General, Regular Army, in 1948.

Brigadier General J. J. O'Hare

I knew General O'Hare in World War II as the Head of the Personnel Division of General Bradley's 12th Armored Group. He was one of the two or three finest staff officers in that headquarters and carried very heavy responsibilities. He was at all times completely informed as to the details of his task and was decisive and effective. More than this, he willingly accepted responsibility. Since the termination of the war, he has been serving in the Personnel Division of the Department of the Army in which position I have found his services invaluable. I consider him a man of great ability and would be more than glad to have him serve with me either in peace or war. I strongly urge that he be considered favorably for promotion to Brigadier General, Regular Army, in 1948.

The three officers described above are mature men who, if not soon promoted, will almost certainly fail to reach a higher permanent grade during their service in the Army. I am writing this letter out of a sense of duty. None of these men has ever spoken to me about the matter, but I request, unless this should violate regulations, that a copy of this letter be placed in the official files of each of these three officers so that it may inescapably come to the attention of the next Promotion Board.[2]

[1] For background on Allen see the previous document; on Caffey, see no. 374. Joseph James O'Hare had graduated from West Point in 1916. Also see Chandler, *War Years*, on all three officers.

[2] These officers would not be appointed Regular Army brigadier generals in 1948. Allen would be promoted to this rank in 1951; Caffey would retire with the rank of brigadier general, RA, in 1950, as would O'Hare in 1953.

2048   *Eisenhower Mss.*

To George Catlett Marshall   *February 7, 1948*

Dear General Marshall: When I received your letter of January 26th concerning decorations for the officers who served under Gillem, I immediately started the Decorations Board to working on the matter.[1]

It now appears that their conclusions will not be presented to me, as I terminate my service as Chief of Staff today.[2] However, I am handing your letter to General Bradley, who, I am sure, will follow it up. *Very sincerely*

[1] Secretary Marshall's letter protested that the board had approved decorations for only a few of those who had served on Marshall's mission to China and who had been recommended by the U.S. commander, General Alvan C. Gillem, Jr. For background on Gillem's and Marshall's service in China see no. 652.

[2] On this, his last day as Chief of Staff, Eisenhower held a press conference at 9:20 in the morning. He spoke mainly about the Army's serious manpower problems (see no. 2039; Eisenhower's own draft of his remarks is in EM, Press Statements and Releases. See also *New York Times*, Feb. 8, 1948). During the morning Eisenhower answered many of the messages he had received congratulating him on his years of service in the Army; these replies, most of which are not printed here, are in EM.

2049 *Eisenhower Mss.*

To Thomas Troy Handy   *February 7, 1948*

Dear Tom: Thank you very much for your fine letter.[1] Bradley is fully aware of our arrangements with respect to you and will notify you in plenty of time.[2]

I think we had better not send Miss Hays until the situation clears up.[3] In great haste,[4] *Sincerely*

[1] Handy's letter of February 2 said (in part): "I do not believe that there is any use for me to tell you that you will always have my undying admiration, respect, and affection. It certainly is my hope that our paths will cross often."
[2] Handy was slated to relieve Clay (see no. 2001).
[3] Warrant Officer Hays was scheduled to leave the Chief of Staff's office for a position with Handy (see no. 2001).
[4] Eisenhower added a postscript: "This is 20 minutes before I am relieved as Chief of Staff."

2050   *Eisenhower Mss.*

To Willard Stewart Paul   *February 7, 1948*

Memorandum for Director, Personnel & Administration: I believe that the special attention of the next General Officers' Selection Board should be called to the case of Colonel Carter Clarke of the Intelligence Division.[1]

Colonel Clarke occupies a very special position in the Army Department, the details of which you can communicate to the members of the Board. It is my belief that because of his unique qualifications for this particular work he should be considered practically in the status of a Special Staff Officer. Consequently I think he should be promoted and kept indefinitely, indeed through his entire remaining period of active service, on the identical job he is now doing.

I know of no other person in the Army who is qualified to fill that position and it will certainly require him a considerable length of time to train someone else who, in turn, should then be kept on the job indefinitely.[2]

[1] For background on Clarke see no. 1008. This letter would be dispatched on February 9.
[2] Clarke would be promoted to brigadier general in 1949.

2051   *Eisenhower Mss.*

To British Chiefs of Staff   *February 7, 1948*
Cable WCL 28833

US MILATTACHE AMEMBASSY London, England from CSUSA
signed Eisenhower: Please pass following message to the British Chiefs of
Staff: Admiral Moore[1] has given me your very gracious message.[2] I am
deeply touched and full of gratitude for the generous sentiments it
contains.

My past associations with the British Chiefs is a source of lasting
pride to me, and I shall ever cherish the cordial friendships born in
common service with stouthearted men and women of the British
Commonwealth.

[1] Admiral Sir Henry Ruthven Moore had entered service as a cadet in 1902 and had
seen fleet duty in both world wars. He was presently head of the British Naval
Mission in Washington, D.C.
[2] In a note of February 5 Moore, in his capacity as Chairman of the Joint Services
Mission, had forwarded the following message from the BCOS: "Your devotion to
and unfailing help in our combined cause, both during the war and in the difficult
years that followed, have been a constant source of inspiration and encouragement." Carroll drafted Eisenhower's reply.

2052   *Eisenhower Mss.*

To Paul Thomas Carroll   [*February 7, 1948*][1]

Dear Carroll:[2] It would be futile for me to attempt to express the depth
of my obligation to you for brilliant and devoted service during the past
many months. I know of no other officer in the Army who could have
been of equal value to me in assisting in the preparation of reports,
speeches, letters and other documents. Your great skill, judgment,
experience and tact have saved me many hours of work and, more than
this, have frequently helped me to present ideas more accurately and
forcefully than I, alone, could have done.

I am delighted that you have volunteered to assist me, on an unoffi-
cial basis, for some time to come. But as I leave the Office of Chief of
Staff, I feel impelled to give to you and to the Department of the Army
some written record of my appreciation of your past services.

You are one of those unusual officers whose capacity for future
usefulness to the Army is unlimited. If I am fortunate enough to live
for another fifteen or twenty years I shall most assuredly be addressing
you as Chief of Staff of the Army. You need only, aside from good

health, to continue adding to a record that is already crowded with fifteen years of splendid achievement.

With warm personal regard, *Cordially*

[1] The typed copy of this letter, with Eisenhower's initials as drafter, is dated February 26, but a handwritten note near the typed date reads, "To be dated 2/7/48." Later in the month Eisenhower would write similar letters to other members of his staff (see EM).

[2] For background on Carroll see no. 533. Eisenhower made numerous revisions in his own draft of this message.

2053   *COS, 1948, 335.18*

To THE AMERICAN SOLDIER[1]   *February 7, 1948*

Cable WCL 28815

Departure today from my present post breaks many ties that are dear to me. But the separation is not complete. I take with me the knowledge that, both by law and in my own heart, my service with you shall not end as long as I live. Assurance of such fellowship is my most prized possession, for no man can have a more worthy comrade and loyal friend than the American soldier.

For thirty-seven years I have been privileged to serve with men who manifested, in their performance of every duty, the stout hearts of Americans and the spirit of our Nation. Pride of service, loyalty to the flag, love of country strengthened them beyond the common strength given to men. Whatever their rank or arm, they were before all else soldiers, heirs to generations of soldierly tradition, distinguished for soldierly virtue. What they have done to preserve their country from its enemies and to free their world from evil tyrannies is written large in human history. My words add nothing to their fame. But I cannot let this day pass without telling them, the fighting men of ground and air—those who have left the ranks and you who still wear the uniform—that my fondest boast shall always be: "I was their fellow-soldier."

[1] This message bore the following heading: USMILATTACHE AMLEGA-TION, Pretoria, Union of South Africa; USMILATTACHE AMEMBASSY, Madrid, Spain; USMILATTACHE AMLEGATION, Stockholm, Sweden; USMILATTACHE AMLEGATION, Bern, Switzerland; USMILATTACHE AMLEGATION, Damascus, Syria; USMILATTACHE AMEMBASSY, Ankara, Turkey; USMILATTACHE AMEMBASSY, Montevideo, Uruguay; US-MILATTACHE AMEMBASSY, Caracas, Venezuela; USMILATTACHE AMEMBASSY, Belgrade, Yugoslavia: Dissemination A. ZI Armies notified direct. From AGAO-S sgd Witsell TAG. Desired that the following message from General of the Army Dwight D. Eisenhower be disseminated to all members of your command.

To Douglas MacArthur   *February 7, 1948*

Dear General: In 20 minutes I shall be relieved as Chief of Staff. I am taking occasion to write you a note because it suddenly occurs to me that in all my years in the Army I served longer directly under your supervision than any other.

Another reason for writing is because of the efforts that some of our cheaper type of columnists have been making to prove that you and I have always been deadly enemies and that even when I wrote a letter walking completely out of the political picture they asserted that I was also trying to take you out. In a recent press conference I emphatically denied all this.[1] I told them that the last person I saw in the Philippines in 1940 was you and that you were the first person I met when I reached Japan in 1946[2] and that I hoped that you treasured our old friendship as much as I do. Moreover, I pointed out that in my public letter I clearly stated: "At least this applies in my case." and I stated further that the determining factor in such cases was every man's sense of some inner compulsion and of qualification.[3]

In any event, this note is merely to say a sort of official Goodbye. It does not imply that I am going to lose any bit of my interest in the Army or in any of my old associates.

Good luck to you, and please convey my very warmest greetings to Jean and to young Arthur.[4]

With lasting regard, *Sincerely*

[1] See *New York Times*, February 6, 1948.
[2] See no. 893.
[3] See no. 1998.
[4] MacArthur's wife and son.

To James Vincent Forrestal   *February 7, 1948*[1]
Personal and confidential

Memorandum for Secretary Forrestal: Complying with your request that I provide you, upon termination of my active service, with a memorandum of observations bearing upon organization and procedures in the Defense Department, the following is submitted:

* * * * * * * * *

In developing organization and administrative practices, it will be wise, in broader issues, to avoid irrevocable decision until time and experience can determine the wisdom of included and progressively established details. There should be no hesitancy in using the "trial and error" method so long as these proceed from minor innovation toward larger and more radical objectives in final result.

Office Staff

A wide variety of subjects, emanating from many different sources, impinge upon the office of the Secretary of Defense. This is merely an index of the degree in which the national security problem is entwined with and a part of our whole national complex. Just as it is almost impossible to deal with the security problem without giving consideration to vital factors involving the political, industrial, economic, and even moral fibre of the United States, so do officials dealing with these other factors find it necessary to take into consideration the responsibilities of the security establishment. This situation makes it desirable, if not necessary, that the Secretary have a small, highly efficient staff, the purpose of which would be *to digest and analyze, and to determine relationships among the various and numerous subjects with which the Secretary of Defense is called upon to deal.*

Manifestly, such a staff requires a head. But for obvious psychological reasons and, indeed, legal prescription, the head of such a staff should not be called a Chief of Staff. My personal choice would be for the title "Administrative Assistant," but he should come from one of the military services. He must, at all costs, be a useful assistant in accumulating, briefing, and presenting to you the opinions and recommendations of military professionals. His rank should not be so high as to cause suspicion on the part of the Joint Chiefs of Staff that he might be tempted to intervene between any of these Chiefs of Staff and yourself. On the other hand, he should be of such experience and rank as to have the respect of everybody in the military services. His personal qualifications should be so apparent that any Department Secretary or Chief of Staff would normally be glad to call him and to lay before him appropriate questions and suggestions with a certainty that these would be properly and intelligently transmitted to the Secretary of Defense. I know of several men in the Army that could fill such position with great value to the Secretary, among whom Lutes is one.[2] In the Air Corps and the Navy are such people as Norstad and Sherman.[3] No man of this caliber would ever overstep the limits of his own responsibilities and authority. This staff would constantly search the full catalogue of Secretarial responsibility to see that no important duty is neglected. Confidence, in this regard, will be invaluable to the Secretary. The group should be small but able, and should be representative of all services and include upon it selected civilians.

This kind of a staff would, I believe, be welcomed by such groupments as the Munitions Board, the National Resources Board, and the Executive of the National Security Council.

Assistants who are personally close to the Secretary of a governmental department always oppose the formation of an advisory and coordinating staff group under a single head, since this development, they feel, thrusts them one step away from the throne. Theoretical argument is that a group of co-ordinate assistants, each charged with a specific function, and with the sum of these functional responsibilities equal to those prescribed for their chief, eliminates the need for an integrated staff. Such words as "over-organization," "red-tape," and "duplication" are used to condemn the idea of staff integration.

These arguments are not sound. First of all, the top man in any organization—and this applies with particular force to cabinet officers in Washington—has "prescribed" responsibilities with respect to the organization he heads; but he has a tremendous number of duties that force him continually to face outward, to represent the interests of his entire organization in all types of conference and frequently viz-a-viz other segments of government. In policy matters only the Secretary can do this effectively, yet the time, thought, and effort consumed leave him no chance to act effectively as the detailed coordinator of his own team. As a result the details fall into confusion; policy cannot be efficiently applied. Moreover, if there is no integrated staff, all principal *operating* subordinates (Secretaries of Services and Chiefs of Staff) are compelled to decide which one of the chief's various "assistants" takes cognizance of a particular subject—and more frequently than not a problem involves the functions of more than one of these special assistants. My own experience has been that once these special assistants understand and begin working in an integrated staff, under a staff chief who is a real leader, they adopt the system whole-heartedly and enthusiastically.

Joint Chiefs of Staff

Under this heading I have one suggestion only, since the functions and legal position of the Joint Chiefs of Staff seem clear. The value of this group to the Secretary of National Defense can conceivably vary within wide limits. If each member comes to regard himself merely as the special advocate or pleader of the service he represents, I fear that in the long run the body will be little more than an agency for eliminating from proposals and projects inconsequential and minor differences—a body of "fly speckers." Major disagreements would, in the long run, have to be decided personally by the Secretary of National Defense, without the confidence that his decision was based upon truly broad analysis and disinterested advice.

I believe, on the other hand, that the Secretary can do much to defeat this natural tendency and to make the body one of the most tremendous value to himself and to the whole problem of security. I suggest that a good method would be for the Secretary to set aside one luncheon hour a week to which he would invite the three service Chiefs of Staff. Except on rare occasions and for special purpose, I think no one else should be present and, ordinarily, *detailed* items of business should not be taken up. The effort should be to promote the concept that the four individuals present, without regard to their respective responsibilities and specific duties, were meeting as a group to talk over broad security problems in an atmosphere of complete friendliness and objectivity. Whenever at such a meeting any individual showed a tendency to become a special pleader, the subject should be skillfully changed and constant effort made to achieve unanimity of conclusion, first upon broad generalities and these gradually brought closer to concrete application to particular problems.

The men composing this staff have reached the pinnacle of their respective careers. They should consider every problem from its broad national viewpoint; but habits of years will have to be overcome by some patience and a sense of humor. If the Secretary habitually and casually brings out into the open, at informal meetings, major controversial issues in the attitude of one seeking *general* professional assistance so that he may make decisions on the basis of the national welfare, he will eventually profit immeasurably. Once this body has achieved the collective conviction that its reason for existence is, as a unit, to serve the Secretary faithfully and intelligently, many inter-service problems will disappear as if by magic.

I do not suggest that the Presidential Chief of Staff should attend these informal and friendly, almost social, meetings, because the primary purpose is to achieve a comradeship and unity among the three service Chiefs, which will be reflected in all the joint planning and other staffs that are responsive to these particular heads.

Composition—Chiefs of Staff

I believe that under the organization prescribed by the Unification Act[4] the inclusion of the President's Chief of Staff in the Joint Chiefs of Staff has become anomalous, in spite of the fact that this is directed by law.

Under the old organization the Presidential Chief of Staff was the only connecting link between the President and his chief military advisers; that function has now been taken over by the Secretary of National Defense.

Quite naturally if, for his own purposes, the President of the United States feels the need of an officer he calls his Chief of Staff, no one can make valid objection. Unfortunately, as I see it, the law prescribes that if the President names such an individual, then the man shall also be a member of the Joint Staff body. The result is that whereas the Secretary of National Defense in his development of plans and recommendations for submission to the President, naturally attempts to coordinate the advice he receives from the Joint Chiefs of Staff with that received from other parts of the whole security organization, there still exists in the person of the Presidential Chief of Staff a direct shortcut to the ear of the President.

The present incumbent of that post has so served since 1942 and is obviously deeply trusted by the President.[5] Consequently, I do not advocate making an immediate issue of this particular point; I would merely try to block the appointment of any new individual to such a post when the present one gives it up.

Some Observations on Functions of Secretary

Implicit in the law setting up the Secretary of National Defense is the hope and intent that there will be developed a security program in which all fields of responsibility will be covered but from which all unnecessary duplications will be eliminated. This applies both to operational and logistical activity. While some improvements in both fields can go ahead hand in hand, functionally and logically a satisfactory development of an agreed operational program defining roles, missions, and framework of organization must provide the basis for logistic economy and efficiency.

The difficulties are partially rooted in the natural human feeling that every man wants under his own hand complete control and authority over every factor or unit that has a possible function in the discharge of his responsibilities. The old saying, "Centralization is the refuge of fear," is true, also, in the sense that commanders are fearful of dependence upon "cooperating arms." For example, in a ground battle every Divisional Commander always wants under his exclusive authority all of the artillery, tanks, mortars, and other supporting weapons that may be necessary to him in the winning of a particular fight. He instinctively opposes the idea of securing this necessary support from groupments and pools directly responsible to a higher commander. This is true in spite of the fact that over and over again there has been proved the economy and efficiency of pooling these supporting arms so as to provide great flexibility in battle and to use them where and when most needed. The same attitude, the same psychological reaction, will show itself in everything you may try to do toward eliminating from any service or arm any element that may be desirable or essential in battle, even when these apparently duplicate the functions of another of the three services.

Always present in any discussion of these possible or apparent duplications is the argument between the Air Force and the Bomber portions of Naval aviation. Oddly enough, I do not believe that this matter would be so important in actual war as it is in peace. In war, the problem is susceptible to solution by designation of a single commander for a given strategic mission. For example, the Air Force might be directed to bomb the industry of a given hostile country. In such circumstances, all bombing planes, no matter from what source they might come, would logically and necessarily be placed under the commander charged with this mission. Otherwise, hopeless confusion and disorganization would result.

However, in the process of peacetime preparatory work, the matter is far from simple. Yet I believe it can be solved. Suggested concrete steps are:

(1) Agreed concept of war (already done).[6]

(2) Determination, in specific terms of tasks to be accomplished in order to achieve aims of strategic concept.

(3) Determination of who is to do each job. This is where the fight centers, and it is my opinion that the Air Force and the Navy never will, by themselves, reach an agreement. Therefore, the next step that must be determined is the *comparative cost and efficiency* of the carrier, together with its supporting vessels of all kinds, as opposed to a land-based field within effective range of the target area selected. Detailed answers to this problem will change as time goes on due to the increasing range and speed of bombers. The problem is to find out how to prepare for the greatest bombing effectiveness at a given point on the earth's surface with the least expenditure of preparatory dollars, and the period that is critical to the solution of this problem is the 2–8 years following upon the time when these carriers could be available.

(4) The problem just stated should be given in specific terms to the Research and Development Board. The study should be exhaustive, calling upon scientists and others for assistance. Additional drain upon the steel industry will be an important factor.

(5) Depending upon the answers made by the Research and Development Board, the Secretary of Defense will decide (3) above.

Even if the Chiefs of Staff should arrive at an agreed answer to (3), I would still suggest having the indicated study made by the Bush Board.[7]

In this way the matter will be taken out of the realm of generality and brought down to specific recommendation.

Always these questions come back to the importance of making the most out of the national security dollar. Another example is found in the question of the scope of responsibility allotted to the Marines and, therefore, to the scale of their preparatory operations and expenditures *in time of peace.* All recognize the need of the Navy for Marines. For certain specific types of operations, it would be uneconomical for the Army to be required to provide ground contingents for use by the Navy. However, once we begin to expand our ideas of the need for Marines to involve heavy and sustained land fighting by large units, each with their supporting arms, then we get into the field of duplicated preparation with all its attendant expenses. In no major amphibious landing, made for the purpose of undertaking a decisive land campaign, is there any need or excuse for special landing divisions. Indeed their presence is a detriment, since presumably they should be removed from the theater once the landing has been made. In many respects an amphibious landing is far from the most difficult type of tactical task an infantry division is called upon to undertake. Again, in war, this problem would not be so difficult because if there were more Marines available than were needed by the fleet for minor landing missions, the entire overage could be allotted by the Secretary of Defense to the Army and used exactly as are normal Army troops. But I repeat that unless we relate our need and our expenditures in all these things to specific requirements, we are going to be *wasting dollars in peace.*

In spite of repeated efforts over the past two years, I have never gotten any significant part of military thought to agree with me that all ocean transport should be organized and operated by the Navy. On the part of the Army staff the same old fear arises that, unless water transportation is operated under its own control, the supply of military forces in the field will be subject to arbitrary decision by the Navy. On the part of the Navy staff there seems to be a fear that to take over this entire responsibility would be tending to classify the Navy as a transportation service rather than as a fighting arm. It is only fair to say that in both staffs there is a contention that this particular item of organization does not involve significant increase in costs.

The Army, of course, operates ports of embarkation and of debarkation and is charged with the proper loading of ships so that supplies carried are most readily available at the using end. However, none of the ships loaded can proceed to sea until Naval escort vessels have been accumulated and the whole convoy goes out under Naval command. In addition, the Navy is compelled to operate a Naval transport service for its own purposes. It would appear again that while the matter may not have too much significance in time of war, it does imply that, in time of peace, two organizations are planning for and maintaining nucleus for the expanded water transport responsibilities of war.

Under General Spaatz the Air Staff has agreed to the principle of depending largely upon the Army for all services common to the two arms. Thus the Air Force has made no attempt to set up separate Engineering, Ordnance, Signal, Medical, and Quartermaster services. However, the same characteristic purpose to be completely independent in all these matters has been implicit in many of the recommendations and studies presented by junior officers. The matter will have to be watched with the closest concern.

Logistics

In the broad field of logistics there will always necessarily be some minor duplications. This is unavoidable but this very fact makes it all the more necessary to work toward the elimination of those that are unnecessary. Some activities offer immediate and obvious examples of what might be done although in these instances it is probable that savings would not be too great. They do have, though, a great value from a public relations viewpoint as well as in educating all of us toward the ideal of a maximum of mutual interdependence in the interests of the common efficiency. Common use of airfields and of hospitals immediately suggest themselves for study. You have undoubtedly seen the report on the San Francisco Bay area recently rendered by the Anderson Sub-Committee of the Armed Services Committee of the House.[8] This committee believed that it found duplication and waste among Army, Navy, Air and Marine installations in that area. All over the world similar areas should be studied. Hospitalization, transportation, storage, and numbers of other functions are involved.

Procurement

I have great faith that the Army-Navy Munitions Board will, under the new set-up, go deeper and deeper into the matter of organized and coordinated procurement. In this instance I believe that the war-time problem is far more important than the peace-time problem. One of the never-ending tasks is to prevent approval of war plans which, in the sum of their requirements, exceed the amounts American industry can provide. I believe that if we support the Army-Navy Munitions Board, constantly increasing its power and authority so that competitive procurement will be eliminated and the equipment and maintenance of each service handled under a strictly coordinated system, tremendous savings will result.

I assume that most of the coordination incident to procurement and supply will fall to the lot of the Army-Navy-Air Force Munitions Board. One field to which the attention of that Board will necessarily be directed will be to provide for the greatest possible economy in those areas where operational needs indicate apparent duplication. For example, assuming that the Air Force and Naval aviation both find need for fast, large bombers, it would appear that by skillful handling much of the research, experimental and development work could be done without competition and duplication. In the matter of fuselage, engine and instrument design, and in related fields, it would seem that much of the cost incident to complete duplication could be avoided. This same observation will certainly apply to many other kinds of development and again I believe that although the Joint Chiefs of Staff will as a body have no responsibility in this matter, they can, by their personal influence, lead their own services to accept and to strive for this type of economy. Again this points up the need for teaching and training the Joint Chiefs of Staff to think and act as a body, not as a group of special advocates.

General

In all these matters, success will largely depend upon the character of the responsible individuals in each service. I believe that the Secretary of Defense will find that his success in achieving the objectives of the recent law will be largely measured by his success in finding and appointing officials whom he has determined in advance to be completely sold on the idea of achieving greater efficiency and economy through a maximum interdependence among the services. This applies first of all to the Secretaries and Assistant Secretaries of the several departments. While I know that the Secretary of Defense is not expected to interfere in detailed administration of the several services, yet if he is successful in getting the right type of men in the top positions, he will also influence the assignment of higher ranking professional officers to key positions. In any event, I believe that the Secretary of Defense has a direct and legal interest in the identity of the individuals appointed as Chiefs of Staff of their respective services because these individuals, as a body, make up his own military staff, called the Joint Chiefs of Staff.

Here I should like to make some short observations of which the truth has been demonstrated to me time and time again. In organizing teams, personality is equally important with ability. Too many people believe that strength of character is synonomous with arrogance and insufferable deportment. Leadership is as vital in conference as it is in battle. The work of the Secretary will never be successful unless the principal members of his team are *friends*. I simply cannot over-stress the importance of this point; I have had personally to relieve officers of ability from high staff positions because of the dislike for themselves they generated among their associates.

In dealing with problems, friends develop among themselves a natural selflessness that is the outgrowth of their regard for each other. Personal antagonism enjoys the defeat of the opponent—consequently, objectivity and selflessness cannot be attained when it is present.

Selected Officers to be Commissioned in the Armed Forces of the United States

This idea is an appealing one. The important thing, now, is that we begin to realize that primary qualifications for the highest command and staff positions in war and in peace do not necessarily include intimate knowledge of specialized methods and techniques peculiar to any of the several arms. To the contrary, I think we should seek, for these positions, men, regardless of service, who have demonstrated a capacity to deal with subjects of the broadest scope; whose reputations and experience give proof that they will never forget for an instant the relationships existing between fighting forces in the field and the complex economic, political and social problems of the area in which they may be called upon to operate. I would, in a great land campaign, cheerfully serve, as a ground force commander, under a *Theater* Commander from either the Navy or the Air Force, provided the individual selected were of the caliber of a Sherman or a Norstad.

Some day it will be possible to give to selected officers of the several services "combined arms" commissions that will transcend in prestige and in public regard anything that they could hold of comparable rank in one of the individual services. The thought injects itself, however, that when this does become possible, *it may no longer be necessary,* because of the perfection of cooperation.

Some progress can be made now by earmarking and utilizing to the best advantage officers of the required capacity and personality. Human nature usually seeks avidly that which is difficult to get, whether it is money, position, or reputation. Assignments as students to certain Army schools are very much sought after because it is well known that such an assignment means a man has been especially selected. Application of this truth to certain positions under the direct control of the Secretary of Defense will have a similar happy effect. Of course, if such an assignment carries along with it an automatic step-up of some kind, whether it would be in temporary rank, or some other material reward, that would be a help. What we must guard against is the feeling, on the part of these officers, that upon return to their own services they will be made to suffer unless, during their tour on Combined Staffs, they act as special pleaders for their respective Departments. I believe that the "follow-up" interest of the Secretary of Defense, if actively demonstrated, will meet this issue. Also, a thought in connection with this matter is that legal opportunity for inter-service transfers might help.

For the moment I would do nothing more than constantly to stress to the several Departmental Secretaries and to the Chiefs of Staff the very great compliment that is paid a man when he is selected for duty in functions that affect all three services.

Incomplete List of Army Officers of Extraordinary Ability

Older Group

General Omar N. Bradley	(54)
General Thos. T. Handy	(55)
Lt. Gen. LeRoy Lutes	(57)
Lt. Gen. Wade H. Haislip	(58)
Lt. Gen. Leonard T. Gerow	(59)
Lt. Gen. W. D. Crittenberger	(57)
Maj. Gen. Manton S. Eddy (nominated for Lt. Gen.)	(55)
Maj. Gen. E. M. Almond	(56)[9]

Intermediate Group

General Lucius D. Clay (will soon retire)	(50)
Lt. Gen. W. B. Smith (now Ambassador)	(52)
Lt. Gen. John E. Hull	(52)
Lt. Gen. A. C. Wedemeyer	(51)
Lt. Gen. M. B. Ridgway	(52)
Lt. Gen. J. Lawton Collins	(51)
Maj. Gen. Charles L. Bolte	(52)
General Mark W. Clark	(51)[10]
Maj. Gen. John Dahlquist	(50)[11]

Younger Group

Maj. Gen. A. M. Gruenther	(48)
Maj. Gen. Maxwell D. Taylor	(46)
Maj. Gen. Lyman L. Lemnitzer	(48)[12]
Maj. Gen. Clinton F. Robinson	(45)[13]
Maj. Gen. A. C. McAuliffe	(49)

Among still younger men, people that have or will certainly make a mark for themselves:

Maj. Gen. James M. Gavin	(40)[14]
Maj. Gen. Robert T. Frederick	(40)[15]

Col. Kilbourne S. Johnston	(41)[16]
Brig. Gen. Gerald J. Higgins	(38)
Lt. Col. John W. Bowen	(37)
Lt. Col. Dan Gilmer	(38)
Lt. Col. Paul T. Carroll	(37)
Lt. Col. J. H. Michaelis	(35)[17]

So far as I know these men are all in good health and the younger ones intend to stay in the Army. All of those named are personally known to me and have served directly under my command. (To secure a more comprehensive list it would be easy at any time to have the Personnel Division of the General Staff select those in each age group-ment whose records show them to be outstanding in every respect.)

Procedure for Coordination of Contacts with Other Departments

Due to established practices and personal acquaintanceships, I find that lower level State Department officials frequently call upon Staff Sections of the Department of the Army (particularly the Operations Division headed by Wedemeyer) for conferences and consultation involving matters that frequently pertain to the Department of National Defense. I think it would be a mistake to break up these informal conferences which will normally serve a most valuable purpose in examination of problems before they come to the direct attention of the highest levels of authority. However, coordination in this matter is mandatory, and a set of simple instructions should be issued by the Secretary's office. These, without sacrificing the advantages deriving from informal conference and friendships, should seek only to eliminate any chance of working at cross purposes.[18]

Special Army Problems

Certain of the Army's problems grow so important that they are rapidly becoming matters for direct attention of the Secretary of Defense.

A—The first of these is manpower. Our present jobs are:
1. Occupation
2. Maintenance of an Emergency Force
3. Construction of Framework for Mobilization.

The problem of manpower affects the Army's performance of all three of these missions. No one has ever questioned our need for some 670,000 officers and men. We are about 100,000 short. No one has ever belittled the importance of the occupation task or failed to appreciate the resulting calamity which failure in these duties would involve. The pinch on manpower is also keeping below strength our modest Emergency Force of 2 1/3 divisions although enlistments for State-side service are far easier to get.[19]

One of two things will now happen:

a. We will succeed in holding our strength at roughly its present level, in which case we might have to dissolve the Emergency Force and some occupation units to conduct UMT[20] if enacted, unless we can enlist a special corps of UMT trainers; or

b. Our downward trend will continue until occupation is no longer possible and the areas involved would have to be abandoned to chaos and communism.

If manpower difficulties continue to worsen, extraordinary measures will become necessary, such as double pay or double service credit for occupation duty. Comparable measures to stimulate enlistments in the home forces would include greatly improved pay, quarters and stations.

In this connection I have been alarmed by the numbers of young, promising officers who would really like to forsake the service for civil life. The pressure on them is great. Both the Air Forces and the Navy have methods (flying pay, submarine pay, sea duty pay) of bolstering up the income of the mass of their officers. The Army's opportunities, in peace, are limited to a relatively few men. Yet, in war, the Ground Division takes the losses—and all know this.

We must insist upon a decent living scale for all our officers.

The problem of Materiel is hardly less serious than that of Manpower. We hear so much of Air and Navy; their dramatic quarrels and stupendous costs fill the press, but the GI still has to participate in wars. His arms and equipment are of more importance than ever before. The present budget split of 40% Navy, 60% Army and Air, seems entirely disproportionate in the light of the Two Billion occupation cost that eats into the Army's portion. This has thrown the relative state of preparedness of the three services entirely out of balance since only a small percentage of the Army's budget can be devoted to its materiel. This unbalance jeopardizes the validity of the whole joint defense concept.[21]

A continuation of such unbalance threatens to undermine the validity of large expenditures for sea and air power unsupportable by adequate land power. Every strategic concept visualizes the readiness of large and efficient land forces to seize bases and constantly to advance these closer to the enemy. The effect of budgets for '46, '47, and '48 have been to render the Army increasingly unable to mobilize effective land power to support air and sea power in any emergency requiring a major mobilization. With certain negligible exceptions we have purchased no new equipment since the war. Consequently, we cannot arm even the few regular combat troops with new weapons developed late in the war but which had not achieved large-scale production. Obviously, we have not been able to equip them with weapons developed since the war. Equipping the National Guard and Reserves with modern equipment is even further out of the question. This destroys readiness; and without readiness in necessary land forces, all so-called retaliatory and even defensive plans are mere scraps of paper.

The people of the United States have appreciated for years that if they expected naval power to be useful in inhibiting wars or in winning wars, we must maintain a fleet in being. The Air Force is rapidly convincing the country that airplanes must be procured in peacetime if they are to be available for war. But the old idea of 'a million men springing to arms overnight' seems to persist in the public and even Congressional mind as the solution to raising the Army required to make our land-sea-air power effective. They do not seem to realize that the production curves for the creation of Army materiel follow the same patterns as those for planes and ships and that, if land forces are to be used in conjunction with planes and ships, then Army equipment must likewise be "in being."

We should be much further along the road toward a fully air-transportable ground force. Lack of modern communications, radar and detection equipment, modern tanks, personnel carriers and other devices are fast reducing our regular land forces to obsolescence. Destruction of our reserve stocks are rapidly making our civilian component mobilization plan a paper fiction. And the curve of our materiel readiness is rapidly dropping.

So that you may be acquainted and fully appreciate the Army's precarious materiel position, I suggest that you receive a staff presentation of this matter at your early convenience.

The time has come when that curve must be made to swing upward. I personally informed the Director of the Budget that I could take no part in defending estimates unless a reasonable amount were included for new ground equipment. $150,000,000 was added as a result of this appeal. But it is only a beginning—it deserves the driving support of the entire Defense Establishment.[22]

---

[1] Eisenhower wrote the date on this document by hand. On February 6 he had submitted to Royall his last formal report as Chief of Staff. A copy of that report (printed on February 7) and various drafts are in COS, 1948, 319.1 Annual Report.

[2] Lutes was now deputy chairman of the executive committee of the Munitions Board. For background on his career see no. 1965.

[3] For information on Norstad see no. 1864. Vice-Admiral Sherman had recently been appointed Commander of Naval Forces in the Mediterranean. For background see no. 610.

[4] On the Unification Act see no. 1675.

⁵ Admiral Leahy (see no. 8).

⁶ See no. 1957.

⁷ Bush chaired the Joint Research and Development Board (see no. 612).

⁸ Jack Zuinglius Anderson, Republican, of San Juan Bautista, had represented the Eighth District in California since 1939. See U.S., Congress, House, Committee on Expenditures in the Executive Departments and Committee on Armed Services, *Surplus Real Property and Consolidation of the Supply Facilities of the Armed Services, San Francisco Bay Area: Hearings on H. Res. 90, H. Res. 100, and H. Res. 303, Part 1,* 80th Cong., 1st sess., Sept. 15–17, 1947.

⁹ On Bradley see the next document, n. 3; on Handy see no. 2001; on Lutes see n. 2 above; on Haislip, no. 1371; on Gerow, no. 1304; on Crittenberger, no. 1032; on Eddy, no. 1300; and on Almond, no. 1144.

¹⁰ On Clay's plans see no. 2003; on Smith's most recent communication see no. 2009; on Hull see no. 1393; on Wedemeyer, no. 1300; on Ridgway, no. 1913; on Collins, no. 1727; on Bolté, no. 1133; and on Clark, no. 1344.

¹¹ Major General John Ernest Dahlquist had been deputy director of P&A since June 1947. During World War II Dahlquist had served as CG of the 70th and 36th Infantry Divisions. He had been a member of the Secretary of War's Personnel Board from November 1945 until he assumed his present position. For further background see Chandler, *War Years*.

¹² On Gruenther see no. 1680; on Taylor, no. 277; and on Lemnitzer, no. 2010.

¹³ Major General Clinton Frederick Robinson (USMA 1924) was now executive assistant to the chairman of the National Security Resources Board. He had been director of the Control Branch at Headquarters, Services of Supply, in Washington, D.C., and in the ETO from 1942 until 1946.

¹⁴ For background on Major General Anthony C. McAuliffe see no. 1990. On Gavin see no. 376.

¹⁵ Major General Robert Tryon Frederick (USMA 1928) had become Army Ground Force observer at the Air University at Maxwell Field, Alabama, in the fall of 1947. He had commanded the PLOUGH Force—that is, the First Special Service Force—during World War II (see Chandler, *War Years*).

¹⁶ Colonel Kilbourne Johnston (USMA 1928) had served during the war as an executive officer and as the commanding officer of Army Service Force bases in the Philippines. Since the war he had held various positions in Washington, D.C., including most recently the post of Chief of the Management Division in the Office of the Chief of Staff.

¹⁷ On Higgins see no. 1163; on Bowen, no. 307; on Gilmer, no. 1731; on Carroll, no. 533; and on Michaelis, no. 1513.

¹⁸ At this point on the copy in EM, Eisenhower wrote, "Submitted to Sec. Forrestal Feb—'48."

¹⁹ For the Army's current problem over troop strength see no. 2039.

²⁰ Universal Military Training (see no. 1980).

²¹ For the Army's budget problems see no. 1493.

²² A note at the bottom of this document indicates that it was sent to Forrestal on February 12. Forrestal's acknowledgment of February 21 is in EM.

To John Sheldon Doud Eisenhower and   *February 7, 1948*
Barbara Thompson Eisenhower

Dear Barbara and Johnnie: This is the last note that I shall write as
Chief of Staff and it seemed eminently fitting that I should address it to
you two.

Within a matter of a few minutes we are to have a ceremony here in
the Pentagon as I turn over the job and General Bradley takes it on. It is
a lot of fuss for very little reason; General Bradley and I attempted to do
it on a very simple basis with only him and me present. We were
defeated.

Pupah[1] is still in bed and will have to stay there for the next two or
three weeks. Mamie has had a case of flu and is now suffering the
reaction from the penicillin.

Min[2] and I are still on our feet and she is now in my office to see the
big ceremony.

Love from all of us to you two.[3] *As ever*

[1] Mr. Doud.

[2] Mrs. Doud.

[3] Precisely at noon General Eisenhower administered the oath of office to his
successor, Omar Bradley. At this ceremony in the office of Secretary of the Army
Royall, President Truman pinned a third Oak Leaf Cluster to Eisenhower's DSM
and then gave him a silver cigarette box as a gift from the President and the service
chiefs, Admiral Denfeld (Chief of Naval Operations since December 1947) and
General Spaatz. Eisenhower's acknowledgments for the gift are in EM; and Bradley's oath of office, signed by the two men, is in COS, 1948, 201 Bradley. See also
New York Times, February 8, 1948.

Bibliography:
Essay on Primary Sources

Most of the research for volumes VI through IX of *The Papers of Dwight David Eisenhower* was of necessity conducted in primary, manuscript sources. As Edwin Alan Thompson stated in the essay on primary sources used for the previous volumes (Alfred D. Chandler, *The Papers of Dwight David Eisenhower: The War Years*, 5 vols. [Baltimore, 1970], vol. V, pp. 17–32), the goal of the project determined the manner of that research. Since we have continued to concentrate our attention on those documents with which Eisenhower was personally involved, we expended most of our effort on his own personal files and the records of those individuals and organizations closest to him.

I

As was the case in the previous volumes, we found that the majority of documents we ultimately selected for publication could be located in the prepresidential Dwight D. Eisenhower Personal Papers (covering the years 1916–53), now in the Presidential Library in Abilene, Kansas. This large collection (often referred to as the Schulz file, after General Robert L. Schulz, Eisenhower's military aide and former custodian of his records) is divided into the Principal Files and the Secondary Files. The most important of the several series that make up the Principal Files is entitled Correspondence with Individuals and Organizations. There are 42 feet of records (approximately 126 boxes; one linear foot of records fills three archives boxes) in this series, and the documents therein are arranged alphabetically by name of corre-spondent. This file must be used with care, since correspondence with an individual may be filed under the name of the organization with which he was affiliated. It has been our practice to cite documents from this file simply as "Eisenhower Mss." (or "EM" in the footnotes).

Two other series in the Principal Files, although less rewarding, have proved useful. One, the Subject File, filling approximately 54 boxes, is arranged alphabetically by subject. Again, some prudence is in order when using this file; for example, a cable from Eisenhower to General Handy about General Gruenther's appointment to the Joint Staff (no. 1680), sent from Alaska to the War Department, is filed under "Trips"; we cite it as "Eisenhower Mss., Subject File, Trips." Also included in the Subject Files are several important groups of cables, which we cite collectively as "Eisenhower Mss., Cable File."

Two separate research aids to the Correspondence with Individuals and Organizations and to the Subject Files are part of the prepresidential manuscripts. The first, a small index, consists of over four thousand five-by-eight-inch cards prepared by The Adjutant General's Office. The second is composed of cross-reference sheets originally interfiled with these two substantive files. Both aids are arranged alphabetically by name or subject; neither is as extensive as might be desired.

A third series in the Principal Files, Family Correspondence and Papers (2 ft.), is arranged alphabetically under the names of the Carlsons, the Douds, and several of the Eisenhowers. We refer to this set of papers as "Eisenhower Mss., Family File." We have also referred to the Miscellaneous Routine Correspondence Series (22 ft.), which comprises correspondence handled by Eisenhower's subordinates, in the Secondary Files. These papers are arranged alphabetically by name of correspondent and are cited as "Eisenhower Mss., Routine Corr."

II

The Eisenhower Manuscripts, while unquestionably the best source for the papers contained in these volumes, must nevertheless be supplemented by papers from an array of official and personal files. Although copies of most letters written by the General may be found among his papers, other types of Eisenhower documents are less likely to appear in this collection. Formal communications to the Joint Chiefs of Staff, for example, usually cannot be found among Eisenhower's records. Brief memoranda, handwritten by the General on reports or summaries, are more often found in official files than among Eisenhower's personal papers. Finally, a number of incoming com-munications, as well as supporting documents containing information about issues with which Eisenhower was involved, also must be located elsewhere.

The task of retrieving information from Army or Army-related files on a particular subject is made easier by the War Department decimal filing system. This system is based upon, and to an extent resembles, the Dewey decimal system used in libraries. While different military organizations occasionally filed papers dealing with the same subject under different decimals, a few decimal numbers were employed in the same way throughout the Army: 000.5 for war crimes; 201 for records concerning individuals; 319.1 for reports; 322 for organizations and tactical units; 334 for boards and committees; and 381 for plans.

Perhaps the richest source of documents and information concerning Eisenhower's role in the American military occupation of Europe is the decimal correspondence file of the Secretary of the General Staff of ETOUSA (European Theater of Operations, United States Army)— designated USFET (United States Forces, European Theater) after July 1, 1945. During the war ETOUSA was the top administrative headquarters for the United States Army. After the dissolution of the inter-allied command, or SHAEF (Supreme Headquarters, Allied Expeditionary Force), USFET SGS was established under Eisenhower as the purely American successor of SHAEF's SGS. The ETOUSA-USFET SGS files contain many SHAEF documents relating to the postwar mission of the American forces in Europe. The bulk of the records, however, were generated during the second half of 1945. Fortunately for the researcher, this file, housed in the Modern Military Records Branch of the National Archives in Washington, D.C., is relatively small (27 boxes). The decimal-file folders in this collection are not in strict numerical order, and there are separate cable and geographical subject files at the end of the regular decimal series. At the beginning of the file is an index that lists the correspondence found under each decimal. There are also some cross references under the 201 decimal series. We have cited documents from this file dated before July 1, 1945, as "ETOUSA SGS" followed by the decimal file number; later items are cited as "USFET SGS."

The records of Eisenhower's last wartime command—Supreme Headquarters, Allied Expeditionary Force (SHAEF)—were screened and consulted for the first part of volume VI. Within this enormous collection, located in the National Archives (Record Group 331), several files proved to be useful. Among them was the SHAEF SGS decimal file, which was maintained for the use of Eisenhower and his Chief of Staff, General Walter Bedell Smith. The existence of drafts, memoranda, and working papers in the SHAEF SGS file makes it particularly valuable for those interested in the process of policy formulation. The records of SHAEF's G–3 are perhaps the most useful of all the General Staff records. G–3's responsibilities included operational and posthostilities planning, as well as the evaluation of current operations. The decimal correspondence file (27 boxes) kept by a subsection of G–3, the Operations A unit, from 1943 to 1945 had several items of interest. Two SHAEF G–3 message files also yielded many important documents: One, a chronologically arranged message file, comprises six boxes of incoming and outgoing cables dated September 1944–November 1945 and includes some top-secret communications. A separate SHAEF G–3 Top Secret Message File comprises two boxes of folders filed alphabetically by subject; some of the cables in this file are dated as late as March 1946.

The records of three other European-based organizations also deserve mention. Located in the National Archives (in Record Group 334) are the files of the United States Military Mission to Moscow, 1943–45. Included in these records are thirty-two boxes of subject files and a cable file. A larger and more unwieldy collection—comprising more than 10,000 feet of materials—is the OMGUS (Office of Military Government [Germany], United States) file in the Washington National Records Center (WNRC), Suitland, Maryland (in Record Group 260). The most commonly used citation for this file includes the box or footlocker number followed by the number assigned to the shipment in which the document was sent to the United States; we have also added the title or number of the folder containing the cited document. Thus, a typical citation would read: "OMGUS, Quadripartite Access to and Control of Berlin, V 201-2/3A, Box 23-2/5," with the last number referring, in this case, to the second part of the twenty-third footlocker, fifth shipment. We also give shorter citations to more manageable collections, such as the OMGUS AG (Adjutant General) decimal file. Another major set of records in the WNRC is the EUCOM (European Command) file. Although EUCOM was established as the successor agency of USFET in 1947, some items in its files date back to 1945.

III

For information on Eisenhower's term as Chief of Staff of the Army, the central files of the Office of the Chief of Staff (Record Groups 165 and 319) should be consulted first. These files, cited here as "COS" (although many writers use the abbreviation WDCSA when referring to Eisenhower's office), are arranged according to the War Department decimal system and are located—as are all of the following files unless noted otherwise—in the Modern Military Branch of the National Archives. The COS files that we have used for these volumes include 373 boxes and are divided into eight parts: four chronological files (1944–45, 1946, 1947, and 1948) and a separate top-secret file for each of the four chronological divisions. Some researchers have complained that the COS files are disappointingly thin, and it is true that many—perhaps most—of the papers that passed through Eisenhower's office did not remain in the office files. The Office of the Chief of Staff functioned in large part as a routing and approving agency; important matters brought to Eisenhower's attention were almost invariably sent elsewhere for preliminary staff work. Often the only COS record of an action is an onionskin copy of a summary sheet and an attached draft letter for the signature of the Chief of Staff or the Secretary of War. These onionskin copies bear a stamp of approval or disapproval and some notation that a communication has or has not been sent out. Additional information about the disposition of a matter may be obtained by consulting the COS indexes. These indexes, which are the most extensive and most detailed of any of the indexes used in connection with these volumes, are divided chronologically in the same fashion as the corresponding decimal files, with separate annual top-secret indexes for the top-secret files. Each item is cross-referenced under several decimal numbers, which appear on each copy of the index sheet. A researcher interested in the occupation of Germany, for example, would consult the index under such decimals as 091 Germany; 201 Clay, Lucius; 334 SWNCC; and 371 ETO. The decimal number on the far left of the sheet is that of the file where the item may be found—that is, if a copy was retained in COS. Each index sheet also gives a summary of the pertinent documents, the office to which a matter was referred for staff work, and in many instances the location of further information in the files of other offices.

A few other files are associated with the COS records that we have cited—the papers of General J. Lawton Collins, Chief of Information from 1942 to 1946 (1 box); a box of COS Secretariat cables and correspondence with the White House (1939–46); and the ETO Trip File. The papers in the latter file were originally interfiled in the 1946 COS decimal series under the heading 311 Varied Topics. Unfortunately, both files have been lost, and there are no index sheets to either, but an attempt at reconstruction is now underway.

The General Staff agency upon which the Chief of Staff relied most heavily was the Operations Division (OPD), later renamed the Directorate of Plans and Operations (P&O). In addition to planning, coordinating, and supervising operations, OPD/P&O was responsible for relations between the War Department and the Joint Chiefs of Staff (JCS), the Combined Chiefs of Staff (CCS), and the State-War-Navy Coordinating Committee (SWNCC). While its authority was slightly reduced after the Eisenhower reorganization of 1946, OPD/P&O's

broad powers in areas central to the most important missions of the Army made it preeminent among the many organizations within the War Department. Consequently, the OPD/P&O records are the richest of all files for the study of high-level policy formulation during the period covered by volumes VII–IX.

The OPD/P&O Unclassified through Secret decimal files covering the 1942–48 period fill 2,110 archives boxes; the OPD portion (Record Group 165, covering the years 1942–45) is over three times as large as the P&O portion (Record Group 319, 1946–48). We also screened 213 boxes in two separate top-secret decimal files, one for 1945 (OPD TS) and another for the years 1946–48 (P&O TS). All four decimal files are divided first according to decimal number and then into cases; each case deals with a particular subject. Cases containing a number of papers are further divided and given case subnumbers. Thus, the citation for a document about proposals for the Army's withdrawal from the Philippines might be given as P&O 381 TS, Case 32/40. In front of each case or subcase is a cover sheet (the Combined Routing-Information-Filing Form), which gives both the decimal under which the documents were to be filed and the decimals under which the documents were to be cross-indexed. Often a memorandum for record—which provides a valuable summary of the background and disposition of an issue—may be found on the reverse side of the cover sheet. At the beginning of each decimal division in the file is a master sheet that lists chronologically all papers filed under the decimal and gives the case and subnumber for each. There is also a set of cross-index sheets that can be used to find items in both the Top Secret and the Secret through Unclassified files. The most valuable of these for our purposes were the sheets under the decimal 201 Eisenhower. A researcher should consult both master and cross-index sheets for a particular decimal, since they are not coextensive. He should also keep in mind that papers on a single subject may be in both the Top Secret and the Secret through Unclassified files.

The most valuable source of information about the formulation of policy within joint (that is, interagency) and combined (international) agencies is the ABC—for American-British Conversations—Decimal File, maintained by the Strategy and Policy (later Plans and Policy) Group of OPD/P&O. The ABC File, which is part of Record Group 319, fills 634 boxes of documents spanning the years 1942–48. Documents directly from the Chief of Staff's office or papers bearing Eisenhower's handwritten comments appear less frequently in the ABC File than in the central OPD/P&O records, but the ABC File is a far better source for messages from Eisenhower to the Joint Chiefs. Indeed, virtually all of the formal, numbered papers circulated by the JCS, the CCS, or the SWNCC, as well as drafts, summaries, transcripts of conversations, and other internal memoranda, may be found here. The ABC File is richest for the period prior to the summer of 1947, when General George A. Lincoln, Chief of the Strategy and Policy Group, left the War Department. The most valuable papers in the collection— aside from the numbered documents, that is—are memoranda to and from Lincoln. Most papers retained in official files tend to be somewhat formal in nature; the value of the ABC File lies in the informal, often conversational notes that bluntly outline the real issues at stake and shed light upon the often murky decisionmaking process. The index for the ABC File (45 feet), which covers the entire 1942–48 period, is arranged alphabetically by subject and contains good summaries of the material in the files. Documents related to the issues covered in a particular JCS, CCS, or SWNCC paper may be readily located through this index, since the papers in each section are filed chronologically. Our citations give the symbol "ABC," the decimal number and other designation, a file date (usually the date when the file was started), a section number, and a subsection number.

A few other OPD/P&O files also proved useful for our research. The division retained a major collection of incoming and outgoing cables in which it had an interest. The Unclassified through Secret OPD/P&O Message File for the years 1946–47 contains 93 rolls of microfilm and is arranged chronologically, with a master list for each day. The top-secret portion of the file, composed of paper messages in binders, runs through the end of 1945. There is also a collection of teletype conferences (cited as "WD Telephone Conversations") that includes unclassified through top-secret documents. Many important messages, transcripts, and other valuable papers are to be found in an informal file kept by the Executive Group of OPD/P&O. This file comprises seventeen major subject categories, in which each principal subdivision (called an item) has been given a number. Most of these records were generated during World War II. We cite material from this collection as "OPD Exec #, Item #, Folder or Envelope #." Finally, a file kept by General Lincoln for his own use, the Action Officers Personal File, contains a number of interesting papers. Broken up at some point and interfiled with the OPD/P&O central decimal files, it is now being reconstituted by William H. Cunliffe, Assistant Chief of the Modern Military Branch, National Archives.

The files of the other General Staff divisions contained less Eisenhower material than the OPD/P&O records. The Unclassified through Secret decimal correspondence files and indexes of the Personnel and Administration Division, G–1, are in WNRC. They are arranged in two chronological subseries: The first covers the period January 1942–June 1946; the second, June 1946–December 1948. A separate

Top Secret G–1 Subject File (12 boxes), covering the years 1943–47, is in the National Archives. The files of the Organization and Training Division (O&T, formerly G–3) are difficult to use. They have no indexes and are divided into several segments, including separate decimal and project decimal files (the latter arranged alphabetically by subject) for three periods: 1942–45, 1946, and 1947. They are, however, remarkably complete and detailed for subjects in which O&T had an interest. Both G–1 and O&T Unclassified through Secret files are arranged chronologically by case under each decimal; our citations give the decimal number and the date of the basic correspondence for the case. Associated with the records of the Service, Supply and Procurement Division (G–4) is the personal subject file of its director, General LeRoy R. Lutes, which contains several important items not located elsewhere.

The most rewarding records of the War Department Special Staff are those generated by the Civil Affairs Division (Record Group 165). CAD was responsible for the formulation and coordination of military-government policy and also assisted Army commanders in their occupation and civil-affairs duties. CAD records include decimal files covering the following periods: January 1945 to June 10, 1946 (51 boxes); June 11, 1946 through 1947 (171 boxes); and 1948 (107 boxes). Each segment has its own separate index; the index for 1945–46, however, begins in August 1945. There are also two separate Top Secret files (for 1946–47 [7 boxes] and for 1948 [8 boxes]) and a separate Top Secret index. Many messages that are hard to find in other files may be located in the 15 boxes of the CAD Top Secret Message File; for example, the first box contains Eyes Only messages, which in most cases are especially difficult to find. A collection of teletype conversations (1946–49) and a set of papers of the Army member of the Combined Civil Affairs Committee (1942–49) also contain useful information.

We found files of other Special Staff divisions to be less valuable. Several files of correspondence and reports in the records of the Legislative and Liaison Division (L&LD), which handled the War Department's relations with Congress, proved less useful than we had anticipated. Fiscal legislation, budgetary planning, and appropriated-fund allocation were all functions performed by the War Department's Budget Division. Its Administrative Section maintained a decimal file (1942–49 [173 boxes]) and indexes that were relatively useful to us. The records of the Chief of Information, Public Information Division (11 boxes), provided little new information about Eisenhower's career. The New Developments Division (NDD) and its General Staff successor, the Research and Development Division (R&D), were responsible for the coordination, and to a certain extent the direction, of plans for technological innovation in the field of military equipment. NDD maintained decimal files for 1945 and January–May 1946; R&D has separate decimal files for 1946 (June–December), 1947, and 1948. There are indexes for these files, and we cite these records by giving the abbreviation of the organization (NDD or R&D), the file date, and the decimal. The decimal and project (that is, subject) files of the Special Planning Division, 1943–46, are available in 123 boxes and contain information about planning for demobilization and the postwar Army. Associated with these records is the Army Patch-Simpson Board File, covering the years 1938–46. This file yielded material about the War Department reorganization efforts, including extensive transcripts of interviews with Eisenhower and other officers.

The office of The Adjutant General (TAG) had among its administrative duties, the responsibility for records management. At one time copies of all official-action papers were to be placed in the AG files (Record Group 407). Although this system was no longer in operation by the time Eisenhower became Chief of Staff, a large number of documents nevertheless found their way into The Adjutant General's office from other War Department agencies. There was apparently no hard and fast rule about which records went to the AG and which did not. The AG files are, however, a likely source for certain formal communications, reports, orders, circulars, and matters concerning more than one agency, department, or government. The AG decimal files are divided into three major segments according to classification: Unclassified, classified (through Secret), and Top Secret. They are further divided chronologically, with the most relevant portions for our purposes being the 1946–47 classified and Top Secret files (194 boxes and 13 boxes, respectively) and a separate 1946–48 Unclassified file (1,776 boxes). The AG indexes are divided into classified (1941–47, on microfilm) and Unclassified (1940–45 and 1946–48, on microfilm and paper, respectively) segments. Unfortunately, the Unclassified cross-index sheets under the 201 decimal series have been destroyed. We cite these files as "AG" followed by the decimal number and the basic date of the case. If the citation is to the Unclassified files, no mention is made of classification; if the classified or Top Secret files are cited, this fact is noted.

In 1942 Chief of Staff George C. Marshall established three major field commands: the Army Air Forces (AAF), the Army Ground Forces (AGF), and the Army Service Forces (ASF; originally the Services of Supply). Although all three commands were functioning when Eisenhower succeeded Marshall, only the Army Ground Forces was still in existence when Eisenhower's term as Chief of Staff ended. The air wing had become a separate service—the United States Air Force—and the ASF had been abolished. The files of these three commands are all in the National Archives. They contain relatively few items not located in the Eisenhower Manuscripts or in the other War Department files. Many AAF-generated records are filed with the records of the Headquarters, United States Air Force, in Record Group 341. The most valuable of these are the several series of files of the Director of Plans, 1942–55. The AAF Plans Division (AC/AS-5) was responsible for operational, joint, and combined air planning; we cite its file as "AF/PD" followed by the decimal number, the file date, and the section. An incomplete microfilm index to the 1945–46 portion of the AF/PD File gives the location of JCS papers written by Eisenhower. The Air Adjutant General maintained the central files of the AAF (Record Group 18). This Air AG File (abbreviated here as "AF/AG"), like the Air Force Plans File, is organized roughly along the lines of the War Department decimal system. The Adjutant General's Section of the AGF also maintained a general decimal file (Record Group 337), which we cite as "AGF" followed by the decimal number, the classification, and the binder and case number, when appropriate. To locate a document in the AGF file, the researcher needs its date as well as the file citation. The last major field command, the Army Service Forces, also maintained a number of files in its headquarters. The general decimal correspondence files of the Control Division, Office of the Commanding General (Record Group 160), have been cited in these volumes as "ASF CG, Control Division, 1945–46." A personal file kept by the ASF commanding general, Brehon B. Somervell, is arranged alphabetically by subject and is cited "Somervell Desk File."

IV

The files of Eisenhower's civilian superiors are generally more difficult to use than the strictly military files. Each secretary, under secretary, and assistant secretary kept more than one set of records, and entirely new files were started after the National Security Act of 1947 brought about a major reorganization of the American military establishment. Since the civilian secretariat controlled a relatively small staff and was forced to depend upon the military bureaucracy, the secretariat files usually do not contain complete sets of papers for any particular issue; however, these records are essential for any study of Eisenhower's activities as Chief of Staff.

The Office, Secretary of Defense (OS/D), was established in 1947, and former Secretary of the Navy James Forrestal was its first chief. Forrestal's office files (Record Group 330), which are arranged according to a system of numerically designated subject headings, reflect his naval background. The OS/D Numeric Files, 1947–49, are divided into unclassified (or Central) and classified portions. The citations for the classified files all have the letters *CD* before the file numbers; the unclassified files use the single letter *D*. These quite voluminous files are very complete with respect to the activities of the first defense secretary; they give a good picture of the enormous problems Forrestal faced in trying to establish his authority over the armed services after unification. For each OS/D file there is a "cardex" index arranged alphabetically by name or subject. Record Group 330 also contains several lesser collections created by officials in OS/D. Among these are the Aides' Chronological Files and the Reading Files. The papers in both are arranged by date under the last name of the aide who kept them.

The files maintained by Secretary of War Robert P. Patterson (1945–47) and Secretary of the Army Kenneth C. Royall (1947–49) are scattered throughout Record Groups 107 and 335. One of the richest collections in these groups is Patterson's small (7 boxes) personal top-secret subject file, which we cite as "OSW/RPP Safe File." The file contains few routine or unimportant papers, and there are a number of letters written by Eisenhower. There is no index, but the file's small size and the alphabetical arrangement of the subject folders facilitate its use. Patterson also kept a decimal and a project decimal file (10 boxes), which we cite as "OSW/RPP Gen. Dec. File" and "OSW/RPP Proj. Dec. File," respectively, followed by a decimal number and, for the project file, the name of a military base or geographical area. A much larger file is that of the Office of the Administrative Assistant to the Secretary of War, Coordination and Records Section (cited here as OSW). There are two chronological segments to the unclassified OSW files: 1943 to January 1946 (175 boxes), and February 1946 to July 1947 (91 boxes). There is a single index for both the unclassified OSW files and for the classified decimal and project decimal OSW/RPP files. These three files continue after July 1947, when the War Department became the Department of the Army. The classified (TS) Central Decimal File of Secretary Royall, 1947–49 (28 boxes), is cited as "OSA/KCR Cent. Dec. File."

The personal and office files of Patterson's subordinates are less systematic than the Secretary of War's records. The papers of Assistant Secretary of War (AS/W) Howard C. Petersen, the War Department member of SWNCC and Patterson's advisor-agent in the areas of civil affairs, war crimes, and race relations, are in a number of overlapping files. There are, to begin with, separate classified and unclassified series of AS/W office decimal files that run from 1940 to 1947. In addition, there are 18 boxes of a classified decimal file covering the years 1945–47. These boxes, which were mislabeled when we first examined them, bore the notation "Office, Special Assistant to the Secretary of War 1942–45." We have cited this file as "OSAS/W 42–45 (AS/W-HCP)" in the hope that this will help researchers locate it. Finally, 6 more boxes of Petersen's top-secret personal files are in Record Group 335 and attributed to "Assistant Secretary of the Army" Petersen. These we cite as "AS/A (HCP) Gen. Dec. File 45–47" or "Gen. Sub. File, 41–51." The records of the Under Secretary of War (US/W) are in a much more coherent state: There is one classified series (1943–47) and one unclassified (1945–47) series. The unclassified files and most of the classified files are arranged according to the War Department decimal system. At the end of the classified files is a project file, arranged by subject. The US/W files are rich in matters of materiel procurement, industrial mobilization, and military justice. There are indexes for both the US/W and the AS/W files, but they are difficult to use. The US/W cross-reference sheets are interfiled with the main body of the records, and the several AS/W indexes do not always specify the portion of the AS/W records in which a particular paper is located.

V

Although the Eisenhower Manuscripts, together with the Army files described above, contain copies of virtually every Eisenhower document that we found, two other sources occasionally furnished a message or piece of information not readily located elsewhere. The files of the Joint Chiefs of Staff (Record Group 218), which only recently have been made available to scholars, are invaluable for any study of military or politico-military policy formulation for the post-World War II era. The largest collection is the subject and geographic decimal file—the CCS File. In the National Archives the CCS file is physically divided into three chronological segments—for 1942–45, 1946–47, and 1948–50. The files run continuously, however, and material from one time period may be found in the files of an earlier or later period. Since the CCS File is organized decimally along the lines of the War Department files, our citations give the symbol "CCS" followed by the decimal number and qualifying designation (if any), the file date, and the section number. Occasionally a citation includes the letters *B.P.*, for "bulky package"; bound volumes or large reports are found in these boxes. Material still classified has been separated from the declassified files, pending review. When we screened the 1946–47 declassified files there were 136 boxes of materials. Most of the JCS, CCS, and SWNCC documents in the CCS File can also be found in the ABC File. The main advantage in using the CCS File is that the smaller volume makes it easier to find particular papers and, as of this writing, more material has been declassified in CCS than in ABC. Unfortunately, the CCS File lacks drafts, working papers, and informal memoranda, and the CCS indexes are open only to authorized researchers. Information from the CCS File can be supplemented by reference to the records of Admiral William D. Leahy, who was Chief of Staff to the Commander in Chief of the Army and the Navy and the President's representative on the JCS throughout the period when Eisenhower was Chief of Staff. In this collection (20 boxes), cited as "JCS, Leahy Files," are a number of important cables and memoranda from Army, Navy, and State Department sources. This file, arranged by subject in 144 folders, has been almost entirely declassified.

The central files of the State Department (Record Group 59) for the 1945–49 period contain approximately 2,700 feet of material. These papers are arranged decimally, but the system used is entirely different from that of the War Department. All documents have a decimal-file subject number followed by a document number that incorporates the date. A smaller and for our purposes more rewarding State Department collection is the file of General George C. Marshall's mission to China, 1945–47 (55 boxes). The Marshall Mission Records are divided into several parts, including War Department records, political-affairs records, military-affairs records, State Department Chinese Affairs Office records, and the records of John Carter Vincent. There are several cable files in this collection, including a complete set of GOLD messages. In our citations to both of these State Department collections (which are administered by the Diplomatic Branch, Civil Archives Division, National Archives) we include the box number and folder title for the paper.

VI

The quality of the personal manuscript collections relevant to our project varies greatly. Certainly one of the most valuable is the Walter Bedell Smith Collection in the Eisenhower Library at Abilene. General Smith, Eisenhower's Chief of Staff at SHAEF and USFET, kept two message files of particular importance: the Cable Log, which summarized or quoted in full messages for Smith, Eisenhower, and their principal assistants; and the Eyes Only Cables, a chronologically arranged set of very sensitive and personal messages. Citations to this collection read: "W. B. Smith Coll." Also at the Eisenhower Library is a collection of draft letters and messages kept by Major Robert J. McDuff, an aide in the Office of the Chief of Staff of the Army. Messages in the McDuff collection bear Eisenhower's handwritten emendations, which often were our only means of determining the nature and extent of Eisenhower's involvement in the voluminous correspondence that went out over his signature.

Of all the manuscript collections in the Library of Congress only two were found to contain a significant amount of Eisenhower material. The Robert P. Patterson Manuscripts (198 boxes) are richer for his legal career and service as under secretary of war than for the years that he was secretary of war. Most of the material dated between 1945 and 1947 also appears in official files located at the National Archives. A more important collection is that of General Carl Spaatz, commanding general of the AAF and first Chief of Staff of the United States Air Force. Among the 329 boxes of his papers are 31 boxes of "diaries" (1915–53), which contain cables, official correspondence, and other documents. The Spaatz Papers also include a cable file (15 boxes), a subject file (1942–45 [195 boxes]), and a Chief of Staff, Air Force, file, (1946–48 [26 boxes]).

Three other manuscript collections, all kept by prominent soldier-statesmen, were employed in our search for primary sources. In the National Archives there are 15 boxes of the personal papers of General Lucius D. Clay, American military governor for Germany and later commander of American forces in Europe. A large number of Clay's papers have been edited for publication by Jean Edward Smith; most of our citations, however, are to the manuscript collection, and we give the number of the box in which the document cited may be found. The papers of General George C. Marshall, Army Chief of Staff, special presidential envoy to China, and secretary of state, are in the George C. Marshall Research Library in Lexington, Virginia. A number of important items were provided to us through the kindness of members of the George C. Marshall Research Foundation. Our citations are to the "Marshall Papers" (as distinct from the Marshall Mission Records) followed by the folder or file title. Finally, the personal papers of General Douglas MacArthur, Southwest Pacific Area commander and later America's proconsul in the Far East, are in the MacArthur Memorial Bureau of Archives, in Norfolk, Virginia. A few messages that we were unable to locate elsewhere were found by members of the MacArthur Memorial staff, who generously supplied them to us. Our citations to such material are given in the form used by the MacArthur Memorial Bureau of Archives.

As the foregoing description suggests, a scarcity of sources is one problem that does not confront an historian interested in modern

American military or diplomatic history. Indeed, the researcher must narrow his field of interest quickly so that he can avoid examining an overwhelming mass of records. It is our hope that these volumes and this essay will ease the task of those who undertake further researches in the subjects covered herein.

DAUN VAN EE

Bibliography:
Secondary Sources Cited

Acheson, Dean. *Present at the Creation: My Years in the State Department.* New York, 1969.

———. *Sketches from Life of Men I Have Known.* New York, 1961.

Alexander, Field Marshal Earl, of Tunis. *The Alexander Memoirs, 1940–1945.* Edited by John North. London, 1962.

Allied Military Government. *Trieste Handbook, 1950.* 2d ed., rev. Trieste, 1950.

Alperovitz, Gar. *Atomic Diplomacy: Hiroshima and Potsdam.* New York, 1965.

Altieri, James. *The Spearheaders.* New York, 1960.

Ambrose, Stephen E. *Duty, Honor, Country: A History of West Point.* Baltimore, 1966.

———. *Eisenhower and Berlin, 1945: The Decision to Halt at the Elbe.* New York, 1967.

———. *The Rise to Globalism: American Foreign Policy, 1938–1970.* Baltimore, 1971.

———. *The Supreme Commander: The War Years of General Dwight D. Eisenhower.* Garden City, N.Y., 1970.

Arango, E. Ramón. *Leopold III and the Belgian Royal Question.* Baltimore, 1961.

Aron, Raymond. "Reflections on the Foreign Policy of France." *International Affairs,* no. 21 (1945), 437–47.

Ayer, Fred, Jr. *Before the Colors Fade.* Boston, 1964.

Bach, Julian, Jr. *America's Germany.* New York, 1946.

Backer, John H. *Priming the German Economy: American Occupational Policies, 1945–1948.* Durham, N.C., 1971.

Baizer, Ashur. "I Was at Lichfield." *The Nation,* June 15, 1946, pp. 715–17.

Balfour, Michael, and Mair, John. *Four-Power Control in Germany and Austria, 1945–46.* Survey of International Affairs, 1939–1946, edited by Arnold Toynbee. New York, 1956.

Banks, Arthur C., Jr. "International Law Governing Prisoners of War during the Second World War." Ph.D. dissertation, The Johns Hopkins University, 1955.
Barker, Carol M., and Fox, Matthew H. *Classified Files: The Yellowing Pages.* New York, 1972.
Barth, Alan. *The Loyalty of Free Men.* New York, 1951.
Baruch, Bernard M. *Baruch: My Own Story.* New York, 1957.
————. *The Public Years.* New York, 1960.
Baxter, James Phinney, III. *Scientists against Time.* Boston, 1946.
Bechhoefer, Bernard G. *Postwar Negotiations for Arms Control.* Washington, D.C., 1961.
Bennett, Jack. "The German Currency Reform." *Annals of the American Academy of Political and Social Science: Military Government* 267 (1950), 43–55.
Bernadotte, Count Folke. *The Curtain Falls.* New York, 1945.
Bernstein, Barton J. "The Quest for Security: American Foreign Policy and International Control of Atomic Energy, 1942–1946." *Journal of American History* 60, no. 4 (1974), 1003–44.
————, and Matusow, Allen J., eds. *The Truman Administration: A Documentary History.* New York, 1966.
Bialer, Seweryn, ed. *Stalin and His Generals: Soviet Military Memoirs of World War II.* New York, 1969.
Bidault, Georges. "Agreement on Germany: Key to World Peace." *Foreign Affairs* 24, no. 4 (1946), 571–78.
Biddle, George. *Artist at War.* New York, 1944.
Blum, John Morton. *From the Morgenthau Diaries.* 3 vols. Boston, 1959–67. Vol. III, *Years of War, 1941–1945.*
————. *Roosevelt and Morgenthau.* Boston, 1970.
Blumenson, Martin. *Breakout and Pursuit.* U.S. Army in World War II, edited by Stetson Conn. Washington, D.C., 1961.
————. *Salerno to Cassino.* U.S. Army in World War II, edited by Stetson Conn. Washington, D.C., 1969.
————. *The Patton Papers.* 2 vols. Boston, 1974. Vol. II, *1940–1945.*
Bowett, D. W. *United Nations Forces.* New York, 1966.
Bowles, Chester. *Promises to Keep: My Years in Public Life, 1941–69.* New York, 1971.
Bradley, Omar N. *A Soldier's Story.* New York, 1951.
Bradshaw, Mary E. "Military Control of Zone A in Venezia Giulia." *Department of State Bulletin* 16, no. 417 (1947), 1257–65.
Brodie, Bernard. "Military Policy and the Atomic Bomb." *Infantry Journal* 59, no. 1 (1946), 23–35.
Brookings Institution. *Major Problems of United States Foreign Policy, 1947: A Study Guide.* Washington, D.C., 1947.
————. *Summary of Developments in Major Problems of United States Foreign Policy* 1, no. 5 (1948), 16; and no. 6 (1948), 15.
Brown, Thomas A. "ANSCOL at the Naval War College." *United States Naval Institute Proceedings* 72, no. 517 (1946), 433–38.
Buhite, Russell D. *Patrick J. Hurley and American Foreign Policy.* Ithaca, 1973.
Bullitt, William Christian. *The Great Globe Itself: A Preface to World Affairs.* New York, 1946.
Bureau of the Budget, War Records Section. *The United States at War: Development*

and *Administration of the War Program by the Federal Government*. Washington, D.C., 1946.

Burgess, Erik. "The Cuxhaven V-2 Tests." *Journal of the American Rocket Society* 64 (December 1945), 22-23.

Bush, Vannevar. *Modern Arms and Free Men: A Discussion of the Role of Science in Preserving Democracy*. New York, 1949.

Butcher, Harry C. *My Three Years with Eisenhower: The Personal Diary of Captain Harry C. Butcher, USNR*. New York, 1946.

Butler, Nicholas Murray. *Across the Busy Years: Recollections and Reflections*. New York, 1939.

Byrnes, James F. *All in One Lifetime*. New York, 1958.

―――. *Speaking Frankly*. New York, 1947.

Campbell, John C. *The United States in World Affairs, 1945-1947*. New York, 1947.

Cannon, M. Hamlin. *Leyte: The Return to the Philippines*. U.S. Army in World War II, edited by Kent Roberts Greenfield. Washington, D.C., 1954.

Caraley, Demetrios. *The Politics of Military Unification*. New York, 1966.

Chalfont, Alun. *Montgomery of Alamein*. New York, 1976.

Chandler, Alfred D., Jr., ed. *The Papers of Dwight David Eisenhower: The War Years*. 5 vols. Baltimore, 1970.

Charters, Werrett Wallace. *Opportunities for the Continuation of Education in the Armed Forces*. Washington, D.C., 1952.

Chase, Joseph Cummings. *Face Value: Autobiography of the Portrait Painter*. New York, 1962.

Cheng, Bin. *The Law of International Air Transport*. New York, 1962.

Childs, Marquis. *Eisenhower, Captive Hero: A Critical Study of the General and the President*. New York, 1958.

Chuikov, Vasili I. *The Fall of Berlin*. New York, 1967.

Churchill, Winston S. *The Second World War*. 6 vols. Boston, 1948-53. Vol. VI, *Triumph and Tragedy*.

Clark, Mark W. *Calculated Risk*. New York, 1950.

Clark, Ronald W. *The Birth of the Bomb*. London, 1961.

Clay, Lucius D. *Decision in Germany*. New York, 1950.

―――. *The Papers of General Lucius D. Clay, Germany, 1945-1949*. Edited by Jean Edward Smith. 2 vols. Bloomington, Ind., 1974.

Clemens, Diane Shaver. *Yalta*. New York, 1970.

Cline, Ray S. *Washington Command Post: The Operations Division*. U.S. Army in World War II, edited by Kent Roberts Greenfield. Washington, D.C., 1951.

―――, and Matloff, Maurice. "Development of War Department Views on Unification." *Military Affairs* 13, no. 2 (1949), 71.

Codman, Charles R. *Drive*. Boston, 1957.

Coffman, Edward M. *The Hilt of the Sword: The Career of Peyton C. March*. Madison, 1966.

Cohen, Jerome B. *Japan's Economy in War and Reconstruction*. Minneapolis, 1949.

Cole, Hubert. *Laval*. New York, 1963.

Cole, Hugh M. *The Ardennes: Battle of the Bulge*. U.S. Army in World War II, edited by Stetson Conn. Washington, D.C., 1965.

Coles, Harry L., and Weinberg, Albert K. *Civil Affairs: Soldiers Become Governors*. U.S. Army in World War II, edited by Stetson Conn. Washington, D.C., 1964.

Conant, James B. *My Several Lives: Memoirs of a Social Inventor*. New York, 1970.

Conn, Stetson; Engelman, Rose C.; and Fairchild, Byron. *Guarding the United States and Its Outposts*. U.S. Army in World War II, edited by Stetson Conn. Washington, D.C., 1964.

Conn, Stetson, and Fairchild, Byron. *The Framework of Hemisphere Defense*. U.S. Army in World War II, edited by Kent Roberts Greenfield. Washington, D.C., 1960.

Craven, Wesley Frank, and Cate, James Lea, eds. *Europe: Argument to V-E Day. The Army Air Forces in World War II*, vol. III. Chicago, 1958.

Dalfiume, Richard M. *Desegregation of the U.S. Armed Forces*. Columbia, Mo., 1969.

Daniels, Roger. *Concentration Camps USA: Japanese Americans and World War II*. New York, 1971.

Daugherty, William E., with Janowitz, Morris. *A Psychological Warfare Casebook*. Baltimore, 1958.

Davidson, Eugene. *The Death and Life of Germany*. New York, 1959.

―――. *The Trial of the Germans*. New York, 1966.

Davie, Maurice R. *Refugees in America*. New York, 1947.

Davis, Franklin M., Jr. *Come As a Conqueror: The United States Army's Occupation of Germany, 1945–1949*. New York, 1967.

Davis, Kenneth S. *Soldier of Democracy: A Biography of Dwight Eisenhower*. New York, 1945.

Davis, Vincent. *Postwar Defense Policy and the U.S. Navy, 1943–1946*. Chapel Hill, 1962.

Deane, John R. *The Strange Alliance: The Story of Our Efforts at Wartime Cooperation with Russia*. New York, 1947.

De Gaulle, Charles. *The War Memoirs of Charles de Gaulle*. 3 vols. New York, 1955–60. Vol. III, *Salvation, 1944–46*, translated by Richard Howard.

De Guingand, Francis. *Operation Victory*. 3d ed., rev. London, 1963.

Dennett, Raymond, and Turner, Robert K., eds. *July 1945–December 1946*. Documents on American Foreign Relations, vol. VIII. Princeton, 1948.

DePorte, Anton W. *De Gaulle's Foreign Policy, 1944–1946*. Cambridge, Mass., 1968.

Derthick, Martha. *The National Guard in Politics*. Cambridge, Mass., 1965.

Dod, Karl C. *The Corps of Engineers: The War against Japan*. U.S. Army in World War II, edited by Stetson Conn. Washington, D.C., 1966.

Donnison, F. S. V. *Civil Affairs and Military Government: Central Organization and Planning*. History of the Second World War, edited by J. R. M. Butler. London, 1966.

―――. *Civil Affairs and Military Government: North-West Europe, 1944–1946*. History of the Second World War, edited by J. R. M. Butler. London, 1961.

Dorn, Walter L. "The Debate over American Policy in Germany in 1944–1945." *Political Science Quarterly* 72 (1957), 481–501.

Dornberger, Walter. *V-2*. New York, 1954.

Douglass, Paul F. *Six upon the World*. Boston, 1954.

Dulles, Allen. *The Craft of Intelligence*. New York, 1963.

Dunn, Frederick S., et al. *The Absolute Weapon: Atomic Power and World Order*. Edited by Bernard Brodie. New York, 1946.

Dusenberry, William. "Foot and Mouth Disease in Mexico, 1946–1951." *Agricultural History* 29 (April 1955), 82–90.

Dziuban, Stanley W. *Military Relations between the United States and Canada, 1939–*

1945. U.S. Army in World War II, edited by Kent Roberts Greenfield. Washington, D.C., 1959.

Eayrs, James G. *In Defence of Canada.* 2 vols. Toronto, 1964–65. Vol. II, *Appeasement and Rearmament.*

Eisenhower, Dwight D. *At Ease: Stories I Tell to Friends.* New York, 1967.

——. *Crusade in Europe.* New York, 1948.

——. *Letters to Mamie.* Edited by John S. D. Eisenhower. New York, 1978.

——. *Mandate for Change, 1953–1956.* New York, 1963.

Eisenhower, John S. D. *The Bitter Woods.* New York, 1969.

——. *Strictly Personal.* New York, 1974.

Eisenhower, Milton S. *The President Is Calling.* New York, 1974.

Eisenhower Medical Center Auxiliary. *Five Star Favorites: Recipes from Friends of Mamie and Ike.* New York, 1974.

Engler, Robert. "The Individual Soldier and Occupation." *Annals of the American Academy of Political and Social Science: Military Government* 267 (1950), 82–83.

Epstein, William. *Disarmament: Twenty-five Years of Effort.* Toronto, 1971.

Esposito, Vincent, J., ed. *The West Point Atlas of American Wars.* 2 vols. New York, 1959. Vol. II.

Falk, Stanley L. *Bataan: The March of Death.* New York, 1962.

Farago, Ladislas. *Patton: Ordeal and Triumph.* New York, 1964.

Feis, Herbert. *The Atomic Bomb and the End of World War II.* Princeton, 1966.

——. *Between War and Peace: The Potsdam Conference.* Princeton, 1960.

——. *The China Tangle: The American Effort in China from Pearl Harbor to the Marshall Mission.* Princeton, 1953.

——. *Churchill, Roosevelt and Stalin: The War They Waged and the Peace They Sought.* Princeton, 1957.

——. *From Trust to Terror, 1945–1950.* New York, 1970.

Fleming, Denna Frank. *The Cold War and Its Origins, 1917–1960.* New York, 1961. Vol. II.

Fleming, Thomas J. *West Point.* New York, 1969.

Floyd, Marcus W. "Displaced Persons." Occupation Forces in Europe Series, 1945–46. Mimeographed. Washington, D.C., 1947.

Foot, Michael R. D. *SOE in France: An Account of the Work of the British Special Operations Executive in France, 1940–1944.* History of the Second World War. London, 1966.

Ford, Corey, and MacBain, Alastair. *Cloak and Dagger: The Secret Story of OSS.* New York, 1945.

Forrestal, James. *The Forrestal Diaries.* Edited by Walter Millis. New York, 1951.

Frederiksen, Oliver J. *The American Military Occupation of Germany, 1945–1953.* Darmstadt, Germany, 1953.

Frey, Richard, ed. *The Official Encyclopedia of Bridge.* New York, 1971.

Friedrich, Carl J. "The Peace Settlement with Germany—Economic and Social." *Annals of the American Academy of Political and Social Science: Peace Settlements of World War II* 257 (1948), 133.

Friend, Theodore. *Between Two Empires: The Ordeal of the Philippines, 1929–1946.* New Haven, 1965.

Furer, Julius Augustus. *Administration of the Navy Department in World War II.* Washington, D.C., 1959.

Gaddis, John Lewis. *The United States and the Origins of the Cold War.* New York, 1972.

Gardner, Lloyd C. *Architects of Illusion: Men and Ideas in American Foreign Policy, 1941–1949.* Chicago, 1970.

Gimbel, John. *The American Occupation of Germany: Politics and the Military, 1945–49.* Stanford, 1968.

———. *The Origins of the Marshall Plan.* Stanford, 1976.

Ginzberg, Eli, and Bray, Douglas W. *The Uneducated.* New York, 1953.

———, et al. *The Ineffective Soldier: Lessons for Management and the Nation.* New York, 1959.

Goodrich, Leland M. *Korea: A Study of U.S. Policy in the United Nations.* New York, 1956.

———. *The United Nations.* New York, 1959.

———, and Carroll, Marie J., eds. *July 1944–June 1945.* Documents on American Foreign Relations, vol. VII. Princeton, 1947.

Gowing, Margaret. *Independence and Deterrence: Britain and Atomic Energy, 1945–52.* 2 vols. New York, 1974. Vol. I, *Policy Making.*

Gray, Alan. "Tommy Atkins through the Ages." *The Contemporary Review* (London), no. 956 (1945), 91–95.

Green, Constance McLaughlin; Thomson, Harry C.; and Roots, Peter C. *The Ordnance Department: Planning Munitions for War.* U.S. Army in World War II, edited by Kent Roberts Greenfield. Washington, D.C., 1955.

Green, Harold P., and Rosenthal, Alan. *Government of the Atom: The Integration of Powers.* New York, 1963.

Greenfield, Kent Roberts. *The Historian and the Army.* New Brunswick, N.J., 1954.

———; Palmer, Robert R.; and Wiley, Bell I. *The Organization of Ground Combat Troops.* U.S. Army in World War II, edited by Kent Roberts Greenfield. Washington, D.C., 1947.

Grodzins, Morton. *Americans Betrayed: Politics and the Japanese Evacuation.* Chicago, 1946.

Groves, Leslie R. *Now It Can Be Told: The Story of the Manhattan Project.* New York, 1962.

Guderian, Heinz. *Erinnerungen eines Soldaten.* Heidelberg, Germany, 1951.

Hammond, Paul Y. *Organizing for Defense.* Princeton, 1961.

Harrington, Charles Willmot, Jr. *The Problem of Disarmament in the United Nations.* Geneva, 1950.

Harris, C. R. S. *Allied Military Administration of Italy, 1943–1945.* History of the Second World War, edited by J. R. M. Butler. London, 1957.

Hata, Donald Teruo, Jr., and Hata, Nadine Ishitani. *Japanese Americans and World War II.* The Forum Series, edited by Franklin Mitchell. St. Charles, Mo., 1974.

Hatch, Alden. *Red Carpet for Mamie.* New York, 1954.

Haynes, Richard F. *The Awesome Power: Harry S. Truman as Commander in Chief.* Baton Rouge, 1973.

Hayward, Edwin J. "Coordination of Military and Civilian Civil Affairs Planning." *Annals of the American Academy of Political and Social Science: Military Government* 267 (1950), 19–27.

Her Majesty's Stationery Office. *Statutory Instruments, 1954.* London, 1955.

Hester, Mildred V. "Redeployment." Occupation Forces in Europe Series, 1945–46. Mimeographed. Washington, D.C., 1947.

Hewes, James E., Jr. *From Root to McNamara: Army Organization and Administration, 1900–1963*. Washington, D.C., 1975.

Hewins, Ralph. *Count Folke Bernadotte*. Minneapolis, 1950.

Hewlett, Richard G., and Anderson, Oscar E., Jr. *A History of the United States Atomic Energy Commission*. Vol. I, *The New World, 1939–1946*. University Park, Pa., 1962.

――――, and Duncan, Francis. *A History of the United States Atomic Energy Commission*. Vol. II, *Atomic Shield, 1947–1952*. University Park, Pa., 1969.

Higa, Mikio. *Politics and Parties in Postwar Okinawa*. Vancouver, 1963.

Hillman, William. *Mr. President*. New York, 1952.

His Majesty's Stationery Office. *Statutory Rules and Orders, 1942*. 2 vols. London, 1943. Vol. I.

Holborn, Hajo. *American Military Government: Its Organization and Policies*. Washington, D.C., 1947.

Honeywell, Roy J. *Chaplains of the United States Army*. Washington, D.C., 1958.

Howard, Harry Nicholas. *Turkey, the Straits and U.S. Policy*. Baltimore, 1974.

Howe, George F. *The Battle History of the 1st Armored Division*. Washington, D.C., 1954.

――――. *Northwest Africa: Seizing the Initiative in the West*. U.S. Army in World War II, edited by Kent Roberts Greenfield. Washington, D.C., 1957.

Howley, Frank. *Berlin Command*. New York, 1950.

Hurwitz, Harold J. "U.S. Military Government in Germany: Press Reorientation." Vol. I. Mimeographed. Washington, D.C., 1950.

Hyneman, Charles S. "The Army's Civil Affairs Training Program." *American Political Science Review* 38 (1944), 342–53.

Inter-Allied Reparation Agency. *Reports of the Secretary General, 1946–1949*. Brussels, 1947–50.

International Military Tribunal. *Trial of the Major War Criminals before the International Military Tribunal*. 42 vols. Nuremberg, 1947–49.

Ismay, Hastings L. *The Memoirs of General Lord Ismay*. New York, 1960.

Jacobs, Clyde Edward, and Gallagher, John F. *The Selective Service Act: A Case Study of the Governmental Process*. New York, 1968.

James, R. Warren. *Wartime Economic Cooperation: A Study of Relations between Canada and the United States*. Toronto, 1949.

Jameson, Henry B. *Heroes by the Dozen*. Abilene, 1961.

Jamieson, John. *Editions for the Armed Services, Inc.: A History*. New York, 1948.

John, Robert, and Hadawi, Sami. *The Palestine Diary*. New York, 1970. Vol. I, *1914–1945;* and vol. II, *1945–1948*.

Jones, Joseph Marion. *The Fifteen Weeks (February 21–June 5, 1947)*. New York, 1955.

Jorgensen, Daniel B. *Air Force Chaplains*. 2 vols. Washington, D.C., 1961. Vol. I, *The Service of Chaplains to Army Air Units, 1917–1946*.

Kahin, George McTurnan. *Nationalism and Revolution in Indonesia*. New York, 1952.

Kennan, George Frost. *Memoirs, 1925–1950*. Boston, 1967.

Kertész, Stephen D., ed. *The Fate of East Central Europe*. Notre Dame, 1956.

Kirby, S. Woodburn. *The War against Japan*. 5 vols. London, 1957–69. Vol. V, *The Surrender of Japan*. History of the Second World War, edited by J. R. M. Butler. London, 1956–76.

Kirkpatrick, Lyman B., Jr. *The Real CIA*. New York, 1968.

Kogan, Norman. *A Political History of Postwar Italy*. New York, 1966.

Kolko, Joyce, and Kolko, Gabriel. *The Limits of Power*. New York, 1972.

Komer, Robert W. "Civil Affairs and Military Government in the Mediterranean Theater." Mimeographed. Washington, D.C., 1948.

Konvitz, Milton R. *The Alien and the Asiatic in American Law*. Ithaca, 1946.

Kornitzer, Bela. *The Great American Heritage: The Story of the Five Eisenhower Brothers*. New York, 1955.

Kousoulas, D. George. *Revolution and Defeat: The Story of the Greek Communist Party*. London, 1965.

Krock, Arthur. *Memoirs: Sixty Years on the Firing Line*. New York, 1968.

Kuklick, Bruce. "The Division of Germany and American Policy on Reparations." *Western Political Quarterly* 23, no. 2 (1970), 276–93.

LaFeber, Walter. *America, Russia, and the Cold War, 1945–1966*. New York, 1967.

Laffin, John. *Tommy Atkins*. London, 1966.

Lane, Arthur Bliss. *I Saw Poland Betrayed*. New York, 1948.

Langer, William L. *Our Vichy Gamble*. New York, 1947.

Larson, Henrietta M.; Knowlton, Evelyn H.; and Popple, Charles S. *New Horizons, 1927–1950: History of Standard Oil Company (New Jersey)*. New York, 1971.

Lasby, Clarence. *Project Paperclip: German Scientists and the Cold War*. New York, 1971.

Latham, Earl. *The Communist Controversy in Washington: From the New Deal to McCarthy*. Cambridge, Mass., 1966.

Leahy, William D. *I Was There*. New York, 1950.

Lee, Asher, ed. *The Soviet Air and Rocket Forces*. New York, 1959.

Lee, R. Alton. "The Army 'Mutiny' of 1946." *Journal of American History* 53, no. 3 (1966), 555–71.

Lee, Ulysses. *The Employment of Negro Troops*. U.S. Army in World War II, edited by Stetson Conn. Washington, D.C., 1966.

Legere, Lawrence J., Jr. "Unification of the Armed Forces." Mimeographed. Washington, D.C., n.d.

Lerwill, Leonard L. "Organization and Administration of the European Theater and Its Headquarters." Occupation Forces in Europe Series, 1945–46. Mimeographed. Washington, D.C., 1947.

Levy, Willy. *Rockets, Missiles, and Space Travel*. New York, 1958.

Lewis, George G., and Mewha, John. *History of Prisoner of War Utilization by the United States Army, 1776–1945*. Department of the Army Pamphlet 20-213. Washington, D.C., 1955.

Lilienthal, David E. *The Journals of David E. Lilienthal*. 4 vols. New York, 1964–69. Vol. II, *The Atomic Energy Years, 1945–1950*.

Lindley, John Mason. " 'A Soldier Is Also a Citizen': The Controversy over Military Justice in the U.S. Army, 1917–1920." Ph.D. dissertation, Duke University, 1974.

Liss, Sheldon B. *The Canal: Aspects of U.S.-Panama Relations*. Notre Dame, 1967.

Luza, Radomic. *The Transfer of the Sudeten Germans*. New York, 1964.

Lyon, Peter. *Eisenhower: Portrait of the Hero*. Boston, 1974.

MacArthur, Douglas. *Reminiscences*. New York, 1964.

———. *Reports of General MacArthur*. Prepared by his General Staff. Washington, D.C., 1966. Vol. I supp., *MacArthur in Japan: The Occupation: Military Phase*.

McCann, Kevin. *Man from Abilene.* New York, 1952.

McClure, Arthur F. *The Truman Administration and the Problems of Postwar Labor, 1945–1948.* Rutherford, N.J., 1969.

MacDonald, Charles B. *The Siegfried Line Campaign.* U.S. Army in World War II, edited by Stetson Conn. Washington, D.C., 1963.

Machado, Manuel A., Jr. *An Industry in Crisis: Mexican–United States Cooperation in the Control of Foot-and-Mouth Disease.* University of California Publications in History, vol. 80. Berkeley, 1968.

McKeogh, Michael J., and Lockridge, Richard. *Sgt. Mickey and General Ike.* New York, 1946.

McLachlan, Donald. *Room 39: Naval Intelligence in Action, 1939–45.* London, 1968.

Mallaby, George. *From My Level: Unwritten Minutes.* London, 1965.

Marshall, George C. "Biennial Report of the Chief of Staff of the United States Army to the Secretary of War, July 1, 1943 to June 30, 1945." In *Marshall, Arnold, King: The War Reports of General of the Army George C. Marshall, General of the Army H. H. Arnold, and Fleet Admiral Ernest J. King,* pp. 141–300. New York, 1947.

———. *Marshall's Mission to China.* 2 vols. Arlington, Va., 1976.

Marshall, Katherine Tupper. *Together: Annals of an Army Wife.* New York, 1946.

Masland, John W., and Radway, Laurence I. *Soldiers and Scholars.* Princeton, 1957.

Matloff, Maurice, and Snell, Edwin M. *Strategic Planning for Coalition Warfare 1943–1944.* U.S. Army in World War II, edited by Kent Roberts Greenfield. Washington, D.C., 1959.

Matthews, W. R., and Atkins, W. M., eds. *A History of St. Paul's Cathedral.* London, 1957.

Matusow, Allen J. *Farm Policies and Politics in the Truman Years.* Cambridge, Mass., 1967.

Meade, Edward Grant. *American Military Government in Korea.* New York, 1951.

Mecham, John Lloyd. *The United States and Inter-American Security, 1889–1960.* Austin, 1962.

Merriam, Robert E. *Dark December: The Full Account of the Battle of the Bulge.* Chicago, 1947.

Michael, Paul, et al., eds. *The American Movies Reference Book: The Sound Era.* Englewood Cliffs, 1969.

Middleton, Drew. *Our Share of Night: A Personal Narrative of the War Years.* New York, 1946.

Millett, Allan R. *The General: Robert L. Bullard and Officership in the United States Army, 1881–1925.* Westport, Conn., 1975.

Millett, John D. *The Organization and Role of the Army Service Forces.* U.S. Army in World War II, edited by Kent Roberts Greenfield. Washington, D.C., 1954.

Montgomery, Bernard L. *Eighth Army: El Alamein to the River Sangro.* Berlin, 1946.

———. *The Memoirs of Field-Marshal the Viscount Montgomery of Alamein, K.G.* Cleveland and New York, 1958.

Moorehead, Alan. *Montgomery: A Biography.* London, 1967.

Moran, Lord John. *Churchill: Taken from the Diaries of Lord Moran.* Boston, 1966.

Morgan, Frederick E. *Overture to Overlord.* New York, 1950.

———. *Peace and War: A Soldier's Life.* London, 1961.

Morgan, Kay Summersby. *Past Forgetting: My Love Affair with Dwight D. Eisenhower.* New York, 1976.

Morgenthau, Henry. *Germany Is Our Problem.* New York, 1945.

Morton, Louis. *The Fall of the Philippines.* U.S. Army in World War II, edited by Kent Roberts Greenfield. Washington, D.C., 1953.

————. *Strategy and Command: The First Two Years.* U.S. Army in World War II, edited by Kent Roberts Greenfield. Washington, D.C., 1962.

Mosely, Philip E. "The Occupation of Germany." *Foreign Affairs* 28 (July 1950), 587–604.

Murphy, Robert. *Diplomat among Warriors.* New York, 1964.

Nadich, Judah. *Eisenhower and the Jews.* New York, 1953.

Nelson, Otto L., Jr. *National Security and the General Staff.* Washington, D.C., 1946.

Nobleman, Eli E. "Quadripartite Military Government Organization and Operation in Germany." *American Journal of International Law* 41 (1947), 650–55.

Norman, Albert. *Operation Overlord: Design and Reality; The Allied Invasion of Western Europe.* Harrisburg, Pa., 1952.

Norton, Garrison. "World Air Transport: Development of United States Policy." *Department of State Bulletin* 15, no. 387 (1946), 1006–10.

O'Ballance, Edgar. *The Greek Civil War, 1944–1949.* New York, 1966.

Pan American Union. *The United Nations Conference on International Organization: Report by the Director General.* Washington, D.C., 1945.

Paterson, Thomas G., ed. *Cold War Critics: Alternatives to American Foreign Policy in the Truman Years.* Chicago, 1971.

Patton, George S., Jr. *War As I Knew It.* Boston, 1947.

Paul, Randolph E. *Taxation in the United States.* Boston, 1954.

Phillips, Harlan, ed. *Felix Frankfurter Reminisces.* New York, 1960.

Playfair, I. S. O., with Molony, C. J. C. *The Mediterranean and Middle East.* Vol. V. History of the Second World War, edited by J. R. M. Butler. London, 1973.

Pogue, Forrest C. *George C. Marshall.* 3 vols. New York, 1963–73. Vol. I, *Education of a General, 1880–1939;* Vol. II, *Ordeal and Hope, 1939–1942;* and Vol. III, *Organizer of Victory, 1943–1945.*

————. *The Supreme Command.* U.S. Army in World War II, edited by Kent Roberts Greenfield. Washington, D.C., 1954.

Pollock, James K., and Meisel, James H. *Germany under Occupation.* Ann Arbor, 1947.

Pomeroy, Earl S. *Pacific Outpost: American Strategy in Guam and Micronesia.* Stanford, 1951.

Ramazani, Rouhollah K. *Iran's Foreign Policy, 1941–1973: A Study of Foreign Policy in Modernizing Nations.* Charlottesville, 1975.

Ransom, Harry Howe. *Central Intelligence and National Security.* Cambridge, Mass., 1959.

Ratchford, B. U., and Ross, William D. *Berlin Reparations Assignment: Round One of the German Peace Settlement.* Chapel Hill, 1947.

Rehn, John W. H. "Africa-Middle East Theater." In *Communicable Diseases,* edited by John Boyd Coates, Jr. Preventive Medicine in World War II, vol. V. Washington, D.C., 1960.

Reischauer, Edwin O. *The United States and Japan.* Cambridge, Mass., 1965.

Report of the President's Advisory Commission on Universal Training: A Program for National Security. Washington, D.C., 1947.

Ridgway, Matthew B. *Soldier: The Memoirs of Matthew B. Ridgway As Told to Harold H. Martin.* New York, 1956.

Ries, John C. *The Management of Defense: Organization and Control of the U.S. Armed Services.* Baltimore, 1964.

Riker, William H. *Soldiers of the State: The Role of the National Guard in American Democracy.* Washington, D.C., 1957.

Risch, Erna, and Kieffer, Chester L. *The Quartermaster Corps: Organization, Supply and Services.* Vol. II. U.S. Army in World War II, edited by Kent Roberts Greenfield. Washington, D.C., 1955.

Roll, Eric. *The Combined Food Board: A Study in International Planning.* Stanford, 1956.

Ross, William F., and Romanus, Charles F. *The Quartermaster Corps: Operations in the War against Germany.* U.S. Army in World War II, edited by Stetson Conn. Washington, D.C., 1965.

Roxan, David, and Wanstall, Ken. *The Rape of Art: The Story of Hitler's Plunder of the Great Masterpieces of Europe.* New York, 1964.

Royal Institute of International Affairs. *United Nations Documents, 1941–1945.* London, 1946.

Rundell, Walter, Jr. *Black Market Money: The Collapse of U.S. Military Currency Control in World War II.* Baton Rouge, 1964.

Ruppenthal, Roland G. *Logistical Support of the Armies,* vol. II, *September 1944–May 1945.* U.S. Army in World War II, edited by Kent Roberts Greenfield. Washington, D.C., 1959.

Russell, Ruth B. *The United Nations and the United States Security Policy.* Washington, D.C., 1968.

Ryan, Cornelius. *A Bridge Too Far.* New York, 1974.

Ryan, Oswald. "International Air Transport Policy." *Air Affairs* 1, no. 1 (1946), 45–66.

Sawyer, Robert K. *Military Advisors in Korea: KMAG in Peace and War.* Edited by Walter G. Hermes. The Army Historical Series, edited by Stetson Conn. Washington, D.C., 1962.

Sceva, Paul H. *Recollections by "The Old Man of the Mountain."* Tacoma, n.d.

Schapsmeier, Edward L., and Schapsmeier, Frederick H. *Prophet in Politics: Henry A. Wallace and the War Years, 1940–1965.* Ames, 1970.

Schechtman, Joseph B. *The United States and the Jewish State Movement: The Crucial Decade: 1939–1949.* New York, 1966.

Schlesinger, Arthur M., Jr. *The Age of Roosevelt II: The Coming of the New Deal.* Boston, 1958.

Schnabel, James F. *Policy and Direction: The First Year.* U.S. Army in the Korean War, edited by Maurice Matloff. Washington, D.C., 1972.

Sheehan, Fred. *Anzio: Epic of Bravery.* Norman, Okla., 1964.

Shelton, William R. *Soviet Space Exploration.* New York, 1968.

Sherry, Michael S. *Preparing for the Next War: American Plans for Postwar Defense, 1941–45.* New Haven, 1977.

Sherwood, Robert E. *Roosevelt and Hopkins: An Intimate History.* New York, 1948.

Shurcliff, William A. *Bombs at Bikini.* New York, 1947.

Smith, Clarence McKittrick. *The Medical Department: Hospitalization and Evacua-

tion, Zone of Interior. U.S. Army in World War II, edited by Kent Roberts Greenfield. Washington, D.C., 1956.

Smith, R. Elberton. *The Army and Economic Mobilization*. U.S. Army in World War II, edited by Kent Roberts Greenfield. Washington, D.C., 1959.

Smith, Walter Bedell. *My Three Years in Moscow*. New York, 1950.

Smyth, Henry DeWolf. *Atomic Energy for Military Purposes: The Official Report on the Development of the Atomic Bomb under the Auspices of the United States Government, 1940–1945*. Princeton, 1948.

Snell, John L. *Wartime Origins of the East-West Dilemma over Germany*. New Orleans, 1959.

———, and Pogue, Forrest C., eds. *The Meaning of Yalta*. Baton Rouge, 1956.

Sokolov, V. L. "Soviet Use of German Science and Technology 1945–1946, Research Program on the USSR." East European Fund Series, no. 72, pp. 1–30. New York, 1955.

Sparrow, John C. *History of Personnel Demobilization in the United States Army*. Department of the Army Pamphlet 20-210. Washington, D.C., 1952.

Stannard, Harold. "Civil Aviation." *International Affairs* 21, no. 4 (1945), 497–511.

Starr, Joseph R. "Operations from Late March to Mid-July 1945." Mimeographed. Washington, D.C., 1950.

———. "U.S. Military Government in Germany: Operations during the Rhineland Campaign." Mimeographed. Washington, D.C., 1950.

Steinberg, Alfred. *The Man from Missouri: The Life and Times of Harry S. Truman*. New York, 1962.

Strauss, Lewis L. *Men and Decisions*. New York, 1962.

Sumler, David E. *Europe and the Cold War*. St. Charles, Mo., 1974.

Summersby, Kay. *Eisenhower Was My Boss*. New York, 1948.

Supreme Commander Allied Powers, Government Section. *Political Reorientation of Japan, September 1945 to September 1948*. Washington, D.C., 1949.

Supreme Commander Allied Powers, Health and Welfare Section. *Public Health and Welfare in Japan, 1948*. Tokyo, 1948.

Swomley, John M., Jr. *The Military Establishment*. Boston, 1964.

Tauber, Kurt P. *Beyond Eagle and Swastika: German Nationalism Since 1945*. 2 vols. Middletown, Conn., 1976. Vol. I.

Taylor, Telford. *Final Report to the Secretary of the Army in the Nuremberg War Crimes Trials under Control Council Law no. 10*. Washington, D.C., 1949.

Tedder, Arthur W. *With Prejudice: The War Memoirs of Marshal of the Royal Air Force Lord Tedder*. London, 1966.

Terrett, Dulany. *The Signal Corps: The Emergency*. U.S. Army in World War II, edited by Kent Roberts Greenfield. Washington, D.C., 1956.

Thompson, George Raynor, and Harris, Dixie R. *The Signal Corps: The Outcome*. U.S. Army in World War II, edited by Stetson Conn. Washington, D.C., 1966.

———, et al. *The Signal Corps: The Test*. U.S. Army in World War II, edited by Kent Roberts Greenfield. Washington, D.C., 1957.

Thompson, Reginald William. *The Montgomery Legend*. 2 vols. London, 1967–69. Vol. II, *Montgomery: The Field Marshal*.

Toland, John. *The Last 100 Days*. New York, 1966.

Tompkins, Peter. *The Murder of Admiral Darlan: A Study in Conspiracy*. New York, 1965.

Truman, Harry S. *Memoirs by Harry S. Truman.* 2 vols. New York, 1955. Vol. I, *Year of Decisions;* and vol. II, *Years of Trial and Hope.*

Truman, Margaret. *Harry S. Truman.* New York, 1973.

Truscott, Lt. General L. K., Jr. *Command Missions: A Personal Story.* New York, 1954.

Tsou, Tang. *America's Failure in China, 1941–1950.* Chicago, 1963.

Underhill, Frank H., ed. *The Canadian Northwest: Its Potentialities.* Toronto, 1959.

United Nations. *Atomic Energy Commission Official Records.* New York, 1946. Nos. 1–10.

————. *Official Records of the First Part of the First Session of the General Assembly: Plenary Meetings.* London, 1946.

————. *Official Records of the First Special Session of the General Assembly: Plenary Meetings.* Lake Success, N.Y., 1947. Vol. I.

————. *Official Records of the Second Part of the First Session of the General Assembly: Plenary Meetings.* Flushing Meadow, N.Y., 1947.

————. *Official Records of the Second Session of the General Assembly: First Committee, Summary Record of Meetings, 16 September–19 November 1947.* Lake Success, N.Y., 1947.

————. *Official Records of the Second Session of the General Assembly: Plenary Meetings, 16 September–29 November 1947.* Lake Success, N.Y., 1947. Vols. I and II.

————. *Official Records of the Second Session of the General Assembly: Resolutions, 16 September–29 November 1947.* Lake Success, N.Y., 1947.

————. *Official Records of the Second Session of the General Assembly, Supplement No. 11: United Nations Special Committee on Palestine.* Lake Success, N.Y., 1947. Vols. I–V.

————. *Report of the Preparatory Commission of the United Nations.* London, 1945.

————. *Security Council Official Records: Second Year.* New York, 1947. Nos. 1–108, supps. 1–20, special supps. 1–4.

United Nations Information Organization. *Documents of the United Nations Conference on International Organization (San Francisco, 1945).* 16 vols. New York, 1945.

U.S. Army. *The Army Almanac: A Book of Facts Concerning the Army of the United States.* Washington, D.C., 1950.

U.S. Army Medical Department. Internal Medicine in World War II. 3 vols. Washington, D.C., 1961–68.

————. *Zone of Interior.* Edited by Robert S. Anderson. Neuropsychiatry in World War II. Washington, D.C., 1966.

U.S. Army, Western Defense Command and Fourth Army. *Final Report: Japanese Evacuation from the West Coast, 1942.* Washington, D.C., 1943.

U.S. Bureau of the Budget. *The Budget of the United States Government for the Fiscal Year Ending June 30, 1948.* Washington, D.C., 1947.

U.S. Department of Commerce. *St. Lawrence Seaway.* Washington, D.C., 1941. Pt. 1, *History of the St. Lawrence Project.*

U.S. Department of State. *The China White Paper, August 1949.* Stanford, 1967.

————. *Foreign Relations of the United States: Diplomatic Papers. Conference of Berlin (Potsdam Conference), 1945.* 2 vols. Washington, D.C., 1960.

————. *Foreign Relations of the United States: Diplomatic Papers. The Conferences at Cairo and Tehran, 1943.* Washington, D.C., 1961.

————. *Foreign Relations of the United States: Diplomatic Papers. The Conferences at Malta and Yalta, 1945.* Washington, D.C., 1955.

———. *Foreign Relations of the United States: Diplomatic Papers, 1942*. 7 vols. Washington, D.C., 1960–63. Vol. VI, *The American Republics*.

———. *Foreign Relations of the United States: Diplomatic Papers, 1944*. 7 vols. Washington, D.C., 1963–67. Vol. I, *General*; vol. II, *General: Economic and Social Matters*; and vol. VII, *The American Republics*.

———. *Foreign Relations of the United States: Diplomatic Papers, 1945*. 9 vols. Washington, D.C., 1965–69. Vol. I, *General: The United Nations*; vol. II, *General: Political and Economic Matters*; vol. III, *European Advisory Commission; Austria; Germany*; vol. IV, *Europe*; vol. V, *Europe*; vol. VI, *The British Commonwealth: The Far East*; vol. VII, *The Far East: China*; and vol. IX, *The American Republics*.

———. *Foreign Relations of the United States: Diplomatic Papers, 1946*. 11 vols. Washington, D.C., 1969–72. Vol. I, *General: The United Nations*; vol. II, *Council of Foreign Ministers*; vol. III, *Paris Peace Conference: Proceedings*; vol. IV, *Paris Peace Conference: Documents*; vol. V, *The British Commonwealth; Western and Central Europe*: vol. VI, *Eastern Europe; The Soviet Union*; vol. VII, *The Near East and Africa*; vol. VIII, *The Far East*; vol. IX, *The Far East: China*; vol. X, *The Far East: China*; and vol. XI, *The American Republics*.

———. *Foreign Relations of the United States: Diplomatic Papers, 1947*. 8 vols. Washington, D.C., 1971–73. Vol. I, *General; The United Nations*; vol. II, *Council of Foreign Ministers; Germany and Austria*; vol. III, *The British Commonwealth; Europe*; vol. IV, *Eastern Europe; The Soviet Union*; vol. V, *The Near East and Africa*; vol. VI, *The Far East*; vol. VII, *The Far East: China*; and vol. VIII, *The American Republics*.

———. *Foreign Relations of the United States, 1948*. 9 vols. Washington, D.C., 1972–76. Vol. II, *Germany and Austria*; vol. III, *Western Europe*; vol. IV, *Eastern Europe; The Soviet Union*; vol. VI, *The Far East and Australasia*; and vol. IX, *The Western Hemisphere*.

———. *A Report on the International Control of Atomic Energy*. Washington, D.C., 1946.

———. *The United Nations Conference on International Organizations, San Francisco, California, April 25 to June 26, 1945: Selected Documents*. Washington, D.C., 1946.

U.S. Department of State, Office of Public Affairs. *The Turkish Aid Program*. Washington, D.C., 1948.

U.S. Military Academy. *Bugle Notes*. West Point, 1966.

U.S. Selective Service System. *Selective Service and Victory*. Washington, D.C., 1948.

Vali, Ferenc A. *Bridge across the Bosporus: The Foreign Policy of Turkey*. Baltimore, 1971.

Vandenberg, Arthur H., Jr. *The Private Papers of Senator Vandenberg*. Boston, 1952.

Van der Beugel, Ernst H. *From Marshall Aid to Atlantic Partnership: European Integration as a Concern of American Foreign Policy*. Amsterdam, 1966.

Varg, Paul. *The Closing of the Door: Sino-American Relations, 1936–46*. Ann Arbor, 1973.

Viorst, Milton. *Hostile Allies: FDR and Charles de Gaulle*. New York, 1965.

Von Braun, Wernher, and Ordway, Frederick I. *History of Rocketry and Space Travel*. New York, 1966.

Von Oppen, Beate Ruhm, ed. *Documents on Germany under Occupation, 1945–1954*. London, 1955.

Wagner, Jean. *Runyonese: The Mind and Craft of Damon Runyon*. New York, 1965.

Walton, Richard J. *Henry Wallace, Harry Truman, and the Cold War*. New York, 1976.

War Assets Administration. *Acceleration of Surplus Disposal: Quarterly Progress Report to the Congress*. Washington, D.C., 1946.

Wassenbergh, Henri Abraham. *Post-War International Civil Aviation Policy and the Law of the Air*. The Hague, 1957.

Watson, Mark Skinner. *Chief of Staff: Prewar Plans and Preparations*. U.S. Army in World War II, edited by Kent Roberts Greenfield. Washington, D.C., 1950.

Wedemeyer, Albert C. *Wedemeyer Reports!* New York, 1958.

Weigley, Russell Frank. *History of the United States Army*. New York, 1967.

Werth, Alexander. *France, 1940–1955*. New York, 1956.

Whitman, Roswell H. "Economic Recovery in Japan." *Military Government Journal* 1 (January 1948), 2–5.

Williams, Mary H. *Chronology, 1941–1945*. U.S. Army in World War II, edited by Kent Roberts Greenfield. Washington, D.C., 1960.

Willoughby, William R. *The St. Lawrence Waterway*. Madison, 1961.

Wingate, Ronald. *Lord Ismay: A Biography*. London, 1970.

Winterbotham, Frederick W. *The Ultra Secret*. New York, 1974.

Wise, David, and Ross, Thomas B. *The Invisible Government*. New York, 1964.

Wohlstetter, Roberta. *Pearl Harbor: Warning and Decision*. Stanford, 1962.

Woodbridge, George. *UNRRA*. 3 vols. New York, 1950.

Yergin, Daniel. *Shattered Peace: The Origins of the Cold War and the National Security State*. Boston, 1977.

Young, Edward H., ed. *Trials of War Criminals before the Nuremberg Military Tribunals under Control Council Law No. 10*. 15 vols. Washington, D.C., 1949–53.

Zhukov, Georgi K. *The Memoirs of Marshal Zhukov*. Translated by the Navosty Press Agency Publishing House. 1st American ed. New York, 1971.

Ziemke, Earl F. *Stalingrad to Berlin: The German Defeat in the East*. Army Historical Series. Washington, D.C., 1968.

———. *The U.S. Army in the Occupation of Germany, 1944–46*. Army Historical Series. Washington, D.C., 1975.

Zink, Harold. "The American Denazification Program in Germany." *Journal of Central European Affairs* 6 (October 1946), 234.

———. *American Military Government in Germany*. New York, 1947.

———. *The United States in Germany, 1944–45*. Princeton, 1957.

Maps

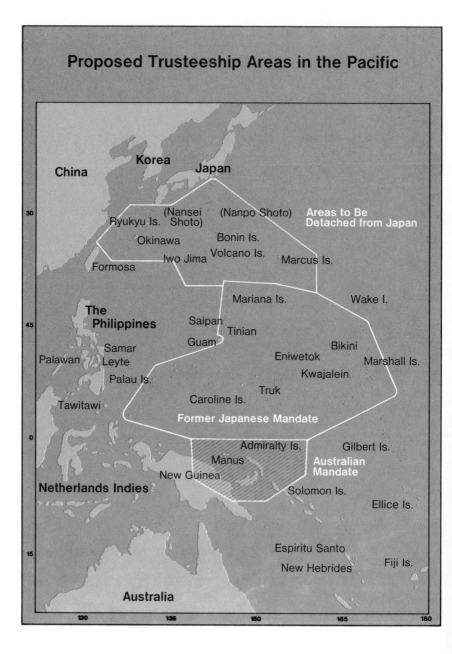

Proposed Trusteeship Areas in the Pacific

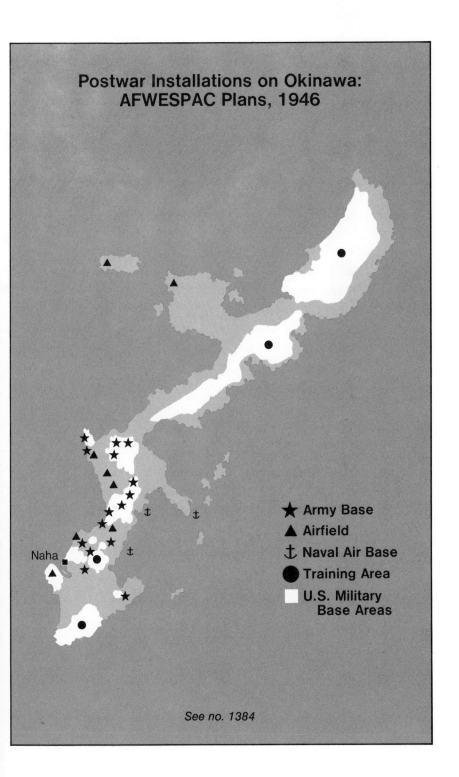

Postwar Installations on Okinawa:
AFWESPAC Plans, 1946

Naha

★ Army Base
▲ Airfield
⚓ Naval Air Base
● Training Area
U.S. Military
   Base Areas

See no. 1384

2293

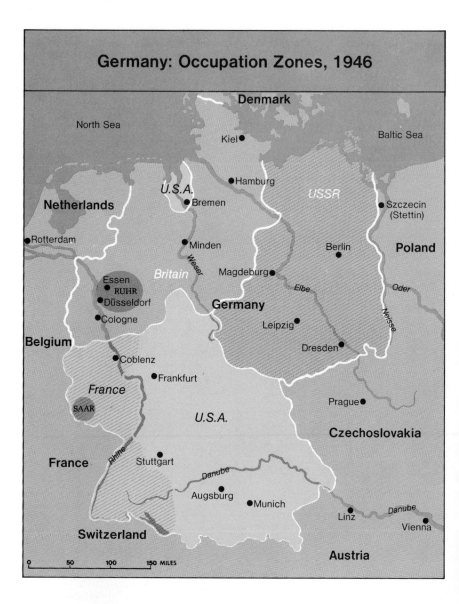

Germany: Occupation Zones, 1946

Denmark

North Sea

Baltic Sea

Kiel●

●Hamburg

U.S.A.

Netherlands ●Bremen

●Szczecin
(Stettin)

●Rotterdam ●Minden

Berlin●

Poland

Essen
● RUHR *Britain* Magdeburg●

Elbe *Oder*

●Düsseldorf

●Cologne **Germany**

Leipzig●

Belgium

Dresden●

●Coblenz

●Frankfurt

France Prague●

SAAR *U.S.A.* **Czechoslovakia**

Rhine

France● Stuttgart●

Danube

Augsburg●

●Munich

Linz● *Danube*

Switzerland Vienna●

Austria

0   50   100   150 MILES

2294

AFWESPAC Plans for Postwar U.S. Army Installations in the Philippines   August, 1946

Laoag
Airdrome
Secondary Port

San Fernando
Alternate Airdrome
Secondary Port
Staging Area 2 Divisions

Camp John Hay
Leave & Rec Center

Subic Bay
(Navy Base)

Limay
Tank Farm
(Bataan Terminal)

Manila
Main Port, Transit Storage
Leave Center
Gen. Depot & Repair Ctr.
Tank Farm

Batangas
AAF Bomb Dump
Secondary Port
Staging Area 2 Divisions

McGuire
Alternate Airdrome

Puerta Princesa
Air Base
Secondary Port

Palawan

Mandurriao
Alternate Airdrome

Moret
Airdrome

Borneo

Tawitawi
(Naval Anchorage)

Fort Stotsenberg
HQ Philippine Ground Force
Command Division Post

Clark Field
Air Base VHB

Florida Blanca
Air Base VLR Fi

Novaliches
GHQ Main
Hq AFWESPAC
Joint Opns Ctr
Manila Post
Communications Center

Fort McKinley
Gen Hospital
HQ Pacusa

Nichols Field
Air Base, Air Depot,
& ATC

Sangley Point
(Naval Air Base)

Tacloban
Alt. Airdrome

Cebu
Secondary Port
Staging Area 1
Division

Mactan Island
AirBase, VHB

Libby
Alternate Airdrome

Luzon

Mindoro

Masbate   Samar

Panay

Iloilo   Cebu   Leyte

Negros

Bohol

Mindanao

Davao

STATUTE MILES
10 0   50   100   50   200
NAUTICAL MILES
10 0   50   100   50   200

2295

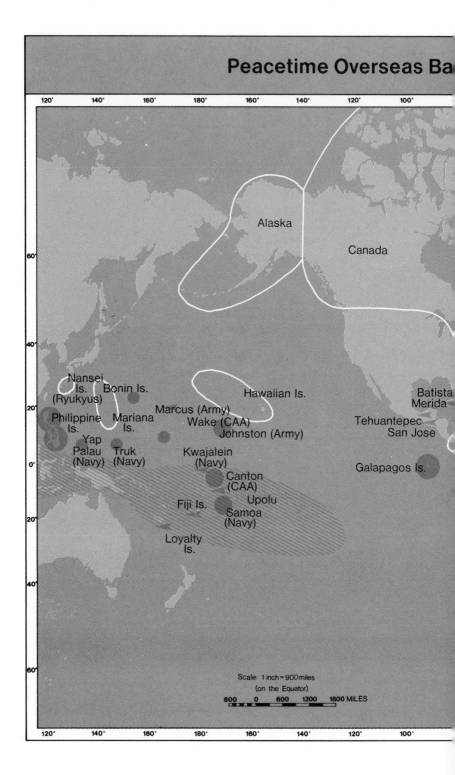

Peacetime Overseas Ba

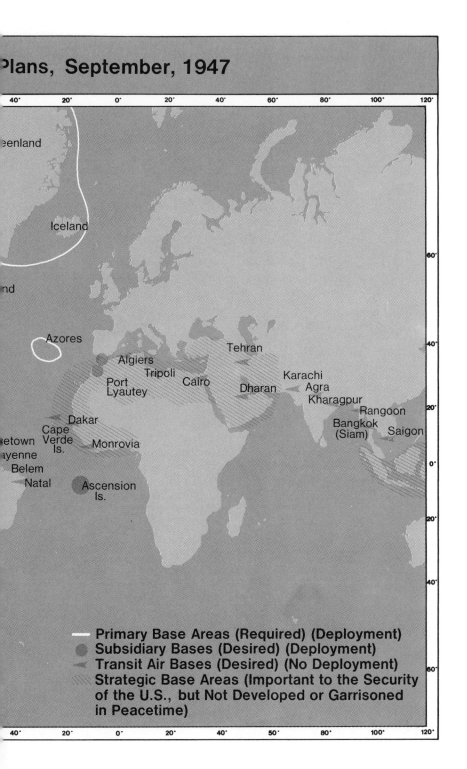

Greenland

Iceland

Azores

Tehran

Algiers

Tripoli

Cairo

Karachi

Port Lyautey

Dharan

Agra

Kharagpur

Rangoon

Dakar

Bangkok (Siam)

Saigon

Cape Verde Is.

Freetown

Monrovia

Cayenne

Belem

Natal

Ascension Is.

— **Primary Base Areas (Required) (Deployment)**
● **Subsidiary Bases (Desired) (Deployment)**
◀ **Transit Air Bases (Desired) (No Deployment)**
▨ **Strategic Base Areas (Important to the Security of the U.S., but Not Developed or Garrisoned in Peacetime)**

2297

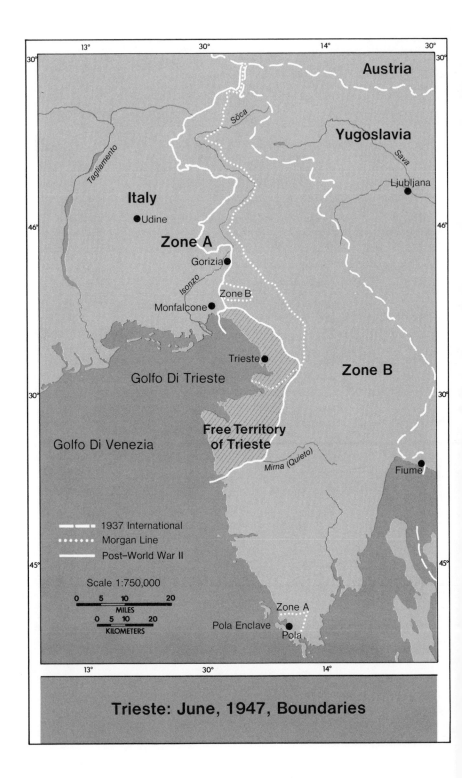

13°   30°   14°   30°

Austria

Yugoslavia

Sava

Ljubljana

Soča

Tagliamento

Italy

●Udine

Zone A

Gorizia●

Isonzo

Zone B

Monfalcone●

Trieste●

Zone B

Golfo Di Trieste

Golfo Di Venezia

Free Territory
of Trieste

Mirna (Quieto)

Fiume●

▬ ▬ ▬ 1937 International
•••••• Morgan Line
▬▬▬▬ Post–World War II

Scale 1:750,000

0   5   10   20
        MILES
0   5   10   20
      KILOMETERS

Zone A

Pola Enclave

Pola●

Trieste: June, 1947, Boundaries

Glossary

AAF	Army Air Forces
ABMC	American Battle Monuments Commission
AC	Allied Commission
	Army Air Corps
ACA	Allied Commission for Austria
ACAN	Army Command and Administrative Network
ACC	Air Coordinating Committee
	Allied Control Commission/Council
A.C. of S.	Assistant Chief of Staff
ADA	Atomic Development Authority
A.D.C.	*Aide-de-camp*
ADC	Alaska Defense Command
AEC	Atomic Energy Commission
A.E.F.	Allied Expeditionary Force
AF	Air Force
AFHQ	Allied Force Headquarters
AFMIDPAC	United States Army Forces, Middle Pacific
AFSWP	Armed Forces Special Weapons Project
AFWESPAC	United States Army Forces, Western Pacific
AG	Adjutant General
AGF	Army Ground Forces
AGRC	Army Graves Registration Command
AGWAR	Adjutant General, War Department
AJDC	American Joint Distribution Committee
AMAG	American Mission for Aid to Greece
AMG	Allied Military Government

AMGOT	Allied Military Government
AMSSO	Air Ministry Special Signals Office
ANCXF	Allied Naval Commander, Expeditionary Force
ANMB	Army-Navy Munitions Board
ANSCOL	Army-Navy Staff College
AP	Associated Press
APO	Army Post Office
ARC	Allied Reparations Commission
ASCOM	Army Service Command
ASF	Army Service Forces
ASR	Adjusted service rating
ATC	Air Transport Command
AUS	Army of the United States
A.W.O.L.	Absent without leave
BACKFIRE	Code name for the test-firing of German V–2 rocket missiles
BCOS	British Chiefs of Staff
B hours	British Double Summer Time (Greenwich mean time plus two hours)
Big Three	Great Britain, Russia, and the United States
BJSM	British Joint Staff Mission
BMM(G)	British Military Mission, Greece
Book message	A message transmitted to two or more addresses that requires no coordinated action by the recipients
BPR	Bureau of Public Relations
BSM	Bronze Star Medal
CAA	Civil Aeronautics Administration
	Civil Aeronautics Authority
CAB	Civil Aeronautics Board
CAD	Civil Affairs Division
CALA	Combined Administrative Liquidating Agency
CAS	Chief of Air Staff
C.B.	Companion of the Bath
C.B.E.	Commander Order of the British Empire
CBI	China-Burma-India Theater of Operations
CC	Chief commander
CCA	Combat Command A
CCAC	Combined Civil Affairs Committee
CCB	Combat Command B
CCOS	Combined Chiefs of Staff
CCS	Combined Chiefs of Staff
CC/S	Combined Chiefs of Staff

CDT	Combined Development Trust
CFB	Combined Food Board
CFM	Council of Foreign Ministers
CG	Commanding general
CGUSAFIK	Commanding General, United States Army Forces, Korea
CIA	Central Intelligence Agency
CIC	Counterintelligence Corps
CID	Criminal Investigation Division
CIG	Central Intelligence Group
CIGS	Chief of the Imperial General Staff
C in C	Commander in Chief
CINCAFPAC	Commander in Chief, Army Forces, Pacific
CINCAL	Commander in Chief, Alaska
CINCARIB	Commander in Chief, Caribbean
CINCEUR	Commander in Chief, European Command
CINCFE	Commander in Chief, Far East
CINCLANT	Commander in Chief, Atlantic
CINCNAVEAST LANTMED	Commander in Chief, United States Naval Force, Eastern Atlantic and Mediterranean
CINCPAC	Commander in Chief, Pacific
CINCPOA	Commander in Chief, Pacific Ocean Area
CIOS	Combined Intelligence Objectives Subcommittee
CL	Light cruisers
CMC	Communications Message Center
CMF	Central Mediterranean Forces
CM-IN	Classified message, incoming
CM-OUT	Classified message, outgoing
CNO	Chief of Naval Operations
CNOB	Commandant of the Naval Operations Base
CNRRA	China National Relief and Rehabilitation Administration
CO	Commanding officer
COMGEN CHINA	Commanding General, United States Forces, China
Committee of Three	George Marshall, the United States President's special representative in China; General Chang Shun, of Nationalist China; and Chou En-lai, of Communist China.
	Secretaries of State, War, and Navy departments
COMNAVEU	Commander, United States Naval Forces, Europe
COMNAVO FRANCE	Commander, United States Naval Forces, France
Com Z; COMZ	Communications Zone

Comzone; Com Zone	Communications Zone
COS	Chief of Staff
COSSAC	Chief of Staff to the Supreme Allied Commander
CPC	Combined Policy Committee
CROSSROADS	Code name for first atomic-bomb test, Bikini, 1946
C/S	Chief of Staff
CVB	Large aircraft carrier
CWO	Chief warrant officer
CZ	Panama Canal Zone
DD	Destroyer
	Duplex drive (common name for an amphibious tank)
D-day	The first day of any military operation
DOUBLE CHECK	Code name for the security control and credentials check to uncover prohibited articles and evidence of black-market operations in the American zone of Germany, October 1945
DP	Displaced persons
DRAGOON	Revised code name for ANVIL, the 1944 invasion of southern France
DSC	Distinguished Service Cross
DSM	Distinguished Service Medal
EAC	European Advisory Commission
Eagle's Nest	Hitler's house on Obersalzberg, overlooking Berchtesgaden in the Bavarian Alps
ECAD	European Civil Affairs Division
EM	Eisenhower Manuscripts
EP	Eisenhower Project, Milton S. Eisenhower Library, The Johns Hopkins University
ETGEC	European Theater of Operations, G–5 (Civil Affairs)
ETO	European Theater of Operations
ETOUSA	European Theater of Operations, United States Army
ETTCG	European theater, theater commanding general
EUCOM	European Command, United States Army
EVERSHARP	Code name for victory celebrations in the United States for returning officers
EXFOR	Cable address for Montgomery's headquarters
FAA	First Airborne Army (United States)
FAAA	First Allied Airborne Army
FAN	Designated cables covering all subjects from CCS to Supreme Commander AFHQ
FBI	Federal Bureau of Investigation
FEA	Foreign Economic Administration

FEC	Far Eastern Commission
FIAT	Field Information Agency, Technical
FLC	Foreign liquidation commissioner
FM	Field marshal
FO	Finance officer
FPHA	Federal Public Housing Authority
G-1	Personnel section of divisional or higher staff
G-2	Intelligence section of divisional or higher staff
G-3	Operations and Training section of divisional or higher staff
G-4	Logistics section of divisional or higher staff
G-5	Civil Affairs section of divisional or higher staff
G-6	Publicity and Psychological Warfare section of divisional or higher staff
GAF	German Air Force
GHQ	General Headquarters, United States Army
G.O.C.-in-C.	General Officer Commanding-in-Chief
GRS	Graves Registration Service
GS	General Staff
HUAC	House Committee on Un-American Activities
IARA	Inter-Allied Reparations Agency
ICD	Information Control Division
I&E	Information and Education
I&ED	Information and Education Division
IG	Inspector General
IGCR	Inter-Governmental Committee on Refugees
IMO	International Meteorological Organization
IMT	International Military Tribunal
INS	International News Service
ISO	International Security Organizations
IT&T	International Telephone and Telegraph Corporation
JAAN	Joint Action of the Army and Navy
JAG	Judge Advocate General
JBUSMC	Joint Brazil-United States Military Commission
JCAC	Joint Civil Affairs Committee
JCB	Joint Communications Board
JCS	Joint Chiefs of Staff
JIC	Joint Intelligence Committee
JIG	Joint Intelligence Group
JIS	Joint Intelligence Staff
JLC	Joint Logistics Committee
JLPG	Joint Logistics Plans Group
JMAC	Joint Munitions Allocation Committee

JMC	Joint Meteorological Committee
JMTC	Joint Military Transportation Committee
JNW	Joint Committee on New Weapons and Equipment
JRDB	Joint Research and Development Board
JSC	Joint Security Control
JSM	Joint Secretariat Memorandum
	Joint Staff Mission (British)
JSP	Joint Staff Planners
JSPC	Joint Strategic Plans Committee
JSPG	Joint Strategic Plans Group
JSSC	Joint Strategic Survey Committee
JUSMAPG	Joint United States Military Advisory and Planning Group in Greece
JWPC	Joint War Plans Committee
KMT	Koumintang party in China
Kommandatura	Inter-Allied governing authority for the Greater Berlin Area, responsible to the Allied Control Council of the Allied Control Authority
LEM	Designated cables covering economic, export, import, and supply matters for northwest Europe from CCAC to G–5, SHAEF
L&LD	Legislative and Liaison Division
LM	Legion of Merit
L of C	Line of Communication
L of M	Legion of Merit
MA	Military attaché
MAAF	Mediterranean Allied Air Force
MAG	Military Advisory Group
MAM	Medium Automotive Maintenance
M-day	Mobilization day
MDW	Military District of Washington, D.C.
MID	Military Intelligence Division
MIS	Military Intelligence Service
MOI	Ministry of Information (London)
MOS	Military occupational specialty
MP	Member of Parliament
MSC	Military Staff Committee to the United Nations
MTO	Mediterranean Theater of Operations
MTOUSA	Mediterranean Theater of Operations, United States Army
NAF	Designated cables covering all subjects from Supreme Commander AFHQ to CCS

NATO	North African Theater of Operations
NATOUSA	North African Theater of Operations, United States Army
NDD	New Developments Division
N.E.I.	Netherlands East Indies
NG	National Guard
NROTC	Naval Reserve Officers Training Corps
NSC	National Security Council
NSRB	National Securities Resources Board
OASW	Office of the Assistant Secretary of War
O.B.E.	Officer Order of the British Empire
OCMH	Office, Chief of Military History
OCS	Office of the Chief of Staff
OER	Officer's evaluation report
OFLC	Office of the foreign liquidation commissioner
OKH	*Oberkommando des Heeres* (German Army High Command)
OKL	*Oberkommando der Luftwaffe* (German Air Force High Command)
OKM	*Oberkommando der Kriegsmarine* (German Naval High Command)
OKW	*Oberkommando der Wehrmacht* (German Armed Forces High Command)
OLC	Oak Leaf Cluster
OMGUS	Office of Military Government, United States
OMGUSZ	Office of Military Government, United States zone
ONI	Office of Naval Intelligence
OPA	Office of Price Administration
OPD	Operations Division
OQMG	Office of the Quartermaster General
ORC	Officers' Reserve Corps
	Organized Reserve Corps
OSRD	Office of Scientific Research and Development
OTB	Occupational Troop Basis
Ourad	Our radio
OVERLORD	Code name for the invasion of northwest Europe in the spring of 1944
OWI	Office of War Information
PA	Philippine Army
P&A	Personnel and Administration Division
PAAC	Philippine Army Air Corps
PACUSA	Pacific Air Command, United States Army
PF	Patrol frigate
PHANTOM	Code name for forward reconnaissance detachment
PI	Philippine Islands

PINCHER	Code name for tentative war plan involving an overall strategic concept and estimate of initial operations
PJDB	Permanent Joint Board on Defense
PM	Prime minister
PMG	Provost marshal general
P&O	Plans and Operations Division
POA	Pacific Ocean Area
POW	Prisoner of war
P&P	Plans and Policy Group
PRD	Public Relations Division
PRO	Public relations officer
PTA	Personal transfer account
PW	Prisoner of war
PWD	Psychological Warfare Division
PX	Post exchange
QMC	Quartermaster Corps
RA	Regular Army
RAF	Royal Air Force
RAMP	Recovered Allied Military Personnel
R&D	Research and Development Division
R-day	Redeployment day
Reur	Reference your radio
Reurad	Reference your radio
RFC	Reconstruction Finance Corporation
ROTC	Reserve Officers Training Corps
SAC	Strategic Air Command
	Supreme Allied Commander
SACMED	Supreme Allied Commander, Mediterranean Theater of Operations
SACSEA	Supreme Allied Commander, Southeast Asia
SANACC	State-Army-Navy-Air Force Coordinating Committee
SANDSTONE	Code name for series of atomic tests proposed by the Atomic Energy Commission for April 1948
SAR	Strength Accounting and Reporting Office
SC	Security Council of the United Nations
SCAEF	Supreme Commander, Allied Expeditionary Forces
SCAF	Designated cables covering all subjects from SCAEF to CCS
SCAJAP	Shipping Control Authority for the Japanese Merchant Marine
SCAP	Supreme Commander, Allied Powers
SCOFOR	Scottish Forces
SEAC	Southeast Asia Command

SFHQ	Special Force Headquarters
SGS	Secretary General Staff
SHAEF	Supreme Headquarters, Allied Expeditionary Force
SHAEF forward; SHAEF main; SHAEF rear	Cable addresses for the three echelons of Eisenhower's headquarters
SHGCT	Supreme Headquarters, G–3 (Operations and Training)
SHPRD	Supreme Headquarters, Public Relations Division
SHSGS	Supreme Headquarters, Secretary General Staff
SO	Special Operations Branch (of the Office of Strategic Services)
SOE	Special Operations Executive
SOP	Standard Operating Procedure
SOS	Services of Supply
SOUTHCO	Southern Command
S&P	Strategy and Policy Group
SPD	Special Planning Division
SPEARHEAD	Code name for British training exercise, May 1947
SS	*Schutzstaffel* (German Elite Guard)
SS&P	Service, Supply and Procurement Division
SWNCC	State-War-Navy Coordinating Committee
SWPA	Southwest Pacific Area
T/3	Technician, 3d class
TAG	The Adjutant General
TALLYHO	Code name for the security control and credentials check to uncover prohibited articles and evidence of black-market operations in the American zone of Germany, July 1945
TERMINAL	Code name for the Potsdam meeting, July 1946
T.H.	Territory of Hawaii
TI&E	Theater Information and Education Division
T/O	Tables of Organization
T/O and E	Tables of Organization and Equipment
TSF	Theater Service Forces
TSFET	Theater Service Forces, European Theater of Operations
UK	United Kingdom
UMT	Universal military training
UNAEC	United Nations Atomic Energy Commission
Undertaking	German surrender document. Preliminary agreement in surrender negotiations
UNESCO	United Nations Education, Scientific and Cultural Organization
UNO	United Nations Organization
UNRRA	United Nations Relief and Rehabilitation Administration

UNSCOB	United Nations Special Committee on the Balkans
UNSCOP	United Nations Special Committee on Palestine
UP	United Press
Urad	Your radio
USAAF in the MTO	United States Army Air Force in the Mediterranean Theater of Operations
USAFFE	United States Army Forces, Far East
USAFI	United States Armed Forces Institute
USAGG	United States Army Group, American Mission for Aid to Greece
USARAL	United States Army, Alaska
USASTAF	United States Army Strategic Air Forces
USCG	United States Coast Guard
USFCT	United States Forces, China Theater of Operations
USFET	United States Forces, European Theater of Operations
USFIA	United States Forces in Austria
U.S.G.C.C.	United States Group Control Council
U.S.G.C.C./A.	United States Group Control Council/American
USJCS	United States Joint Chiefs of Staff
USMA	United States Military Academy
	United States military attaché
USSR	Union of Soviet Socialist Republics
USSTAF	United States Strategic Air Forces
VA	Veterans Administration
V-E Day	Victory in Europe Day
VHB	Very heavy bomber
VIP	Very important person
V-J Day	Victory in Japan Day
V-weapon	German vengeance weapon; the V–1 and V–2 rocket bombs
WAA	War Assets Administration
WAC	War Activities Committee
	War Assets Corporation
	Women's Army Corps
WAR	War Department
WARCAD	War Department Civil Affairs Division
WD	War Department
WDGAP	War Department General Staff, G–1 (Personnel)
WDGS	War Department General Staff
WDSS	War Department Special Staff
WFTU	World Federation of Trade Unions
WMO	World Meteorological Organization
WO	War Office (British)

WOJG	Warrant officer, junior grade
WPD	War Plans Division
WRNS	Women's Royal Naval Service
WSA	War Shipping Administration
WVS	Women's Voluntary Services
ZI	Zone of the Interior
Z time	Greenwich mean time

Chronology

The chronology for volumes VI–IX begins when Eisenhower assumed the post of Chief of Staff of the U.S. Army in 1945 and ends when he left that position to become president of Columbia University in 1948. During these years Eisenhower maintained a complex schedule, which made accurate accounts of his daily appointments and frequent trips away from Washington necessary. His staff kept two separate desk calendars; one was written in anticipation of coming events, and the other, which was written after the fact, incorporated cancellations and other changes in the Chief of Staff's schedule. We relied heavily upon these calendars in compiling this chronology. We included references to those telephone calls that were logged in December 1945 and the first months of 1946. It is unlikely that these were the only outgoing and incoming calls the Chief of Staff made during these months, but we have included them to supplement our picture of Eisenhower's daily contacts.

We were unable to locate appointment schedules for the months between the German surrender in 1945 and General Eisenhower's first days as Chief of Staff. During the spring of 1945 Eisenhower's headquarters moved from Reims to Frankfort, and the General made trips to London, Paris, and the United States, the last of which included stops in Washington, New York, Kansas City, and Abilene. After a brief vacation in White Sulphur Springs, West Virginia (June 25–July 5), Eisenhower returned to Frankfort; he made subsequent trips to Berlin, Moscow and Leningrad, Belfast, Brussels, Rome, Warsaw, Amsterdam, Prague, and London. These trips are covered in detail in the notes to these volumes. On November 10 Eisenhower left his headquarters in Frankfort for the last time and returned to the United States. After brief visits to Boston, Washington, and Chicago he entered Ashford General Hospital on November 22 and did not leave the hospital until early December, when he returned to Washington, D.C.

As was the case in the *War Years,* we have given the full names and identities of those persons not so identified in these volumes. Shortened names are used for persons already identified, and we have added initials to distinguish between persons with similar names and ranks.

1945

December   1   Ashford General Hospital.

2   Ashford General Hospital.

3   Washington. Attends morning meeting of War Council. Afternoon visits to Admiral King and the White House.

4   Washington. Telephone calls to Senator Thomas and Congressman May. Morning appointments with Generals Paul and Lutes; General Gordon Edmund Textor (SPD); F. W. McCullough (vice-president of Chesapeake and Ohio Railroad). To General Arnold's office. Afternoon appointments with General Persons; General Edwards; American Legion delegates. Presents DSM to General Guy Venor Henry, Jr. (head of Inter-Allied Personnel Board and senior Army member of U.S., Canadian, and Mexican defense commissions).

5   Washington. Morning appointments with P&O and G–2; General Groves; Admirals King and Nimitz. Noon briefing by Generals Surles, Textor, and Edwards. Afternoon appointment with Admiral Richard Stanislaus Edwards (Deputy Chief of Naval Operations). Staff meeting in Secretary of War's conference room. Appointment with General Sultan. Views film in Projection Room 2.

6   Washington. Morning telephone conversation with Senator Thomas. Morning appointments with General Edwards; General Hilldring; General Textor. Noon appointment with General Irwin. Luncheon (coordinated by General Richards) with West Point Class of

December   1915. Afternoon conference re demobilization with Generals Paul and Lincoln.

7   Washington. Morning telephone conversation with Senator Austin, followed by filming of a newsreel. P&O-G-2 meeting in Deputy Chief of Staff's office. JCS luncheon. Photographed in office. Appointments with General Eddy; representatives of the BCOS.

8   Washington. Luncheon with Senate Military Affairs Committee in Secretary of War's mess.

9   Washington.

10   Washington. Morning appointments with P&O and G-2 re strength of the permanent military establishment; General Haislip; General Kirk. Presentation by representatives of AGF. Lunch in office with General Vaughan. Afternoon presentation by Simpson Board. Appointment with Admiral Fenard. To Secretary of War's office for conference on UMT.

11   Washington. Morning presentation by P&O on strength of the permanent military establishment. First official visit to White House. Afternoon appointments with Frank Page; Colonel T. D. Campbell; General William F. Sharp (who commanded U.S. forces on Mindanao, Philippine Islands, surrendered to the Japanese in May 1942, and was released in August 1945); Cabell Phillips (of the *New York Times*); Jack Brooks Beardwood and Miss Hansen (of *Life* magazine).

12   Washington. Morning appointments with P&O and G-2; Congressmen James Hardin Peterson (Florida), George W. Gillie (Indiana), and J. Harry McGregor (Ohio). Lunch in office with Admiral Turner. Afternoon appointments with General De Witt; General Cramer; General Allen Russell Kimball (CG, Schenectady General Supply Depot); General Richards; General Maxwell. To Projection Room 4 for viewing of film on destruction of Hiroshima and Nagasaki.

13   Washington. Morning appointments with General Bradley; General Maxwell. Afternoon appointments with General Levin Hicks Campbell, Jr. (Chief of Ordnance); General Witsell; Colonel W. D. Brown;

December	General Paul. Attends American Society of Newspaper Editors dinner.
14	Washington. Morning appointments with P&O and G–2. To White House ceremony awarding DSM to Admiral King. Briefing by Colonel Juskalian on JCS papers. Noon telephone conversation in Secretary of War's office with John Stelle (national commander of the American Legion). JCS luncheon. Afternoon appointment with General Hodges. Telephone conversation with former Ambassador Davies. Appointments with General Hilldring; Colonel R. H. Smith. Telephone conversation with Speaker Frederick B. Willis, (of the Massachusetts House of Representatives).
15	Washington. Appointment with General T. H. Green. Telephone conversation with Congressman May. Appointments with General Eichelberger; General H. J. Casey; Arthur Hays Sulzberger (publisher of the *New York Times*). Luncheon with House Military Affairs Committee. Sees General Marshall off to China. Gridiron Club dinner.
16	Washington.
17	Washington. Morning appointments with General Lanham; General A. R. Wilson. Meeting of P&O and G–2 in General Handy's office. Meeting with American Legion delegates. Decorates Generals J. S. Bradley and Palmer. Lunch in Secretary of War's office with Secretary Patterson, Secretary Forrestal, and Admiral Nimitz. Afternoon conference with American Legion representatives; appointment with General Devers. Meeting with General Groves in Secretary of War's office to discuss atomic bomb.
18	Washington. Telephone conversation with Senator McMahon. Morning appointments with Dr. Dunning; Admiral Hill; General Arnold; General J. F. Williams; General Edward Sedley Bres. Medal of Honor ceremony at White House. Lunch in office with former Ambassador Davies. Afternoon appointments with Rabbi Barnett Robert Brickner and six other representatives of the Jewish Welfare Board; General Betts; General E. B. Howard.
19	Washington. Morning appointments with General

December   Paul; P&O and G–2. War Council meeting. Telephone conversation with Secretary of the Interior Ickes. Lunch in office with Milton S. Eisenhower. Afternoon appointments with General Donald Armstrong (commandant of the Army Industrial College); L. F. Kimball. Telephone conversation with General D. Armstrong. Sketched by *PM* artist. Appointment with General Holmes. Dinner at home of Senator McMahon.

20   Washington. Morning appointment with General Shelley Uriah Marietta (commanding officer of Walter Reed General Hospital and Army Medical Center). Telephone conversation with Congressman William Richard Thom (Ohio). Appointment with General Larkin. ASF presentation by General Lutes, followed by luncheon with ASF staff in Secretary of War's mess. Afternoon appointment with H. C. Butcher. Views newsreel depicting Chief of Staff's activities. Appointment with General Bonesteel. Telephone conversation with Governor Tobin. Appointment with General McCoy. Conversation with Carl Bernard Wall (newspaperman, formerly a correspondent in the European theater).

21   Washington. Morning appointments with Generals Lutes and Gregory; Oscar Berger (caricaturist for *Life* magazine); P&O and G–2. JCS luncheon. Presented with Paper Troopers Medal by Secretary Patterson in Secretary of War's office. Afternoon appointment with Field Marshal Wilson and Admiral Moore. Telephone call to General Vaughan. General Arnold's Christmas party. Presents LM to Major L. J. Hansen. Evening party given by P&O at Army and Navy Club.

22   Washington. Records message for overseas troops. Appointment with General Collins. Lunch in office with Milton S. Eisenhower and H. C. Butcher. Dinner at the apartment of G. E. Allen at the Wardman Park Hotel.

23   Washington.

24   Washington. Morning appointment with General Frederick. Telephone conversation with Senator Capper. Appointments with General Bergin; OPD and

December	G–2. Telephone conversation with General Vaughan. Afternoon visit to veterans at Walter Reed General Hospital.
25	Washington.
26	Washington. Morning appointments with General Hershey; General Richard Kerens Sutherland; General Wheeler. Afternoon appointments with Generals L. D. Miller and William Donoghue Cleary (chaplains); General Borden; Oscar Berger and General Lanahan.
27	Washington. Morning appointments with General Eaker; General Harmon; General Hilldring; Colonel Duncombe re Pearl Harbor investigation. Afternoon appointments with General Malony; General Sidney Parker Spalding (Deputy Executive Chairman of the Army and Navy Munitions Board); Colonel Muller; Colonel Waters; Colonel C. W. Thompson; Oscar Berger; General Lanahan.
28	Washington. Morning appointments with General Hull; M. W. Childs; General Bessell. JCS luncheon.
29	Washington. Morning appointment with General Somervell. Telephone call to Admiral Nimitz. Appointments with Mark Skinner Watson *(Baltimore Sun* correspondent); the Honorable Wei Tao-ming (Chinese Ambassador to the United States); General H. A. Craig; J. Pelley; General Guy Venor Henry, Jr.; Generals Paul and Hull. Lunch in office with Colonel and Mrs. E. R. Lee.
30	Washington.
31	Washington. Morning appointments with General Simpson; General Spaatz; Ambassador Pearson. Lunch in office with Generals W. B. Smith and Gerow. Telephone call from Ambassador Pearson.

1946

January	1	Washington.
	2	Washington. Morning appointment with P&O and G–2. Telephone conversation with Secretary of State

Byrnes. Lunch at Blair House with Secretary Byrnes. Afternoon appointments with General Joseph Wilson Byron (Director, Special Services Division); Colonel Westray Battle Boyce (Director, Women's Army Corps); Donald Bennett Adams (on duty with committees for reserve and retirement affairs).

3 Washington. Early morning duck shooting with General W. B. Smith. Morning appointment with General Hilldring. Afternoon telephone conversation with Dr. Clothier. Afternoon appointments with General Paul William Baade (incoming Director of Training, ASF); Doris Fleeson (Washington correspondent for Bell Syndicate); General Paul.

4 Washington. Morning appointment with General Casey. Telephone conversation with Captain Dugan. Appointments with Mrs. E. D. Barlow re UMT; P&O and G-2; General Arnold. JCS luncheon. Afternoon appointments with Mr. Gordon (Department of Commerce); Generals Spaatz and Richards re the budget; C. L. Burgess; Colonel Ennis.

5 Washington. Presentation of citations to Majors Charles G. Heitezberg and Howard Ellsworth Sommer. Appointments with General David Goodwin Barr (G-1, AGF); Sophie Gurevick; General Horkan. Telephone conversation with Admiral Nimitz. Appointment with Duke Shoop (journalist, *Kansas City Star*). Lunch with Dr. E. L. Bowles. Afternoon appointment with General Prichard. General Arnold's game dinner at Bolling Field.

6 Washington.

7 Washington. Morning appointment with Admiral Kirk. Telephone call from Secretary of State. Appointment with General D. Armstrong. P&O-G-2 presentation. Award of citations to P&O personnel. Afternoon presentation of decorations to Generals Gerow and Betts. Appointment with General Paul.

8 Washington. Morning appointments with General A. J. Browning; Captain Dugan; Field Marshal Wilson. To White House to attend presentation of DSM to General Arnold. Afternoon appointment with General Paul. Late afternoon train to Canada, accompanied by

January	Mrs. Eisenhower, Major Schulz, Captain Cannon, and Sergeant Dry.
9	Morning arrival in Ottawa. Greeted by Prime Minister King and Ambassador Atherton. Luncheon at Government House. Dinner with the Prime Minister. Overnight guest of the Governor General and Princess Alice.
10	Ottawa. To U.S. Embassy. Press conference at the Parliament with the Prime Minister. Tour of Houses of Parliament. Luncheon with the Ottawa Canadian Club (Eisenhower's speech is broadcast). Calls on the Prime Minister at his home. Dinner given by Ambassador and Mrs. Atherton. Overnight at the U.S. Embassy.
11	Ottawa. Call on the Chief of the Canadian General Staff. Places wreath at the National War Memorial. Luncheon given by Minister of National Defence and attended by Canadian military leaders. Evening reception by Ambassador and Mrs. Atherton, followed by a ball given by the Governor General and Princess Alice at Government House. Departure (11:00 P.M.) by train for Toronto.
12	Toronto. Press conference at the Royal York Hotel. Wreath-laying ceremony at City Hall. Luncheon given by the University of Toronto, followed by convocation and award to Eisenhower of an honorary Doctor of Laws degree (Eisenhower's remarks are broadcast). After a reception by the Lieutenant Governor of Ontario, the Eisenhower party leaves for Washington by train at 6:05 P.M.
13	Morning arrival in Washington. Lunch in office with Admiral Nimitz.
14	Washington. Morning conference at White House re demobilization.
15	Washington. Morning appearance before members of Congress re demobilization. Conference with McCloy. Telephone conversation with Congressman Herbert Covington Bonner (North Carolina). Telephone conversation with Congressman May. To Constitution Hall for evening program by the Don Cossack Chorus.

January 16   Washington. Morning presentation by P&O and G–2. Telephone conversations with Congressman May and Admiral Nimitz. Afternoon telephone conversation with Congressman Forest Arthur Harness (Indiana). Afternoon appointments with Charles Guy Bolte (organizer of American Veterans Committee); Congressman Wadsworth; Congressman William Joseph Green, Jr. (Pennsylvania); S. Hillman; General Betts.

17   Washington. Morning appearance before a subcommittee of the Senate Committee on Military Affairs. Telephone conversations with Admiral Nimitz; Secretary Forrestal. Afternoon appointment with R. A. Lovett. Telephone conversation with Admiral Nimitz.

18   Washington. Morning appointments with Congressman Wadsworth; General North; P&O and G–2; General W. M. Robertson. JCS luncheon. Afternoon appointments with Governor E. Martin; General Levin Hicks Campbell, Jr.; General Wainwright. Evening radio broadcast (CBS) on demobilization.

19   Washington. Morning appointment with General Hilldring. Telephone conversation with Senator James Edward Murray (Montana). Appointments with General Littlejohn; Stilwell Board; Samuel Hamilton Kaufman (of Senator Murray's office). Lunch in office with Albert Wayne Coy (assistant to the publisher, *Washington Post*, and executive vice-president, WTNX Broadcasting Company). Afternoon appointments with A. Krock; General Paul; General Hull. Cocktails at Willard Hotel suites of Arthur Grover Newmyer (public relations consultant) and F. Page, followed by Alfalfa Club dinner.

20   Washington. Attends memorial service for General Patton at Washington Cathedral.

21   Washington. Morning appointments with General Lutes and Provost Marshal General; Mrs. Harold Hitz Burton (president of the Congressional Women's Club); P&O and G–2. Afternoon appointment with William Cameron Forbes (former governor general of the Philippine Islands [1909–13]). To White House for presentation of medals to Selective Service offi-

January | cials. Appointments with General Betts; General Bissell.

22 | Washington. Morning appearance before House Military Affairs Committee. Lunch in office with General Harmon. Afternoon appointments with General R. N. Young; Alaskan delegation, led by Ernest Gruening (C in C, Alaskan Territorial Guard); General Edward Postell King, Jr. (Japanese POW for three years, released in August 1945); Henry Clarence Cassidy (Associated Press foreign news editor), accompanied by Miss Clayton. Accompanied by General Surles to evening cocktail party for Duke Shoop.

23 | Washington. Morning appointment with P&O and G–2. To White House for presentation of Army and Navy Medal of Honor awards. Lunch in office with J. E. Hoover and Under Secretary of War Royall. Afternoon appointments with Admiral Joseph Francis Farley (commandant of the U.S. Coast Guard Academy); Admiral H. W. Hill; Frank Bane (Executive Director, Council of State Governments); A. Frieder. To closing ceremonies of the Stage Door Canteen in the evening.

24 | Washington. Morning appointments with General Crittenberger; General Milton A. Reckord (adjutant general of Maryland); Gillem Board. Luncheon with General Lutes for service commanders. Afternoon appointments with M. McKeogh; General Herron; General Paul and a delegation of women calling for the demobilization of fathers; General F. B. Wilby; General Taylor. Texas State Society dinner at the Mayflower Hotel.

25 | Washington. Telephone conversation with B. Baruch. Morning appointments with General Robert F. Blodgett; General Larkin, who presents award from New York Film Critics Association; P&O and Colonel Juskalian, for briefing on JCS matters; General Lutes and service commanders. JCS luncheon. Afternoon appointment with Hanson Baldwin. Saint Andrews Society dinner at the Mayflower Hotel accompanied by Mrs. Eisenhower.

26 | Washington. Morning appointment with Ralph

January		Lucier. To Secretary of War's office. Returns to office to present decorations to several officers. Appointment with Bernard Kantor. Lunch in Secretary of War's mess with members of the Senate Appropriations Committee. Afternoon appointments with Eugene Meyer (editor and publisher of the *Washington Post*); Mrs. Frances Anderson; Dr. Gilchrist and Speaker Rayburn; E. Kemper Carter. Accompanied by Mrs. Eisenhower to Walter Reed General Hospital for a dinner given by General and Mrs. Kirk.
	27	Washington.
	28	Washington. Morning appointment with P&O and G–2. Lunch in office with Herbert Hoover. Afternoon appointments with Rabbis Wise and Bernstein; H. C. Butcher; son of Doctor Hamilton Holt.
	29	Washington. Morning appointment with General Levin Hicks Campbell, Jr. Conference on demobilization. Appointment with General Walter Ernst Lauer (retiring after commanding several infantry divisions during World War II). Lunch in office with former Ambassador Davies and General W. B. Smith. Afternoon appointment with Marine Sergeant Mary Hacker (former employee of Edgar Eisenhower). To Secretary of the Navy Forrestal's office for cocktails and dinner.
	30	Washington. Telephone conversations with Secretary Byrnes and Senator Tom Stewart. Lunch in Senate dining room with Senator William Abner Stanfill (Kentucky). Afternoon appointments with Admiral William Harrison Standley, ret. (former CNO); General Charles Andrew Willoughby (G–2, Southwest Pacific); General E. Morgan. Telephone conversation with Congressman May. To Duke Shoop's for cocktails. Departure by train for Boston (11:00 P.M.).
	31	Morning arrival in Boston. Inspection tour of Fort Devers, including Lovell General Hospital. Guest speaker at testimonial dinner in honor of Dr. D. L. Marsh, on his twentieth anniversary as president of Boston University, at the Statler Hotel. Train to Washington (11:00 P.M.).
February	1	Morning arrival in Washington. To Secretary of War's press room to swear General Witsell in as Ad-

February   jutant General. Morning appointments with General Paul; General F. E. Morgan. Telephone conversations with Senator Burnet Rhett Maybank (South Carolina) and Senator Capehart. JCS luncheon. Addresses meeting of Congressional Women's Club. To Secretary of War's office to discuss Simpson Board report. Swearing-in of W. S. Symington as Assistant Secretary of War for Air. To the Statler Hotel for cocktails and National Rifle Association dinner.

2   Washington. Morning appointments with G–1 and G–4 officers for demonstration of blue dress uniform; K. S. Davis; Senator Capehart. Luncheon with members of House Appropriations Committee.

3   Washington.

4   Washington. Morning appointments with General Groves; P&O and G–2. Lunch in office with General E. S. Hughes. Afternoon appointments with General Milton A. Reckord, Governor Edward Martin, and General Ellard A. Walsh (adjutant general of Minnesota); Herbert H. Rogge and S. R. Marsh (of Westinghouse); Postmaster General Hannegan; General Surles, for presentation of award from War Department to B'nai B'rith.

5   Washington. Morning appointments with General Beightler; General Paul and Colonel W. B. Boyce; Elizabeth Williams Fulbright (wife of Senator James William Fulbright [Arkansas]) and Mrs. Bacon; Kansas delegation, led by Senator Capper and Congressmen Edward Herbert Rees, Clifford Ragsdale Hope, and Frank Carlson. Afternoon appointments with General Miltonberger, General R. E. Truman, and General John Augustus Harris (adjutant general of Missouri); Congressman Clyde Doyle (California); J. L. Hennessy and H. C. Blunck. To General Surles's quarters for informal evening meeting with newspaper group.

6   Washington. Morning appointments with General Leavey; Dr. Bowles; Generals Hull and Hertford. To White House for presentation of DSM to Admiral Leahy. Lunch in office with Under Secretary Acheson. Afternoon appointments with a group of film

February executives; General Ladd; Major Roland McKinley Buffington (Eisenhower's cousin).

7 Washington. Morning appointments with Generals I. D. White and Wyman; General Joyce; Reverend Hazen; L. Whitman. Lunch at Fort Myer with General Haislip. Afternoon meeting of War Council. Appointment with Dr. Hutchison.

8 Washington. Morning appointments with General Sayler; General Lutes and Colonel Hamilton; Colonel Bowen and staff re congressional presentation; Mrs. Francis Biddle; General Lincoln for briefing on CCS matters. JCS luncheon for BCOS. Afternoon presentation of OLC to DSM to General Barney McKinney Giles (commanding general of Pacific Ocean Area, AF). To dinner for Field Marshal and Lady Wilson.

9 Washington. Morning appointments with General John Dudley Lavarack (head of the Australian Military Mission); Congresswoman C. B. Luce. Afternoon appointment with General Snyder. To White House for Women's Press Club dinner for President and Mrs. Truman.

10 Washington. Addresses the graduating class of American University in the afternoon. Evening call on Admiral and Mrs. Nimitz.

11 Washington. Morning presentation of OLC to DSM to General I. H. Edwards. Conference with Generals Handy, Hull, Hoge, Wheeler, and Maxwell. Accompanied by Mrs. Eisenhower to luncheon for former Prime Minister Churchill at the British Embassy. To Arlington Hall with General Vandenberg for inspection. Appointment with General Handy to discuss guided missiles.

12 Washington. Morning appointments with Congressman May and two constituents, Mr. Price and Mr. Conover; Captain Frank Hayes (who served as an engineer in the ETO). Lays wreath at the Lincoln Memorial. Afternoon appointment with General Paul. To Treasury Department to be photographed in connection with bond drive. Informal dinner at Secretary and Mrs. Patterson's home.

February 13   Washington. Morning appointments with General Raymond Oscar Barton (CG of 4th Infantry Division during most of World War II, retiring on February 28, 1946); General Paul; P&O and G-2. Afternoon appointment with General V. Evans, General Edward Sedley Bres (on duty with the War Department General Staff Committee on National Guard and Reserve Policy), and General Leslie Chasemore Hollis (Senior Assistant Secretary in office of British War Cabinet). To White House.

14   Washington. Early morning departure for Kansas City, Missouri, first stop on inspection tour of Army facilities in the West. Addresses luncheon of the Military Order of World Wars. Visits 7-11 Club. Spends evening with Arthur Eisenhower.

15   Kansas City. Inspection trips to Fort Leavenworth and Fort Riley, Kansas. Afternoon visit with Edna Eisenhower in Junction City, Kansas. Evening and overnight at the home of Milton S. Eisenhower in Manhattan, Kansas.

16   Manhattan. Leaves for Abilene after lunch, to spend the afternoon and night with mother, Ida Stover Eisenhower.

17   Abilene. Departure by auto for Salina, Kansas, and from there by plane to Denver. Inspection of Fitzsimmons General Hospital, followed by luncheon. Afternoon inspection of Lowry Field. Overnight in Denver.

18   Denver. Early morning plane to Salt Lake City for inspection of Headquarters, 9th Service Command, and Tooele Ordnance Depot at Fort Douglas. Overnight in Salt Lake City.

19   Salt Lake City. Early morning plane to Tacoma, Washington. Lunch at McChord Field, followed by inspection. Overnight at home of Edgar Eisenhower.

20   Tacoma. By auto to Fort Lewis for inspection and luncheon. Afternoon inspection of Madigan General Hospital. Overnight at home of Edgar Eisenhower.

21   Tacoma. Morning departure for San Francisco. Afternoon inspection of Letterman General Hospital. Overnight in San Francisco.

February 22   San Francisco. Morning inspection of San Francisco Port of Embarkation. Flight to Salinas, California, followed by auto trip to Fort Ord for inspection. Return to Salinas for flight to Long Beach. Inspection of Air Transport Command Base at Long Beach, followed by auto trip to Los Angeles. Overnight in Los Angeles.

23   Los Angeles. Inspection and luncheon at the separation center at Fort MacArthur. Afternoon inspection of Los Angeles Port of Embarkation. Overnight in Los Angeles.

24   Los Angeles. By auto to Long Beach for morning flight to El Paso, Texas. Overnight in El Paso.

25   El Paso. By auto to Fort Bliss, Beaumont General Hospital, and Biggs Field for inspections. Luncheon at Biggs Field. By auto to Randolph Field in San Antonio, Texas, where Mrs. Eisenhower is visiting the Gordon Moores. Overnight in San Antonio.

26   San Antonio. Morning inspections of Kelly Field and Fort Sam Houston. Afternoon inspection of Randolph Field. Overnight in San Antonio.

27   San Antonio. General and Mrs. Eisenhower at the Gordon Moores'.

28   San Antonio.

March 1   San Antonio.

2   San Antonio. By plane to Washington, arriving late afternoon.

3   Washington.

4   Washington. To Secretary of War's office in afternoon for P&O presentation. Appointment with Admiral Nimitz.

5   Washington. To Secretary of War's office for a briefing by General Norstad on the congressional hearings on unification. Appointment with Generals Vandenberg and H. A. Craig. Secretary of War's press conference. Afternoon appointments with General De Witt; General Surles and Colonel Stack; Frank Bane; Assistant Secretary of War Petersen.

6   Washington. Morning appointments with General North; Generals Lincoln and H. A. Craig, with Colo-

March   nel Bowen, on the Army's missions and roles; General Paul, with Colonel Bowen, on demobilization; P&O and G-2; Admirals Nimitz and Radford. Afternoon appointments with General Richards for briefing on congressional budget hearings; General Paul; General J. W. Byron and Mrs. J. R. Eden.

7   Washington. Morning appointment with Assistant Secretary of War Symington. Appears at House Appropriations Committee hearings on nonappropriated funds of the Secretary of War. War Council meeting. Afternoon appearance before a subcommittee of the Senate Military Affiars Committee to testify on unification. To the White House.

8   Washington. With Mr. and Mrs. Winston Churchill and Sarah Churchill to Richmond, Virginia, by train. Churchill and Eisenhower address Virginia legislature. To Williamsburg by auto. Tour of Colonial Williamsburg and William and Mary College. Dinner at the Williamsburg Inn as guests of Mr. and Mrs. John D. Rockefeller III. Return by train to Washington.

9   Washington. Morning appointment with General Paul. Evening reception with Secretary of War, followed by dinner for Churchill at Quarters One.

10   Washington.

11   Washington. Morning appointments with General Groves for briefing on meeting with Senator McMahon; F. H. LaGuardia. To the White House for afternoon meeting with the President. Dinner with Senator McMahon and other members of the Special Committee on Atomic Energy.

12   Washington. Morning appointments with General Paul on general officer program; H. Hoover; Jack Brooks Beardwood, and General Surles. Lunch in office with General W. B. Smith. Afternoon appointments with R. Simon and Colonel Stack; A. Harriman.

13   Washington. Morning appearance before the House Military Affairs Committee. Appointment with P&O and G-2. Afternoon appointments with Generals Spaatz and Hull on roles and missions of the Armed

Forces; Miss Fanny Holtzman; Field Marshal H. M. Wilson; Charles Christian Wertenbaker (chief of foreign correspondents, *Time* and *Life* magazines). Evening address to the Public Administration Group.

14 Washington. Morning appointments with Congresswoman Bolton and Congressman Carl Thomas Curtis (Nebraska); General Paul on disability retirements; Joseph Wright Alsop, Jr. (author and syndicated columnist); S. Hillman; T. J. Watson. Presents LM to General Harry Farnham Germaine Letson for his service as Chairman of the Canadian Joint Staff Mission. Lunch in office with Generals Letson and Hull. Afternoon appointments with General Benicio (Brazilian military attaché); R. W. Bliss. To Secretary of War's buffet dinner for congressmen.

15 Washington. Morning briefing by General Lincoln and Colonel Juskalian on JCS matters. JCS luncheon. Afternoon appointments with General R. Q. Brown; Colonel K. R. Greenfield; General Stratemeyer; Egbert White (advertising executive and publisher, wartime edition of *Stars and Stripes*, Mediterranean); Mrs. Ruth Boyd (antique dealer), who presents Eisenhower with a gift. To Colonel Stack's quarters in the evening.

16 Washington. Morning appointments with General Ridgway and Colonel Carroll; Colonel George Wilbur Cocheu, ret. (an instructor of Eisenhower's at West Point); Sir Forbes, delivering a letter from Marshal Tedder; General Snyder.

17 Washington.

18 Washington. Morning appointment with General Kenner. Afternoon appointments with Dr. Bowles to discuss atomic energy; W. Lippmann with Colonel Stack; Congressman Daniel Knagg Hock (Pennsylvania). To dinner for Field Marshal and Lady Wilson.

19 Washington. To Secretary Byrnes's office at the State Department. Morning appointments with General Paul re the general officer program; Congressman Plumley; Major Paul Roudokoff, delivering a message from Marshal Zhukov. Afternoon appointments with Generals Simpson, Devers, Hull, and Bolté to

March   discuss the Simpson Board report; General E. S. Hughes with Colonel Stack. Accompanied by Mrs. Eisenhower to the Statler Hotel for an evening meeting of the Kansas State Society of Washington.

20   Washington. Morning appointments with Air Marshal Robert Leckie (Chief of the Royal Canadian Air Staff); Eugene Meyer with Colonel Stack; General Paul; P&O and G–2. Lunch in office with Air Marshal Leckie. Afternoon appointments with Philip Fox La Follette (lawyer and former governor of Wisconsin); Judge Edwin Owen Lewis (of the Court of Common Appeals in Philadelphia, and honorary president for life of the General Society of Sons of the Revolution).

21   Washington. Accompanied by General Persons to Capitol Hill to testify before the House Military Affairs Committee hearings on selective service. Lunch at the Army-Navy Club with Colonel George Wilbur Cocheu. To afternoon testimony before Senate Military Affairs Committee with General Spaatz. To Secretary of War's buffet supper for congressmen at the Pentagon.

22   Washington. Morning appointments with General Saltzman and Colonel Stack; General North; General Lincoln for briefing on JCS matters. JCS photographed, followed by JCS luncheon. Afternoon appointment with General Shang Chen (chief of the Chinese delegation to the United Nations).

23   Washington. Morning appointments with General North; General Paul re general officers; Eugene Meyer, Herbert Berridge Elliston (editor, *Washington Post*), P. L. Graham, and Generals Surles and Collins. Accepts, with General Bradley, a special award from the Army and Navy Union. Appointments with Edward Lewis Bartlett (Alaskan delegate to Congress); Grace Moore. Dinner with Mrs. Eisenhower and T. J. Davis at the Shoreham Hotel.

24   Washington. Accompanied by Mrs. Eisenhower to luncheon at the home of Admiral and Mrs. Stark.

25   Washington. Secretary of War's luncheon for pub-

March   lishers and editors. Afternoon appointment with Generals Handy, Spaatz, and Richards re the budget.

26   Washington. Morning appointment with William Watts Chaplin (NBC news commentator). Luncheon with Senator Richard Brevard Russell (Georgia) and members of the Georgia Bar Association. Afternoon appointments with L. Lambert; General Cardenas Guzman; Bradley Dewey (president of Dewey and Almy Chemical Company and chairman of the JCS Guided Missiles Committee). To the White House office of John Wesley Snyder (Director, Office of War Mobilization and Reconversion). Evening Spanish class with Captain Cannon.

27   Washington. Morning appointments with F. Page; W. F. White; General Handy and Dr. Thortin Rusten Hogness (professor of chemistry, University of Chicago) to discuss atomic energy; P&O and G-2. To the Capitol for luncheon with the Texas delegation in the Speaker's dining room. Photographed for cover of *Newsweek*. Secretary Patterson presents LM to General P. J. Hurley.

28   Washington. Accompanied by Mrs. Eisenhower to Richmond by auto. Receives honorary degree at the University of Richmond. Evening return to Washington.

29   Washington. Morning appointments with Field Marshal Wilson; Dr. Ernest Orlando Lawrence (Nobel prize-winning physicist) to discuss the atomic bomb. Briefing on JCS matters. JCS luncheon.

30   Washington. Morning appointments with General G. C. Beach, Jr.; General Valdes; Mr. Conway and photographers from the Cleveland Air Show. Lunch with former Ambassador Davies.

31   Washington. Accompanied by Mrs. Eisenhower to supper party at quarters of General and Mrs. Surles.

April 1   Washington. Morning appointment with Doolittle Board. Lunch with Secretary Forrestal. Afternoon appointments with General H. O. N. Brownfield (Commander of the Canadian Joint Staff in Washington);

April Leland Stowe (journalist, lecturer, radio commentator); Secretary of War re retired officers. Evening broadcast over radio station WOL on the American Cancer Society fight against cancer.

2 Washington. Accompanied by Mrs. Eisenhower to New York City by train. Luncheon and reception at Metropolitan Museum of Art with T. J. Watson. Visit to restaurant of M. Snyder and J. Schwarz. Acceptance of plaque at Freedom House. To the Knickerbocker Club as guests of Arthur Wilson Page (vice-president of American Telephone and Telegraph Company) in the evening. Overnight in New York City.

3 Early morning return to Washington. Morning appointments with Generals Spaatz and Lincoln for JCS briefing; P&O and G-2; members of the British Air Staff. Lunch with George Fielding Eliot (author, journalist, and military analyst for Columbia Broadcasting System). JCS meeting. Appointment with Generals Handy and Richards re the budget. Accompanied by Mrs. Eisenhower and Ambassador and Mrs. Davies to dinner for Senator Tydings.

4 Washington. Morning appointments with Air Chief Marshal Harris for presentation of DSM; Robert G. Woodside (Vice-Chairman of the American Battle Monuments Commission). War Council meeting. Appointment with Senator H. F. Byrd and delegation from Virginia American Legion. Luncheon with General and Lady Gale, Field Marshal and Lady Wilson, General and Mrs. Holmes, General and Mrs. Nevins. To the White House. To Quarters One to see W. A. Burpee.

5 Washington. Morning appointments with General Truscott; Congressman John Parnell Thomas (New Jersey). Presents DSC to Colonel Andrew Jackson Goodpaster, Jr. (S&P, P&O). Appointment with Under Secretary of War Royall to discuss the Lichfield trials. Secretary of War's luncheon for radio commentators. Late afternoon train for Chicago with President Truman and General Spaatz.

6 Early morning arrival in Chicago. Review of Army

April   Day parade. Address at Soldier Field Stadium. Late afternoon train for Washington.

7   Early morning return to Washington. Accompanied by Mrs. Eisenhower to evening tea with Major and Mrs. Parker Whitney West.

8   Washington. Morning briefing by G–1 and L&LD for congressional appearance. Accompanied by General Persons to testify before the Senate Military Affairs Committee. Lunch with General Gordon Nevil Macready (former Chief of British Army Staff in Washington) and the Right Honorable Leslie Hore-Belisha (former member of the British War Cabinet). Afternoon appointments with Mr. and Mrs. Quentin Reynolds; Congressman Bernard William Kearney (New York), who presents Eisenhower with portrait pictures; Colonel T. D. Campbell with Colonel Stack.

9   Washington. Morning appointments with S. Stone to sit for portrait; General Earl McFarland (superintendent), Colonel Steele, and Captain Peyton (all of Staunton Military Academy); Brazilian Ambassador Carlos Pereira e Sousa Martins and General Vandenberg; General Paul and Colonel Christian Gingrich Foltz (of the War Department Board) re new efficiency-report forms. Lunch with John D. Rockefeller III and Captain Cannon. Afternoon appointments with Generals Milton A. Reckord and E. A. Evans; Mrs. Ogden Reid; Dr. Joseph Clinton Todd (educator and ordained minister of Disciples of Christ Church), Arthur Wilson Eckman (general counsel, First Church of Christ, Scientist, Boston), and Dr. Robert Wyckoff Searle (minister and general secretary of the Greater New York Federation of Churches); War Department Advisory Committee on Military Justice.

10   Washington. Appointment with Lady Astor. Presents DSM to General Littlejohn and LM to General Persons. Appointments with General P. Lincoln Mitchell; Basil O'Connor; P&O and G–2. Afternoon appointments with Colonel H. W. Riley; General A. R. Harris. To Secretary of War's office for meeting re Harford Engineering Works. War Council meeting.

April 11   Washington. Mid-morning plane for Cleveland, Ohio. Attends Cleveland Air Show and Aviation Club dinner. Late night plane for Washington.

12   Washington. Afternoon appointments with Ambassador Messersmith; Senator Saltonstall; Ambassador Harriman; General Bonesteel. Telephone call to General Hull.

13   Washington. Morning appointments with General Hanford MacNider (on active duty in the Pacific during World War II, now president and general manager of Northwestern States Portland Cement Company); Generals Collins and North re Mountbatten dispatch; General Handy, Colonel Trichel, Bradley Dewey, and Dr. Edwin Richard Gilliland (professor of chemical engineering and deputy dean of engineering at M.I.T.) to discuss guided missiles. Telephone conversation with Congressman Gordon Canfield (New Jersey). Afternoon appointments with General Wedemeyer; L. W. Douglas. To the Statler Hotel for Gridiron Club dinner.

14   Washington.

15   Washington. Morning appointments with Wing Commander Campbell-Johnson, with message from Lord Mountbatten; B. Baruch; R. Roberts. Luncheon with General Ridgway and Inter-American Defense Board at the Mayflower Hotel. Afternoon appointment with Gerow Board re the Army school system. Accompanied by Mrs. Eisenhower to dinner at home of Colonel and Mrs. Fahnstock.

16   Washington. Morning appointments with M. Chase; F. H. LaGuardia. To CAA hangar for helicopter demonstration. Lunch with Secretary of War. Afternoon appointments with William Sholto Douglas (Marshal of the Royal Air Force); H. H. Lehman.

17   Washington. Morning appointments with Sidney M. Shalett (of the *New York Times*); General George Henry Decker (Deputy Commander and Chief of Staff, U.S. Army, Pacific); General William Curtis Chase (CG, 1st Cavalry Division); P&O and G–2; the Honorable Wilhelm Thorleif Munthe Morgenstierne (Norwegian Ambassador) to receive the Order of Olaf.

April   Afternoon appointments with General Haislip; General Hull for briefing on JCS 1656, "U.S. Security Interests in the Disposition of Tripolitania." To office of Secretary of State Byrnes for further discussion of JCS 1656.

18   Washington. Morning appointments with Admiral H. W. Hill re National Service Schools; Dr. H. W. A. Hanson; General Paul re efficiency-report forms. War Council meeting. Noon meeting with General Wickersham. Appointment with Assistant Secretary H. C. Petersen and Jonathan Worth Daniels (journalist and former press secretary to the President) re press job in Berlin. Lunch with Speaker Rayburn in the Speaker's office.

19   Washington. Morning appointments with General Somervell; General Leonard Russell Boyd (formerly CG of the 93d Infantry Division); Field Marshal Wilson; General Lincoln for JCS briefing; General Surles. Luncheon with the American Society of Newspaper Editors at the Presidential Room of the Statler Hotel.

20   Washington. Early morning plane for Dennison, Texas. Visit to Eisenhower's birthplace, followed by a parade, speech at the reviewing stand, barbecue, and press conference. Late afternoon flight to College Station, Texas, to receive honorary degree from Texas A & M College.

21   College Station. Addresses sunrise muster service for Texas A & M men who died in World War II. By plane to Washington.

22   Washington. Morning appointments with General Collins; General Joseph Wilson Byron to discuss Boy Scouts of America; General Mikhail Romanovich Galaktionov (military editor of *Pravda*); General Spaatz; General F. R. McCoy. Accompanied by several officers to luncheon with Under Secretary of State Acheson at Blair House. Afternoon appointment with E. F. Colloday, delivering letter from former Governor A. M. Landon re procurement of pipe. Kansas State College Alumni Association dinner.

23   Washington. Morning appointments with General

April	Ridgway; Major Poniatowski; General Parks and Charles A. Merrill (assistant managing editor of the *Boston Globe*); G-3 for briefing on ROTC policy; General Beightler. Lunch with Major Poniatowski. Afternoon appointment with General Richards. To see H. D. Smith, Director of the Bureau of the Budget, with the Secretary of War and General Richards. Appointments with B. House; General Spaatz.
24	Washington. Morning appointments with General North; General Devers and Army commanders; General Hertford and Colonel Bertollo; General Paul; General Persons; P&O and G-2. Luncheon with General Commission of Army and Navy Chaplains at the Statler Hotel. Afternoon train for New York City to speak at the William Allen White Memorial Dinner. Overnight in New York City.
25	New York City. Lunch at Time, Inc., with Charles Christian Wertenbaker. To the wedding and reception for Sergeant F. N. Smith and Captain B. N. Johnson (both of whom served under Eisenhower at SHAEF headquarters). Formal address at the annual dinner of the American Newspapers Publishers Association. Departure by train for Washington.
26	Early morning arrival in Washington. JCS luncheon.
27	Washington. Morning appointments with Chaplain L. D. Miller; General Hull; Under Secretary of War Royall; General Collins; Congressman Paul Joseph Kilday (Texas); General Paul; General Persons. Afternoon appointment with Assistant Secretary of War H. C. Petersen.
28	Washington. Departure by plane for Pacific inspection trip. Late afternoon arrival in San Francisco. Dinner with General Arnold. Late plane for Hawaii.
29	Early morning arrival at Hickam Field, Honolulu. Visit to Tripler Army Hospital and inspection of various Army and Navy installations. Press conference.
30	Honolulu. Inspection of various installations.
May 1	Honolulu. Inspection of various installations. Addresses to the chamber of commerce and at Wheeler Field and Schofield Stadium. Late evening departure for Guam, with stop at Kwajelein, Marshall Islands.

May 2   Kwajelein. Inspection of preparations for forthcoming Bikini bomb tests. Late afternoon arrival in Guam.

3   Guam. Morning inspection of Army posts. Afternoon plane to Saipan, with brief stop at Tinian. Inspection of installations and return to Guam by plane. Late flight to Manila, Philippine Islands.

4   Manila. Inspection of various installations. Dinner with President-elect Roxas.

5   Manila. Inspection of various installations.

6   Manila. Inspection of various installations.

7   Manila. Inspection of various installations. Overnight at Baguio.

8   Manila. Morning plane to Okinawa. Addresses several thousand men at a boxing show. Overnight in Okinawa.

9   Okinawa. Early morning plane for Nanking. Meeting with General Marshall and visit to MAG. Luncheon with Marshall and Generalissimo and Mrs. Chiang Kai-shek. By plane to Shanghai for dinner with General Gillem and return to Nanking for the night.

10   Nanking. Morning departure for Tokyo. Conference with General MacArthur. Inspection of various installations.

11   Tokyo. Inspection of various installations.

12   Tokyo. Review of 1st Cavalry Division.

13   Tokyo. Inspection of various installations.

14   Tokyo. Inspection of various installations.

15   Tokyo. Morning plane to Seoul, Korea. Inspection, followed by luncheon with General Hodge. By plane to Iwo Jima. Buffet supper. By plane to Wake Island for the night.

16   Wake Island. Morning departure for Honolulu.

17   Honolulu.

18   Honolulu. Early morning plane to Sea Island, Georgia (for vacation), with stop in San Francisco. At Sea Island through May 23.

24   Sea Island. Late afternoon plane to Washington, arriving early evening.

May 25   Washington.

26   Washington.

27   Washington. Early morning departure by auto with Mrs. Eisenhower for Gettysburg College to accept honorary degree and address graduating class. Evening return to Washington.

28   Washington. Morning appearance before House Foreign Affairs Committee. To the White House at midday. Afternoon appointments with General Ridgway; General Bull; General Handy and Colonel Trichel to discuss coordination of military research; General Paul.

29   Washington. Early morning plane to Oklahoma City. Luncheon, speech, and discussion at governors' conference. Late evening plane to Washington.

30   Washington. Morning appointments with General North; General Paul. Accompanied by Mrs. Eisenhower to Memorial Day service at Arlington Amphitheater.

31   Washington. Early morning plane to West Point. Review of corps of cadets. Luncheon with the corps, followed by address to the graduating class. Midafternoon return to Washington. To Secretary of War's office to make newsreel for D-day anniversary.

June 1   Washington. Morning appointments with General Bradley; General Swift. To Under Secretary of War Royall's office to swear in General E. S. Hughes; Colonel Parmentier. Early evening train for Chicago.

2   Early afternoon arrival in Chicago. Addresses the Reserve Officers Association convention at the Congress Hotel.

3   Chicago. Morning train for Detroit to attend the meeting of the Army Ordnance Association, arriving mid-afternoon. Press conference. Early evening meeting with twelve heads of Detroit industry, followed by informal discussion with other guests, dinner, and address to the Association.

4   Detroit. Morning plane to Washington, arriving at noon. Appointment with General Horkan. To the White House to see President Truman re unification.

June   Appointment with McCloy and Geddy. Accompanied by Mrs. Eisenhower to dinner given by Assistant Secretary of War and Mrs. Symington.

5   Washington. Morning appointment with General Richards re appearance before House Appropriations Committee. Testifies before the committee. To general officers lounge for Secretary of War's luncheon with women editors. Afternoon appointments with General von der Becke; Generals Paul, Milton A. Reckord, and E. A. Evans. Late evening train for Boston.

6   Morning arrival in Boston. To Harvard University to accept honorary degree. Midafternoon plane to Washington. Appointment with General Collins, F. W. McCullough, and Mark Skinner Watson. To the White House to see the President.

7   Washington. Morning appointments with General De Witt; General Gilbert Richard Cook (of the Advisory Board to the Chief of Staff) with General Paul; General Echols; General Paul; General Lincoln for briefing on JCS matters. To the Pentagon Court at noon to hear a Michigan high-school choir. JCS luncheon. Late afternoon appointment with General O. N. Bradley. To Secretary of War's conference room for presentation by General Littlejohn of a flag.

8   Washington. Morning appointments with General Larkin; Polish Military Attaché General Isydor Modelski with Colonel Bowen. Late afternoon train for Northfield, Vermont.

9   Early morning arrival at Montpelier Junction. By auto to Norwich University to receive honorary degree and address graduating class. After luncheon, afternoon plane to Washington.

10   Washington. Morning appointments with W. A. Wood, Jr. (at request of Senator James Oliver Eastland [Mississippi]), re West Point; Colonel Godwin Ordway, Jr.; General Paul. To fifth-floor auditorium to speak briefly on the deactivation of ASF. Lunch in office with General Nevins. Afternoon appointments with General H. B. Lewis; Theodore M. Richle (president-elect of the Economic Club of New York);

June   Lieutenants R. L. Gruenther and Harlan Gustave Koch (1946 graduates of West Point); Mrs. Anna Rosenberg.

11   Washington. Morning appointments with G–3 officers for briefing on ROTC policy; Lloyd Eugene Hedberg (executive secretary of the Association of Military Colleges and Schools of the United States); General R. E. Porter and Colonel Barker (SPD) for briefing on postwar ground forces. To Secretary of War's conference room to be photographed with ETO banner. Afternoon appointments with General Emmons; General Richard Kerens Sutherland. To conference in office of Secretary of State Byrnes. To the Pan American Room of the Statler Hotel for evening cocktails with Mr. Elson.

12   Washington. Morning appointments with Assistant Secretary of War Symington; Congresswoman E. N. Rogers; General Bor-Komorowski; General Paul; P&O and G–2. Afternoon appointments with Generals Spaatz, Handy, and Aurand; General Ridgway with Colonel Bowen.

13   Washington. Morning appointments with General Bonesteel; General R. N. Young. Briefing on JCS papers. Noon JCS meeting, followed by JCS luncheon.

14   Washington. Morning appointments with General Paul; Senator Mead and Joseph Henry Biben (president of Jewish Ledger Publishing Company), to receive the American Hebrew Annual Medal Award; Colonels Cossens and C. H. Wilson. To the White House to attend Medal of Honor ceremony. Luncheon with Under Secretary of State Acheson, Mr. Braden, and Generals Handy, Norstad, and Chamberlin. Afternoon appointments with General McCoy; General St. Clair Streett (SAC). To view newsreels of Eisenhower's D-day statement.

15   Washington. Morning appointment with Colonel Carlos Aldana (Chief of Staff of the Guatemalan Army).

16   Washington. Supper and bridge with Colonel and Mrs. Nevins.

17   Washington. Morning appointments with General

June   O. N. Bradley and G–3 re ROTC policy; Colonel John Callan O'Laughlin (publisher of the *Army-Navy Journal*). Afternoon appointments with R. Simon; Generals E. S. Bres and Donald Bennett Adams.

18   Washington. Morning viewing of film on musk ox. Appointment with Field Marshal Wilson. Afternoon appointment with Robert S. Peare (vice-president of General Electric).

19   Washington. Morning appointments with General T. D. Campbell; General Matthew John Gunner (MacArthur's G–1); P&O and G–2. Luncheon in Secretary of War's office with editors going overseas. Afternoon appointment with General Gerald Walter Robert Templer (Director of Military Intelligence, British War Office).

20   Washington. Morning appointments with Major Gentile; Colonel J. M. McHugh (USMC, ret.); Colonel Leon Dostert (French interpreter in Africa); General Edward Sedley Bres with Colonel Stack to discuss Navy ROTC. To luncheon given by J. C. Black for Colonel Castle at the Carlton Hotel. Afternoon appointment with Juan-Terry Trippe (president) and Harold McMillian Bixby (vice-president, Pan American Airlines). To Secretary of War's office for presentation of Medal of Merit to B. F. Fairless.

21   Washington. Morning appointments with F. Page and Colonel Stack; General Paul re general officers; General Lutes. JCS luncheon. To Walter Reed General Hospital accompanied by General H. M. Snyder, Sr. Buffet supper for Generals Hull and H. A. Craig at the Army War College.

22   Washington. All-day fishing trip with General Horkan.

23   Washington. To the Dominion Boat Club in Alexandria, Virginia, in the afternoon to meet former Ambassador and Mrs. Davies.

24   Washington. Morning appointment with General Paul and Colonel Stack. To Secretary of War's office for conference on integration of reserves into Regular Army. Appointment with F. H. La Guardia. Noon presentation of report of the Supreme Commander to

June   representatives of the American Legion and the Veterans of Foreign Wars. Appointment with General Edward Poole (Deputy Chief of Staff, South African
Defence Forces). Lunch with Assistant Secretary of
War Symington. To General Paul's office for presentation of civilian award to Mrs. Gruber. Appointments
with Colonel Louis Curtis Tiernan, chaplain (at request of President Truman); Generals Handy and
Paul re general officers.

25   Washington. Appointments with W. E. Meyers and
son Peter; Generals Handy and Richards for briefing
on congressional appearance. Testimony before the
Senate Appropriations Committee. Afternoon appointments with Colonels Carroll and Mitchell of
G–1; Field Marshal Wilson; General Persons, Bergin, and Swift for briefing on June 27 congressional
appearance.

26   Washington.

27   Washington. Morning appointment with General
Ridgway. Telephone conversation with Admiral
Nimitz. Testimony before the Senate Military Affairs
Committee re increased officer strength. Lunch with
former Ambassador Davies. Afternoon conference on
legislation for Medical Corps officers with Generals
Kirk, Persons, Bergin, and Swift and Mr. Voorhees.
Appointment with Air Marshal Thomas Walker Elm-
hurst (Director of Intelligence, British Air Ministry
to the United States). To evening cocktail party for
General Aleid Van Tricht (Netherlands Mission).

28   Washington. Morning briefing on JCS papers. JCS
luncheon. Afternoon appointment with Colonel
Blaik, delivering a letter from General Taylor.

29   Washington. Morning appointments with Lincoln
Freeman (of *Fortune* magazine). Late morning departure from office for engagement with J. C. Black.

30   Washington.

July 1 Washington. Accompanied by Mrs. Eisenhower to the
House of Representatives for noon commemorative
service for F. D. Roosevelt. Afternoon appointments
with General Ward; General Horkan; Colonel

July   "Lefty" Parker. To the National Theater with Mrs. Eisenhower in the evening.

2   Washington. Morning appointments with Dr. Duncan Black MacDonald Emrick (historian) to discuss Eisenhower's recent report; T. F. Boyle, with Captain Cannon, re Colonel Reeder. Luncheon with Drew Pearson, Generals Collins and Parks, and Colonel Stack. Afternoon appointments with Admiral Halsey, with Captain Cannon; Generals Norstad and Harding. To the Carlton Hotel for Speaker Rayburn's evening cocktail party.

3   Washington. Morning appointments with General Chamberlin; General Collins. Lunch with George Kennan. Afternoon appointments with General Bergin; Grace Moore.

4   Washington.

5   Washington.

6   Washington. Morning appointment with Homes Bannard, introducing R. H. Clare.

7   Washington.

8   Washington. Morning appointments with Colonel Thiele; Colonel Westray Battle Boyce; Dr. Marian E. Kenworthy. Lunch with Colonel J. I. Greene. Afternoon appointment with four Swiss journalists—Drs. Eugene Diedtschi, Carl Doka, Hugo Kramer, and James Sietz.

9   Washington. To Secretary of War's office for conference with Senator Downey. Appointment with President Truman's brother and cousin, John Vivian Truman and General Truman. Film on atomic-bomb tests at Bikini. Lunch with Milton S. Eisenhower and John D. Rockefeller III. Afternoon appointment with General Bergin to discuss reserve general officers eligibility list. Dinner at Army and Navy Country Club.

10   Washington. To the Capitol to testify before the House Military Affairs Committee on legislation to authorize 25,000 additional Army officers. To Secretary of War's luncheon for the Belgian delegation. Leaves office (10:00 P.M.) for trip to Amherst, Massachusetts.

July 11 Amherst. Receives the American Alumni Council Award of Merit and returns by afternoon plane to Washington.

12 Washington. Morning appointment to discuss the integration of twenty-five thousand additional officers with General Bergin and Drs. Robert James Wherry (Assistant Chief for Research, Personnel Research Section, The Adjutant General's office) and Henny. Briefing on JCS papers, followed by JCS luncheon. Golf at Chevy Chase Club with Generals Gasser and Parks in the afternoon.

13 Washington. Morning appointments with General Alexander Papagos (commander of the Greek Armed Forces during the Albanian campaign); J. S. McDaniel (a personal friend from New York); Generals Handy, Persons, and Collins. Lunch with Generals Handy and Styer. Evening departure for reunion with brothers in Big Lake, Wisconsin. Remains at Big Lake through July 21.

22 Returns to Washington.

23 Washington. Morning appointments with General Persons; General Stoner with Colonel Bowen. Afternoon appointments with General Styer; Robert Merriam.

24 Washington. Morning appointments with Senator Taft; Field Marshal Wilson; P&O and G-2. Afternoon appointments with Congressman John Crain Kunkel (Pennsylvania) and three men from Lykens, Pennsylvania, re a Labor Day invitation; General Egbert Frank Bullene (CG, Army Chemical Center, Edgewood Arsenal, Maryland). Accompanied by Mrs. Eisenhower to Under Secretary and Mrs. Royall's home in the evening.

25 Washington. Morning presentation of LM to Colonel Raymond Bradner Marlin. Presentation of uniforms by Tim White of QMC. Appointments with General Ho Ying-chin (Chinese representative to the United Nations and head of the Chinese Military Mission); General Gray. To the White House for a meeting with the President. Lunch with Colonels Greene and DeWeerd. Afternoon appointments with General

July   Ridgway and Colonel Bowen; West Point Chaplain Murdock with Captain Cannon; General Ingles with Colonel Carroll.

26   Washington. Morning appointments with General Chamberlin; Ambassador Elizalde; T. Rovelstad re St. Paul's Cathedral in London; General Devers for briefing on Installation Board; Fred Benham (a friend of E. Oliphant). Briefing on JCS papers, followed by JCS luncheon. Golf at Chevy Chase Club with Generals Parks and Collins in the afternoon.

27   Washington. Morning appointments with General Chapman; Jean Dixon; Yousuf Karsh. Accompanied by Mrs. Eisenhower to an afternoon wedding at Fort Myer.

28   Washington.

29   Washington. Morning appointment with Generals Hines and Bolté. To the new War Department Building for a meeting of the Army-Navy Munitions Board, accompanied by Richard Redwood Deupree (chairman). Photographed at Bureau of Public Relations. Luncheon with Generals Parks and Gasser and three civilians. Afternoon appointment with General Paul and Colonel Stack.

30   Washington. Morning briefing by General Malony, then meeting with twenty-five members of the Historical Group. Briefing by General Richards, followed by a meeting in the White House with the Advisory Board to the Director of War Mobilization and Reconversion. Lunch with Milton S. Eisenhower. Afternoon appointments with General Baber Shum Shere Jung Bahadur Rana (senior commanding general of the Nepalese Army); General Paul with Colonel Stack; General De Witt with Colonel Stack; Dr. Bowles.

31   Washington. Morning appointments with General Collins re the budget; General Miltonberger; P&O and G–2. Lunch with Generals Spaatz, Handy, and Aurand.

August 1   Washington. Early morning departure with Mrs. Eisenhower for trip to Latin America. Stop at Morrison Field, Florida, for Army Air Forces Day

August	speech. Departure and subsequent arrival at Berinquen Field, Puerto Rico. Reception and dinner at the officers club, followed by brief news conference and overnight stay at the base.
2	Berinquen Field. Morning departure for the air base in Belem, Brazil. Upon arrival, brief interview by the press. Overnight at the base.
3	Belem. Departure for Natal Air Base, Brazil.
4	Natal. Early morning departure for Rio de Janeiro. Upon arrival, greeted by Brazilian officials and U.S. Ambassador and Mrs. Pawley. Call on President Dutra. While in Rio, the Eisenhowers stay at the private villa of Roberto Marinho (a Rio publisher).
5	Rio de Janeiro. Accompanied by Ambassador Pawley on official calls. Luncheon with the Brazilian War Minister. Evening reception given by the Pawleys.
6	Rio de Janeiro. Visits various military establishments. Receives decoration from the Air Minister. Luncheon with the National Association of Newspaper Editors. President and Mrs. Dutra present decorations to General and Mrs. Eisenhower. Banquet and reception given by President and Mrs. Dutra.
7	Rio de Janeiro. Visit to military academy at Rezende. American Society reception, at which Eisenhower and Ambassador Pawley speak, in the evening.
8	Rio de Janeiro. Addresses special session of the National Constituent Assembly. Evening reception given by the War Minister.
9	Rio de Janeiro. Press conference in Ambassador Pawley's office. Luncheon with President and Mrs. Dutra. Evening reception at the U.S. Embassy; makes farewell remarks and receives an honorary degree from the University of Brazil.
10	Rio de Janeiro. Departure for Natal Air Base. Overnight at the base.
11	Natal. Departure for the U.S. air base at Atkinson Field, British Guiana. Brief news conference upon arrival. Dinner at the officers club. Overnight at the base.

August 12   Atkinson Field. Departure for Albrook Field, Panama Canal Zone, arriving in the afternoon. Evening reception by General and Mrs. Crittenberger, attended by President Jiménez. While in the Canal Zone, the Eisenhowers stay with the Crittenbergers.

13   Canal Zone. By open car to visit President Jiménez, who accompanies Eisenhower on the return trip. Dinner given by President and Mrs. Jiménez, at which Eisenhower is presented Panama's highest decoration, the Order of Vasco Nuñez de Balboa in the degree of grand master.

14   Canal Zone. Morning inspection trip to the Atlantic side of the Canal Zone. Luncheon given by Ambassador and Mrs. Hines and attended by President and Mrs. Jiménez. Evening reception given by Ambassador and Mrs. Hines and the American Society of Panama. Dinner at the governor's house in Balboa Heights.

15   Canal Zone. Departure for Mexico City, arriving in the afternoon. Parade through the streets. Receives the Civic Merit Medal. While in Mexico City, the Eisenhowers stay at the U.S. Embassy as guests of Ambassador Thurston.

16   Mexico City. Morning call on President Camacho and General Urquizo. Afternoon reception by President and Mrs. Camacho. Press conference at the U.S. Embassy, followed by meeting with the Mexico City chapter of the American Veterans Committee. Evening reception given by General and Mrs. Urquizo at the Military Club.

17   Mexico City. Visits to Military Camp No. 1 and military academy. Luncheon at the Academy Club. Evening reception at the U.S. Embassy, then to performance of the opera *Rigoletto*.

18   Mexico City. Early morning departure for San Antonio, Texas. Overnight in San Antonio.

19   San Antonio. Departure for Washington arriving late in the afternoon.

20   Washington.

21   Washington. Morning appointments with General

August		Paul and Colonel Stack; P&O and G–2. Noon appointment with Assistant Secretary Symington and General Spaatz. Lunch with Admiral Nimitz. Afternoon appointment with T. Rovelstad re the American roll of honor in St. Paul's Cathedral in London. To Griffith Stadium for baseball game.
	22	Washington. Morning appointments with P&O re equipment for Brazil; General Devers with Colonel Stack; General Moseley; Field Marshal Wilson re Field Marshal Montgomery's visit. To Blair House for lunch with Dean Acheson.
	23	Washington. Morning presentation of decoration to General Wedemeyer. Appointment with General Ridgway. Briefing on JCS papers, followed by JCS luncheon.
	24	Washington. Morning briefing by General Handy and P&O re handling of domestic disturbances.
	25	Washington.
	26	Washington. Ill in quarters.
	27	Washington. Ill in quarters.
	28	Washington. Morning appointments with General Edwin Logie Morris (British Army representative on the MSC, UN); P&O. Afternoon appointment with Assistant Secretary Symington. Evening engagement with General and Mrs. Haislip.
	29	Washington. Morning appointments with General Paul re strength of the Army; General Bonesteel to say good-by. Noon appointment with General Wedemeyer. Afternoon appointments with General Parks and ten people from the press; Generals Spaatz and Norstad.
	30	Washington. JCS luncheon, with BCOS as guests.
	31	Washington.
September	1	Washington. Early morning plane for Des Moines, Iowa. By car to Boone to visit the Carlsons. Return to Des Moines. Late morning plane for Lincoln, Nebraska. Reception and luncheon at Hotel Cornhusker, followed by a visit to the fairgrounds for a parade and speech. Late afternoon plane to Des Moines and then by car to the Carlsons' in Boone. Overnight at the Carlsons'.

September 2   Boone. Departure by auto to Des Moines and then by air to Washington. Midnight train for Boston, Massachusetts.

3   Early morning arrival in Boston. Afternoon speech to convention of Veterans of Foreign Wars. Night train to Washington.

4   Morning arrival in Washington. Morning appointments with Mrs. Nell Henry; General Ridgway; P&O. Noon meeting with Richard Redwood Deupree. Lunch with Albert Wayne Coy. To Secretary of War's office for meeting with Senator Hill and then to Walter Reed General Hospital.

5   Washington. Morning conference with General Collins and others re the postwar Establishment. War Council meeting. JCS luncheon. Afternoon appointment with Generals Handy and Richards. To Griffith Stadium for baseball game in the evening.

6   Washington. Morning appointment with General Paul. Conference on the postwar Establishment. To the White House to see the President. Noon recording of message for U.S.O. Lunch with Generals Handy and Wedemeyer. Afternoon appointment with Air Vice Marshal Hugh Pughe Lloyd (senior instructor at the Imperial Defence College). To Walter Reed General Hospital in the late afternoon.

7   Washington. Morning conference on the postwar establishment. Lunch with former Ambassador Davies.

8   Washington.

9   Washington. Morning conferences on the postwar establishment: Reserve, National Guard. Lunch with Secretary of War. Afternoon appointments with Dr. Hutchison; Dr. Pogue.

10   Washington. Morning appointments with General Ridgway and Colonel Stack; H. Baldwin. Lunch with J. Hennessy. Afternoon appointment with Assistant Secretary Symington. To the White House with Secretaries of War and Navy and Admiral Nimitz. To ATC terminal to meet Field Marshal Montgomery in the late afternoon.

11   Washington. To Secretary of War's conference room to attend address by Field Marshal Montgomery, then

September	returns to office for briefing by staff officers. Press conference with Montgomery. To Secretary of War's dining room for luncheon for Montgomery. Evening reception for Montgomery at Quarters One. Evening train for Abilene, Kansas.
12	Abilene.
13	Abilene. Attends funeral services for his mother, Ida Stover Eisnehower. Spends night in Manhattan, Kansas, with Milton S. Eisenhower.
14	Abilene.
15	Abilene.
16	Returns to Washington. To Secretary of War's office for morning conference on the postwar Army with Generals Collins and Hodes. Appointment with General M. W. Clark. To the Washington Navy Yard to board the U.S.S. *Sequoia* for luncheon and afternoon cruise with Admiral Nimitz and Field Marshal Montgomery. Late afternoon telephone call from Air Marshal Robert Victor Goddard.
17	Washington. Testifies before court of inquiry. Afternoon meeting with General Paul re strength of the Army.
18	Washington. Morning telephone conversations with Senator Howard Alexander Smith (New Jersey); H. J. Taylor. Appointment with Dr. Bowles.
19	Washington. Morning appointments with General Styer and Captain Cannon; General Ridgway; Senator Carl Trumbull Hayden (Arizona), who brings a message from the governor of Arizona. War Council meeting. Luncheon with Generals Handy, Norstad, and Persons and several congressmen. To Fort Myer to attend formal review for Field Marshal Montgomery and then to ATC to bid Montgomery farewell.
20	Washington. Morning appointments with Philip Bucknell (of *Stars and Stripes*); AGF and G-3, re postwar divisions. Briefing on JCS papers. Appointment with General Collins and Mr. Mowrer (correspondent from Trieste). JCS luncheon. To the White House to see the President.

October 21 Washington. Morning appointments with H. J. Taylor; Mrs. O. Reid; a committee from Bloomfield, New Jersey (at the request of Senator H. Alexander Smith); General Bull. Noon train with Mrs. Eisenhower for Halifax, Nova Scotia, to board H.M.S. *Queen Mary* for Europe. Talks with H. J. Taylor at the station in Washington, and in response to a large crowd at a stop in Boston, appears even though in pajamas and robe.

22 Halifax. Evening boarding of the *Queen Mary*, followed by an informal meeting with the press.

23 Halifax. Because of fog the departure delayed until early evening.

24 Aboard the *Queen Mary*.

25 Aboard the *Queen Mary*. Afternoon press conference.

26 Aboard the *Queen Mary*. Afternoon tea with officers in the officers wardroom. Evening cocktails with the captain and guests.

27 Aboard the *Queen Mary*. Liner docks in Southampton, England, in midafternoon. Captain John Eisenhower joins his parents. Overnight on ship.

28 Morning debarkation from the *Queen Mary*. Motor to Stoney Cross, and from there by plane to Frankfort, Germany. Briefing by USFET officials. Press conference. Evening and night at Teves House.

29 Frankfort. Morning plane for Luxembourg. Visits graves of Generals Patton and Betts at Hamm Cemetery. Calls on Grand Duchess Charlotte at Royal Palace. Early afternoon return to Frankfort. Dinner with General and Mrs. McNarney. To Berlin to General Clay's home.

30 Berlin. Addresses a group of enlisted men. Press conference at OMGUS. Luncheon at Harmack House and then to meeting of ACC. Evening reception at General Clay's home.

October 1 Berlin. Morning plane to Prestwick, Scotland. Press conference and then to Culzean Castle for the night.

2 Culzean Castle. Morning departure by auto for Murdostoun Castle, Newmains, Lancashire, residence of

October		Captain and Mrs. Stewart, where the Eisenhowers spend the night.
	3	Newmains, Lancashire. By auto to Edinburgh. Acceptance of honorary degree, followed by address, at Edinburgh University. Luncheon in the City Chambers and formal presentation of the appartment at Culzean Castle. Attends christening of Lord and Lady Tedder's son. Ceremony at Scottish-American Memorial, followed by reception at North British Hotel by British Legion and then other brief meetings before return to Culzean Castle.
	4	Culzean Castle. Presented with letters of historical interest as souvenirs of visit to Culzean.
	5	Culzean Castle. By auto to Maybole, Scotland, to receive Freedom of the City and to make short address. By plane to Balmoral Castle. Overnight guests of the King and Queen.
	6	Balmoral Castle. By plane to Culzean Castle.
	7	Culzean Castle.
	8	Culzean Castle.
	9	Culzean Castle. Visit to AAF base unit at Prestwick Airport before flying to St. Andrews Golf Club near Edinburgh. Return to Culzean Castle. Late evening train from Kilmarnock for London.
	10	Early morning arrival in London. To home of U.S. Ambassador. Address to Imperial Defence College. Visit to Air Marshal Portal. Dinner with Prime Minister Attlee at 10 Downing Street.
	11	London. Morning auto to Cambridge to receive honorary degree. Evening press conference at U.S. Ambassador's residence. Evening cocktail party.
	12	London. Calls on Queen Mary. Luncheon with Lord and Lady Tedder. Visits places of interest, including Telegraph Cottage.
	13	London. Late morning plane to Frankfort. Supper with General and Mrs. McNarney. Late evening train for Munich.
	14	Morning arrival in Munich. Review of troops. Visit to Headquarters, OMGUS, in Bavaria, followed by at-

October   tendance at export show in Munich. Visits two displaced-persons camps.

15   Munich. Review of troops. By train to Salzburg to inspect troops. By train to Italy.

16   Early morning arrival in Torvisio, then by auto to Gorizia to inspect 88th Division. Early evening train to Frankfort.

17   Frankfort. Conference with senior USFET officers. Dinner with General and Mrs. McNarney.

18   Frankfort. Brief press conference before departure by plane for Washington. Overnight stop in the Azores.

19   Azores. Continuation of flight to Washington, with stop in Bermuda. Mid-evening arrival in Washington.

20   Washington.

21   Washington. Morning telephone call to Senator Wherry. Afternoon appointments with General Bevins; General Almond; General Collins.

22   Washington. Morning appointments with General Styer; General Truscott; the governor of Szechenan Province, China; General Paul. Lunch with Admirals Nimitz and Leahy. Afternoon appointments with Generals Handy and Lutes re shipment of dependents overseas; Air Marshal Arthur Penrose Martyn Sanders (commandant of the RAF School). Dinner with General and Mrs. O. N. Bradley.

23   Washington. Morning appointments with General Ridgway; P&O for Intelligence presentation. To Walter Reed General Hospital at noon for overnight stay.

24   Washington. Noon return to office. Appointments with General Collins and twenty press representatives; General Larkin. Presentation of LM to Bob Hope (comedian). Appointment with Field Marshal Wilson.

25   Washington. Morning briefing re presentation at the White House. Presentation of citation to Irving Geist (of New York City). Afternoon appointments with General North; General Moore.

26   Washington. Morning appointments with Generals North and Horkan and Leslie L. Biffle (Secretary of

October		the Senate) re American cemeteries. To NBC in the afternoon to see television broadcast of Army-Duke football game.
	27	Washington. Afternoon train to New York City, arriving early evening. To Theodore Roosevelt House to address the Roosevelt Memorial Association and to receive its medal of honor. Early morning train to Washington.
	28	Morning arrival in Washington. Appointments with Assistant Under Secretary of State Benton; General Groves; General Adcock.
	29	Washington. Accompanied by the Secretary of War to see the President at the White House in the morning. To the new War Department Building in the afternoon, to meet with the Advisory Committee of the Army-Navy Munitions Board. Afternoon appointment with G–3 for analysis of General Reckord's report. To the Secretary of War's office to meet with eleven editors just returned from overseas. To Fort Myer Chapel in the early evening to attend wedding of Lieutenant Chick.
	30	Washington. Morning appointment with P&O. Afternoon train to New York City to address the *Herald Tribune* Forum at the Waldorf-Astoria Hotel. After the speech and a buffet supper, departs for Washington after midnight by train.
	31	Washington. Morning arrival. Appointments with A. S. Goss; General Gerhardt; General Herron; General Paul. Lunch with General Gray.
November	1	Washington. Morning train to Bethlehem, Pennsylvania, and then by auto to Lafayette College in Easton. Address and acceptance of honorary degree. Overnight at the home of President Hutchison.
	2	Easton. Morning departure by auto for West Point to attend Army-West Virginia football game. By car to Jersey City, New Jersey, then by early evening train to Washington, arriving at 11:30 P.M.
	3	Washington. Evening cocktails at the home of Colonel (ret.) and Mrs. Clark Lynn.
	4	Washington. Morning appointments with Assistant

November   Secretary Symington; G–3, to discuss plan for UMT demonstration unit; General John A. Appleton (vice-president of Pennsylvania Railroad). Accompanied by Mrs. Eisenhower to dinner at the Belgain Embassy.

5 Washington. Morning appointments with General Merritte Weber Ireland (Army Mutual Aid Society); Generals Handy and Richards re the budget; Generals Spaatz, Chamberlin, and Charles Henry Caldwell (military attaché to Argentina). Noon appointment with General Wedemeyer. Lunch with James Edwin Webb (Director of the Bureau of the Budget). Afternoon appointment with Congressmen Henry Dominique Larcade, Jr., and Asa Leonard Allen (both of Louisiana) to discuss Camp Polk.

6 Washington. Morning appointments with General Mehaffey. P&O Intelligence presentation. Lunch with Secretary Harriman. Afternoon appointment with General North. Dinner with General and Mrs. Lutes at the Army and Navy Town Club.

7 Washington. Morning appointment with Dr. Ernest Stacey Griffith (Director of Legislative Reference Service, Library of Congress). To the Secretary of War's office accompanied by General Reckord. War Council meeting. Luncheon at Quarters One with fourteen members of USMA Class of 1915. Photographed by *National Geographic* photographer in the afternoon. Appointment with Generals Handy, Norstad, Hall, and Persons re National Guard and Reserve.

8 Washington. Morning appointments with Mrs. Kermit Roosevelt; General Reckord.

9 Washington. Early morning train for New York City to attend Army-Notre Dame football game at Yankee Stadium. Dinner with General and Mrs. Taylor and Colonel and Mrs. Stack at the Waldorf-Astoria Hotel, followed by the theater. Post-midnight train to Washington.

10 Early morning arrival in Washington. To dinner at Ambassador Pawley's home in Plains, Virginia.

11 Washington.

12 Washington. Morning appointments with General

Ridgway and Major Cannon; Field Marshal Wilson. Noon appointment with Mrs. Anna Rosenberg. Lunch with Ambassador Pawley, Milton S. Eisenhower, and General Clay. Afternoon appointment with General Robert Edward Laycock (Br. Chief of Combined Operations). To General Handy's office to sit for photograph. Presentation of G–3 reorganization of War Department based on unification plan.

13 Washington. Morning appointments with General Parks and Colonel Stack; General Kenner; General Clay with Colonel Stack; P&O. Afternoon appointment with Maxwell Cohen. Report by R&D chiefs on 1946 expenditures and 1948 program.

14 Washington. Morning appointment with James Coggeshall, Jr. (executive vice-president of First Boston Corporation). To Saint Thomas Apostle Church to attend funeral services. Luncheon address to Advisory Council of Women's Interest Unit of PRD at general officers dining room. Afternoon appointments with General Lutes; General Richards. To the White House for a conference with the President and others. Dinner at Quarters One with guests.

15 Washington. Morning appointment with Colonel John K. Borneman (chaplain). To the Pentagon for review of survey of Army as blue-uniform team. Appointments with General Paul; General Richards. Afternoon appointment with General Ridley. To Secretary of War's office to discuss technical services.

16 Washington. Morning appointment with Joseph Wright Alsop, Jr., for off-the-record talk. Dinner with General and Mrs. Snyder.

17 Washington.

18 Washington. To Secretary of War's luncheon for National Guard and wing commanders. Afternoon appointments with Walter Lippmann; Dr. Freeman. To Mayflower Hotel for evening reception for foreign military and air attachés and heads of missions.

19 Washington. Morning appointments with Generals Persons, Lutes, and Reber re Camp Croft, South Carolina; John Alfred Davenport (of *Fortune* magazine); Herb Landes, of Salt Lake City and

November   Abilene. Lunch with Dr. Grosvenor and Franklin L. Fisher, both of *National Geographic* magazine. To Pentagon auditorium for showing of the film *Best Years of Our Lives*. To the Symingtons' to attend a dinner for the Vinsons.

20   Washington. Early morning train for Atlantic City, New Jersey, to address CIO. To New York City by train to speak at Economic Club dinner. Post-midnight train for Washington.

21   Early morning arrival in Washington. Morning appointments with General Persons; G–3 for presentation of comments on proposed divisional organization for infantry and armored divisions. War Council meeting. Address to key personnel and state directors of Selective Service. Afternoon conference with General Richards and others on FY 1948 budget. To Secretary of War's office for conference with General Snyder and medical consultants.

22   Washington. Morning appointment with Ambassador Elizalde. To the Mayflower Hotel to address a meeting of the National Council of the Reserve Officers Association. Late afternoon departure for Aberdeen, Maryland, for overnight hunting trip with General Hughes.

23   Aberdeen. Early evening return to Washington.

24   Washington. To cocktail party given by General and Mrs. Collins and then bridge with General and Mrs. Sayler.

25   Washington. Morning appointments with General Stoner and Colonel Stack; General Truscott with Colonel Bowen. Afternoon appointments with General McLain; General Norstad with Colonel Stack. To Secretary of War's office for meeting with Ambassador McNutt.

26   Washington. To the National War College to address class. Noon appointment with General Ridgway and Major Cannon, followed by appointment with General McLain re the American Legion convention. Discussion of budget for Ordnance and Air Force. To White House dinner for diplomatic corps.

27   Washington. Morning appointments with R. L.

November		Davies; B. Andrews. Appointment with General Mc-Lain at 12:30 P.M., followed by lunch with P. H. Griffith. Afternoon appointment with General Paul. Dinner at Quarters One with H. J. Taylor.
	28	Washington.
	29	Washington. Early morning train for New York City to address luncheon of Saints and Sinners at Waldorf-Astoria Hotel. Brief talk with J. Linen after the luncheon. Mid-afternoon train for Washington, arriving in early evening.
	30	Washington. Morning appointment with General Paul.
December	1	Washington.
	2	Washington. Morning appointment with General Paul. To Fort Myer chapel for funeral of Colonel Helms. Appointment with Field Marshal Wilson. Afternoon appointments with Walter Sherman Gifford (president of American Telephone and Telegraph Company); W. Dillingham. Lunch with Assistant Secretary Symington and Generals Spaatz and Norstad. Afternoon conference re organization and concept of airborne divisions. Appointment with General Chamberlin.
	3	Washington. Late morning train for New York City to address the Calvin Bullock Forum at 1 Wall Street. To the Waldorf-Astoria Hotel to receive the Churchman Award in the early evening. After a visit by Mrs. Rosenberg, post-midnight train for Washington.
	4	Morning arrival in Washington. Morning appointments with Assistant Secretary Petersen; General Obino; General Ingles; General Paul. To Secretary of War's mess for luncheon honoring General Obino. Afternoon appointment with General Groves.
	5	Washington. Morning presentation of budget. War Council meeting. Lunch with General Fox Conner.
	6	Washington. Morning briefing on JCS papers. Appointment with former Ambassador Davies. Noon appointment with General Donald Bennett Adams. JCS luncheon. Afternoon appointment with General Paul.

December 7   Washington. Noon session with press representatives and photographers. Mid-afternoon train to Florida, arriving at Pratt General Hospital in Miami on December 8 and remaining in Florida for rest and recreation until January 12, 1947.

1947

January 12   Miami. Mid-afternoon return to Washington.

13   Washington. Morning appointments with General Paul re promotion list; General North. Lunch with General Craig. Afternoon appointment with General Paul and others re selective service.

14   Washington. Morning appointments with General Ridgway and Colonel Stack; Robert Sherwood; General Cramer; Colonel E. Clark. To Secretary of War's luncheon for editors and commentators going overseas. Afternoon appointments with General Arthur Gilbert Trudeau (Chief of Manpower Control, War Department); P&O; W. Lippmann. Dinner given by Under Secretary and Mrs. Royall for the Max Gardners (Ambassador to Court of St. James) at the Pentagon.

15   Washington. Morning appointment with Bishop Peabody to discuss availability of a general officer to head Manlius Military School. To fourth-floor dining room for Army Day filming and recording. Appointment with General Dahlquist re promotion plan. Noon briefing on JCS papers, followed by JCS luncheon. War Council meeting.

16   Washington. Morning briefing by Generals Collins and McLain re the President's Advisory Commission, followed by a meeting of the commission at the White House. Luncheon for the Prince of Saudi Arabia at the White House. Afternoon appointments with G–3 officers to discuss allotment of personnel and grade spread to various branches; Ambassador Messersmith.

17   Washington. To the White House for conference on unification. Morning plane for Chicago. Addresses

January   dinner meeting of various military associations. Overnight in Chicago.

18   Chicago. University of Illinois Stabilization Committee dinner. Late train for Washington.

19   Late afternoon arrival in Washington.

20   Washington. Morning appointments with Congressman Olin E. Teague (Texas) and Dr. Gilchrist; G–3 for conference on Infantry and armored divisions; Field Marshal Wilson. To Statler Hotel for luncheon of conference of mayors. Afternoon appointment with General Spaatz. Conference in office with G–3 and high-ranking staff officers re postwar Army. To the Carlton Hotel for Dr. Bush's dinner.

21   Washington. To Walter Reed General Hospital for overnight stay.

22   Washington. Late morning return to office. Afternoon briefing by General Norstad on Army commanders' conference. To the Secretary of War's conference room to address Army commanders. Appointment with Dr. Cutler. To Secretary of War's office for discussion of report of American Bar Association.

23   Washington. Morning appointments with Assistant Secretary Symington; General Collins and McLain for briefing on UMT conference. Addresses UMT conference. Appointment with General Bissell. Early afternoon train to New York City. To the Waldorf-Astoria Hotel. Meeting with General D. Sarnoff. Addresses Bond Club dinner, Starlight Roof. Overnight in New York City.

24   New York City. Late afternoon train to Washington, arriving mid-evening.

25   Washington. Morning appointments with General Paul to discuss nomination list for first increment of Regular Army integration program; G–1 for presentation concerning selective service (high-ranking staff officers attending); the Secretary of War and Generals Handy and Richards. To Secretary of War's luncheon for new congressmen.

26   Washington.

January 27   Washington. To the Sapphire Room of the Mayflower Hotel to attend Women's Press Club luncheon.

28   Washington. Morning appointments with Assistant Secretary Symington; General Handy and Dr. Bowles. Lunch in office with General Marshall. Afternoon appointments with General Lutes; W. Dillingham.

29   Washington. Morning briefing on regulation of armaments and JCS matters. To General Marshall's office to discuss regulation of armaments. JCS luncheon. Afternoon appointment with General Snyder. To the Chinese Room of the Mayflower Hotel for Business Advisory Council dinner.

30   Washington. Morning conference with staff officers to discuss Selective Service. Briefing by General Hall on allocation of grades, followed by a conference on the subject. To Secretary of War's office for Senate Armed Forces Committee luncheon and briefing. Afternoon appointment with A. Houghton. To the Wardman Park Hotel for dinner with Senator and Mrs. Tydings.

31   Washington. Morning appointments with General Persons; General Ingles with Major Cannon. Presents General Hall with OLC to DSM. Appointment with Field Marshal Wilson. To luncheon given by General Spaatz for board of control of Air Forces Project. To cocktail party given by Senator Bridges for Senate Appropriations subcommittee at the Carlton Hotel, then to F Street Club to attend dinner given by Congressman Andrews for House Armed Services Committee.

February 1   Washington. Morning appointment with Hans Von Kaltenborn (radio commentator). To the White House to discuss Secretary of War's letter on selective service. To the general officers dining room for Secretary of War's luncheon with new congressmen. To the Statler Hotel for Radio Correspondents Association dinner.

2   Washington. To Fort Myer Chapel for afternoon christening of Captain and Mrs. Hall's daughter.

3   Washington. Morning appointment with Mrs. Richard Long Harkness re invitation to speak to the

convention of the Women's Action Committee for Lasting Peace. Lunch in office with J. L. Hennessy. Afternoon conference with high-ranking staff officers re report of Hennessy Food Committee.

4 Washington. Morning appointment with H. Gibson. Noon round-table discussion with Hennessy Food Committee. To Secretary of War's luncheon for the Hennessy Committee. Afternoon appointment with Assistant Secretary Petersen, Frederick Leonard Devereux (special assistant, OMGUS), and Arthur Stanhope Barrows (a Sears official serving as deputy director of the Economic Commission, OMGUS). Accompanied by Mrs. Eisenhower to White House dinner and reception for Army and Navy personnel, followed by cocktails with A. Harriman at the Shoreham Hotel.

5 Washington. Morning P&O Intelligence presentation. Appointment with Governor General Alexander of Canada. To Fort Myer Chapel in the afternoon to attend funeral of Admiral Marc Andrew Mitscher. Appointment with George Eisenhower (a distant cousin). To dinner at the British Embassy for Governor General and Viscountess Alexander.

6 Washington. Morning appointments with Generals Norstad and Lincoln; Mr. and Mrs. M. Mueller; Field Marshal Wilson; General Wei Li Huang. War Council meeting. Lunch in office with Senator Cain. To Blair House in late afternoon for informal cocktail party given by the Governor General of Canada. Dinner at the Canadian Embassy for Governor General and Viscountess Alexander.

7 Washington. Morning appointment with General Richards. To Secretary of War's office to meet with Congressman Engel. Appointments with General Parks for Army Week radio recording; General Norstad and others for conference on reduction of strength. To General Paul's luncheon for Admiral Denfeld. To dinner-dance given by former Ambassador and Mrs. Davies and Senator and Mrs. Tydings for the Parmentiers.

8 Washington. Dinner with General and Mrs. Haislip.

February 9 Washington.

10 Washington. Morning appointment with Colonel William Lee. To evening farewell party for Lieutenant Donnan at the Statler Hotel.

11 Washington. Morning appointment with General Ridgway. To Secretary of War's office to discuss luncheon. To the Capitol to see Senator Bridges. To Secretary of War's luncheon for the House Armed Services Committee. To the Highlands for dinner with General Frank Sherwood Cocheu.

12 Washington. Morning appointments with Generals Persons, Surles, Collins, and Parks; General Norstad. Afternoon G–4 presentation by General Lutes.

13 Washington. Morning appointments with General Lincoln for briefing re joint mobilization plan; General Chamberlin; General Bertello; Field Marshal Wilson; General Malony re Dr. Pogue's mission to London. To White House for luncheon in honor of the president-elect of Uruguay, Thomás Berreta.

14 Washington. Morning appointment with General Richards to discuss appearance before House Appropriations Committee. Afternoon appointment with Ambassador Steinhardt. To the admiral's house, Naval Observatory, for buffet supper given by Admiral and Mrs. Nimitz.

15 Washington. Morning appointment with L. Lambert. To dinner given by the George Morrises.

16 Washington.

17 Washington. Morning appointments with General Devers and Colonel Stack; Generals Spaatz, Devers, Norstad, Hall, and Paul; G–3 for presentation re airborne division. Afternoon appointment with Colonel Anderson.

18 Washington. Morning appointments with Colonel Abbott and Major Cannon; General Ridgway; General Parks and General Frederick Elwood Uhl (CG, Replacement Command, AFWESPAC); General Vollin. Afternoon appointment with Charles Guy Bolté.

19 Washington. Morning briefing on JCS matters. Appointment with General Hall re hearings before the

February House Subcommittee on War Department Appropriations, followed by appearance before the subcommittee. JCS luncheon. Afternoon appointment with General Swift re hearings before the House Armed Forces Committee on Retirement of Regular and Reserve Officers.

20 Washington. Morning appointment with General Paul re efficiency reports. War Council meeting. Appointment with General Vandenberg. Lunch with General Joyce. Afternoon appointment with General Paul to continue discussion re efficiency reports.

21 Washington. Morning train to New York City. Early afternoon arrival at Columbia University to attend reception, luncheon, and convocation and to receive an honorary degree. Late afternoon train to Washington, arriving at 12:30 A.M.

22 Washington. Morning appointment with General Richards. Afternoon appointment with General Collins.

23 Washington. To Shoreham Hotel for United Jewish Appeal luncheon. Early evening train for St. Louis, Missouri.

24 Early afternoon arrival in St. Louis, followed by a parade, visit to Soldiers Memorial, visit with committee at Symington home, and press conference. Evening reception and dinner given by St. Louis Chamber of Commerce. Late evening visit with Mr. Calhoun and W. R. Cox, (of the Log Cabin Club). Overnight at Symington home.

25 St. Louis. To Washington University for morning review of ROTC and impromptu talk. Return to Symington home. Early evening train to Washington.

26 Late afternoon arrival in Washington. To the Army and Navy Town Club to attend the 76th and 77th Club dinner.

27 Washington. Morning appointments with General Ridgway and Colonel Stack; Generals Handy and Allen re civilian manpower; Senator James Oliver Eastland and Congressman John Bell Williams (Mississippi); G–1 and Dr. Churchill for presentation of medical-department plan. Afternoon appointments

February   with General Eaker and Lieutenant Cavnar; Joseph Curran (vice-president of the CIO). Dinner with General and Mrs. Surles on their thirty-second anniversary (Mrs. Eisenhower is unable to attend due to illness).

28   Washington. Morning appointment with Generals Larkin and T. H. Green. To the Statler Hotel to give brief welcome to conference of adjutant generals. To Secretary of War's office for noon discussion of civilian manpower. Afternoon appointments with Generals Norstad, Lincoln, and Lemnitzer; General Chamberlin and staff officers to discuss CIC and CID.

March 1 Washington. Morning appointments with Admiral Nimitz and General Spaatz; General Truscott. To the White House to see the President. To the Statler Hotel for White House Correspondents Association dinner.

2 Washington. To Constitution Hall in the evening for American Red Cross Drive meeting.

3 Washington. Morning appointments with Generals Spaatz and Norstad to discuss the Moscow Conference; General Wyche. Noon appointment with Field Marshal Wilson. Lunch in office with Ambassador Douglas.

4 Washington. Morning farewell call by General Ridley. Appointments with Mrs. Mary Sobolta; General Larkin. To luncheon given by Eugene Meyer.

5 Washington. Morning appointments with General Hawley; Generals Handy and Bull; P&O and Intelligence. Noon appointment with General Paul re WAC director. Afternoon appointment with General Wyman.

6 Washington. Morning appointment with R. W. Bliss. Noon War Council meeting. Lunch in office with Albert Wayne Coy. To the Statler Hotel to attend VFW dinner for members of Congress.

7 Washington. Morning appointments with Dr. Case; Generals Chamberlin and Walter Edwin Todd (Deputy Director of Intelligence). Lunch with General O. N. Bradley.

8 Washington. To Mrs. George Mesta's dinner.

March 9 Washington.

10 Washington. Morning appointments with General Parks and David Cohen; Generals Devers and Hall; General Paul re general officers. Afternoon appointments with Bryant Baker (Br. sculptor); Ambassador Lane; Sergeant McCall and Private Mitchell, from Camp Lee, Virginia.

11 Washington. To the office of the U.S. Army Recruiting Service for brief address. Appointment with R. Cline and Major Donald Howard Richardson. Afternoon appointments with General Handy and G–2 for presentation re German scientists; Congressman Celler (New York) re model homes for veterans in Brooklyn.

12 Washington. Morning appointment with Generals Paul, Dahlquist, Collins, and Persons for presentation re promotion bill. Afternoon appointment with Air Marshal Charles Roderick Car (formerly Air Officer Commander-in-Chief, India).

13 Washington. Morning appointments with Mrs. E. F. Wood, Jr., to present posthumous award to her husband, Lieutenant Wood; Hall Board; Generals Paul and St. Clair Streett re recruiting. Afternoon appointment with Colonel Haw.

14 Washington. Morning appointment with General Wainwright. Afternoon presentation by the Hall Board in the Office of the Secretary of War.

15 Washington. Morning appointment with Congressman Rayburn. Views newsreels at noon.

16 Washington.

17 Washington. Morning appointments with General Perez-Damera (Chief of Staff of the Cuban Army); Generals Hall and Allen. Views Army Day film. Afternoon appointment with General Larkin and George M. Mardikian (food specialist). To luncheon for General de Guingand. Dinner at Quarters One for General de Guingand.

18 Washington. Morning appointment with Colonel MacNinch. Noon appointment with Assistant Secretary Symington. Afternoon appointments with Gen-

eral Kirk; Bolivian Ambassador Señor Ricardo Martínez Vargas. To the Roger Smith Hotel for 78 Club dinner.

19 Washington. Morning appointments with Colonel Robert Alan (AAF) for briefing re appointment with Juan-Terry Trippe; Mr. Trippe and Mr. Pryer (vice-president of Pan American Airlines). P&O Intelligence presentation. Noon appointment with Generals Hall and Richards re National Guard budget cuts. Afternoon appointment with former Congressman Edward Gay Rohrbough (West Virginia).

20 Washington. To Secretary of War's office for conference on currency. To the Statler Hotel for Henry Luce's luncheon and preview of film *The New America*. Afternoon appointment with Field Marshal Wilson. War Council meeting. To British Embassy to receive the Sword of Honor.

21 Washington. Morning appointments with General North; General Tom Campbell; General Guillermo Barrios Tirado (Commander in Chief, Chilean Army). Lunch with General Barrios Tirado.

22 Washington. Morning appointments with General Conklin; General Ridgway with Colonel Stack.

23 Washington.

24 Washington. Morning appointment with General Groves. Afternoon viewing of film *Seeds of Destiny*. Dinner with Field Marshal and Lady Wilson.

25 Washington. Morning briefing by Generals Handy, Norstad, Surles, and Persons for Senate committee appearance. To the Capitol to testify on unification bill before Senate Armed Services Committee. National Press Club luncheon. To General and Mrs. Snyder's for cocktails.

26 Washington. Morning appointment with General Ridgway. Briefing on JCS matters. P&O Intelligence presentation. JCS luncheon. Afternoon appointments with General Malony; Generals Chamberlin and Vandenberg; Ambassador Pawley.

27 Washington. Morning appointments with Senator Gurney; General Paul re efficiency reports; Siamese

March	Military Mission members; Congressman Henry Dominique Larcade, Jr., and Mrs. Michie; General Hodge. Lunch with W. Bullitt. To afternoon seminar by the Historical Division. Dinner with General and Mrs. Gruenther.
28	Washington. Morning appointments with General Kirk; General Parks for presentation on public relations; General Paul re new efficiency reports; Rufus Stanley Woodward and W. E. Robinson, both of the *New York Herald Tribune*. Afternoon appointment with Generals Handy, Norstad, and Bull re the Civil Defense Board. To dinner of the Women's Action Committee for Lasting Peace at the Mayflower Hotel.
29	Washington. Morning appointments with H. Baldwin; Otis Bryan (vice-president, Trans World Airlines). To luncheon with Kansas congressional delegation.
30	Washington. Morning departure for inspection trip of bases in southeastern United States. Late afternoon arrival at Fort Bragg, North Carolina, where for the next four days General and Mrs. Eisenhower are guests of General and Mrs. Irwin.
31	Fort Bragg. Morning conferences and inspections at the base. Golf in the afternoon.
April 1	Fort Bragg. Various conferences and inspections at the base, followed by afternoon trip to Chapel Hill to visit with Captain Hazlett. Return to Fort Bragg for the night.
2	Fort Bragg. Inspection of 82d Airborne Division. To Pope Field to meet the oldest enlisted man in the Army. Meets with editor of the Fayetteville newspaper. Press conference.
3	Fort Bragg. Mid-morning departure for Fort Jackson, South Carolina, arriving in midafternoon. General and Mrs. Eisenhower are guests of the commanding general.
4	Fort Jackson.
5	Fort Jackson. Departure for Fort Benning, Georgia.
6	Fort Benning.

April 7 Fort Benning. To Atlanta, Georgia, for Army Day speech. Overnight in Atlanta.

8 Atlanta. To Maxwell Field, Alabama.

9 Maxwell Field.

10 Maxwell Field. Departure for Anniston Army Air Field, Alabama, then to Fort McClellan. Return to Anniston and then to Fort Benning.

11 Fort Benning.

12 Fort Benning.

13 Fort Benning. Departure for Chattanooga, Tennessee, with stop in Rome, Georgia. Overnight in Chattanooga.

14 Chattanooga. Departure for inspections in Asheville, North Carolina, with stop in Knoxville, Tennessee. Overnight in Asheville.

15 Asheville. Departure for Roanoke, Virginia, with stop in Winston Salem, North Carolina. Overnight in Roanoke.

16 Roanoke. Departure for Fort Myer, Virginia.

17 Washington. Morning appointment with General Beightler. War Council meeting. Appointments with Field Marshal Wilson and General W. D. Morgan; General Collins. Lunch in office with A. Nielsen. Afternoon appointments with Generals Paul and Kirk re general officers; Generals Handy, Collins, Persons, and Norstad re unification. Dinner with General and Mrs. North.

18 Washington. Morning appointments with General Paul; Generals Handy, Collins, Persons, and Norstad to review unification progress; Haislip Board for briefing on UMT. Lunch with R. Roberts. To the White House to discuss UMT with the Compton Committee.

19 Washington. Morning appointments with General Akin; General Surles and Colonel Carroll; G-3 officers for presentation of revised budget figures re total officers. Noon appointment with Mrs. John Nicholas Brown of the American Aid to France Committee.

April   Lunch with Mrs. A. Rosenberg. Afternoon address to the American Society of Newspaper Editors. Early evening visit with Senator Tydings at the Wardman Park Hotel, followed by attendance at dinner of American Society of Newspaper Editors.

20   Washington. Supper and bridge with the Saylers.

21   Washington. Morning appointments with G–3 officers for presentation of Air Force troop basis; Mrs. McCarthy-Morrogh; General North. To lunch with Field Marshal Wilson and General W. D. Morgan. Evening party in honor of Field Marshal Wilson at the Army and Navy Town Club.

22   Washington. Morning appointments with General Ridgway; Colonel E. N. Clark; General Devers with Major Cannon; Dr. Pogue; General Bliss. To the White House to see the President. To luncheon with the Advisory Committee of the Historical Divsion. Afternoon appointments with Egyptian Chief of Staff and party; General Lemnitzer; General O. N. Bradley. Dinner with General and Mrs. North.

23   Washington. Morning appointment with General Emmons. P&O Intelligence presentation. To Union Station to say good-by to Field Marshal Wilson. Afternoon appointment with Generals Handy and Dahlquist re the five-star promotion bill. Dinner with French Ambassador and Madame Henri Bonnet.

24   Washington. Morning conference re permanent ranks in Secretary Forrestal's office. Appointment with Mr. Nicolay. To the Naval Gun Factory for the Annapolis-West Point Class of 1915 luncheon. Afternoon briefing in office on unification hearings in the House. To Secretary of War's office for briefing on atomic energy.

25   Washington. Morning appointments with Miss Patricia McClary and father; Mrs. D. G. Hughes. To Secretary of War's luncheon with Secretary Forrestal, Admiral Nimitz, and General Spaatz. Afternoon conference with P&O re special planning.

26   Washington. Morning appointment with General Doolittle. To Chevy Chase Club with General Gasser for golf in the afternoon.

April 27   Washington.

    28   Washington. Morning appointment with General Paul re warrant officers and enlisted men. To luncheon for Lord Trenchard. Afternoon appointment with Ward Canady (of Toledo, Ohio).

    29   Washington. Morning appointment with General Richard Amyatt Hull (commandant of the British Staff College). Meeting with the Advisory Council of the ANMB. To Secretary of War's luncheon for Senate Armed Services Committee. Afternoon appointment with General Vandegrift. To the White House for stag dinner given by the President for President Alemán of Mexico.

    30   Washington. Morning briefing on JCS matters. Appointments with P&O for Intelligence presentation; a Texas mayor. JCS luncheon. To the Mexican Embassy dinner and reception for the president of Mexico.

May 1   Washington. Morning War Council meeting. Appointments with General Crawford and Colonel Stack; General Snyder re the dispensary. Lunch in office with W. Lippmann. To National War College to attend evening cocktail party for the Kruegers.

    2   Washington. Morning appointments with Mrs. Vincente Lim (of the Philippines); J. Ashton Devereux and John Marshall Bosne (chairman and vice-chairman of the Army Advisory Committee, Baltimore, Maryland). To Secretary of War's office for briefing on post-occupation Regular Army. To Chevy Chase Club for golf with Colonel Allen in the afternoon.

    3   Washington. Morning appointment with General Bull re General O. N. Bradley's DSM. To Burning Tree Club for lunch with General Bradley and Mr. Black.

    4   Washington. Late evening train for New York City.

    5   Early morning arrival in New York City. Attends Kaltenborn's luncheon for Radio News Analysts. Appointment with H. B. Swope. Wings Club dinner at the Waldorf-Astoria Hotel. Late evening departure for Washington.

    6   Morning arrival in Washington. Morning appoint-

May   ment with Generals Handy, Spaatz, Norstad, and Persons for briefing on congressional unification hearings. To Chevy Chase Club for golf with Mr. L. Eakin in the afternoon.

7   Washington. Morning appointments with General Lincoln for briefing on JCS matters; General Eddy. To the Capitol to testify on unification before the House Armed Services Committee. Lunch in office with Generals Handy, Collins, and Sumter de Leon Lowry, Jr. (artillery officer, 131st Infantry Division). Afternoon appointment with General Devers. To Secretary of War's office to discuss promotion bill. To House Armed Services Committee informal stag buffet supper, then to dinner given by General and Mrs. Marshall for Ambassador Smith at the Alibi Club.

8   Washington. Morning appointment with General R. E. Truman. To the Capitol to testify on unification before the House Expenditures Committee. Dinner at Quarters One with Lord and Lady Halifax, General Smith, and Milton S. Eisenhower.

9   Washington. Receives life membership from representatives of the Third Division Society. Morning appointment with General Paul.

10   Washington. Morning viewing of school safety-patrol parade. Appointment with General Aurand. Lunch in office with Ambassador Smith and Mr. and Mrs. Marx. To the Statler Hotel for Gridiron Club dinner.

11   Washington.

12   Washington. To Tom's Auto Service to meet T. Amatucci in the morning. Appointment with Generals Collins and Persons re legislation priorities; General Bull re European theater DSM war cases. To Chevy Chase Club for golf with General Parks in the afternoon.

13   Washington. To the Capitol to testify on unification before the House Expenditures Committee. Lunch in office with General Marshall. Afternoon appointments with General Ridgway; General North; General Parks, General Herbert Jay Brees, ret.

14   Washington. Morning appointment with General

May   Truscott. JCS briefing. Appointments with General Spaatz; Generals Handy, Haislip, Collins, and McLain; P&O for Intelligence presentation. JCS luncheon. To the Statler Hotel for WAC anniversary tea in the evening.

15   Washington. Morning appointments with General Baptista Duffles Teixeira Latt (Brazilian military attaché), bringing message from General Obino; L. Lambert. War Council meeting. Dinner with Senator and Mrs. McMahon.

16   Washington. Morning appointments with Generals Collins, Parks, and O'Hare; Ira F. Lewis (president of the *Pittsburgh Courier*); General Grejales (Chief of Staff of the Mexican Secretariat of National Defense to the United States). To informal talk by Ambassador Smith.

17   Washington. To Columbia Golf and Country Club for luncheon and golf tournament. To Metropolitan Club for Senator Taft's cocktails and buffet.

18   Washington.

19   Washington. Morning appointment with Robert Behar (of London). Receives decoration from and attends luncheon given by the Egyptian Military Mission. Purchase in office of first poppy from the American Legion's Women's Auxiliary. To Constitution Hall for evening meeting of convention of Daughters of the American Revolution.

20   Washington. Morning presentation of OLC to DSM to General Milton A. Reckord. To the Capitol to testify before the House Foreign Affairs Committee. Lunch at the Capitol with Colonel Stack and Leslie V. Biffle. To Chevy Chase Club for golf with General Parks in the afternoon.

21   Washington. Early morning departure by car for Carlisle Barracks, Pennsylvania, for graduation address, presentation of diplomas, and luncheon. Mid-afternoon departure by car for Fort Myer, Virginia, arriving late afternoon.

22   Washington. Morning appointment with A. Houghton. To studio of Augustus Vincent Tack (ar-

May   tist). Afternoon appointments with L. H. Brown; General Richards.

23   Washington. Morning appointment with General W. D. Morgan. Presentation of OLC to DSM to General O. N. Bradley, followed by lunch in office with General Bradley. To Chevy Chase Club for golf with S. Early and Colonel Allen in the afternoon.

24   Washington. To studio of Augustus Vincent Tack. To Chevy Case Club for golf with Colonel Allen in the afternoon.

25   Washington.

26   Washington. Morning appointments with General Paul; Colonel Ford Trimble (Field Artillery); General Sayler. To Secretary of War's Affiliation Conference. Appointment with General Ridgway. To Under Secretary Royall's luncheon for members of the Affiliation Conference. Afternoon appointment with General Whitlock. To Walter Reed General Hospital to meet Mrs. E. N. Rogers.

27   Washington. Morning train to New York City to address a dinner meeting of the Fire Underwriters National Board at the Hotel Commodore. Late evening train for Washington.

28   Early morning arrival in Washington. Morning acceptance of Guatemalan Medal from Colonel Lopez (military attaché). Briefing on JCS papers. Appointment with General M. Clark. JCS luncheon. To Secretary of War's office in late afternoon, to attend presentation of LM to Mrs. Rosenberg. Dinner with the Cliffords.

29   Washington. Views newsreels of golf tournament in the morning. To the District Court Building to testify in the May case. Appointment with General Huang (Chinese director of I&E, U.S.A.). Presentation of second OLC to DSM to General M. Clark, followed by lunch with Generals O. N. Bradley and Clark and W. Benton. To the Egyptian Embassy to receive award. Evening cocktails with General and Mrs. Truscott.

30   Washington.

May 31   Washington. Morning appointment with General Sturdee. Dinner with the Julius Holmeses.

June 1   Washington. Early morning train to West Point, arriving in the afternoon. Accompanied by Mrs. Eisenhower to Class of 1915 dinner party at Bear Mountain Inn.

2   West Point. Attends alumni exercises at Thayer Monument and review of corps by alumni. Class of 1915 stag dinner at West Point Army Mess.

3   West Point. Gives address at graduation exercises. Luncheon at superintendent's quarters. Early afternoon train for Washington, arriving in the evening.

4   Washington. Morning appointments with Jim Shepley (of *Time* magazine) and General Parks; General Cipriano Olivera (Chief of Staff, Uruguayan Army); H. J. Taylor; P&O for Intelligence presentation; General W. D. Morgan. Noon appointment with Dave Breger (cartoonist) and Mrs. Breger. To Chevy Chase Club for golf with General Parks in the afternoon.

5   Washington. Morning appointments with General Paul; Colonel Johnny Bevan (Br., Allied Chief of Deception in World War II). To Capitol to testify on medical-procurement legislation before House Armed Services Committee. War Council meeting. Appointments with Admiral Kirk; Joseph Wright Alsop, Jr. To Columbia Golf and Country Club for luncheon and golf with Mr. Moorman and William Thomas Faricy (lawyer).

6   Washington. Morning departure by plane with the President to attend the reunion of the 35th Division in Kansas City, Missouri. Address at evening D-day celebration. Overnight in Kansas City.

7   Kansas City. Morning departure for day's visit to Abilene, Kansas. Late afternoon return to Kansas City. To Mission Hills Club dinner. Overnight in Kansas City.

8   Kansas City. Late afternoon plane to Washington.

9   Washington. Morning conference with Generals

June	Handy, Richards, and Persons. Morning departure by car for Fort Monroe, Virginia, to attend wedding of Captain John S. D. Eisenhower.
10	Fort Monroe. Afternoon wedding of Captain Eisenhower and Barbara J. Thompson. Reception afterwards at the Beach Club.
11	Midmorning return to Washington. Morning appointment with P&O for Intelligence presentation. Afternoon appointments with Robert Gros (lecturer); General Gillem. To Secretary of War's office for presentation of decoration to General Gillem.
12	Washington. Morning appointments with General Paul; General Miltonberger; General Groves. Presentation of OLC to DSM to General McLain. Appointment with Air Vice-Marshal George E. Wait (Canadian Joint Staff Mission) and General H. O. N. Brownfield. Lunch in office with General O. N. Bradley. To Secretary of War's office to meet group of newspapermen.
13	Washington. Morning presentation of second OLC to DSM to General Eaker. Appointment with General W. D. Morgan. Presentation of bust of B. Baruch to Army War College, followed by luncheon with Admiral Hill.
14	Washington. Luncheon in office with L. Marx's daughter Barbara and four of her friends.
15	Washington.
16	Washington. Morning appointments with Generals Handy, Collins, and Persons; General Truscott. War Council meeting.
17	Washington. Early morning plane with Mrs. Eisenhower and President and Mrs. Truman to Princeton University to receive honorary degree. Late afternoon plane to Washington.
18	Washington. Morning plane for Philadelphia to receive honorary degree from University of Pennsylvania. Mid-afternoon plane to Washington.
19	Washington. Morning appointments with Captain Summersby; Dr. W. A. Groves; General Paul. Noon

June   appointment with General Edmund Bower Sebree (Assistant Division Commander, 35th Infantry Division). Afternoon at Burning Tree Club for golf with William Thomas Faricy and Mr. Moorman. Dinner at Quarters One for aides and wives.

20   Washington. Morning appointment with Lynn Upshaw Stambaugh (lawyer and member of the board of the Export-Import Bank). To the National War College for graduation exercises. Appointments with General Conklin; Colonel Ordway. Noon appointment with Dr. Bush. Afternoon appointment with Justice and Mrs. Burton. To White House garden party for disabled veterans.

21   Washington.

22   Washington.

23   Washington. Morning appointment with General Wedemeyer. To Secretary of War's office in the afternoon to meet clergymen. Afternoon appointments with General W. D. Morgan; General Josef Robert Sheetz (deputy military governor of Korea); General Larkin.

24   Washington. Morning presentation of OLC to DSM to General Ridgway. Morning appointments with Judge Rifkind re displaced persons and Palestine; G–3 for presentation on Compton report (with Secretary of War and others attending). Noon meeting with His Excellency Abdel Rahman Azzam Pasha (Secretary General of the Arab League), accompanied by General Chamberlin. To general officers dining room for R&D luncheon.

25   Washington. To Secretary Forrestal's office to receive Navy DSM. To hearings on the Inter-American Military Cooperation Act. To the White House. After return to office, appointments with Congressman George W. Gillie and delegates; Congressman Joseph Patrick O'Hara (Minnesota) and delegates; A. Houghton.

26   Washington. Morning appointments with General Ridgway; General Persons; General Paul; Eugene Meyer; G. Kennan. Noon appointment with Senator

| June | | Kilgore and Colonel Louis Johnson. To Secretary of War's luncheon for General Olivera. To Statler Hotel for party for Colonel Stack, and then to the Army and Navy Town Club for party given by P&O for General and Mrs. Lincoln. |

27 Washington. Afternoon viewing of newsreels. To Secretary of War's conference room for press conference. To White House for meeting with the President and others. To Chevy Chase Club with Mr. Barnett in late afternoon.

28 Washington. Morning briefing by General Richards for Senate Appropriations Committee appearance. To Capitol for interview with Senator Bridges, and then testifies before the Senate Appropriations Committee. Return to office for appointment with P. McNutt. Lunch in office with R. A. Lovett.

29 Washington.

30 Washington. To seminar on history of P&O. Appointment with General W. D. Morgan. Noon appointment with General Herney (Canadian). Lunch in office with Dr. Lilienthal. Afternoon appointments with Colonel Stack; General Collins.

July 1 Washington. Morning visit to O&T Division. Appointments with W. Bullitt; Mr. Kolitz (at the request of Congresswoman Bolton); General Hughes; Gilbert Bailey (*New York Times Magazine*), accompanied by General Parks. Afternoon appointments with General Hull; Dr. Conant.

2 Washington. Morning appointments with General Wedemeyer; Captain Killick; Dr. Gans. To the Capitol to testify on WAC legislation before the House Armed Services Committee. Returns to office for noon appointment with General Crittenberger.

3 Washington. Morning appointments with General Handy; Generals Handy and Devers; General O'Hare. Late morning plane for Vicksburg, Mississippi, arriving in afternoon. After buffet dinner, to the *General Newton* (Mississippi River Commission boat) for the next two nights.

4 Aboard the *General Newton*. To shore for recruiting and press conference, parade, radio broadcast.

July 5 Aboard the *General Newton*. Early morning departure by car to Jackson Army Air Base and then by plane to Washington, arriving in late afternoon.

6 Washington.

7 Washington. Morning conference on UMT bill. To Capitol to testify before Senate Foreign Relations Committee re trusteeship of Pacific Islands. Noon War Council meeting. Lunch with General Collins and Colonel William Haynie Neblett (lawyer and reserve officer on active duty with the Air Corps). Visit to P&A Division and then to Army War College for talk to Food Service Conference. Returns to office for appointment with P. McNutt.

8 Washington. Morning appointment with B. Hedges. To Secretary of War's conference room to discuss recruiting with Generals Paul and Streett. Appointments with Assistant Secretary Symington; General Arthur Lynn Lerch (military governor of Korea). Afternoon appointment and lunch with G. Allen and H. V. Smith, who presents Eisenhower with scrapbook.

9 Washington. Morning appointment with Paul A. Lawrence (Adjutant General, VFW), L. David Leroy, and H. N. Hennshey. Visit to P&O Division. Appointment with Generals Handy, Norstad, Groves, and Brereton. Noon briefing on JCS matters in General Handy's office. Lunch in office with Mrs. Eisenhower and Mr. and Mrs. Doud.

10 Washington. Morning appointments with General Dahlquist; General Bull; General Paul and staff officers re uniforms. To Navy Department for lunch with Secretary Forrestal.

11 Washington. Morning appointments with Kenneth Gale Crawford (*Newsweek* journalist); Captain Atkeson; General Van Tricht, who introduces Captain Stram (Navy representative from the Netherlands Mission). Lunch in office with W. Benton.

12 Washington. Morning appointments with Generals Cramer and Miltonberger; Generals Persons and Paul.

13 Washington.

14 Washington. Morning appointments with General

July	Chamberlin; Dr. Butts; General Dahlquist and Colonel Dinsmore for briefing on military-justice bill.
15	Washington. Accompanied by General Persons to Capitol to testify on military-justice legislation before the House Armed Services Committee. Appointment in office with Robert S. Peare. To Secretary of War's office for luncheon. Golf with Generals O. N. Bradley and Parks in the afternoon.
16	Washington. Morning appointment with Generals Persons and Paul. To the Capitol to discuss promotion bill. Returns to office for appointment with Raymond F. Kohn (president of Penn-Allen Broadcasting Company) and his brother. Noon appointment with Ambassador Messersmith. Afternoon appointment with former Senator Robert Marion La Follette, Jr. (Wisconsin). Evening cocktail party for Food Service Conference at the Statler Hotel.
17	Washington. Morning briefing by General Collins for appointments with Markel and Baldwin. Appointment with General Brooks. Visit to Intelligence Division. Appointments with Lester Markel (Sunday editor, *New York Times*); H. Baldwin. Accompanied by General Snyder to Walter Reed General Hospital in the afternoon. To Secretary of War's stag buffet for Congressman Thomason.
18	Washington. Morning appointments with Colonel E. N. Clark; Vicente Villamin (Philippine lawyer and economist). Visit to SS&P Division. Noon presentation of commission to Colonel Florence Aby Blanchfield (Superintendent, Army Nurse Corps). Lunch in office with McCloy.
19	Washington. Morning appointments with General Truscott; General Crittenberger. To Capitol to testify before Joint Congressional Committee on Atomic Energy.
20	Washington. Evening cocktail party at the B. F. Caffeys'.
21	Washington. Morning appointments with Generals Norstad, Collins, and Persons; General Bull re decora-

July   tion policy. War Council meeting. Afternoon appointment with General Bull to complete discussion. Evening cocktails at the quarters of General and Mrs. Hall.

22   Washington. Morning visit to R&D Division. Appointments with General Paul; Paul Miller (former chief of Washington bureau of Associated Press) and Relman Morin (Miller's successor). Noon appointment with Marshall Andrews (of the *Washington Post*).

23   Washington. Morning appointments with General Paul; P&O. Accompanied by Mrs. Eisenhower to Secretary Forrestal's home for dinner given jointly by Secretary Forrestal and Under Secretary of War Royall for Secretary of War Patterson.

24   Washington. To Secretary of War's conference room for farewell address by Secretary Patterson. To Secretary of War's office for swearing-in of Secretary Royall. To Secretary Harriman's office to address a meeting. Afternoon appointment with G. Allen. To evening farewell buffet given by General Staff for Secretary Patterson.

25   Washington. Morning appointments with Carl Sandburg (poet) and Dr. Duncan Black MacDonald Emrich; General Collins and Lawrence Edmund Spivak (editor and publisher, *American Mercury*). Noon appointment with Dr. Diedder (of Abilene). To National Airport in the afternoon for Secretary Patterson's send-off. To the White House.

26   Washington. Morning appointment with Colonel McCawley (O&T) re Reserve Officers Association resolutions.

27   Washington. Morning departure by plane for trip to Alaska. Arrival in early afternoon at Fort Riley, Kansas. By auto to Manhattan, Kansas, to spend the night with Milton S. Eisenhower.

28   Manhattan. By auto to Fort Riley. By plane and auto to Billings, Montana, to inspect wheat farm. By car to Great Falls, Montana. Overnight at Great Falls.

July 29	Great Falls. Early morning departure for Fort Richardson, Anchorage, Alaska, with stop at Fort Nelson. Overnight at Fort Richardson.
30	Fort Richardson. Inspection of Elmendorf Field and Fort Richardson.
31	Fort Richardson. Morning departure by car for Lake Louise. Fishing and bridge at Lake Louise through August 3.
August 4	Lake Louise. Morning departure for Ladd Field, Fairbanks. Overnight at Ladd Field.
5	Ladd Field. Inspection.
6	Ladd Field. Morning departure for Point Barrows. After a three-hour stay, on to Nome Air Base for the night.
7	Nome Air Base. Morning departure for Adak, arriving in mid-afternoon. Overnight at Adak.
8	Adak.
9	Adak. Early morning departure for Naknek Army Air Base. Fishing and bridge.
10	Naknek Army Air Base. Fishing and bridge.
11	Naknek Army Air Base. Afternoon departure for Fort Richardson. Dinner and speech to Anchorage civic groups.
12	Fort Richardson. Morning plane for McChord Field, Washington, then by auto to Fort Lewis, Washington.
13	Fort Lewis. Review of 2d Division and the post.
14	Fort Lewis. Rest.
15	Fort Lewis. Morning plane for Lowry Field, Colorado, arriving in late afternoon.
16	Lowry Field. Morning plane for Washington, arriving in early evening.
17	Washington.
18	Washington. Morning appointments with Admiral Hill; General Schuyler for briefing on JCS matters. War Council meeting. JCS luncheon, followed by meeting of the JCS with the President's Air Policy Committee.

August 19   Washington. Morning appointment with Generals
Lutes and R. A. Wheeler for briefing on stevedores
and district engineers in Alaska. To the White House
for off-the-record conference on unification. To lunch
with Secretary Forrestal. Afternoon appointment with
Dr. Lucius Junius Desha (professor of chemistry and
dean of Washington and Lee University) and M. E.
Rogers.

20   Washington. Morning appointments with General
Paul re general-officer appointments; General W. D.
Morgan. Lunch in office with S. Symington and General Spaatz.

21   Washington. Morning appointment with P&A re
selection procedures.

22   Washington. Morning appointment with General
Glen Edgar Edgerton (recently returned Director of
UNRRA in China). Lunch with G. Allen. To Fort
Myer Chapel to attend funeral services for General
James Guthrie Harbard, ret. (honorary chairman of
Radio Corporation of America).

23   Washington. To Chevy Chase Club for golf with
Colonel Allen in the afternoon.

24   Washington.

25   Washington. Morning appointments with General
Kibler, reporting for General Ridgway; Joseph Wright
Alsop, Jr.; Admiral Gilbert Jonathan Rowcliff, ret.
(now in charge of the Washington office of Fitch Investors Service). Presents General Handy with OLC
to DSM. Luncheon with Mrs. Eisenhower, General
and Mrs. Handy, and their daughter. Buffet supper at
Colonel E. B. Howard's.

26   Washington. Morning appointments with General R.
A. Wheeler; Frank Smithwick Hogan (District Attorney for New York City and president of Columbia
College Association); A. Page. To Burning Tree Golf
Club with Congressman Arends for afternoon golf.

27   Washington. Morning appointment with General
Herron. Lunch with Secretary Forrestal. To Secretary
of War's office for O&T briefing on Army strength.

28   Washington. Morning train to Raleigh, North

August	Carolina, arriving in late afternoon. Party at governor's mansion, followed by speech to meeting of Farmers and Farm Women's Convention at North Carolina State College. Late evening train for New York City.
29	Morning arrival in New York City. Mid-afternoon address to American Legion National Convention. Train for Washington, arriving late evening.
30	Washington. Morning appointment with General De Witt. To Secretary of War's office for conference with General Norstad and Assistant Secretary of State Lovett. Lunch with Admiral Ramsey and General Norstad. Afternoon appointment with Admiral H. R. Moore. To Chevy Chase Club with Secretary Forrestal and General Sayler.
31	Washington. Afternoon plane for Minneapolis, Minnesota, with stop in Chicago.
September 1	Minneapolis. To state fairgrounds for press conference, informal talk to 4-H Club, visit to exhibits, luncheon, formal address, and dinner with B. Mintener and C. Gray. Late evening train for Superior, Wisconsin.
2	Early morning arrival in Superior. To Cedar Island. Fishing at Cedar Island Lodge for the next two days.
3	Cedar Island. Fishing.
4	Cedar Island. To Superior by car in the morning, and then by train to Minneapolis, arriving in early afternoon. By plane to Chicago to address meeting of the American Meat Institute at the Statler Hotel. Overnight in Chicago.
5	Chicago. Morning plane to Washington, arriving just after noon. Evening farewell dinner for General Handy.
6	Washington. Morning appointments with Generals Collins and Paul to discuss personnel matters; Admiral Earle Watkins Mills (Chief, Bureau of Ships), H. S. Merrick, and Colonel Edwin Sumner Bettelheim, Jr. (Assistant Chief of Staff, Military District of Washington)—all members of Columbia Alumni Association.

September 7 Washington.

8 Washington. Morning appointments with General Pee; W. Lippmann; General Taylor. Presentation of Medal for Merit to H. B. Swope, followed by luncheon with Swope and others. Afternoon budget presentation by General Richards and staff directors.

9 Washington. Morning appointments with Senator Sparkman; Generals Spaatz and Collins re separation of the Air Force. To Burning Tree Golf Club for afternoon golf with J. R. Black and Dr. Carl Milton White (director of libraries and dean of School of Library Science, Columbia University).

10 Washington. Morning appointments with Vance Packard (of *American* magazine), accompanied by General Parks; Committee on National Guard and Reserve Policy; Dr. Baxter. Afternoon press conference. Post-midnight train with Mrs. Eisenhower for three-day visit to New York City.

11 Morning arrival in New York City. Breakfast with T. J. and Jane Watson. Inspection of residence of president of Columbia University, press conference in Low Library, visit to several houses for sale, dinner with the Watsons and guests.

12 New York City. Inspection of houses for sale. Formal dinner at the Watsons'.

13 New York City. Morning visit to Connecticut farm. Informal lunch at the Watsons'. Evening cocktail and tea party at estate of Mr. and Mrs. Gayer Bardner Dominick.

14 New York City. Early morning departure for Washington.

15 Washington. Morning appointments with General Perez-Damera. Lunch with Mr. and Mrs. D. Middleton. Early afternoon plane for Columbus, Ohio, to speak to the Air Force Association. Overnight in Columbus.

16 Columbus. Morning plane to Washington, arriving in late morning. Afternoon appointments with General Collins; Dr. Bush.

September 17 Washington. Morning appointments with General Ridgway; Dr. Lilienthal. To Secretary Forrestal's office for swearing-in ceremony, meeting on unification, and luncheon.

18 Washington. Morning appointments with C. M. Potter; Colonel Brewster for conference on Turkish General Staff defense plans; Colonel Bingham. Acceptance of Grand Order of Yung Fei, Cloud and Banner, 1st class, from Generals Pee and Ho Ying-chin. To Secretary Forrestal's office to attend swearing-in ceremony for Secretaries Symington and Sullivan. Lunch with Colonel Norman Jay Boots (West Point classmate).

19 Washington. Morning appointments with E. Booz and James Lane Allen (management consultant with Booz, Allen, and Hamilton); Mrs. Ogden Reid; General Chamberlin; Lawrence Laybourne (of *Time* and *Life*), who presents drawing of *Time* cover; General T. D. Campbell. Noon appointment with Commander Powell, who presents a copy of Karsh's book *Faces of Destiny* (Chicago, 1946) and Manila photographs. Lunch in office with H. C. Butcher.

20 Washington.

21 Washington. Afternoon plane with Secretary Marshall and others for Mitchell Field, New York, and then by auto to Huntington, Long Island, to attend birthday supper for former Secretary Stimson. Evening departure for Washington, arriving in mid-evening.

22 Washington. Morning appointments with General Paul; General Wedemeyer. Lunch with Senator Gurney and General Persons. Afternoon appointments with Generals Collins and Haislip to review Haislip Report; General J. C. H. Lee: His Royal Highness Prince Olaf of Norway. To Secretary Forrestal's office.

23 Washington. Morning appointment with Assistant Secretary of State Benton. Morning plane for Morgantown, West Virginia, to receive honorary degree and address convocation at the University of West Virginia. Late afternoon plane to Washington.

September 24   Washington. Morning appointment with General Aurand. Departure by plane for vacation trip to Savannah, Georgia, and coastal area. In Savannah through October 4.

October   5   Savannah. By plane to Washington.

6   Washington. Army War Council meeting. Lunch with A. Nielsen. Afternoon appointment with Kemp Crawford.

7   Washington. Morning appointments with General R. E. Porter; General Wedemeyer; C. M. Potter, Paul Hunter, and General Parks. Lunch in office with Dr. Hutchins. Afternoon appointment with Secretary Forrestal. Co-hosts dinner for Turkisk Chief of Staff and party at the Shoreham hotel.

8   Washington. Morning appointments with members of the Turkish mission; Colonel E. N. Clark; General W. D. Morgan. Luncheon at Turkish Embassy for Turkish Chief of Staff. Dinner at Quarters One with Ambassador W. B. Smith.

9   Washington. Morning appointments with John Crain; General Fox Conner; General Officers Selection Board; Generals Truscott and Harmon. Lunch with General Eichelberger. Afternoon presentation of Soldiers Medal to Sergeant Wylie Bell, of the air crew.

10   Washington. Morning appointments with General Schuyler re joint U.S.-Canadian defense; Colonel Clark Wallace Thompson (USMC, ret., now congressman from Texas); A. Hatch; General North; General Bull. Noon appointment with Generals Handy and Hodges. To the White House for presentation to General Guy Venor Henry, Jr. Afternoon briefing on JCS matters. JCS meeting on Palestine. Appointment with J. Hennessy.

11   Washington. Morning briefing re National Guard in Secretary of War's office. Appointment with P&O and Intelligence. To Burning Tree Golf Club for golf with General O. N. Bradley in afternoon.

12   Washington.

13   Washington. Morning appointments with General

October	Ridgway; Mrs. Rosenberg; John A. McCone (business executive and member of the President's Air Advisory Committee); Twelve Mexican cadets. Lunch with Ambassador Douglas and General O. N. Bradley. Afternoon appointment with D. Pearson.
14	Washington. Morning presentation of report by Advanced Study Group, P&O. To the Netherlands Embassy to accept sword given by Queen Wilhelmina. General Eisenhower's fifty-seventh birthday.
15	Washington. Morning appointments with Admiral Nimitz and General Spaatz; C. Lanier (of Senator Hoey's office), with delegation from North Carolina; Dr. Holt; Mrs. Summersby. Lunch with General Leslie Chasemore Hollis.
16	Washington. Morning appointments with Jim Lucas (Scripps-Howard); General De Witt. Afternoon plane to Manchester, New Hampshire, for dinner at a country club and speech to Community Forum at the armory. Overnight at home of L. Finder.
17	Manchester. Morning plane for Washington, arriving just before noon. To Secretary Forrestal's luncheon for Air Chief Marshal Garrod and Air Marshal Robert Victor Goddard. Conference with Mr. Bard. Appointments with General Hull; W. E. Robinson.
18	Washington. Morning appointments with General Bull; Colonel Allen; W. H. Lancaster and Colonel Hawr (of Johnson City, Tennessee); S. Houston. To Chevy Chase Club for golf with General Parks in the afternoon.
19	Washington.
20	Washington. Morning appointments with General Charles Henry Caldwell; Frank Eleazer (of UP). Army War Council meeting. Noon appointment with Dr. Roelif Hasbrouck Brooks (rector of St. Thomas Church, New York City).
21	Washington. Morning appointment with R. P. McElroy, who presents National Civic Award of Fraternal Order of Eagles. To Secretary of Defense's War Council meeting. Appointments with S. Mink; R. L. Simon. To Chevy Chase Club for golf in the after-

October   noon. To Army-Navy Country Club for cocktails and dinner honoring 12th Army Group Organization Day.

22   Washington. Morning appointment with Ray H. Brannaman (national commander of VFW). JCS briefing. Noon appointment with Assistant Secretary of the Treasury E. H. Foley. JCS luncheon.

23   Washington. Morning appointments with F. Coykendall; Elder Michaux; General Hurley. Afternoon appointments with General K. W. D. Strong; Mr. and Mrs. Coykendall.

24   Washington. Morning departure by plane for visit to Kansas State College, Manhattan, Kansas. Stays at home of Milton S. Eisenhower.

25   Manhattan. Parade and Kansas-Nebraska football game. Speech on peace and foreign aid.

26   Manhattan. To Abilene to visit boyhood home and present mementoes to Eisenhower Memorial Foundation.

27   Manhattan. Morning plane from Fort Riley for Washington, arriving in afternoon.

28   Washington. Morning appointments with General Ridgway; O&T for conference on reorganization of the Task Force. Noon appointment with B. Hibbs, B. W. Smith, and M. Summers.

29   Washington. Morning appointment with General W. M. Robertson. To Secretary of Army's office to pose for group picture. Appointment with P&O. JCS briefing, followed by JCS luncheon.

30   Washington. Morning appointment with General Salih Omurtak (head of the Turkish Military Mission). To ceremony for returned war dead at Arlington Cemetery. Appointment with Lewis Morgan Parsons (assistant to vice-president, U.S. Steel Corporation of Delaware). Lunch with Dr. Bush and Devereux Colt Josephs (president, Carnegie Corporation of New York). To Turkish Embassy for evening reception given by General Omurtak.

31   Washington. Morning appointment with General K. W. D. Strong. To G–2 conference room for off-

October		the-record talk with J. J. McCloy, Secretary Royall, and Secretary Forrestal. Appointments with Mr. McIntosh upon his retirement; Colonel John Callan O'Laughlin. Noon appointment with General Crittenberger. Lunch with H. Blunck.
November	1	Washington. Early evening departure by train for trip to Fort Worth, Texas, and Little Rock, Arkansas, via Chicago.
	2	Morning arrival in Chicago. Leaves for Fort Worth.
	3	En route to Fort Worth.
	4	Fort Worth. Unveils bronze statue of Will Rogers and horse. Buffet dinner, then late train for Little Rock.
	5	Little Rock. Addresses Little Rock veterans. By train to Washington.
	6	Mid-evening arrival in Washington.
	7	Washington. Lunch with Colonel E. N. Clark and M. R. Moore. Informal speech on steps of Treasury Building on behalf of Community Chest drive. Dinner with General and Lady W. D. Morgan.
	8	Washington. Morning appointments with Carver Seal Committee to receive first block of stamps; G. Bye. Afternoon golf with General Parks. To Guggenheim dinner.
	9	Washington. Afternoon bridge and mah-jong with Mrs. Eisenhower and Colonel and Mrs. Matchett.
	10	Washington. Morning appointments with John A. McCone; M. W. Childs; Theodore Silkman Rapplier (advertising executive and president of the Advertising Council). Afternoon appointments with Dr. Hutchinson; Tim White re uniform; General Bull; General Richards; General Collins. To Secretary of Army's office for report of joint committee on pay. To dinner with Mrs. Eisenhower and Secretary Forrestal.
	11	Washington. Morning appointment with Dr. Gregg Manners Sinclair (president of the University of Hawaii). To Arlington Cemetery for Armistice Day ceremonies at Tomb of Unknown Soldier. Noon appointment with Ernest Kennedy (Ayrshire Society), followed by appointment with Secretary Symington.

November   Lunch with A. Nielsen. Afternoon appointment with General Frederick. Off-the-record discussion with Air Advisory Committee. To General Hughes's for dinner.

12   Washington. Morning appointments with Major George Fielding Eliot; Generals Collins and Lutes for equipment presentation; P&O; General Malony. JCS luncheon. Afternoon appointment with William S. Paley.

13   Washington. Poses for pictures with General Officers Selection Board. Appointment with Mrs. Mary Lord (of the National Civilian Advisory Committee to the Chief of Staff). To Agriculture Building for retake of newsreel pictures. Lunch with Colonel E. N. Clark, W. Davenport, and William Ludlow Chenery (publisher of *Collier's Weekly*). Golf.

14   Washington. Morning appointments with General Collins and Lutes re construction in Alaska; J. H. G. Pierson; Mrs. Ogden Reid; Stacey Jones. Afternoon appointment with Colonel John Richard Nygaard. Swearing-in of WOJG Margaret Hayes. To office of Eric Allen Johnston (president, Motion Picture Association) for luncheon for S. Goldwyn. Evening birthday party for Mrs. Eisenhower.

15   Washington.

16   Washington. Accompanied by Mrs. Eisenhower to dinner at General and Mrs. G. Young's.

17   Washington. Morning appointments with General John Alden Crane; former Secretary of War Woodring. Noon appointment with Reuben Alexander Lewis, Jr. (publisher of *Finance* magazine). Lunch with George Houk Mead (chairman of the board of the Mead Corporation and member of the Commission on Reorganization of the Executive Branch of Government).

18   Washington. To Secretary of Defense's War Council meeting. To National Press Club luncheon to present Medal of Freedom to General Parks. Afternoon appointments with Morris Duane (lawyer), Walter Simonds Franklin (railway official), and Geoffrey S.

November		Smith (lawyer)—members of Associated Harvard Clubs of Philadelphia; Ambassador Pawley.
	19	Washington. Morning appointments with representatives of Philadelphia high schools—Dr. Alexander Jerry Stoddard (superintendent), Dr. Hart, and Mr. Harkins; P&O for briefing on JCS matters. JCS luncheon.
	20	Washington. Begins series of tests at Walter Reed General Hospital. Evening reception at Secretary Forrestal's.
	21	Washington. Early evening reception for General Ferenbaugh, then to dinner with General and Mrs. Hall.
	22	Washington. To General and Mrs. Sayler's dinner for Dr. Holton (of Savannah, Georgia).
	23	Washington. Afternoon bridge and mah-jong with General and Mrs. Thompson at the Army and Navy Club.
	24	Washington. To special morning meeting of Secretary of Army's War Council.
	25	Washington.
	26	Washington. Morning JCS briefing. Afternoon appointments with General Collins; General Paul and the General Officers Selection Board. Early evening telephone broadcast to West Point corps of cadets.
	27	Washington.
	28	Washington. Morning appointment with Congressman Wright Patman (Texas). Poses for Christmas Seal photo. To Secretary of Army's office to meet National Guard recruiters. To National Guard recruiting luncheon. Dinner at Quarters One with the Walkers and Haislips.
	29	Washington. To Philadelphia for the Army-Navy game.
	30	Washington.
December	1	Washington. Morning appointment with Dr. George Keith Funston (president of Trinity College). Army War Council meeting. Lunch with former Ambassador Davies. Afternoon appointments with Con-

December gressman Arends; General Paul, who introduces Colonels Selection Board.

2 Washington. Morning briefing for War Council meeting luncheon. Dinner at Quarters One with the Walkers and Haislips.

3 Washington. Morning briefing with R. Slocum and H. Hawkins, of Poor Richard Club of Philadelphia; Congressman Frederic René Coudert, Jr. (New York). Noon appointment with Major Ethel Westermann.

4 Washington. Morning appointments with Ben Pearse (*St. Louis Post-Dispatch*); General Lucius Ray Holbrook, ret. Intelligence briefing on Syria. Lunch with J. Gunther. JCS meeting. Appointments with Congressmen Abe McGregor Goff (Idaho) and former Congressman Hamilton Fish (New York). Dinner at Netherlands Embassy.

5 Washington. JCS meeting. Appointment with W. E. Robinson. Lunch with James Black. To dinner given by Mr. and Mrs. John Gross and J. Edwin Durham at the F Street Club.

6 Washington. Morning appointment with Kaltenborn. Dinner with former Ambassador Davies.

7 Washington. Mah-jong and bridge at the Saylers' in the evening.

8 Washington. Morning appointment with General Mast. To Secretary of Army's office to confer with General Van Tricht and General Moget. Appointment with Generals Paul and Collins. Lunch with former Ambassador Davies. To Fort Myer in the afternoon to attend funeral services for General Surles. To National Theater in the evening to see *Sweethearts*.

9 Washington. Morning train for New York City to attend funeral of Dr. Butler. Early afternoon return to Washington. Afternoon appointments with General North; Generals Devers and Collins; Sir John Maud. To F Street Club for dinner with General and Mrs. Vandenberg.

10 Washington. Morning appointment with E. R. Murrow. JCS briefing. Appointment with General De

December   Witt. JCS luncheon. Afternoon appointments with R. L. Simon and M. L. Schuster; John G. Bennett.

11   Washington. Morning appointments with General Paul; Ted Huggins (of San Francisco Press Club); General Gruenther; Messrs. Fenton and Walker, of the Association of Columbia Graduates; Edward Lewis Bartlett and Ernest Gruening. To Secretary of Defense's office. Afternoon appointment with James Kimble Vardaman, Jr. (member of the board of governors, Federal Reserve System). To White House for presentation of DSM to Admiral Nimitz, followed by reception for Nimitz and General Vandegrift at the Hotel Carlton. To Paramount Studio in the evening to see *Bishop's Wife*.

12   Washington. Morning appointments with General James Kerr Crain, ret.; C. Canfield; Colonel (formerly commanding officer of the SHAEF secretarial detachment) and Mrs. B. B. Smith; R. C. Leib. To home of former Ambassador Davies for luncheon. Afternoon appointment with General Paul. To the White House. Dinner at Quarters One with General Cocheu and Mrs. A. T. Smith.

13   Washington. Late morning train for New York City for Pennsylvania Society dinner. Train departure for Washington shortly before midnight.

14   Morning arrival in Washington. To Fort Myer.

15   Washington. Morning appointment with Colonel Terrazas (Chief of Staff, Bolivian Army). To Secretary of Navy's office for changeover ceremony for Admirals Nimitz and Denfeld. Lunch with G. Allen. To Secretary of Defense's office. Appointment with C. P. Fletcher. To the Hotel Carlton for dinner with the Van Trichts.

16   Washington. To Secretary of Army's office for briefing. Meeting of Secretary of Defense's War Council. Appointment with Dr. Marvin. To Secretary of Defense's office for luncheon. Afternoon appointment with Ambassador Steinhardt. Dinner at General Aurand's.

17   Washington. Morning appointments with Con-

December   gressmen Albert MacDonald Cole and Rees and Mr. Patterson (all of Kansas) to discuss the Van Winkle case; Senator Hoey and delegation; Arthur Gardner (assistant to Secretary Snyder); P&O-Intelligence-JCS briefing. JCS luncheon. Afternoon appointment with Mrs. K. Roosevelt.

18   Washington. Morning appointments with General Groves; W. D. Fuller and B. Hibbs; Congressman Leroy Johnson (California) and Mrs. Eleanor McClatchy (of California). Afternoon appointment with Generals Milton A. Reckord and Ellard A. Walsh.

19   Washington. Morning appointments with General W. D. Morgan; Joseph A. Moller re Chicago speech; Tim White. Luncheon with Generals Collins, Aurand, Wheeler, Hughes, Akin, and Leavey. Afternoon appointment with Colonel Carroll.

20   Washington. Luncheon with General Mast, General Maurice Mathanet (military attaché of the French Embassy), and others.

21   Washington.

22   Washington. Morning appointments with W. E. Robinson; James Kimble Vardaman, Jr.; E. Booz, Mr. Browning, and Mr. Olsen for presentation of Columbia survey.

23   Washington. Morning appointment with Advanced Study Group. Luncheon in office with General O. N. Bradley and eight others. Early evening cocktails at the Haislips'. To the Horkans' for dinner.

24   Washington. Morning appointments with J. L. B. Williams. Christmas baskets presentation. Appointment with R. L. Simon.

25   Washington.

26   Washington. Morning appointment with Hugh Joseph Kelly (senior vice-president and director of Whittlesay House).

27   Washington.

28   Washington.

29   Washington. Morning appointment with General

December		Eddy. Luncheon with W. E. Robinson, D. M. Black, K. D. McCormick, and D. Richberg. To early evening at-home at General and Mrs. Kenner's.
	30	Washington. Morning briefing for Army program, also attended by Secretaries of Defense and Army and Deputy Chief of Staff, followed by Army program presentation. Luncheon with W. E. Robinson and associates and D. Richberg.
	31	Washington. Morning P&O-Intelligence-JCS briefing. To Veterans Administration to attend afternoon swearing-in of General Gray.

1948

January	1	Washington.
	2	Washington. Morning appointment with General William Clayton Rose, ret. (vice-president of Hawaiian Sugar Planters Association). Lunch with Admiral Sherman. Afternoon meeting in Secretary Forrestal's office.
	3	Washington.
	4	Washington.
	5	Washington. Morning appointments with Richard Halworth Rovere (writer and editor) re article for *Harper's* magazine; Milton S. Eisenhower. Meeting of Secretary of Army's War Council. Staff luncheon in office with Generals Parks, Persons, Lanham, Richards, Noce, McLain, Russel Burton Reynolds (Chief, Special Services), and William Henry Kasten (Chief of Finance).
	6	Washington. Morning appointments with Congressman Javitz; H. M. Schley; Otto C. Smith (of Topeka); General Wedemeyer. Afternoon appointments with L. H. Brown; Congressman W. G. Andrews.
	7	Washington. Morning P&O-Intelligence-JCS briefing. Appointment with General Curits. JCS luncheon.

January 8   Washington. All appointments canceled due to illness. At home through January 11.

12   Washington. Morning appointment with Robert R. Gros (of Palo Alto, California). Lunch with K. McCormick. Afternoon appointments with Dr. James Kerr Pollock (professor of political science and chairman of the Social Science Division, University of Michigan); A. Frieder.

13   Washington. All appointments canceled due to illness. At home.

14   Washington. Morning appointments with General Arnold; Joseph Wright Alsop, Jr.; P&O-Intelligence-JCS briefing. Secretary Forrestal's luncheon for Brooke Claxton (Canadian Minister of National Defence). Afternoon appointment with General Lucas. Meeting with Gillem Board.

15   Washington. Morning presentation by Sir Alwyn Douglas Crow (head of scientific and technical services, British Supply Office, Washington) of Medal of Freedom with Bronze Palm. Late morning train to New York for Columbia College alumni dinner honoring Dr. Fackenthal at the Waldorf-Astoria.

16   New York City. Late night train for Philadelphia.

17   Morning arrival in Philadelphia. Receives Poor Richard Club 1948 Medal of Achievement. Afternoon departure for Washington.

18   Washington. Morning appearance at trustees room.

19   Washington. Morning appointments with General Persons; General Bull. To Secretary Forrestal's office for conference with Admiral Denfeld and General Spaatz re Air Force. Appointment with K. McCormick. Afternoon appointment with Congressman Case and Mr. Morgan.

20   Washington. Morning briefing, followed by meeting of Secretary of Defense's War Council. Lunch with Secretary Symington. Afternoon appointments with General David Goodwin Barr; General Legge. Secretary Marshall's dinner at Alibi Club.

21   Washington. Morning appointment with Generals

January Bradley, Collins, Lutes, and Aurand. P&O-Intelligence-JCS briefing. JCS luncheon.

22 Washington. Morning appointment in Secretary Forrestal's office. Staff luncheon.

23 Washington. Morning appointments with General Clifton Bledsoe Cates (CG of USMC schools); General Paul. Luncheon with Generals Spaatz and Wedemeyer and Mr. Elihu Root, Jr. (lawyer). Afternoon meeting with Dr. Bush in Secretary Royall's office. Appointment with H. C. Butcher.

24 Washington. Morning appointments with Mr. Fred Winant; Colonel Wendell Westover (Executive for Reserves and ROTC Affairs).

25 Washington.

26 Washington. Morning swearing-in of Generals Collins, Paul, Chamberlin, and Aurand. UMT briefing in Secretary Royall's office. Appointments with General Lutes; Colonel Robert Moore Fletcher, ret. Lunch with J. Black. Afternoon meeting with Mr. Edward Nichols re Mr. Borden. Dinner at Army and Navy Club given by General William Clayton Rose.

27 Washington. Morning appointment with General Ridgway. UMT presentation in Secretary Forrestal's office for Senate Armed Services Committee, followed by buffet luncheon. Afternoon appointment with M. W. Childs. Evening reception at the White House for Army, Navy, and Air.

28 Washington. Morning appointments with Mr. Ted Young (architect); P&O and Intelligence. Afternoon appointment with James Kimble Vardaman, Jr., and Dr. Sonier.

29 Washington. Morning appointment with L. Whitman. Lunch with Joseph Wright Alsop, Jr., and Geoffrey Crowther (editor of the *Economist*). Dinner for USMA Class of 1915.

30 Washington. Morning appointment with Anna Lea Lelli (Italian scholar and lecturer). Lunch with Albert Wayne Coy. Afternoon appointment with E. N. Clark.

January 31 Washington. Morning conference re AGF with General O. N. Bradley and staff. Interview by Leon Philipson. Appointment with Mr. Ohly. Cocktails at Army and Navy Club with General and Mrs. Aurand. Dinner with the Cannons.

February 1 Washington.

2 Washington. Early morning departure for Norfolk, Virginia, to address incoming class at Armed Forces Staff College. Late afternoon return to Washington.

3 Washington. Morning briefing for meeting of Secretary of Defense's War Council, followed by meeting. Appointment with General J. A. Chapman. Lunch with Mr. Black. Afternoon appointments with B. Baruch; C. A. R. Dunn.

4 Washington. Morning appointments with Colonel F. A. Allen; Duncan Black MacDonald Emrick. P&O-Intelligence-JCS briefing, followed by JCS luncheon. Evening reception for foreign representatives to meet Generals Eisenhower and Bradley.

5 Washington. Morning appointments with T. J. Watson, Sr.; General W. D. Morgan. Afternoon meeting with Generals Bradley and Parks at National Press Club. Presentation ceremony for Colonels Bowen and Carroll and Major Cannon. To Secretary of the Army Royall's office for presentation of award to Richard Redwood Deupree. Appointment with Admiral Moore. Evening farewell party for Eisenhower in Secretary Royall's office.

6 Washington. Morning presentation ceremony for Hays, Marsh, and Murray. Historical Division luncheon. Evening staff party for Eisenhower.

7 Washington. Morning press conference, followed by newsreels, still pictures, and recorder. Noon swearing-in of General Bradley in Secretary Royall's office, succeeded by pictorial coverage of event. Lunch in Secretary Royall's dining room.

Index

Adoration of the Mystic Lamb, return of, to Belgium, 305-6
Advisory Commission on Universal Military Training. *See* President's Advisory Commission on Universal Military Training
AEF Clubs, closing of, 296
Aero Digest, 1749
Aeronautical Board, joint JCB-JRDB-Aeronautical Board Communications systems planning, 1788-89, 1966-97
Africa, ATC routes to and over, 1304-6
Agriculture, Department of: grain exports, control of, 975; nominations for service with, 1741
Ailsa, Lord. *See* Kennedy, Charles
Air-base defense, number of troops available for, 1011-12
Airborne Corps, XVIII, 49, 51, 91-92, 141
Airborne Divisions: 82d, 82, 107, 508; 101st, 508, 2023
Airborne units, postwar retention, 91-92, 508
Air commands, territorial organization, 1006
Air Coordinating Committee, policy for Europe, 265-66
Air Corps (*see also* Air forces; Army Air Forces; Arnold, Henry Harley), officers, assignment to W.D. posts, 336
Aircraft: AAF, government officials travel in, 734-35; Germany, destruction by, 27; jets, Soviet reliance on, 2156; liaison, military characteristics for, 2170-71; loudspeakers on, 751-52; research and development, economy in, 2250; Soviet Union, estimate of development by, 744; transport, number available for M-Day, 1947-48
Air defense, forces for, 789, 791, 1442
Air Defense Command, agreement on unity of command, 1362
Air defense units, policy for assignment to Pacific, 219
Air defense weapons (*see also* Missiles and rockets), Soviet reliance on, 2156
Air depots, retention and inactivation, 1652
Air Division, 2d, 107
Airey, Terence Sydney: background, 1741; SACMED, assignment to, 1740-41
—Trieste Free Territory: establishment and boundary delineation, 1907-8; report on administration, 2158-59; Yugoslav role in administration, 2092
Airfields, Berlin requirements, 229; interservice use of, 2249
Air Force, Department of the (*see also* United States Air Force): activated, 1867; atomic weapons, systems coordination, 2048; budgets, coordination with other services missions, 2052-53; command and control, unified, 1968

Air Force, U.S. *See* United States Air Force
Air Force Association, address by E., 1915, 1921
Air forces (*see also* Air Force, Department of the; Air Corps; Army Air Forces; Arnold, Henry Harley; United States Air Force): antisubmarine mission, 930, 976-77; Army, separation from, 1914-15; autonomy for, 1005-6, 1063-64; cost estimates, 812; effect of growth on operations, 929; low-score personnel, screening by, 1024-26; Marine Corps, continuance of, 930; overstrength, 1025; Pacific theater, command and control, 858, 861; reconnaissance missions, 977; roles and missions, 215-17, 369-71, 701-2, 789-91, 927-32, 976-77, 997, 1005-6, 1057-59, 1063-64, 1360, 1466-67, 1528-29, 2037-39, 2247; service support units for, 1005-7, 2249
—Strategic: international regulation, 1485; support of under unified command, 1409-12
Air Forces (units): Fourth, 1361-62; Sixth, 1301; Ninth, 63
Air-ground cooperation. *See* Tactical air support
Air Inspector, AAF, Shanghai Enlisted Men's Committee, 959
Air Intelligence Group, Army representation on, 2046
Air Ministry Special Signals Office (British), 1
Air mobility, need for developing, 2255
Air operations, potential developments in, 1447-48
Air Policy Board, 1948
Air-raid defenses. *See* Civilian defense
Air-space channels: agreement on, 526; U.S. violations of, 521-22, 526, 1237-38
Air systems, JCS definition, 1304
Air Transport Command: Africa, routes to and over, 1304-6; aircraft available for M-Day, 1948; India, routes to and over, 1304-5; Thailand, continuing operations in, 1304-6
Air travel: Europe, policy on, 264-66, 1212-13; Germany, policy on, 264-66; Soviet interruption to, 521, 525-26
Air University, 1646
Air warning systems, responsibility for, 789, 791
Akin, Spencer Ball, 621; Chief Signal Officer, assignment as, 1977
Alamogordo Air Base, 204
Alamo pilgrimage, 1656
Alanbrooke of Brookeborough, Baron. *See* Brooke, Alan Francis
Alaska, 2014-15

Alaska Command, Air Force Chief of Staff as JCS executive, 1893, 1983; commander, grade for, 1869–70, 1872; unified command and missions, 1274–76, 1298–1300, 1409–12

Alaska Department: Army Exchange Service stocks for, 1893; Canol oil distribution system, 1382–84; cost-plus contracts in, 1445–46; district engineer, relationship to commander, 1870–71, 1892; inspection tour by E., 1459–60, 1522, 1537, 1548, 1624, 1685–86, 1724, 1739, 1744, 1748, 1753, 1755, 1764, 1769–70, 1779, 1795, 1800, 1814, 1820, 1833, 1841, 1843, 1845, 1847, 1851, 1854, 1869–70, 1892–93, 1901; railroad construction in, 1893; redesignated U.S. Army, Alaska, 1983

Albania, censured by UN for support of Greek guerrillas, 1999

Albright, John Johnson, 1812

Alcoholic beverages. See Liquor

Aldrich, Winthrop Williams, 2211–12

Alemán, Miguel, 1662, 1675

Alexander, Frank Samuel, 162

Alexander, Harold Rupert Leofric George: American Legion, address to, 1839–40; Army-Navy game, attendance at, 1884, 1903–4, 2016, 2101, 2108–9, 2131, 2147; background, 36; Canada, appointment as governor general, 237–38; Chief of Imperial General Staff, appointment as, 238; comments on service by, 1488–89; decoration for, 36; Germany, withdrawal from Soviet zone, 167; Italy, French withdrawal from, 48–49, 62; Military Academy, visit to, 1548; officers, retention on active duty, 345; Pantelleria seizure, role of air forces in, 2112, 2187; peerage appointment, congratulations from E. on, 719; troop units, redeployment plans, 154; Venezia Giulia, occupation by Yugoslavia, 57–59, 62–64, 66; visit with E., 1489, 1548, 2101; visit with Truman, 1489; visit to U.S., 1488–89; war reports, review by E., 2101, 2111–12, 2187–88

—Austria: British zone in, 63; British zone, movement into, 167; nonfraternization policy, 178; prisoners of war problem, 63, 66–68; refugees problem, 63, 67–68

Alexander, Roger Gordon, 1663

Algiers, 296

Alice, Princess of England, 717, 746

Alien property, litigation over, 737–38

Aliens, policy on marriage, 179

Alien Spouse Act, 179

Allegheny-Pittsburgh Coal Co., 323

Allen, Ellen Gordon, 2235–38

Allen, Frank Albert, Jr.: background, 34–35; commendation by Pinkley, 89; evaluation of and promotion for, 2235–38; press relations assignment for, 59–60, 78; troop unit, assignment for, 78

Allen, George E., 1088, 1430

Allen, Leven Cooper, 487, 637

Allen, Robert Sharon, 1974–75, 2018; background, 1974

Allen, Terry de la Mesa, 73; background, 73; evaluation as combat commander, 1893–95; Sobolta, information on death of, 1950

Allied club in Algiers, 296

Allied Commission on Reparations, 260–61

Allied Control Council, 52; activation, 53; air-space channels, agreement on, 526; air travel in Europe, policy on, 265–66; British and U.S. predecessors formed, 31–32; civilian representation on, 437, 461–63, 478–80; Czechoslovakia, restitution of transportation equipment, 464, 466; E. as U.S. representative, 113, 189; deterioration of meetings, 527; first meeting agenda, 228–29; formation, 31–32, 52–53, 66, 68, 112–14, 125; JCS relation to, 1299; Jodl, clemency for, 1319–20; meetings with E., 53, 125, 135–38, 1312; Poland, liaison mission to Berlin, 447–48; reparations policy, responsibility for, 261, 526–27; SHAEF liaison element, 32; signing ceremony, 132–33; U.S. representation on, 166; war criminals, prosecution of, 644; Yalta agreement on, 32

—Berlin: coal supplies for, 229, 282; food supplies for, 229; French sector, movement into, 229

—France: opposition to agencies, 620; representation on, 32

—Germany: banned book index, 509; children, Swedish food supplies for, 489; coal production, accelerating, 894; control machinery, U.S. proposals, 229; documents captured, use in intelligence operations, 96; nonfraternization policy, 179; troop units strength authorizations, 1747

Allied Expeditionary Force: commendation by E., 16–17; disparagement of accomplishments, 825; farewell by E. on SHAEF inactivation, 184–85

Allied Force Headquarters (see also Supreme Commander, Allied Expeditionary Force): British Chiefs, decision to retain, 405; British element, renamed GHQ, Central Mediterranean Forces, 405; final dinner, message from E., 1796; inactivation, 838–40, 918, 1796; JCS decision to retain, 405; MTOUSA, separation from, 405

—Austria: troop operations lines, 65; U.S.

Armistice Day (1918): discontinuing observance, 1166–67; remark by E. on, 75–76; Truman proclamation on, 1167

Armistice Day ceremonies: attendance by E., 500–502, 515, 535, 557; message from E., 2055

Armored Divisions: 1st, 627; 2d, 82, 107, 249; 3d, 107, 204, 253, 777–78; 4th, 107; 6th, 107; 7th, 508; 10th, 71; 79th (British), 322; Pacific theater, assignment to, 219

Arms, bureaus, and services: chiefs, inactivation of, 98, 330, 332, 336, 518; chiefs, liaison with, 576

Arms and equipment (see also Materiel): Canada, standardization with; civilian assistance in R&D, 1046–50; development and use, predictions on, 1424–25, 1441–43, 1446–48; international regulation and reduction, 1483–86, 1550–52; postwar needs, study of, 91–92; release of information to U.S., 1418–19; reserve components, 2255; Soviet Union development, estimate of, 744; United Kingdom, standardization with, 1418–19; UNO, regulation by, 1392–94

Army, Department of the (see also War Department): activated, 1867; Argentina, military assistance to, 2043–44, 2167; atomic weapons, custody and maintenance, 1937–38; Austria, economic assistance for, 2142; Caribbean Command, activation, 1968–69; cooks and bakers schools, authority over, 2220; Defense Department, representatives at orientation meeting, 1975–78; families, transport overseas, 1945; FECOM, troop units strength authorizations and reductions, 2229–30; Germany, documents captured, classification downgrading, 2073–75; Greece, coordination of U.S.-U.K. missions, 2103–4; Japan, U.K. withdrawal from, 2163–64; reserve components, quotas for joint colleges, 2188–89; soldiers, conduct standards for, 1944; transport aircraft, number available for M-Day, 1947–48; World War II records, public access to, 2136–37, 2112–13

—World War II history: citation of JCS and OCS documents in, 2098–99; publication project, 2072, 2098

Army, U.S. See Army of the United States; Ground forces; Regular Army; Troop units

Army Air Forces (not United States Air Force, q.v.; see also Air Corps; Air forces; Arnold, Henry Harley; Spaatz, Carl): aircraft, government officials travel in, 734–35; commendation by E., 214; commissions policy, 1167–68; congratulated by

E., 272; discharge pin, distinctive, 645; football competition, 535; general officers, evaluation and selection, 1182–83; Italy, retention of units in, 839–40; Japanese navy, vessels as test targets, 580; missiles and rockets, responsibility for R&D, 1152–53; publications, activities in, 434; roles and missions (see Roles and missions); service units, battle credit for, 645

—officers: allocation to, 1585–87; assignment to WDGS, 336, 1005, 1007

—recruiting programs, 679–80, 1026; standards, 1024–26, 1185

—troop units: manning and operating, 602; strength authorizations and reductions, 371, 680–81, 1518–19

Army and Air Force Vitalization and Retirement Equalization Act (1948), 1696

Army and Navy Journal, 1256

Army Command and Administrative Network, 939

Army Day and Army Week, 1646

Army Education Program, 426 (see also Information and education programs)

Army Exchange Service: Alaska theater, stocks for, 1893; currency control by, 1605–6; families travel overseas, 475; reorganization, 1224

Army General Classification Test, scores, 1184–86

Army Ground Forces (see also Devers, Jacob Loucks): congratulated by E., 912–13; mission and reorganization, 339, 518

Army Groups: 6th, 91; 12th, 50–51, 55, 91, 117, 138–44, 418, 1574, 1680, 2040–41; 15th, 166, 168–69, 1680; 21st, 50–51, 55, 143–44, 165, 188, 212, 1068–72, 1574; grades for commanders, 1676

Army Hour, 501

Army Industrial College (see also Industrial College of the Armed Forces): activation, 332, 1018; attendance at, 1450, 1463–64

Army of the United States (distinct from Regular Army, q.v.): demobilization program, 140–41; Germany, mission in, 436; mobilization, plans for future, 742–45; reserve components, commissions policy, 948; soldiers, percentage commissioned in, 948; troop units strength, periodic, 1290; wartime burden on, 1676

—National Guard: as element of AUS, 937; percentage of officers commissioned in, 948

—officers: number in war service, 649, 951; release of, 1323–24

Army-Navy Club of Manila, honorary membership for E., 621

Army-Navy games: attendance by E., 566–

67, 1391, 1406, 1425–27, 1903–4, 2016, 2089, 2101, 2108–9, 2147; continuing, 535, 555
Army-Navy Liquidation Commission, 464–65
Army-Navy Munitions Board: arms and equipment, potential developments in, 1425; atomic weapons, potential developments in, 1447–48; industry, scattering for security, 1289; interservice agency, recognition as, 1868; materiel procurement by, 2249–50; organization and functions, 795–96; unification, role in, 1315
—mobilization, industrial: planning for, 2067–68; strategic guidance in planning, 1582–85
Army-Navy Petroleum Board, staff augmentation and reduction, 1607–8
Army-Navy-Public Health Service Medical Officer Procurement Act, 1623
Army-Navy Staff College (see also Armed Forces Staff College): activation, 332, 335; AWC building use by, 802–3; curriculum and student standards, 800–803; dictionary, joint Army-Navy, 1271; name proposed, 1117; NWC, transition to, 723; student allocations, 803; State Department students at, 332, 803
Army–Notre Dame games: attendance by E., 1356, 1370; terminating, 1331–32
Army Ordnance Association, 1094, 1111, 2024–25
Army Remount Service, 1637–38
Army Reserve. See Reserve components; Reserve officers
Army Service Forces (see also Services of Supply; Somervell, Brehon Burke): civilians, housing on military posts, 842–43; dismemberment proposed, 339; division of functions, 339; inactivation, 1006, 1111; officers, allocation to, 1585–87; reports on domestic situation, 597–98
Army Talks, 257
Army university at Biarritz, 256–57
Army War College: ANSC use of building, 802–3; reactivation, 330, 332, 335
Army-West Virginia game, 1359
Arnold, David Lee, 836–37
Arnold, Henry Harley (see also Air Corps; Army Air Forces), 609; air service units, battle credits for, 645; Army, postwar organization and strength, 680; atomic bomb, decision to use, 205; China, postwar policy in, 623–24; Columbia presidency, congratulations to E. on, 1811; demobilization, plans for, 680; intelligence agencies, reports on domestic situation, 597; Japanese army, repatriation of, 623–

24; Japanese navy, vessels for test targets, 580–81; Northwest Europe Operations Report, presentation copy, 618; Pacific islands, administration of bases in, 587–88; postretirement personal services, 1144–45, 1165–66, 1219, 1235; retirement, 428; son, AAF aircraft personal use, 836; Soviet Union, report of military mission to, 835–36; training programs, troops awaiting discharge, 670–72; troop units, discharge acceleration, 600; White House, liaison with, 617
—AAF: organization and strength, postwar, 680–81; recruiting and public relations programs, 679–81
Arnold, Richard R., 544, 1036
Around-the-world flight, 1490
Arthur, Joseph Dogan, Jr., 1822–23
Articles of War. See Courts-martial; Military Justice
Art treasures, return of, to Belgium, 306
Ashby, George Franklin, 1130
Asheville, N.C., 1645
Ashford General Hospital, return of, to owners, 715–16
Asia region: future threat from, 1100–1101; troop units, commitment to, 1584, 1603–4
Assembly Air Command, 50, 299
Assistant Secretaries of War. See War Department
Assistant Secretary of War for R&D, 1005
Associated Press, 434, 492–93; security breach by, 12, 264, 1193–94
Association of Radio News Analysts, 1728
Athenaeum Club, 351
Atherton, Ray, 746
Athlone, Earl of, 717, 746
Atkins, Tommy, 612, 615
Atlanta, Ga.: homecoming celebrations, 98; visit by E., 1645, 1733
Atlanta Journal, 632
Atlantic Command: activation, 1967–69; Atlantic Fleet, redesignated from, 1968; unified command for, 1968–69
Atlantic Fleet: Atlantic Command, redesignation as, 1968; naval command designation, 1968
Atlantic islands. See Antilles Command; Caribbean Command
Atomic Energy Act (1946), 641, 1525, 1937, 2020
Atomic energy plants, of Canada and U.K., effect on U.S. security, 1525–26
Atomic weapons: aggression by, defining, 2047; Air Force, systems coordination by, 2048; Army Chief of Staff as JCS executive, 1994–95; attack, U.S. vulnerability to, 1448; Azores as storage site, 1077; bases

warning to E. against, 736; tribute to by E., 1308-9; universal military training, 735-36, 766-67; veterans employment, 765-66; war, elimination of, 1093
—UNO: armaments regulation by, 1393-94; Commission on Atomic Energy, appointment to, 636, 1078
Bass, Michael A., 607
Batangas, demonstration by soldiers, 753
Bates, Raymond Henry, advancement of, 913-14
Battle credits: AAF service units, 645; citation policy, 106-7
Baudoin, Prince of the Belgians, 152
Baugh, Sammy, 2055
Baughey, Robert Martin, status as officer, 958
Bavaria: civil government in, 117; denazification program, 307-9, 351-52, 374-76, 391-92; liquor issue and purchase policy, 494-95
Baxter, James Phinney, III, 2039-40, 2139; background, 2040
Beach, Coral, 76
Beach, George Corwin: background, 1579; ETO, assignment to, 76; Surgeon General of U.S., nomination for, 1578-79
Beach, James Keller, 2132
Beale, Betty, 694
Bear Mountain Inn, 1745
Beattie, James S., 2054-55
Beaver, Edna R., 1566-67
Beaverbrook, William Maxwell Aitken, 561
Beck, Clyde McKay: background, 1420, 1579; hunting invitation to E., 1735; RA commission for son, 1735-36; retirement grade for, 1695-96; Surgeon General of U.S., nomination for, 1578-79; visit with E., 2088-89
Beck, Dorothy Coors, 1735-36
Beck, James A., RA commission for, 1735-36
Becke, Carlos von der, 1094-97, 1147-48
Behn, Sosthenes, 939
Beightler, Robert S., 992-93; background, 993; BAMBOO, attendance at, 2207
Belchem, Ronald Frederick King, 1571-75
Belfast, honorary burgess and reception for E., 240, 247, 290, 292, 310
Belgium: art treasures returned to, 306; currency exchange, black market in, 388; decoration to E., 291; government return to, 152; honors to E., 254-55; tribute by E. on SHAEF inactivation, 185
Bell, Homer G., 1209
Benes, Edouard, 457
—Czechoslovakia: Soviet economic demands on, 451-52; transportation problems, 464;

U.S. troop units strength, 452-53; U.S.-Soviet withdrawal from, 450-52
Benfield, Edgar L., discharge of, 947-48
Benfield, Pauline, 947-48
Benignus, Albert, 192
Bennett, Andrew Carl, commendation by E., 954
Benson, Clarence Corinth, 428-29
Benton, William: address, comment by E. on, 1486-87, 1730; background, 1882; gift to E., 1881-82; visits with E., 1730-31, 1802, 1882
—Columbia University: Booz study of special problems, 1929; congratulations to E. on presidency, 1801-2
Berchtesgaden, 95, 294-95, 326
Bergin, William Edward, 981
Berlin, Irving, 1421
Berlin (see also Clay, Lucius Du Bignon; Military government; Potsdam conference): access rights to, 166-67, 382-83, 522, 526; air-space channels, U.S. violation, 521-22; air travel, Soviet interruption, 521, 525-26; blockade by Soviets, 2196, 2200; British sector, movement into, 164-65, 167-68; civil administration, 137; Clay retention in, 1363; coal supplies for, 229, 282; currency exchange, black market in, 244-45; damage assessment, 95; flag-raising ceremony, 204; food supplies for; hunger and disease in, 504-5; importance to U.S., 1498; industrial equipment removal from, 260; infant mortality, 504; move by E. to, 248; OMGUS move to, 116, 132, 438; Polish liaison mission to, 447-48; Potsdam conference, arrangements for, 163-65; radio communications with, 158; Red Cross girls for, 250; rehabilitation task, 88; sectors, delineation and agreements on, 52, 125, 133, 137; Soviet currency exchange practices, 245, 389; surrender signing, 7, 12-13; U.K. airfield requirements, 229; U.K. mission in, 438; U.K.-U.S. sectors delineation, 166; U.S. sector, movement into, 164-65, 167-68; USFET headquarters move to, 1340-41, 1350
—drive to, 287, 1679-80; Soviet film on, 320; Stalin explanation, 286-87
—French sector: delineation, 210-11, 229; movement into, 167-68, 229
Berlin Airlift (1948), 526
Bernadotte, Folke, 488-89; background, 489
Bernstein, Philip Sidney, 688
Berry, Kearie Lee, RA appointment as brigadier general, 1179-80
Berry, Robert Wallace, 1906
Berryman, Clifford Kennedy, 1834

Carlson, Carolyn, 1250, 1415
Carlson, Eda Wilhelmina, 34, 492, 1250, 1415, 1783; birthday message from E., 1055–56; illness of, 1248
Carlson, Frank, 1803–4
Carlson, Joel E., 34, 1250, 1415
Carlton, Don E.: background, 394; Third Army, assignment to, 394
Carney, Francis, 442–43
Caroline Islands, administration of, 587–88
Carr, Charles R., 187
Carr, Dorothy, 1640
Carroll, Earl J., 978–79, 1262–63, 1335
Carroll, Frederick Aloysius, 455–56
Carroll, John Wallace, 1302–3
Carroll, Marie Madeleine, 170, 794–95; background, 170, 914
Carroll, Paul Thomas, 615, 847, 1727, 2240–41; evaluation by E., 2253
Carsley, Demetrios, 909
Carter, Amon Giles, 792–93, 1032, 1392, 2150
Carter, Doniphan, 1381–82; assignment for, 1175; background, 1175, 1718
Carter, E. Kemper, 816
Carter, Marshall Sylvester, 1112, 1718; promotion for, 1610–11
—China theater: map coverage of, 1367–68; shipping for, 1054–55
Carter, Minnie Meacham (Smith), 2150
Case, Charles Augustine, 152–53, 922, 1420, 1739
Case, Clifford Phillip, 2190
Case, Everett Needham, 1423, 1633, 1656–57
Case, Francis Higbee, 948–50, 1528–29, 1793–94
Case against the Admirals (Huie), 909–10
Casey, Hugh John: background, 331; reassignment for, 329
Casey, Katheryn P., 1902–3
Caspian Sea area, as Soviet industrial center, 1584
Cass, Lewis, 1219
Cassidy, Thomas Edward, 1808–9
Castellano, Giuseppe, 458; background, 459
Caste system. See Doolittle Report; Officers, relations with enlisted soldiers
Castle, Benjamin Frederick, 1152
Castle, Benjamin Walker, 1152
Castle Mountain, 747
Casualties. See Dead
Causen, Janis Eisenhower, 1437
Cavalry Division, 1st, 1060
Cedargates, 1745
Cedar Island Lodge, 1904
Celebes Islands, 752
Celler, Emanuel, 1514, 1602
Cemeteries, national: accomodations for visitors, 395–96; administration and maintenance, 230, 323–25; number of burials in, 325; number in service, 325; sites in foreign countries, 1689–91
Censorship: Austria, termination in, 1905–6; directives on, 42, 158; Germany, policies in, 115, 442; Kennedy, breach by, 12–13, 264, 1193–94; newsmen charge of, 865–66; Poland, 444; Stars and Stripes, alleged censorship, 905–6; USFET, 434
Central America: alternate canal routes in, 1705–6; highways system improvement, 1373–74
Central Intelligence Agency: activation, 699, 1466, 1483, 1868; German documents, access to, 2075; mission, 667, 1868; NSC supervision of, 1483; plans for, 667; psychological warfare, research, planning, and training in, 2063
Central Intelligence Group: atomic weapons explosions, long-range detection, 1918–19; reorganization, 1481–83
Central Pacific theater, unified command and missions, 1259, 1298–1300
Centre College, 1745
Ceski, 6
Chadwick, James, 1476–77
Chamberlain, Frederick R., Jr., 317; DSM award for, 316–17
Chamberlain, William, 2219–20
Chamberlin, Stephen Jones: background, 331; Becke, conference with E., 1148; Clarke, promotion and retention, 1187–88; intelligence reports on domestic situation, 598; Latin America, mutual defense plans, 1399; reassignment of, 329; WDGS, assignment to, 855, 1059–60
—Greece: military advisory group for, 1997, 2000; military assistance to, 1996–2001
Chandor, Douglas, 1202
Chang Chun, conference with MacArthur, 1361
Chapel Hill, N.C., 1645, 1729, 1840
Chapel Hill Weekly, 786
Chapels, surplus, disposal of, 1862
Chapin, William Wallace, 2066–67
Chaplains: commissions, policy on, 533; return to civilian communities, 844–45; tribute to by E., 306–7, 844–45, 1168–69
Chapman, John Austin, 2225
Chapman, Mary K., 1004
Chapultepec, Act of (1945), 821–22, 878, 1148, 1399
Charcoal drawing of E., 993–94
Charles, Prince of the Belgians, 152
Charlotte, Grand Duchess, 1312
Charter Club, 149
Chase, Joseph Cummings, 1841

Compton, Karl Taylor, 1440–43, 1692–93, 2020; background, 1442

Conant, James Bryant, 1786; Harvard degree for E., 1133; national security commission, 772, 814; World War II history, joint U.S.-U.K. publication, 2139
—atomic weapons: fallout, future danger from, 1686; forecast of development, 1992–93

Concentration camps, E. on exposing, 154

Conduct standards. *See* Discipline; Morale; Soldiers; Training programs

Conference of Foreign Ministers. *See* Moscow Conference of Foreign Ministers

Congress (*see also* House of Representatives; Senate): address to and testimony by E., 156–57, 162–63, 501, 534–35; Air Policy Board, 1948; Atomic Energy Act, request for review, 2020; Central America, alternate canal routes in, 1705–6; command and control, unified, 861, 862; criticism of, forbidden by E., 1793–94; European Recovery Plan, 2143; fathers deferment and discharge, 784; France, currency exchange rates, 209; Greece, military assistance to, 1998; intelligence agencies, centralization of functions, 863; Japan, troop units reduction, 1516–20; Korea, troop units reduction, 1516–20; materiel, liquidating surplus, 714; missiles and rockets, test sites for, 1031; Navy Department appropriations, 814; Pearl Harbor attack, investigation of, 843–44, 861–63, 1084, 1258, 1327–28; reserve components, provision for, 908; Roosevelt (Kermit) Fund, 1385; St. Lawrence Seaway, legislation for, 955; Texas delegation, address by E., 901; universal military training, 120, 766, 908, 1442; Voice of America, 1665; War Department budget appropriations and reductions, 814, 1807
—armed services: pay increases, 1161; unification, 1057, 1062–64, 1282–83, 1314
—atomic weapons: commission to evaluate tests, 961; international regulation, 576–77, 639–42, 1078; national policy on, 2047; U.K., release of information to, 1525
—general officers: Regular Army, special appointment in, 1179–80; retirement grades for, 1695–96
—officers: attendance at civilian colleges, 971–1017; disability retirement, investigation of, 2104–6; industry, tours with, 971
—Regular Army: officer strength augmentation, 1119–20; pay increases, 1241; recruiting programs, 463, 475
—Selective Service: extension of, 908, 1087, 1169, 1215, 1337, 1442, 1520; termination, pressure for, 599, 605

—troop units: discharge acceleration, 599, 605; strength authorizations, 605, 1087

Congressional Club, 816

Congress of Industrial Organizations, 1336, 1412, 1922–23

Coningham, Arthur, 187; background, 36; decoration for, 35, 45–46

Conklin, Helen, 1540

Conklin, John French, 1540; background, 1540; decoration for, 317

Connally, Tom (Thomas Terry), 652

Connecticut, contemplated as residence by E., 1838, 1921

Connelly, Matthew James, 1211, 1219–20; background, 1211

Conner, Fox, 564

Connolly, Jack S., 132

Conolly, Richard Lansing, assignment to Eastern Atlantic and Mediterranean, 1969

Conscientious objectors, 1694

Conscription. *See* Selective Service; Universal military training

Constabulary, Germany: local manpower for, 600, 604, 767; need for, 604; reorganization plans, 1861, 1885–86

Construction program, moratorium on, 1240

Cook, Everett Richard, 1921–22

Cook, Ross K., 372

Cooks and bakers schools: authority over, 995, 1509–10, 2220; instructors for, 995

Cooper, Kent, 264

Cooper, Prentice William, Jr., 1302

Cooperative Defense Agreement (1942), 1301

Coors, Giles Augustus, 740, 1735

Copenhagen: air-space channel for, 526; visit by E., 483, 489–90, 492, 515, 539

Corinthia, 58

Corlett, Charles Harrison, 1741–42, 1831–32; background, 1742

Cornwall-Jones, Arthur T., 789, 983

Coronet, 1420

Corps: II (Polish), 293, 2040, 2112; III, 141; V, 63, 141; VI, 532; VII, 141; X (British), 776; XII (German), 72; XIII (British), 141, 405, 838–39; XVI, 140–41; XXIV, 1054

Correspondence, E. personal: compassion in, 613; preparation and dispatch, 615–16

Correspondents. *See* Newsmen

Corson, Allen, 1463–64, 2233

Cosmopolitan, 1924

Cossacks, 67–68

Cossens, John Bisp, 1120–23, 1169

Cost of living, E. on government controls on, 1921–22

Cost-plus contracts in Alaska theater, 1445–46

Cota, Norman Daniel, 422

Cotentin peninsula, seizure of, 1070

Cotten, Joseph, 914

Coughlin, William Leo, 1117–18
Council of Common Defense, proposed, 1466
Council of Foreign Ministers, 453; Czechoslovakia, motor vehicles for, 466; Korea, trusteeship for, 857; Trieste Free Territory, establishment, 1188–90, 1720–21; UNO, commission on atomic energy, 579; Venezia Giulia, dispute over, 839–40
—Germany: coal production, accelerating, 894; disarmament and demilitarization, 841; troop units strength authorizations, 1746
Counterintelligence Corps: command and control, 1545–46; curtailment of activities, 1359
COURIER. See Truman, Harry S.
Courts-martial (see also Military justice): enlisted soldiers service on, 832; sentence remission, transfer of power to JAG, 1790–91; sentences review, 145–46, 147–48
Cowan, Walter Henry, 47–48
Cowles, Gardner, 1881
Cox, Albert Lyman, 1767
Cox, Willard R., 1198, 1909–10
Coykendall, Frederick, 1787; background, 1776; Butler, death of, 2121–22; visit with E., 1925, 2055, 2057
—Columbia: aides detail to, 2056–57, 2078–79; inauguration of E. as president, 1951, 2079–80; presidency offer to E., 1775–76; trustees meeting with E., 1925–26; trustees support assured, 2057
Coykendall, Mary Beach (Warrin), 2056–57, 2080
Craig, Howard Arnold: Alaska theater district engineer, relationship to commander, 1871, 1892; Army Exchange Service stocks for Alaska, 1893; armed services unification, 705–6; cargoes, unloading by union stevedores, 1892; executive branches, coordination of information with, 658; intelligence agencies, centralization of functions, 697, 699, 862–63; Pacific theater, administration of bases, 1056–57; promotion for, 1869–70; reserve components, authority and responsibility for, 1893; Stars and Stripes, alleged censorship, 905–6
Craig, Louis Aleck, 992
Cramer, Kenneth Frank: background, 1763; National Guard Bureau chief, nomination for, 1762–63
Craney, Edward, 1726
Crawford, Robert Walter, 1812, 1814; arms and equipment, study of postwar needs, 91; background, 495, 1768; invitation to E., 1767–68; liquor, policy on issue and purchase, 495
Creative Age Press, 190–91

Crerar, Henry Duncan Graham, 154–55, 187; background, 19; decoration for, 19, 35
Criminal Investigation Division, command and control, 1545–46
Crittenberger, Josephine Frost (Woodhull), 1208
Crittenberger, Willis Dale: Argentina, military assistance for, 2043–44, 2166–67; Caribbean Command, assignment to, 1969, 2043; Chile, visit to, 1286–87; evaluation by E., 2252; invitation to E., 1208; Moore, quarters in Panama for, 2159; Panama defense sites, withdrawal from, 1286–87; recruiting program, intensifying, 1311–12; training programs, troops awaiting discharge, 670–72; troop units, discharge acceleration, 600
Croke, Cy C., 1452–53
Cross-Channel attack, comments by E. on, 1570–71
CROSSROADS (see also Atomic weapons tests): release of information on, 2019–20, 2048; report of evaluation board, 2045–48
Cross-training among services, 1048–49, 1601
Crowder, Charles W., 945
Crutcher, John Flowers, 101–2
Cryptography: joint U.S.-U.K. planning, 1344; security measures in, 819
Cuba: invitation to E., 985; treatment of representatives, 1713–14
Cub Scouts, 1576–77
Culbertson, Ely, 2086–87, 2162–63
Culin, Frank Lewis, Jr.: Agriculture Department, assignment to, 1741–42; background, 1742
Culzean Castle (see also Gault, James Frederick): apartment presented to E., 483, 496, 540–41, 647–48, 667–70, 792, 1310–11; cottages for veterans at, 668–70, 1310–11; guests welcome at, 1172–73, 1199, 2208; painting by Colville to E., 1964–65; visit by E., 1173, 1313
Cunningham, Andrew Browne, 29–30, 897; background, 30, 48
Cunningham, John Henry Dacres, decoration for, 36
Currency exchange rates: Army Exchange Service role in, 1605–6; Austria, policy for, 386–89, 2200–2201; black market operations in, 244–45, 386–89; cigarettes as medium, 1358; civilians, policy for, 387; finance officers role in, 386–87; Italy, policy for, 389; Netherlands, black market operations, 388; officers, policy for, 387; Poland, policy for, 444; prisoners of war, policy on, 1606; USFET, policy for, 244–45, 386–89, 441; war

dential aspirations, 2191–94, 2197, 2202–3, 2205, 2209–12, 2216–17, 2225, 2227–28, 2232–33; visit with E., 1953, 2203
Finkelstein, Louis, 306–7
Finland, resistance to Soviet attack, 1594
First Deficiency Appropriation Act (1945), 538
Fischl, Ignatius, 1424
Fisher, Grant, 1899–1900
Fitzgerald, Francis Valentine, 77–78; background, 716; retirement, 716–17
Fitzpatrick, Henry Davidson, discharge of, 421–22
Fiume, 58
Flag officers. *See* General officers
Flags, issue to civilians, 991
Fleet admiral, appointment statute, 1145
Fleming, Robert Vedder, 173–74
Flensburg, 95, 97
Fletcher, Cassius Paul, 2147
Flight officers, point credit system for, 345
Florida, hospitalization of E. in, 1367, 1370–71, 1381, 1384, 1392, 1396–97, 1411, 1414–15, 1419, 1423, 1427–29, 1437, 1439, 1444, 1467, 1473, 1523
Flying bombs (*see also* Missiles and rockets): equipment, testing and removal, 144; launching sites, capture and destruction, 143–45
Foggia air base, 840
Fond du Lac, Wis., memorial service at, 1088–89
Food service (*see also* Cooks and bakers schools): as morale factor, 1511; complaints by soldiers, 1117–18; Hennessy report on, 994–96, 1509–12, 2220; improvement in, 995–96, 1509–12, 2220; messes, visits by E., 1313; officers, 901–2
Football, E. views on benefits of, 566–67, 598–99
Football players, point system circumvention for, 656
Forbes, Bertie Charles, 1895
Ford, Hamer Pace, 386–89; background, 388
Ford, Henry, II, 2135
Foreign Liquidation Commissioner: China theater, shipping for, 1054–55; Korea, coast guard for, 1073–74; surplus materiel, liquidating, 1060–61
Foreign Ministers Conference. *See* Moscow Conference of Foreign Ministers
Foreign policy, E. on public information on, 1105–7
Foreign Policy Association, 1535
Foreign service. *See* Overseas tours
Foreign Trade Policy Committee, 1646–47
Forester, Cecil Scott, 924

Forgan, James Russell: background, 130; commendation by E., 129
Formosa, map coverage of, 1368
Forrestal, James Vincent (*see also* Defense, Department of; Navy, Department of the): Alaska theater district engineer, relationship to commander, 1871; arms and equipment, predictions on development and use, 1448; Army-Navy agencies, secretariat to coordinate, 796; Austria, food supplies for, 2143; Bush, armed services reorganization plan, 1039; Commercial Club of Chicago, address by E., 2222; communications systems, security of, 938–40; Defense Department, orientation meeting of executives, 1975–78; Eagle's Nest destruction, 294–95; Edie Co. political developments analysis report, 1906; European Recovery Plan, economic assistance for, 2218–20; final memorandum from E., 2242–57; five-star admirals, postretirement services for, 1145, 1166; general officers grades, disparity among services, 1677; Groves, promotion for, 2108, 2123–24; Guam, reversion to Navy administration, 1056–57; Huie book charges against Navy, 909–10; Latin America, mutual defense plans, 878–79; MacArthur statement on unification, 1087; Marine Corps roles and missions, 1063–64; materiel overstocks, 2068–69; Mediterranean Sea region, naval forces commitment to, 1597; National Security Act, corrections in, 1868; naval air service roles and missions, 1063–64; Negroes, integration policy, 1514–15; Oahu Railway and Land Co. abandonment, 1493; petroleum products storage in abandoned mines, 2071; Princeton Club invitation to E., 1001; psychological warfare, research, planning, and training in, 2062–63; R&D, coordination among services, 707–8; St. Lawrence Seaway, security of, 954–55; Selective Service, extension of, 1520; Soviet ships, sudden clearances from ports, 963–64; tactical air support, command and control of, 2037–39; Turkey, military assistance to, 1592–97; World War II history, joint U.S.-U.K. publication, 1878–80, 2139–40; yacht trip with E., 1842
—air forces: autonomy for, 1063–64; separation from Army, 1914–15
—armed services: roles and missions, 1063–64, 1528–29; unification, 217, 410, 703, 1001, 1062–64, 1282–83, 1466–67, 1633
—atomic weapons: custody and maintenance, 1937–38; destruction of excess stocks, 1827–29; international regulation, 1858
—atomic weapons tests: commission to

Gill, Richard, Jr., 950–51, 1965
Gillem, Alvan Cullom, Jr.: background, 81, 1503; BAMBOO, attendance at, 2207; Boy Scouts executive, nomination for, 1502–3; dinner with E., 1059; Negro troops, report of board on utilization, 672–73; PANDORA, attendance at, 2207; promotion for, 79, 347; Third Army, assignment to, 1670
—China MAG: assignment to, 762–63; decorations for officers of, 2238
Gillette, Edward Clinton, III, 1034
Gillmore, William Nelson: background, 81; promotion for, 80
Gilmer, Dan: background, 1919; evaluation by E. and promotion for, 1919, 2253
Glasgow Ayrshire Society, 973
Glass, Ralph Rigby, 589
Gleeson, William L., 1749–50
Globe Radio Co., 938
Glover, Cato Douglas, Jr., 1818
Godchildren, number for E., 1550
Goddard, Robert Hutchings, 1020
Godfrey, John T., 793–94; background, 794
Goedecke family, 639
Goering, Hermann, 42, 306
Gold, Mitchell, 1379–80
Goldstein, Israel, 415, 417
Goldwyn, Samuel, 131, 208, 243, 1391
Golf, 1729, 1732, 2170
Goodell, Joseph Edward, 900
Good Neighbor Foundation: award to Baruch, 2097; award to E., 2096–97
Good neighbor policy, E. stress on, 1217
Goose Bay, base at, 1416–18
Goren, Charles Henry, 1882–83, 2087; background, 1883
Gorizia, 58, 1313
Gorman, Lawrence Clifton, 1543
Goshaw, George Roland, 1083
Goss, Albert S., 1674
Gousev, Feodor Tarasovitch, 113; background, 113
Government agencies: coordination among, 2253; officials travel in AAF aircraft, 735; permanent assignment for E. proposed, 437, 439; secretariat for, 795–97, 2149
Government employees. See Civilian employees
Governors Conference, 1088
Governors Island, First Army move to, 987
Govorov, L. A., 295
Grace, Porter, 1812
Graham, Charles Lemach, 2160–61; background, 2161
Graham, Emmett Schwedner, 1280, 1744
Graham, Miles William Arthur Peel, 484; background, 484
Graham, Philip Leslie, 1732
Grain exports, Agriculture Department control of, 975

Grandes Conférences Catholiques, 255
Grant, Robert M., 648, 670, 792
Grant, Ulysses Simpson, evaluation by E., 1172, 1372–73
Granville, capture of, 1069
Graves, Sidney Carroll, 2006; background, 2008
Graves registration service, 229–31, 323–25, 1949; assignment of head, 324
Gray, Carl Raymond, Jr., 1904, 1911, 1927; congratulations from E. on VA appointment, 2107–8
Gray, Gordon, 1977
Graybar Electric Co., 372–73
Greater Hessen, civil government in, 117, 494–95
Greatest moment, recollection of, by E., 694–95
Great Falls, Mont., 1870
Great Lakes region, security of, 954–55
Greece: coordination of U.S.-U.K. missions, 2102–4; guerrilla forces, suppression of, 1900, 1998, 2103; Italian attack, resistance to, 1594; MAG for, 1997, 1999–2001; military assistance for, 1593, 1596–97, 1700–1703, 1761, 1900–1901, 1996–2001, 2102–4; military mission, activation, 2185; mission chief, nominations for, 2184–86, 2230; security of, importance to U.S., 1702; troop units, commitment to, 2001; UNO, efforts to end hostilities in, 1999
—Soviet Union: extension of influence in, 1593; pressure on government by, 1900
—United Kingdom: coordination of U.S.-U.K. missions, 2103–4; withdrawal from, 1872, 1900–1901
Green, Clarence McKinley, 1729–30
Green, Dwight Herbert, 992, 1203–4
Green, John Frederick, assignment to Military Academy, 1687
Green, Theodore Francis, 146
Green, Thomas Henry (see also Judge Advocate General): background, 832; Boy Scouts, legality of Army officer on board, 1766; commanders, authority to suppress subversion, 1985–86; five-star generals, retirement of, 1166; military justice, criticism of, 832
Greenbrier Hotel, return to owners, 715–16
Greene, Joseph Ingham, 1197; background, 1197
Greene, Ward, 1807, 2184
Greenland: base rights in, 490–91; security of, importance to U.S., 1298
Greenwich, Conn., contemplated as residence by E., 1910
Greenwich Country Club, membership for E., 1941

Greenwood, Lord: Pilgrims of Great Britain, 313–14

Gregory, Edmund Bristol: background, 713; QMG, nomination for, 712–13; WAC director, nomination for, 757; War Assets Corporation, appointment to and resignation, 714, 1118

Greig, Louis, 2208; Butcher book, indiscretions in, 827–28; letters to and from E., 624–25, 648, 670, 688, 792; W. B. Smith, visit with, 2129; *Sunday Despatch*, letter by E. to, 827–28

Grew, Joseph Clark, 159

Grewe, Henry E., 1262–63

Grey, Irving M., 742

Gridiron Club, 1002–3, 2018

Griffin, Edward, 752

Griffith, Clark Calvin, 1029

Griffith, John Allison, Jr., 1628

Griffith, John Sharpe, 386–89; background, 388

Griffith, Paul Howard, 1839–40; background, 1839

Grimm, Pete, 2195

Griswold, Dwight Palmer, Greece, assignment to, 2104

Griswold, Oscar Woolverton: background, 1670; hospitalization, 1669–70; Third Army, relief from, 1669–70

Grosvenor, Gilbert Hovey, 1386

Ground forces: amphibious operations, role in, 977, 1057–58; officers, allocation to, 1586; roles and missions, 215–17, 339, 369–71, 518, 701, 743–45, 927–32, 976–77, 997, 1057–59, 1360, 1466–67, 1528–29, 2038, 2248

Ground Forces Reinforcement Command, 200

Ground operations, potential developments in, 1448

Groves, Leslie Richard: background, 581, 636, 1497, 1503, 2124; Boy Scouts executive, nomination for, 1502–3; Japanese navy vessels for atomic tests, 581; promotion for, 1386–87, 2108, 2123–24; replacement for, 1104–5; retirement, 1387, 2124

—AFSWP: organization and mission, 1731–32; release of information on, 1497

—atomic weapons: Bikini tests, 919; international regulation, 641, 761–62, 1078; target ships positioning in tests, 919–20; UNO, release of information on, 634–36

Groves, Walter Alexander, 1745

Gruenther, Alfred Maximilian, 678–79, 1117, 2006; ANSC, assignment as deputy commandant, 802; background, 223–24; birthday message from E., 1549; bridge skill, E. on, 552, 2006, 2086; budgets, coordination of missions in, 2053; Chief

of Staff, title as Presidential adviser, 1639; Defense Department, Army representatives at orientation meeting, 1977; Earle, comment on book by, 1512–13; evaluation by E., 2252; Military Academy, nomination as superintendent, 222–24; Parker Pen vice president, nomination for, 989–90, 1161; promotion for, 347; reports of E. Presidential candidacy, 2162–63; Roosevelt (Kermit) Fund, 1385–86

—Joint Staff: assignment as director, 1873–74, 1966, 1970; organization and functions, 1971

Gruenther, Donald Alfred, 224

Gruenther, Grace Elizabeth (Crum), 552

Gruenther, Richard Lewis, 224

Grummon, Arthur Ray, 1184–86

Grunert, George, 630

Guam: demonstrations by soldiers, 752; memorial in, 1691; reversion to Navy administration, 1056–57; troop units strength authorizations, 1057; unified command and missions, 1410–11; visit by E., 1050

Gubbins, Colin McVean: background, 130; commendation by E., 129

Guided missiles. *See* Missiles and rockets

Guided Missiles Committee, 1152

Guide to Germany, 87–88

Gunther, John, 1854–55; background, 1854

Gurley, Fred, 816, 1811

Gurney, John Chandler, 586–87, 1683, 1806–7, 1854

Gurney-Wadsworth Bill, 120

Guzmán Cárdenas, Cristóbal, 984–85

Haakon, King of Norway, decoration for E., 490–91, 492, 515

Haffner, Charles Christian, Jr., 1454, 1522

Hague, The, 417

Haig, Margaret, 687–88

Haight, Edward M., 993–94; background, 994

Haislip, Alice Jennings (Shepherd), 343

Haislip, Wade Hampton: background, 56, 220, 1117, 1342; evaluation by E., 2252; Fourth Army, nomination as commander, 56; Korea, nomination for assignment to, 2100; Personnel Board, assignment to, 342–43; promotion for, 99, 347; quarters for at Fort Myer, 1059; Rhine River crossing, staff work in, 99; Seventh Army, assignment to, 99, 343; soldiers, overseas tour by, 294; Third Army inactivation, 1351; USFIA, assignment as CG, 1342; War Department policies and programs study (*see* Haislip Board)

—Germany: coal and fuel shortage, 281–83; displaced persons, employment for, 281–83; housing shortage, 281–83; lumber and

wood products shortage, 281–83; military government, civilian control of, 220–22; prisoners of war, employment for, 281–83; transportation problem, 281–83
Haislip Board: activation and mission, 1586; budgets, coordination of missions in, 2053; confidence of E. in, 2123–24; membership, 2090, 2124, 2162; proposals, implementation of, 2053; UMT, proposals for, 2053
—general officers: National Guard, promotion policies, 1454; Regular Army, evaluation and promotion policies, 2089–90, 2123–24, 2162
Haiti, decoration for E., 176–77
Hale, Nathan, 1933
Halifax, Earl of. *See* Wood, Edward Frederick Lindley
Hall, Charles Philip: armed services, roles and missions, 1528–29; assignments for, 329, 855, 956–57, 1058; background, 855, 957; Montgomery, training doctrine critique by, 1294–95; officers, allocation to ground forces, 1586; reserve components, RA cooperation with, 1669; supply agencies reorganization, 1315
Hall, Isabel Durand (Mayer), 957
Hall, John, 837
Hall, William Evens, 1618, 1666–67, 1914; background, 1617–18
Hamblen, Archelaus Lewis: background, 1081; retention of grade, 1080–81
Hamburg, air space channel for, 526
Hammer, Olive W., 2054
Hammond, Elton Foster, decoration for, 317
Handy, Thomas Troy: Adcock, promotion for, 261–62; airborne units, postwar retention, 508; Air Force, separate services for, 1667; air forces, UNO maneuvers by, 1083; atomic weapons tests, target ships positioning, 920; background, 82, 331, 336; Bonesteel, assignment as CIG director, 1037; Bor-Komorowski, conference with E., 1107–9; Brazil, national defense college for, 1718; Bush, armed services reorganization plan, 1039; cadet-midshipman cruise, invitation to E., 1846; Camp Peary, Army acquisition of, 1135; cargoes, unloading by union stevedores, 1872–73; Chamberlin, assignment to WDGS, 1059–60; command and control, unified, 1328, 1411–12; commendation by E., 1949; currency exchange rates policy, 388; Dawley, promotion for, 337; dead, repatriation of, 323–25; Deputy Chief of Staff, relief from, 1915; Doolittle, RA commission for, 1079; economy program, stress on, 1240–41; Eichelberger, assignment to Sixth Army, 1329–30; EUCOM, assign-

ment as commander, 2195–96, 2199; evaluation by E., 2252; families, movement overseas, 918; food service, Hennessy report on, 995–96; Fourth Army, assignment to, 980, 1949; Frye, biography of Marshall, 1265–66; General Staff reorganization plan, 1007; Gruenther, assignment to Joint Staff, 1873–74; Haislip, quarters for at Fort Myer, 1059; Hall, assignment to WDGS, 1059–60; Hays, assignment for, 2173–74, 2195–96, 2239; Hoge, assignment to Philippines, 142–43; Huie book charges against Navy, 910; Hull, assignment to AFMIDPAC, 1060–61; Joint Brazil-U.S. Military Commission, pay equalization with Navy, 1349–50; Kilian, promotion denied, 1336; Latin America, mutual defense plans, 878–79; Lee, retirement of, 918; Lichfield courts-martial, 979; Lutes, quarters for at Fort Myer, 1059; McLain, RA commission for, 1079; Military Academy, nomination for superintendent, 223; missiles and rockets, coordination of R&D, 873, 1319; Montgomery, visit to U.S., 1208; NWC, intelligence supply to, 1923–24; naval forces, transport mission, 1177; Navy officers, decorations for, 1319; Okinawa, retention of bases in, 1604; Palestine, establishment of Jewish state in, 1778–79; personal staff of E., assignments for, 2173–74, 2195–96; Philippine Scouts, retention in RA, 1052–53; Philippines, withdrawal from bases in, 1051–53; Poland, military assistance for, 444–45; prisoners of war, repatriation of, 1060–61; reduction in grade, 2228, 2239; progress reports from E. to, 435; promotion for, 347; Regular Army, peacetime organization and strength, 1211; reports, reducing number of, 1694; R&D, centralization in WDGS, 1000, 1045; Ryukyu Islands, administration of, 720, 1056; Secretary of Defense, advisory group for, 1235; Secretary of War, proposals for, 1062–64; Selective Service, extension of, 1321; service commands, inactivation of, 337, 903; service ribbons, separate for ETO and MTO, 81–83; Shanghai Enlisted Men's Committee, 960; Silvester, relief and reduction, 1614; staff officers, college for, 1015–16; Stilwell, hospitalization and death of, 1319; surplus materiel, liquidating, 713–15; tribute to by E., 1949, 2239; United Kingdom, troop units reductions in Europe, 1872; universal military training, 123; Vienna-Klagenfurt-Udine route, armed escort for, 1238; war criminals, postmortem dissection, 925; War Department reorgani-

1104–5; requirements by armed forces, 1954–55
—Groves: promotion for, 2123–24; replacement for, 1104–5
Hickerson, John Dewey, 1108
Hickey, Dale Overton, 778
Higgins, Gerald Joseph: background, 1357; evaluation by E., 2253; Military Academy, psychology and leadership courses at, 1357
High school students: press conference by E., 1463–64; recruiting programs in, 2070
Hill, Harry Wilbur, 1117, 1783–84; background, 802
—ANSC: curriculum proposed, 800–802; student allocations, 803
—NWC: graduation, invitation to E., 1756; intelligence materials for, 1923–24
Hill, Lister, 934–35, 1057–59, 1910; background, 1058
Hill, Luther Lyons, 190–91; background, 191
Hill, Wolfram, 1148–49
Hilldring, John Henry, 609; Assistant Secretary of State, appointment as, 892; background, 283, 620; newsmen, daily releases to, 434
—Germany: coal and fuel shortage, 283; displaced persons, responsibility for, 418; food supplies for, 974; occupation by non-Allied forces, 768
—military government: civilian administration, transfer to, 675–76, 732; civilian head for, 461–63, 478–79; public relations program for, 863–66
Hillenkoetter, Roscoe Henry, 2077–78; background, 2078
Hillman, Sidney, 435, 437; background, 437
Hills, Jedediah Huntington, 632
Hines, John Leonard, 85
Hines, John Leonard, Jr.: background, 86; decoration and promotion for, 85
Hinshaw, David, 847
Hiroshima, atomic bomb dropped on, 204–5, 272
Hirschfeld, Abraham Bernard, 1795
Historical Division, WDSS: activation, 429; mission, 615; Montgomery ETO report, review of, 1224
History, E. on value of studying, 1330–31
Hitler, Adolf, 940
Hitler Youth, 213
Hobart, Percy Cleghorn Stanley, 322
Hobbs, Leland Stanford, 630
Hobert, Chester A., 1590
Höchst, 116
Hocking, John Elwood, 1377
Hodes, Henry Irving: background, 481; command and control, unified, 1362;

economy board chairman, 1240; Frye, biography of Marshall, 1265–66; intelligence reports on domestic situation, 597; missiles and rockets, coordination of R&D, 873; poem sympathizing with generals, 742; reports, reducing number of, 1694; ROTC, horses with units, 1634–35; training programs, troops awaiting discharge, 672; troop units demobilization acceleration, 754
—War Department: movement from Munitions Building, 747; reorganization plans, 481–82
Hodge, Charles, 1728
Hodge, John Reed, 1062; background, 856–57
—Korea: command chain in, 1659; invasion from north, plans for meeting, 1708–10; military government, policy delineation, 1660; political situation, clarification, 856–58; relief from, 2100–2101
Hodges, Carl G., 1420
Hodges, Courtney Hicks: Atlanta homecoming, 22, 96; background, 22, 1835; China, nomination for assignment to, 762–63; Clark, E. N., assignment and promotion for, 1835–36, 1874–76; First Army, assignment to, 980; food service, improvement in, 1509–12; reduction in grade, 2228; SHAEF inactivation, letter from E. on, 187; USFIA, nomination for assignment, 1342
Hodges, Frank, 1957
Hodges, George Hartshorn, death of, 1957
Hodges, James Pratt, 682
Hodgson, Anne, 182, 1752, 2007, 2086, 2235
Hodgson, Paul Alfred, 506, 889–900, 2005, 2008, 2086–87; background, 182
Hoey, Clyde Roark, 2149; background, 1982
Hoge, William Morris: background, 142–43; Philippines, assignment to, 142–43
Holloway, James Lemuel, Jr., 1467–68; background, 1468
Hollywood, investigation of communism in, 2014–15
Holman, Eugene, 1187
Holmes, Julius Cecil, 2129; background, 2130
Holt, Andrew David, 1876
Holt, Hamilton, 1980
Holt, Joseph E., 248
Homecoming plans by E., 22, 60–61, 70, 156, 162–63, 342
Home Insurance Co., 1850–51
Honduras, policy toward, 877
Hoof-and-mouth disease control, 1444–45, 1629, 1831–32
Hoover, Calvin B., 467–69
Hoover, Herbert Clark, 869–70, 973–75,

1562-63
Hoover, John Edgar, 963, 2055; background, 848
Hopkins, Harry Lloyd: Berlin, access to U.S. sector, 166-67, 382-83; background, 1068; death of, 808-10; health, concern by E. over, 406; memoirs publication by E., recommendation for, 406-7; memorial service for, 1067-68; Moscow visit by E., 229; Soviet zone, withdrawal from, 166-67, 382-83; tribute to by E., 1067-68; Zhukov, visit to U.S., 229
Hopkins, Louise Macy, 808-9
Horkan, George Anthony: background, 713, 1163, 1165; decoration for, 628-29; QMG, nomination for, 612; WAC director, nomination for, 757
Horkan, Mary Thompson, 629, 2169
Hornbeck, Stanley Kuhl, 419-20
Horridge, Richard Malcolm, 1007
Horses: budget request for, 1638; elimination from Army, 1634-35; with ROTC units, 1634-35; sales by remount service, 1637-38; at service schools, 1634-35
Hospitalization and medical treatment of E., 357, 430, 501-2, 537-38, 539-45, 549-50, 552, 557, 561, 624-25, 637, 833, 1252-53, 1266-67, 1310, 1337, 1367, 1370-71, 1381, 1384, 1392, 1396-97, 1411, 1414-15, 1419, 1423, 1427-29, 1437, 1439, 1444, 1453, 1457, 1462, 1523, 2054, 2057-58, 2080, 2089, 2094, 2127, 2129, 2188, 2194, 2206
Hospitals, interservice use of, 2249
Hot Springs, Ark., 2106, 2194, 2206
Houghton, Amory: Boy Scouts chief executive, nominations for, 1502-3, 1765-66, 1781-83; Boy Scouts executive conference, E. attendance at, 1816-17
House, Bromley, 1201, 1268-69, 1280-81
House of Representatives: armed services unification, 537, 1683; atomic weapons, national policy for (see May-Johnson bill); commanders, removal of judicial review from, 1790-91; general officers grades, disparity among services, 1677; Greece, military assistance for, 1999, 2001; intelligence agencies, centralization of functions, 1481-83; Japan and Korea occupation, troop units required, 1519; Mexico, hoof-and-mouth disease control, 1742; military justice, changes proposed, 832, 1790-91; OWI budget reduction, 159; Rapido River crossing, criticism of, 981-84, 1172; San Francisco area, investigation of waste in, 2249; Selective Service, extension of, 1014; tactical air support, command and control of, 2038; universal military training, 120, 501, 535, 736; UNRRA, ap-

propriations for, 536-38, 543; USFET, E. as commander, 439; WAC, integration into services, 1853-54; War Department budget, appropriations and curtailments, 1807
—officers: Officer Personnel Act (1947), 1798-99; retired, wartime grades for, 1797-98
Housing programs: civilians on military posts, 842-43; veterans, 834-35, 842-43, 1514, 1533, 1568-69, 1898
Houston, Herbert Sherman, 1990
Howard, Edwin Britain, 678-79; assignment for, 1457-58; background, 390; NWC, assignment to, 1457-58
Howard, George, 649
Howard, Jane Pluck, 390-91, 1457-58
Howard, Nathaniel Richardson, 1002, 1019-20
Howard, Roy Wilson, 1947
Howe, Joe W., 2168; background, 2168
Ho Ying-chin: China decoration for E., 1940-41; thanks from E., 1086
Hoyt, Edwin Palmer, 1882
Huebner, Clarence Ralph, 1345; background, 81, 1341; Berlin, assignment to, 1340-41, 1350; 1st Infantry Division, assignment to, 1894; promotion for, 80, 1506-7; USFET, assignment as deputy CG, 1507
Huff, Marion H., 727, 2226-27
Huff, Sidney Lauren, 727
Hughes, Everett Strait, 517, 540, 1319, 1736-37; background, 390-91; Chief of Ordnance, appointment as, 586; WDGS, appointment to, 585
Hughes, Gladys Wigner, 1665-66
Hughes, John Hendricken, 561
Huie, William Bradford, charges against Navy, 909-10
Hulbert, Elizabeth Gaylor, 1783
Hulbert, Robert, 751-52
Hull, Dale Sayler, 833-34, 1655, 1847
Hull, John Bowler, 2170; assignment as E. aide, 833-34; background, 834, 1218, 1848; illness and retirement, E. concern over, 1847-48
Hull, John Edwin, 609; AFMIDPAC, assignment to, 1060-61; armed services roles and missions, 997; background, 197, 331; CCS, release of E. report to, 1071-72; China MAG, nomination for, 762; China theater, shipping for, 1054-55; evaluation by E., 2252; Guam, administration of, 1056-57; Huie book charges, 909-10; Imperial Defence College, attendance by U.S. officers, 723; intelligence agencies, improving efficiency of, 667; Japanese navy vessels for atomic tests, 580; Latin America, mutual defense plans, 878-79;

Lend-Lease issues, limitations on France, 196–98; Marine Corps roles and missions, 1058; Oahu, joint maneuvers at, 1614–15; Pacific theater, troop units authorizations and reductions, 1061; prisoners, military, guards ages for, 993; promotion for, 347; reassignment of, 329, 404, 472; recruiting programs, standards raising, 1026; R&D, centralization in War Department, 1000; Smith, W. B., assignment as UNO representative, 473; Soviet hostilities, plans for meeting, 1106–7; strategic plans, guide to facilitate, 850; troop units, demobilization acceleration, 754–55
—atomic weapons: international regulation, 642, 1078; test joint task force, assignment as commander, 1995
—UNO: air forces, maneuvers by, 1083; assignment as representative, 472; troop units, signal communications for, 818–19; troop units, weather service for, 820
Hulme, Henry Rainsford, 1686
Humelsine, Carlisle Hubbard, 609
Humphrey, Hubert Horatio, 1569
Hungary, Soviet troop units authorizations, 1563
Hunt, John H., commendation by E., 176
Hunter, Frank A., assignment to ETOUSA, 76–77
Huntington, Ellery Channing, Jr., 1633–34
Huntington, N.Y., 1751, 1939
Hurd, George Arthur, 2138
Hurd, Maud Rogers, 1777–78, 2137–38
Hurley, Patrick Jay, 2050; decoration for, 2050; resignation as ambassador to China, 590
Huse, Doris F., 1114–15
Hutchins, Robert Maynard, 1972–73; background, 1972
Hutchison, Chester, 551
Hutchison, Ralph Cooper, 1781; gift of books to E., 1371–72, 1395–96; Lafayette College, alleged fee to E., 1623–24; Lafayette College degree for E., 852
Hutter, Collie, 1650
Hutter, Howard Joseph, Jr., RA commission for, 1650
Hyde Park, N.Y., 247

I. G. Farben office, 100–101
Iberian peninsula, bridgehead in, 1010
IBM war memorial dedication, 1800–1801
Iceland: security of, importance to U.S., 1298; withdrawal from, 1013
Ichauway plantation, 1760
Ickes, Harold Le Claire: background, 1934; congratulations to E., 589; government service, permanent assignment for E., 437, 439; military government, civilian

control of, 437, 439; Presidency, advice on proposals for E. candidacy, 1933–35, 1954; Sherman, reference to, 1935; Smith, W. B., appointment to National Parks, 473; Summers, commendation by Ickes, 431
Illinois University YMCA, 1450
Imperial Defence College, 723: address by E., 1313; attendance by U.S. officers, 722–24; visit by E., 724; visit to by U.S. officers, 2207
Import-export policy for Japan, 1333–34
Independence, U.S.S., 1181
India: ATC routes to and over, 1304–6; Japanese war criminals in, prosecution of, 738–39; U.S. war effort in, 2230–31
India-Burma theater, troop units strength authorization, 2230–31
Indochina: estimate of French control reestablishment, 744; policy toward, 877; republic proclaimed, 690
Indoctrination programs, E. on importance of, 122–23, 355, 459
Industrial College of the Armed Forces (see also Army Industrial College), 332; command and control, study of deficiencies in, 1329; education, integrating, 802; instructors, diplomas for, 1404–5; mission, 1015; quotas for, 2188; reserve components, quotas for, 2188–89
Industrial mobilization. See Mobilization, industrial
Industry: association with in R&D, 1046–50; E. on contribution to war effort, 2024; officers tours with, 971; scattering as security measure, 1288–89
Infantry Divisions: Pacific theater, policy for assignment to, 219; 1st, 82, 107, 238, 429–30, 1009, 1893–95; 2d, 107, 508, 856, 1871; 3d, 82, 106–8; 9th, 107; 13th (Yugoslav), 64; 28th, 422; 29th, 107; 30th, 107; 35th, 1487, 1685–86, 1698–99, 1719, 1744, 1747, 1759–60; 36th, 82, 107, 290, 775–76, 981–83; 43d, 1129; 45th, 82, 107; 66th, 140; 69th, 107; 75th, 140; 84th, 204, 253; 86th, 141; 88th, 1313, 1943, 1946; 89th, 140; 90th, 107; 91st, 64; 95th, 141; 97th, 141; 100th, 607–8; 104th, 73, 141, 1893–95
Infantry Regiments: 4th, 1114–15; 15th, 964; 19th, 192; 361st, 64
Infantry School conference, 1030
Infantry units. See Ground forces
Inflation, distortion of E. remarks on, 2132–33, 2146, 2183, 2203
Information and Education Division, ETO, 104, 257
Information and Education Division, War Department (see also Information and edu-

cation programs), education program, survey in ETO, 426

Information and education programs, 104–5, 256, 875; Com Z, ETO, 200; films, use in, 104; Germany, 409; implementation, 199–200, 425–26, 459; radio broadcasts use in, 104; schools, number in operation, 426; Soviet Union, indoctrination on, 198–99, 257–58; stress by E. on, 104–5, 199–200, 1486–87; students, number enrolled, 426; suspension of, 875–86; uniform wearing, 1277

Information Bulletin, 257

Ingersoll, Ralph McAllister: background, 1071; book by, comment by E. on, 1070, 1072, 1121, 1131

Ingles, Harry Clyde, 937–40, 1478–79

Inglis, Thomas Browning, 699

Inland Daily Press Association, 2092–93

Insinger, Frederic Nettleton: background, 420; decoration for, 419–20

Inspection tours, E. on value of, 1725

Inspector General, War Department (*see also* Wyche, Ira Thomas): food service, Hennessy report on, 994–95; Lichfield courts-martial investigation, 1334–36; Shanghai Enlisted Men's Committee, 959

Instructors: civilian, procurement of, 875; cooks and bakers schools, 995; diplomas for AFSC and ICAF, 1404–5

Integration of armed services. *See* Armed services, unification of

Intelligence agencies: for atomic weapons, 2047–48; centralization of functions, 697–99, 862–63, 1328, 1481–83; efficiency of, improving, 665–67; national unified, plans for, 666; reorganization plans, 340, 518, 578; stepchild status, 666
—United Kingdom: coordination of functions with, 698; U.S. reliance on, 667

Intelligence Division, WDGS: international communications systems, security of, 936–40; universal military training, 906–7

Intelligence operations and reports: Ardennes counteroffensive, 654; British Chiefs, coordination with, 657; Canada, exchange with, 1688–89; documents captured, use in, 96; domestic situation, 597–98; executive branch, coordination with, 658; France, requests by, 1388; Germany (*see* Field Information Agency, Technical); instruction in, 1328; NWC, supply to, 1923–24; postwar world situation, estimate of, 744; Soviet Union, requirements for, 1106; State Department, coordination with, 658
—Combined Chiefs: coordination among, 657

—JCS: clearance with, 1233–34; coordination with executive branches, 656–58

Intelligence tests. *See* Army General Classification Test

Inter-Allied Governing Authority (*Kommandatura*), 137

Inter-Allied Reparation Agency, 261

Inter-American Conference for Maintenance of Peace and Security. *See* Rio de Janeiro Conference (1945)

Inter-American Conference on Problems of War and Peace. *See* Mexico City Conference (1945)

Inter-American Defense Board: E. address to, 1002–3; hemispheric defense developments, 821–22; Inter-American Military Defense Council, organization and missions, 1657–58

Inter-American Military Agency, 822

Inter-American Military Cooperation Act, 2043–44

Inter-American Military Defense Council, organization and missions, 1657–58

Inter-American Treaty of Reciprocal Assistance. *See* Rio de Janeiro Agreement (1947)

Inter-Governmental Committee on Refugees, 267

Interim International Information Service, 159

Interior, Department of the: Alaska Command, railroad construction in, 1893; Pacific theater, administration of bases in, 1056–57

International affairs, E. comments on, 1130, 1249–50, 1477, 1479, 2014, 2021–22

International amity, E. plea for, 1938, 1953

International Atomic Development Authority, 1078, 1127

International Meteorological Organization, 820

International Military Tribunal, 643

International News Service, 434

International Rapids, 955

International Red Cross, 481

International Relief Organization: UNRRA functions transfer to, 1279

International Telephone & Telegraph Co., 938–39

Interpreter, for E., 258

Interstate Commerce Commission, 1492–93

Invasion of U.S., E. on likelihood of, 849

Inventories. *See* Materiel

Inverchapel, Archibald John Kerr Clarke Kerr, 1206–7, 1241

Investment services offer to E., 1847

Invitations: E. on volume and burden of, 143, 483, 510, 1155–56, 1184, 1460, 1523, 1840, 1851, 2015, 2030, 2079

Joint Committee of Ground, Air and Navy, 795

Joint Committee on New Weapons and Equipment: British committee on guided missiles, U.S. representation on, 1378–79; missiles and rockets, coordination of R&D, 707–8, 872–73, 1030–31; missiles and rockets, Navy test site for, 1031, 1050

Joint Communications Board: joint JCB-JRDB-Aeronautics Board communications systems planning, 1788–89, 1966–67; joint U.S.-U.K.-Canada communications systems planning, 1464–65; UNO troop units, communications service for, 818–19

Joint Export-Import Agency, 442

Joint Intelligence Committee (British), 788

Joint Intelligence Committee (U.S.): activation, 1971; Anderson, quotations from E. by, 1307–8; atomic weapons tests, release of information to U.K., 1146–47; charter revision, 1481–83; dictionary, joint Army-Navy, 1270–71; German documents, access to, 2074–75; intelligence agencies, Army-Navy centralization, 863; mission, 1233; National Archives, access to JCS-CCS war records, 2136; need for, 697–98; scientists and technicians, exploitation and recruitment, 823–24, 1178–79; Soviet Union, report of military mission to, 835–36; State Department representation on, 1482–83; World War II history, citation of JCS documents in, 2099

—intelligence operations and reports: clearance with JCS, 1233–34; instruction in, 1328

Joint Intelligence Group, 1483, 1971

Joint Intelligence Staff: charter revision, 1481–83; intelligence reports, clearance with JCS, 1233

Joint Logistics Committee: Canol, abandonment in Alaska supply, 1383–84; Foreign Trade Policy Committee, JCS representation on, 1646–47; industry, scattering for security, 1289; Korea, coast guard for, 1072–74, 1139–41; Lend-Lease, return of materiel, 595–96; materiel, enemy, requests for, 631–32; mobilization, industrial, strategic guidance in planning, 1582–85; National Archives, access to JCS war records, 2136; naval forces, transport mission, 1177; St. Lawrence Seaway, security of, 955

—Central America; alternate canal routes in, 1706; highways system, improvement of, 1373–74

Joint Logistics Plans Committee: activation, 1971; industry, scattering for security, 1289

Joint Logistics Plans Group, 1971

Joint Meteorological Committee, 820

Joint Military Transportation Committee: Japan and Korea, shipping in support of occupation, 1401; naval forces, transport mission, 1177

Joint Munitions Allocation Committee, 595–96

Joint Planning Committee, 795

Joint Research and Development Board: atomic weapons tests, report of evaluation board, 2046; interservice agency, recognition as, 1868; joint JCB-JRDB-Aeronautics Board communications systems planning, 1788–89, 1966–67; joint U.S.-U.K.-Canada communications systems planning, 1465; missiles and rockets, coordination of R&D, 1152; neuropsychiatric cases, research into, 2083; R&D, coordination among services, 708, 1315; roles and missions, determination by, 2247; U.K. guided missiles committee, U.S. representation on, 1378

—research and development: coordination among services, 708, 1315; security measures in, 1829

Joint Research and Development Committee, 708

Joint Security Control: inactivation, 1971; mobilization, industrial, strategic guides in planning, 1583, 1585; National Archives, access to JCS war records, 2136; Northwest Europe, Report of Operations, publication of, 788; NWC, intelligence materials for, 1923–24; R&D, security measures in, 1829

—atomic weapons tests: commission to evaluate, 961–62; release of information on, 2019–20

—JCS: documents, citation in war histories, 2098–99; documents, downgrading security classification, 1697–98

Joint Staff: activation, 1868; budgets, coordination of services missions, 2052–53; commands, study of missions, 2230; communications systems, joint agency for, 1966–67; Italy, withdrawal from, effect of, 2012–13; organization and functions, 1969–71; reserve components, quotas for joint colleges, 2188–89; troop units, study of allocations, 2230

Joint Staff Planners: antisubmarine operations, plans for, 1583; arms and equipment, potential developments in, 1425; Asia region, commitment of troop units to, 1584, 1604; Atlantic Command, activation, 1967–69; budgets, coordination of services missions, 2053; Canada, mutual defense plans, 1416–18; China, postwar

Kretschmar, Philip C., 1568–69
Krieger, Mary Jane, 551
Krock, Arthur, 994, 1803, 2132–33
Kronberg Castle, 1148–49
Kroner, Hayes Adlai; background, 956; decoration for, 955–56
Krueger, Walter, 630, 1662–63; leave, adjustment of, 1260–61; temporary-duty assignment for, 759
Krupps test center, 144
Kuomintang, activities of, against Communists, 589–90
Kutz, Harry Russell, 561
Kwajalein, 1050
Kyle, William Harvey, 1751

Labor organizations. *See* Unions
Labrador, security of, importance to U.S., 1298
Lacey, Thomas M., 964
Ladd, Florence Von Kanel, 430, 1326, 1708
Ladd, Jesse Amos, 1708; AGF board, assignment to, 1325–26; background, 430, 1326
Ladd Field, 1870
LaFarge, Louis Bancel, 306
Lafayette College, 1623–24; degree for E., 852, 1358, 1365, 1431–32
La Gorce, John Oliver, 1386
La Guardia, Fiorello Henry: background, 171; death of, 2042; New York reception for E., 171–73; relatives removal from Berlin, 544–45; Selective Service, extension of, 778; troop units, demobilization acceleration, 778; UNRRA, reorganization by, 1279
La Guardia, Marie Fisher, 2042
Lahey, Edwin Aloysius, 2183; background, 2183
Lake, Stuart N., 1371–72
Lake Charles, La., 562
Lake Louise, 1870
Lake Superior. *See* St. Lawrence Seaway
Lambert, Betty, 2195
Lambert, Lloyd Washington, 2195
Lambert, Marion J., 1198
Lanahan, Francis Henry, Jr., 517
Landers, Jean Dobbs, 1538
Landing ship, tank: in Japanese army repatriation, 1400–1401; in Bikini tests, 1091–92; in support of Japan and Korea occupation, 1400–1401, 1538–39; unloading railway equipment from, 1927
Landon, Truman Hemple, ANSC, assignment as deputy commandant, 802
Lane, Arthur Bliss, 325, 396, 444–48, 1912–13
Langer, William Leonard, 2139–40
Language school: courses at, proposal for, 781; site, 903

Lanham, Charles Trueman, 609, 670–72; background, 671–72
Lanier, Con, 1982
Larkin, Thomas Bernard, 2006; background, 74, 346, 356; dead, repatriation of, 1501; E. class reunion, 74; flags, issues to civilians, 991; gift to E., 517; point credit system, 354–56; promotion for, 347; QMG, appointment as, 757; Second Service Command, nomination as commander, 346, 356; troop units redeployment program, 354–56; TSFET, assignment as commander, 345–46, 356; uniform, changes in, 1561
Larrabee, Eric, 1630–32
Larsen, Roy Edward, 1920
Larson, Hubert G., 2097–98
Larson, M. Burneice, 1896
Lascelles, Alan Frederick: background, 313, 2184; E. visit to England, 1327; George VI, Christmas message to E., 2183–84; invitations to E., 313; misidentification of son by E., 837; U.K., popularity of E. in, 837
Laski, Harold Joseph, 244
Latin America (*see also* Caribbean Sea region; Central America): Inter-American Military Defense Council, 1657–58; mutual defense plans, 177, 821–23, 877–79, 1094–97, 1147–48, 1300, 1398–99, 1700–1703, 2043; tour by E., 1162, 1164, 1172, 1187, 1192, 1200, 1202, 1208, 1213, 1215, 1217, 1221–22, 1232, 1234, 1236, 1239, 1243, 1247, 1249, 1267, 1271–72, 1285–86, 1287
Lattre de Tassigny, Jean de (*see also* France): Allied Control Commission, formation and signing, 113, 130; background, 7; decoration proposed by E., 19, 35; decoration from Truman, 193; decoration from Zhukov, 135, 138; German surrender, role as signatory, 7, 12; SHAEF inactivation, commendation by E. at, 193
Latvia, displaced persons, repatriation of, 360
Laval, Pierre, arrest of, 231
Lavant River, 65
Leadership: courses at service schools, 593; E. on importance during demobilization, 670–72; improving, studies on, 592–94; lack of seen by E., 934; Military Academy, courses at, 710–11; stress by E. on practice, 1860
League for National Unity, 251–52
League of Nations, 1098
Leahy, William Daniel: background, 13; Biddle, delay in reaching Berlin, 458; Bonesteel, assignment as CIG director, 1037; China, postwar policy toward, 623–24; civilians, travel permits for, 507; command and control, unified, 1411–12;

confidence of Truman in, 2246; Germany, effect of withdrawal from, 2076; Indochina, policy toward, 879; Japanese army, repatriation of, 623–24; Latin America, mutual defense plans, 1702; liaison with E., 576; pushbutton warfare, dispelling impressions of, 1425; Soviet hostilities, plans for meeting, 1157–59; United Kingdom, arms and equipment standardization, 1418–19; UNO, armaments regulation by, 1394

—atomic weapons: bomb, decision to use, 205; excess stocks, destruction of, 1828; international regulation, 1128, 1858; tests, commission to evaluate, 961

—Canada: arms and equipment standardization, 1418–19; mutual defense, plans for, 1416–18, 1702

—Pacific theater: trusteeships for islands, 1100–1101; unity of command in, 1276–77, 1338

Leahy, William E., 171

Lear, Ben: background, 207–8; commendation by E., 207

Leaves: personal use by E., 101, 103, 115, 128, 131, 133, 139, 141–42, 147, 153, 155–56, 161, 163, 225, 326, 352, 383, 899, 1045, 1384, 1950–51, 1953, 2016, 2030,2059, 2095, 2107, 2127, 2129, 2141, 2146, 2175, 2194, 2203, 2206, 2216, 2223, 2233; terminal, policy on, 1260–61, 2196, 2199

Leavey, Edmond Harrison, 1977

Leckie, R. W., 669

Lee, Clark, 1894–95

Lee, Dwight Eisenhower, 1550

Lee, Ernest Rose, 225, 247, 355; background, 77, 142, 227, 546, 927; child, congratulations on by E., 1281–82; commendation by E., 692, 926–27, 1945–46; Creative Age Press, proposal of book by E., 191; decoration for, 582; diary for E., 226; gift to E., 517; godchild, gifts from E. to, 1550; Negro troops, help extended by E., 830; personal affairs of E. handled by, 545–46; Summersby and E. appointments diary, 755; tribute to E., 926–27; Wasserman fund transaction, 471

Lee, Eve B. (Ellis), 918

Lee, Hermien, 927, 1281–82, 1550

Lee, John Clifford Hodges (see also European Theater of Operations, United States Army; Mediterranean Theater of Operations, United States Army): Airey, assignment to SACMED, 1740–41; Antwerp and Liège, presentation of SHAEF award to, 740–41, 918; automobile purchase by E., 496; background, 40, 356, 1502; Blood, assignment to USFET, 1618; Boy

Scouts executive, nomination for, 1502–3; Brown, W. D., services of declined, 413–14; chauffeurs, reports of misuse, 1961; Dasher, nomination for Military Academy assignment, 1618–19; denazification program, 351–52; E. class reunion, 74; extravagant living, charges of, 1943, 1946; France, currency exchange rates policy, 210, 386–89; fraternal organizations, reports of pressure to join, 1961; Gaither, assignment to Trieste, 1618; gift to E., 517; graves registration service, 325; Hamblen, retention in grade, 1080–81; Harding, relief from SACMED, 1740; Italy, consolidating Allied functions in, 838–40; Jaynes, assignment to SACMED, 1618, 1740–41; Legge, assignment for, 1619; Lichfield courts-martial, 1080–81; Magruder, assignment as deputy, 346; Moore, B. E., assignment to Trieste, 1618; Moore, Grace, performances for soldiers, 1173–74; MTOUSA, assignment as commander, 740–41, 918; nonfraternization policy, 127; prisoners, military, reports of mistreatment, 1080–81, 1961; promotion for, 347; recreation facilities, discrimination in, 351–52; Regular Army recruiting program, 476; retirement, 918, 1538, 1544, 1619, 1715–16, 1945, 1947; SACMED, assignment as commander, 1720; St. Paul's Cathedral, memorial to U.S. dead, 446–47, 740–41; Second Service Command, nomination for assignment, 346, 356; SHAEF inactivation, letter from E. on, 187; Sixth Army, nomination for assignment to, 1538, 1544; Soviet ships, sudden clearances from ports, 963; *Stars and Stripes*, censorship alleged, 905–6; Thrasher, position with UNO, 1243; Trieste Free Territory, establishment and boundary delineation, 1720–21, 1740, 1765, 1907–8; troop units, redeployment program, 140–41, 284–85; United Kingdom, tribute to transport workers, 1135; venereal diseases, repression of, 252; Vienna-Klagenfurt-Udine route, armed escort for, 1236–38; visit with E., 1312

—AFHQ: dinner, message from E. to, 1796; inactivation, 838–40

—soldiers: charges of mistreatment, 1942–46, 1961; overseas tours by, 294

—TSFET: assignment as commander, 345–46, 356; commander's authority, scope of, 299–300

Lee, Robert Edward, 1172

Leeds, 313–14

Leeds University, degree for E., 779, 792

Leeper, Kathryn Elizabeth (Blevins): 1621–22

fied command and missions, 1276; armed services unification, 1062, 1064, 1086–87; Asiatic-Pacific Campaign Medal, presentation of first, 2147; assignment offers to, 1338; background, 272; Bonin Islands, command and control, 1411; businessmen, objection to visit by, 718; Chamberlin, assignment to WDGS, 855, 1059–60; Chang Chun, conference with, 1361; China, postwar policy in, 624; Christmas message from E., 1430; CINCFE, scope of command and control, 1410–11; clearance of statements, 799; command and control, unified, 1409–12; comment on by E., 1066; congratulations from E., 271–72; decorations, policy for awards, 1711–13; dual command, SWPA and CINCAFPAC, 860; FECOM, naval command structure, 2010; Formosa, map coverage of, 1368; friction with E., alleged, 2242; Hall, assignment to WDGS, 855, 957; Hoge, assignment to Philippines, 142–43; Hull, assignment to AFMIDPAC, 1060–61; Izu Islands, military government transfer to Army, 720; Jones, assignment as Philippines MAG head, 1243–44; letter of thanks from E., 1065–66; Mariana Islands, command and control, 1411; Marquat, retention in grade, 986; naval forces, control of, 705; Negro troops, assignment to Pacific theater, 1339; Philippine Scouts, troop units strength and pay, 798, 800; point credit system, cuts in, 753–54; prisoners of war, repatriation of, 1060–61; prostitution, suppression of, 699–701; newsmen exclusion message leak, 1412–13; Regular Army, troop units authorizations and reductions, 1713; Richardson Board, testimony at, 1062; Ryukyu Islands, military government administration by Navy, 720; Selective Service, extension of, 1062, 1064, 1080, 1086; Sheridan charges against Eichelberger, 1293; Soviet ships, sudden clearances from ports, 963; training programs, troops awaiting discharge, 670–72; tribute to by E., 2242; troop units demobilization acceleration, 604–5, 753–54; uniform, identical for all services, 556; venereal diseases problem, 252; visit by E., 797, 800, 1065–66; visitors to headquarters, authorization, 717–18; Volcano Islands, command and control, 1411; WAC, integration into regular forces, 1734–35; war criminals, postmortem dissection, 925–26; War Policies Commission report, 181; Whitlock, retention in grade, 986
—China theater: command and control in, 1410–11; shipping for, 1054–55
—general officers: evaluation and reduction,

986; FECOM, assignment to and transfer from, 1661
—Japan: army, repatriation of, 1400–1401; civilian employees, criticism of, 1518; directive on surrender, 690; doctors, prosecution of, 926; import-export policy, 1333–34; industrial facilities, removal from, 1539; invasion, plans for, 1276; military assistance for, 2010; reformation of occupation features, 1520; reparations from, 1539; shipping in support of occupation, 1400–1401, 1538–39; troop units, strength authorizations and reductions, 605, 798–99, 1512–20, 1710, 1958–59, 2214, 2229–30; U.K. withdrawal from, 2163–64; withdrawal from, 1710
—Korea: civilian employees, criticism of, 1518; coast guard for, 1072–74, 1139–41; command termination in, 1659; invasion from North, plans for meeting, 1708–10; military government policy delineation, 1658–60; occupation, necessity for, 1520; police force, equipment for, 1073; political situation, clarification of, 856–58; shipping in support of occupation, 1400–1401, 1538–39; troop units, strength authorizations and reductions, 798–99, 1516–20, 1710, 1746, 1958–59, 2229–30; withdrawal from, 1710
—Military Academy: honor code, 711; Taylor article on, 1754
—officers: retention on active duty, 345; saluting, tradition of, 1059–60
—Pacific theater: command structure and missions, 858–62, 1258–60, 1272–77, 1297–1300; troop units, strength authorizations and reductions, 605, 798–99, 1337–40
—Philippines: bases in, withdrawal from, 1368–70, 1402–4; civilian employees, reduction in number, 1520; conduct of U.S. soldiers, 1338–40; neutrality for, 1403
—SCAP: command authority, 860; separation from Pacific theater, 860–62
MacArthur, Jean Faircloth, 837–38, 1087, 1339, 2242
MacArthur-Northcott Agreement, 2163–64
McAuliffe, Anthony Clement, 2252; background, 333, 2185; Greece, nomination for mission chief, 2184
McCain, John Sidney, Jr., 954
McCann, Kevin Coyle: background, 1515; appointment as Columbia aide, 1758, 1929, 2056–57, 2079
McCarthy, Frank, 419
McCarthy, Joseph Raymond, 499
McCarthy-Morrogh, Vera, 202
McChord Field, 1814, 1871
McClean, C. H., 372

McClean, William R., 373
McClelland, George William, 1455, 1480
McCloy, John Jay, 119; Alexander, comments on by E., 1488-89; atomic weapons, international regulation, 577; Babelsberg meeting, 204; background, 120, 552, 1810; Berlin, French sector delineation, 211; Camp Peary, Army acquisition of, 1134-35; congratulations and tribute to E., 551-52, 1809-10; *Foreign Affairs* article, clearance of, 1888; Germany, coal and fuel shortage, 283; High Commissioner for Germany, appointment as, 552; military government, civilian administration, transfer to, 459, 675-76; *Pocket Guide for Germany*, 529; visit with E., 1810
McClure, James Gore King, 2065
McClure, John Elmer, 1202-3, 2095-96
McClure, Robert Alexis: background, 213, 404, 1764, 2063; gift to E., 517; Murphey, radio job for, 1841-42; PANDORA, attendance at, 2207
—Germany: publications ban, reports of, 44; relaxing controls in, 212-13
—psychological warfare: book on, plans for, 403-4; research, planning and training in, 1764, 2062-63
McClure, Robert Battey: background, 764; China MAG, nomination for, 763-64
McCoach, David, Jr., 538
McConaughy, James Lukens, 1762-63; background, 1763
McCormack, John V., 1376-77
McCormack, John William, 148, 750-51
McCormick, Kenneth Dale, 2160, 2175
McCoy, Frank Ross, 757-59; background, 758-59
McCreery, Richard Loudon, 366
McCutcheon, Currie, 706
McDermott, John A., 1862
McDonald, P. McCracken, 972-73
McDonald, Stuart Clarence, 804
McDuff, Robert Joseph, 615-16; background, 615
McElwain, James Franklin, 2095
MacEwen, Norman Duckworth Kerr, 484
McFarlan, Frederick M., 1787-88
McFarland, Andrew Jackson Briggs, 623-24, 633; background, 576
McFarland, Ernest William, 830-31
McGarraghy, Joseph C., 171
McGeer, Gerald Grattan, 1753
McGhee, Joseph, 147-48
McGovern, John Terence, 1263-64; background, 1264
McGowen, Sheila Burton, 1143-44
McGrail, Thomas Martin, 355, 396, 514; background, 396

MacKay Cable & Wireless Co., 98
McKeldin, Theodore Roosevelt, 200
McKellar, Kenneth Duncan, 159, 988; background, 988
McKelway, Benjamin Mosby, 1796
McKeogh, Michael James (Mickey), 163, 247-48, 838, 1430; background, 31; book by, foreword by E., 176, 519-20; book, parady on, 1113; farewell letter from E., 176; radio tribute to E., 225, 227; visit with E., 563; welfare, E. interest in, 1183-84, 1475-76, 1626-27
McKeogh, Pearl Hargrave, 30, 176, 247, 519-21, 1430, 1475, 1627
McKinney, Walter Hastings, 846-47
McLain, Bernard F., 584
McLain, Raymond Stallings, 362; background, 81, 361-62, 1079; hospitalization, 361; promotion for, 79, 427; Regular Army, commission in, 1079
McLaughlin, H. R., 876
McLean, Robert, 1193, 2131-32
McMahon, Brien, 1730-31; atomic weapons, national policy for, 641, 762, 1101-2, 1354
McMahon, William Claude, 85-86, 502-3; background, 502-3
McMahon Act (*see* Atomic Energy Act)
MacMillan, Harold, 146, 779; background, 146
McMillen, Rolla Coral, 484-85; background, 485
McMillen, Thomas R., 485
McNair, Clare Huster, 1017-18
McNarney, Helen Wahrenberger, 1341
McNarney, Joseph Taggart (*see also* Operations Division, WDGS; United States Forces in the European Theater of Operations): Antwerp and Liège, SHAEF award to, 741; background, 19, 22; civilian schools, students on detached service at, 875-76; civilians, unauthorized confinement of, 1262-63; Clark, assignment as USFIA commander, 87; command and control, unified, 1409, 1458-59; Czechoslovakia, restitution of transportation equipment, 466; ETO, departure from, 150; Fellowship of U.S.-British Comrades, 1122, 1169-70; FIAT, withdrawal from, 817; France, Communist disorders in, 1012; Frankfort, arrivals and departures, 542; general officers, evaluation and reductions, 678; Gibson, visit to USFET, 1477-78; Huebner, promotion for, 1506-7; information and education program, suspension of, 875-86; Italy, U.K. troop units redeployment, 366; Jews, emigration of, 1138; Jodl, clemency for, 1320; Keyes, assignment as USFIA com-

Mangum, Hal L.: Corlett, assignment to hoof-and-mouth disease control, 1831–32; invitations to E., 1200–1201, 1231–32, 1370–71, 1444–45; invitation to John Eisenhower wedding, 1682; Mexico, hoof-and-mouth disease, control of, 1444–45, 1629, 1742; photograph of E. for, 1629; wedding present for John Eisenhower, 1831–32

Manhasset, N.Y., contemplation as residence by E., 1797–98

Manhattan, Kan., visits by E., 816–17, 874, 1870, 2009, 2014, 2030

Manhattan District. See Groves, Leslie Richard

Manhattan Project. See Armed Forces Special Weapons Project

Manila: demonstration by soldiers, 753; extent of destruction, 88–89; visit by E., 1050, 1052

Manitou, Colo., 1935

Manpower (see also Troop units; Universal military training), conservation of, 1185–86

March, Fredric, 1391

March, Peyton Conway, 1431–32

Marcus, Jacob Rader, as Jewish religious leader, 562–63

Marcus Island, trusteeship for, 1097–1101

Mariana Islands: administration of, 587–88; command and control, 1275, 1297–1300, 1338, 1410–11

Marine Corps. See United States Marine Corps

Marquat, William F., 585, 621; background, 585, 621, 987; retention of grade, 986

Marriage to aliens, E. on policy, 179

Marseilles, 299; base operations at, 1573; berth for U.K. shipping, 365; venereal disease rate, 252

Marsh, Daniel Lash, 750–51

Marshall, George Catlett (see also Chief of Staff, U.S. Army; State, Department of; War Department): AAF, strength proposed, 371; ADB conversations, testimony on, 844, 1084; air forces roles and missions, 369–71; air officers, assignment to WDGS, 336; airborne units, postwar retention, 92; Allen, press relations assignment for, 59–60; American Campaign Medal, presentation of first to, 2147; American Legion convention, E. attendance at, 500–501, 535; ANSC activation, 335; Argentina, policy toward, 1468–70; Army, concern over image of, 373; around-the-world flight of B–29 aircraft, 1490; AWC reactivation, 330, 332, 335; background, 13; Baruch, tribute from, 735–36; Biddle, delay in reaching Berlin,

457–58; biennial report by, 391–92; Boston, Armistice Day participation by E., 500–501, 535; Bowen, assignment as SGS, 329–30; Bronze Star, policy on awards, 291–92; Brown, W. D., restoration to grade, 531; Butcher book, War Department clearance, 264; Cannon, homecoming timing, 22; Carter, promotion for, 1610–11; Chicago, invitation to E., 501; chickens, concern over health of, 852, 1131–32; chiefs of arms, bureaus and services, inactivation of, 98, 330, 332, 336, 518; Chief of Staff, assignment of E., 309–10, 328–30; China theater, shipping for, 1053–55; civilian clothes wearing by occupation forces, 377–78; civilians, travel permits for, 507; Clark, homecoming timing, 22; Clay, assignment to State Department, 419; Committee of Three member, 1361; commendation of E. by, 14–15; conference with E., 1059, 1085–86; Conference of Foreign Ministers, attendance at, 1523; confidence in E., 482, 1008; Copenhagen, visit by E., 515; Council of Foreign Ministers, attendance at sessions, 1468–69, 1492, 2166; Cuba, treatment of representatives, 1713–14; Davis, assignment as ATAG, 336; decorations policy for foreign officers, 19; demobilization, personal touch in, 670; Deputy Chief of Staff, air officer assignment as, 336; Devers, homecoming timing, 22; De Witt, successor for at ANSC, 331–32; Dill Memorial Committee, 945; dinner by E., attendance at, 1665; displaced persons camps, inspection of, 458–59; divisions, number required in peacetime, 369; Doolittle, promotion for, 428; Eichelberger, nomination for Deputy Chief of Staff, 336; Eisenhower, J. S. D., accompanies E. to U.S., 133, 139; ETO, absorption of ComZ proposed, 97–98; executive branch, coordination of intelligence with, 658; expenses fund allotment, 1112; families, joining ETO troops, 134–35, 150, 474–75; Fitzpatrick, discharge of, 422; flying bombs, launching sites destruction, 143–45; Formosa, map coverage of, 1368; Frye biography, 1265–66; garrisons overseas, manning, 369; Germany, permanent assignment of E. to, 435, 437; Gillem, assignment to China MAG, 762–63; graves registration service, 229–31; ground forces roles and missions, 369–71; Handy, reassignment of, 331; Henry, relief from G–1 assignment, 393; Hines, decoration award and promotion for, 85; Hodge, retention in Korea, 2100–2101; homecoming tour plans for E., 22, 156, 162–63; ill-

cancer research, interest in, 943; coin for Marshall, 93–94; gift to E., 1719; invitations to E., 254, 1184; Kansas State College, endowment for, 911–12, 942–44; Ross, admission to George Washington University, 1825, 1838–39; toys, gifts to Army children by, 2102; visits with E., 1665, 1716, 1748–49, 2101–2

Marx girls, 1838–39

Masaryk, Jan Garrigue, 457

Massachusetts, Fort Devens transfer to, 1129–30

Massigli, René, 320–21

Mast, Charles Emmanuel, 1733–34

Masters, Harris Kennedy, 1863

Matchett, Henry Jeffrey, 1927–28, 2006; background, 1928

Materiel (see also Arms and equipment, or by type): ANMB, procurement by, 2249–50; disparity in apportioning to services, 2254–55; enemy, requests for, 630–32; Lend-Lease, return of, 594–96; overstocks of, 2068–69; procurement, E. on economy in, 2249–50; reserve stocks, destruction of, 2255; surplus (see also War Assets Administration), inventory value, 714; surplus, liquidation, sale and loan, 464–67, 603, 713–15, 798, 1060–61, 1862

Mathews, Frank Asbury, Jr., 689–91

Matthews, Frederick S., 317

Matthews, H. Freeman, 316

Matthews, Ronald Wilfred, 240–41

Maud, John Primatt Redcliffe, 2127, 2137; background, 2128

Maunsell, Raymund John: background, 112
—FIAT: role in administration, 111–12; U.S. withdrawal from, 817

Maxwell, Russell Lamonte, 609

Maxwell Field, 1645

May, Andrew Jackson: atomic weapons, national policy for, 1101–2; court-martial sentence, investigation of, 1683; Fitzpatrick, discharge of, 421–22; Rapido River crossing, criticism of, 983; trial, subpoena served for, 1682–83

Maybole, Scotland, 1313

May-Johnson (atomic energy) bill, 577, 1101–2

Mayer, Arno J., 945–46

Mayfield Baptist Sunday School, 991

M-Day, defined by E., 745

Mead, James Michael, 684, 851–52, 867–68

Meader, George, 1498

Meadows, Clarence Watson, 715–16, 1942

Medical Corps: commissions in, policy on, 533; legislation for improving attractiveness, 1849; qualifications for chief, 1413–14

Medical officers: civilian professors to train, 1849; qualifications for, 1628–29; shortage of, relieving, 1618, 1623, 1625

Medical services: amalgamation of federal agencies, 1580, 1617, 1623, 1624–26; interservice use of, 2249; separate for Air Force, 1616–18

Medical technicians, point credit system for, 345

Mediterranean Allied Air Force, 63

Mediterranean Sea region: lines of communication, safeguarding, 1581–83, 1593–94; naval forces commitment to, 1597; pipeline route from Persian Gulf, 2002–3; security of, importance to U.S., 2013; Soviet bases in, 1013; Soviet threat to, 1900; submarine threat in, 1584; U.K., decline of influence in, 1593

Mediterranean Theater of Operations, United States Army (see also Lee, John Clifford Hodges; McNarney, Joseph Taggart): inactivation, 840; inactivation, E. message on, 1796; investigation of soldiers's treatment, 1942–47, 1960–61; lines of communication, safeguarding, 1583–84; memorial for campaigns in, 1690; naval command activation, 1967–69; reenlistment rate, 1943; separation from AFHQ, 405

Medjez-el-Bab, E. on defense of, 1307–8

Mein Kampf, 509

Melberg, Reinold, assignment as military attaché, 769

Memoirs of E.
—negotiations for publication and serialization: American Newspaper Alliance, 2151–52; Barker, Le Baron, Jr., 855–56; Bye, George T., 204, 243, 1956; Canfield, Cass, 243, 406–7, 2184; Davies, Joseph Edward, 2148, 2153, 2159–60, 2174–75; Doubleday & Co., 243, 855–56, 1994, 2159–60, 2174–75, 2184; Greene, Ward, 1807, 2184; Harper & Brothers, 243, 406–7, 2184; Lippincott (J. B.) Co., 204, 243; McCormick, Kenneth Dale, 2160, 2175; New York Herald Tribune Syndicate, 1994, 2148, 2153, 2159–60, 2174–75, 2184; New York Times Co., 2184; North American Newspaper Alliance, 243, 2184; Quinzburg, Harold K., 2151; Robinson, William E., 1994, 2148, 2153, 2159–60, 2174–75, 2184; Saturday Evening Post, 2130–31, 2148; Schuster, Max Lincoln, 203–4; Simon, Richard Leo, 1151, 1222–23, 2148, 2204; Simon & Schuster, 203–4, 243, 516, 2148; Wheeler, John Neville, 2151–52, 2184; Williams, John L. B., 2151
—tax aspects, 2153, 2160, 2174–75, 2183

—administration and authority, division of, 165–66; inefficiency in charged, 434
—SCAEF: enactments on, 132; responsibility for, 68, 150–51
—State Department: policy on, 482; transfer of administration to, 462, 675–76, 729–33
Military Government Weekly Information Bulletin, 434
Military Intelligence Division, War Department, reports on domestic situation, 598
Military justice (*see also* Courts-martial): appeal rights under, 791; changes proposed, 832, 1790–91; clemency and review under, 1496; commanders, removal of judicial review from, 1790–91; criticism of, 660, 767–69, 831–32, 863–66; study by American Bar Association, 831–32
Military occupation specialties, critical categories, 345
Military Order of the Purple Heart, 2009
Military Order of the World Wars, membership for E., 816–17, 874
Military Personnel Procurement Service, 1025–26
Military policy: proposals by E. for postwar, 214–17; role by E. in, 575–77
Military Staff Committee, UNO: air forces, maneuvers by, 1082–83; armaments regulation, 1392–94; JCS representation on, 1780–81; organization and mission, 473; Security Council, additional members for, 633–36
—atomic weapons: effect on armed services organization, 760; international regulation, 1552, 1077–79, 1093, 1128
—troop units: command and control, 1021–23; commitment to UNO, 1190, 1936–37; signal communications for, 818–19; weather service for, 820
Miller, Dale, 793, 1975
Miller, Ernest Frederick, 1213, 2209; background, 1213
Miller, Francis Trevelyan, 189–90
Miller, Harold Blaine, 910
Miller, Henry Jervis Friese, reduction in grade, 1600
Miller, Lois Mattox, 1112–13
Miller, Luther Deck, 1977–78
Millikin, Eugene Donald, 1498
Mills, Katherine, 2061
Milton, Hugh Meglone, II, 2059–60; background, 2059–60
Miltonberger, Butler Buchanan: background, 1204; retirement, 1762
Milwaukee Journal, 1963
Mines, abandoned, petroleum products storage in, 2071
Ministerial Control Center, 96

Ministerialrat, 118
Ministry of Information (British), 245–46
Mink, Samuel J., 2005
Minneapolis, Minn., visit by E., 1835, 1851, 1904, 1909, 1911, 1981
Minneapolis Club, 1835
Minneapolis Tribune, 115
Minnesota State Fair, visit by E., 1835, 1851, 1904, 1909, 1911, 1981
Minocqua, Wis., visit by E., 1198, 1745, 1820–21, 1910
Minor, Harry S., 992
Mintener, James Bradshaw, 2171–73; background, 2172
Missiles and rockets: Germany, launching sites destruction, 143–45; international regulation, 1485; JB-2 system, 790–91; Navy Department test site for, 1031, 1050; operation, responsibility for, 789–90; potential developments in, 578, 1448; Soviet development, estimate of, 744; test sites for, 1030–31
—research and development: coordination of, 789–90, 872–73, 1030–31, 1152–53, 1319; responsibility for, 1152–53
—United Kingdom: collaboration with, 1378–79; committee on, U.S. representation on, 1378–79
Missing persons, searches for, 751–52
Mission Hills Country Club, 1744
Missouri Pacific Railroad, 172
Mitchell, Curtis, 246
Mitchell, William De Witt, 843–44
Moaney, John Alton, 1183, 1475, 1717–18; background, 545–46, 991; Columbia, detail to, 2174; personal affairs of E., care of, 545, 547
Mobilization, industrial: planning for, 2067–68; security measures in planning, 1583; strategic guidance in planning, 1581–85, 1606, 1609–10; War Policies Commission report on, 180–81
Mobilization, military: AUS, plans for future, 742–45; interference with by enemy, 2156–57; M-Day defined by E., 745; manpower, effect on, 2253; million-men-springing-to-arms fallacy, 2255; National Guard, strength required for, 811; periodic increments in, 849; plans for future, 121–23, 742–45, 850; public conception of, 2255; regional plan, 851; shipping needs, review of, 2068; speed required, 1694; time required, 908; total, need for, 849–50, 2215; transport aircraft, number available for, 1947–48; troop units, number required, 1011, 1441
—Regular Army: future plans for, 742–45; mission in, 743; numbers required, 811
—reserve components: numbers needed, 811, 1441; plans for future, 1669, 2259

program, 814–15; maintenance programs, 105
Morale Services Division, War Department, 529
Moravska Ostrava, 287
Morcom, James Stewart, on soldier's opinion of E., 349–50
Morgan, Frederick Edgworth: background, 18, 85; book by, foreword by E. and clearance, 1450, 1597–99, 1663–64, 2165–66; Brown, commendation by Morgan, 1278–79; Christmas message from E., 2166; commendation by E., 17; confidence of E. in as UNRRA administrator, 722–23; decoration for, 19, 35; Fellowship of U.S.-British Comrades, 1170; Germany, food supply situation, 54; Jews, migration into U.S. zone, 723; Presidency, proposal of E. candidacy, 2165–66; reassignment of, 84–85; SHAEF inactivation, letter from E. on, 187; UNRRA, assignment to and relief from, 85, 1279; visit with E., 1184
Morgan, Hugh J., 699; background, 700
Morgan, Kay Summersby. See Summersby, Kay
Morgan, Thomas Alfred, 1187
Morgan, Thomas Ellsworth, 1862
Morgan, William Duthie (see also Mediterranean Theater of Operations; Supreme Allied Commander, Mediterranean): AFHG inactivation, 839; Alexander, attendance at Army-Navy game, 1884; background, 64, 412, 2104; British Joint Staff Mission, assignment to, 2023, 2104; Greece, coordination of U.S.-U.K. missions, 2102–4; Hamblen, retention in grade, 1081; Trieste, dispute over, 839; Venezia Giulia, dispute over, 839–40
—SACMED: assignment as, 64, 412; British preference for as deputy, 405
—Yugoslavia: ammunition supply to, 1348–49; intelligence reports on, 839
Morgan Line, establishment in Venezia Giulia, 64, 1721
Morgantown, West Va., 1942, 1952, 1957
Morgenthau, Henry, Jr., 2122–23; plan for Germany, E. disassociation from, 424–25, 529–30, 1877–78
—book by: on treatment of Germany, 424–25, 1877–78; Roosevelt use of, 424
Morgenthau plan, 1877–78
Morningside Drive, residence for E. at, 1916–17, 1921, 2122
Morris, Brewster Hillard, 327
Morris, George Maurice, 2180
Morris, Milton Arthur, 991
Morris, William Henry Harrison: background, 1351; USFIA, nomination as commander, 1350–51

Morrison, Leo, 131, 209, 349, 510
Morrison, Ray, 598–99
Mortgage Bankers Association, 2011
Moscow, visit by E., 31–32, 135–38, 228–29, 246–47, 258, 262, 271, 284, 292, 295, 342, 352, 1530
Moscow Conference of Foreign Ministers: Far Eastern Commission, activation, 731; UNO, commission on atomic energy, 634–35
—Germany: hostilities by, collective defense against, 1604; occupation, troop units strength authorizations, 1562–63
Moscow Declaration (1943), 58
Moseley, George Van Horn, 585, 595, 791–92, 1904–5
Moses, Herbert, 1272
Moses, Raymond George, 637
Mothers, tribute to, by E., 1665–66
Motor convoy, E. role in transcontinental test (1919), 1952
Motor vehicles (see also by type): driving, caution by E. on, 528; unauthorized use of, 1945, 1959–61
Mount, William H., 585
Mountbatten, Edwina Cynthia Annette (Ashley), 596–97, 719
Mountbatten, Louis Francis Albert: background, 99, 1575, 1992; congratulations from E., 99, 272; congratulations to E., 596–97; disloyalty against, 1084; Pogue interview, E. comments on, 1570–71; SEAC report, review and publication, 1083–85, 1355, 1991–92, 2230–32; Stilwell, friction with, 2230; on U.S.-U.K. amity, 596–97
Mountbatten, Philip, 2039
Mount Eisenhower, 747
Mount Rainier, Md., 2186–87
Mount Union College, 1220
Mudge, Verne Donald: Agriculture Department, assignment to, 1741–42; background, 1742
Mueller, Merrill, 88, 1507–9; decoration for, 1852–53
Mueller, Nancy, 785
Mulde River, 8, 125
Muller, Walter Joseph, 317; decoration for, 317
Mundt, Karl Earl, 437, 439
Munich, 71, 97, 306; denazification program in, 392; visit by E., 1313
Munitions Building, War Department movement from, 747
Münster, 151
Murphey, Harvey Dixon; background, 1842; radio job for, 1841–42
Murphy, Marian M., 644–45
Murphy, Robert Daniel, 2200; background, 133; Darlan agreement, account of, 1303;

588, 1056–57; unified command in, 1276–77, 1299–1300
—research and development: coordination among services, 707–8; security measures in, 1829
Nazis, reported coddling, 71
Neal, Benjamin Edwards, 2096–97
Nebraska State Fair, 917
Negro troops (*see also* Race relations): Doolittle Board, lack of representation on, 985–86; enlistments suspended, 1339; feeling of E. toward, 764–65; help extended to by E., 830; integration, opposition to, 672; National Guard, desegregation in, 1515; Navy Department integration policy, 1514–15; Pacific theater, assignment to, 1339; report of Gillem Board on, 672–73; segregation and integration, 672, 1514–15; transfer to labor units, 830; Truman desegregation order, 1515
Nelson, Horatio, 1422
Netherlands: currency exchange rates, black market in, 388; German surrender in, 10; SHAEF inactivation, E. tribute to on, 185; UNO, nomination as nonpermanent member, 633–34
Netherlands East Indies: Japanese army, repatriation from, 690; military jurisdiction by SEAC, 689–91; prisoners of war and internees in, 690–91
Neumayr, Friedrich Wilhelm, 1637–38
Neuropsychiatric cases, E. on research into, 2082–84
Neville, Robert, 934
Nevins, Allan, 2139; background, 2139
Nevins, Ann, 430, 1813
Nevins, Arthur Seymour, 430; advice from E. on employment, 1221; background, 35, 430, 1221, 2182; Czechoslovakia, U.S. troop units strength in, 452–53; gift to E., 517; memoirs, association with, 1813, 2181–82; testimonial from E. for job, 1813; troop duty, assignment to, 34
New America, 1615–16
Newcomb, Paul, 562
Newfoundland: security of, importance to U.S., 1298; motor vehicles, illicit sale of, 1149; visit by E., 247
New Hampshire, Republican pledge to E. in primary, 2191–94, 2202–3, 2205, 2209–12, 2216–17, 2225, 2227–28, 2232–33
New Mexico, 2146
New Mexico Military Institute, 2059–60
New Orleans, La., 144
New Republic, proposal of articles by E., 493–94
News and information services, E. on control of, in Germany, 158–59
Newsmen (*see also* Censorship): announce-

ments to, 515; atomic weapons tests, representation at, 1089–90; British, criticism of E. by, 326; censorship, charges by, 865–66; comments on by E., 82, 104, 114–15, 1987; criticism of E. by, 433–35, 436–37, 439, 483, 1375–77; daily releases to, 60, 433–35, 515; decorations for, policy on, 1852–53; denazification program, criticism of, 308; Eichelberger, unfavorable reports on, 1546; FEC tour exclusion message leak, 1412–13; nonfraternization program, criticism of, 39–40, 42; freedom of expression for, E. insistence, 44; French, criticism of E., 532; German surrender, discontent over news release, 13; Japan tour by, 1803; leaks to, 909, 1364; MacArthur exclusion message leak, 1412–13; military government policies and practices, improving image of, 863–66; OMGUS, relations with, 865–66; periodic reports to, 60, 433–35, 443–44, 1641; publications ban in Germany, criticism of, 43; pushbutton warfare, dispelling impressions of, 1424–25; relations with, improving, 1032–34; service troops, commendation of treatment by, 253; Smith, W. B., commendation of, 2129; soldiers' conduct, criticism of, 529; tribute by E. to, 172–73, 497
—Soviet Union: criticism of U.S., 1609–10; exchange with, 522–23, 526, 559; visit to U.S. by, 998
Newsome, Florence T., 576
Newspaper, offer of publishing job to E., 1530
Newspaper Guild, 497
Newspapers, Army, criticism of, 1033
Newspapers, civilian. *See* Newsmen
Newsreel, 1114
New York, U.S.S., 1181
New York Central Railroad, 172
New York City: dislike of by E. as home, 1757, 1759, 1775, 1799, 1837–38, 1884–85; move to, 2122, 2191, 2198, 2224, 2234; Soviet ships, sudden clearance from, 963; visits by E., 162–63, 171–73, 953, 975, 1002–3, 1035, 1187, 1370, 1462, 1472, 1530, 1535, 1716, 1737–38, 1748–49, 1756–57, 1759–60, 1816, 1839, 1851, 1890–91, 1895, 1897, 1903, 1920, 2058, 2080–81, 2097, 2102, 2145, 2188
New Yorker, 75–76, 1883
New York *Herald Tribune,* 389, 2150
New York Herald Tribune Forum, 302–3, 392, 409, 478, 1350
New York Herald Tribune Syndicate, 1994, 2148, 2153, 2159–60, 2174–75, 2184
New York Times, 42, 50, 123, 171, 246,

information on, 2020, 2048; target ships positioning, 919–20; United Kingdom, release of information to, 1146–47

—Canada: ally, question of position as, 2158; arms and equipment standardization, 1418–19; mutual defense plans, 1416–18

—Japan: army, repatriation of, 1400–1401; occupation, shipping in support of, 1400–1401, 1539; prisoners of war, repatriation of, 1061

—JCS: agencies of, staffs augmentations and reductions, 1606–8; documents, downgrading security classification, 1698

—Korea: coast guard for, 1074, 1139–41; occupation, shipping in support of, 1400–1401, 1539

—Marine Corps: aviation, continuance of, 930; roles and missions, 702, 704–5, 932, 997, 1057; troop units strength authorizations, 932

—naval forces: operations by, future applications, 1360; roles and missions, 702, 927–32, 977, 997, 1360

—Pacific theater: command structure and missions, 858–62, 1258–60, 1276–77; trusteeships for islands, 1099–1101

—United Kingdom: arms and equipment standardization, 1418–19; atomic energy plant in, effect on U.S. security, 1525–26; guided missiles committee, U.S. representation on, 1378–79

1925 F Street Club, 2132–33, 2146, 2183, 2203

Nixon, Thomas Hay, decoration for, 317

Noble, Edward John, 2065–66; background, 2066

Noble, Robert Ernest, 599

Noce, Daniel, 378, 1836; background, 1836

Nome, Alaska, 1871–73

Nonfraternization program: Austria, 178–79; Germany, 40, 87–88, 105, 126–27, 177–79; newsmen criticism of, 39–40, 42

Nordhausen Caverns, flying bombs launching site, destruction of, 143–45

Norfolk, Va., 2223

Normandy campaign: Bradley role in, 1069, 2040–42, 2234; British Army role in, 1069; Canadian army role in, 1068–72; commemoration of, 127–28, 1114; comments on by E., 1058, 1570–71, 2165; Dempsey role in, 1068, 1071; development of plans for, 1598–99; justification of conduct, 1068–72; memorial to, 1691; Montgomery role in, 423–24, 1068–72, 1571–72; security measures in, 456–57; SHAEF direction of, 1572; 6th Army Group link-up with, 1573, 1575

Norris, John G., 1948

Norstad, Lauris: Armed Forces Special Weapons Project, release of information on, 1497; armed services unification, 1063–64, 1283, 1466–67; arms and equipment, international regulation, 1483–86; background, 790, 2064; cadet-midshipman cruise, invitation to E., 1846; cemeteries in foreign countries, 1689–91; China, military assistance to, 1702; commendation by E., 2063–64; Darlan agreement, confirmation of, 1303; deceptive measures, research and training in, 1763–64; Defense Department chief executive, nomination for, 2243; Fellers, nomination for Philippine MAG head, 1244; Greece, MAG for, 2000; Japan, prisoners of war repatriation, 1061; Marine Corps roles and missions, 1283; monuments in foreign countries, 1689–91; naval air service, antisubmarine role, 1283; Okinawa, retention of bases in, 1603–4; Pacific theater, unity of command in, 1299–1300; Palestine, establishment of Jewish state in, 1778–79; Philippines, military assistance for, 1608–9; promotions for, 1977; Ryukyu Islands, withdrawal from bases in, 1603–4; psychological warfare, research, planning and training in, 1763–64; staff officers, college for, 1015–16; UNO, commitment of troop units to, 1936–37

—air forces: roles and missions, 790–91; UNO, maneuvers by, 1083

—atomic weapons: international regulation, 1078, 1128, 1678; custody and maintenance, 1937–38

—Soviet Union: hostilities by, joint U.S.-U.K. plans for meeting, 1354; hostilities by, plans for meeting, 1157–59

North, Dorothy Gatewood, 1962

North, Earl, 1961–62; background, 1962

North, Thomas: background, 788, 1223, 1254; Encyclopedia Britannica, article for, 925; Marshall reports, role in, 925; Montgomery ETO report, review and publication, 1224; Normandy campaign, changes in official history of, 1071; Rapido River crossing, comment on, 983; St. Paul's Cathedral, memorial to U.S. dead, 1253–54; World War II history, joint U.S.-U.K. publication, 924

North Africa campaign: commemoration, 529; E. on cross-Channel attack, 1376–77, 1571; E. on forebodings over, 2166; memorial for, 1690; rebuttal by E. to Middleton account, 1374–77; surviving associates of E., 1717; U.S.-U.K. roles in, 2111–12

North America, confinement of operations to, 849

motion and retirement, 174–75, 248–49, 511, 779–83, 1191, 1631; female, fraternizing with enlisted soldiers, 29; fraternal organizations, pressure on to join, 1944, 1959–61; ground forces, allocations to, 1586; hospitalized, promotion policy, 1007–8; industry tours for, 971; Imperial Defence College, attendance at, 723; inept, eliminating, 780–81, 1008–9, 1324; JAG commissions, policy for, 533; JCS, assignment to, 2245; mess arrangements, 901–2; misconduct charges against, 1109–10; morale and efficiency, improving, 814–15; Navy General Line School, attendance at, 897–98; Officer Personnel Act (1947), 1798–99, 1822; overseas tours, policy on, 1324, 1455–56, 1462, 1611–12, 1615; Patterson tribute to, 2167; privileges, soldier grievances against, 902; promotion policies, 781, 985, 1008, 1195, 1631, 1798–99; public statements, E. caution on, 1948; quarters, exclusion of women from, 1100; redeployment program, 345; resignations, policy on, 2169; retired, wartime grades for, 1797–98; saluting, tradition of, 1059–61; scientific training for, 1046–50; specialists, retention in service, 319; strength authorizations and reductions, 1215, 1807; time in grade for promotion, 782; training, E. tribute to, 20; tribute by E. on war service, 951, 1860
—AAF: allocation to, 1585–87; commissions, policy on, 1167–68; WDGS, assignment to, 336
—AUS: number in war service, 649, 951; release of, 1323–24
—efficiency reports: basis for promotion, 1283; first recorded, 1219
—enlisted soldiers: percentage commissioned, 948; relations with, 649–50, 933–34, 948–50, 951–52, 1003, 1026–27, 1031–32, 1033, 1159
—foreign: decorations and awards policy, 19; treatment of, 1713–14
—German: fraternization with, 39–43, 126; preferential treatment alleged, 1908
—living standards: criticism of, 1563–66; improving, 2254
—medical: commissions, policy on, 533; relieving shortage of, 1625
—National Guard: civilian clothes wearing by, 1504; commissions, policy on, 533, 936–37, 1589–90; percentage commissioned in AUS, 948; promotion, policy on, 1203–4
—nurses: commissions, policy on, 2014–15; fraternization with enlisted soldiers, 29, 93
—Regular Army: allocation to, 1585–87;

commissions, policy on, 533–34, 781–82, 934–35, 1650, 1684–85, 1862, 2224; inept, eliminating, 782; integration into, 1684–85; strength authorizations and reductions, 781, 783, 815, 1119–20, 1585–87, 1798–99
—reserve components: commissions, policy on, 533, 937; percentage commissioned in AUS, 948; return to active duty, 958
Officers' clubs, eligibility for membership in, 2008
Officers Reserve Corps. See Reserve components; Reserve officers
Ogilvie, Eain G., 172
O'Hare, Joseph James, evaluation of and promotion for, 2237–38
Oil supplies. See Petroleum products
Okinawa: retention of bases in, 1602–4; troop units strength authorizations, 799; trusteeship for, 1099; visit by E., 1056
Old, Archie, 1056
Old Guard of New York City, 1424
Oliphant, Elmer Quillen, 506–7, 551; background, 506
Olympics Association, 1263–64
Omaha, Neb.: Army facilities for civilian use, 1130; homecoming for E., 156; service command inactivation, 903
Omaha Beach, landing at, 1058
Omurtak, Salih, 1920
O'Neal, Emmet, 485
Operations Division, WDGS (see also Handy, Thomas Troy; McNarney, Joseph Taggart; War Department; War Plans Division): AAF organization and strength, postwar, 680; ANSC curriculum, 802–803; armed services roles and missions, 997; atomic weapons, international regulation, 641; China, map coverage of, 1367–68; Fairchild-Noce board report, comments on, 796; Japanese troops, use against Java insurgents, 690; reliance by E. on, 575–76; shipping, priorities for, 317–19; Stars and Stripes, censorship alleged, 906; stragetic plans, guide to facilitate, 849–51; universal military training, 906–7; visitors to headquarters, authorization for, 718; war criminals, prosecution of, 644; World War II history, joint U.S.-U.K. publication, 924
—atomic weapons tests: security of, 920; target ships positioning, 920
—UNO: Security Council, additional members for, 633; troop units, command and control, 1023
Opinion poll on Soviet Union, 257
Oppenheimer, Bernard S., 1795
Orange Bowl game, 1439
Ord, Emily, 175

Ord, James Basevi, 175
Order of Yun-Fei, decoration for E., 1940–41
Ordnance Department, R&D responsibility for missiles and rockets, 790
Ordway, Godwin, Jr., 1873
Ordway, John Gilman, 1904
Organization of American States: activation, 1658; charter adopted, 822
Organized Reserves. *See* Reserve components; Reserve officers
Orne River, drive to, 1069
Osaka, 699
Osborne, Lithgow, 431, 491
Osborne, Ralph Morris, 112
Oslo, visit by E., 483, 490–91, 492, 515
Osobka-Morawski, Edward Boleslaw, 444–45; background, 292–93
Osteopathic Profession, 733
Ostraw, 287
Our World, 830
Outdoors life, E. on benefits of, 2025
OVERLORD. *See* Normandy campaign
Overseas service, E. attitude toward, 1221
Oxford University, degree for E., 247, 314, 380, 445–46, 481

Pacific Air Command, United States Army, 861, 1065–66
Pacific Fleet: CINCPAC, separation from, 1412; command and control, 1298; congratulations from E., 271
Pacific National Exhibition, 1753
Pacific Ocean Areas, Navy command and administration, 860
Pacific theater: air defense units, policy for assignment to, 219; air forces, command and control of, 858, 861; armored divisions, policy on assignment to, 219; assignment to, policy for, 219; bases, administration of, 587–88, 720, 1056–57, 1099–1101, 1273–74; bases, security of, 1298–1300; comforts denied soldier in, 88; command and control, unified, 705, 858–62, 1258–60, 1272–77, 1296–1300, 1338; command of sea as factor, 1273; congratulations from E., 271–72; dead, repatriation of, 1501; general officers, redeployment from, 329–31; infantry divisions, policy for assignment to, 219; inspection tour by E., 900, 984, 1001, 1002–3, 1009, 1035, 1036–38, 1040, 1045, 1050, 1085–87, 1090; Japan, importance to security of, 1297–1300; memorial in, 1691; military government for islands, 587–89, 1056–57, 1097–1101; missing persons, searches for, 752; names of commands, disagreement on, 1409; naval operations, plans for, 1584; Negro troops, assignment to, 1339; Philippines, important to security of, 1297–1300; SCAP, separation from, 860–62; service units, assignment to, 219; shipping, redeployment to, 66, 285, 605; submarine threat in, 1584; trusteeships for islands, 587–89, 1097–1101; unity of command for, 859, 1258–60, 1272–77, 1296–1300, 1338
—troop units: redeployment to, 50, 218–20, 284–85; strength authorizations and reductions, 605, 798–99, 1060–61, 1337–40
Pack units, retention of, 1634–35
Page, Frank Copeland, 1186–87, 2225; illness, concern by E. over, 2224; international communications systems, security of, 910–11, 937–40
Page One Award, 497
Paget, Bernard Charles Tolver, 1571, 1575
Paget, Frank A., 1910
Painting, as hobby for E., 1748
Palau Islands, administration of, 587–88
Palekh, USSR, 721
Palestine: Jewish state establishment in, 1778–79; Jews, resettlement in, 268–69, 358; partition plan, 2122–23; trusteeship for, 1137–38
Paley, William Samuel, 1841–42; background, 1187, 1880, 2062, CBS directorship offer to E., 1880–81; psychological warfare operations, research, planning, and training in, 2062–63; visits with E., 1880–81, 2062
Palmer, John McAuley, 120; background, 772; commendation by E., 1001; mobilization, time required, 908; National Guard, role in Army reorganization, 908; national security council, proposal for, 771–72; Regular Army, appropriation for and postwar strength, 811–14; Switzerland, study of UMT in, 908
—reserve components: cost estimates, 908; manning plans, 907–8; role in Army reorganization, 908; UMT, role in, 908
—universal military training: advisory commission for, 906–8; proposals for, 772, 814
Palmyra Island, administration of bases in, 588
Panama, Republic of: decoration for E., 1208; defense sites in, withdrawal from, 1286–87, 1706; number of military facilities in, 822
Panama Canal: security of, 821–22, 1298, 1300–1302, 1705–6, 1984; West Indies role in security of, 1300–1302
Panama Canal Department: command and control, 1967–69; inspection tour by E.,

Pershing, John Joseph: birthday message from E., 1296; "Black Jack," reference to origin, 1176; heads Battle Monuments Commission, 324; radio program to honor, 218; Taylor article on Military Academy, 1754; tribute to, 20–21, 1296; visit with E., 163

Persian Gulf: pipeline route to Mediterranean, 2002–3; Soviet threat to, 1597

Personal accounts of E., verification of, 830

Personnel. *See* Officers; Soldiers; Troop units

Personnel carriers, lack of, 2255

Personnel Division, WDGS. *See* Paul, Willard Stewart

Persons, Wilton Burton, 609, 716, 988

Peru, negotiations for air bases, 1300–1302

Petersen, Howard Charles: background, 761, 2179; Germany, food supplies for, 973–75; military government, public relations program for, 864; Negro troops, desegregation policy, 1515; recreation center, inept commander at, 1346–47; resignation, 1857; universal military training, 2179
—atomic weapons: effect on armed services organization, 761; international regulation, 1855–58
—atomic weapons tests: security of, 918–20; target ships positioning, 918–20
—Japan: civilian relief, 1519; navy vessels for atomic tests, 918–20
—Korea: civilian relief, 1519; coast guard for, 1141

Petrillo, Edward G., 1981

Petroleum products: France, issue to, 196–98; control of in Middle East, 1138; storage in abandoned mines, proposed, 2071

Philadelphia, Pa., visits by E., 1088, 1541, 2131–32, 2179, 2188

Philadelphia Club Printing House Craftsmen, award to E., 2005

Philippine Army Air Corps, wings presented to E., 558

Philippines: as atomic bombs storage site, 1077; civilian employees, number in, 1518; conduct of U.S. soldiers, 1338–40; health problems in, 583; independence proclaimed, 1053, 1604; inspection tour by E., 1050, 1052; memorial in, 1691; military assistance for, 1518, 1608–9; military assistance group, nominations for, 1243–44; Navy song on recovery of, 2106–7; neutral, assumption of position as, 1403; neutrality declaration proposals, 1403, 1888; recollections of service by E., 2186, 2194; relation to Pacific theater security, 1297–1300; relations with U.S., deterioration of, 1369, 1389, 1403; troop units strength authorizations and reductions, 799
—bases: administration of, 588; agreement on, 1404; withdrawal from, 1051–53, 1368–70, 1388–90, 1402–4, 1518, 1603–4

Philippine Scouts: retention in Regular Army, 1052–53; troop units strength and pay, 798, 800, 1053

Philipy, Tom R., 1488

Phillipson, Irving Joseph, 192

Philpot, Sheppard Blunden, 1548

Physical disability of E. as cadet, 1034–35

Physical therapists, point credit system for, 345

Pickett, Clarence E., 237

Pickett's charge, 1172

Pierre Hotel, 1910

Pierson, John Herman Groesbeck, 2064–65; background, 2065

Pike, Edwin Benjamin, amity with Soviet Union, 1664

Pilgrims of Great Britain, 314

Pilsen, 6, 450

PINCHER. *See* Soviet Union, hostilities by

Pinehurst proposition. *See* Marshall, George Catlett, Secretary of State, appointment as

Pinkley, Virgil M., 89

Pittsburgh Courier, 765

Pius XII, audience with E., 352, 689

Plans, strategic: guide to facilitate, 848–51; security of, 1013

Pleven, René Jean, 209

Plue, Russell J., RA commission for, 2224

Plumley, Charles Albert, 1526–27

PM (newspaper), 115

Pocket Guide for Germany, 529

Pogue, Forrest Carlisle, 1209–11, 1570–75; background, 1210

Pogue, Lloyd Welch, 264–66; background, 265

Point Barrow, Alaska, 1871, 1873

Point credit system: Combat Infantryman Badge as basis for, 644–45; cut in credits, 753–54; decorations and awards feature in, 645; football players, circumvention for, 656; implementation, 50, 53, 285, 318–19, 345, 354–56, 398–99, 600, 738, 754, 783, 868–69, 1115; indoctrination in, 355; officers, grades calculation method, 345; policy on, 354–56

Point Mugu, Calif., 1030–31

Pola Enclave, 58, 1721

Poland: air travel to, Soviet interruption, 521–22, 525–26; atomic weapons, international regulation, 1485; Berlin, liaison commission to, 447–48; currency exchange rates policy, 444; Czechoslovakia, troop units movement into, 447–48; decoration for E., 292–93, 326; displaced persons, repatriation of, 358, 360, 414; economic assistance for, 444–45; elections in,

UNO; training programs, troops awaiting discharge, 670–72; troop units, demobilization acceleration, 600
—UNO: air forces, maneuvers by, 1082–83; armaments regulation by, 1394; troop units, command and control, 1021–23; 1936; troop units commitment to, 1190, · 1662, 1936–37
Ridley, Clarence Self, retirement of, 1506–7
Rifkind, Simon Hirsch, 1778–79; background, 470; personal advisor to E., 267, 269, 469–70
Riley, Hugh Willard: background, 1162; Parker Pen vice president, nomination for, 1160, 1162
Rio de Janeiro Agreement (1947), 822
Rio de Janeiro Conferences (1942, 1945), 822, 1095
Riordan, Mame McInerney, 2144
Ripple, Richard Wilkins, 99–100
Ritter, Charles P., 2071
Riverside Church, 1815
Riviera, villa leased by E., 250, 352–53
Rizzo, Sam A., Jr., military aspirations of, 1630
Roanoke, Va., 1645, 1655–56
Robb, James Milne, 188, 1846–47; background, 36, 1847; commendation by E., 45; decoration for, 35, 45–46
Robb, Walter Johnson, 2186
Roberts, George H., 2160–61
Roberts, Owen Josephus, 1496
Roberts, Roy Allison, 1747–48, 1767, 1909, 2216–17
Roberts, Shirley N., 2160–61
Robertson, Absalom Willis, 626, 1110–11
Robertson, Brian Hubert, 523, 526–27
Robertson, Paul Melville, 856
Robinson, Clinton Frederick: background, 2256; evaluation by E., 2252
Robinson, J. French, 2081
Robinson, Trula B., 1438–39; as companion for Ida Eisenhower, 557–58, 638, 693; letter to E., 622
Robinson, William Edward: background, 1994; negotiations for E. memoirs serialization, 1994, 2148, 2153, 2159–60, 2174–75, 2184; visits with E., 2148, 2175
Rockefeller, John Davison, Jr., 1134–35
Rockefeller, John Davison, III, 810, 999
Rockefeller Foundation, 999
Rockets. *See* Missiles and rockets
Rock Hill Herald, 2225–26
Rockne, Knute Kenneth, boxing bout with E., alleged, 1420, 1475
Rogers, Edith Nourse, 1129–30
Rogers, H. Mead, 1103–4
Rogers, Helen Crampton, 1366

Rogers, Robert Sterling, death of, 1366
Rogers, William Penn Adair (Will), 2030–31
Rohrbach, John Grandin, 1990–91
Roles and missions: Air forces, 215–17, 369–71, 701–2, 789–91, 927–32, 976–77, 997, 1005–6, 1057–58, 1063–64, 1360, 1466–67, 1528–29, 2037–39, 2247; armed services, 215–17, 339, 369–71, 518, 701–2, 743–45, 927–32, 976–77, 997, 1039, 1057–59, 1060, 1063–64, 1291–92, 1360, 1528–29, 2037–39, 2246–49, 1466–67, 1867–68; coastal air command, 702–3, 705; determination of, 2247; E. on, 215–17, 339, 369–71, 518, 701, 743–45, 927–32, 976–77, 997, 1039, 1057–59, 1060, 1291–92, 1360, 1466–67, 1528–29, 2037–39, 2246–49; ground forces, 215–17, 339, 369–71, 518, 701, 743–45, 927–32, 976–77, 997, 1057–59, 1360, 1466–67, 1528–29, 2038, 2248; JCS on, 743, 927–32, 976–77, 997, 1360, 1441, 1443, 1466–67, 1528–29, 2247–48; Marine Corps, 369, 702, 704–5, 928–32, 976–77, 997, 1056–60, 1063–64, 1283, 1467, 2248; National Guard, 937; naval forces, 215–17, 369–71, 702–4, 927–32, 976–77, 997, 1057–59, 1063–64, 1360, 1466–67, 1528–29, 2247–48
Rolling stock. *See* Railroads
Rollins College, degree for E., 1980
Romania: displaced persons, repatriation of, 358; Soviet Union troop units, strength authorizations, 1563
Romanick, John M., 536
Rome, Ga., 1645
Rome, Italy, 352
Rome Air Depot, closing of, 1652
Rommel, Erwin, E. on command ability of, 940
Romulo, Carlos P., 558
Rooks, Lowell W., 35
Roosevelt, Anna Eleanor, 868–69, 1496, 2009
Roosevelt, Belle Willard, 1385–86
Roosevelt, Elliott, 1202, 1427–29
Roosevelt, Franklin Delano: atomic energy, peacetime control proposals, 576–77; decorations, policy for awards, 1711; Japanese-Americans, displacement from homes, 1985; Malta garrison, citation for, 1751; Morgenthau book, use by, 424; Nottingham Memorial Scholarships Fund, 442–43; Philippines neutrality declaration opposed by, 1888; tomb, visit by E., 163; warmongering charged to, 1155
Roosevelt, Franklin Delano, Jr., 1067–68
Roosevelt, Theodore, Jr., 996

156; VA hospital in, 1533; visit and address by E., 1533, 1537, 1539–40, 1548–49, 1587–89
St. Nazaire, battles at, 940, 1573
St. Paul, Minn., 1834–35
St. Paul's Cathedral, memorial to U.S. dead, 446–47, 740–41, 1253–54, 1322
Saipan, 1050
Sakawa, H.I.M.S., 581
Sakier, A. H., 836–37
Salerno, landing at, 1058
Salinas District air base, negotiations for, 1300–1301
Salisbury, N.C., 2162–63
Salt Lake City, Utah, service command headquarters inactivation, 903
Salt Lake City, U.S.S., 1181
Saltonstall, Leverett, 1133
Saltzman, Charles Eskridge: background, 1162; Parker Pen vice president, nomination for, 1161–62, 1286
Salute, 1480
Saluting, E. on amending regulations on, 1159; tradition of, 1059–61
Salvati, Raymond Earnest, 1942
Salvation Army, rally, 2065–66
Salzburg, 1313
Samoa, administration of bases in, 588
Samuel, Bernard, 2005
San Antonio, Tex.: contemplated as residence by E., 1654–55, 1671–73, 1721–22; Eisenhower for President Club, 239; visit by E., 854, 875, 881–82, 950–57
SANDSTONE. *See* Atomic weapons tests
San Francisco, Calif.: investigation of waste and duplication, 2249, 2256; Soviet ships sudden clearance from, 963; visits by E., 899, 1656
San Francisco Chronicle, 1113, 2186
San Gerononimi, 1831
Sangley Point, 1402
Santa Claus Mail Association, 2054
Sarafian, Sue. *See* Jehl, Sue Sarafian
Saratoga, U.S.S., 1181
Sarnoff, David, 585, 1529–30
Saturday Evening Post: articles by E., 1797; articles by E. proposed, 460, 1963–64; articles by Smith, W. B., 2084; Butcher book serialization, 433, 516, 685, 733, 825, 827; international affairs, editorial on U.S. attitude, 1130; negotiations for memoirs serialization, 2130–31, 2148; military government, criticism of, 863, 865; officers living standards, article on, 1564, 1566; Rangers, article on, 1194–96; Reeder, article on, 851; SHAEF, charges of prolonging war, 2015
Saturday Review of Literature, 1973–74
Sauer, John Edward, assignment to Military Academy, 1687

Sauerkraut recipe, 2172–73
Saunders, Charles D., 1130
Saunders, J. Maryon, 349
Savannah, Ga., visit by E., 1064–65, 1074, 1090, 1917, 1920, 1941–42
Save the Children Fund International Union, 403
Sawyer, Charles, 254–55, 290–91, 305–6
Sawyer, Raymond, 1809
Sayler, Dale, 833–34
Sayler, Henry Benton, 2006; background, 804, 834
Sayler, Jessie Dale (Dixon), 1421–22, 2170
Sayler, John Milton, 1421–22, 1902
Schaefer, Julius Earl: armed services unification, 1162; atomic weapons, international regulation, 1128; congratulations to E., 621; service in war effort, 203; XL-15 liaison aircraft development, 2170–71
Schaerbeek, 291
Scheiberling, Edward Nicholas, 333–34, 538
Scheva, Paul H., 1537
Schlatter, David Myron, 132, 517; background, 133
Schlosberg, Hyman Carol, 1506
Schmidt, William Richard: background, 406, 1341; SACMED, nomination for, 405–6; Third Army, assignment as chief of staff, 1340–41
Schmitt, Heinz, 1827
Schoeneman, George Jeremiah, 2153
Schoeppel, Andrew F., 142
Schoerner, Ferdinand, arrest of, 23–24
Schofield Stadium, 1067
Scholarships, E. proposal of, for ROTC cadets, 1692–93
Schools, civilian. *See* Colleges, civilian
Schools, service (*see also* Colleges, service): attendance by civilians, 801; commandants as War Department advisors, 336; exchange of U.K.-U.S. officers, 723; foreign, exchanges with, 781, 803; horses at, 1634–35; information and education programs, number in operation, 426; leadership courses at, 593; tribute to by E., 20
Schow, Robert Alvin, 637
Schuck, Arthur Aloys, 1503
Schlitz, A. L., 1820–21
Schultz, Edwin, 917
Schultz, Sigrid, 71–72
Schulz, Robert L., 750; appointment as Columbia aide, 1758, 1929, 2056–57, 2079, 2174; background, 746
Schuster, Max Lincoln, 203–4
Schutzstaffel, reported coddling, 71–72
Schuyler, Cortland van Rensselaer, 1968, 1969, 2053; background, 1830
Schwartz, Erich, sentence commuted by E., 309
Schwartz, Joseph Joshua, 267

Schwarz, John, 838
Schwarzschild, Leopold, 1696
Schwerin, 6
Scientific information, exchange among nations, 1486–87
Scientists and technicians: association with in defense planning, 1315; association with in R&D, 1046–50, 1264–65, 1512–13; exploitation and recruitment, 823–24, 1178–79, 1826–27; disposition of enemy, 261; intelligence on (*see* Field Information Agency, Technical); surrender of enemy, 261
Scott, Richard Underhill, 2197, 2198–2199
Scott-Bailey, Victor E., 646–47
Scottish Trust. *See* National Trust for Scotland
Scrivner, Errett P., 1184
Sea Islands, Ga., leave taken by E. at, 1045, 1064–65, 1068, 1074, 1090, 2095
Secretaries of Chambers of Commerce, 1769–70
Secretary for Co-Action, 1038–39
Secretary of Agriculture. *See* Anderson, Clinton Presba
Secretary of Defense (*see also* Defense, Department of; Forrestal, James Vincent): advisory group for, 1235; final memorandum to by E., 2242–57; functions, E. views on, 2246–49; mission and powers, E. proposals for, 1064, 1617–18, 1633, 1666; proposals for office, 1038, 1062–64, 1283, 1466; secretaries and assistant secretaries, selection of, 2250–51
Secretary of State. *See* Acheson, Dean Gooderham; Byrnes, James Francis; Marshall, George Catlett
Secretary of the Army (*see also* Army, Department of the; Royall, Kenneth Claiborne), final memorandum to by E., 2255
Secretary of the General Staff, organization and functions, 615–16
Secretary of the Interior. *See* Interior, Department of the
Secretary of the Navy. *See* Forrestal, James Vincent; Navy, Department of the
Secretary of the Treasury. *See* Morgenthau, Henry, Jr.; Treasury, Department of the
Secretary of War. *See* Patterson, Robert Porter; Stimson, Henry Lewis; War Department
Security measures (*see also* Intelligence agencies; Intelligence operations and reports): Associated Press, breach by, 12, 264, 1193–94; atomic weapons and tests, 575, 577–78, 634, 640, 918–20, 960–61, 1146–47; Butcher story on breaches,

1627–28; Canada, atomic energy plant in, effect on, 1525–26; Chief of Staff to Supreme Allied Commander, 456–57; Congress, admissions to, 1084; cryptography, 819; disarmament, effect on, 1550–52; Far East sea communications, 844; flying bomb sites destruction, 143–45; geographical, fallacy of, 1431–32; Germany, check of credentials and premises, 513–14; Great Lake region, 954–55; Greece, importance to U.S. security, 1702; Greenland, importance to U.S. security, 1298; headquarters scattering, 1289; industrial mobilization planning, 1583; industry scattering, 1288–89; Italy, importance to U.S., 1702; Japan, importance to U.S., 1702; JCS documents, classification downgrading, 1697–98; leaks, investigation of, 1413; loyalty checks, policy on, 1898–99; Mediterranean Sea region, importance to U.S., 2013; MTOUSA lines of communications, 1583–84; national, problems in, 1448; national security, UMT importance to, 1440–43, 2027, 2179, 2254; necessity for, 89; Pacific theater bases, 1298–1300; Panama Canal, 821–22, 1298, 1300–1302, 1705–6, 1984; Report of Operations in Northwest Europe, 788; in research and development, 1829; St. Lawrence Seaway, 954–55; SHAEF, 456–57; Soviet Union in Poland, 744; Strait of Gibralter, importance to U.S., 2012; in strategic planning, 1013; troop units, indoctrination in, 1526; Turkey, importance to U.S., 1702; United Kingdom, importance to U.S., 1702; West Germany, importance to U.S., 1702; Western Europe, importance to U.S., 1702, 2217
—communications systems: scattering, 1289; international, 937–40
Segregation of Negro troops. *See* Negro troops
Seine River, drive on, 654, 1070–71
Selective Service: age limits changed, 1014, 1087, 1169; continuation unresolved, 603; draft suspensions, 1014, 1519; draftees, discharge of, 1519–20; draft termination, 1806–7, 2229; extension of, 778, 798–800, 908, 994, 1003, 1013–14, 1025, 1060-62, 1064, 1086–87, 1169, 1215, 1337–38, 1442, 1520, 2229; fathers, exemption from, 1014; term of service limited, 1014; termination, pressure for, 599, 605
Selective Training and Service Act (1940). *See* Selective Service
Selfishness, E. on evils of, 2144–45
Sellew, Waldo W., 1795
Senate (*see also* Congress): armed services

Souers, Sidney William, 698–99, 1045
Sous-les-Vents, 505
South Africa. *See* Union of South Africa
South America. *See* Caribbean Command; Latin America
South Carolina Bar Association, 583–84
South East Asia Command: Mountbatten report, review and publication, 1084–85, 1355, 1992, 2232; NEI, military jurisdiction over, 689–91; troop units strength authorizations, 799
Southeast Asia region, estimate of nationalism diminution, 744
Southeastern posts, inspection tour by E., 1523, 1590, 1602, 1616, 1624, 1639–40, 1645, 1648, 1671, 1673
Southern France campaign, 1069, 1071; Balkans vs. Southern France concept, 1678–79
Southwest Pacific Area, Army command and administration, 860
Soviet Russia Today, proposal of article by E., 498
Soviet Union (*see also* Stalin, Joseph; Zhukov, Georgi Konstantinovich): aggressive policy by, 1800, 1933–34, 2021, 2084–85; aircraft, estimate of development, 744; air-defense weapons, reliance on, 2156; air travel, interruption by, 521–26; Allied Control Council, E. as first chairman, 229; amity with, 498–99, 915, 1664; army, junction with, 5–8, 1679–80; aspirations, E. concern over, 481; Baltic states, occupation by, 360; Black Sea region as industrial center, 1584; Bornholm Island occupied by, 491; bureaucrats, behavior of, 1216, 1428; Caspian Sea region as industrial center, 1584; CCS existence, concern over by, 1532; China, occupation of northern area, 589–90; commanders, consultation with E., 53; cooperation with, 282; Danube navigation rights, disagreement on, 398, displaced persons, repatriation from, 398; distrust by E. of intentions, 1855–57; Dodecanese Islands, bases in, 1013; economic assistance to, 524; economic rehabilitation, estimate of, 744–45; enigma of, 836; European recovery, obstruction by, 1524; Finland, resistance by, 1594; flying bomb launching sites, capture of, 145; foreigners, distrust of, 836; general officers, decorations for, 262; Hungary, troop units strength authorization, 1563; indoctrination program on, 198–99, 257–58; intelligence on required, 1106; jet aircraft, reliance on, 2156; joint SHAEF secretariat, 138; Lend-Lease, continuance to, 198, 527; liaison with army commander by E., 182; Manchuria, occu-

pation by, 589–90; Mediterranean Sea region, bases in, 1013; military assistance for, 596; military government, enactments on, 132; military mission to, report of, 835–36; military-political policy integration, 115; missiles and rockets, estimate of development by, 744; nationals, repatriation of, 360; navy, capability of, 2156; Oder River, drive to, 1679; officers, decorations for, 262; opinion poll on, 257–58; Prague, occupation by, 450; relations with, 314–15, 498–99, 527, 1105–7, 1596; Romania, troop units strength authorization, 1563; scientists and technicians, exploitation and recruitment, 823–24, 1178–79; ships sudden clearance from ports, 962–64; soldiers' attitude toward, 198–99; Spain, potential control by, 1584; submarine fleet, expansion of, 2156; Suez Canal, threat to, 1597; threat of aggression by, 1552, 1567–68; Tripolitania, bases in, 1013; Truman Doctrine, denunciation of, 2085; Turkey, pressures on, 1593–94, 1596–97; universal military training in, 766; V-E Day proclamation, 13; Venezia Giulia, occupation by Yugoslavia, 57–59, 64; Western Europe, potential seizure by, 1584; Yugoslavia, release of shipping from control of, 398
—arms and equipment: estimate of development by, 744; international regulation, 1485–86
—atomic weapons: intelligence on production by, 744, 1857, 1919; international regulation, 123, 215, 368, 554, 861, 1485, 1855–58; tests, observers at, 920; unfinished stocks, destruction of, 1828
—Austria: AEF troop operations lines in, 65; demands for withdrawal from, 1550; elections protested, 678; hostilities continued by, 24; reparations from, 1544; troop units strength authorizations, 1563
—Berlin: air access interruption by, 521, 525–26; blockade of, 2196, 2200; currency exchange practices in, 245, 389; industrial equipment removal from, 260
—Chemical-biological-radiological weapons: estimate of development, 744; potential use by, 2156–57
—Czechoslovakia: economic demands on, 451–53; occupation of, 449; shipping, release from control by, 398; troop units strength in, 451–52; withdrawal from, 449–52
—Germany: armed forces liquidation, 94–96; cargo handling through zone, 398; civil agencies, investigation of, 94; denazification program, 439; documents captured, access to, 95–97; European Advi-

Transportation: Czechoslovakia, equipment restitution to, 464, 466; Germany, problems in, 281-83, 464-67; interservice use of, 2249

Trans World Airlines, 1767, 1777

Travis, Robert Jesse, 936-37

Treadwell, George, 443

Treasury Department of the (see also Morgenthau, Henry, Jr.): Coast Guard, control by, 1074; France, currency exchange rates policy, 209-10; Germany, currency exchange rates policy, 245, 441-42, 1605-6; Korea, coast guard for, 1072-74, 1139-41; rulings on E. memoirs, tax aspects, 2153, 2160, 2174-75, 2182; USFET, currency exchange rates policy, 389

Trees, Merle Jay, 2222

Tregor, Nisson Alexander, 1325

Trenchard, Hugh Montague, 357, 446-47, 561; World War II history, joint U.S.-U.K. publication, 1878-80, 2139-40

Tresch, Ernest Hiram, 561

Tresch, N. J., 561

Trichel, Gervais William: background, 1045-46; R&D, assignment as acting director, 1045

Trieste Free Territory: Airey report on administration, 2158-59; award to Italy, 1189, 2158-59; establishment and boundary delineation, 1188-90, 1720-21, 1739-40, 1764-65, 1907-8; governor, appointment of, 2159, SCAEF, control by, 58; threat of clash in, 962; troop units strength authorizations and reductions, 2092, 2125; withdrawal from, 1189-90, 1720-21; Yugoslavia, role in administration, 2091-92

Trigg, Father (unidentified): surplus chapel for, 1862

Trigg, Ralph, 1832

Tripartite Merchant Marine Commission, 526

Tripartite Naval Commission, 526

Triphibious warfare, E. comments on, 553-54

Tripolitania, Soviet bases in, 1013

Trohan, Walter, 908-9

Troop units (see also Service units; Regular Army; Soldiers): air-base defense, number available, 1011; allocations, study of, 2229-30; battle credit citation policy, 106-7; camps for UMT, reduction in, 1246; Christmas messages from E., 676-77, 1431; civilian clothes wearing by, 377-78; commands, study of missions, 2229-30; courtesy, observance of, 528; demobilization program (see Demobilization program); employment and transfers, 66; general officers, assignment to, 34-35,

1341, 1506; Haislip Board proposals, 2053; homecoming timing, E. concern over, 21-22; missions, study of priorities, 603, 2229-30; mobilization (see Mobilization, military); NATO jurisdiction over, 477; Negroes, opposition to integration of, 672; numerical designation, 1494; overseas bases, 369, 812-13; overstrength, 1320-21; point credit system (see Point credit system); quarters for, 367; redeployment program (see Redeployment program): Regular Army organization and strength, periodic: 334, 336-41, 368-71, 480-82, 486, 517-19, 679-81, 742-45, 811-14, 1211, 1958; security measures, indoctrination in, 1526; special units for veterans, 987; strength authorization and reductions, periodic, 140-41, 369-71, 599-605, 1011, 1087, 1211, 1321, 1441, 1518-19, 1585-86, 1651, 1713, 1806-7, 1958, 2229, 2253-55; strength, effect on Army mission, 2253-55; United Kingdom, court jurisdiction over, 476-77; UNO, commitment to, 1936; voting procedures, 288-89

Truck Companies: 3534th, 1494; 4378th, 218-20

Trucks. See Motor vehicles

"True Glory" film, 245-46, 383, 389-90, 432

Truman, Harry S.: AAF aircraft for government officials travel, 734-35; Alexander, visit with, 1489; Armistice Day proclamation, 1167; Army-Navy Munitions Board, organized by, 796; Arnold, personal services for, 1235; Atomic Energy Act signing, 1102; Atomic Energy Commission, establishment, 577; Babelsberg meeting, 204, 253; Baruch, decoration for, 1874; Bonesteel, assignment as CIG director, 1037, 1045; Burning Tree Club, invitation to, 1088; Bush armed services reorganization plan, 1039; Byrnes, dissatisfaction with, 1086; Canada, mutual defense plans, 1416-18; Carter, promotion for, 1611; Chicago, visit to, 992; civilian clothing, wearing by officers, 1278; civilian employees loyalty program, 499; civilians, travel permits for, 507; Clark, appointment as high commissioner in Austria, 1200; command and control, unified, 1299, 1411-12, 1453-59; company commander, demands on, 815; Czechoslovakia, withdrawal from, 452-54; decorations, policy on awards, 1832; Defense Department organization proposals, 1235; Dodds, visit with, 1763; economy program, directive on, 1239-41, 1245; European Recovery Plan, economic assistance for, 2220; executive branches and agencies, coordination among, 658, 741–42; families accompanying overseas troops, 150; fathers, discharge of, 784; Fond du Lac, attendance at memorial service, 1088–89; Frankfort, visit to, 252; Greece, military assistance to, 1596–97, 1701–3, 1761, 1999; Groves, promotion for, 1387; Herald Tribune Forum, invitation from, 303; industry, scattering for security, 1288–89; intelligence agencies, centralization of functions, 697–99; intelligence reports, exchange with Canada, 1688–89; Jews, treatment of, 353–54, 357–61, 414–48; Kilian, promotion denied, 1336; Lattre de Tassigny, decoration for, 193; Lauley, nomination as Under Secretary of Navy, 947; Leahy, confidence in, 2246; Littlejohn, appointment as War Assets Administration head, 1118–19; McNarney, assignment to USFET, 310; materiel, enemy, claims for, 631; medical officers, relieving shortage of, 1623; missiles and rockets, coordination of R&D, 1030–31; Montgomery, visit to U.S., 1206; national defense committee chairman, 684; National Intelligence Authority, activation, 698; National Press Club, attendance at dinner, 535; National Security Act signing, 1867–68; Navy, personnel strength authorizations, 371, 1520; Negroes, integration order on, 1515; newsmen, freedom of expression for, 44; Northwest Europe, Operations Report, presentation copy, 618; Okinawa, retention of bases in, 1604; OPA, controls removed, 1187; OWI, activities transfer to State Department, 159; Patterson, resignation accepted, 1751; Philippines, withdrawal from bases in, 1403–4; Princeton University, degree from, 1763; prisoners of war, repatriation of, 785–86; psychological warfare, research, planning and training in, 2063; QMG, nominations for, 756–57; redeployment program, 65; Royall, nomination as Secretary of War, 1751; scientists and technicians, exploitation and recruitment, 1179; Smith, W. B., appointment as ambassador to Soviet Union, 582; soldiers, demonstrations by, 754, 815; Stimson, birthday celebration for, 1751; 35th Division reunion, attendance at, 1487, 1685–86, 1698–99, 1719, 1744, 1747, 1759–60; Truman, L. W., visit with, 253; Truman Doctrine, enunciation of, 1596, 1701–3; Soviet denunciation of, 2085; Turkey, military assistance for, 1596–97, 1701–3, 1761, UNRRA, appropriations for, 537; Vandenberg, nomination for CIG director, 1045; Van Fleet, as-

signment to Greece, 2230; V-E Day proclamation, 13; Venezia Giulia, occupation by Yugoslavia, 58–59, 64; veterans, postwar employment for, 455; Vienna, U.S. sector delineation, 166; Vienna-Klagenfurt-Udine route, armed escort for, 1237–38; WAC, integration into regular services, 2214; war criminals, prosecution of, 642–44; Zhukov, visit to U.S., 229, 998
—admirals: five-star, permanent commissions for, 1144–45, 1166, 1220; five-star, personal services for, 1219–20
—air forces: autonomy for, 1063; roles and missions, 1063–64
—armed services: appropriations for, 813; organization and strength, postwar, 679; roles and missions, 1867; unification, 370, 410, 706, 1045, 1057–59, 1062–64, 1086–87, 1282–83, 1466–67, 1528–29, 1684, 1867
—atomic weapons: bomb, decision to use, 204–5; authority to order use, 1937, 2020, 2047; international regulation, 577, 1078, 1092–93; national policy for, 1101–2; stockpiling, 1606; UNO, releasing information to, 579
—atomic weapons tests: approval of, 1995; commission to evaluate, 960–62; observers at, 920; release of information on, 2019–20; release of information to U.K., 1147, 1354; target ships positioning, 1181–82
—Austria: civil relief and rehabilitation, 2143; troop units redispositions, 167–68; U.S. zones delineation, 166
—Berlin: flag-raising ceremony, 204; U.S. sector, movement into, 167; U.S.-U.K. sectors delineation, 166
—Bradley: Chief of Staff, nomination and appointment, 2080, 2129, 2194; general grade, retention of, 1677; VA head, appointment as, 55–56, 72
—budgets: Army and Navy, coordinating, 1292; cuts in, 1517
—China: MAG for, 762–63; military assistance for, 1338; postwar policy in, 623
—displaced persons: admission to U.S., 418; treatment in U.S. zone, 267, 357–61, 414–48
—Eisenhower: Columbia presidency, offer of, 1757; decorations for, 163, 2257; birthday message from E., 1055; birthday message to E., 1325; Canada visit by, 717; Chief of Staff, appointment as, 310, 537; Chief of Staff, retirement from, 2194; Christmas message to, 675; commendation of, 25; condolences to, 1725; felicitations to mother, 25; Germany, permanent assignment in, 435, 439; gifts to, 1536, 2257; globe presented by E., 289–90;

Tunisia campaign, 940, U.S.-U.K. roles in, 2112

Turkey: amity with, 1584; armed services strength, 1595; economic assistance for, 1595; military assistance to, 1592–97, 1701–3, 1761; security of, importance to U.S., 1158, 1702; Soviet pressures on, 1593–94, 1596–97

Turner, Harold Rathbun, 1600

Turner, Richmond, Kelly, 1082–83; background, 1082

Tweed, Thomas, 1648–49

Twining, Nathan Farragut, Alaska Command, assignment as commander, 1983

Tydings, Millard Evelyn, 947, 1172–73

Tyler, William Royall, 794

Udine Province, 405–6

Ulio, James Alexander, 533–34, 617; background, 86

ULTRA. See Code-breaking, U.S.-U.K. in wartime

Underground forces. See Partisan forces

Underhill, Adna H., 934

Underhill, Charles M., 1156

Under Secretary of War. See War Department

Unification of armed services. See Armed services, unification; Armed services, roles and missions

Unified command. See Command and control, unified

Uniform: blue, plans for, 1277–78, 1561; changes in proposed, 1503–4, 1561; civilians, wearing by, 1277–78; discipline in wearing, 528; distinctive design for, 1277–78; German prisoners of war, 377; occupation forces, 377–78; standardizing for all services, 555–56, 1278

Uniform Code of Military Justice, revision of, 1791

Union League Club, 1794

Union of South Africa, assumption of neutral position by, 2157

Union of Soviet Socialist Republics. See Soviet Union

Union Pacific Railroad, 172

Unions, 120; cargoes unloading by, 1872–73, 1892; German, relaxing controls on, 213; United Mine Workers strike, 1432

Unit citations, Marine Corps policy, 106–7

United Air Lines, 2014–15

United Hospital Fund, 1920

United Jewish Appeal, 1460–61

United Kingdom (see also British Army; British Commonwealth; War Office [British]): Allied Control Council formation, 1122–13; ally, assumption of position as, 2154–58; amity with encouraged, 149, 161, 442, 493–94, 596–97, 773–74,

826, 828, 849, 853, 896, 914, 944–45, 1120–21, 1191–92, 1525, 2166; army (see British army); atomic energy plant in, effect on U.S. security, 1524–26; Austria, troop units strength authorizations, 1563; cemetery for U.S. dead, 357; CBS weapons, enemy, requests for, 631–32; code-breaking, wartime, 1147; cryptography, joint U.S.-U.K. planning, 1344; currency exchange rates policy, 389, 441; deceptive measures, joint U.S.-U.K. planning, 1344; economic assistance to, 1532; Egypt, withdrawal from, effect of, 1593; electronics, joint U.S.-U.K.-Canada planning, 1464–65; Europe, troop units reductions in, 1872; FIAT, participation in, 111–12, 817; flying bombs launching sites destruction, 143–45; guided missiles committee, U.S. representation on, 1378–79; housing shortage, E. concern over, 1310–11; international policy, estimate of, 1552; Japan, withdrawal from, 2163–64; joint planning with U.S., 1157–59, 1344–45; Lend-Lease, continuance of, 198; materiel, enemy, requests for, 631–32; Mediterranean region, decline of influence in, 1593; memorial to U.S. dead, in 1690; military assistance for, 596; neutral, assumption of position as, 2157; newsmen, criticism of E. by, 326; North Africa campaign, role in, 2111–12; Pacific islands, administration of bases in, 588; plans, strategic, U.S. cooperation in, 1012; popularity of E. in, 837; radar systems, joint U.S.-U.K.-Canada planning, 1464–65; radio communications, joint U.S.-U.K.-Canada planning, 1464–65; scientists and technicians, exploitation and recruitment, 824, 1178–79; security of, importance to U.S., 1702; severe winter in, 1531–32; shipping priorities for, 355, 399; Soviet hostilities, plans for meeting, 1157–59, 1344–45; staff committee system, E. comment on, 1084; subordination of E. to, alleged, 1154–55; technical activities, access to, 1345–46; transport workers, tribute to, 1135; "True Glory" film, 390; Turkey, economic assistance to, 1592, 1595–96; victory anniversary commemoration, 1123; visits by E., 894–95; 988–89, 1120–22, 1247, 1266, 1278–79, 1285, 1310–11, 1322, 1327, 1355–56, 2208; World War II history, joint U.S.-U.K. publication, 923–24, 1878–80, 2139–40

—arms and equipment: international regulation, 1485; release of information to, 1418–19; standardization with U.S., 1418–19

—atomic weapons: cooperation in developing

(*see* Truman-Attlee-King declaration); international regulation, 575–79, 1127

—atomic weapons tests: observers at, 920; release of information to, 1146–47, 1354, 1476–77, 1524–26

—Berlin: airfield requirements, 229; sector delineation, 166, 229; Soviet sector delineation, 229

—communications systems: joint U.S.-U.K.-Canada planning, 1464–65; joint U.S.-U.K. planning, 1344

—Germany: armed forces liquidation, 94–96; currency exchange rates policy, 1605–6; denazification program, 439; documents captured, access to, 96; documents, removal from, 261; European Advisory Commission declaration on control, 112–13; imports-exports, U.S.-U.K. cooperation in, 468; nonfraternization policy, 178; public health conference, plans for, 70–71; railroad facilities, priorities for, 365–66; railroads, priorities for, 365–66; troop units strength authorizations, 1563, 1746–47, 1872

—Greece: coordination of U.S.-U.K. missions, 2102–4; economic assistance for, 1593, 1596; withdrawal from, 1872, 1900–1901

—intelligence agencies: coordination among, 698; U.S. reliance on, 667

—Italy: air force rehabilitation by U.K.-U.S., 1667–68; troop units redeployment program, 366; withdrawal from, 1872, 1900–1901

—Java: use of Japanese troops in, 689–91; use of U.S. equipment in, 690–91

—missiles and rockets: collaboration with U.S. on, 1378–79; committee, U.S. representation on, 1378–79

—Palestine: establishment of Jewish state in, 1778; trusteeship for, 1138, 1593; withdrawal from, 2122–23

—service schools: exchange of U.S.-U.K. officers, 723; U.S. officers attendance at, 1620

—training exercises: joint U.S.-U.K. 1817–19; U.S. officers attendance at, 1620, 1725, 1817–19, 1847, 1971–72, 2206–7

—Trieste Free Territory: Airey report on administration, 2158–59; establishment and boundary delineation, 1764–65, 1907–8; Italy, award to, 1189, 2158; Yugoslavia, role in administering, 2092

—troop units: court jurisdiction over U.S. troops, 476–77; priorities for, 355, 365–66; railroad transportation for, 366; redeployment program, 355, 365–66, 399

—UNO: secretary-general, proposal of E. for, 634; troop units, command and con-

trol, 1023; troop units, commitment to, 1394, 1936–37

—Venezia Giulia: occupation by Yugoslavia, 58–59, 67; safeguarding rights in, 839

United Mine Workers, strike by, 1432

United Nations (Allies): congratulations from E., 271; War Crimes Commission, 643

United Nations Organization: air forces, maneuvers by, 1082–83; Albania, censure for Greek guerrillas support, 1999; armaments regulation by, 1392–94, 1485–86; Australia, as nonpermanent Security Council member, 633; Balkans, special committee on, 2000; Brazil as nonpermanent Security Council member, 633; Bulgaria, censure for Greek guerrillas support, 1999; Canada as nonpermanent Security Council member, 633; charter, adherence to, 998; charter members, 633; Commission on Atomic Energy, 579, 634–36, 640, 1077–79, 1127–28; effectiveness, 878–79; Egypt as nonpermanent Security Council member, 633–34; Greece, efforts to end hostilities in, 1999; Korea, elections in and withdrawal from, 2099–2100; Military Staff Committee (*see separate entry*); organizational meeting, 821–22; permanent site for, 1363; power to prevent war, 2157; regional defense agreements, resolution on, 821–22; secretary-general, appointment of E., proposed, 382, 493, 634; Security Council, additional nonpermanent members proposed, 633–34; Soviet Union, bar of commission from North Korea, 2229; Trieste Free Territory, establishment, 1188–90, 1720–21; trusteeships, exclusion from inspection, 1098; Yugoslavia, censure for Greek guerrillas support, 1999

—atomic weapons: control by, 760; excess stocks, destruction of, 1828; regulation and reduction, 1485–86; release of information to, 575, 578–79, 634–36, 1093

—Palestine: establishment of Jewish state in, 1778, 2122–23; partition plan, 2122–23

—troop units: command and control, 743, 812, 818, 1021–23; commitment to, 743, 812, 818, 1190, 1392, 1394, 1936–37; communications systems for, 818–19; estimate of reliability, 744; formation and plans for use, 635, 1083; signal communications for, 818–19; weather service for, 819–20

United Nations Relief and Rehabilitation Administration: appropriations hearings, 536–38, 543, 722; Austria, civil relief and rehabilitation, 2143; Czechoslovakia: motor vehicles and railroad rolling stocks supplied to, 465; displaced persons, responsibility for, 268, 359, 416–18; Germany,

zone, U.S. troop movements in, 320–21; Heller, clearance for U.K. visit, 244; letter from E., 650; troop units, U.K. court jurisdiction over, 476–77

Winchell, Walter, commendation by E., 1500–1501

Wings Club, 1684, 1696, 1706–7, 1749

Winston-Salem, N.C., 1645

Wise, Stephen Samuel: background, 269; special advisor to E. on Jews, 266, 269

Wismar-Schwerin-Domitz line, 6

Witsell, Edward Fuller: command and control, study of deficiencies in, 1329; missing persons, searches for, 1473; officers, policy on commissions, 533–34; recruiting programs, advertising on radio, 1749–50; soldiers' records, transfer to VA, 1570, 1637; veterans, reenlistment of disabled, 1285

Wittenberge, 151

Wives. See Families

Woehler, Otto, arrest of, 23–24

Wogan, John Beugnot, 407, 550; background, 407; decoration for, 503–4, 956

Wolf, Alfred M., 1981

Wolfsberg, 65

Women: E. on drafting for service, 340; female officers, fraternization with enlisted soldiers, 29; as peace crusaders, 1640–41; tribute by E. as peace crusaders, 1640; tribute by E. to war service, 1853, 2215; writers, address to by E., 1112–13

Women Appointed for Voluntary Emergency Service (WAVES), integration into regular service, 1854

Women's Action Committee for Lasting Peace, 1640

Women's Armed Services Integration Act (1947), 1853

Women's Army Corps: integration into regular services, 1734–35, 1853–54, 2213–16; nominations for director, 757; point credit system for, 345, 398; tribute to by E., 2215

Women's Patriotic Conference on National Defense, 1486–87, 1515–16

Women's Press Club of London, 687–88

Wood, Carol, 564–65

Wood, Edward Frederick Lindley, 810, 1665

Wood, Robert Jefferson, commendation by E., 1831

Woodall, Harding Chambers, 1009

Woodring, Harry Hines, 1470

Woodruff, Robert Winship, 1760

Woodrum (Clifton Alexander) Committee: armed services postwar organization, 216; national security council, proposals for, 772; universal military training, 119–24

World Jewish Congress, 723

World Meteorological Organization, 820

World War II: books read by E., 1889; dead, number of, 1501; German documents, downgrading classification, 2073–75; history (see World War II history); JCS records, public access to, 2136; records, public access to, 2071–75, 2135–37, 2212–13

World War II history: Army publication project, 428–29, 2072, 2098; CCS documents, citation in, 2098–99; civilians role in writing, 429; E. on distortions and inaccuracies in, 773, 807, 2015, 2084–85; Germany, compilation terminated, 1908–9; JCS documents, citation in, 2088–89; joint U.S.-U.K. publication, 923–24, 1878–80, 2139–40

World Zionist Organization, 723

Worley, Francis Eugene, 1742

Wright, J. H. (Mrs. Frank), 1114

Wyche, Ira Thomas, 1335–36, 1413, 1943–46; background, 1335

Wylie, Robert H., 804

Wyman, Ethel Mae (Megginson), 1648, 1834

Wyman, Willard Gordon, 1647–48, 1834

XL–15 liaison aircraft, E. on development of, 2170–71

Yale Daily News, 1990–91

Yalta conference: allied Control Council, agreement on, 32; Germany, agreement on zones, 52, 137; reparations, agreement on, 260; Soviet nationals, agreement on repatriation, 360; Soviet Union as host, 164

Yank (magazine), 321–22

Yokohama, demonstration by soldiers, 753

Young, Dorothy Mills, 2061

Young, Gordon Russell, 1788

Young, Howard, 1198, 1745

Young, John, 621

Young, John Russell, 171

Young, Milton Ruben, 765

Young, Robert Nicholas, 36, 60–61; background, 37; MDW, assignment to, 37

Younger, James Wellington, graves registration chief, 230

Youth Day Committee, 2054

Yugoslavia: air-space channels, U.S. violation, 1236–38; air transport service, attacks on, 1236–38; ammunition supply to, 1348–49; Austria, claims for zone in, 58–59, 64; displaced persons, repatriation of, 414; intelligence reports on, 839; shipping, release from Soviet control, 398; UNO censure for Greek guerrillas support, 1999

—Italy: peace treaty ratification, 1901; potential action against, 2125

Library of Congress Cataloging in Publication Data (Revised)

Eisenhower, Dwight David, Pres. U.S., 1890-1969.
  The papers of Dwight David Eisenhower.

  Vol. 6 edited by Chandler and L. Galambos; v. 7- by Galambos.
  Includes bibliographies.
  CONTENTS: v. 1-5. The war years.—v. 6. Occupation, 1945.—v. 7-9. The chief of
staff.
  1. United States—Politics and government—20th century—Sources. 2. World War,
1939-1945—Sources. 3. Eisenhower, Dwight David, Pres. U.S., 1890-1969. I. Chandler,
Alfred Dupont, ed. II. Galambos, Louis, ed.

E742.5.E37 1970   940.54′012   65-27672
ISBN 0-8018-1078-7 (v. 1-5)
ISBN 0-8018-2061-8 (v. 6-9)